THE

PHYSICS OF

IMMORTALITY

FRANK J.
TIPLER

DOUBLEDAY

New York   London   Toronto   Sydney   Auckland

THE
PHYSICS
OF
IMMORTALITY

Modern Cosmology,

God and the

Resurrection of the Dead

PUBLISHED BY DOUBLEDAY
a division of Bantam Doubleday Dell
Publishing Group, Inc.
1540 Broadway, New York, New York 10036

DOUBLEDAY and the portrayal of an anchor with a dolphin are
trademarks of Doubleday, a division of Bantam Doubleday Dell
Publishing Group, Inc.

Book design by Claire Naylon Vaccaro

Some of the material in the Appendix for Scientists is based on articles the author has
published in various scientific journals over the last seventeen years:

"Black Holes in Closed Universes." *Nature* **270:** 500–501 (1977); "Causally Symmetric
Spacetimes." *Journal of Mathematical Physics* **18:** 1568–1573 (1977); "General Relativity,
Thermodynamics, and the Poincaré Cycle." *Nature* **280:** 203–205 (1979); "Maximal
Hypersurfaces and Foliations of Constant Mean Curvature in General Relativity." (with
J. E. Marsden) *Physics Reports* **66:** 109–139 (1980); "Penrose Diagrams for the Einstein,
Eddington-Lemaitre, Eddington-Lemaitre-Bondi, and anti-De Sitter Universes." *Journal of
Mathematical Physics* **27:** 559–561 (1985); "Closed Universes: Their Future Evolution and
Final State." (with John D. Barrow) *Monthly Notices of the Royal Astronomical Society* **219:**
395–402 (1985); "The Closed Universe Recollapse Conjecture." (with John D. Barrow
and Gregory G. Galloway) *Monthly Notices of the Royal Astronomical Society* **223:** 835–844
(1986); "Interpreting the Wave Function of the Universe." *Physics Reports* **137:** 231–275
(1986); "Cosmological Limits on Computation," *International Journal of Theoretical Physics*
25: 617–661 (1986); "Achieved Spacetime Infinity." *Nature* **325:** 201–202 (1987); "Action
Principles in Nature." (with John D. Barrow) *Nature* **331:** 31–34 (1988); "The Omega
Point as *Eschaton:* Answers to Pannenberg's Questions for Scientists." *Zygon* **24:** 217–253
(1989); "The Ultimate Fate of Life in Universes Which Undergo Inflation." *Physics Letters*
B286, 36–43 (1992); "A New Condition Implying the Existence of a Constant Mean
Curvature Foliation" appeared in a 1993 Conference Proceedings published by Cambridge
University Press; "God in the Equations." *Nature* **369:** 198 (1994).

Library of Congress Cataloging-in-Publication Data
Tipler, Frank J., 1947–
   The physics of immortality: modern cosmology, God and the resurrection of the
dead/by Frank J. Tipler.—1st ed.
      p. cm.
   1. Cosmology. 2. Physics—Religious aspects. 3. Omega Point.
4. Eschatology. 5. God—Proof, Cosmological. I. Title.
QB981.T57 1994
215′.3—dc20   93-45046
                                                                        CIP

To the grandparents of my wife, the great-grandparents of my children

JÓZEFA BASAREWSKA and ADAM ROKICKI
Shot to death by the Nazis in 1940, for the crime of being Poles.

JÓZEF BASAREWSKI
Tortured by the Gestapo, and died shortly thereafter.

All three being citizens of Toruń, Poland, the birthplace of
Copernicus.

Who died in the hope of the Universal Resurrection,
and whose hope, as I shall show in this book, will be fulfilled near
the End of Time.

Eternal must that progress be
Which Nature through futurity
Decrees the human soul;
Capacious still, it still improves
As through the abyss of time it moves,
Or endless ages roll.

Its knowledge grows by every change;
Through science vast we see it range
That none may here acquire;
The pause of death must come between
And Nature gives another scene
More brilliant, to admire.

Thus decomposed, or recombined,
To slow perfection moves the mind
And may at last attain
A nearer rank with that first cause
Which distant, though it ever draws,
Unequalled must remain.

from "On the Powers of the Human Understanding"
by Philip Freneau (1752–1832),
known as the
"poet of the American Revolution"
and as the
"founder of American poetry"

P R E F A C E

It is quite rare in this day and age to come across a book proclaiming the unification of science and religion. It is unique to find a book asserting, as I shall in the body of this book, that theology is a branch of physics, that physicists can infer by calculation the existence of God and the likelihood of the resurrection of the dead to eternal life in exactly the same way as physicists calculate the properties of the electron. One naturally wonders if I am serious.

I am quite serious. But I am as surprised as the reader. When I began my career as a cosmologist some twenty years ago, I was a convinced atheist. I never in my wildest dreams imagined that one day I would be writing a book purporting to show that the central claims of Judeo-Christian theology are in fact true, that these claims are straight-forward deductions of the laws of physics as we now understand them. I have been forced into these conclusions by the inexorable logic of my own special branch of physics.

I obtained my Ph.D. in 1976 in the area of global general relativity. This branch of physics, created in the late 1960s and early 1970s by the great British physicists Roger Penrose and Stephen Hawking, enables us to draw very deep and very general conclusions about the structure of space and time by looking at the universe in its *totality* in both time and space.

Now one might think that such a view of the universe is the view of all cosmologists, but this is not so. Almost all cosmologists concern themselves with what is called the *visible universe:* that part of the universe whose past can be seen from Earth. Since the universe came into existence about 20 billion years ago, and since nothing can go faster than light, we can in principle see the pasts of galaxies which are now about 20 billion light-years away: the visible universe is thus a sphere about 20 billion light-years across.

But to anyone regarding the universe in its total extent in space and especially in time, it is immediately obvious that the visible universe is only a tiny fraction of reality. The universe is almost certain to continue to exist for another 100 billion years, and probably much longer. In other words, the part of the spacetime which can be seen from Earth is relatively insignificant in comparison to the part which lies in our future; we humans have come into existence in the very early childhood of the cosmos. Hence, as a global relativist, I realized that I would have to study the future of the universe, since the future comprises almost all of space and time. It is not possible to look at the universe in its totality in both time and space while ignoring almost all of space and time.

But how does one calculate the behavior of the universe in the far future? My colleague, the British astrophysicist John D. Barrow, has proved that this behavior would be chaotic, which means that the evolution of the universe becomes unpredictable after a time short in cosmological scales. It is now known that chaotic evolution is common on all astronomical scales: on the scale of the solar system, on the scale of the galaxies, on the scale of clusters of galaxies, and so on up to the scale of the entire universe itself.

Furthermore, a simple calculation shows that, since chaos occurs on all size scales, intelligent beings would be able to use these instabilities to manipulate the motion of matter on the very largest scales. In other words, the possible presence and actions of intelligent life cannot be ignored in any calculation of the evolution of the far future. This would appear to make calculation of the universe's future even more impossible, since the behavior of humans is notoriously unpredictable. We shall have chaos in the society of intelligent living beings added to the chaos in the Einstein equations.

Interestingly, this is not true. The two sources of chaos cancel out.

What happens is that intelligent life, in order to survive, must use the chaos in the physical laws to force the evolution of the universe into one of a very restricted number of possible futures. Its very survival requires life to impose order on the universe. Taking biology into account allows us to do the physics of the far future.

But in order to do calculations, it is essential to translate basic biological concepts into physics language. It is necessary to regard all forms of life—including human beings—as subject to the same laws of physics as electrons and atoms. I therefore regard a human being as nothing but a particular type of machine, the human brain as nothing but an information processing device, the human soul as nothing but a program being run on a computer called the brain. Further, all possible types of living beings, intelligent or not, are of the same nature, and subject to the same laws of physics as constrain all information processing devices.

Many people find this extreme reductionist approach to life not only wrong but repulsive. I think, however, that their hostility is not to reductionism as such but to what they mistakenly believe to be consequences of reductionism. They are convinced that regarding people as machines would mean that people would have no "free will," that there is no hope of individual life after death, that life itself is a totally insignificant part of "an overwhelmingly hostile universe."[1]

In fact, the exact opposite is true. The very fact that humans are machines of a very special sort allows us to *prove* that we humans probably have free will, that we shall have life after death in an abode that closely resembles the Heaven of the great world religions, and that life, far from being insignificant, can be regarded as the ultimate cause of the very existence of the universe itself. How this works as a matter of physics is the subject of this book. The fact that all of these assertions are a consequence of physical reductionism has come as a great surprise to me also. As I said above, I never imagined when I began my career as a physicist that I would one day be writing, *qua* physicist, that Heaven exists, and that we shall each and every one of us enjoy life after death. But here I am, writing what my younger self would regard as scientific nonsense. Here I stand—as a physicist, I can do no other.

One naturally wonders why it is only in the last decade of the twentieth century that these ideas have appeared in physical cosmology. A good question. Part of the reason is that the mathematical techniques to analyze the global structure of the universe did not exist until about twenty-five years ago. But a deeper reason is that almost all physicists have ignored the future of the physical universe. There seemed to be a tacit consensus that the future is not as real as the present and the past, in spite of the fact that *all* fundamental physical theories advanced in the past three centuries—Newtonian mechanics, general relativity, quantum mechanics, string field theory—have insisted that there is no fundamental distinction between past, present, and future. Hence, the future is just as real as the present. Fifty years ago, the early universe was an equally taboo subject. As the Nobel-prize-winning physicist Steven Weinberg put it:

> . . . I think . . . the "big bang" theory did not lead to a search for the 3°K microwave background because it was extraordinarily difficult for physicists to take seriously *any* theory of the early universe. (I speak here in part from recollections of my own attitude before 1965.) . . . [The early universe is] so remote from us in time, the conditions of temperature and density are so unfamiliar, that we feel uncomfortable in applying our ordinary theories of statistical mechanics and nuclear physics.
>
> This is often the way it is in physics—our mistake is not that we take our theories too seriously, but that we do not take them seriously enough. It is always hard to realize that these numbers and equations we play with at our desks have something to do with the real world. Even worse, there often seems to be a general agreement that certain phenomena are just not fit subjects for respectable theoretical and experimental effort.[2]

I take the far future of the universe as seriously as I do the early universe. The equations of physics tell us to take the far future seriously, and until I have experimental evidence to the contrary, I shall believe what the equations say. I hope my fellow physicists will do the same. I intend to show in this book that, by ignoring the far future, they are passing up opportunities to do physics as they previously did by ignoring the early universe.

. . .

It is more surprising to me that theologians have ignored the ultimate future of the cosmos. This ultimate future supposedly is the chief concern of the two main Western religions, Christianity and Islam. The central discipline for both religions should therefore be *eschatology,* which is the study of "last things." Eschatology has traditionally dealt with questions of whether to expect life after death, what the afterlife will be like, and how God will provide for humankind in this afterlife.

I have been interacting with theologians and professors of religious studies for some six years now, and I have gotten the impression that, with only a few exceptions, they are quite ignorant of eschatology. Let me justify my accusation by recounting one of my recent experiences. In the fall of 1990 the annual meeting of the American Academy of Religion happened to be held in New Orleans. I attended a plenary lecture by a famous Columbia University historian of the Middle Ages, who spoke on medieval beliefs about life after death. She discussed at length an analysis by St. Thomas Aquinas, the greatest of the medieval theologians, of a technical problem which arises with the idea of the resurrection of the dead: if the universal resurrection is accomplished by reassembling the original atoms which made up the dead, would it not be logically impossible for God to resurrect cannibals? Every one of their atoms belongs to someone else! The audience, several hundred theologians and religious studies professors, thought this quaint "problem" hilarious, and laughed loudly.

I didn't laugh. When I first read Aquinas' analysis, which I came across when I first began to consider seriously the technical problems associated with a universal resurrection, I did laugh. But I soon realized that Aquinas' cannibal example was subtly chosen to illustrate the problem of personal identity between the original person and the resurrected person; establishing this identity is the central problem to be solved in any theory of resurrection of the dead. Any scholar who has seriously thought about the resurrection of the dead would almost certainly have come across Aquinas' analysis, be completely familiar with the cannibal example, and not laugh when it was mentioned. I infer that the typical American theologian/religious studies professor has never seriously thought about the resurrection of the dead. Eschatology has been left to the physicists.[3]

We physicists are by and large an extremely arrogant group of scholars. Our arrogance stems from the reductionist perception that ours is the ultimate science, and from our undoubted achievements over the past few centuries. What we promise, we generally deliver. Whatever one thinks of social significance of the nuclear bomb, there is no doubt that it works. Solar eclipses occur exactly when we predict they will. As one who has spent his entire life as a physicist or as a physicist *manqué,* I not surprisingly share this arrogance. In my previous publications on religion and physics, I have attempted to conceal this arrogance (not very successfully). In this book, however, I have not bothered, mainly because such concealment in the past has prevented me from presenting the strongest case for reductionism. And reductionism is true. Furthermore, accepting reductionism allows one to integrate fully religion and science.

Many of my fellow physicists have strongly advised me to avoid using words like "God," "Heaven," "free will," and the like. My friends believe these words have been debased by philosophers and theologians into synonyms for "nonsense." The "Omega Point" is a beautiful pure physics construct, and it should not be sullied by calling it "God." My friends have a point, but the old theological words retain a rough coherence in the popular language, and I propose to reintroduce them as technical terms which, as the reader will see in the chapters of this book, have roughly their popular meaning. "Resurrection of the dead" has a clear and unequivocal meaning to the person in the street, and if physics predicts such an event will one day occur, it seems unreasonable to adopt a new vocabulary to describe it. Another reason for their well-intended advice is that my fellow physicists are as a general rule atheists, believing that religion is a phenomenon of a prescientific world view. They are convinced that the God hypothesis is one which was refuted long ago.

But on rare occasions we physicists find we must reconsider long-rejected theories. Copernicus was perfectly aware that he was resurrecting a theory that had been rejected by astronomers nearly two thousand years before. As his student Rheticus reported in 1539: "My teacher [Copernicus] is convinced, however, that the rejected method of the Sun's rule in the realm of nature must be revived. . . ."[4] Copernicus himself in his own book, published four years after Rheticus wrote these words, emphasized that the ancient astronomers had considered and then rejected the Sun-centered solar system.

It is time scientists reconsider the God hypothesis. I hope in this book to persuade them to do so. The time has come to absorb theology into physics, to make Heaven as real as an electron.

Fort Walton Beach, Florida
July 1993

TABLE OF CONTENTS

TABLE OF CONTENTS

A C K N O W L E D G M E N T S

Much thanks are due to many friends and colleagues who have commented on earlier versions and individual sections of this book, and who have discussed various technical points with me. I am particularly indebted to Peter C. Aichelburg, Robert Beig, Jacob Bekenstein, Frank Birtel, Brice Cassenti, David Deutsch, Willem Drees, George F. R. Ellis, Dieter Flamm, Antony Flew, James Force, Robert Forward, Martin Gardner, Thomas Gilbert, K. Hidaka, Christopher Hill, the late Sidney Hook, Bei Lok Hu, Morris Kalka, Andrei Linde, Val A. McInnes, Peter Moore, Heide Narnhofer, Joseph Needham, John Polkinghorne, Frank Quigley, Sir Martin Rees, Helmut Rumpf, Robert John Russell, Nathan Sivin, Walter Thirring, Jolanta Rokicka Tipler, John Updike, and John A. Wheeler. I learned a great deal from the Tulane students of the Omega Point Colloquium, held in the fall 1990 term at Tulane University. I should like to thank these students, and also the scholars who traveled to New Orleans to participate in the Colloquium, especially Willem Drees, Antony Flew, Philip Hefner, Ella Moravec, Hans Moravec, and Robert J. Russell.

I am especially grateful to Professor Wolfhart Pannenberg for an exchange of letters which played a crucial role in the improvement of this book. Pannenberg is a very rare exception among twentieth-century theologians: he bases his theology on eschatology, and for him "Heaven" is not just a metaphor but something that shall actually exist in the future. He is therefore one of the very few modern theologians to truly believe that physics must be intertwined with theology, and makes a serious effort to understand modern science. My very critical remarks directed against modern theologians do not apply to him. My intellectual debt to him will be apparent in what follows.

But my greatest intellectual debt, and hence my deepest debt of gratitude, goes to my colleague and coauthor (of many research papers and one book), Professor John D. Barrow, with whom I published an earlier version of the Omega Point Theory. John's seminal work on chaos in general relativity provided an essential foundation stone for the Omega Point Theory, as will be made clear in the text.

Writing the book and research on the Omega Point Theory were supported in part by the Fonds National de la Recherche Scientifique of Belgium, the Tomalla Stiftung of Switzerland, the Tulane Honors Program, the Tulane Judeo-Christian Chair, the Fundacion Federico's Gravitation and Cosmology Project, and the Austrian Bundesminister- ium für Wissenschraft und Forschung under grant number GZ 30.401/1-23/92.

MATHEMATICS
AND CONVENTIONS
IN THIS BOOK

This is intended to be a popular book. However, I shall attempt in it to solve the most important problems of human existence by using the most up-to-date knowledge of modern mathematics and physics. The most advanced mathematics and physics are impossible to present to a popular audience in a completely rigorous way. So at first blush it appears that this cannot be a popular book.

I've tried to make it a popular book by isolating the really tough math in an Appendix for Scientists at the very end. The main body of the book will contain *no formulas at all* (except for $E = mc^2$, which hopefully no one will have trouble with), so no prior deep mathematical knowledge will be required in this main part. But I'll assume in the main body of the book that the reader is familiar with scientific notation for numbers: instead of three million or 3,000,000 I'll simply write

$$3 \times 10^6$$

The 6 is called an "exponent," and 10^6 just means "1 followed by 6 zeros." More generally, 10^n means "1 followed by n zeros." If you are a bit rusty in your algebra, recall that the symbol "n" represents any number. Thus, 3×10^6 means "three multiplied by 1 followed by 6 zeros," or 3 million. Finally, 3×10^{-6} means "three multiplied by 1 *over* one million." I shall find it necessary to deal with numbers that are so large they must be expressed as double exponentials, for example, 10^{10^6}. This means "1 followed by 10^6 zeros (one million zeros)." The largest number I shall use is $10^{10^{123}}$, which is "1 followed by 10^{123} zeros."

I shall generally use metric system units. The units for mass are the *gram*, which is roughly $1/30$ of an ounce, and the *kilogram*, which is roughly two pounds. The units for length are the *meter*, which is roughly a yard, and the *kilometer*, which is roughly half a mile.

Cosmology will play a central role in this book, so I shall assume that my reader has some knowledge of distances in astronomy. The basic unit is the *light-year*, defined to be the distance light can travel in a year. Since light travels 3×10^8 meters per second, a light-year is 9.46×10^{15} meters. A light-year is huge by human standards: it's 63,000 times the distance from the Earth to the Sun. But really large astronomical distances are usually given not in light-years, but in parsecs. A *parsec* is 3.26 light-years. I shall use the terms 1 kiloparsec = 1 thousand parsecs; 1 megaparsec = 1 million parsecs; 1 gigaparsec = 1 billion parsecs; and 1 teraparsec = 1 trillion parsecs. The center of our Galaxy is 10 kiloparsecs away from us. The nearest large galaxy, the Great Nebula in Andromeda, is about 1 megaparsec away. The edge of the visible universe is about 3 gigaparsecs away, and I predict that the other side of the universe is currently between 1 and 10 teraparsecs away.

In the main part of the book I'll describe in rough outline the basic ideas in the Appendix for Scientists, so anyone willing to do some hard thinking and with a high school education should be able to understand the main part.

I'll use three of the many different English translations of the Bible: KJV stands for King James Version, RSV stands for Revised Standard Version, and NEB means New English Bible.

THE
PHYSICS OF
IMMORTALITY

I.

INTRODUCTION

THIS BOOK IS A DESCRIPTION OF THE Omega Point Theory, which is a testable physical theory for an omnipresent, omniscient, omnipotent God who will one day in the far future resurrect every single one of us to live forever in an abode which is in all essentials the Judeo-Christian Heaven. Every single term in the theory—for example, "omnipresent," "omniscient," "omnipotent," "resurrection (spiritual) body," Heaven—will be introduced as pure physics concepts. In this book I shall make no appeal, anywhere, to revelation. I shall appeal instead to the solid results of modern physical science; the only appeal will be to the reader's reason. I shall describe the physical mechanism of the universal resurrection. I shall show exactly how physics will permit the resurrection to eternal life of everyone who has lived, is living, and will live. I shall show exactly why this power to resurrect which modern physics allows will actually exist in the far future, and why it will in fact be used. If any reader has lost a loved one, or is afraid of death, modern physics says: "Be comforted, you and they shall live again."

The resurrection theory requires us to accept that a human being is a purely physical object, a biochemical machine completely and exhaustively described by the known laws of physics. There are *no* mysterious "vital" forces. More generally, it requires us to regard a "person" as a particular (very complicated) type of computer program: the human "soul" is nothing but a specific program being run on a computing machine called the brain. I shall show that accepting this allows us to show not only that we shall be resurrected to eternal life, but also that we have free will—we are indeed machines, but we, in contrast to the machines we ourselves have built, possess true free will.

That we have free will, that God exists, and that He will one day resurrect each and every one of us to eternal life is not what one expects to be the message of physics, to say the least. One is accustomed to hear instead that the message of science is: we are mechanistic puppets of blind, impersonal, and deterministic natural laws; nothing remotely like a personal God exists; and when we're dead, we're dead, and that's the end of it. The latter has indeed been the message of science for a very long time now.

This has now changed. The cause of the change is that cosmologists have finally asked the fundamental question: how *exactly* will the physical universe evolve in the future? What *exactly* will be the final state of the cosmos? In particular, do the physical laws permit life to continue to exist until this final state, or is the extinction of life inevitable?

It is obvious that these questions are questions of physics, and that physical science cannot be considered complete until they are answered. Heretofore, science has concerned itself with what the universe is like now and what it was like in the past. But the universe has existed for only 20 billion years, whereas if the physical laws as we understand them are even remotely correct, the universe will continue for at least another 100 billion years, and almost certainly much longer. In other words, *almost all of space and time lies in the future.* By focusing attention only on the past and present, science has ignored almost all of reality. Since the domain of scientific study is the whole of reality, it is about time science decided to study the future evolution of the universe.

A problem immediately arises. The basic equations physicists use in cosmology, the Einstein field equations, are maximally chaotic.[1] This means that, without further assumptions, it becomes impossible to say anything at all about the state of the universe, after a time which is short in cosmological terms. But which additional assumptions should we make?

The assumption which I consider the most beautiful, the most fruitful, and which is the basis of this book, was proposed by the physicists J. B. S. Haldane, John Bernal, Paul Dirac, and Freeman Dyson: let the universe be such that life can continue until the end of time, literally forever. I pointed out in the Preface that chaos itself makes this assumption plausible, and that said assumption solves the prediction problem. As will be seen, this assumption clears up a huge number of puzzles in physics—such as which boundary condition to impose on the universal wave function, and even why the universe exists at all. The assumption also leads inexorably to the above theological conclusions. Physics has at last invaded the territory of theology.

But a moment's reflection shows that this latter development was inevitable. Either theology is pure nonsense, a subject with no content, or else theology must ultimately become a branch of physics.

The reason is simple. The universe is defined to be the totality of all that exists, the totality of reality. Thus, by definition, if God exists, He/She is either the universe or part of it. The goal of physics is understanding the ultimate nature of reality. If God is real, physicists will eventually find Him/Her. I shall argue in this book that physics may have in fact found Him/Her: He/She is actually everywhere; we have not seen Him/Her only because we have not looked at the universe on a sufficiently large scale—and have not looked for the Person in the machine.

The Omega Point Theory will require looking at God in a non-traditional way, but I think this new way is already present in modern theology. Paul Tillich,[2] for example, has emphasized that it is incorrect to think of God as *a* being; rather, God is being itself. God is ultimate reality. But Tillich adds—an all-important addition—that this ultimate reality is *personal*. This crucial constraint on ultimate reality, that it must be personal, is the distinguishing feature of theism as opposed to pantheism.[3] The personality constraint is what makes Tillich's definition nontrivial. It is a terrible mistake to think of God as apart from the everyday world, to be Wholly Other. That is the road to gnosticism, to the dualist idea that the physical world was created by an evil God.[4] The orthodox Christian God gets His/Her hands dirty. He/She is in the world, everywhere, and is with us, standing beside us, at all times. The love of the Christian God for His/Her creatures requires such

Presence. But such Presence means that God must be discoverable by physicists. As St. Paul put it: "His invisible attributes, that is to say his everlasting power and deity, have been visible, ever since the world began, to the eye of reason, in the things he has made." (Romans 1:20, NEB.)

In one unfortunate and crucial respect, Tillich's model of God remains pre-nineteenth century. Following the pre-nineteenth-century physical cosmologies, Tillich pictured God's mode of being as static, unchanging. However, biblical scholars began to realize in the late nineteenth century that such a view of God was utterly foreign to the New Testament. Jesus' picture of God, as demonstrated by the theologian-missionary doctor Albert Schweitzer among others, was based on seeing Him as the ruler of the *coming* Kingdom of God, that is, on regarding His mode of being as the power of the *future*. The essential Christian message was in its *eschatology,* which is the study of the ultimate future. Some major late twentieth-century theologians have understood this, most importantly the German theologian Wolfhart Pannenberg: "Jesus proclaimed the rule of God as a reality belonging to the future. This is the coming Kingdom. . . . [I]n a restricted but important sense, God does not yet exist. Since his rule and being are inseparable, God's being is still in the process of coming to be."[5] We shall see in the later chapters of this book how physics makes the Tillich-as-modified-by-Pannenberg model of God precise.

Some scholars have argued that this view of God, that He/She is to be considered primarily a future being, was already present in the very beginning of ancient Judaism. When God spoke to Moses out of the burning bush, Moses asked Him for His Name. According to the King James translation of the Bible, God replied "I AM THAT I AM . . . say unto the children of Israel that I AM hath sent me [Moses] unto you" (Exodus 3:14). However, in the original Hebrew God's reply was *"Ehyeh Asher Ehyeh."* In Hebrew, the word *Ehyeh* is the future tense of the word *haya,* which means "to be." That is, God's reply to Moses should be translated "I WILL BE WHAT I WILL BE. . . . Tell the children of Israel that I WILL BE sent me to you." (Most scholarly English translations[6] of the Bible point out this true translation of the original Hebrew in their footnotes to Exodus 3:14.) The Jewish German philosopher Ernst Bloch[7] and the Catholic German theologian Hans Küng[8] have both pointed out this true future tense translation, and emphasize that the God of Moses should be regarded as an "End- and Omega-God." The Omega Point God described in the physics of this book is definitely a God Who exists mainly at the end of time.

Many theologians are nevertheless reluctant to admit that physics could have anything to say about this Personal Ultimate Reality. They tend to think of physics as concerned with *finite* reality, whereas ulti- mate reality is fundamentally infinite. In fact, Tillich himself is one example of such a theologian: "The main argument against naturalism in whatever form is that it denies the infinite distance between the whole of finite things and their infinite ground. . . ."[9] However, mathematical physicists (primarily Penrose and Hawking) have devel- oped in the past thirty years the intellectual tools to analyze an actual infinity. Physics is no longer limited to the finite; technical advances inside physics itself have forced physicists to become concerned with the physics of the infinite. As we shall see, many properties—e.g., its eternity—of the physical universe are actual infinities.

Most contemporary scientists agree with the above-mentioned theologians that science and religion can have nothing to do with one another. For example, the Council of the U. S. National Academy of Sciences decreed in a Resolution dated 25 August 1981: "Religion and science are separate and mutually exclusive realms of human thought whose presentation in the same context leads to misunder- standing of both scientific theory and religious belief."[10] What scien- tists who make statements like this really mean is that religion is emo- tional nonsense, expressing nothing but our fear of death and the primitive view that the natural world is animate. Such scientists regard any attempt to fully integrate science and religion as a reactionary throwback to a prescientific model of reality.

But on occasion the advance of science itself requires us to recon- sider and finally accept a physical theory which earlier generations considered refuted for all time. The best-known example is the helio- centric theory of the solar system, first proposed in antiquity by the Greek astronomer Aristarchus of Samos,[11] but rejected early in the Christian Era in favor of the geocentric model of Ptolemy. Precisely four hundred and fifty years ago, in 1543, Nicolaus Copernicus brought back the Sun-centered solar system, reactionary throwback though it was, in the form of a powerful mathematical model able to account for more of reality than the Ptolemaic theory. Many of Copernicus' contemporaries[12] were perfectly aware that the Copernican theory was a return to a long-rejected model. Martin Luther, for instance, called Copernicus a ". . . fool [who] wishes to *reverse* [my emphasis] the entire science of astronomy. . . ."[13] Galileo, one of the strongest supporters of Copernican revolution—Galileo was severely punished by the Inquisition for this support[14]—also knew the Copernican theory had been rejected in ancient times. But in his classic study of the relationship between religion and science, *Letter to the Grand Duchess Christina*, Galileo correctly called Copernicus the theory's "restorer and confirmer,"[15] and Galileo went on to discuss at length[16] the support which the heliocentric theory had enjoyed in antiquity. Medicine provides another example of science having to reconsider a previous theory which had been rejected, apparently for all time. Under the influence of a new (but wrong) theory of inflammation, surgery retrogressed in the first half of the nineteenth century: mortality after operations became much higher than in previous centuries, because the new theory rejected the antisepsis practiced unknowingly by the earlier surgeons, who used cauterizations by fire, boiling liquids, and other disinfectants. But Pasteur, Lister, and others in effect brought back the earlier theory, in a much more powerful formulation, based firmly on the results of physical science.[17]

So a refusal to reconsider a previously rejected theory in the light of new data is bad science. The modern attempt to keep religion strictly separate from science is also bad theology. The idea that religion and science must be integrated was accepted in all Christian countries by all the great theologians—for example, St. Paul, Origen, Augustine, and Aquinas—prior to the twentieth century: *ubique, semper, ab omnibus* (believed everywhere *[ubique]*, always *[semper]*, and by everyone *[ab omnibus]*) is the ultimate authority in Christian theology just as experiment is the ultimate authority in science. In fact, the rule *ubique, semper, ab omnibus* is theology's version of "experiment." In science, the only valid experiment is one which can be reproduced by anyone *(ab omnibus)*, anywhere on Earth *(ubique)*, at any time in

Earth's history *(semper)*. The reason for this emphasis on experiment in science is to let Nature, not mere human opinion, be the ultimate authority of science. Nature is never wrong, whereas human scientists often are. Similarly, the intent of *ubique, semper, ab omnibus* is to let God, not mere human opinion, be the ultimate authority of theology. Only a truly universal belief about God could be a true belief about God.

Of course, the real reason modern theologians want to keep science divorced from religion is to retain some intellectual territory forever protected from the advance of science. This can only be done if the possibility of scientific investigation of the subject matter is ruled out a priori. Theologians were badly burned in the Copernican and Darwinian revolutions. Such a strategy seriously underestimates the power of science, which is continually solving problems philosophers and theologians have decreed forever beyond the ability of science to solve. In the Preface to the Second Edition and in the Introduction to his *Critique of Pure Reason,* the German philosopher Immanuel Kant[18] declared science forever incapable of solving the three fundamental problems of metaphysics: God, freedom, and immortality; that is, Kant contended that physics can never determine if God exists, if we have free will, or if God will grant us immortal life.

I disagree. By turning these "problems of metaphysics" into problems of physics, I shall argue in the body of this book that these questions can be answered, and that the answers to all three are *probably* He does exist, *probably* we have free will, and *probably* He will grant us eternal life after we have died. I say "probably" because science is not in the business of giving an absolutely certain-to-be-true answer, valid for all time. Science can only give "probably true" answers, as witness the fate of the geocentric hypothesis of Ptolemy, discussed above. But I firmly believe it is better to have the "probable" answers of science than the "absolutely certain"—i.e., wrong—answers of metaphysics. As the Scots philosopher David Hume put it at the very end of his *An Enquiry Concerning Human Understanding:*

> If we take in our hand any volume; of divinity or school metaphysics, for instance; let us ask, *Does it contain any abstract reasoning concerning quantity or number?* No. *Does it contain any experimental reasoning con-*

cerning matter of fact and existence? No. Commit it then to the flames: for it can contain nothing but sophistry and illusion.[19]

In answering "yes" to the immortality question, science at last invades the central keep of theology. In his own attempt to establish partial independence of science from theology, Galileo defended[20] an opinion he ". . . heard from an ecclesiastic of the most eminent degree (Cesare Cardinal Baronio): 'The intention of the [Bible] is to teach us how to go to heaven, not how the heavens go.' " Science now tells us how to go to Heaven.

Galileo got into serious trouble when he dared to invade the turf of the philosophers and theologians.[21] However, as I implied by my earlier description of the domain of physics—the whole of reality—an invasion of other disciplines by physicists is inevitable, and indeed the advance of science can be measured[22] by the extent of the conquest of other disciplines by physics. Louis Pasteur advanced science and human welfare when he introduced the experimental methods of physical chemistry into medicine, against the fierce opposition of the medical profession: "a majority of physicians and surgeons considered that it was a waste of time to listen to 'a mere chemist'[23] . . . who was poaching on the preserves of others."[24] Like medicine, religion is simply too important to be left to its traditional professionals. Indeed, both medicine and religion are vital to humankind in the literal sense of the word "vital." The Spanish philosopher/novelist Miguel de Unamuno devoted an entire book, *Tragic Sense of Life,* to a passionate argument for the proposition that the emotional foundation of all religion is the hunger for immortality. "Talking to a peasant one day, I proposed to him the hypothesis that there might be a God who governs heaven and earth, [but who does not grant immortality]. He replied: 'Then wherefore God?' "[25] The "tragedy" in Unamuno's title came from the divorce between human nature, which desperately wants immortality, and human reason, which in the past has claimed that there is no such thing. If the Omega Point Theory is correct, this divorce between emotion and reason is at an end.

The divorce will end soon, one way or the other. As Aristotle said more than two thousand years ago, a human being is at bottom a thinking animal, a creature whose distinguishing feature and chief survival mechanism is its ability to consider the world rationally. In the end, reason will sway emotion. If science continues to find no evidence for the existence of God, and for an afterlife, first the scientists will become atheists, and then the laity of all churches.[26] People will find a philosophy which will allow them to face the inevitability of their own very final and permanent deaths, the deaths of their children, their civilization, the death of all life in the cosmos and of everything they care about.

This advance of atheism can be documented in the history of twentieth-century biology. The Cornell historian of biology William B. Provine[27] has pointed out that in the 1920s many, probably most, evolutionists were religious. At that time Darwinian evolution theory was in eclipse, having been temporarily replaced by the hypothesis of a purposive force which was evolving life toward more complexity. The dean of the American evolutionists, Henry Osborn, head of the American Museum of Natural History, called this force "aristogenesis"; the French philosopher Henri Bergson called it *élan vital;* the French evolutionist Pierre Teilhard de Chardin called it "radial energy." The terms were different but the evolutionary mechanism was the same: there was a nonphysical cosmic force guiding evolution. The existence of such a force was the consensus belief[28] of evolutionists in the 1920s, and it was a small step to identify the force with God.

The consensus opinion returned to Darwinism in the 1930s and 1940s with the development of the Modern Synthesis, which invokes nonpurposive mechanisms—natural selection, random genetic drift, mutation, migration, and geographic isolation—to account for evolution. Organisms are created by blind deterministic mechanisms combined with others that are effectively random. (Here, I might add, is another example of science returning to a previously rejected theory. A return for which I am glad, since the Omega Point Theory presupposes the truth of the Modern Synthesis; indeed its truth is essential for the free will model developed in Chapter V.) By the end of the 1940s, all trace of God had been eliminated from evolutionary biology.

Provine remarks, "My observation is that the great majority of modern evolutionary biologists are atheists or something very close to that. Yet prominent atheistic or agnostic scientists publicly deny that there is any conflict between science and religion. Rather than simple intellectual dishonesty, this position is pragmatic. In the United States, elected members of Congress all proclaim to be religious; many scientists believe that funding for science might suffer if the atheistic implications of modern science were widely understood."[29] Provine's opinion is confirmed by Steven Weinberg's 1987 congressional testimony[30] asking for money to build the SSC, a $10 billion device to be constructed in Texas. (Funding has since been cut off.) A congressman asked Weinberg if the SSC would enable us to find God, and Weinberg declined to answer. But eventually the atheistic implications of modern science will be understood by the general public, who will themselves become atheists. The majority of Western Europeans and a large minority of Americans have already become effective atheists: they rarely if ever go to any church, and a belief in God plays no role in their daily lives. The evidence is clear and unequivocal: if scientists have no need for the God hypothesis, neither will anyone else. Were theologians to succeed in their attempt to strictly separate science and religion, they would kill religion. Theology simply *must* become a branch of physics if it is to survive. That even theologians are slowly becoming effective atheists has been documented by the American philosopher Thomas Sheehan.[31]

As I stated above, it is definitely true that the universe will exist for billions of years in the future. In fact, the evidence that the universe will continue to exist for 5 billion more years is at least as strong as the evidence that the Earth has already existed for 5 billion years. There is simply no way our extrapolations could be so wrong as to falsify this prediction of longevity. Furthermore, if the standard cosmological models are approximately accurate, then the universe, if closed, will continue to exist at least another 100 billion years (in proper time), and, if open or flat, will continue to exist for literally infinite (proper) time. In either case, we are seeing the universe in a very early stage in its history. Most of the physical universe lies in our future, and we cannot truly understand the entire physical universe without understanding this future. But we can study this future reality, in particular the ultimate future which constitutes the end of time, only if in some way this final state of the physical universe makes an imprint on the present.

I shall obtain a hold on this future reality by focusing attention on the physics relevant to the existence and behavior of life in the far future. I shall provide a physical foundation for eschatology—the study of the ultimate future—by making the physical assumption that the universe must be capable of sustaining life indefinitely; that is, for infinite time as experienced by life existing in the physical universe. All physical scientists should take this assumption seriously because we have to have *some* theory for the future of the physical universe—since it unquestionably exists—and this is the most beautiful physical postulate: that total death is not inevitable. *All* other theories of the future necessarily postulate the ultimate extinction of everything we could possibly care about. I once visited a Nazi death camp; there I was reinforced in my conviction that there is nothing uglier than extermination. We physicists know that a beautiful postulate is more likely to be correct than an ugly one. Why not adopt this Postulate of Eternal Life, at least as a working hypothesis? I shall show in Chapter II that the universe is in fact capable of sustaining life at least another million trillion years. Specifically, I shall demonstrate that it is technically feasible for life to expand out from the Earth and engulf the entire universe, and that life *must* do so if it is to survive.

Nobel laureate Paul Dirac was the first physicist to argue for the Postulate of Eternal Life: "With my assumption . . . life need never end. There is no decisive argument for deciding between [certain] assumptions. I prefer the one that allows the possibility of endless life. One may hope that some day the question will be decided by direct observation."[32] It turns out that the Postulate of Eternal Life imposes rather stringent requirements on the future. It also makes some predictions about the present, because the physics required to sustain life in the far future must be in place now, since the most fundamental laws of physics do not change with time. I shall describe the experimental tests of the postulate in Chapter IV. In rough outline, Chapter II will be concerned with the evolution of life between now and the time when the universe expands to its maximum size; Chapter III will present a history of various theories of the universe's ultimate future, thereby deepening the reader's insight into the meaning of eternal life for the biosphere as a whole, and with this insight Chapter IV will trace out the future history of life from the time of maximum expansion to the end of time, the ultimate and infinite future.

But the really fascinating consequence of the eternal life assumption is what it implies if life really does exercise its option to exist forever: there must exist in this future (but in two precise mathematical senses, also in the present and past) a Person Who is omnipotent, omniscient, omnipresent, Who is simultaneously both transcendent to yet immanent in the physical universe of space, time, and matter. In the Person's immanent temporal aspect, the Person is changing (forever growing in knowledge and power), but in the Person's transcendent eternal aspect, forever complete and unchanging. How this comes about as a matter of physics will be described in Chapters II–IV. The physics shows the Person to have a "pointlike" structure in the ultimate future, so I will call Him/Her the *Omega Point*. Mathematically speaking, the Omega Point is the *completion* of all finite existence. It will turn out that all finite existence is included in this completion, but the completion is more than all finite existence.

A fundamental question remains: is this Omega Point God (assuming said Person actually exists) *the* God? It is generally felt that *the* God must be the uncreated Creator of the physical universe, a Being Who not merely exists but Who exists necessarily, in the strong logical sense of "necessity"; i.e., the Person's nonexistence would be a logical contradiction. Only if God is not in any sense contingent can one avoid regress posed in the query, who created God? I shall tackle the question of necessary existence in Chapter VIII. I shall analyze the notion of contingency in classical general relativity and in nonrelativistic quantum mechanics in Chapter V, and extend this analysis to quantum cosmology in the following chapter. In both chapters, I shall discuss in what sense modern cosmological models can be said to sustain themselves in physical existence. Finally, in Chapter VIII, I shall use the ideas developed in the preceding three chapters to argue that the universe necessarily exists—and necessarily sustains itself in existence—if and only if life and the Omega Point exist therein. If this argument is accepted, then the Omega Point exists necessarily, and further, ultimate reality is Personal. The Omega Point is in essence the Tillich-Pannenberg God: Being itself, but the mode of Being is futurity. This establishes the Omega Point as *the* God, for there cannot be more being than all Being, and this Being has all of the traditional divine attributes.

I shall show in Chapter VII that—contradictory though it may seem—this necessary existence of the universe, the necessary existence of the events that comprise it, and the omniscience of God, can nevertheless be consistent with human free will. Basically, I shall do this by showing that the American philosopher William James's definition of indeterminism and free will might be physically realized in quantum cosmology. This physical indeterminism can arise only in the context of quantum gravity, and thus it is completely different from the "indeterminism" arising from the uncertainty principle. (Nonrelativistic quantum mechanics is in fact deterministic.) This new type of physical indeterminism was first discovered in the early 1980s and is in essence a consequence of Gödel's Incompleteness Theorem. I shall end Chapter VII by showing that, by carefully defining in physics language each of the three words in the phrase "God's free decision," one can prove that in the Omega Point Theory the universe (= all that exists) is contingent in the special sense that it depends on (is generated by) God's free decision(s), in spite of existing necessarily. One avoids the seeming contradiction between contingency and necessity by avoiding the traditional sharp distinction between God and the rest of reality. This sharp distinction cannot be drawn in the Omega Point Theory, and as I argued above, the sharp distinction inevitably leads to the gnostic heresy. Or rather, it *is* the gnostic heresy: the idea of a wholly other God wholly divorced from our mundane world. It also leads indirectly to the Problem of Evil, and I shall show in Chapter X how this problem is naturally resolved in the Omega Point Theory.

Wolfhart Pannenberg has suggested[33] that there may exist a previously undiscovered universal physical field (analogous to Teilhard's "radial energy") which can be regarded as the source of all life, and which can be identified with the Holy Spirit. There are no undiscovered "energy" fields of significance to biology; conservation of energy and the size of the energy levels in biology preclude it. However, I shall argue in Chapter VI that the *universal* wave function (provided it satisfies an "Omega Point" Boundary Condition) is a universal field with the essential features of Pannenberg's proposed new "energy" field.

The Omega Point Boundary Condition (which makes the wave function explicitly Personal) and Tillich's insight on the relation between God and Being suggest identifying the personalized wave function with the Holy Spirit. If this identification is made, it becomes reasonable as a matter of physics to say God is in the world, everywhere, and is with us, standing beside us, at all times. I pointed out above that such Presence is a key property of the Christian God. (This does not mean, however, that God intervenes in human history in a supernatural way.)

The emphasis in Chapters II–VIII will be the physics—the nuts and bolts—of infinite continued survival. But the Christian God is a great deal more than the God of the philosopher-physicist. The former is a God of love and mercy, a God Who grants eternal life to each individual human being. The Swiss theologian Karl Barth has pointed out that "Without any doubt at all the words 'resurrection of the dead' are, for [St. Paul], nothing else than a paraphrase of the word 'God.' "[34] I shall show in Chapters IX and X that the Omega Point has the physical power to resurrect all humans who have ever lived and grant them eternal life. In brief, the physical mechanism of individual resurrection is the emulation of each and every long-dead person—and their worlds—in the computers of the far future. I shall show in Chapter IX that we and our computer emulations *are* the same persons. I shall give in Chapter X a plausibility argument based on the mechanism of survival of any form of life in the far future—an argument based on (1) game theory as applied to biological evolution and (2) microeconomics—for believing the Omega Point will in fact resurrect us and grant us eternal life. Remarkably, the argument boils down to a proof that we will be granted eternal life because it is probable that the Omega Point loves us! Thus the ultimate cause of eternal life for humans in the Omega Point Theory is exactly the same as it is in the Judeo-Christian-Islamic tradition: God's selfless love, which is called *agape* (ἀγάπη) in New Testament Greek. Each of us shall live again in a new Heaven and a new Earth.

According to both modern physics and ancient Semitic natural philosophy, the human personality is not naturally immortal: it dies with the body. As Wolfhart Pannenberg, discussing the generally agreed-upon meaning of the Christian resurrection hope, puts it:

The contrast to the Greek way of thinking (which was only able to conceive of life beyond death as the continued life of the soul, separated from the body) is expressed by the particular stress of the [Apostles'] creed's formulation when it talks about the resurrection of the *body*.[35]

Hence, both the Omega Point Theory and Christianity assert that we would die never to rise again except for the conscious future act of God, the Omega Point's act of "personal condescension and absolutely gratuitous clemency to man," to quote the definition of "grace" given by the famous German Catholic theologian Karl Rahner.[36] I shall discuss in Chapter XI the view of life after death in early Taoism, Hinduism, Judaism, Christianity, and Islam. All of these envisaged the afterlife as involving the resurrection of some sort of body, and so are, broadly speaking, consistent with the resurrection model in the Omega Point Theory.

I shall analyze in Chapters IX and X the physical nature of the resurrection body and the type of life enjoyed by the resurrected individuals. I shall show that St. Paul's phrase "spiritual body" aptly describes the resurrection body: it is simultaneously material and immaterial. This is because—in the language of computer science—the resurrection body is our current body at a higher level of implementation (what exactly this means will be discussed in Chapters II and X). In fact, the resurrection body has many key features in common with Jesus' post-Easter body as described in the gospel of Luke. The life of the resurrected dead will be of a much higher quality than the life experienced by virtually anyone today or in the past; God's love for us ensures this. However, the precise nature of this life depends on whether the Omega Point chooses to suspend our innate finiteness. If He/She does, the resurrected life could be a life of continued individual becoming, an exploration into the inexhaustible reality which is the Omega Point. In either case, I show that realms which can be accurately described as "Heaven" and "Purgatory" will exist in the far future. "Hell" may or may not exist, depending on whether human finiteness is suspended, and whether a certain finite dual game with perfect information has winning pure strategy for a particular player.

Maps can be provided for realms which really exist. Every library has maps of Florida, China, Italy. The people of the Middle Ages truly believed that Heaven, Hell, and Purgatory were as real as Italy and China. In fact, *The Divine Comedy* was quite seriously intended by Dante to be a road map for Heaven, Hell, and Purgatory, and *The Divine Comedy* was so regarded by Dante's contemporaries. Since, if the Omega Point Theory is true, Heaven, Purgatory, and possibly Hell will actually exist in the far future, a rough spacetime map of these realms can be made. Such will be provided in Chapter X.

A Christology can be developed in the Omega Point Theory, but it does not really appear naturally in the model, and in any case the Christology depends on some unlikely possibilities in quantum cosmology. I shall discuss in Chapter XII the question of whether the religion most discussed in the West, Christianity, can be incorporated into the Omega Point Theory. The short answer is, not easily. But, as discussed above, the aspects of Christianity which most people seek in a religion—a Personal Being Who shall one day resurrect themselves and their loved ones to eternal life in Heaven—are basic features of the Omega Point Theory. I shall in fact demonstrate in Chapter XI that the Omega Point Theory is consistent with only those features of religion which are found in all of the great world religions. No single religion can be singled out as most consistent with the Omega Point Theory.

Instead, the Omega Point Theory can be a solid foundation of support for all of the great human religions. The core of all religions is a belief in a Supreme Personal God, and a belief that He/She will somehow provide individual immortality for all of us. Similarly, the core chapters of this book are Chapter IV—where the basic physics of the Omega Point is described—and Chapter IX—where the mechanism of individual resurrection to immortal life is outlined.

Let me emphasize again that the Omega Point Theory, including the resurrection theory, is pure physics. There is nothing supernatural in the theory, and hence there is no appeal, anywhere, to faith. The genealogy of the theory is actually atheistic scientific materialism: the line of research which led to the Omega Point Theory began with the Marxist John Bernal, as I shall discuss in Chapter III. The resurrection mechanism was independently discovered at about the same time by myself,[37] the computer scientist Hans Moravec,[38] and the philosopher Robert Nozick.[39] This simultaneous discovery strongly suggests that "eternal life as physics" is an idea whose time has come. The key concepts of the Judeo-Christian-Islamic tradition are now scientific concepts. From the physics point of view, theology is nothing but physical cosmology based on the assumption that life as a whole is immortal.

II.

THE ULTIMATE LIMITS
OF SPACE TRAVEL

·———·

Space Travel by Man and Intelligent Machine

IF THE HUMAN SPECIES, OR INDEED ANY part of the biosphere, is to continue to survive, it must eventually leave the Earth and colonize space. For the simple fact of the matter is, **the planet Earth is doomed.** The Sun is becoming more luminous every day, and in about 7 billion years its outer atmosphere will have expanded to engulf the Earth. Owing to atmospheric friction, the Earth will then spiral into the Sun, and the Earth will vaporize. If life has not succeeded in moving off the planet before this occurs, life also will be doomed. But the physical destruction of the entire Earth is not the only danger the biosphere faces. As the luminosity of the Sun increases, the surface of the Earth heats up, making it too hot for life and, in addition, silicate rocks weather more readily, causing atmospheric carbon dioxide to fall below the critical level for photosynthesis. One of these two effects will wipe out the entire biosphere between 900 million and 1.5 billion years from now.[1] These numbers are admittedly enormous by human standards, but in this book we are considering ultimate questions, so we must address the question of what the biosphere must do to ensure its ultimate survival. The answer is clear and unequivocal: it must leave the Earth and colonize space.

Let us follow many environmentalists and regard the Earth as *Gaia,* the mother of all life (which indeed she is). Gaia, like all mothers, is not immortal. She is going to die. But her line of descent *might* be immortal. Indeed, every being now alive on the Earth is the direct lineal descendant of one-cell organisms that lived 3.5 billion years ago. The age of the lines of descent of those ancient organisms, our ancestors, is a substantial fraction of the age of the entire universe, about 20 billion years. So Gaia's children might never die out—provided they move into space. The Earth should be regarded as the womb of life— but one cannot remain in the womb forever.

What I shall do in this chapter is describe the movement of life from the Earth-womb into the cosmos at large. I shall provide a fairly detailed analysis, showing that it is physically possible, using technology just slightly in advance of what we now possess, for life to engulf the entire universe and gain control of it. Life will have to have accomplished this by the time the universe reaches its maximum size (which, for reasons I shall give in Chapter IV, will be between 5×10^{16} and 5×10^{18} years in the future). I shall show in this chapter exactly how this can be done. This chapter will outline the history of life, if it is to survive, between now and the time of maximum expansion. In Chapter IV, I will continue the story all the way into the end of time, the Omega Point.

We already have the rocket technology capable of exploring and colonizing the galaxy. Indeed, several of our space probes have already left the solar system and have begun traveling in interstellar space. What we lack is not propulsion technology but computer technology.

Since the stars are separated by light-years, any interstellar vehicle, manned or unmanned, must be completely self-sufficient. Even at the speed of light, it would take years to send any spare parts and orders on how to react to unforeseen events in the other stellar systems. The ability to make decisions on the spot would require either a manned spacecraft or else a robot probe controlled by a computer with human-level intelligence. A completely self-sufficient manned spacecraft would require an enormous payload mass, so an intelligent robot probe is preferred. But an intelligent robot probe would be sufficient to seed other star systems with life, because the machine could code DNA sequences for humans and other terrestrial life forms in its memory, and then use this information to create living cells of these life forms in the star systems.

Can a Machine Be Intelligent?

The assumption that we humans can eventually build an intelligent machine is called the Strong AI Postulate, where AI is short for "artificial intelligence." I've noticed in conversations with nonexperts in computer science that a majority, perhaps a large majority, are quite dubious[2] about this assumption—and assumption it is, because obviously we are currently unable to build such a machine. Let me first address the technical feasibility of constructing an intelligent machine, and then address the utterly unfounded Frankenstein monster fear: that even if we could construct such a machine, we should not, because it would turn on us, its creators.

First of all, how would we know if we succeeded? How could we tell if a computer *was* intelligent? For that matter, how do we know if a human being we see is intelligent? Maybe he is suffering from brain damage, and so is unable to think. Unfortunately, there are such people. The answer in the case of humans is simple: talk to them. If they make a coherent reply to a question you pose, then you immediately conclude that they probably have full human intelligence. But of course there are mental defects which are not apparent in a single exchange. So you talk with the other person some more. After days and weeks and *years* of talking with the other person, you would now *know* whether any mental defects are present.

The great British computer scientist Alan Turing proposed that we apply the same criteria to computer intelligence: if you can talk to the machine—*really* talk to it, carry on a conversation with it just as you would with another normal human being—then the machine *is* intelligent. If after interacting for years with the machine it acts as if it has a personality, has consciousness (and a conscience), then it really does. This algorithm[3] (procedure) for determining whether a computer is intelligent is called the *Turing Test*. When Turing first proposed the Turing Test in the 1950s, computers were incapable of generating spoken language; they were only capable of printing out a response to a question on paper or displaying it on a computer screen. So Turing proposed his test in the following manner. Suppose we have two rooms, one containing a human being and the other containing a computer. There is a computer screen and keyboard outside the two rooms. Wires lead from this screen and keyboard to the inside of both rooms, and the wires are connected to another computer screen and keyboard in the room containing the human, and directly to the computer in the other. The rooms are isolated, so a person outside does not know which room contains the computer and which the human being.

A human on the outside now tries to guess which is which by typing questions on his keyboard and analyzing the replies. If after days and weeks and *years* of typing in messages and receiving answers, the human outside cannot tell which room contains the computer and which the human being, then the computer passes the Turing Test: a human has "talked" with the computer for years on end and it acts just like a person, so it *is* a person. The essential idea of the Turing Test is that what counts for personhood is behavior: if it behaves in all respects like a person, then it *is* a person. Regrettably, there have been people in the past who believed that physical form was a relevant factor in determining whether or not a being was a "person" with full human rights. In the nineteenth century, many white European males were convinced that non-Europeans, and women of all human races, were not fully human, and denied them full human rights. Even many scientists (all white European males) believed that women and non-Europeans were not fully human. What ultimately changed these scientists' minds was the Turing Test applied to women and non-Europeans: given the opportunity, women and non-Europeans could perform any intellectual task as well as (or better than) any white European male. Therefore, if white European males were fully human, so were women and non-Europeans. One hopes we can learn from our mistakes, and come to view intelligent machines as persons. For, as will be seen, the creation of such intelligent machines will be a matter not of "man playing God," but rather of humanity ensuring a union with God.

However, no computer today can pass the Turing Test. I feel free to smash my desktop computer any time I wish, without having to fear being arrested for murder. The question is, will a computer *ever* be able to pass the Turing Test, and if it is technically feasible to build such a machine, how long will it be before we do?

To answer this question, we must get an estimate on the complexity of the human brain *qua* computer. Roughly speaking, a computer's complexity can be described by two numbers: one giving how much information its memory can store, and the other telling how fast it can process information.

The human brain storage capacity is obtained as follows.[4] The human brain has about 10^{10} neurons, each of which has about 10^5 connections with other neurons. Assuming each *neuron* codes one bit gives 10^{10} bits. Assuming each *connection* codes one bit gives 10^{15} bits, since an upper bound[5] to the number of synaptic connections in the cerebral cortex and cerebellum is 10^{15}. The consensus view[6] among neurophysiologists is that the information in the brain is stored (somehow) in the synaptic connections. Measurements by neurophysiologists[7] of the actual amount of information stored yield between 10^{13} and 10^{16} bits for children, and between 10^{14} and 10^{17} bits for seventy-year-olds. I obtained this estimate of between 10^{13} and 10^{17} bits from my colleague at the University of Vienna Theoretical Physics Institute, Dieter Flamm. (When I was a visiting professor at the University of Vienna in 1992, I showed Dieter the above calculation of between 10^{10} and 10^{15} bits, and he called a neurobiologist friend of his to see what biologists thought of these numbers. Dieter's friend replied: "You physicists! You are always trying to quantify the unquantifiable! And anyway, the storage capacity is not between 10^{10} and 10^{15} bits, it's between 10^{13} and 10^{17} bits!" The computer scientist Jacob Schwartz[8] estimates one byte (8 bits) per synapse, and he gets about 10^{17} bits for the storage capacity of the brain.)

The other number we need is the speed of information processing of the brain. Computer speeds are generally given in flops, which stands for floating point operations per second. A floating point operation is the addition, subtraction, multiplication, or division of two numbers expressed in scientific notation. For example, suppose we add 3.02×10^{10} and 5.74×10^9. We move the decimal point in the second number to get the same power of 10 in the exponent (the decimal point "floats") and add, getting 3.59×10^{10}. (We drop the 4 because we only have three significant digits.) If you are a bit rusty with scientific notation, this calculation may have taken you ten seconds, in which case your speed for doing this calculation is $1/10$ flops.

Standard computers are a bit faster. Your desktop computer can do a few megaflops (that's one *million* flops) and in 1986, when I first started writing about computers and brains, the fastest supercomputer then available, the Cray-2, had a speed of 1 gigaflop (that's one *billion* flops). By 1990, the speed of the fastest supercomputer had reached 10 gigaflops. In January 1992, Thinking Machines Inc. shipped a 100-gigaflop machine, the CM-5, to Los Alamos research labs. The cost of this machine was $10 million, a standard price for a state-of-the-art supercomputer. Danny Hillis, the chief scientist for Thinking Machines, announced at the time that his company was ready to build a 2-teraflop (that's two *trillion* flops) any time someone would come up with the money to pay the $200 million price. (A teraflop computer is sometimes called an *ultracomputer.*)

So how rapidly does the brain process information? Well, about 1% to 10% of the brain's neurons are firing at any one time, at a rate of about 100 times per second. If each neuron firing is equivalent to a flop, the lower number gives 10 gigaflops. If each synapse is equivalent to a flop at each firing, then the higher number gives 10 teraflops. Jacob Schwartz[9] estimates 10 million flops as an upper bound to the amount of power required to simulate a single neuron. If this is the actual requirement, then 100,000 teraflops would be required to simulate the entire brain. As Schwartz admits, this is probably an overestimate. The computer scientist Hans Moravec,[10] on the basis of a careful analysis of the information processed in the retina and optic nerve, estimates that the entire human brain processes information at 10 teraflops.

Let's use 10^{15} bits and 10 teraflops as the best available estimates for the storage capacity and speed of information processing of the human brain, respectively. We already have machines that can code 10^{15} bits, so speed is the real barrier to making a machine that can pass the Turing Test. How long will it take to reach 10 teraflops?

Not long. The general consensus[11] of the experts is that our fastest supercomputers should be in the 1,000-teraflop range by 2002. This is consistent with the factor of 100 increase in the past seven years.

Moravec[12] has shown that computer speeds have increased over the past forty years by a factor of 1,000 every twenty years. So we should see computers with human-level information processing capacity by the end of the decade. Moravec[13] has also pointed out that the power of desktop machines follows the power of the fastest available machines with a delay of about thirty years. If this trend continues in the future for as long as it has continued in the past, then we can expect to see personal computers with human-level information processing capacity, at current personal computer prices of a few thousand dollars, by the year 2030. This is within the lifetime of most people who are middle-aged and younger. Notice that if I'm wrong about the upper bound, and a Turing Test–passing computer needs 10^{17} bits and 100,000 teraflops (as some computer scientists and neurobiologists think), then since my estimates are too low by a mere factor of 100, it will take us only *seven* more years to develop computers with the necessary power and memory. Obviously, seven years doesn't make much difference: it took evolution at least 3.5 *billion* years to make us from one-cell organisms.

There are, of course, many people who think we will never be able to make an intelligent machine. The arguments of two such scholars, the mathematical physicist Roger Penrose and the philosopher John Searle, are the most often discussed, so I will consider them here.

Penrose points out, correctly, that Gödel's Theorem proves all computers, no matter how powerful, are subject to fundamental limitations. He then claims, I think incorrectly, that human beings are not subject to the same limitations.

Gödel's Theorem is actually based on a remark which St. Paul made in a letter to Titus: "One of themselves . . . said, 'Cretans are always liars. . . .' " (Titus 1:12 RSV.) The interesting thing about this claim which Paul attributes to a Cretan is that, if it is true, then it is false. Consider the similar sentence: "This statement is false." Once again, if the statement is true, then it is false, but in addition, if it is false, then it is true. In both cases, the paradoxes arise from self-reference: the two sentences are trying to say something about themselves.

What the logician Kurt Gödel did in the 1930s was to show that the full theory of arithmetic—the theory of arithmetic we are all familiar with, which includes addition, subtraction, multiplication, and division—contains a self-reference statement equivalent to: "This statement is unprovable." If it is true, then the statement itself is unprovable, and arithmetic is incomplete—a theory is said to be *incomplete* if it contains a true statement which cannot be proven from the axioms of the theory. On the other hand, if the statement is false, then, since it is equivalent to a statement of arithmetic, arithmetic would be logically inconsistent. A further consequence of this argument is that arithmetic, if consistent, must be incomplete, and hence must be undecidable—a theory is said to be *undecidable* if there is no algorithm which, given any statement in the theory, can tell you whether the statement is true or false. An *algorithm* is just a procedure which will give you the answer if there is one. For example, if I ask you, "What do you get if you multiply 52 times 27?" an "algorithm" you can use to get the correct answer 1,404 is just the procedure you were taught to use as a child to multiply two numbers together. A problem for which there exists an algorithm to solve it is said to be *solvable*. The problem of multiplying two numbers together is solvable, and you know an algorithm for doing so. An *unsolvable problem* is one for which no algorithm exists for solving it.

What has Gödel's Theorem got to do with the limitations of computers? It turns out that Gödel's Theorem is essentially equivalent to the unsolvability of the computer *Halting Problem.*

If we want to solve a mathematical problem using a computer, what we do is pick a computer program, load the program in the computer, type in the problem, and hit the "start program" key. If the problem is solvable, and if we've chosen the right program, then after a while the computer prints out the answer and stops. We say the program has *halted*. However, suppose the computer has been grinding away at the problem for days on end and no answer is in sight. We begin to get worried. Maybe the problem is unsolvable, or maybe we've chosen the wrong computer program. If either is true, then the computer will grind away *forever* and never end up with the right answer: it will *never* halt. What we would like to do is solve the Halting Problem: find a single algorithm which will tell us if a given program, working on a given problem, will eventually halt.

Turing proved that the Halting Problem is unsolvable: there is no algorithm for deciding whether or not a program ever halts. It is easy to prove that the Halting Problem is unsolvable. Consider all "computable functions"—a *function* is a rule f that assigns to any whole number N another whole number f(N), and a *computable function* is one for which the number f(N) can be calculated by some program for any N. Since any computer program is just a finite sequence of numbers, we can put all such programs in an ordered list $\{1, 2, \ldots\}$ where 1 is the first program, 2 is the second, and so on. If a function is a computable function, it must also be expressible as a finite sequence of numbers, and so we can list all computable functions just as we list all programs. Let's define a special self-referenced function G(N) to be either one more than the value of the Nth computable function in the list applied to the number N, or else the number zero if this value is undefined because the Nth computer program never halts when the number N is its input. First, we note that G(N) cannot be a computable function itself, because if the Nth computer program calculated it, then we would have G(N) equaling G(N) + 1, which is impossible. But the only way that the function G can fail to be computable is for it to be impossible to decide if the Nth program halts when N is its input.

If you've gone through this argument, and realized that it is valid (which it is), then you have "out-Gödeled" the machine you have analyzed. That is, you have understood something that the machine cannot. Penrose concludes from this that we humans have an insight into logic which no machine can have, and hence it is impossible for any computer, no matter how powerful, to pass the Turing Test. The problem I see with Penrose's argument is that there are machines which can out-Gödel us.

In my opinion (and that of virtually all other computer experts) Penrose's argument is in essence the same as an argument put forward years ago by the Oxford University philosopher John Lucas. An interesting exchange[14] concerning the validity of the Lucus-Penrose argument occurred during a debate on "The Nature of the Mind" held in 1972 at the University of Edinburgh among the philosopher Anthony Kenny, Lucas, and the physicist-cognitive scientist Christopher Longuet-Higgins:

KENNY: . . . You remember that John Lucas argued that minds were not machines because, given any machine working algorithmically, we could produce something which would be like a Gödelian formula, that is to say, we could present it with a formula which we could see to be true, but the machine couldn't prove to be true. When John first produced this argument, one of his critics, I think it was Professor Whiteley, made the following objection: he said, "Take this sentence: 'John Lucas cannot consistently make this judgment.' Now," he said, "clearly any other human being except John Lucas can see this is true, without inconsistency. But clearly John can't make this judgment without inconsistency, therefore that shows that we all have a property which he doesn't have, which makes us as much superior to him as we all are to computers. . . ."

LONGUET-HIGGINS: . . . [Lucas was] suggesting that there was some superiority attached to human beings because they could always out-Gödel a machine, but by implication, but never explicitly, [Lucas claimed] a machine could never out-Gödel them. But actually, I could write a program to print out [Whiteley's] question to you [Lucas], and that would out-Gödel you.

KENNY: Well, now he's withdrawn [to the position that] the difference between men and computers [is] only like the difference between one man and the next man, one computer and the next computer.

LUCAS: This is enough, though—if I am unlike any computer as I am unlike Kenny, then I can be sure that I am what I always thought I was.

Penrose's own version of this argument was demolished in a review of *The Emperor's New Mind* by the famous computer scientist John McCarthy, the inventor of the important computer language LISP:

The Penrose argument against AI . . . is that whatever system of axioms a computer is programmed to work in, e.g. Zermelo-Fraenkel set theory, a man can form a Gödel sentence for the system, true but not provable within the system.[15]

The simplest reply to Penrose is that forming a Gödel sentence from a proof predicate expression is just a one-line LISP computer program. Imagine a dialogue between Penrose and a mathematics computer program:

PENROSE: Tell me the logical system you use, and I'll tell you a true sentence you can't prove.

PROGRAM: Tell me the logical system *you* use, and I'll tell you a true sentence *you* can't prove.

PENROSE: I don't use a fixed logical system.

PROGRAM: I can use any system you like, although mostly I use a system based on a variant of ZF and descended from the 1980s work of David McAllester. Would you like me to print you a manual? Your proposal is like a contest to see who can name the largest number with me going first.

Penrose has another argument for thinking that the human mind cannot be a computer program: he finds it difficult to imagine how such a program could have originated. But Penrose *himself* describes the mechanism.

If we suppose that the action of the human brain . . . is merely the acting out of some very complicated algorithm, then we must ask how such an extraordinarily effective algorithm actually came about. The standard answer, of course, would be "natural selection." As creatures with brains evolved, those with the more effective algorithms would have a better tendency to survive, and therefore, on the whole more progeny. . . . [O]ne . . . might imagine some kind of natural selection process being effective for producing *approximately* valid algorithms.[16]

However, Penrose "finds this very difficult to accept"[17] because he believes (1) any selection can work only on the outputs of the algorithms and not on the algorithms themselves, and (2) "the slightest 'mutation' of an algorithm would tend to render it totally useless, and it is hard to see how actual *improvements* could ever arise in this random way."[18]

The problem with both of these reasons is that, if valid, they would disprove the modern theory of biological evolution. All living beings are generated by programs coded in DNA molecules. These DNA programs originated in exactly the manner Penrose finds "very difficult to accept." Biological natural selection can indeed act only on the whole biological organism, and not on the DNA programs directly. Furthermore, a mutation of a gene is almost always a change for the worse. Nevertheless, it was natural selection acting on such mutations (and other random changes in the gene pool) that generated the human genotype. Even leaving out the complexity of the human mind, the human body by itself is a marvelously complex machine, more complex, more in accord with reality (i.e., fitted to survive), and more beautiful than any creation of the human mind. So beautiful and so complex is the human body that, until Darwin demonstrated to the contrary, it was believed to have been created directly by a superhuman Person, God Himself. Since we *know* that natural selection acting on random mutations can be and has been more creative than any human mind, it seems perfectly plausible that the human mind can create ideas and be itself created by the same mechanism.

Penrose realizes that his reasons for disbelieving in the natural formation of a mind program would also apply against modern biological evolution theory:

> To my way of thinking, there still is something mysterious about evolution, with its apparent "groping" towards some future purpose. Things at least *seem* to organize themselves somewhat better than they "ought" to, just on the basis of blind-chance evolution and natural selection. It may well be that such appearances are quite deceptive.[19]

Indeed, appearances are quite deceptive. The algorithms of the human mind and of human DNA are both created by "blind-chance evolution and natural selection." The development of random algorithms like "genetic algorithms" demonstrate just how deceptive appearances can be. Genetic algorithms are computer programs to find solutions by just the mechanism Penrose finds "very difficult to accept." And on the average, such algorithms find solutions more rapidly than standard deterministic algorithms.

Over the past ten years, scholars in a wide variety of disciplines have come to realize that randomness plays a much larger role in change than previously thought. The paleontologist David Raup[20] has presented convincing evidence that most species extinctions were due to unpredictable events like the impact of giant meteors with the Earth (now the favored mechanism to explain the disappearance of the dinosaurs some 70 million years ago). The evolutionist John Maynard Smith has argued for even more randomness in evolution than Raup:

> If one was able to replay the whole evolution of animals, starting at the bottom of the Cambrian (and, to satisfy Laplace, moving one of the individual animals two feet to its left), there is no guarantee—indeed, no likelihood—that the result would be the same. There might be no conquest of the land, no emergence of mammals, certainly no human beings.[21]

The economist Paul Krugman[22] revolutionized international trade theory in the 1980s by establishing that a country may come to be the dominant producer of certain goods by having the sheer luck of being the first to produce them. For example, there is no good reason for supposing that Seattle in the United States is the best place on Earth for producing large commercial aircraft, yet most such aircraft are currently being manufactured there. The most likely reason Seattle is the location of the main producer is that, since the R&D costs for manufacturing such machines is so enormous, there are likely to be only one or two producers worldwide, and Seattle is where the main producer just happens to be. The logic of technology and economics requires the manufacture of large aircraft to be concentrated *somewhere*, and Seattle just happens to be that somewhere. In short, I think that Penrose drastically underestimates the importance of randomness in evolution and in human creativity.

But my main argument against Penrose's anti-AI claim is the Bekenstein Bound, according to which there is an upper bound to the number of distinct quantum states that can be in a region of finite size and energy and an upper bound to the rate at which a change of state can occur. The Bekenstein Bounds will be discussed in more detail in Chapter IX and in the Appendix for Scientists, so I shall just summarize them now. According to quantum mechanics, any physical system is *exhaustively* described by its quantum state. That is, a system *is* its quantum state. The physicist Jacob Bekenstein showed that quantum systems—and according to physics, everything in sight is a quantum system—have only a finite number of states. In particular, a human being can be in one of $10^{10^{45}}$ states at most, and can undergo at most 4×10^{53} changes of state per second. These numbers are of course enormous, and as a matter of fact I'm sure the actual numbers of states and changes are much less than these upper bounds. But these bounds are nevertheless finite, and firmly based on the central laws of quantum mechanics. They thus prove that a human being is a finite state machine, and *nothing but* a finite state machine. Penrose, being a very good physicist, naturally accepts[23] the validity of the Bekenstein Bounds. But together they refute his claim that a human being cannot be a machine.

Penrose, needless to say, disagrees. The reader of this book will rightly infer that I have an immense regard for Roger Penrose. He created the field of global general relativity which is my main area of research. Indeed, the basic idea of the Omega Point is built on Penrose's concept of "c-boundary," as I shall discuss in Chapter IV.

Roger first told me of his disbelief in 1984 while we were having lunch together at an astrophysics conference in Jerusalem. At another astrophysics conference, this time in Berkeley, California, in 1992, I had a fierce debate with Roger over Strong AI—again over lunch, but P. C. W. Davies joined us to moderate. (Paul is essentially neutral on Strong AI, but leans toward Roger's skepticism. Strong AI is a bit too "reductionist" for Paul.)

In our debate, Roger granted the validity of the Bekenstein Bounds, but argued that Gödel's Theorem rules out determinism, and that the number of possible states for humans allowed by the Bekenstein Bound is too enormous for a purely random evolution between states to be able to explain progress in mathematics. Therefore, Roger contended, there must be something governing the jumps between quantum states besides quantum mechanics, and hence we are not finite state machines.

I grant both of Roger's arguments, but I don't accept his conclusion. It still seems to me that the judicious mixture of chance and necessity postulated by modern evolutionary theory to explain the creation of human beings is sufficient to explain also the evolution of mathematics. It means of course that the evolutionary history of mathematics is no more inevitable than the evolution of *Homo sapiens*. In the Omega Point Theory, progress is inevitable, but the precise history of this progress is not. There can even be retrograde periods. Even if there were a mechanism unknown to physics causing jumps between quantum states, as postulated by Penrose, the two Bekenstein Bounds still imply that we are finite state machines.

Computer theory distinguishes two radically different types of machines: finite state machines and infinite state machines. Since this distinction is absolutely essential to the theses of this book—the fact that we are finite state machines is crucial to the proof that one day an infinite state machine will resurrect us—I must describe these two types in detail.

A *finite state machine* is finite in two ways. First, the machine has only a finite number of states. Second, in so far as the machine is concerned, time comes in discrete steps. It might be that time actually varies continuously, but a finite state machine cannot see this continuity. Its clock is digital.

The human visual system has long been known to be digital. A movie or VCR film actually consists of a series of discrete snapshots, shot at the constant rate of about 25 pictures per second. When these still snapshots are shown on the movie screen or the television set, the action appears to be continuous. It's not. The VCR, the movie projector, and your mind are finite state machines. For all finite state machines, time comes in whole numbers: $t = 1, 2, 3, \ldots$.

A finite state machine is thus defined by giving its internal state $S(t)$ at time t, and by giving how it will respond to any external stimulus. Since the machine is finite, there are only a finite number of possibilities for $S(t)$, no matter what the time: $(s_1, s_2, s_3, \ldots s_n)$ are the only possibilities. At any time t, $S(t)$ must be one of these n possibilities.

The response output $R(t+1)$ the finite state machine will make at time $t+1$—remember, this is the immediate time instant after time t— can depend[24] only on the external input $I(t)$ at time t, and the internal state $S(t)$ of the machine at time t.

An external input $I(t)$ can cause a change of internal state of the machine. Again, because time comes in discrete intervals, the internal state $S(t+1)$ at time $t+1$ can depend[25] only on the input $I(t)$ at time t and the internal state $S(t)$ at time t.

A finite state machine is completely defined by giving the two transition functions $S(t+1)$ and $R(t+1)$. Each of these functions is defined by only a finite number of input values, so each can be represented by a table with a finite number of entries. For example, let us consider a simple machine with only two states, s_1 and s_2, and suppose that it can accept only two inputs, which we will label with the numbers 0 and 1. Let this machine do nothing but keep track of the parity (the evenness or the oddness) of the number of 1's it has received. The transition tables are

	state $S(t)$	
$S\ (t+1)$	i_1	i_2
input 0	i_1	i_2
$I(t)$ 1	i_2	i_1

	state $S(t)$	
$R\ (t+1)$	i_1	i_2
input 0	0	1
$I(t)$ 1	1	0

These tables show that the state S and the output R remain the same when a 0 is the input, but changes when 1 is the input. So an even number of 1's will cause no net change of state. This is a very boring machine, but all finite state machines are, broadly speaking, similar; they differ only in having longer transition tables. Since a human brain can store 10^{15} bits, and as will be discussed in Chapter IX, this means the number of possible distinct brain states is $10^{10^{15}}$, so even though a human being is a finite state machine, its transition table for the function $S(t)$ alone contains $10^{10^{15}}$ entries.

Now that we have a precise definition of a finite state machine, it is clear that we are still finite state machines even if Penrose's mysterious quantum jumping force were real. (As I have indicated, I don't think this force exists.) For the effect of any such force can be described exactly by a suitable choice of what has been called the "external input."

One can prove some very general theorems about the limits of finite state machines. One such theorem[26] is: *any finite state machine, in the absence of an external stimulus, will eventually enter a state after which it will repeat endlessly a perfectly periodic sequence of states.* To prove this theorem is simple. Since the machine has only a finite number of states, it will after a finite number of time steps return to a state it has been in previously. But since there is no external stimulus to distinguish the return from the first time it was in this state, it will go to the state it went to from the first time it was in this state, and so on. This is the first example of what I shall call *Eternal Return Theorems.* An Eternal Return Theorem says that a physical system must return to a previous state, and return again, and again, and again . . . Even with an external stimulus, we see that a finite state machine, if run forever, must return eternally. But if the external stimulus is not itself periodic, then the sequence of states which a finite state machine executes won't be periodic either. But it will eventually return to its previous states. A finite state machine, ultimately, is a boring machine. Infinite machines are fundamentally more interesting.

A *Turing machine* is the prototype of all infinite state machines. It is a finite state machine (called the *head*) which is connected to an *infinite* paper tape. (Here "infinite" means "unlimited" or "potentially infinite" rather than "actually infinite.") A Turing machine is shown in Figure II.1. The paper tape is divided up into squares of the same size. The head can do five and only five things. First, it can write one of a fixed and finite number of symbols on the square it is on (two symbols, say 0 and 1, can be shown to be sufficient). Second, it can read what is written on that square. Third, it can remember what it read (there are only a finite number of possibilities it could see on the square). Fourth, it can erase what is on that square (and replace it with another symbol). Fifth, it can move the tape exactly one square to the right or one square to the left. As with finite state machines, time is discrete. Each of the above operations is considered to take one unit of discrete time.

The tape acts as the memory of the Turing machine. Since the

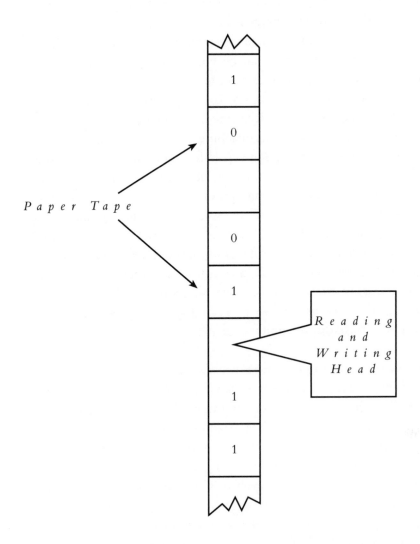

FIGURE II.1: *A Turing Machine, the simplest machine which can compute anything, and which can be made to emulate any other machine. It consists of two parts; (A) a paper* tape *(which is of unlimited length in both directions) and (B) a* head, *which is a finite state machine that does five and only five things: (1) it can write one of a finite number of symbols on each square of the tape; (2) it reads what is written on each square of tape; (3) it can remember what it read; (4) it can erase what is written and print some other symbol; and (5) after doing one or more of the other four things, it moves the tape one square to the left or right.*

tape is infinite, a Turing machine has capabilities far beyond any finite state machine. One of the things it can do is simulate any finite state machine. Since the transition table for any finite state machine is finite, it is clear that these numbers can be coded in the tape of a Turing machine. In addition, these numbers can be coded so that the Turing machine can use them to compute the response of any finite state machine to any stimulus. In a deep sense, the transition table numbers so coded in the tape of a Turing machine *are* the finite state machine. Anything which a real finite state machine with the same transition table does, its numerical counterpart in the Turing machine tape does. The "machine" which exists as numbers in a Turing machine (or other computer) and not as real hardware is called a *virtual machine*. The virtual machine, which has the same transition tables as a real world machine, is a perfect computer simulation of the real world machine. A perfect simulation is called an *emulation*. Most computer simulations are not emulations, of course. Only simple machines have been emulated to date, because the computer memory and speed required to emulate can be enormous. But all finite state machines can be emulated by Turing machines.

Turing machines can emulate other Turing machines. In fact, there is one Turing machine, called the *universal Turing machine,* which can emulate all Turing machines, including itself. We can thus have a hierarchy of machines emulating other machines. Turing machine T_0 may be a real machine, but inside it there is a virtual Turing machine T_1, and inside T_1 there is virtual machine T_2, which in turn codes virtual machine T_3, and so on. These levels of virtual machines inside virtual machines are called *levels of implementation.* The higher-level machines operate completely obliviously of the machines on lower levels. For nothing happens to the higher levels if one or more of the lower-level machines are replaced by other completely different machines—provided, needless to say, that the replacement machines are capable of emulating the higher-level machines at the same speed. As a general rule in computers, machines from various levels do not mix, but this is done to simplify life for human computer programmers rather than something required by the mathematics. If a machine is transferred to a higher level of implementation, it is said to be *uploaded,* and if it is transferred to a lower level of implementation, it is said to be *downloaded.*

There are an infinity of machines which are completely equivalent to the universal Turing machine, and hence can emulate any other machine. Dozens of these machines have been described in the technical computer literature,[27] but here I will mention only two: the billiard ball computer and the Game of Life.

The billiard ball computer[28] is made up of balls which do nothing but collide with each other and bounce off rigid walls, with both the collisions and the bounces being governed by standard Newtonian mechanics. The balls move on an infinite plane with constant velocity except when they encounter a wall or another ball. The whole of the plane upon which the balls move is divided up into squares, and the presence or absence of a ball in a square is considered to be a 1 or 0, respectively. [The division of the plane into squares is] equivalent to the infinite tape of the Turing machine, the balls are equivalent to the symbols which the head writes on the tape, and the collisions and bounces play the same role as the head. A rigorous analysis[29] shows that an appropriate collection of balls and walls can compute anything a Turing machine can compute.

The Game of Life[30] is a simple computer game which was invented by the English mathematician John Conway. As with the billiard ball computer, an infinite plane is divided up into squares. Each square is either blank or contains a single dot. From one unit of discrete time to the next, one of only three things can happen to each square: (1) a dot is added to a blank square; (2) a dot is erased from a square which contained a dot; and (3) a dot which was in a square remains in the square. The rule for determining which of these three possibilities will occur is exceedingly simple: a given square has eight neighboring squares. A dot will be added to the square if exactly three of these eight neighboring squares have dots. If the square already has a dot, it will keep the dot so long as either two or three of its eight neighbors have dots, otherwise the dot will be erased. An example of the behavior of a particular collection of dots—called a "glider"—evolving through five time steps under these rules is given below. The "glider" changes its shape over time, but in the fifth time step it has the same shape as it did in the first time step, and the entire glider has moved so that its tip occupies the square with the O by the fifth time step.

	★																						
		★			★		★				★				★					★			
★	★	★				★	★		★		★				★	★				★			
			O		★		O		★	★	O		★	★	O			★	★	★			
1				2				3				4				5							

By making structures like the glider in the Game of Life, one can simulate and emulate any machine that a universal Turing machine can emulate, and conversely.[31] After some sixty years of looking, no one has ever been able to think of a machine which can compute something that a universal Turing machine cannot. This strongly suggests that no such machine exists.

The hypothesis that no such machine exists or, to phrase it another way, the hypothesis that a universal Turing machine (or its equivalent) can emulate any machine is called the *Church-Turing Thesis*. The Halting Theorem discussed above applies to the universal Turing machine, so no machine whatsoever can solve the Halting Problem.

The fact that many machines are universal has misled John Searle, a University of California philosopher, into constructing a widely discussed argument[32] against Strong AI, the Chinese Room Experiment. Let us imagine, says Searle, that I am in a room full of books which collectively code a computer program capable of passing the Turing Test—in the Chinese language. We know that the running of any program is equivalent to opening a book, reading what is written, erasing some of what is written, remembering some of what is written, and going from one book to another. (This procedure is yet another universal machine.) Suppose that someone passes under the door a piece of paper with Chinese writing on it. Now I (Searle) know no Chinese, so to me the writing is just meaningless scratch marks on paper. However, if we are to believe the strong AI proponents, then simply by following the instructions in the books (and modifying the books appropriately) I can make marks on another piece of paper—meaningless marks to me—which will be correctly recognized as coherent Chinese by Chinese-speaking humans outside the door. In fact, by passing such papers back and forth under the door, a conversation will be conducted, and the Chinese-speaking humans outside will believe that there is a Chinese speaker inside the room. Therefore, says Searle, I have passed the Chinese-Speaking Turing Test. If the Turing Test were a valid test of intelligence, we would have to conclude that I understand Chinese. But I have already said that I do not understand Chinese. Hence the Turing Test is fundamentally flawed and, furthermore, we see that "understanding" is not a property of computer simulations: no computer, no matter how complicated, can think.

I think it is Searle's basic premise, not the Turing Test, that is fundamentally flawed. A human being could no more hand-simulate a program that could pass the Turing Test than she could jump to the Moon. Everyone knows jumping to the Moon is impossible, but it will prove instructive to show, using the laws of physics, just why this is impossible. It is a simple calculation, and it nicely illustrates how physicists are able to rule out processes as physically impossible, even in principle. I shall then use an analogous calculation to show that the hand simulation of a Turing Test–passing program is also physically impossible, thus refuting Searle's argument.

To reach the Moon, it is necessary to have a speed sufficient to escape the Earth's gravitational field. This so-called escape velocity is seven miles per second. To achieve this speed over a single meter distance—in a typical jump, the jumper extends herself one meter, from a crouching to a standing posture—would mean an acceleration of *six million* gravities. This much acceleration would squash a human being flat. Even the astronauts in taking off from Earth experience only about six gravities. Most people black out if the acceleration goes much above ten gravities. (The record for human endurance of "high" acceleration is about twenty gravities.) The energy of motion (kinetic energy) of a 50-kilogram (110-pound) person moving at seven miles a second is 760,000 Calories. Since the average person needs about 2,000 Calories per day (about 100 watts), this energy—expended in a tenth of a second—is the average person's energy expenditure over an entire year. A kilogram of fat has a food energy value of 9,290 Calories per kilogram (protein and carbohydrates about half this[33]), so even if the 50-kilogram jumper's *entire body* were used as food for the jump, there would only be at most 460,000 Calories available. A human being cannot jump to the Moon. But of course this is obvious to everyone without a calculation.

It is less obvious that it is equally impossible to hand-simulate a computer program of sufficient complexity to pass the Turing Test. The reason it is not obvious is that, although practically everyone has experience with jumping, very few have actually tried to hand-simulate a program. If my earlier estimate that the human brain can code as much as 10^{15} bits is correct, then since an average book codes about 10^6 bits (this book has a little under 10^7 bits) it would require more than 100 million books to code the human brain. It would take at least thirty five-story main university libraries to hold this many books. We know from experience that we can access any memory in our brain in about 100 seconds, so a hand simulation of a Turing Test–passing program would require a human to be able to take off the shelf, glance through, and return to the shelf all of these 100 million books in 100 seconds. If each book weighs about a pound ($^1/_2$ kilogram), and on the average the book moves one yard (one meter) in the process of taking it off the shelf and returning it, then in 100 seconds the energy consumed in just moving the books is 3×10^{19} joules; the rate of energy consumption is 3×10^{11} megawatts. Since a human uses energy at a normal rate of 100 watts, the power required is the bodily power of 3×10^{15} human beings, about a million times the current population of the entire Earth. A typical large nuclear power plant has a power output of 1,000 megawatts, so a hand simulation of the human program requires a power output equal to that of 300 million large nuclear power plants. As I said, a man can no more hand-simulate a Turing Test–passing program than he can jump to the Moon. In fact, it is far more difficult. Penrose[34] has suggested that perhaps one does not need the full capacity of the human brain in order to simulate "the occurrence of a single mental event." We now know that a substantial fraction of the entire brain is truly required, because dynamic brain scans of a thinking human being show that at least 1%, and probably more, of the brain is activated during "a single mental event." (Recall that in my estimate of the brain's computation rate I assumed that only 1% to 10% of the brain was active at any particular time.) The dynamic brain scans are done with a fast M.R.I. (Magnetic Resonance Imaging) machine, which can distinguish between oxygenated and deoxygenated blood on scales of one square millimeter in the surface of the brain. Active nerve cells use oxygen at a faster rate than inactive ones, and so the draining of oxygen in a region indicates the presence of activity in that region. Since these scans do not detect electrical activity directly, they just give a lower bound to the size of the region which is activated. As the number of items imagined by the person increases, so does the percentage of the brain activated in total. It is clear from this brain scan work that passing the Turing Test would require most of the brain.

The calculation I just gave assumes sequential computation, which is what we would have if a single human being were doing the hand simulation. But the first computer to have the necessary computing power to run a Turing Test–passing program will undoubtedly be a parallel machine. A sequential machine does only one step at a time, while a parallel machine does many steps at a time, in parallel. In this vein, Searle has proposed using the entire population of India (800 million people) to hand-simulate the program. Now this is more feasible, but it would require the entire human race to come close to equalling the power of the 10 billion neurons which make up the human brain. However, such a modification destroys Searle's argument, because it is obvious to everyone that the entire human species can "know" things which no individual human knows. For example, no individual human being has sufficient knowledge to make an automobile. Making an automobile does not mean merely assembling the parts. It also means making the parts, and mining and refining the metals required to make the parts. And it means knowing in detail how to do this, not just knowing in rough outline. No individual human has this knowledge, yet the human race collectively does. So it is perfectly reasonable that the human race (or the population of India) collectively *could* speak Chinese, even though no one individual human doing the hand simulation does. An analogue of this occurs in the brain: no individual neuron can think, but the integrated collection of neurons in the brain certainly does. Furthermore, a 10-teraflop computer, be it sequential or parallel, can search a memory of 10^{15} bits in 100 seconds, and do it with power of less than a kilowatt. So it is perfectly reasonable to think a 10-teraflop machine can run a Turing Test–passing program.

Searle has also suggested that the energy required can be reduced by internalizing the Turing Test–passing program. That is, the human in the Chinese room "memorizes the rules in the ledger and the data banks of Chinese symbols, and he does all the calculations in his head." Memorize the entire contents of 100 million books? Impossible! Besides the sheer number of books, remember that the contents of each book consist entirely of tables of numbers. Even a human with a photographic memory would require at least an hour per book, and since there are a little less than 10,000 hours per year, memorizing the entire collection would require 10,000 years, assuming no time off to eat and sleep. Once again, it cannot be done. Searle's Chinese Room Experiment requires us to imagine a logical contradiction: a normal human being doing what a normal human being cannot do.

Searle's central point in the Chinese Room Experiment is "A computer has a syntax, but no semantics."[35] That is, all the program does is manipulate symbols according to certain formal rules (syntax). It has no *understanding* of what the symbols *mean* (semantics). True enough, symbol manipulation per se gives no understanding. However, when a program is written, it is designed for an environment in which a certain series of symbols will result in the hardware doing certain things. For example, "5546" might result in valve number 46 being opened if the computer program is in control of an oil refinery. Thus the symbol "5546" *means* "Open valve number 46." In a different environment—if the oil refinery program were run on my desktop computer for example—nothing would happen if %%$^ appeared. The string of symbols %%$^ is *meaningless* in the environment of my desktop computer. ("Where did %%$^ come from?" you probably asked. "We were talking about 5546!" So we were. %%$^ is what you get if you type 5546 while depressing the shift key on the keyboard. A slight change of environment turns a meaningful sequence of symbols into a meaningless one.) In summary, the meaning in the symbols comes from how the symbols in the program are connected through the computer hardware to the environment, not from the manipulation of the symbols themselves. A computer program being run on a computer coupled to an oil refinery doesn't merely simulate controlling an oil refinery, it really does control the oil refinery.

If a Turing Test–passing program were being run on a 10-teraflop computer in the Chinese room, and the papers the computer read and printed were meaningful exchanges in Chinese, then we can conclude that the program had been run *previously* in an environment that allowed it to interact with humans and learn what the words in at least one human language *mean*. An intelligent program would have to learn what various words mean just as children learn what words mean. I have two daughters—in 1993 their ages are four and seven—and I have watched them learn to speak. Their first use of a word was often inappropriate, but as they interacted with people and with the world, hearing others speak and noting the context, their word use slowly became more accurate, and their vocabularies grew. My children have learned, and are still learning, the referents of words in the real world; they are learning what the sounds they make *mean*. So it would be with a Turing Test–passing program. The aim of the Strong AI program is to make a computer program which, if it is run on computer hardware that will enable it to interact with the world, will be able to bootstrap itself into intelligence. That is what my children have done: they have created themselves, and I have watched them do it. Before the age of one, neither of my children could have passed the Turing Test. Now both can pass it with ease.

So the evidence is overwhelming that in about thirty-odd years we should be able to make a machine which is as intelligent as a human being, or more so. Should this be permitted? I am arguing that to prevent men and women who are capable of creating an intelligent robot from doing so is shortsighted, a product of fear and ignorance, not rational deliberation. We ourselves are "intelligent machines." Indeed, there is a powerful practical argument for creating intelligent machines. *Such machines will enhance our well-being, even if they are our superiors in every way.* One of the most solidly founded theorems of economics is the Theory of Comparative Advantage, which justifies free trade. It says that, if two individuals, nations, or races differ in their relative efficiencies for producing goods, it will benefit both to engage in trade, even if one can do everything better than the other. This applies to the human—intelligent-robot interaction as well as to trade between nations. Of course, it would not be wise for humans to try to enslave intelligent machines, or to murder them. In the original Frankenstein novel by Mary Shelley, the "monster" was more intelligent than any human being, and was innately friendly and good. It began to attack humans only after they attacked him first.

But the fundamental reason for allowing the creation of intelligent machines is that, without their help, the human race is doomed. With their help we can and will survive forever. To see this, let us first see how they could help us colonize space.

How to Build an Interstellar Robot Probe

In the colonization of space, it is wise to adopt a strategy which maximizes the probable rate of star systems colonized and minimizes the cost subject to the constraints imposed by the level of technology. Costs can be minimized in two ways: first, "off-the-shelf" technology should be used as far as possible to reduce the research and development costs; second, resources which could be used for no other purpose should be utilized as far as possible. The resources available in uninhabited stellar systems cannot be utilized for any human purpose (or the purpose of any other living being) unless a space vehicle is first sent; indeed from the economics point of view, materials which cannot be used at all are valueless by definition. Therefore, any optimal colonization strategy must utilize the material available in other stellar systems as far as possible. With present-day technology, such utilization cannot be very extensive, but with the level of computer technology assumed in the previous section, these otherwise useless resources can be made to pay for virtually the entire cost of the exploration program.

What one needs is a self-reproducing universal constructor: a machine capable of making any device, given the construction materials and a construction program.[36] By definition, it is capable of making a copy of itself. A universal constructor is analogous to the universal computer discussed in the previous section: a universal computer can compute anything that can be computed, and a universal constructor can construct anything that can be constructed. Turing showed how to build a universal computer, and Von Neumann[37] has outlined how to build a universal constructor. A special NASA study[38] in 1980 estimated that robot universal constructors could be built within twenty years if funds were provided for the project. In fact, like universal computers, all sorts of machines are universal constructors: a human being is just such a universal constructor specialized to perform on the surface of the Earth. Thus, a manned interstellar colonization program will be just a special case of a colonization strategy to be carried out by universal constructors.

The payload of a probe to another stellar system would be a self-reproducing universal constructor with human-level intelligence—I have elsewhere[39] termed such a probe a *von Neumann probe*—together with an engine for slowing down once the other stellar system is reached, and an engine for traveling from place to place within the target stellar system—the latter could be an electric propulsion system,[40] or a solar sail.[41] The von Neumann probe would be instructed to search out construction material with which to make several copies of itself and the original probe propulsion system. Judging from observations of our own solar system, what observations we have of other solar systems, and most contemporary solar system formation theories, such materials should be readily available in virtually any stellar system in the form of meteors, asteroids, comets, and other debris left over from the formation of the stellar system. Recent observations of huge amounts of dust around the star Vega and other stars indicate that such materials are indeed present around many, if not all, stars. Whatever elements are necessary to reproduce the von Neumann probe, they should be available from some source in a stellar system. For instance, the material in the asteroids is highly differentiated; many asteroids are largely nickel-iron, while others contain large amounts of hydrocarbons.

As copies of the original von Neumann probe are made, they would be launched toward stars near the original target star. For example, we will probably send the original von Neumann probe to Proxima Centauri. The copies could be launched toward Alpha Centauri (the star nearest Proxima Centauri; sometimes Proxima Centauri is considered an outlying member of the Alpha Centauri system) and/or at Sirius, Epsilon Eridani, Tau Ceti, and Procyon. When these new probes reached those stars, the process would be repeated, and repeated again, until the probes had covered all the stars in the entire Galaxy. The exponential growth of the von Neumann probe expansion is shown in Figure II.2.

Once a sufficient number of copies had been constructed, the von Neumann probe could be programmed to explore the stellar system in which it found itself, and relay the acquired information back to Earth. It could also be programmed to use the resources in the stellar system to conduct scientific research which would be too expensive or too dangerous to conduct in our own solar system.

The von Neumann probe would then colonize the target stellar system with human beings and other terrestrial life. Even if there were no planets in the target stellar system—the target could be a binary star system containing only asteroid-like debris (the Alpha Centauri system may be of this type)—the von Neumann probe could be programmed to turn some of the available material into an *O'Neill colony*,[42] a self-sustaining human colony in space which is not located on a planet but is rather a space station. Inhabitants for the colony could be synthesized by the von Neumann probe. All the information needed to manufacture a human being or any other terrestrial life form is contained in the genes of a single cell of the life form. Thus, once we possess the knowledge to synthesize a single cell—some biologists have claimed the human race could develop such knowledge within thirty years; the Human Genome Project is a major step in this direction—then we would be able to program a von Neumann probe to synthesize a fertilized egg cell of any terrestrial species. For the seeds of plants or the eggs of birds the synthesis of a single egg cell would be sufficient to give adults of these forms of life in a short time. For humans, the fertilized eggs would have to be placed in an artificial womb—such technology is currently in the beginning stages of development—in which case the target solar system would have human beings in that system within nine months after the fertilized human eggs were placed in the artificial womb. These children could be raised to adulthood by

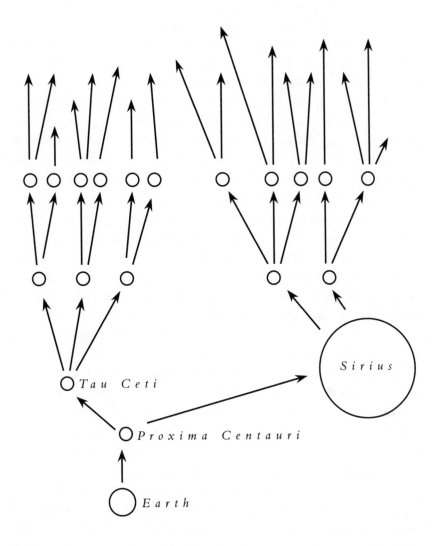

FIGURE II.2: *The exploration of the universe using a von Neumann probe, a self-reproducing space-craft. A single probe is launched from Earth, which travels to the nearest star system (Proxima Centauri). Using the material available in the star system, the probe creates two copies of itself, which are sent to Tau Ceti and Sirius. The probes sent to the Tau Ceti and Sirius stellar systems in turn make copies of themselves, which are sent to still other star systems. This process repeats until all the star systems in the galaxy (ultimately the entire universe) has a probe resident in it. The entire Galaxy has been explored for the cost of a single probe.*

robot nannies, after which the adult humans could have further children by the traditional method.

Hence the problem of interstellar travel has been reduced to the problem of transporting a self-reproducing universal constructor to another stellar system. This can be accomplished by present-day rocket technology. A number of rocket experts[43] pointed out in the 1960s that, by using a Jupiter swing-by to approach the Sun and then adding a velocity boost at closest approach to the Sun, a solar system escape velocity of about 90 km/sec (about $3 \times 10^{-4}c$ is possible with present-day chemical rockets ("c" is the letter scientists use to denote the speed of light: $c = 3 \times 10^5$ km/sec = 186,000 miles per second). The Voyager spacecraft that passed by Neptune a few years ago now has a solar escape velocity of about $0.6 \times 10^{-4}c$. At these velocities, the transit time to the nearest stars is between 10^4 and 10^5 years.

Robot space probes with very small mass are now recognized as the standard, making them much cheaper relative to their capabilities than was the case with the Voyager. The Pluto Fast Flyby Mission,[44] currently scheduled for launch in February 1999, is based on a spacecraft with a mass of 110 kilograms (220 pounds). This spacecraft, costing about $400 million, will take seven years to reach Pluto, compared with the twelve years which the Voyager probe took to reach Neptune. After completing its pass by Pluto, the probe will have a solar system escape velocity of about 20 kilometers per second (about $0.6 \times 10^{-4}c$), which means it will cover a distance of five light-years—the average distance between stars in the neighborhood of our solar system—in 80,000 years. The nearest star, Proxima Centauri, is 4.3 light-years away. Proxima Centauri is part of a triple star system (three stars bound together by their mutual gravity), and so it is unlikely to have Earthlike planets, though the star system probably has debris in the form of asteroids left over from its formation. The two nearest single stars which have a power output like our Sun are Tau Ceti (11.3 light-years away) and Epsilon Eridani (10.7 light-years away). The Pluto probe, were it aimed at Proxima Centauri, would take 70,000 years to reach it. So, if we could make instrumentation that could last several tens of thousands of years, and if we were very, *very* patient, we could even today launch an interstellar probe.

But with modern computer technology we can do much better.

The trick is to make the instrumentation *very* small, using nanotechnology[45] to make every single atom in the payload useful. *(Nanotechnology* means technology on the scale of individual atoms, which are roughly a nanometer in size. We know such technology is feasible, and in fact several hundred million dollars are currently being spent by private companies to develop this technology.) Let's assume a payload mass of 100 grams—I'll show in a moment that this is actually a gigantic payload mass if every payload atom is utilized. But a 100-gram payload is tiny from the point of view of space propulsion systems. Such a small payload mass makes it easy to design an affordable interstellar probe that travels at 90% of the universal speed limit, the speed of light. At this speed, the probe would cover the distance to Proxima Centauri in only five years, and the distance to Tau Ceti or Epsilon Eridani in about twelve years. Since radio signals travel at the speed of light, we could receive information about Proxima Centauri in only nine years after launch, less time than we had to wait for information about Neptune from Voyager. With a speed of 0.9c, interstellar probes become plausible.

The problem with using rockets to accelerate a spacecraft to extremely high speeds is that the rocket fuel must also be accelerated. Thus, with rockets, almost all the mass of the spacecraft must be rocket fuel. The solution is clear: the engine propelling the spacecraft must not be part of the spacecraft. It is known that light itself exerts pressure, and so a spacecraft consisting mainly of a giant sail can be propelled by the light reflected from it. In fact, NASA had originally planned to send out just such a probe to the comet Halley during its closest approach to the Sun in 1986, but the mission was canceled because the money was needed to cover cost overruns on the space shuttle. In the proposed Comet Halley Mission, the Sun would have been the light source. The Sun, however, provides insufficient energy to accelerate a sail to 0.9c, so for interstellar probes an extremely powerful stationary laser would provide the light.

The problem with using a laser to accelerate an interstellar probe is slowing the probe down once the target star is reached. The American physicist Robert Forward[46] has solved this problem. He has suggested that the sail reflecting the light of the laser be in two parts which separate when the star is reached. One part then reflects the laser light *back* onto the other (which contains the payload), slowing it down. One can modify Forward's detailed proposal to obtain the following numbers for an interstellar probe. I shall assume a payload mass of 100 grams, and a total mass, including both sections of sail, of 1 kilogram. The total unit would be a sail in the form of a hexagon 8 kilometers across, and the central part of this hexagon would be another hexagon 3 kilometers across. This central hexagon would be the part containing the payload. The outer part of the hexagon would be the part that decelerates the smaller hexagon at the target star.

Using a 250-gigawatt (250 million kilowatts) laser to accelerate the probe would give an acceleration averaging eight gravities, bringing the probe up to 0.9c in about one and a half months. Detailed engineering plans for a 10-gigawatt laser exist—such lasers were worked on in the 1980s as part of President Reagan's Strategic Defense Initiative —so a 250-gigawatt laser should be technically feasible. One would need a huge Fresnel lens one billion kilometers in diameter to focus the light on a spot smaller than the size of the larger hexagon at 4.3 light-years, the distance of Proxima Centauri. Although the lens is enormous in size (larger than the diameter of the Sun) it would consist of a fine mesh in orbit around the Sun, and thus the entire lens would have a total mass of only 2 trillion tons, about the size of a small asteroid. (The Doppler shift at 0.9c is about 4, so deceleration at the target star will be slightly less than eight gravities unless a more powerful laser is used.) To power such a laser would require a solar collection area about 40 kilometers square; clearly the laser and its power source would have to be in orbit around the Sun just like the lens.

Since the entire probe would have to be constructed in space, by a well-developed space manufacturing base, it is difficult to be precise about the cost of the probe. However, the cost of the probes will be roughly equal to the cost of construction material alone, since von Neumann probes can make themselves—they are universal constructors, after all—and the original research and development costs would be small because intelligent self-reproducing machines would have been originally developed for other purposes.[47] We know that a 1-gigawatt nuclear power plant costs (in 1993 dollars) about $1 billion U.S. The lens needs to be made of metal, but large iron-nickel asteroids of the necessary size exist. Let us guess that such an asteroid would cost $10 billion. If the cost of the entire probe is approximated by the cost of this asteroid and the present-day cost of sufficient nuclear power plants to power the laser, then the cost of a 0.9c interstellar probe would be $260 billion, about five times the cost of the Apollo program, and about one half the estimated cost of the proposed manned mission to Mars. Thus the cost of an interstellar probe with an acceptable mission duration is reasonable when compared with standard present-day interplanetary missions.

This is true provided that the payload of a von Neumann probe can be only 100 grams. As I said above, such a tiny payload mass would require that every atom in the payload be utilized. Drexler has done a detailed study[48] of how nanotechnology can be used to enable a machine to use every atom. He concludes that machines capable of universal construction are feasible using less than a few billion atoms— these are molecular-sized universal constructors. Furthermore, it is possible in principle[49] to store about 1 bit per atom in an extended array. Physicists[50] at NEC in Japan have already discovered how to code 1 bit per 20 atoms. Now 100 grams of matter contains about 10^{24} atoms if the material is an element lighter than iron, so it should be possible to store about 10^{24} bits of information in such a probe, and equip it with sufficient devices to make it capable of self-reproduction using the materials available in the target star. To get an idea of what can be coded with 10^{24} bits of information, recall that in the previous section I showed that a human-level intelligent being can probably be simulated with 10^{15} bits. Assuming that a simulation of the biosupport system for this being will require 100,000 times more memory, a simulation of a human with a biosupport system would require 10^{20} bits. Thus this 100-gram probe could carry a simulation of a complete city of 10,000 people! (Another essential feat performed by the universal constructors in the payload is reconfiguring the sail during the transit to reduce the cross-sectional area of the probe. At speeds of 0.9c, the effect of a collision with a dust mote could be serious. Even collisions with the gas molecules in the interstellar medium would wear down the sail at this speed.[51])

In earlier discussions of interstellar travel, one of the primary reasons for speeds near the speed of light is to make use of what is called "relativistic time dilation," namely the fact that time slows down for objects moving near the speed of light. For a spacecraft moving at 0.9c, time would pass at a little less than half the rate it would pass for someone staying behind on Earth. If such a spacecraft traveled to Proxima Centauri and returned to Earth at this speed, 9.6 years would have passed on Earth, but only 4.2 years according to the people on the spacecraft. This motivation for speeds near the speed of light disappears when people are traveling as emulations rather than at the current lowest level of implementation: the simulation can be carried out at any speed one pleases relative to universal time. The simulation could be run much slower than life proceeds on Earth, so that, to the people being emulated on the spacecraft, the trip would take only a few hours or days.

In these days of government budget deficits, $250 billion may seem an impossible sum to raise. However, the costs of materials relative to wages has been dropping exponentially with a time constant of fifty years for the past hundred and fifty years. This means that the average person is about twenty times wealthier than the average person of a hundred and fifty years ago. If this trend continues for the next four hundred years, the $250 billion probe would appear as expensive to people in that era as an $80 million probe does to us today. There are several hundred people in the world today whose net worth is greater than $80 million, so I conclude that an interstellar probe will definitely be launched within a few centuries.

It is also highly likely that the estimated costs will come down. When I first began researching interstellar travel in the late 1970s, the most detailed interstellar travel proposal was the 1978 Project Daedalus study of the British Interplanetary Society. A von Neumann probe using the Daedalus engine (a nuclear pulse rocket, which moves by tossing nuclear bombs behind it and setting them off) would travel between the stars at just 0.16c, and would cost $200 *trillion,* based on the fuel cost alone. A von Neumann probe using the Forward laser sail mechanism and nanotechnology to reduce payload mass would travel six times faster and cost a thousand times less. Nanotechnology and laser sail propulsion are new ideas from the 1980s. The 1990s should bring more ideas for bringing down the price.

A new rocket propulsion idea from the 1980s, combined with nanotechnology, might be sufficiently cheap. The key to rocket propulsion is getting a lot of energy to the exhaust gas. Now the greatest source of energy available is mass, as everybody knows from Einstein's famous formula $E = mc^2$. Chemical reactions are grossly inefficient: the energy released by exploding one megaton of TNT is equivalent to only about 50 grams of mass. Even nuclear reactions convert less than 1% of the original mass into energy. In matter-antimatter annihilation reactions, however, *all* of the mass is converted into energy. Thus, the ultimate rocket will use matter-antimatter annihilation as the energy source.

Antimatter is still a bit exotic, so a brief review of its properties is in order. It is a law of physics that all material comes in two forms: particles and antiparticles. An antiparticle is just like its corresponding particle, except that it has an electric charge of the opposite sign. For example, the electron has a negative charge, and thus its antiparticle, the positron, has a positive charge but otherwise is just like the electron. The proton has a positive charge, and so the antiproton has a negative charge. Just as a proton combines with an electron to give one atom of electrically neutral hydrogen, an antiproton can combine with a positron to give one antiatom of electrically neutral antihydrogen. In principle, antiatoms of any type can be made, although only antihelium has actually been made to date in the laboratory. With more effort we could make anticarbon, antiiron, and so forth.

Antimatter is difficult to store because if a particle comes into contact with its antiparticle the two immediately annihilate in a burst of radiation. If an antihydrogen were released into air, the positrons would be electrically attracted to the electrons in the air atoms, and the electrons and positrons would annihilate. The antiprotons would be electrically attracted to the protons in the air atoms, and annihilate. Nevertheless, we now know how to manufacture and store large amounts of antimatter. Many billions of antiprotons have been manufactured at the CERN laboratory in Geneva, Switzerland, and have been stored for months at a time in ion traps. Antiprotons can now be purchased commercially; the current price is about one dollar per billion.[52] Detailed plans[53] have been made for factories that can produce milligrams of antihydrogen per year, with a cost as low as $1 million per milligram[54] once large-scale production gets under way.

Forward[55] has proposed using ordinary hydrogen as the rocket exhaust gas, while heating this hydrogen by adding a tiny amount of antihydrogen. Such a rocket with a payload of 100 grams would require only 1.6 kilograms of liquid hydrogen for the exhaust and 3.6 milligrams of antihydrogen for the energy source, assuming that the rocket accelerated to 0.1c, coasted at this speed to the target stellar system, and then decelerated to zero speed at the target stellar system. Assuming as before that the cost of the probe would be essentially the cost of the construction materials, the cost of the probe would be only about $4 million, almost all of it for the antihydrogen. At this price, there are at least a million people now living on the Earth who could afford to pay it. And the buyer could hold her interstellar von Neumann probe in the palm of her hand! Fairly detailed theoretical studies of the Forward antimatter rocket now exist, and several laboratories have announced that they are ready to begin experiments which will lead to the manufacture of the engine. We could launch a 0.1c interstellar probe by the end of the decade if we had the necessary computer technology, namely the molecular-size universal constructor and the atomic-size computers. Given the rate of development of nanotechnology, I would expect that the necessary computer technology will in fact exist by the time we have a computer capable of passing the Turing Test. As I showed in the previous section, this should occur by the year 2030. A von Neumann probe could be launched by the middle of the next century.

A von Neumann probe, once launched, will require only between five to ten years to travel between the stars. The question now is, how long will it take for the probe to make a copy of itself? If we compare a von Neumann probe to the only self-reproducing machines in our current experience, namely human beings, it would require between twenty and thirty years for the machine to reproduce itself. If we compare the von Neumann probe to an entire technical civilization, then about three hundred years is the time required to build up the United States into an industrial nation. Most of this time was required to develop the necessary technical knowledge, not the machines themselves. Possessing the necessary knowledge, Japan and Germany rebuilt their industries in a single decade after World War II, requiring only minor investments from outside. The late physicist Gerard O'Neill[56] estimates that space colonies could be self-sufficient and ready to make more space colonies in less than a century. I will thus make the reasonable assumption that a von Neumann probe would start making copies of itself within fifty years after reaching the target stellar system. If it sent copies of itself to all stars within ten light-years of itself, colonization of the galaxy could proceed at the rate of ten light-years per sixty years, or $1/6$ light-year per year. Since the galaxy is about 100,000 light-years in diameter, it would thus take about 600,000 years to colonize the entire Milky Way Galaxy. Such colonization could begin by the middle of the next century.[57]

A Space Traveling Species Can Ultimately Engulf and Control the Entire Universe

The nearest large galaxy, the Andromeda galaxy, is 2.7 million light years away, so the biosphere can engulf it also in about 3 million years, using only the 0.9c probe described in the previous section. The nearest large cluster of galaxies, the Virgo Cluster, is about 60 million light years away, so the biosphere can engulf it in about 70 million years. In both cases the reproduction time is small compared with the travel time, even at 0.9c, so it can be ignored.

For galaxies farther away than this, it is necessary to take into account the expansion of the universe when computing the average speed of the spacecraft. Hubble's Law says that the farther a galaxy is from Earth, the faster it is moving away from us. Therefore, a spacecraft launched with a given speed relative to the Earth will have a slower speed relative to a distant galaxy when it finally reaches that galaxy. I show in the Appendix for Scientists that the ratio of the spacecraft momentum at the Earth relative to its momentum at the distant galaxy is equal to the ratio of the radius of the universe when the spacecraft reaches the galaxy to the radius of the universe now. I shall show in Chapter IV that the latter ratio is at most about 300,000 when the universe is at its maximum size (this ratio could be as small as 3,000). The upper bound of 300,000 implies that, to expand throughout the universe, arriving at the other side of the universe with speed 0.9c by the time of maximum expansion (a speed of 0.9c means its total energy is equal to about twice its mass), will require giving spacecraft payloads an initial energy equal to 600,000 times their mass. I show in the Appendix for Scientists that such a spacecraft is technically feasible if one uses a matter-antimatter annihilation rocket. With payload of 100 grams, the rocket would have an initial total mass of ten billion tons, half of it antimatter. Such an amount of antimatter will not be cheap. At $1 million a milligram, a billion tons of the stuff would cost $10 trillion trillion, about one billion times the current GNP of the entire world. Sending a probe directly from our Galaxy to the other side of the universe will require the resources of an entire stellar system. But it can be done.

A better strategy would be to send a probe from one galaxy to the next rather than try to go directly to the antipodal point. However, this becomes more and more difficult as the universe expands and the galaxies move farther apart. I show in the Appendix for Scientists that, in a universe which is between 3×10^3 and 3×10^5 times its present size at the time of its maximum expansion, the antipodal point is currently between 1 and 10 teraparsecs away (a teraparsec is 10^{12} parsecs), and the universe will reach maximum expansion between 5×10^{16} and 5×10^{18} years from now (in proper time). The material content of the universe will have changed significantly over this period of time, as shown in the following table.

IMPORTANT EVENTS IN FUTURE HISTORY

EVENT	TIMESCALE (IN YEARS)
Sun expands to engulf the Earth	7×10^9
Galaxies evaporate from clusters of galaxies	10^{11}

Stars cease to form; all massive stars have become either neutron stars or black holes	10^{12}
Longest-lived stars use all their fuel and become white dwarfs	10^{14}
Dead planets are detached from dead stars via stellar collisions	10^{15}
White dwarfs cool to black dwarfs at 5 degrees K	10^{17}
Neutron stars cool to 100 degrees K	10^{19}

This table assumes that life will not interfere with the evolution of matter. In reality, of course, life will. For example, rather than let the Earth be vaporized seven billion years from now, our descendants would have long before taken the entire planet apart in order to use the material to expand the biosphere. (Dyson has shown that taking a planet apart is technically feasible, if you are willing to take a few million years to do it.) Allowing nature to take its course and destroy the Earth will merely allow what is left of the biosphere on Earth to be wiped out to no purpose. If instead the Earth is taken apart, its material can be used to construct O'Neill colonies where life can continue. In fact, more life and a more diverse biosphere would be possible if the Earth is taken apart than would be the case if the Earth were to remain whole, because with a whole Earth life can use only the atmosphere and the first few kilometers of the Earth's crust. If the Earth were taken apart, *all* the Earth's material can provide habitat. The same argument applies of course to the other planets and indeed to the Sun itself. In the very long run, first the entire solar system, then the entire Galaxy, then the entire Virgo Cluster of galaxies, and finally the entire universe of matter will be taken apart and converted into habitat for the expanding biosphere.

Remember that in the very long run life has no choice: it *must* take the natural structures apart if it is to survive. So I conclude that it will.

A light ray sent out from the Earth's location at the beginning of the universe would arrive at the other side of the universe at the time of maximum expansion, so a spacecraft launched in the next few billion years with the above energy would arrive just a little behind the light ray, just after the universe had begun to contract. I conclude that engulfing the entire universe by this time is technically feasible, using technology which we should possess within about fifty years. A computer simulation of the biosphere engulfing the entire universe is pictured in Figure II.3, Figure II.4, and Figure II.5.

The first frame, Figure II.3, shows the universe 10^{16} years from now. The universe is about three thousand times larger than it is now. On this scale, the entire universe at the present time is about the size of the period at the end of this sentence. The universe is represented as a two-dimensional sphere with the Earth located at the North Pole of the sphere. The other side of the universe—the antipodal point—is thus the South Pole. The dark circle on the sphere represents a flash of light which left the Earth in 1993. The light has reached the equator of the sphere. This means the light has been able to cover only half the distance between the Earth and the antipodal point in the 10^{16} years since it left the Earth. The darkened area on the sphere is the biosphere. It has engulfed about a third of the universe.

The second frame, Figure II.4, shows the universe 10^{17} years from now. The universe is still expanding, and it has become larger than in the previous figure. Life has now engulfed about three fourths of the universe. The light which left the Earth 10^{17} years before has still not reached the antipodal point, although it is closer. The expanding biosphere is just slightly behind the light.

The third frame, Figure II.5, shows the universe 10^{18} years from now. The universe is still expanding, and it has become larger than in the previous figure, but it is now very close to its maximum size. Life has now engulfed about 90% of the entire universe. The light which left the Earth 10^{18} years before has almost reached the antipodal point.

The fourth frame, Figure II.6, shows the universe 10^{19} years from now. The universe is past the time of maximum expansion and is now contracting. The universe is now smaller than it was in the previous frame. Life has now engulfed the entire universe. A dark circle is still pictured. As in the previous figures, this circle represents light which

left the Earth in 1993, but now the light has passed through the antipodal point and is on its way back to the Earth.

The next question is, can life gain control of the entire universe
once it has engulfed it? To put it another way, can our descendants run
the universe, or will they just be along for the ride? The answer is, they
can indeed control the future motion of the entire universe. The
mechanism they will use is chaos in the equations governing the universe's dynamics.

There are many definitions of the word "chaos" in physics, but the
crucial one is "chaos means instability." That is, if a small change is
made in the initial conditions of a chaotic system, the future motion

FIGURE II.3: *A frame from a computer simulation of life expanding to engulf the entire universe. This figure shows the universe 10^{16} years from now. The universe is about three thousand times larger than it is now. The universe is represented as a two-dimensional sphere with the Earth located at the North Pole of the sphere. The other side of the universe—the antipodal point—is thus the South Pole. The biosphere—represented in this figure as a darkening of the spherical grid—has engulfed about a third of the universe. A dark circle represents a beam of light sent out from the Earth in 1993. This light has reached the equator of the sphere. This means the light has only been able to cover half the distance between the Earth and the antipodal point in the 10^{16} years since it left the Earth.*

deviates exponentially from the expected evolution. Stable evolution, in contrast, would mean that, if the initial conditions are changed slightly, then the future motion of the system will be fairly close to the future without the change. For an example of stable motion, suppose we move a particle two meters to the left. Then after one second the particle is one meter from where it would have been if it had not been moved; after two seconds, the particle is half a meter from where it would have been if it had not been moved; after three seconds the particle is one fourth meter from where it would have been if it had

FIGURE II.4: *Second frame from the computer simulation of life expanding to engulf the entire universe. It shows the universe 10^{17} years from now. The universe is still expanding, and it has become larger than in the previous figure. The biosphere, expanding at an average velocity of 90% the speed of light, is just behind the light beam which left the Earth in 1993. Life has now engulfed about three fourths of the universe. The light which left the Earth 10^{17} years before has still not reached the antipodal point, although it is closer.*

not been moved; and so on. Thus we see that "stability" means a tendency for the precise values of the initial conditions to be unimportant. The system, so to speak, has made up its mind where it wants to go and is determined to go there no matter what we do to it. We can make such a system go elsewhere, but it would take an enormous amount of energy to do so. To make this particle be one meter to the left after sixty seconds, we would have to move its initial position a hundred light-years to the left.

FIGURE II.5: *Third frame from the computer simulation of life expanding to engulf the entire universe. This frame pictures the universe 10^{18} years from now. The universe is still expanding, and it has become larger than in the previous figure, but it is now very close to its maximum size. Life has now engulfed about 90% of the entire universe. The light which left the Earth 10^{18} years before has almost reached the antipodal point.*

For an example of unstable chaotic motion, suppose when we move the initial position of a particle two meters to the left, and after one second the particle is four meters from where it would have been without the move; after two seconds it is eight meters from where it would have been without the move; after three seconds it is sixteen meters from where it would have been without the move, and so on. The deviation of this chaotic system from its position without the

FIGURE II.6: *Fourth frame from the computer simulation of life expanding to engulf the entire universe. This frame shows the universe 10^{19} years from now. The universe is past the time of maximum expansion and is now contracting. The universe is now smaller than it was in the previous frame. Life has now engulfed the entire universe. A dark circle is still pictured. As in the previous figures, this circle represents light which left the Earth in 1993, but now the light has passed through the antipodal point and is on its way back to the Earth.*

change is 2^t, where t is the time in seconds. It is clear that after a very small time the location of the particle is going to be enormously far from where it otherwise would have been: after sixty seconds this hypothetical particle is about a hundred *light-years* away from where it would have been without the change. (This is obviously a hypothetical example only, because *nothing* can go faster than light.) Making such a chaotic unstable system go where we want it to is very easy and requires very little expenditure of energy. To make this hypothetical particle be one meter to the left after sixty seconds, we would have to move it to the left a tiny fraction of the size of an atom.

On the largest scales, gravity is the most important force, and large systems of particles governed by gravity are almost always chaotic. The best example is our own solar system. The gravitational attraction of the other planets to the Earth makes the location of the Earth in its orbit chaotic. That is, the shape and size of the Earth's orbit does not change very much, but the precise position of the Earth in its orbit is very unstable: it varies as 2^t, just as in the hypothetical example above, except that now t is the time in multiples of 3.5 million years.[58] The implications of this chaos in Earth's orbit can be put dramatically. Suppose a *butterfly* decides to move one meter to go from one flower to another. The effect of this single movement by this single butterfly is to *move the entire Earth from one side of the Sun to the other in 500 million years.*

If a single butterfly[59] can move the Earth from one side of its orbit to the other in 500 million years, then it is not unreasonable that our descendants, once they have engulfed the entire universe, can control the evolution of the entire universe over timescales of 10^{16} years.

Like the butterfly and the Earth, our descendants will not be able to control all aspects of the future motion of the universe. Just as the butterfly cannot change the shape and size of the Earth's orbit, so our descendants cannot change the fact that, once the universe reaches its maximum size and starts to collapse, it will collapse to zero size in about 10^{18} years of proper time. What our descendants can do, however, is change *how* the universe collapses. The universe can collapse faster in some directions than others, and my colleague John Barrow[60] has shown that the rate of collapse of the universe in the various directions *is* chaotic. In particular, life in the far future can easily force the universe to collapse very rapidly in two directions while remaining the same size in the third direction. They can do this, and they *must* do this.

They must force the universe to move in this way because only if the universe does move in this way will life in the far future have sufficient energy to survive. To understand this future source of energy, think about the source of energy used by the biosphere today. This source is the Sun, and the Sun is a possible source of energy only because it happens to be hotter than interstellar space. The biosphere is run because green plants take energy from a hot spot in the sky (the Sun) and dump their waste heat into interstellar space. Actually, the atmosphere dumps it for the plants, but let's not worry about this technicality. The key point is that biological activity is possible on Earth only because energy is taken from a high-temperature source and dumped at a low-temperature sink.

Consider now the collapsing universe. We know that as gas expands it gets cooler, and as it contracts it gets hotter. This is how a refrigerator works. Gas is made to expand in the cooling coils, thus becoming cooler than the air in the refrigerator. Heat thus passes from the air to the colder coil gas. This heated coil gas is then taken outside the refrigerator, where it is compressed, making it hotter, and the heat thus passes to the air outside the refrigerator. In the universe, radiation acts just like the gas in a refrigerator: it cools off as the universe expands, and will get hotter when the universe starts to contract.

If, however, the universe stays the same size in one direction while it contracts in the other two directions, radiation in the latter directions will become hotter than in the stationary direction. This means that the directions of contraction will be hot spots in the sky and the other direction will be a cold spot. This temperature difference in different directions will power life in the far future just as the hot spot in the sky called the Sun powers life on Earth today.

The universe will naturally tend to collapse more rapidly in one direction than another. But almost always this natural tendency will be checked before the temperature difference is large enough for life to get sufficient energy. But if life uses the chaos in the directional collapse rates, detailed calculations (see the Appendix for Scientists) show life *can* get sufficient energy. So, as I said, life *must* force the universe to move in this unlikely way.

Furthermore, life must engulf the entire universe if it is to have the power to force the universe to move in this unlikely way. Think again about the butterfly and the Earth. Although the butterfly *can* move the Earth, it probably won't, because another butterfly on the other side of the Earth can cancel out the motion of the first if it moves in the opposite direction. The chaotic effect will be cumulative only if the butterflies act together, which of course they won't. In the case of the universe, it will move in the right direction only if individual living beings act together everywhere in the cosmos. If life has engulfed the universe, and if the universe is still approximately homogeneous when it reaches maximum expansion, then it is extremely likely that living beings will act in just the right way everywhere over the universe, even though they cannot communicate when they start to act. (Recall that light will be able to go from the Earth to the antipodal point only once before the universal collapse begins, so there will not be time for light to go back before life has to start acting.) The reason that life will probably act coherently is that, if the universe is more or less homogeneous, then the universe will start to collapse at different rates in different directions, but these different directions will be the same everywhere. That is, the hot spots will be in the same direction no matter where in the universe life is. Thus everywhere life will try to enhance the temperature in the same direction, and thus life will automatically act coherently. Life will move the universe.

I shall continue this story of how life will act in the collapsing phase of the universe in Chapter IV, but first let me show what might happen if life fails to act in concert. There are two possible dire fates awaiting life in this case: the Eternal Return and the Heat Death.

III.

PROGRESS AGAINST THE
ETERNAL RETURN AND
THE HEAT DEATH

THE OMEGA POINT THEORY IS BASED ON
the Eternal Life Postulate. In Chapter IV, I shall formally state the
Eternal Life Postulate in the form of three conditions which must hold
if we are to say that life continues forever. It will turn out that these
conditions are basically a claim that *progress* will continue indefinitely,
literally to infinity in all standard measures. I have already shown in
Chapter II that, in order to survive, life must eventually expand beyond
the Earth. This requires progress, specifically the advance of technology. Without progress, the complete and total extermination of all life
is inevitable. Even though this fact has been appreciated (at least by
physicists) since the middle of the nineteenth century, progress has not
always been regarded as inevitable, or even as a good thing. There are
two major philosophical and scientific doctrines which have been opposed to the idea of progress: the *Eternal Return* and the *Heat Death*.

The Eternal Return says that all events in nature repeat themselves
in exact detail again and again. In particular, in the future an exact
copy of you, the reader, will read an exact copy of this book again.
And this will be repeated again, and again, and again, without limit.
There are only a finite number of possibilities, and these will be eternally repeated. Thus there cannot be any continued progress. All measures of progress may advance for a period, but then they will show a

decline, until the universe returns to its original primitive state, and the advance repeats once again.

It was thought until recently that the Eternal Return was a consequence of physics. Both classical Newtonian mechanics and nonrelativistic quantum mechanics indeed have "recurrence theorems" as consequences: that is, it can be proven that "permanently finite" systems obeying the laws of classical and nonrelativistic quantum mechanics must indeed return again and again to a previous state. However, I shall outline in this chapter—and prove rigorously in the Appendix for Scientists—that the laws of *general* relativity and quantum gravity will not permit the entire universe to be "permanently finite." I also shall show in this chapter that the Eternal Return is a very old idea, but nevertheless it has had some extremely negative consequences in the twentieth century.

The Heat Death is an invention of nineteenth-century physics. According to the Second Law of Thermodynamics, a quantity called *entropy*—a physical quantity which is a measure of disorder in a system—always increases or remains the same. It can never decrease. Thus, if the amount of entropy which can be generated in the universe is finite, there must come a time in the future after which no further change is possible. If there were a temperature difference between any two parts of the universe, it would be possible to increase entropy still more, so this final state of maximum entropy would be a state of universal constant temperature. In such a situation, all the energy in the entire universe is in the form of *heat;* there is no more "available" or free energy in existence. Thus all life must cease and never arise again for all future time. Hence, this uniform-temperature, constant-entropy, no-free-energy final state is called the *Heat Death.* This very unappealing universal final state was first predicted by the great German physicist Hermann von Helmholtz[1] in an article first published in 1854.

·———·

The Heat Death of
Nineteenth-Century Physics

The Heat Death, which many nineteenth-century physicists thought was implied by the Second Law of Thermodynamics, appalled the believers in perpetual progress. Charles Darwin originally believed that his theory of evolution by natural selection implied such progress. As he expressed it in the concluding pages of his *Origin of Species:*

> As all the living forms of life are the lineal descendants of those which lived long before the Silurian epoch, we may feel certain that the ordinary succession by generation has never once been broken, and that no cataclysm has desolated the whole world. Hence we may look with some confidence to a secure future of equally inappreciable length. And as natural selection works solely by and for the good of each being, all corporeal and mental endowments will tend to progress towards perfection.[2]

Such a hope for the future is also the conclusion of the Omega Point Theory. Darwin was also correct about the past. We now know that we are the descendants of one-cell organisms that evolved more than 3.5 *billion* years ago, and that life probably evolved only once on Earth (more precisely, it is highly probable that life arose less than ten times).[3]

But Darwin did not believe that it would be *Homo sapiens* who would carry on progress. Rather, he knew that we would eventually be replaced by our more advanced descendants:

> Judging from the past, we may safely infer that not one living species will transmit its unaltered likeness to a distant futurity.[4]

Once again, Darwin was correct: of all the species that have evolved in Earth's history only one species in a thousand still exists.[5]

Unfortunately, as his life drew to a close, Darwin's optimism was severely shaken by the prospect of the Heat Death, which he learned about from disputes with physicists on the age of the Earth. As Darwin recorded in his *Autobiography:*

> [consider] . . . the view now held by most physicists, namely that the sun with all the planets will in time grow too cold for life, unless indeed some great body dashes into the sun and thus gives it fresh life —believing as I do that man in the distant future will be a far more perfect creature than he now is, it is an intolerable thought that he and all the other sentient beings are doomed to complete annihilation after such long-continued slow progress.[6]

The implications of an inevitable Heat Death for progress and an optimistic world view were eloquently expressed by the English philosopher Bertrand Russell in a famous passage written in 1903:

> Such, in outline [an outline of a world in which God is malevolent], but even more purposeless, more void of meaning, is the world which science presents for our belief. Amid such a world, if anywhere, our ideals henceforward must find a home. That man is the product of causes which had no prevision of the end they were achieving; that his origin, his growth, his hopes and fears, his loves and his beliefs, are but the outcome of accidental collocations of atoms; that no fire, no heroism, no intensity of thought and feeling, can preserve an individual life beyond the grave; that all the labors of the ages, all the devotion, all the inspiration, all the noonday brightness of human genius, are destined to extinction in the vast death of the solar system, and that the whole temple of Man's achievement must inevitably be buried beneath the debris of a universe in ruins— all these things, if not quite beyond dispute, are yet so nearly certain that no philosophy which rejects them can hope to stand. Only within the scaffolding of these truths, only on the firm foundation of unyielding despair, can the soul's habitation henceforth be safely built.[7]

Russell's sentiments have been echoed in the closing years of this century in an equally famous passage in a popular book on cosmology, *The First Three Minutes,* by the American physicist Steven Weinberg:

It is almost irresistible for humans to believe that we have some special relation to the universe, that human life is not just a more-or-less farcical outcome of a chain of accidents reaching back to the first three minutes [of the universe's existence], but that we were somehow built in from the beginning. . . . It is very hard to realize that [the entire Earth] is just a tiny part of an overwhelmingly hostile universe. It is even harder to realize that this present universe has evolved from an unspeakably unfamiliar early condition, and faces a future extinction of endless cold or intolerable heat. The more the universe seems comprehensible, the more it also seems pointless.[8]

If one believes in the Heat Death, there are two responses one can have. The first is to accept it—accept that human life is meaningless in the long run—and look for meaning only in the short run, finding solace that man, though he is doomed, faces this inevitable doom bravely. As Weinberg puts it: "The effort to understand the universe is one of the very few things that lifts human life a little above the level of farce, and gives it some of the grace of tragedy."[9] Russell, on the other hand, advises us to take the short-run view:

I am told that [the Heat Death prediction] is depressing, and people will sometimes tell you that if they believed that, they would not be able to go on living. Do not believe it; it is all nonsense. Nobody really worries much about what is going to happen millions of years hence. . . . Therefore, although it is of course a gloomy view to suppose that life will die out—at least I suppose we may say so, although sometimes when I contemplate the things that people do with their lives I think it is almost a consolation—it is not such as to render life miserable. It merely makes you turn your attention to other things.[10]

However, it turns out that the Heat Death does not really follow from the Second Law of Thermodynamics. The Heat Death can be shown to occur only if one assumes in addition (1) that the universal temperature is bounded below away from zero, and (2) that the available energy is finite. As I have discussed in the previous chapter, neither of these additional assumptions is true, so as a matter of physical fact the Heat Death is *not* inevitable. It is remarkable that this was realized as early as 1914 by one of the greatest nineteenth-century French experts in thermodynamics, Pierre Duhem:

> The deduction [of the Heat Death] is marred in more than one place by fallacies. First of all, it implicitly assumes the assimilation of the universe to a finite collection of bodies isolated in a space absolutely void of matter; and this assimilation exposes one to many doubts. Once this assimilation is admitted, it is true that the entropy of the universe has to increase endlessly, but it does not impose any lower or upper limit on this entropy; nothing then would stop this magnitude from varying from minus infinity to plus infinity while the time itself varied from minus infinity to plus infinity; then the allegedly demonstrated impossibilities regarding an eternal life for the universe would vanish.[11]

This is the basic mechanism I shall employ in the Omega Point Theory to avoid the Heat Death: I have shown that there is a free energy source—the differential collapse of the universe—which will allow the entropy and information processed and stored to diverge to plus infinity as the final state of the universe, the Omega Point, is approached. This source of free energy diverges to infinity as the Omega Point is approached. I should, however, point out to the reader that Duhem was wrong about entropy increasing from minus infinity in the infinitely distant past. We now know that, since the beginning of time at the Big Bang singularity to the present, there has been only a finite of entropy generated, and most of it is in the form of cosmic background radiation. Furthermore, the entropy is now known to be a measure of the number of microstates of a physical system consistent with the observed macrostate. This means that the entropy of a system cannot be less than zero.

Duhem unfortunately had a great weakness as a scientist: he subscribed to a nineteenth-century philosophy called "positivism," which discouraged belief in the applicability of physical laws much beyond the areas where they had previously been found to apply. Such a scientist is constitutionally unable to generalize the results of his experiments and thus is unable to make really significant discoveries in science. The most influential positivist of all time, the nineteenth-century

Austrian physicist Ernst Mach, denied the existence of atoms to his dying day. Thus not surprisingly Duhem denies that the Second Law of Thermodynamics applies to the universe as a whole:

> So it goes with any long-term prediction. We possess a thermodynamics which represents very well a multitude of experimental laws, and it tells us that the entropy of an isolated system increases eternally. We could without difficulty construct a new thermodynamics which would represent as well as the old thermodynamics the experimental laws known until now, and whose predictions would go along in agreement with those of the old thermodynamics for 10 thousand years; and yet, this new thermodynamics might tell us that the entropy of the universe after increasing for a period of 100 million years will decrease over a new period of 100 million years in order to increase again in an eternal cycle.[12]

Yes, such a new thermodynamics could be constructed—and it would be perfectly useless in predicting anything. The "100 million years" Duhem chose was, as he himself would have acknowledged, completely arbitrary. One could just as easily have chosen 100 thousand years or 100 billion years. But as a matter of historical fact, some thirty years after Duhem wrote that thermodynamics could not be trusted to apply to the universe on a timescale longer than 10 thousand years, the American physicists Ralph Alpher and Robert Herman[13] trusted that the Second Law of Thermodynamics *did* apply to the universe as a whole, and further that it held over a period of 10 *billion* years. Using the Second Law in an essential way, they made in 1948 one of the most extraordinary predictions of twentieth-century science: that the cosmic background radiation had to exist with a present-day temperature of about 5 degrees on the Kelvin scale. This radiation, discovered in 1965 (with a temperature of 2.7 degrees), is proof that the universe began in the Big Bang.

In this book I shall follow Alpher and Herman rather than Duhem: I shall assume that the Second Law of Thermodynamics applies in all circumstances whatsoever. In particular, I shall assume that it will apply at all times in the future, all the way into the Omega Point. The physics of the Omega Point Theory is based in an absolutely essential way on the Second Law of Thermodynamics (which is why I capitalize it). The lesson of history is clear: until an experiment shows otherwise, a scientist should always assume that the firmly established laws of physics are true in all circumstances. This is the methodology I shall consistently follow in this book.

The famous nineteenth-century Scots physicists Balfour Stewart and P. G. Tait realized that an infinite energy source could enable life to avoid the Heat Death. In their immensely popular book *The Unseen Universe: or Physical Speculations on a Future State,* published anonymously in 1875 (though they acknowledged authorship in the following year[14]), Stewart and Tait argued that, although the Second Law of Thermodynamics implied that the visible material universe must necessarily end in a Heat Death, the "Principle of Continuity" implied that there must exist a higher order of reality, an "unseen universe." This unseen universe consisted of an infinite hierarchy of levels, with energy transfer occurring between the levels. The observed material universe is the lowest level, and as radiant energy travels out into interstellar space, it is gradually transferred to the next higher level. The entire hierarchy of levels, which they called "the Great Whole," thus ". . . is infinite in energy, and will last from eternity to eternity."[15]

Unfortunately, optimistic views about the Heat Death, such as those held by Duhem and by Stewart and Tait,[16] were very much in the minority. As the American historian of science Stephen Brush[17] has emphasized, the Heat Death idea had a profoundly negative effect on the meliorism of the late nineteenth and early twentieth centuries. The popular books in cosmology, *The Nature of the Physical World,* by Sir Arthur Eddington[18] and *The Universe Around Us,* by Sir James Jeans[19] both well-known British astronomers, were particularly important in making the general public aware of the Heat Death in the 1930s.

.———.

The Eternal Return in Philosophy, Religion, and Politics

Historically, the most important idea opposed to the idea of progress is not the Heat Death—the idea that the universe is degenerating—but rather the idea of the Eternal Return. According to the world view of the Eternal Return, time is not unidirectional and linear, but rather cyclic. If this is true, then progress without limit is obviously impossible. Progress is possible for a limited period, but because the universe must eventually return to its earlier states again and again without limit (this is what is meant by "Eternal Return") human advancement must necessarily reach a maximum, and then regress to its previous primitive state again and again, without limit. As in the Heat Death cosmology, there can be no ultimate point to human striving in the Eternal Return cosmology.

The concept of the Eternal Return apparently[20] played a key role in the cosmological thought of humankind as far back as 6500 B.C. Ideas in this period were based on such common-sense phenomena as the cycle of the seasons, the rhythm of human life from birth to adulthood to death, and the numerous periodicities in the heavens, such as the phases of the Moon, the annual motion of the Sun through the constellations, and the periodic near return of the planets (the planets were thought[21] to be gods) to previous positions in the sky. Under these circumstances, a cyclic notion of time is more natural than linear time, and it was cyclic time that dominated[22] the thought of the so-called primitive peoples.

The early agricultural civilizations—Sumerian, Babylonian,[23] Indian,[24] Mayan,[25] and in China the Shang-Chou[26]—retained and elaborated the notion of cyclic time. The Babylonians, for instance, based their time on the periodicities of the planets. In their view, the lifetime of the universe, or Great Year, lasts about 424,000 ordinary years. The summer of this Great Year would be marked by the conjunction of all the planets in the constellation Cancer, and would be accompanied by a universal conflagration; the winter would occur when all the planets have a conjunction in Capricorn, and this would result in a universal flood. The cycle then repeats and in some accounts[27] the next cycle is an exact reproduction of the preceding ones. The ancient Indians (Hindus, Buddhists, Jains) extended this basic structure of a single Great Year into an entire hierarchy of Great Years. For example, a destruction and recreation of individual forms and creatures (but not of the basic substance of the universe) occurred every *Kalpa* or day of Brahma. Each day of Brahma—God—had a duration of about 4 billion years. The elements themselves, together with all forms, undergo a dissolution into Pure Spirit, which then reincarnates itself back into matter every lifetime of Brahma, which lasts about 311 trillion years.[28] The lifetime of Brahma is the longest cycle in the Indian system, and the cycle is repeated endlessly.

Among the Greeks, the Stoics were the most fervent believers in the Eternal Return. They claimed that all objects in the universe were bound together in an absolutely determinate web of actions and reactions, and that this determinism led to a precise return of *all* events. That is, no event is unique and occurs once and for all, but rather every event has occurred, occurs, and will occur, perpetually; the same individuals have appeared, appear, and reappear in every return of the cycle. In each and every cycle Socrates will be tried, condemned, and executed. Cosmic duration is thus repetition and *anakuklesis,* Eternal Return.[29]

This Stoic idea of *palingenesia*—that is, the reappearance of the same people in each cycle[30]—carried the idea of the Eternal Return to its logical extreme, and went much further than the above-mentioned earlier thinkers were willing to go, or indeed than Aristotle and Plato were willing to go.

Aristotle was intrigued by the notion of *palingenesia.* He noted that if it were true it would obscure the usual idea of before and after, for it would imply,[31] as Aristotle[32] pointed out, that he himself was living as much before the fall of Troy as after, since the Trojan War would be reenacted and Troy would fall again. However, although Aristotle accepted the cycles, he was reluctant to accept the exact identity of events in each cycle, arguing[33] that the identity was only one of a kind.

Plato's cosmology[34] was also cyclic, with a periodic destruction and recreation of the universe in conjunction with various astronomical events. Indeed, it is through Plato's writings that the notion of the

Great Year entered later Western thought. However, scholars[35] disagree as to whether Plato's view of the cycles went to the extreme of *palingenesia*. The idea of the Eternal Return came to dominate thought in the pre-Christian, later Roman Empire. It was also prominent on the other side of the *oikoumene* in this period, namely in Han dynasty China. As the world's leading authority on ancient Chinese science, Joseph Needham,[36] has pointed out, the popular religious Taoism of the Han period was millenniarist and apocalyptic; the Great Peace was clearly in the future as well as in the past. In the Canon of the Great Peace (written between 400 B.C. and A.D. 200) can be found a theory of cycles that issued fresh from chaos (considered as a state of complete undifferentiation, which is similar to modern ideas of maximum entropy), and then fell slowly until the day of doom (maximum entropy in another guise).

In contrast, the Christian world view was from its very beginning extremely hostile to the idea of the Eternal Return. In his most important book, *The City of God,* Augustine explicitly attacked the Stoic version of the Eternal Return, arguing that Christian philosophy (and its Jewish predecessor) required a *linear* concept of time. In Augustine's own words:

> God forbid that we should believe in [the Eternal Return]. For Christ died once for our sins, and rising again, dies no more.[37]

God created the world *once,* Christ died *once,* and will rise again *once.* (It is, however, not completely clear that cyclic time was absent from the thoughts of the Old Testament writers. In Ecclesiastes 1:9, for example, we find the words "The thing that hath been, it is that which shall be; and that which is done is that which shall be done: and there is no new thing under the sun.")

With the triumph of Christianity over its competitors in the Roman Empire, the notion of linear time became dominant over cyclic time in the West until the rise of modern science, although a few medieval scholars, such as Bartholomaeus (A.D. 1230), Siger of Brabant (A.D. 1270), and Pietro d'Acono (A.D. 1300), were willing to at least entertain the Eternal Return idea.[38] In medieval China, however, the Neo-Confucian school, which flourished from A.D. 1100 to A.D. 1300, and which was influenced by both the Buddhist ideas on recurrence and the above-mentioned ideas of ancient Taoism, accepted[39] the idea that the universe passed through alternating cycles of construction and dissolution. For instances, the Sung scholar Shen Kua (A.D. 1050) discussed[40] recurrent world catastrophes, and later the Ming scholar Tung Ku held[41] that a world period had a beginning, but not the endless chain of all world periods. Joseph Needham has argued[42] that in fact the linear notion of time dominated over the cyclic view in later Chinese thought, but other experts[43] on Chinese science disagree. However, there is no question that linearity dominated Christian thought, and many thinkers[44] have contended that this notion of time played a key role in the rise of modern science.

With the beginning of modern science in the late sixteenth century, philosophy and science began to go their separate ways. But philosophers were aware of the authority of science in the mind of the average person, and as a consequence philosophers who believed in the Eternal Return attempted to formulate scientific-sounding arguments for recurrence.

The attempt by the German philosopher Friedrich Nietzsche to prove recurrence is interesting because it is *almost* a valid argument, given certain (untrue) presuppositions about the nature of the physical universe. That is, Nietzsche's proof contains all the essential ideas needed for a rigorous proof of recurrence of a finite physical system evolving in a particular chancelike way. Nietzsche began his "proof" of recurrence as follows:

> . . . we insist upon the fact that the world as a sum of energy must not be regarded as unlimited—we forbid ourselves the concept of infinite energy, because it seems incompatible with the concept of energy.[45]

Thus Nietzsche argues for the finiteness of energy of the universal system. This is indeed an essential assumption in any valid proof of recurrence. Nietzsche's argument for finiteness has a parallel in modern physics. According to general relativity, only in spacetimes where the total energy is necessarily finite (in the so-called asymptotically flat spacetimes) does "energy" have a well-defined meaning. In particular, total energy does not have a meaning in a closed universe (and I shall use this fact in my proof that infinite progress is possible in closed universes).

Nietzsche also argues that the universe must be infinite in both the past and the future:

> We need not concern ourselves for one instant with the hypothesis of a created world. The concept "create" is today utterly indefinable and unrealistic: it is but a word which hails from superstitious ages. . . .[46]

Actually, in his "proof," Nietzsche does not really need to rule out "creation," he just needs to rule out the idea that the universe has existed for only a finite time. Unfortunately for Nietzsche, the evidence for the Big Bang is overwhelming. That is, the universe has existed for only a finite time—about 20 billion years—even if it is "uncreated." One can find the evidence for this finiteness in time discussed in any book on cosmology. Furthermore, in Chapter VIII, I shall show that the idea of God creating the universe can be given a meaning in modern physics.

Nietzsche claims that recurrence of all states follows from the finiteness of energy (and the space wherein this energy acts), by which he meant a finite number of possible states of the universe, the infinity of elapsed time, and a chancelike evolution:

> If the Universe may be conceived as a definite quantity of energy, as a definite number of centers of energy—and every other concept remains indefinite and therefore useless—it follows that the Universe must go through a calculable number of combinations in the great game of chance which constitutes its existence. In infinity, at some moment or other, every possible combination must once have been realized; not only this, but it must once have been realized an infinite number of times. . . .[47] If all possible combinations and relations of forces had not already been exhausted, then an infinity would not yet lie behind us. Now since infinite time must be assumed, no fresh possibility can exist and everything must have appeared already, and moreover an infinite number of times.[48] That a state of equilibrium

has never been reached, proves that it is impossible. [But it must have been reached] in spherical space.[49] Only when we falsely assume that space is unlimited, and that therefore energy gradually becomes dissipated, can the final state be an unproductive and lifeless one.[50]

I shall show in the section on Physics and the Eternal Return that Nietzsche's world model can be compared fairly closely to a system undergoing a particular type of random evolution—a Markov chain— whose state must recur.

Both Nietzsche[51] and the German philosopher Martin Heidegger, one of the most influential philosophers of the twentieth century, regarded the Eternal Return idea as the basic foundation of the entire corpus of Nietzsche's philosophy; the Eternal Return was not merely an incidental appendage. As Heidegger put it: "Nietzsche's basic metaphysical position may be defined by two statements. First, the basic character of beings as such is 'will to power.' Second, Being is 'eternal recurrence of the same.' "[52] However, Heidegger believed[53] that the Eternal Return was a metaphysical idea, not a proposition of physical science. This is not true, as I mentioned above. Furthermore, Nietzsche himself regarded his proof of the Eternal Return as a scientific proof, and the Eternal Return itself as ". . . the *most scientific* of all possible hypotheses."[54] In fact, Nietzsche had devoted several years to the study of physics for the purpose of learning how to construct such a proof.[55]

Nietzsche both realized and accepted the full implications of the Eternal Return. First, it meant[56] that there was and could be no ultimate purpose to life; existence is useless, senseless, and absurd. This recognition that life leads to nothing was called *nihilism* by Nietzsche. (*Nihil* is the Latin word for "nothing.") Second, the idea of progress was a delusion; Nietzsche contemptuously called it ". . . merely a modern idea, that is a false idea . . . development is *not* by any means necessarily an elevation. . . ."[57] Third, God could not exist—even if He did, He would be as absurd as the universe He created. "God is dead" is Nietzsche's famous expression[58] for this pessimistic form of atheism. Some forms of atheism are optimistic: those forms, like Marxism, which embrace the idea of progress. Optimistic atheism regards the disappearance of the belief in God as a manifestation of progress itself: a prescientific belief preventing us from taking charge of human existence is being eliminated. Nietzsche's atheism was utterly different. One is not happy that God does not exist; one is in *despair* because God does not exist. No longer is there a loving Guide for humans in this absurd universe.[59] The knowledgeable man—Nietzsche called him the "Overman" (German *Übermensch)*—is the one who accepts the absurdity of reality implied by the Eternal Return.[60] (Nietzsche regarded tragedy as the highest form of art.) For Nietzsche, the true Overman does more than merely accept the ultimate meaninglessness of reality implied by the Eternal Return; the Overman is able ". . . not only to bear the necessity [of the Eternal Return], even less to conceal it . . . but to *love* it."[61] In his notes for his most famous book, *Also Sprach Zarathustra,* Nietzsche wrote: *"After the vision of the Übermensch* in a gruesome way the doctrine of the *recurrence:* now *bearable!"*[62]

Fourth, since the universe is irrational at its most basic level, the distinction between objective science and subjective emotion disappears. "Truth" is now culture- and race-dependent, a manner of opinion rather than being the same for all. Science and technology are no longer good things. Since they are inextricably bound together with progress, and progress is a delusion, scientific progress is also a delusion. Nietzsche's follower Max Weber, the famous German sociologist, extolled this reactionary antiscience irrationalism: ". . . though a naive optimism may have celebrated science . . . as the path which would lead to happiness, I believe I can leave this entire question aside in light of the annihilating critique which Nietzsche has made. . . . Who, then, still believes in this, with the exception of a few big babies in university chairs or in editorial offices?"[63] Indeed, science and technology are fundamentally evil since, by promising escape from the absurdity of the cyclic universe, they lead away from the knowledge of the Eternal Return which defines the Overman.

Fifth, the Eternal Return implies racism. As Nietzsche put it, "The *goal of humanity* cannot lie in the end [which is where the goal would lie in a progressive cosmos], but only in *its highest specimens."*[64] ". . . the goal of development [is] in single great human beings [who are not] . . . the last ones in time [but rather are] scattered and accidental existences."[65] Nietzsche was even more explicit in his book *The Antichrist:* "Not with what shall succeed humanity in the sequence of beings is the problem which I pose . . . but what type of man one should *breed.* . . ."[66] These great human beings, who should be bred, were Nietzsche's Overmen. In his last book, *Ecce Homo,* Nietzsche said[67] that only "scholarly oxen" could interpret his Overman Darwinistically as a member of a species superior to man. He denied that there could even be a species superior to man. He asserted, "Man as a species does not represent any progress compared to any other animal"[68] in the section appropriately entitled "Anti-Darwin" of his book *The Will to Power.* This is a consequence of the Eternal Return: if there is no progress at all, then in particular there can be no progress in evolution. Every species should look after its own interest rather than hoping for the betterment of all. There is no betterment of all.

Nietzsche's philosophy has had an enormous effect on twentieth-century culture. The existentialist philosopher Karl Jaspers has said that Søren Kierkegaard and Friedrich Nietzsche have determined between them the starting point of all twentieth-century philosophy. Nietzsche's Eternal Return has spawned a number of cyclic theories of human history, most notably that of the German Oswald Spengler in his *Untergang des Abendlandes* (translated into English as *Decline of the West),* and that of the Englishman Arnold Toynbee, developed in his multi-volume *A Study of History.* In the Preface to his *Decline of the West,* Spengler explicitly said that he owed "everything" to Goethe and Nietzsche. Both Spengler and Toynbee believed that human history is characterized, not as endless progress from a primitive society to advanced civilization, but instead as an endless cycle of birth, growth, decay, and death of civilizations. The title of Spengler's book expressed his belief that Western civilization was in its decaying phase. Both Spengler and Toynbee disliked science and thought that the advance of modern science was nearing its end. This is a typical view of Eternal Return believers, as the historian of science (and physicist) Gerald Holten of Harvard has recently pointed out.[69]

The classical epitome of the Eternal Return is the myth of Sisyphus, a Greek condemned by the gods to push a heavy stone up a mountain in Hell. When Sisyphus finally succeeded in getting the stone up the mountain, the stone immediately fell back to the bottom of the mountain. Sisyphus must then go down the mountain and push the stone up again. This process repeats, eternally. Sisyphus' efforts are doomed to failure; all his efforts come to naught, and always have, and always will. The senselessness of his effort—and his knowledge of its senselessness—is Sisyphus' punishment. If the Eternal Return were true, it would be ours also.

Reflecting on the myth of Sisyphus, the French novelist Albert Camus realized that in an Eternal Return universe, "There is but one truly serious philosophical problem, and that is suicide. Judging whether life is or is not worth living amounts to answering the fundamental question of philosophy. . . . Does the Absurd dictate death?"[70] The only argument for life Camus could find was: "The struggle itself toward the height is enough to fill a man's heart. One must imagine Sisyphus happy."[71]

I have no difficulty imagining Sisyphus happy. Human beings have learned how to find happiness even in the most appalling circumstances. But they would be *happier* knowing that one day there would be better conditions, that the universe was not in point of fact absurd, but rather full of meaning. Sisyphus would be much happier knowing that one day his rock would remain at the top of that mountain, that his toil served some purpose, and that one day he would be free to climb still higher mountains, climb all the way to God Himself. People can find meaning in their lives even believing that they, their children, and all their descendants will eventually die, never to rise again. But they would find *more* meaning in their lives if they believed what the Omega Point Theory claims to be the case, namely that one day they and their children will rise from the dead, never to die again. They would find *more* meaning in their lives if they believed that the Eternal Return is not true. And it is in fact not true, as I shall show below. Camus's happy Sisyphus reminds one of Nietzsche's Overmen, who could "love" the "gruesome" Eternal Return: "Pain, too, is a joy . . . "[72]—thus spoke Nietzsche's character Zarathustra about the Eternal Return.

The political consequences of Nietzsche's Eternal Return philosophy have been catastrophic. Perhaps the simplest way to show this is to point out that the Eternal Return is sufficiently ancient and important a concept in philosophy and religion to have its own symbol. The old Anglo-Saxon word for the symbol of the Eternal Return is *fylfot*. So dominant had the idea of progress—the antithesis of the Eternal Return—become in England that, when the English encountered the Eternal Return symbol again in the twentieth century, they had, to their credit, forgotten their ancient word for it. Instead, they used the Sanskrit word for the symbol: SWASTIKA.

From the very beginning the Nazis affirmed a deep connection between Nazism and Nietzsche's philosophy. The Nazi philosopher Alfred Bäumler asserted that "whoever says 'Heil Hitler!' salutes Nietzsche's philosophy at the same time."[73] Bäumler, professor of philosophy at the University of Berlin from 1933 to 1945, was an important figure in Nazi philosophical circles. He was the chief spokesman for Alfred Rosenberg, the editor-in-chief of the official Nazi party newspaper *Völkischer Beobachter*. Rosenberg[74] himself was in Hitler's cabinet with the title of Nazi party ideologue; he was sentenced to death by the Nuremberg War Crimes Tribunal, and hanged in 1946. It has often been pointed out[75] that Nietzsche himself was not a vulgar racist like the Nazis—in fact, Nietzsche admired the Jews and Poles (two of the Nazis' most hated nationalities). Furthermore, Nietzsche loathed anti-Semitism, and felt that German nationalism as it was developing in the late nineteenth century would result in the ". . . extirpation of the German spirit in favor of the 'German *Reich.*' "[76] However, the Nazis who were aware of these attitudes of Nietzsche emphasized that, in so rejecting racism, Nietzsche was rejecting the implications of his own Eternal Return idea. In this one and only aspect of philosophy the Nazis are correct; I thus reject the Eternal Return.

Heidegger can be considered the most influential Nazi philosopher of all. It is well known that he was a member of the Nazi party before Hitler took power in Germany, but many of Heidegger's later followers have attempted to argue that this was incidental to his philosophy. This is false.[77] When Heidegger's own student Karl Löwith (driven out of Germany in the 1930s because he was half Jewish) told Heidegger that his philosophical work was being damaged by his politics, Heidegger disagreed, claiming[78] that in fact the idea of "historicity," as outlined in Heidegger's most famous work, *Being and Time,* was the justification for his Nazism. And "historicity" as understood by Heidegger was repetition, Eternal Return.

Heidegger considered[79] technology to be the greatest danger facing humankind, for it threatened to change the very essence of personhood. The two nations with the greatest admiration for technical progress, the United States and the Soviet Union, must therefore be opposed. Since both capitalist democracy and Marxist totalitarianism believed in technical progress without limit, they were equally suspect in Heidegger's eyes. Heidegger hoped that the Nazis could provide the necessary restrictions on technology; indeed, he believed that the very essence of Nazism was its desire to keep technology within its proper bounds. As he put it in his *Introduction to Metaphysics,* published *after* World War II, "the inner truth and greatness of National Socialism must be sought in the encounter between global technology and modern man."[80]

In 1976 the German mass circulation magazine *Der Spiegel* published a remarkable posthumous interview with Heidegger. The interview was actually conducted in 1966, with the understanding that it would be printed only after Heidegger's death. Heidegger was allowed to edit the interview, and in fact made extensive modifications to the original interview typescript. *Der Spiegel* published the interview as modified by Heidegger. Thus we know that Heidegger had complete control of the interview and that he intended it to be the final summary of his life's work.

In the interview, Heidegger repeated his belief that the main goal of Nazism was the control of technology:

> HEIDEGGER: . . . For me, I do not understand the problem of man in the world of planetary technology as an unexplainable curse from which we are to escape. I believe that within its proper limits thought ought to help man establish a satisfying relationship with technology. National Socialism certainly took that road. . . .[81] Technicity in its essence is something that man does not master by his own power."[82]

Heidegger also affirmed that his philosophy was racist:

DER SPIEGEL: You attribute to the Germans a special task?

HEIDEGGER: Yes . . .

DER SPIEGEL: Do you believe that Germans have a special qualification for this conversion?

HEIDEGGER: I am thinking of the special inner kinship between the German language and the language of the Greeks and their thought. This is something the French confirm for me again and again today. When they begin to think, they speak German. They assure [me] that they do not succeed with their own language.[83]

Needless to say, this is nonsense. Any thought can be expressed equally in French, German, English, or any other of the human languages. We say that all human languages are *universal languages*. It is true that some ideas are easier to express in some universal languages than others. Although in principle all the technical ideas of the Omega Point Theory can be expressed in plain English, it takes vastly less space to express them in the universal language of mathematics, and thus I have confined the most detailed description of the Omega Point Theory to the Appendix for Scientists. Heidegger realized that, in the future, thought would in fact be expressed in mathematics, a development he deplored since it was a manifestation of the growth of technology:

HEIDEGGER: The sciences, i.e., even for us today the natural sciences (with mathematical physics as the fundamental science), are translatable into all the languages of the world—or to be exact, they are not translated but the same mathematical language is spoken [universally]. . . .[84] [P]hilosophy will be unable to effect any immediate change in the current state of the world. This is true not only of philosophy but of all purely human reflection and endeavor. Only a God can save us. . . .[85] The role of philosophy in the past has been taken over today by the sciences. . . . Philosophy [today] dissolves into individual sciences: psychology, logic, political science.[86]

DER SPIEGEL: And what now takes the place of philosophy?

HEIDEGGER: Cybernetics.

Heidegger has correctly identified his opponent, the opponent of the Eternal Return, the opponent of Nazism and all that these stand for: the book you hold in your hands is a work on cybernetics—the old word for "computer science." Hopefully, those of Heidegger's ilk will indeed fail to effect any change in the development of technology. In which case a God—the Omega Point—will save us.

I have discussed the social and political implications of the Eternal Return at length because I want it to be clearly understood why I explicitly reject such a view. As we shall see in the next chapter, the rejection of the Eternal Return is expressed in the third of three postulates which I shall claim codify in mathematical language what is meant by "eternal life." Since it is this anti-Eternal Return Postulate that gives the Omega Point Theory its real predictive power, it is very important to justify the postulate in detail.

A rejection of racism, that is, a belief in the inherent superiority of any group of intelligent beings—as I showed above, a notion intimately connected with the Eternal Return—is also essential for the Omega Point Theory. As I demonstrated in the previous chapter, a crucial step toward the Omega Point is the colonization of the universe by intelligent robots, by self-reproducing machines. Many humans (including many who should know better) regard the creation of such people—I call intelligent robots "people," because that is what they are—with horror, and initially feel that the creation and reproduction of such machines (people) should be prohibited by law. For example, when I first proposed colonizing the galaxy with von Neumann probes, the astrophysicist Carl Sagan demurred:

> . . . the prudent policy of any technical civilization must be, with very high reliability, to prevent the construction of interstellar von Neumann machines and to circumscribe severely their domestic use. If we accept Tipler's arguments, the entire Universe is endangered by such an invention; controlling and destroying interstellar von Neumann machines is then something to which every civilization—espe-

cially the most advanced—would be likely to devote some attention.[87]

This is a position of fear and ignorance, a definition by exclusion: that which is unlike me is not worthy of existence. A "person" is defined by qualities of mind and soul, not by a particular bodily form. Adolf Hitler disagreed with this definition, of course. He defined "person" in terms of bodily form and tried to prevent the reproduction of all people who were not "Aryans." He nearly succeeded in preventing Jewish reproduction: when the Second World War had ended, 70% of all the Jews in Europe were dead. If one rejects the philosophical basis of racism, one must accept the implications of such rejection: one must oppose any laws restricting the creation or reproduction of intelligent machines. Ultimately, intelligent machines will become more intelligent than members of the species *Homo sapiens,* and will thus dominate civilization. So what?

There will be people who in their heart of hearts remain human supremacists. To those people, let me point out the consequences of your position: your permanent and very final death, and the death of your children. I began Chapter II with a proof that the Sun and the Earth are doomed. Our civilization and our biosphere must ultimately leave the solar system if they are to survive. I shall show in the next chapter that in the very far future, near the end of time, only robots can survive in the extreme conditions that will prevail over the entire universe. *But*—if the robots survive, they can keep us alive also, as emulations in the computers of the far future. Exactly how this can work will be the subject of later chapters; for the moment let me just note that it is possible *only* if we now reject antipathy to the idea of intelligent robots.

Fortunately for the human species and the terrestrial biosphere, the Japanese do not share the fear of robot intelligence which is common in the West.[88] The Japanese welcome robots into their factories. They see these machines not as competitors but as helpmates. They do not fear the arrival of robots with human-level intelligence and beyond; Japanese roboticists are provided lavish financial support for their goal of creating computers and computer programs capable of passing the Turing Test. The Japanese are of course aware of the hostility which the idea of an intelligent machine often faces in the West, and they opine that it is due to a difference in religious tradition and to a different historical experience with machines. The dominant religions in Japan are Shintoism and Buddhism. Both of these religions lack the sharp contrast between living and nonliving beings that is present in Christianity and Judaism. Instead, the Japanese tend toward animism: the belief that everything in existence has a touch of life in them, and that gods *(kami)*—beings superior to humans—are everywhere. Westerners tend to see intelligent robots as soulless hunks of metal, emotionless and therefore innately dangerous, while the Japanese tend to see them as living beings just like everything else, and hence innately good. The leading Japanese roboticist Masahiro Mori[89] wrote an entire book, *The Buddha in the Robot,* to espouse the idea that robots have, like humans, the potential to attain buddhahood, and that humans and robots should work together to help each other become buddhas ("enlightened ones"), just as the Indian Buddha of the sixth century B.C. devoted his life to helping all humans attain buddhahood. Mori asserts that ". . . to learn the Buddhist way is to perceive oneself as a robot."[90] In the West, machines are often the cause (or the excuse) for throwing people out of work, whereas in Japan a worker whose job is automated is simply assigned other (more productive) work. So the Japanese have never had cause to regard robots as a threat.

A third reason for refuting the idea of the Eternal Return is to undermine Nietzsche's cultural relativism, which is based upon it. The Omega Point Theory is a purely scientific theory, founded on the principle that physical science is *universal,* not culturally or even species-based. During the past thirty years almost all claims that physics is no more objective than politics or traditional religion have been based, not on Nietzsche's work directly, but rather on the work of the American philosopher of science Thomas Kuhn. In his bestselling book, *The Structure of Scientific Revolutions,* Kuhn explicitly denies that successive physics theories ". . . grow ever closer to, or approximate more and more closely to, the truth."[91] Kuhn's contention is based on his theory of how scientific revolutions occur, of how one fundamental theory is replaced by another. Since Kuhn first published his book in 1962, a revolution in fundamental physics has occurred. Over the period 1961 to 1974, the theory which is now called the Standard Model of particle physics was created, and by 1980 it had completely swept away all previous theories of particle physics. We can thus test Kuhn's theory by seeing whether this new scientific revolution occurred in the way he predicted it would.

Kuhn's theory has been decisively refuted. Steven Weinberg[92] and Sheldon Glashow,[93] two of the main creators of the Standard Model—revolutionaries, according to Kuhn—have both sharply criticized Kuhn's theory, pointing out that the Standard Model revolution did *not* occur the way Kuhn would lead one to expect. A *former* leading proponent of a non-Standard Model theory, John Polkinghorne—an antirevolutionary, according to Kuhn—has said[94] exactly the same thing. All three physicists agree that the physics community accepted the Standard Model on purely objective, rational grounds. They all present evidence that the Standard Model is in fact a theory closer in accord with objective reality than all other theories which have been developed to date. Polkinghorne, in his book *Rochester Roundabout: The Story of High Energy Physics,* has given a particularly elegant defense of this thesis, showing great sensitivity to the philosophical issues involved. Scientific progress is *real.* We can confidently place our faith in science. In particular, I shall assume in this book that the Standard Model and general relativity are objectively true.

Physics and the Eternal Return

Modern physics—specifically the Newtonian world picture—contained both linear and cyclic temporal aspects from the very beginning. Newton himself was worried that his model of the solar system, which was based on a linear time coordinate, was gravitationally unstable in the long run. (He was correct, but this was not proven[95] until 1989.) To compensate for the instability, he suggested a cyclic process whereby the planets would be replaced by God when they were periodically perturbed from their orbits by the gravitational action of one another.[96] The great mathematical physicists of the eighteenth century, such as Euler, Laplace, and Lagrange, showed that the solar system was in fact stable to first order, the perturbations which worried Newton leading merely to a *cyclic* oscillation of the planetary orbits. The periods of the oscillations were of the order of a few thousand years, and the astronomers of the nineteenth century concluded that the solar system was stable for at least this length of time.

The debate on the question of cyclic versus linear then shifted from astronomy to geology and thermodynamics.[97] The problem in geology was whether the internal heat of the Earth could power geological cycles indefinitely, or whether the Earth would eventually cool to a "state of Ice and Death," as the Scots scientist John Murray[98] put it in 1815. This question in part stimulated research in thermodynamics;[99] by the end of the nineteenth century, Kelvin and others had formulated the Heat Death idea which I have discussed at length above. Not only was the Heat Death believed to rule out cyclic time, but Kelvin and P. G. Tait argued[100] that the Second Law of Thermodynamics implied that the universe had a beginning in time.

However, other physicists, for instance the Swede S. Arrhenius,[101] were unwilling to grant unlimited validity to the Second Law, arguing that creation of the universe would violate the First Law of Thermodynamics, which is the Law of Conservation of Energy. Thus it was claimed that somehow the energy dissipated by thermodynamic processes must be periodically reconcentrated into usable form. The British physicist Rankine,[102] for instance, suggested that heat radiated into space would reach a sort of "ether wall," where the radiant heat would be totally reflected and reconcentrated into various "foci." Thus the history of the universe would be cyclic in the long term. Rankine was basically trying to show that mechanics and the Second Law were inconsistent. The first fully rigorous theorem along these lines was the Recurrence Theorem which was proved by the great French mathematical physicist Henri Poincaré in 1890.

THE POINCARÉ RECURRENCE THEOREM

The Poincaré Recurrence Theorem results from two assumptions: first, the conservation of energy, and second, the postulate that the volume of the total *phase space* available to the system is finite and bounded.

The second assumption requires a little explanation; in particular, it requires a definition of "phase space." Let us first consider a very simple physical system, a single particle with no properties besides its position in space and the rate of change of its position. The key point to notice here is' that even such a simple object requires *six* numbers to describe its state at any given time: three numbers—how high above or below us, how far to the east or west of us, and how far to the north or south of us, for example—to describe its spatial location, and three additional numbers to describe how rapidly each of the numbers giving the spatial location is changing. For technical reasons that won't concern us here, it is usual to give the last three numbers as *momenta* rather than velocities, where the "momentum" of a particle in a given direction is the mass of the particle times the velocity in that direction. The three numbers giving the particle's spatial location define a three-dimensional *configuration space*.

At each instant of time, the state of this single particle is completely described by six numbers. As time advances, the state of the system changes, and this change is completely described by the change of these six numbers. Each of these six numbers can be thought of as a dimension, just as height, length, and breadth are the usual three dimensions of ordinary space. The other three numbers, the momenta, describe the "position" of the particle in "momentum space." The "state space" of the particle is thus six-dimensional: the three dimensions of ordinary space, and the additional three dimensions of momentum space. As the particle changes its state from instant to instant, it "moves" in this six-dimensional state space. A "point" in this state space thus represents the complete description of the particle at any instant of time. A trajectory in this six-dimensional state space represents the history of the particle's states throughout time. This state space is the particle's *phase space*.

Now let us consider a more complicated physical system: a system consisting of N particles just like the single particle we previously considered. ("N" is just some arbitrary whole number.) The state space—the phase space—of this more complicated system has 6N dimensions, and as before, the state of the entire system at any instant of time is a point in this 6N-dimensional space. The state of this physical system is completely described by giving its location in this 6N-dimensional space. As before, a trajectory in this 6N-dimensional phase space is a history of the system's states over time.

Now think what it means for the volume of the system's accessible phase space to be finite and bounded. The phase space is 6N-dimensional, and it will be finite and bounded if and only if both the momentum space and the configuration space are finite and bounded. The latter just means that the N particles are constrained to be always within a finite distance of where they now are. This would be the case, for example, if the particles happened all to be inside a box. The momentum space is finite and bounded only if all the momenta are constrained to be less than a certain number for all time. This would be the case only if all forms of energy available to the particles were bounded.

Neither the configuration space nor the momentum space need be finite and bounded. For example, suppose the system consists of two particles with no interactions between them, and suppose the two particles are located in infinite space. If one particle is moving to the left with a certain velocity and the other particle is at rest, then the two particles will continue to move apart forever with the velocity of the first particle. In this case, the accessible momentum space is finite and bounded, but the accessible configuration space is infinite: the first particle just moves to the left out to spatial infinity. On the other hand, suppose the system consists of two particles with the Newtonian gravitational interaction between them. If they are initially one meter apart, and are initially stationary, they will start to move toward one another, since gravity is attractive. However, since the gravitational potential energy is negative and inversely proportional to the distance between the two particles, the closer the two particles are to each other the more negative will be the potential energy: the potential energy goes to *minus infinity* as the distance between the two particles goes to zero. Since the total energy of this two-particle system is conserved, the kinetic energy must go to *minus infinity*. Now the kinetic energy is proportional to the square of the particle momentum, so the momenta of each particle go to plus infinity in finite time. Thus, in this case, the configuration space is finite and bounded, but the momentum space is not.

The key point to keep in mind is that the state space of any physical system is phase space, not just configuration space. It is thus possible for the accessible state space to be infinite and hence unbounded even if the configuration space is bounded, provided the momentum space is infinite. It is even possible for the state space to be infinite even if the volume of the configuration space is going to zero, provided the momentum space goes to infinity faster than the configuration space goes to zero. As we shall see, this is just what happens near the Omega Point: the available gravitational energy near the Omega Point diverges to infinity in a way quite analogous to the way the Newtonian gravitational potential energy of two point particles diverges.

Conservation of energy has an important implication: if we take any volume in phase space and look at the change of that volume in time, we find that there isn't any: this is called Liouville's Theorem. This doesn't mean that the volume can't change its shape. It just means that an increase in one phase space dimension must be precisely compensated by a decrease in another dimension. In general, we would expect an initially simple phase space volume to become very complicated with time—this would happen, for example, if the motion were chaotic—but nevertheless, the volume cannot change if the energy is conserved.

So the total phase space available to the system is assumed finite, and any given phase space volume cannot change with time. These two facts immediately imply the Poincaré Recurrence Theorem. To see this, pick any tiny volume in phase space around the initial point (remember, this initial point in phase space represents the state of the entire system at the initial instant of time). A short time later, this tiny volume has moved to a different position in phase space, and in doing so, it has swept out a small "tube" in phase space. This tube is also a volume in phase space. Consider the big phase space tube generated by the initial tiny volume over its entire future (infinite) history. Since the phase space available is finite by assumption, this tube must have finite volume, even though future time is infinite.

Now look at another "big" phase space tube, the one generated by allowing the tiny volume *in its second temporal position* to sweep out *its* entire future history. Again, the volume of this second tube must be finite. In fact, the volumes of the two tubes must be equal. For, if the two tubes had different volumes, the second would have to be the smaller of the two, since the first tube contains the second. But if the second tube were smaller, this would mean that phase space volumes decreased with time, since the second tube contains the entire future history of the first except for the small tube connecting the two. This would contradict Liouville's Theorem.

The same argument shows that both tubes must contain all the points in the initial tiny volume, except possibly for a set which has zero volume. Since the initial tiny volume can be arbitrarily small, this means that the system will eventually come arbitrarily close to its initial position in phase space, which in turn means that it will eventually return arbitrarily close to its original state. Thus, we have proven the Poincaré Recurrence Theorem (I'll give another proof in the Appendix for Scientists). This same argument can be modified slightly to show that the system must return arbitrarily close infinitely often.

With a system which can vary its state continuously, both in time and in state space, the time between arbitrarily close returns is not fixed but can vary. If the time between returns is fixed, the system is periodic. Most systems which evolve under Newtonian laws are not periodic, but *chaotic,* which means (among other things) that the future evolution is unstable: a tiny change in the initial conditions results in an enormous change in the system state after a long time.

Ludwig Boltzmann, a University of Vienna professor who was the grandfather of my colleague Dieter Flamm, was the next major physicist after Poincaré to consider the problem of recurrence. Boltzmann originally hoped to deduce the Second Law of Thermodynamics from the Newtonian mechanics of atoms. However, Max Planck's student Zermelo pointed out that the Poincaré Recurrence Theorem implies that this is impossible: if the entropy is a function of the system state, as it must be, it would necessarily have to begin decreasing eventually. Boltzmann then suggested[103] that the universe as a whole had no time direction, but individual regions in it did, when by chance a large fluctuation from thermodynamic equilibrium (Heat Death) should produce a region with low entropy. These reduced entropy regions would then evolve back to the more probable state of maximum entropy—the Heat Death—and the process would repeat in accordance with Poincaré's theorem.

Once it became clear that a finite system of atomic *particles* would be recurrent and not irreversible in the long run, Planck considered whether irreversibility could arise from a *field* theory such as electromagnetism. His idea was to try to derive irreversibility from the interaction of a continuous field with the discrete particles. Planck began a series of papers on this question in 1897, a series that culminated in his discovery of quantum mechanics in 1900. Boltzmann, however, pointed out that, if we regard the field as a system with an infinite number of degrees of freedom, this would be analogous to a mechanical system with an infinite number of molecules, and in either case we would have an infinitely long Poincaré recurrence time; in either case we could have agreement with the Second Law. However, Boltzmann emphasized[104] that for the thermodynamics of fields in a confined space it is more appropriate to regard the field not as a continuous quality governed by differential equations, but rather as a large but finite number of "vector ether atoms" whose equations of motion are obtained by replacing the usual differential equations with finite difference equations. To this system, the recurrence theorem would apply.

PROBABILISTIC MARKOV RECURRENCE

I mentioned above that Nietzsche's proof of the Eternal Return closely resembles the proof of recurrence in Markov chains. A *Markov chain* is a system for which the probability of transition to the next state depends only on its present state. It does not depend on its past history, except in so far as that history is coded in its present state. A finite Markov chain is one involving a system with a finite number of possible states, for which transitions occur only at discrete intervals. A finite Markov chain is a finite state machine which has no information coming in from the outside. In a Markov chain, one has a collection of transition probabilities for going from a given state to another. For example, suppose we have a system with just three states $\{1,2,3\}$ and even odds for going from any state to any other. So if we started in state 1, we would transit to 2 with probability 1/2, and transit to 3 with probability 1/2. It is certain that we go somewhere, and "certain" means "probability 1" so the transition probabilities must add up to one, as they do: $1/2 + 1/2 = 1$. If we started in state 2, we would transit to 1 with probability 1/2, and to 3 with probability 1/2. Finally, if we started in state 3, we would transit to 1 with probability 1/2 and to 2 with probability 1/2. Since the past history is irrelevant, this list of four transition probabilities is sufficient to describe the entire future history of the system.

It is possible that we will return to state 1 after two transitions. We could go from 1 to 2, and then back to 1, or from 1 to 3 and then back to 1. The probability for one or the other of these two possibilities to occur is $(1/2)(1/2) + (1/2)(1/2) = 1/2$. Or we could return to 1 after three transitions: 1 to 2 to 3 to 1 and 1 to 3 to 2 to 1 are the possible sequences. Thus, the probability that we return to the state 1 after three transitions is $(1/2)(1/2)(1/2) + (1/2)(1/2)(1/2) = 1/4$. The probability of returning to the state 1 either after 2 transitions or after 3 transitions is $1/2 + 1/4 = 3/4$. On the fourth transition, we must necessarily return to a previously occupied state, though it might not be the state 1 where we started. The possible transitions leading to the state 1 again for the first time after four transitions are 1 to 2 to 3 to 2 to 1 and 1 to 3 to 2 to 3 to 1. The probability that one of these sequences occurs is $1/16 + 1/16 = 1/8$, and the probability that we return to state 1 by the fourth transition is 7/8. It is intuitively clear that if the number of trials is infinite, the probability that we eventually return to 1 is 1; which is to say, it is essentially certain. Furthermore, if we return to the state 1 once, we can repeat the calculation again— since for Markov chains the past history does not affect the future— and conclude that the probability is once again 1 that we will return again. Repeating this argument again and again, we infer that the probability for returning an infinite number of times to the state 1 is also 1. Hence, we have eternal recurrence. With Markov chains, we can compute the average time between returns, something we could not do in general with Poincaré recurrence. In the simple Markov chain I've just described, the average number of time steps between returns to same state is 5. I give a proof of recurrence in Markov chains with an arbitrary number of states and with arbitrary transition probabilities in the Appendix for Scientists. In the more general case, one has to assume that the Markov chain does not have a subset of states which it can leave never to return. If such a subset exists, one can prove that the probability is 1 that a system which has already been in operation for infinite time has already left the subset, and so, following Nietzsche, this subset can be ignored.

A deterministic sequence is also a Markov chain, though a boring one: 1 to 2 to 3 to 1 is the only possibility, and each transition probability is 1. Here a return necessarily occurs every third transition. But what forces the return in Markov chains is not probability vs. determinism, but finiteness: a finite number of states and discrete time steps.

QUANTUM MECHANICS IS ALMOST PERIODIC

In both Poincaré recurrence and Markov recurrence, the system will eventually return to its present state, but the system need not be exactly periodic. That is, the time between returns can vary enormously from one return to the next. In contrast, an exactly periodic system has the time between returns exactly the same from one cycle to the next. As I said above, the typical system governed by classical Newtonian mechanics is chaotic. I used this classical chaos in Chapter II to show that it is possible for an intelligent species which has engulfed the universe to control the future evolution of the entire universe. What I shall now show is that a quantum system which is bounded both in space and in energy is almost periodic. This means that such a system *cannot* be chaotic.

In quantum mechanics, the state of a system is given by a function of space and time called the *wave function,* and the square of the wave function's magnitude gives the probability that the system will be at the given location at the given time. Now the wave function varies continuously with space and time, so we can't expect to show that, in general, the wave function will return *exactly* to its previous value, as was the case in Markov recurrence. All we could expect to show is that the wave function returns arbitrarily close to its previous state. Recall that this is what the Poincaré Recurrence Theorem proved for bounded classical systems. Furthermore, in actual experiments we cannot distinguish between the values of any continuous variable at two points which are arbitrarily close together. What our instruments really do is measure *averages* over finite regions of the continuous variables. So physically, what a return of a quantum system to its present state would mean is that there exists some later time such that the average of the wave function now minus the wave function at this other time is arbitrarily small.

The Quantum Recurrence Theorem thus asserts that (1) if the spatial volume where the system is confined is finite (this means that the wave function is nonzero only in this volume, because the probability is zero that the system is outside the volume), and (2) if the energy the system can be measured to have is both discrete and bounded above by some finite number, then the wave function must return in the average sense I just defined. But it does more than return once; its return is almost periodic.

To understand what "almost periodic" means, let us first recall exactly what "periodic" means. Consider a typical periodic system: an old-fashioned mechanical alarm clock. As everyone knows, this device has a period of twelve hours, which means that the hour and minute hands return to their exact positions every twelve hours. Furthermore, the hands return to previous positions every whole-number multiple of twelve hours: that is, the hands return to their previous positions every twelve hours, every twenty-four hours, every thirty-six hours, and so on. All of these periods can be written in the form 12n, where n is 1,2,3, etc. So, if f(t) represents the position of the hands at any time t, then we have $f(t) = f(t + 12n)$, for *any* time t whatsoever. This just means that, whatever time t we happen to pick, the positions of the two hands return to their exact positions twelve, twenty-four, thirty-six, and so forth hours later. If t were eleven o'clock, for example, then the clock would again show eleven o'clock twelve hours later, twenty-four hours later, and so forth. This will also be true whatever time t we pick, 12:36, or 5:24, or anything. Exactly twelve hours, twenty-four hours, etc., later, the clock will once again show 12:36, 5:24, or whatever we originally chose. The numbers {12n} for all n are said to be *relatively dense* in the set of all numbers, because there exists a finite number L such that, in any interval of numbers of length L or greater, there will be at least one of the numbers $\{12n\}$. The number L is in the case of the clock *any* number greater than 12, which is the "period" of the clock.

An *almost periodic* system is one for which the state of the system f(t) at any time t is arbitrarily close to the state of the system $f(t + N_i)$ at the time $t + N_i$, where $\{N_i\} = \{N_1, N_2, \text{etc.}\}$ is a relatively dense collection of numbers, for *all* times t. Thus periodic systems are almost periodic also, but the converse need not be true, since the relatively dense set of numbers $\{N_i\}$ need not be whole-number multiples of each other, and furthermore, the system need not return exactly to its previous states, just arbitrarily close.

What the Quantum Recurrence Theorem says is that $|f(t) - f(t + N_i)|$ can be made arbitrarily small, for some relatively dense set $\{N_i\}$ and for *all* times t, where f(t) represents the wave function and the vertical lines represent the average of the wave function. The crucial phrase in this theorem is "for *all* times t." I have emphasized the word "all" because it means that the system doesn't just return; it also repeats its entire history again and again between returns over the whole of infinite future time, and these repeats are arbitrarily close to one another in detail.

This is in sharp contrast to the returns of classical mechanics and to the returns of Markov chains. In both cases, the subsequent history could vary enormously from one return to the next. Thus, this almost periodicity of finite quantum systems means in particular that they *cannot be chaotic.* This fact has troubled quite a few experts in chaos theory, because all physical systems are quantum systems: classical mechanics is just an approximation to quantum mechanics. Hence, if quantum systems are not chaotic, then chaos theory cannot really apply to any physical system whatsoever.

I shall give a formal mathematical proof of the Quantum Recurrence Theorem in the Appendix for Scientists, but it's easy to explain why bounded quantum systems have to be almost periodic. Quantum mechanics has a discreteness to it that is lacking in classical mechanics. Consider phase space in quantum mechanics. As in classical mechanics, an N particle system has a 6N-dimensional phase space, 3N dimensions of configuration space, and 3N dimensions of momentum space. But in quantum mechanics configuration space and momentum space are *not* independent: one indication of this is that the wave function, which completely describes the state of a quantum system, depends *only* on the configuration space variables. In classical mechanics, the system state is specified by its location in configuration space *and* in momentum space. There is a fundamental minimum scale in quantum phase space: Planck's constant h, which has dimensions of (momentum) times (spatial length). Planck's constant thus divides the whole of the phase space available to a quantum system into 6N-dimensional boxes with phase space volume h^{3N}. This gives quantum mechanics a fundamental discreteness, because if two systems are in the same box in phase space, *they are in the same state*. No experiment, even in principle, can distinguish between the two systems. This means that if the total phase space volume assessable to the system is V, then the total number of truly distinct system states is just V/h^{3N}, which is a finite number if the total phase space volume is finite. This total volume will be finite if the maximum energy the system can have is finite (this makes the volume finite in the momentum dimensions) and if the system is restricted to a finite region of space (this makes the volume finite in the configuration space dimensions).

So the state space of a bounded quantum system is finite like that of a finite Markov chain; this alone would give recurrence. But the time evolution of the wave function is deterministic like the system evolution of classical mechanics, as I shall discuss in more detail in Chapter V. This determinism added to the finite state space is what makes quantum mechanics almost periodic.

As we shall see in Chapter IX, this fundamental discreteness of the quantum mechanical state space is what makes the eventual universal resurrection of humanity physically possible. On the other hand, if the Quantum Recurrence Theorem held in the large, then the universal resurrection could not result in eternal life, because we would have to return to our present state eventually. Furthermore, as I pointed out in Chapter II, chaos must occur on cosmological scales in order to enable life to gain control over the entire universe, which as I shall show in the next chapter is required for life as a whole to be eternal. We need part but not all of the Quantum Recurrence Theorem to hold in actual reality.

We can indeed have our cake and eat it too, simply by keeping the quantum discreteness—there is overwhelming evidence for it—and showing that the phase space available to the universe is *not* finite. Such will be the case in a universe governed by general relativity.

No-Return Theorems in General Relativity

When I first gave a lecture on the Omega Point Theory at a physics conference in the early 1980s, and pointed out that it implied eternal progress, the Nobel-prize-winning theoretical physicist Eugene Wigner jumped up and said: "This theory can't be right; it contradicts the Poincaré Recurrence Theorem!" Wigner was wrong, and the reason he was wrong is that a spatially finite universe governed by the gravitational theory of Einstein, general relativity, cannot have an Eternal Return. In brief, the reason it cannot is that the Einstein field equations will not allow the phase space to be finite. In a fundamental sense, the universe in modern cosmology *must* be infinite, even if it is spatially finite.

The analogue in modern cosmology of the finite-sized box assumed in the Poincaré Recurrence Theorem is the closed universe, which is a universe that is finite in volume, but without boundary. The standard model of a closed universe is a three-dimensional version of a sphere, called a "three-sphere." I discussed this model at length in the preceding chapter. If the material sources of gravity are such as to make gravity always attractive, then such a universe starts from an initial "Big Bang" singularity where time begins, expands to a maximum size, and then recontracts to a final "Big Crunch" singularity where time comes to an end. As the universe approaches the final singularity, the volume goes to zero. The spatial part of the phase space is certainly bounded and finite; not only is it bounded and finite, it goes to zero.

But the phase space is *not* going to zero. In general relativity, the analogue of momentum for classical gravity is roughly a mathematical expression which is proportional to the rate of change of the radius of

the universe—the "velocity" with which the universe expands or contracts—divided by the radius of the universe. Thus, if we multiply the
radius of the universe by this momentum, we get the phase space size
to be proportional to the "velocity" of universal expansion or contraction. Since gravity is always attractive and gets stronger as the universe
gets smaller, this "velocity" diverges to infinity as the size of the universe goes to zero. The size of the phase space goes to infinity as the
universe approaches the end of time. Since the phase space in cosmology is infinite, the crucial assumption required for an Eternal Return
does not hold.

Another way to think about why Eternal Returns cannot occur in
a closed universe governed by general relativity is to recall that such
universes must begin and end in singularities of infinite density. There
is no time before or after these singularities; it is thus meaningless to
ask what came before or what will come after these singularities.
(Many people find it difficult to understand just why these questions
are meaningless. Think of it this way. General relativity is called "general" because the field equations are the same in *any* coordinate system.
In particular, *any* timescale is as good as any other. This being so, let us
use as our timescale the "momentum" defined above. This timescale is
called "York time" after the American relativist James York, who
showed that using such a timescale simplifies the mathematics of the
field equations. But York time goes from minus infinity at the initial
singularity to plus infinity at the final singularity; in York time the
universe has always existed and always will. Thus to ask what happened
before the initial singularity is the same as asking what happened before
an eternal universe came into existence. A meaningless question,
surely.)

Since time is bounded by the initial and final singularities, and
since between these two singularities the universe is evolving without
repeating itself—during its expansion phase, it is always expanding,
always getting larger, while during its contraction phase, it is always
contracting, always getting smaller—there is no way the universe could
repeat itself.[105]

Three assumptions have to be made in the No-Return Theorem.
First, we have to assume that gravity is never repulsive. If it were sometimes repulsive, say when the universe is very small, then the universe

could "bounce" when it had contracted to a sufficiently small size, and reexpand to a maximum size, and contract again, this sequence of expansions, contractions, and bounces being repeated ad infinitum. In such a universe, an Eternal Return would be a real possibility. As I indicated above, this cannot happen if gravity is always attractive, because attractive gravity will always pull a contracting universe into a final singularity.

Second, we have to assume that the universe is not so special that it remains forever static. Einstein's original cosmological model, the Einstein static universe, was of this type. A static universe means that it returns the next instant. This is a return, but clearly not one which can occur in our own universe. An infinitesimal fluctuation anywhere in the Einstein universe would cause it to expand forever or contract to a singularity, another indication that the Einstein universe return is unphysical.

Third, we have to assume that the evolution of the universe is deterministic. This assumption is also made in the Quantum Recurrence Theorem and in the Poincaré Recurrence Theorem, but not in the Markov Recurrence Theorem. What is remarkable is that, in general relativity, determinism leads to no-return, rather than return. This is probably not an essential assumption because, as my discussion of the three recurrence theorems makes clear, return really comes from the finiteness of the state space rather than from determinism. But the assumption of determinism makes the mathematics easier.

In general relativity the analogues of position and momentum are continuous variables, so any return or no-return theorem must be stated in terms of averages, as in the Quantum Recurrence Theorem. What the No-Return Theorem says is that, if the above three assumptions hold, then the average of the initial data which define the state of the universe at any time can never again be close to the average of the initial data now. I shall give a proof of this theorem in the Appendix for Scientists.

The Triumph of Progress

If the Eternal Return is not allowed by modern physics, and if the Heat Death can also be avoided, then eternal progress is possible. The main thrust of this book is to prove that such eternal progress is not only possible but inevitable, and will result ultimately in our salvation. By "progress" I mean that, on the average, life is improving. For the biosphere as a whole, progress means an increase, on the average, in the number of ecological niches with time and an increase in the intelligence of the most intelligent species which exists at any given instant in the universe. From the human standpoint, progress means an increase with time of per capita wealth, an increase in the average life span, an improvement in the health of the typical person, more generally an increase in the standard of living. Furthermore, progress means an increase of knowledge. "Eternal" progress means that progress will continue literally without limit. Knowledge will grow without bound, per capita wealth will increase to infinity.

Progress does *not* mean there can never be any setbacks. The Earth has been periodically bombarded by large meteorites, and on occasion these impacts have annihilated huge portions of the biosphere. The dinosaurs were probably destroyed in such a blast some 70 million years ago, and it took mammals millions of years to refill the ecological niches emptied by this mass extinction. But the biosphere has more than made up the losses suffered by this destruction. The most intelligent animal currently on Earth, *Homo sapiens,* has a much larger brain as compared to its body size than any dinosaur ever had. We also know from human history that knowledge has not always increased. Aristarchus developed his Sun-centered astronomy centuries before the birth of Jesus, and Greek mathematical astronomy was sufficiently advanced by the third century A.D. to take the step that the European astronomers in fact took in the late sixteenth and early seventeenth centuries. But this "next" step was *not* taken in the third century. Instead, Greek mathematics and astronomy were largely forgotten in the West after the fall of the Roman Empire, and the next step had to wait for Copernicus some thirteen centuries later. But that next step *was* eventually taken, and today our scientific knowledge is enormously superior to any age before us. What the idea of progress means is not that advance is monotonic, but rather that the advance will *eventually* occur. Our own civilization may fail to build the SSC and learn whether or not the Higgs particle exists—as we shall see in Chapter IV, the existence of the Higgs particle at a particular mass is a prediction of the Omega Point Theory—but if we do fail, a future civilization will succeed.

Progress has been a powerful idea in the West ever since the Greeks in the fifth century B.C., as the distinguished historians Nisbet[106] and Himmelfarb[107] have demonstrated, but it came to full flower in the late nineteenth century. Two thinkers of that period, Herbert Spencer and Friedrich Engels, epitomize this faith in ultimate progress. These men represent the two main branches of the progressive movement.

Herbert Spencer believed that continued progress would come from the continued expansion of the free market. He was an uncompromising defender of laissez-faire capitalism. He strongly opposed child labor and minimum wage laws, arguing that such laws would hinder progress (and incidentally make worse off the very people these laws were designed to aid). According to Spencer, the driving force of progress was increasing heterogeneity. A free market society would allow the maximum growth of heterogeneity, or diversity, manifested in the division of labor. A more diverse society would contain more net knowledge than a homogeneous society. Spencer, like Darwin, was quite worried about the Heat Death. He recognized there is nothing more homogeneous than an entire universe at the same uniform temperature. However, in *First Principles,* a book wherein he summarized his philosophy, Spencer argued[108] that, although the solar system would ultimately end in homogeneity, the force of gravity would generate inhomogeneity on the scale of the stars, and thus progress could (possibly) continue on these larger scales. As to whether this would mean progress could continue forever, Spencer admitted he did not know. There was always the possibility that the sidereal system was limited, that there was a limit to the reach of the "ether" (which nineteenth-century scientists believed carried light rays), in which case the universe would not be progressive but cyclic on the largest time-scales. Spencer did not follow the logical implications of this predicted

Eternal Return, as Nietzsche did. He explicitly denied that the cycle, if it occurred, would indicate a return to an identical previous state. Instead, he saw the cycles as ". . . ever the same in principle, but never the same in concrete result."[109] With his unshakable belief in progress, Spencer felt that something had to be wrong with both the Heat Death and the Eternal Return predictions. He emphasized that knowledge was too limited in the late nineteenth century to take seriously either the Heat Death or the Eternal Return. As we shall see, the mechanism suggested by Spencer for prolonging progress beyond the death of the solar system, namely the effect of gravity on the entire stellar system which is the universe, will work. Gravity operating on cosmological scales is the ultimate power source in the Omega Point Theory.

Friedrich Engels is with Karl Marx the founder of the socialist branch of the progressive movement. Both Marx and Engels were primarily concerned with human social organization, not natural science, but in *Dialectics of Nature,* Engels addressed the question of eternal progress:

> . . . eternally repeated succession of worlds in infinite time is the only logical complement to the co-existence of innumerable worlds in infinite space. . . . It is an eternal cycle in which matter moves. . . . But however often, and however relentlessly, this cycle is completed in time and space, however many millions of suns and earths may arise and pass away, however long it may last before the conditions for organic life develop, however innumerable the organic beings that have to arise and to pass away before animals with a brain capable of thought are developed from their midst, and for a short time find conditions suitable for life, only to be exterminated later without mercy, we have the certainty that matter remains eternally the same in all its transformations, that none of its attributes can ever be lost, and therefore, also, that with the same iron necessity that it will exterminate on the earth its highest creation, the thinking mind, it must somewhere else and at another time again produce it.[110]

At first sight, this passage sounds like Nietzsche arguing for the Eternal Return, rather than a defense of eternal progress. This interpretation, however, misses Engels' main point. Engels is actually trying here to offer an alternative to the Heat Death rather than establish the Eternal Return. He wants to oppose the hopelessness of eternal death foreseen in the Heat Death with the hopeful idea that the eternity of matter and energy *guarantees* life cannot disappear forever from the cosmos. He overlooked the fact—which Nietzsche did not overlook—that the Eternal Return is not a good solution to the Heat Death problem, for the Eternal Return just replaces one form of despair with another. However, *Dialectics of Nature* was never written up in final form, because Engels died before completing the book. So it is quite possible that Engels would have modified the quoted sentences with a passage predicting that one day physicists would find a way to make progress as eternal as matter. J. B. S. Haldane, one of the leading geneticists of the twentieth century and also a Marxist, claimed in his Notes to the first English edition of *Dialectics of Nature* that Engels was very close to doing just that:

> At present [Haldane was writing in 1940] physicists are divided on this question [the ultimate fate of the universe]. A few take Engels' view that the universe goes through cyclical changes, entropy being somehow diminished by processes at present unknown (e.g., formation of matter from radiation in interstellar space). Others think as Clausius did, that [the universe] will run down. But there is a third possibility[111] . . . in 1936–1938 Milne and Dirac independently arrived at the conclusion that the laws of nature themselves evolve, and in particular (according to Milne) that chemical changes are speeded up . . . in relation to physical changes. If so it is at least conceivable that this process may be rapid enough to compensate for the cooling of the stars, and that life may never become impossible. . . .[112] [This] suggests that the universe as a whole has a history, though probably an infinite one both in the past and the future. It is almost certain that Engels would have welcomed this idea. . . .[113]

Edward A. Milne was a distinguished British cosmologist in the 1930s, the holder of the Rouse Ball professorship at Oxford University (the chair that Roger Penrose now holds). Milne was aware of the fact that general relativity allowed any time coordinate to be used, and that the proper time which is the most appropriate time in the environment here on Earth might not be the most appropriate physical time for the universe as a whole. He argued[114] that, although the universe might exist for only a finite proper time in both the past and the future, in entropic time the universe might have an eternity in both the past and the future. Milne is correct as regards the future but, as we shall see, it is not necessary to imagine that the laws of physics slowly change in order for this to occur.

In addition to the above remarks, Haldane had earlier defended unlimited technical progress in a book, written just after World War I, entitled *Daedalus*. A far more extensive discussion of indefinite progress appeared in *The World, the Flesh, and the Devil*, by John Desmond Bernal, a British crystallographer. Bernal, like Haldane, was an ardent Marxist. His ideas are the ultimate source of the Omega Point Theory, because *The World, the Flesh, and the Devil* inspired Freeman Dyson[115] to develop the first detailed physical theory of how life could survive forever, and Dyson's work inspired mine. Bernal realized, as did Spencer before him, that survival forces life to leave the solar system:

> Sooner or later this pressure [the exhaustion of material resources in the Solar System], or perhaps the knowledge of the imminent failure of the Sun, would force some more adventurous [space] colony to set out beyond the bounds of the Solar System. . . .[116] [It] is unlikely that man will stop until he has roamed over and colonized most of the sidereal universe. . . . Man will not ultimately be content to be parasitic on the stars but will invade them and organize them for his own purposes.

Bernal was the first to suggest that the stars—and in particular the Sun —were, from the point of view of life, very wasteful of energy. He argued that this waste should stop.

> A star is essentially an immense reservoir of energy which is being dissipated as rapidly as its bulk will allow. . . . [The] stars cannot be allowed to continue in their own way, but will be turned into efficient heat engines.[117]

Bernal is correct about this. In the end, the Earth itself must be transferred from what I shall call "ultimate reality" into a virtual reality, from real space into a cyberspace in a computer's memory. If this is not done before the Sun leaves the main sequence, not only will much of the Sun's total energy reserve be wasted, but the Earth will be completely destroyed by the expanding Sun to no purpose. The Earth's annihilation in real space is certain. The only question is whether this destruction serves the ultimate purpose of biospheric survival or whether it is merely pointless. We shall see in later chapters how the Earth's destruction can contribute to biospheric survival.

However, Bernal was not sure the Heat Death could be avoided:

. . . The Second Law of Thermodynamics which, as Jeans delights in pointing out to us, will ultimately bring this universe to an inglorious close, may perhaps always remain the final factor. But by intelligent organization the life of the universe could probably be prolonged to many millions of millions of times what it would be without organization. Besides, we are still too close to the birth of the universe to be certain about its death.[118]

Bernal was right to be dubious about the Heat Death. The Second Law still remains the final factor but, as I shall show in the following chapter, the energy of gravitational shear near the Omega Point is sufficient to avoid the Heat Death. Bernal's view of the dominant form of life in the ultimate future is quite similar to the ideas I shall develop in later chapters:

The new life [intelligent beings fitted to survive in space without encumbrances like spacesuits] would be more plastic . . . more variable and more permanent than that produced by the triumphant opportunism of nature. Bit by bit the heritage in the direct line of mankind—the heritage of the original life . . . —would dwindle, and in the end disappear effectively, being preserved perhaps as some curious relic, while the new life which conserves none of the substance and all the spirit of the old would take its place and continue its development. . . .[119] Finally, consciousness itself may end or vanish in a humanity that has become completely etherialized, losing the close-knit organism, becoming masses of atoms in space communicating by radiation, and ultimately perhaps resolving itself entirely into light. . . .[120] Mankind—the old mankind—would be left in undisputed possession of the Earth, to be regarded by the inhabitants of the celestial spheres with a curious reverence.[121] The world [the Earth] might, in fact, be transformed into a human zoo, a zoo so intelligently managed that its inhabitants are not aware that they are there merely for the purposes of observation and experiment.[122]

The Earth, too, shall pass away in ultimate reality. It will be preserved in computer memories, but it will not become a zoo. Instead, we humans have a much more exciting future than mere zoo animals: all of us will be resurrected in the far future to participate in the evolution of the entire universe into the Omega Point.

The term "Omega Point" is not taken from the work of physicists like Bernal or Dyson, but rather from the work of the paleontologist Teilhard de Chardin. (Providing the term is Teilhard's *only* scientific contribution to this book. He is not mentioned in the Appendix for Scientists.)

In addition to being a scientist, Teilhard was also a Roman Catholic priest, a member of the Jesuit order. He had begun in the 1920s to lecture about his speculations on combining Catholicism with evolution. The leaders of the Jesuit order exiled him to China to prevent any further discussion of these ideas in his native France. He was forbidden to publish any of his philosophical works in his lifetime. When the chair of paleontology became vacant at the Collège de France, he was not allowed to apply for the position. He moved to New York City, where he died in 1955. Exiled even in death, he is buried in the cemetery of a Jesuit novitiate some fifty miles from New York, far from his beloved France.[123] When Teilhard's ideas on evolutionary Christianity were published in the year of his death, his friends spread far and wide the pathos of his life story. Undoubtedly, this resulted in his ideas being given a vastly more sympathetic hearing than they might otherwise have received.[124] (Or deserved.)

Teilhard opens what is generally regarded as his most significant philosophical work, *The Phenomenon of Man,* with the statement: ". . . if this book is to be properly understood, it must be read not as a work on metaphysics, still less as a sort of theological essay, but purely and simply as a scientific treatise."[125] His scientific critics—for instance the evolutionist George Gaylord Simpson and the zoologist Sir Peter Medawar—have taken him to task for this statement. Teilhard indeed wrote the book in a language more commonly found in mystical religious tracts than in scientific treatises. Medawar was so put off by the language that he charged that the book ". . . cannot be read without a feeling of suffocation, a gasping and flailing around for sense . . . the greater part of it is nonsense, tricked out by a variety of tedious metaphysical conceits, and its author can be excused of dishonesty only on the grounds that before deceiving others, he had taken great pains to deceive himself."[126]

Most of Teilhard's book is just a poetic description of the evolutionary history of the Earth's biosphere. The description is the standard one of the late 1930s when the book was cast into final form: some one-cell organisms develop into metazoans, some phyla of which in turn develop organisms with complex nervous systems, and one lineage of these finally acquires intelligence: the "hominization" of the world has at last occurred. Simpson and Medawar did not dispute this statement of the evolutionary facts. What they disagreed with was Teilhard's proposed mechanism driving the ascent of life.

Teilhard argued that "energy" existed in two basic modes, "tangential" and "radial." The former is essentially the energy measured by the physicist, while the latter can be regarded as a sort of psychic or spiritual energy. Teilhard's motivation for introducing the latter variety was twofold: first, his cosmological system evolves into higher and higher order in its biota as time proceeds, and this seemed to him to be forbidden by the Second Law of Thermodynamics (it's not), which he admits governs the evolution of the usual variety of energy.[127] Furthermore, the eventual Heat Death predicted by the physicists would undermine any hope of having Ultimate Intelligence in the physical cosmos. Teilhard is well aware that if the Heat Death occurs, and if intelligence is at bottom completely dependent on tangential energy, it must be doomed to extinction in the end, no matter how powerful it becomes. His radial energy is subject to a universal law contrary to the Second Law: radial energy becomes more concentrated, more available with time, and it is this concentration that drives the evolution of life to man, and beyond.[128] Radial energy—psychic energy—is as ubiquitous as tangential energy. It is present in all forms of matter, at least to a rudimentary extent, and so all forms of matter have a low-level sort of life.[129]

To modern scientists this vitalism seems archaic, even occult, and hence unscientific. And indeed, Teilhard's vitalism is completely wrong. However, in justice to Teilhard, it must be said that we now know he planned *The Phenomenon of Man* in the autumn of 1938, and had actually begun writing it down beginning in the autumn of 1939. He finished it in the spring of 1940. Furthermore, Teilhard had written earlier versions[130] of his masterwork, in 1916, in 1928, and in 1930. According to Ernst Mayr,[131] one of its creators, the Modern Synthesis—the modern, purely mechanistic theory of evolution—was developed in the period 1936–47. Almost all of the major books on evolution written in the 1920s and 1930s—and the totality[132] of all those written by French evolutionists—rejected Darwinism. A French historian of biology, Ernest Boesiger, has said that, as recently as the 1970s, "France . . . [was] a kind of living fossil in the rejection of modern evolutionary theories: about 95 percent of all biologists and philosophers [were] more or less opposed to Darwinism."[133] A Darwinian was not appointed[134] to the chair of evolutionary biology in the Paris Faculty of Science—the very top of the French university system —until 1965(!), even though the chair was created in 1887. One of the very few Darwinians in France, Georges Teissier, said[135] in 1958: "In the years of my studies at the University, Darwinism was usually considered an *obsolete* [my emphasis] theory and no biologist in France really believed in natural selection." Thus notions like "radial energy" were in effect the consensus view of most evolutionists at the time Teilhard wrote his book, and still the consensus view of Teilhard's fellow French evolutionists at the time of his death in 1955. One can hardly claim a scientist is being unscientific when he adopts the consensus view of his colleagues, no matter how wrong.

According to Teilhard, ". . . the idea of the *direct* [his emphasis] transformation of one of these two energies into the other . . . has to be abandoned. As soon as we try to couple them together, their mutual independence becomes as clear as their interrelation."[136] So "radial energy" is not really "energy" in any sense that a physicist would recognize. We shall see in a later chapter that "radial energy" is actually quite analogous to another physics concept, information. In fact, Medawar himself pointed out in his review of *The Phenomenon of Man* that ". . . Teilhard's radial, spiritual, or psychic energy may be equated to 'information' or 'information content' in the sense that has been made reasonably precise by communication engineers."[137]

In Teilhard's cosmology, evolution does not end with mankind. Just as nonsapient life covered the Earth to form the *biosphere,* so thinking life—*Homo sapiens*—has covered the Earth to form what Teilhard terms the *noosphere,* or cogitative layer. At present the noosphere is only loosely organized, but its coherence will grow as human science and civilization develop, as "planetization"—Teilhard's word—proceeds. Finally, in the far future, the radial energy will at last become totally dominant over, or rather independent of, tangential energy, and the noosphere will coalesce into a supersapient being, the *Omega Point.* Thus the Omega Point is the ultimate goal of the tree of life and in particular its current "leading shoot," the human species. As Teilhard put it:

> This will be the end and the fulfillment of the spirit of the Earth.
>
> The end of the world: the wholesale internal introversion upon itself of the noosphere, which has simultaneously reached the uttermost limit of its complexity and centrality.
>
> The end of the world: the overthrow of equilibrium [the Heat Death], detaching the mind, fulfilled at last, from its material matrix, so that it will henceforth rest with all its weight on God-Omega.[138]

This is nice poetry, but the science is a bit unclear. Teilhard claimed to be writing *qua* scientist in *The Phenomenon of Man,* and in fact some properties of his Omega Point can be gleaned from other passages in the book.

First property of the Omega Point: it allows humankind to escape death in general and the Heat Death in particular:

> The radical defect in all forms of belief in progress, as they are expressed in the positivist credos, is that they do not definitely eliminate death. What is the use of detecting a focus of any sort in the van of evolution if that focus can and must one day disintegrate? To

satisfy the ultimate requirements of our action, Omega must be independent of the collapse of the forces with which evolution is woven. . . . Thus something in the cosmos escapes from entropy. . . .[139]

Second property of the Omega Point: it is in the ultimate future, not in time, but on the *boundary* of all future time, and is the limit of all temporal sequences which it pulls into itself:

> . . . Omega itself is . . . at the end of the whole process, in as much as in it the movement of synthesis culminates. Yet we must be careful to note that under this evolutive facet Omega still only reveals *half of itself.* While being the last term of its series, it is also *outside all series.* Not only does it crown, but it closes . . . If by its very nature it did not escape from time and space which it gathers together, it would not be Omega.[140] [Teilhard's emphasis.]

Third property of the Omega Point: it can be regarded as analogous to the *singularity* at the point forming the sharp end of a cone (which is why Omega is called a "point"):

> . . . taking a series of sections from the base towards the summit of a cone, their area decreases constantly; then suddenly, with another infinitesimal displacement, the surface vanishes leaving us with a *point* [Teilhard's emphasis] . . . what was previously only a centered surface became a center. . . .[141]

Fourth property of the Omega Point: it can only arise in a *finite and bounded* geometrical system like the surface of the Earth, because only in such environments is mankind forced to coalesce into the Omega Point: only a bounded system is unlimited and hence only in such a system is ceaseless communication possible:

> . . . there intervenes a fact . . . the roundness of the Earth. The geometrical limitation of a star closed, like a gigantic molecule, upon itself . . . what would have become of humanity, if, by some remote chance, it had been free to spread indefinitely on an unlimited surface, that is to say left only to the devices of its internal affinities? Something unimaginable. . . . Perhaps even nothing at all, when

we think of the extreme importance of the role played in its development by the forces of compression.[142]

The "forces of compression" about which Teilhard writes are the social forces which arise from human beings communicating with each
other. Again, it is this limitless communication that drives humanity
into the Omega Point, and thus generates the Omega Point.

Teilhard's bounded world was the finite Earth. He did not believe
that space travel would ever be an important factor in the future evolution of humanity. Indeed, as the immediately preceding passage makes
clear, were humanity to be freed from the confines of the finite Earth,
it would probably never combine into the Omega Point. In 1951,
Teilhard emphasized this in a private conversation with Jean Hyppolite,
a professor of philosophy at the Sorbonne:

> Following in the steps of Haldane, the neo-Marxist tends to escape
> into the perspectives of a vital *expansion,* in other words into a *vital-
> ization* of the Totality of stellar *Space.* Let me stress this second point a
> little. From his own viewpoint, the Marxist will approach willingly
> and with an open mind the idea of an eschatology for a classless
> society in which the Omega Point is conceived as the point of natu-
> ral convergence for humanity. But suppose we remind him that our
> Earth, because of the implacable laws of entropy, is destined to die:
> suppose we ask him what will be the outcome allowed humanity in
> such a world. Then he replies—in terms that H. G. Wells has already
> used—by offering perspectives of interplanetary and intergalactic
> colonization. This is one way to dodge the mystical notion of a
> Parousia, and the gradual movement of humanity towards an ecstatic
> union with God.[143]

Not being a cosmologist, Teilhard was unaware of the possibility that
the universe itself might be closed. And furthermore, that its closure
would allow an escape from the Heat Death. As we shall see in the
next few chapters, life in a closed universe will be forced, by the very
requirement of survival, to converge upon itself and end time in an
Omega Point-God, an Omega Point having *exactly* the key four
properties listed above. For these reasons, in honor of Teilhard's origi-

nal conception, I am calling my cosmological model the *Omega Point Theory*.

Although Teilhard's work inspired the name of the Omega Point Theory, the actual content of the theory was inspired by Freeman Dyson's extraordinary 1979 paper *Time Without End: Physics and Biology in an Open Universe*. This paper is important because it is the first attempt to *calculate* in a rigorous way, using the known laws of physics, what life must do in order to survive forever. Where Bernal, Haldane, and Teilhard speculated, Dyson computed. His mathematics established beyond question that infinite survival is very difficult: it cannot occur in just any universe. But thereby Dyson established the field of physical theology, because this very difficulty means the Eternal Life Postulate has experimental consequences: only if our own universe has certain very special properties can the postulate be true. Dyson attributes the Eternal Life Postulate to Bernal (and, to a lesser extent, Haldane), but he claims[144] the idea of applying it to the remote future he got from a 1977 paper[145] by the Muslim astrophysicist Jamal Islam, who comes from and now lives in Bangladesh. What Islam did was to calculate how matter would evolve in universes which expand forever. Dyson then asked what life would have to do in order to exist on matter that behaves in this way.

The phrase "open universe" in the title of Dyson's paper has a technical meaning. There are three basic types of universe models: the open universe, the flat universe, and the closed universe. A *closed universe* is what I have hitherto considered our own universe to be: it has finite spatial volume, but no boundary—it is a three-dimensional analogue of a sphere. A closed universe will start from an initial singularity, expand to a maximum size, and recontract to a final singularity. An *open universe* is the model Dyson considers. It is infinite in spatial extent, and although it begins in an initial singularity, it expands forever (in proper time). There is very little matter in an open universe, so in its later stages it expands very fast: the separation between galaxies grows linearly with proper time. Separation increasing linearly means that gravity is not slowing down the expansion at all. A *flat universe* is just like an open universe—it is infinite in spatial extent and expands forever from an initial singularity—except that it has just enough matter so that gravity is always significant in slowing the expansion down, but never strong enough to stop the expansion. The separation of galaxies in a flat universe grows as the square root of the proper time.

Interestingly, Dyson's "philosophical bias" was the exact opposite of Teilhard's, who believed, as I do, that life can evolve into infinity only in a finite closed universe. Dyson dismissed the idea of life continuing forever in a closed universe in a single paragraph:

> The end of a closed universe has been studied in detail by Rees.[146] Regrettably I have to concur that in this case we have no escape from frying. No matter how deep we burrow into the Earth to shield ourselves from blue-shifted background radiation, we can only postpone by a few million years our miserable end. I shall not discuss the closed universe in detail, since it gives me a feeling of claustrophobia to imagine our whole existence confined within a box. I can only raise one question which may offer us a thin chance of survival. Supposing that we discover the universe to be naturally closed and doomed to collapse, is it conceivable that by intelligent intervention, converting matter into radiation to flow purposefully on a cosmic scale, we could break open a closed universe and change the topology of spacetime so that only a part of it would collapse and another part would expand forever? I do not know the answer to this question.[147]

But I do know the answer to Dyson's question: it's not possible. More precisely, I shall prove in the Appendix for Scientists that if a closed universe starts to collapse, if gravity is always attractive, and if determinism holds, then every part of the entire universe, without exception, collapses in finite proper time to zero volume while the temperature goes to infinity. There is no way life could stop this collapse.

But stopping the collapse is the last thing life would want to do. It is the very collapse of the universe itself which permits life to continue forever. Dyson's mistake was to assume that the collapse would necessarily have to occur at the same rate in all directions. If this happened it would in fact doom life but, as I pointed out at the end of Chapter II, it will not happen. Chaos in the Einstein equations means that collapse at the same rate in all directions is a very unstable and thus a very improbable future history. Collapse at different rates in different directions (this is called "gravitational shear") means a temperature difference in different directions, and this temperature difference means power for life. Unlimited temperature means unlimited power. Finite temperature means finite power. But of course life will have to change its form to survive the ever increasing temperature near the Omega Point.

Dyson realized that life could not continue in its present form forever, even in universes which do not collapse but instead expand forever. These universes get ever colder as they expand, and life must adapt to an ever colder environment. He therefore had to find a definition of "life" which would apply not only to terrestrial life but to life in any environment whatsoever.

I think his definition was much too crude to allow one to draw any general conclusions. He realized that life was a physical object which is "complex," and that complexity is appropriately measured by the number of possible alternative states a system can be in. Now all physicists know that the system entropy is also a measure of the number of alternative states of the system, so Dyson argued that the complexity of a living being should be proportional to the negative of its entropy. I think he is on firm ground this far.

However, he then computed the entropy of a human being by multiplying the rate at which a human dissipates energy (about 100 watts, as I proved in Chapter II) by the human body temperature and by one second, the time being his estimate of the length of a "moment of consciousness." This product of three numbers, converted into bits of information, Dyson called "Q." For a human, $Q = 10^{23}$. Dyson's procedure seems to me rather arbitrary. For one thing, most of the human energy dissipation occurs to keep our body temperature constant. We are warm-blooded animals, but surely warm blood is not an essential defining quantity of life. However, this particular method of computing complexity, rather than complexity itself, underlies Dyson's entire theory. He infers from this method that the rate at which energy is used for life must be proportional to the square of the temperature, and that the rate at which life has new experiences is proportional to the temperature. There is no reason, however, to think either of these generally holds.

Dyson was nevertheless correct in regarding life as a form of complexity, and in regarding the appropriate timescale to be not proper time but the rate at which life has new experiences. But both the rate of complexity change and the complexity can be measured directly without having to bother with Dyson's method of computing it. I shall thus use these standard measures in my own definition of Eternal Life Postulate in the next chapter, and we shall see that these standard measures invalidate many of Dyson's conclusions. For example, with the subjective timescale proportional to the temperature, according to Dyson there would be only a finite amount of subjective time between now and the Big Crunch in a collapsing closed universe. I shall show, however, that, using the standard physics measure of complexity, it is possible for an infinite amount of complexity to be produced, and hence an infinite amount of subjective time, between now and the Omega Point, even though there is only a finite amount of proper time. Progress *can* continue forever in a closed universe.

Dyson's "philosophical bias" against the spatially closed universe inspired the title of his popular book describing his Eternal Life theory, *Infinite in All Directions*.[148] However, the open universe is *not* infinite in all directions. Although it is spatially infinite, it is *finite* in momentum space: there is a universal upper bound to the energy everywhere in this universe. This is important, because the state of the universe is given by its phase space position, not merely by its configuration space position. Complexity can increase without limit in a closed universe by using higher and higher energy states to code information. Also, from life's point of view the infinity of the configuration space is an illusion. If the universe is roughly the same everywhere, then if life travels sufficiently far in any direction it will run into some other life form's territory. Thus the amount of material available to our descendants is finite, unless they take it away from someone else. This won't happen in a closed universe because the momentum space our descendants will eventually use is currently unoccupied by anybody. And the total energy available diverges to infinity, so there is plenty for everybody.

Some contemporary evolutionists have gone beyond the rejection of a mechanism that drives life toward higher forms (there is no such mechanism in the Modern Synthesis) to reject the idea of progress itself. The most sustained attack on the idea of progress in evolution is

by the Harvard paleontologist Stephen J. Gould: "Progress is a nox-
ious, culturally embedded, untestable, nonoperational, intractable idea
that must be replaced if we wish to understand the patterns of history."[149] Gould asserts that the paleontological data do not support the
idea that progress has occurred in evolution. I claim on the contrary
that the very data Gould cites contain evidence of "progress" in the
sense this term is used in this book: that is, information stored in the
biosphere increases with time, at least on the average. Gould misses the
progress in his data because, as a paleontologist, he lacks the knowledge
of mathematics and physics which is required to interpret his data correctly.

Gould's central argument against progress in the fossil record is
illustrated by his treatment of temporal change in the frequency distributions for EQ (encephalization quotient, which means the ratio of
brain weight to body weight, normalized to the average for the class in
the time period under study) for carnivores and ungulates during the
Tertiary. (Roughly speaking, the higher the EQ, the "smarter" the
animal is.) What is observed is that the EQ frequency distributions are
at all times truncated gaussian distributions (truncated because the EQ
of any animal must be positive—it is not possible for a brain weight to
be negative).

However, although the means of the distributions increase with
time, so do the standard deviations. At all times, there are always some
members of the group with EQ near zero. As Gould puts it:

> To be sure, the distributions do shift—medians as well as means; but
> the main feature of change is a flattening and expansion in the range
> of the frequency distribution, not a general increase for all lineages
> within the clade. . . . Life began in simplicity; this fact of structure
> provided the "entity machine" with but one open direction, for
> complexity is a vast field, but little space exists between the first
> fossils and anything both simpler and conceivably preservable in the
> geological record. Where else but up for the right tail by asymmetri-
> cal expansion of variance?[150]

The answer to Gould's question is of course "down." What could
happen is that the frequency distribution could be cyclic in time: it

could start with a small mean and narrow spread, increase its mean and spread to a maximum, and then decrease its mean and spread until the frequency distribution returned to it original distribution. In other words, an Eternal Return is logically possible. An example of a frequency distribution which behaves in just this cyclic manner is the probability distribution of a quantized harmonic oscillator in one dimension. I have placed a detailed mathematical exposition of this model in the Appendix for Scientists, but the upshot is simple: the data quoted by Gould are most directly interpreted as *linear* progress. Gould's data are *not* cyclic; the Eternal Return of the harmonic oscillator frequency distribution is not present, although in principle it could have been.

It is interesting that Gould himself cannot resist using "progressive" language when describing the very work—Jerison's—he references to *attack* the notion of progress:

> South America provides a natural experiment to test this claim [that the increase of brain size in most mammals was driven by an "arms race" in brains between herbivores and the carnivores who preyed on them]. Until the Isthmus of Panama rose just a couple of million years ago, South America was an isolated island continent. *Advanced* [my emphasis] carnivores never reached this island, and predatory roles were filled by marsupial carnivores with low encephalization quotients. Here, the herbivores display no increase in brain size through time. Their average encephalization quotient remained below 0.5 throughout the Tertiary; moreover, these native herbivores were quickly eliminated when *advanced* [again, my emphasis] carnivores crossed the isthmus from North America.[151]

Gould did not use the word "advanced" to describe the mammalian carnivores which invaded South from North America because there was no other word choice. The word "placental" could have been used in place of "advanced," and would have contained the same information. Rather, his slip of the pen was due to his tacit realization that the placental carnivores were more sophisticated machines than the marsupial carnivores which inhabited South America until the rise of the isthmus of Panama.

I might add that Gould even gives the mechanism that drove the progress in encephalization quotient:

> Animals that make a living by catching rapidly moving prey seem to need bigger brains than plant eaters. And, as the brains of herbivores grew larger (presumably under intense selective pressure imposed by their carnivorous predators), the carnivores also evolved bigger brains to maintain the differential.[152]

(However, it's not clear to me why the same mechanism would not also apply to the interaction between the marsupial herbivores and carnivores in South America. For some reason, the South American mammals did not engage in the same type of arms race.)

In another article, Gould tells the story of the attempt by the great nineteenth-century Swiss-American naturalist Louis Agassiz to disprove Darwin's theory of evolution. Agassiz believed that the deep oceans provided a constant environment over the whole of terrestrial history, and so he thought Darwin's theory would imply that the organisms in the deeps would be the most primitive creatures of any group. Gould remarks: "The persistence of simple forms in a constant deep environment would have satisfied Darwin's evolutionary theory as well as Agassiz's God [true]. But the depths are not constant, and their life is not *primitive*[153] [my emphasis, and true again, though Gould would never admit it]."

Most contemporary evolutionists are not antiprogressive reactionaries like Gould. The most outstanding British evolutionist is probably John Maynard Smith, who in a recent review of Gould's work explicitly disagreed with him on progress: "I do think that progress had happened, although I find it hard to define precisely what I mean."[154] Commenting on Gould's data, Maynard Smith came close to the definition I shall be using over and over in this book: "This looks like progress . . . in the sense of an increase of information transmitted between generations."[155] Virtually all modern evolutionists are agreed on the contingency of evolution—the evolution of "cognitive creatures" is not inevitable, for instance.

What tends to increase over time (on the average) is the complexity, or equivalently the information coded, by the most complex species of a given genus, order, class, etc.[156] The evolutionist Raup has argued[157] for progress in this sense: taxon longevities are observed to increase over geological history, and this means an increase in the ability not to fail, because of an improved ability to deal with environmental change, in turn because of more complexity in the nervous system. I completely agree—and, as I argued in the preceding chapter, it is the complexity of the human nervous system that will enable life to escape the greatest environmental challenge of all, the destruction of the Earth by the Sun. I also showed in the preceding chapter that life can continue for the next 10^{18} years. Now I shall show it can go on forever.

PHYSICS NEAR THE FINAL STATE: THE CLASSICAL OMEGA POINT THEORY

.———.

Computer Definitions of "Life," "Person," and "Soul"

IN ORDER TO INVESTIGATE WHETHER LIFE can continue to exist forever, I shall need to define "life" in physics language. I claim that a "living being" is any entity which codes information (in the physics sense of this word) with the information coded being preserved by natural selection. Thus "life" is a form of information processing, and the human mind—and the human soul—is a very complex computer program. Specifically, a "person" is defined to be a computer program which can pass the Turing test, which was discussed in Chapter II.

This definition of "life" is quite different from what the average person—and the average biologist—would think of as "life." In the traditional definition, life is a complex process based on the chemistry of the carbon atom. However, even supporters of the traditional definition admit that the key words are "complex process" and not "carbon atom." Although the entities everyone agrees are "alive" happen to be based on carbon chemistry, there is no reason to believe that analogous processes cannot be based on other systems. In fact, the British biochemist A. G. Cairns-Smith[1] has suggested that the first living beings—our ultimate ancestors—were based on metallic crystals, not carbon. If this is true, then if we insist that living beings must be based on carbon chemistry, we would be forced to conclude that our ultimate ancestors were not alive. In Cairns-Smith's theory, our ultimate ancestors were self-replicating patterns of defects in the metallic crystals. Over time, the pattern persisted, but was transferred to another substrate: carbon molecules. What is important is not the substrate but the pattern, and the pattern is another name for *information*.

But life of course is not a static pattern. Rather, it is a dynamic pattern that persists over time. It is thus a process. But not all processes are alive. The key feature of the "living" patterns is that their persistence is due to a feedback with their environment: the information coded in the pattern continually varies, but the variation is constrained to a narrow range by this feedback. Thus life is, as I stated, information preserved by natural selection.

This definition of life has some counterintuitive consequences. In 1986, John Barrow and I pointed out[2] that it meant automobiles were alive. They self-reproduce in automobile factories using human mechanics. Granted, their reproduction is not autonomous; they need a factory external to themselves. But so do male humans: to make a male baby, an external biochemical factory called a "womb" is needed. Granted, their reproduction requires another living species. But so does the reproduction of the flowering plants: such plants use bees to pollinate and animals to disperse their seeds. Viruses require the entire machinery of a cell to reproduce. The form of automobiles in their environment is preserved by natural selection: there is a fierce struggle for existence between various "races" of automobiles. Japanese and European automobiles are competing with native American automobiles for scarce resources—money for the manufacturer—that will result in either more American or more Japanese and European automobiles being built. By my definition of life, not only automobiles but all machines—in particular computers—are alive. (Though of course automobiles are not "persons.")

In the same year that Barrow and I published our claim that automobiles were alive, the leading biologist Richard Dawkins of Oxford University published exactly the same claim. On page one of his famous book, *The Blind Watchmaker*, Dawkins wrote: "computers and cars . . . in this book will be firmly treated as biological objects. The reader's reaction to this may be to ask, 'Yes, but are they *really* biological objects?' Words are our servants, not our masters." In the same book, Dawkins refers to machines as "honorary living things."[3] In an earlier book, *The Selfish Gene,* Dawkins says that ideas in the human mind which are preserved by natural selection ". . . should be regarded as living structures, not just metaphorically, but technically."[4] The biologist Dawkins has reached the same definition of life that I shall use: life is information preserved by natural selection. Any attempt to reduce life to physics will inevitably end up with the same definition.

It is extremely important that my definition of life not be misunderstood. Most people's immediate reaction to my definition is typically, "Surely there is more to life than mere information processing, to punching data into a computer, and letting the machine grind away. This may be sufficient for a machine—or a computer hacker—but real people are far more complex. They work for a living, they listen to music, they enjoy conversations with other people, they reflect on the meaning of existence, they worship God, they develop deep and loving relationships with others, they raise children. An infinity of time spent doing nothing but playing with a computer—what a horrid thought!"

I completely agree. It *is* a horrid thought. But it is not the eschatology I am proposing. The crucial point is that, at the most basic nuts-and-bolts physics level, all of the above-mentioned activities of "real" people, indeed *all* of the possible activities of people, are in fact types of information processing. The human activities of listening, enjoying, reflecting, worshiping, and loving are mental activities, and correspond to mental activity in the brain. In other words, at the *physics* level, they are information processing, and nothing but information processing. But at the *human* level, they are not cold and austere "information processing," but warm and human listening, enjoying, reflecting, worshiping, and loving. Furthermore, the essential nature—at the physics level—of all other human activities can be shown to be information processing. The upshot is that the laws of physics place constraints on information processing, and hence on the activities and existence of life. If the laws of physics do not permit information processing in a region of spacetime, then life simply cannot exist there. Conversely, if the laws of physics permit information processing in a region, then it is possible for some form of life to exist there. These limitations and opportunities are analogous to those imposed by food at the biological level. At the human level, it is certainly not possible to reduce all human experience to eating; eating is just one of many human actions, and in fact other things are more important (to most of us, anyway). But having enough to eat is a prior condition for these other activities. There will be no listening, enjoying, reflecting, worshiping, and loving without food. Similarly, a discussion of the future of life must be consistent with regarding life as information processing at the physics level.

So I shall assume that life goes on forever if machines of some sort can continue to exist forever. The pattern is what is important, not the substrate.

There is actually an astonishing similarity between the mind-as-computer-program idea and the medieval Christian idea of the "soul." Both are fundamentally "immaterial": a program is a sequence of integers, and an integer—2, say—exists "abstractly" as the class of all couples. The symbol "2" written here is a *representation* of the number 2, and not the number 2 itself. In fact, Aquinas (following Aristotle) defined the *soul* to be "the form of activity of the body." In Aristotelian language, the *formal* cause of an action is the abstract cause, as opposed to the material and efficient causes. For a computer, the program is the formal cause, while the material cause is the properties of the matter out of which the computer is made, and the efficient cause is the opening and closing of electric circuits. For Aquinas, a human soul needed a body to think and feel, just as a computer program needs a physical computer to run.

Aquinas thought the soul had two faculties: the agent intellect *(intellectus agens)* and the receptive intellect *(intellectus possibilis),* the former being the ability to acquire concepts, and the latter being the ability to retain and use the acquired concepts. Similar distinctions are made in computer theory: general rules concerning the processing of information coded in the central processor are analogous to the agent intellect; the programs coded in RAM or on a tape are analogues of the receptive intellect. (In a Turing machine, the analogues are the general rules of symbol manipulation coded in the device which prints or erases symbols on the tape versus the tape instructions, respectively.) Furthermore, the word "information" comes from the Aristotle-Aquinas' notion of "form": we are "informed" if new forms are added to the receptive intellect. Even semantically, the information theory of the soul is the same as the Aristotle-Aquinas theory.

What Does It Mean for Life to Exist Forever?

Now we know how to define life using the language of information theory. We will need relativity theory to define "forever." Recall that, in relativity, space and time are integrated into a single entity called spacetime. It is conventional to represent spacetime by a Minkowski Diagram, pictured in Figure IV.1.

In a Minkowski Diagram, the vertical axis is time and the horizontal axis is space. Since space and time are the same thing, we should measure both in the same units. Time is measured in years, so space will be measured in light-years. In these natural units, the speed of light is unity: $c = 1$, because light moves at a rate of one light-year per year. The history of a light ray thus appears in a Minkowski Diagram as a straight line inclined at 45 degrees off the vertical (time) axis. The history of an object that doesn't move at all is a vertical line in a Minkowski Diagram. An object that is either stationary or moves less than the speed of light—all real objects are in this category because nothing can go faster than light—is a curve whose tangent is always less than 45 degrees off the vertical. This curve in spacetime is called a *worldline*.

Of course, Figure IV.1 is rather deceptive. It has only one spatial axis. In reality, there are three spatial dimensions and one time dimension, so spacetime is four-dimensional. In Figure IV.2 an attempt is made to be more realistic: two spatial dimensions are shown, together with the vertical axis, which is time.

The collection of all histories of light rays that go out from a point in spacetime—such a point is called an *event*—form a cone. If the cone is a set of light rays moving into the future, the cone is called the *future light cone*. If the cone is the set of light rays moving into the past from an event, it is called the *past light cone*. A worldline can also define past and future light cones. As can be seen in Figure IV.2, the set of all spacetime events which can influence (send signals to) the worldline is just all the events inside and on the past light cone of the worldline, and the set of events which the worldline can influence is all the events inside and on the future light cone of the worldline. No event (spacetime point) which is outside the past light cone of the worldline can influence the worldline because nothing can go faster than light. To see this, imagine that the worldline is your own history. If you are between twenty and forty years of age, you have another fifty or sixty

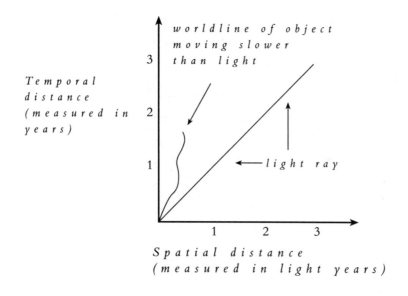

FIGURE IV.1: *Minkowski Diagram for spacetime. The vertical axis is the time direction and the horizontal axis is one of the space directions. The figure uses "natural units" in which distance is measured in light-years and time in years. In these units, the speed of light is 1 (light-years per year). Therefore, a light ray starting at the origin of coordinates moves up one unit of time for every one unit of space. This means a light ray is represented as a line with unit slope: it is a line inclined 45 degrees off the vertical. An object that is either stationary or moving less than the speed of light is a curve everyhere inclined less than 45 degrees off the vertical. Such a curve is pictured, and this curve thus represents the history of the object in spacetime. Such a curve is called a* worldline.

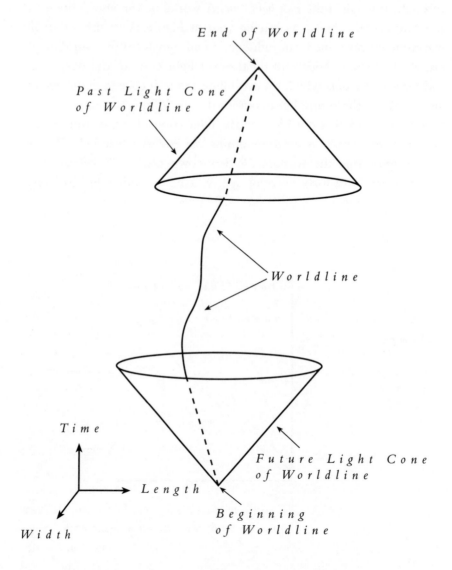

FIGURE IV.2: *A worldline with its future and past light cones. In this figure, another spatial dimension has been added to the Minkowski Diagram of the previous figure. The two horizontal axes are the two spatial dimensions, and the vertical axis is the time dimension. The light which goes out from a point in spacetime is no longer a line as in the previous figure, it is now a cone, the light cone. A worldline of an object which exists for only a finite time is pictured—think of this worldline as the worldline of a human being. The boundary of all spacetime points which can send signals to the human is formed by his past light cone, which is pictured. The boundary of all spacetime points to which he can send signals is formed by his future light cone, also pictured.*

years left on your worldline. Suppose that a person in orbit around the star Betelgeuse decided to signal Earth today. Since Betelgeuse is about 500 light-years away from us, it will take at least 500 years for this signal to reach us, because the signal must travel at light speed or less. You will be long dead by this time. Thus the spacetime event "now at Betelgeuse" is outside your worldline's past light cone.

Your worldline has a definite end point in spacetime: your worldline is terminated by your death. But we can imagine worldlines which have no such end point. Such worldlines are called *future-endless*. Future-endless worldlines, like your own worldline, define past light cones. The past light cone of your own worldline is exactly the same as the past light cone of the end point of your worldline (see Figure IV.2). However, this will not be true for future-endless worldlines: they have no end point in spacetime, by definition. We can nevertheless think of these future-endless worldlines defining "points"—these points are not events *in* spacetime, rather they are points on the boundary of spacetime. They are points which define the end of time. Now two future-endless worldlines can have different past light cones, or they can have the same past light cone. Roger Penrose has proposed that we use this difference to define the collection of points of this boundary of spacetime. Specifically, Penrose says that two future-endless worldlines hit the same point on the future *c-boundary* of spacetime if both worldlines define a the same past light cone. If the two worldlines define different past light cones, they hit different points on the future c-boundary. More precisely, a future c-boundary point *is* the past light cone of a future-endless worldline, considered as a unity. (Recall that, for a worldline with an end point in spacetime, the past light cone was defined by its future end point. The light cone is defined uniquely by the end point, and conversely, the end point is defined uniquely by the light cone. Thus each point in spacetime could be regarded as identical to the past light cone itself. But when we make this identification, the light cone must be considered as a unity, not as being made up of its individual points.) Figure IV.3 illustrates the c-boundary (the letter "c" is short for "causal" because the points are defined by the light cones, which divide events into those that can have a causal effect on worldlines and those that cannot.)

So, life is information processing, and obviously it must make it all the way to the c-boundary if it can be said to go on forever. This leads to the

DEFINITION: I shall say that life continues forever if:

(1) information processing continues indefinitely along at least one worldline γ all the way to the future "c-boundary" of the universe; that is, until the end of time.

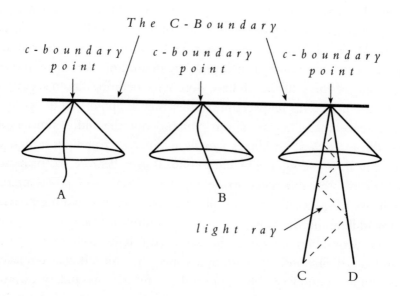

FIGURE IV.3: *The Penrose c-boundary. Worldlines that go all the way to the end of time define points on the c-boundary. Such worldlines are called* future-endless. *The thick black line is the future c-boundary. Two future-endless worldlines define distinct points on the c-boundary if the two worldlines have distinct past light cones. Four distinct worldlines are pictured, as are three distinct c-boundary points. Worldlines A and B have different past light cones, and so define two different c-boundary points. Worldlines C and D, however, have the same past light cone, and so define the same c-boundary point. The dashed lines connecting worldlines C and D are light rays going back and forth between these two worldlines. Two distinct future-endless worldlines will have the same past light cone if and only if light can pass back and forth between the two worldlines an infinite number of times. Thus such worldlines are always in causal contact. The future c-boundary will be a single point if and only if every future-endless worldline is always in causal contact with every other future-endless worldline.*

(2) the amount of information processed between now and this future c-boundary is infinite in the region of spacetime with which the worldline γ can communicate; that is, the region inside the past light cone of γ.

(3) the amount of information stored at any given time τ within this region diverges to infinity as τ approaches its future limit (this future limit of τ is finite in a closed universe, but infinite in an open one, if τ is measured in what physicists call "proper time").

The above is a rough outline of the more technical definition given in the Appendix for Scientists. But let me ignore details here. What is important are the physical (and ethical) reasons for imposing each of the above three conditions. The reason for Condition 1 has already been given: it simply states that there must be at least one history in which life (= information processing) never ends.

Condition 2 tells us two things: first, that information processed is "counted" only if it is possible, at least in principle, to communicate the results of the computation to the history γ. This is important in cosmology, because event horizons abound. In the closed Friedmann universe, which is the standard (but oversimplified) model of our actual universe (if it is in fact closed), every comoving observer eventually loses the ability to send light signals to every other comoving observer, no matter how close. Life obviously would be impossible if one side of one's brain became forever unable to communicate with the other side. Life is organization, and organization can only be maintained by constant communication among the different parts of the organization. The second thing Condition 2 tells us is that the amount of information processed between now and the end of time is actually infinite. I claim that it is meaningful to say that life exists *forever* only if the number of thoughts generated between now and the end of time is actually infinite. But we know that each "thought" corresponds to a minimum of one bit being processed. In effect, this part of Condition 2 is a claim that time duration is most properly measured by the thinking rate, rather than by proper time as measured by atomic clocks. The length of time it takes an intelligent being to process one bit of information—to think one thought—is a direct measure of "subjective" time, and hence is the most important measure of time from the perspective of life. A person who has thought ten times as much, or experienced ten times as much (there is no basic physical difference between these options) as the average person has in a fundamental sense lived ten times as long as the average person, even if the rapid-thinking person's chronological age is shorter than the average.

The distinction between proper and subjective time crucial to Condition 2 is strikingly similar to a distinction between two forms of duration in Thomistic philosophy. Aquinas distinguished three types of duration. The first was *tempus,* which is time measured by change in relations (positions, for example) between physical bodies on Earth. *Tempus* is analogous to proper time; change in both human minds and atomic clocks is proportional to proper time, and for Aquinas also, *tempus* controlled change in corporeal minds. But in Thomistic philosophy, duration for *incorporeal* sentient beings—angels—is not controlled by matter, but rather is measured by change in the mental states of these beings themselves. This second type of duration, called *aevum* by Aquinas, is clearly analogous to what I have termed "subjective time." *Tempus* becomes *aevum* as sentience escapes the bonds of matter. Analogously, Condition 2 requires that thinking rates are controlled less and less by proper time as τ approaches its future limit. *Tempus* gradually becomes *aevum* in the future.

The third type of Thomistic duration is *aeternitas:* duration as experienced by God alone. *Aeternitas* can be thought of as "experiencing" all past, present, and future *tempus* and *aevum* events in the universe all at once. In fact, the classical definition of *aeternitas* was given by the Christian philosopher Boethius (A.D. 480–524) in his book *Consolation of Philosophy* (which he wrote while in prison awaiting execution for treason): *"Aeternitas igitur est interminabilis vitae tota simul et perfecta possessio . . . . :* Eternity therefore is the complete and perfect possession of unlimited life all at once."[5] But more of *aeternitas* later.

Condition 3 is imposed because, although Condition 2 is necessary for life to exist forever, it is not sufficient. If a computer with a finite amount of information storage—recall from Chapter II that this means the computer is a *finite state machine*—were to operate forever, it would start to repeat itself over and over. The psychological cosmos would be that of Nietzsche's Eternal Return. Every thought and every sequence of thoughts, every action and every sequence of actions, would be repeated not once but an infinite number of times. I have shown at length in the previous chapter that such a universe would be morally repugnant or meaningless. Even earlier than St. Augustine (whose attack on the Eternal Return I quoted in the preceding chapter), the first great Christian theologian, Origen, rejected[6] the idea that "Jesus will again come to visit this life and will do the same things that he has done, not just once, but an infinite number of times according to the cycles." The early Church father St. Clement also rejected the Eternal Return for exactly the same reason.[7] All Christian theologians are in universal agreement: the Christian cosmos is progressive.

Only if Condition 3 holds in addition to Condition 2 can a psychological Eternal Return be avoided. Origen emphasized that such a psychological Eternal Return would make human goals meaningless (and this led him to reject the idea of reincarnation[8]). Also, it seems reasonable to say that "subjectively" a finite state machine exists for only a finite time even though it may exist for an infinite amount of proper time and process an infinite amount of data. A being (or a sequence of generations) that can be truly said to exist forever ought to be physically able, at least in principle, to have new experiences and to think new thoughts.

Let us now consider whether the laws of physics will permit life/information processing to continue forever. John von Neumann and others have shown that information processing (more precisely, the irreversible storage of information) is constrained by the First and Second Laws of Thermodynamics. Thus the storage of a bit of information requires the expenditure of a definite minimum amount of available energy, this amount being inversely proportional to the temperature (see the Appendix for Scientists for the exact formula). This means it is possible to process and store an infinite amount of information between now and the final state of the universe only if the time integral of P/T is infinite, where P is the power used in the computation, and T is the temperature. Thus the laws of thermodynamics will permit an infinite amount of information processing in the future, provided there is sufficient available energy at all future times.

What is "sufficient" depends on the temperature. In the open and flat ever expanding universes, the temperature drops to zero in the limit of infinite time, so less and less energy per bit processed is required with the passage of time. In fact, in the flat universe, only a *finite* total amount of energy suffices to process an infinite number of bits. This finite energy just has to be used sparingly over infinite future time. On the other hand, closed universes end in a final singularity of infinite density, and the temperature diverges to infinity as this final singularity is approached. This means that an ever increasing amount of energy is required per bit near the final singularity. However, almost all closed universes undergo "shear" when they recollapse, which means they contract at different rates in different directions. As I mentioned in Chapter II, this shearing gives rise to a radiation temperature difference in different directions, and this temperature difference can provide sufficient free energy for an infinite amount of information processing between now and the final singularity, even though there is only a *finite* amount of proper time between now and the end of time in a closed universe. Thus, although a closed universe exists for only a finite proper time, it nevertheless could exist for an infinite subjective time, which is the measure of time that is significant for living beings.

In most closed universes, the shear will not be sufficient to generate the necessary power. There is, however, a special type of closed universe in which the energy from the shear is sufficient. These are closed universes which collapse in one direction only while remaining essentially the same size in the other two directions. Such universes are called *Taub universes,* after the University of California mathematician Abraham Taub who first discovered them. (I had the good fortune to be Abe's postdoctoral assistant in the late 1970s.) Figures IV.4 and IV.5 illustrate the collapse of a Taub universe, and also picture the temperature difference in the Taub universe.

Figures IV.4 and IV.5 picture a collapse in the same direction. The universe becomes more and more like a squashed sphere (the technical term is "oblate spheroid"). This is actually a very unstable form of collapse. What would almost always happen is that the universe would first shear like this for a short time, then return to a more spherical shape, and then start a Taublike collapse in another direction, as pictured in Figure IV.6.

However, *if* life has already engulfed the universe before the Taub collapse begins, it can use this instability to continue the Taub collapse in the same direction, with the universe becoming much more flattened—more oblate—than is likely to happen without the intervention of life. Life will want to do this—life will *have* to do this—in order to maximize the temperature difference in the different directions. Recall from Chapter II that the ratio of the temperatures is equal to the ratio of the sizes of the universe in the different directions. The greater the

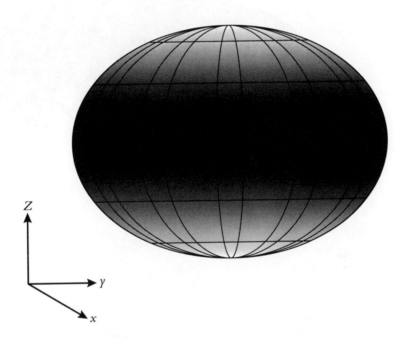

FIGURE IV.4: *A contracting closed universe with shear. The universe contracts at different rates in different directions, leading to a "squashed sphere" shape. (The techincal term is "oblate spheroid.") The shape corresponds to a so-called Taub universe collapse, in which the universe collapses in one direction while retaining the same size in the other two directions. The temperature is higher in the shorter direction than in the longer directions, and it is this temperature difference that provides the energy for life to exist forever in subjective time. The lighter the shading, the higher the temperature. The equator is black, so it is at the lowest temperature. The north and south poles are white, so they are at the highest temperature.*

temperature difference, the greater the energy available for life. As I discussed in Chapter II, the energy for life is ultimately coming from the collapse of the universe as a whole. The available energy diverges to infinity as the universe goes to zero size and infinite temperature and density. Paradoxically, the universe *must* end in a final singularity in finite proper time if life is to survive for infinite subjective time.

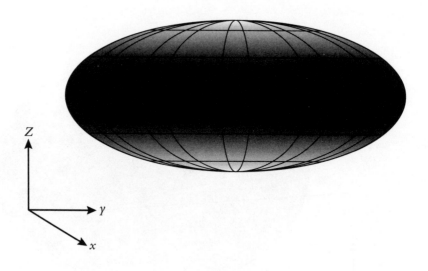

FIGURE IV.5: *Second figure illustrating the collapse of a Taub universe. The universe has gotten smaller in one direction than is was in the previous frame, but the other directions have remained the same size. The north and south poles are hotter than in the previous figure, while the equator is at the same temperature as before.*

Experimental Tests of the
Omega Point Theory

But although the laws of thermodynamics permit Conditions 1 through 3 to be satisfied in open and flat universes, this does not mean that the other laws of physics will. As I discussed in Chapter III, Freeman Dyson pointed out[9] that, although the energy is available in open and flat universes, the information processing must be carried out over larger and larger proper volumes. This fact ultimately makes impossible any communication between opposite sides of the "living" region in a flat universe, because the redshift implies that arbitrarily large amounts of energy must be used to signal, and Dyson showed that only a finite

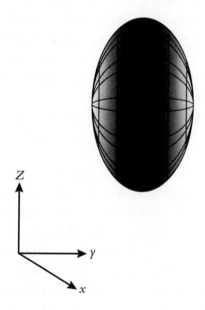

FIGURE IV.6: *Third frame illustrating the collapse of a universe with shear. The universe is now smaller in all directions than it was in the previous two figures. As in the two previous figures, the universe is collapsing in the Taub universe manner, but now another direction corresponds to the collapsing direction. As in the two previous figures, the lighter the shading, the higher the temperature.*

amount of energy is available. On the other hand, open universes expand so fast in the far future that it becomes impossible for structures to form of sufficiently larger and larger size to store a diverging amount of information. This gives the

First Testable Prediction of the Omega Point Theory: the universe must be closed.

However, there is a communication problem in most closed universes—event horizons typically appear, thereby preventing communication. *Event horizons* are surfaces in spacetime which divide spacetime into regions which can communicate with an observer from regions which cannot. The event horizon for any future endless observer is thus his past light cone, as is clear from Figure IV.3. If the universe is closed, then at present it is very close to being the same size in all three directions—we say that it is *isotropic*. If it were to remain isotropic for the rest of its history, then its c-boundary would have the same topology as its spatial sections: it would be a three-dimensional sphere. A *Penrose Diagram* is a convenient way of picturing the totality of spacetime. A Penrose Diagram for a matter-dominated closed Friedmann universe is pictured in Figure IV.7.

A *Friedmann universe* is a spacetime which is isotropic and homogeneous everywhere. *Matter-dominated* just means that all the gravitational attraction is due to the rest mass of matter. There are no pressures to speak of on large scales. Our universe appears to be of this sort, and in such a universe it is possible for light rays or relativistic rockets to reach the other side of the universe just slightly after the recollapse begins, as discussed in Chapter II. If, on the other hand, most of the gravitating matter were in the form of light, we would be in a *radiation-dominated universe*. Such a universe would expand more rapidly than a matter-dominated universe: light and relativistic rockets would be able to go only half of the way to the antipodal point before collapse began. This would be bad news for life. It would not be in a position to control the universe's evolution at the crucial time at the beginning of recollapse. If we did not know that the universe is matter-dominated, I would add this as a prediction.

Almost all closed universes have event horizons. The Taub universe

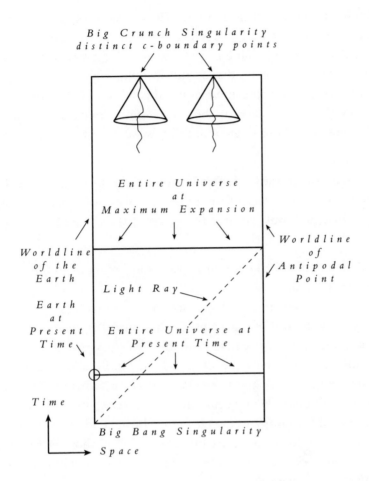

FIGURE IV.7: *Penrose Diagram for a matter-dominated Friedmann universe with spatial topology S^3, a three-dimensional sphere. A Penrose Diagram pictures the entire universe in both its spatial and temporal dimensions. The vertical dimension is time, and the horizontal dimension is space. The initial Big Bang singularity, where time began, is represented as a thick horizontal line. The two vertical lines represent the worldlines of the Earth and the antipodal Point, respectively. The thin horizontal line near the bottom of the figure represents the entire universe as it is now. The circle located at the intersection of the Earth's worldline and the universe now is thus the Earth now. In a Penrose Diagram, as in the Minkowski Diagram, light rays are represented as lines inclined at an angle of 45 degrees. A light ray which leaves the Earth's location at the Big Bang arrives at the antipodal point at the time of maximum expansion, as shown. At the very top of the Penrose Diagram, the Big Crunch final singularity is represented as a thick horizontal line. All worldlines must hit the Big Crunch. Time thus ends at the Big Crunch. Two worldlines of objects moving slower than light are pictured hitting the Big Crunch singularity. The two worldines are enclosed by their past light cones. Since these cones are clearly distinct, they define different c-boundary points. It is obvious that each distinct vertical line defines a distinct past light cone at the Big Crunch singularity, and thus the topology of the Big Crunch singularity is the same as the topology of the entire universe now: a three-dimensional sphere. The initial Big Bang singularity is also a three-dimensional sphere. This is shown using future light cones in the place of past light cones.*

also has them. But there is a rare class of closed universes which don't have event horizons. The absence of event horizons means by definition that every worldline can always send light signals to every other worldline. This implies that all the worldlines have the same past light cone, which therefore must equal the whole of spacetime. But this means the c-boundary of these rare closed universes without event horizons must be a single point. Thus we have the

Second Testable (?) Prediction of the Omega Point Theory: the future c-boundary of the universe consists of a single point; call it the **Omega Point.** (Hence the name of the theory.)

The Penrose Diagram for a spacetime ending in an Omega Point is shown in Figure IV.8.

I have given in the Appendix for Scientists a simple Friedmann universe with an Omega Point. Such a model is, however, unphysical because it requires negative pressures, which means that gravity must become repulsive near the Omega Point. I also show that any Friedmann universe with an Omega Point necessarily has negative pressures, so if an Omega Point occurs in our universe, it means that it must deviate from isotropy in the far future. I might add that horizon disappearance reinforces the First Prediction: I shall show in the Appendix for Scientists that, if the future c-boundary is a single point, then the universe is necessarily closed.

But we know that the universe will deviate from isotropy in the future. It will collapse at different rates in different directions. The American physicist Charles Misner has figured out a way of getting a single c-boundary point in a closed universe with only positive pressures. A Taublike collapse does more than provide a temperature difference for life. It also eliminates horizons. Or rather it eliminates them in one direction. If a light ray were to be sent out in the direction of collapse of a Taub universe, it would circumnavigate the universe infinitely many times in that direction before the final singularity. That is, there is no event horizon in that direction. Unfortunately, event horizons still occur in the other two directions. Misner's idea was to imagine a universe which undergoes a Taublike collapse in one direction

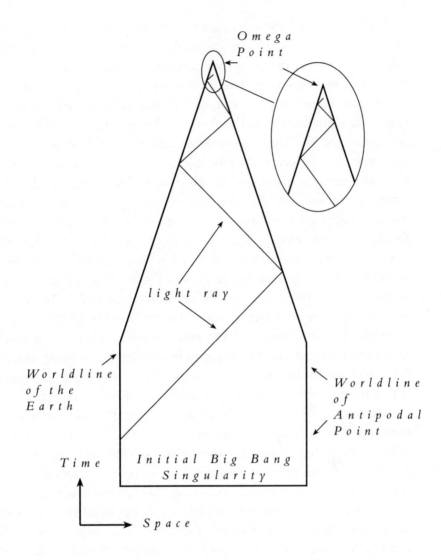

FIGURE IV.8: *Penrose Diagram for a Friedmann universe with spatial topology S³ but with an omega point for the final singularity. The diagram begins just like the previous figure, but the Earth's worldline approaches the worldline of the antipodal point. A light ray starting out from the Earth in 1993 reaches the antipodal point and returns, and then goes back and forth between the Earth and the antipodal point. Light can go back and forth between the Earth's location and the antipodal point an infinite number of times between now and the final singularity. This means that the entire spacetime is a single past light cone; there is only one point in the final singularity. The final singularity is thus an omega point.*

sufficiently far for light to circumnavigate the entire universe in that direction, then become more spherical, and then undergo a Taublike collapse in another direction sufficiently far to allow light to circumnavigate in that direction. This process repeats in the third direction.

Repeating this triple series of Taublike collapses an infinity of times will eliminate the horizons totally, because light will be able to circumnavigate the entire universe an infinite number of times in all directions. Misner originally proposed this series for the beginning of time, but he later abandoned his proposal when he realized that it is extremely improbable that the universe will go from one extreme Taublike collapse to another. I say "extreme" Taub because, in order for light to circumnavigate just once in the collapsing direction, the size of the universe in that direction has to decrease by a factor of about 70. In passing from Figure IV.4 to Figure IV.5, the universe has shrunk in the collapse direction by less than a factor of 2. And even if by luck the universe in fact decreased in one direction by this factor of 70 while the other directions remain constant, it is unlikely it would then decrease in yet another direction by another factor of 70 with the other two directions remaining constant. What almost always happens is that the universe decreases in all directions simultaneously.

However, life can use the instabilities to *force* the universe to move from one extreme Taub collapse to another. Chaos exists in the Einstein equations in precisely the right place to allow this. Life will thus force the universe into one extreme Taublike collapse after another for two reasons: first, a Taublike collapse maximizes the available energy, and second, it is the only way to eliminate horizons when all pressures are positive. But life must engulf the universe in order to force the universe to move in this way. If it tries to force a Taublike collapse on any scale except the entire universe, horizons will form and force life into a region which shrinks much more rapidly than the universe as a whole. Information processing can continue only in closed universes that end in a single c-boundary point, and only if the information processing is ultimately carried out throughout the entire closed universe. In other words, if life is to survive at all, at just the bare subsistence level, it must necessarily engulf the entire universe at some point in the future. It doesn't have the option of remaining in a limited region. Mere survival dictates expansion. But if it does engulf the universe, it then has the option of existing at a much wealthier level. The future history of life is illustrated on a Penrose Diagram in Figure IV.9.

It is possible to obtain other predictions. For example, a more

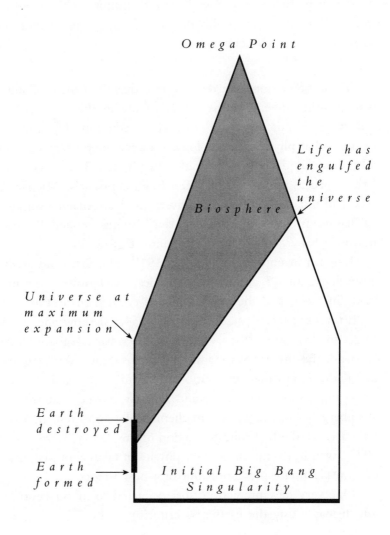

FIGURE IV.9: *Penrose Diagram of the future of life in the universe. The thick vertical black line is the entire history of the Earth. The cross-hatchd region is the biosphere. The biosphere begins to expand out into the universe now (on the scale of the figure, "now" means any time in the next few million years). The biosphere engulfs the entire universe slightly after maximum expansion.*

detailed analysis (given in the Appendix for Scientists) of how energy must be used to store information leads to the

Third Testable Prediction of the Omega Point Theory: the density of particle states must diverge to infinity as the energy goes to infinity, but nevertheless this density of states must diverge no faster than the cube of the energy.

These predictions just demonstrate that the Omega Point Theory is a scientific theory of the future of life in the universe. They are unfortunately not very strong or useful predictions, but it must be kept in mind that physical eschatology is a very young science, and that it takes time to develop a new idea in physics. The story goes that a British prime minister visited the English physicist Michael Faraday, who had just made a major discovery in electromagnetism, and asked, "What use is electricity, Mr. Faraday?" Faraday replied, "What use is a newborn baby? You have to wait until it grows up."

Einstein invented cosmology in 1917. The first solid prediction in cosmology, the 3-degree cosmological background radiation, was made in 1948, and the prediction was confirmed in 1965. Yang and Mills invented local gauge theory in 1954, Glashow applied the ideas to get an electroweak theory in 1961, but as particle masses were put in by hand, the theory was manifestly inconsistent. Weinberg and Salam added the Higgs mass generation mechanism to Glashow's theory in 1967 and 1968 respectively, and t'Hooft proved that the Glashow–Weinberg-Salam theory was mathematically consistent in 1971. Neutral currents, the first solid prediction of the theory, were discovered in 1973. Even in twentieth-century physics, it takes about twenty years to get a really useful prediction out of a new theory.

One very new prediction, that occurred to me in February 1992, which may satisfy the usefulness criterion is the

Fourth Testable Prediction of the Omega Point Theory: the mass of the top quark must be 185 ± 20 GeV, and the mass of the Higgs boson must be 220 ± 20 GeV. These numbers imply that the width of the Higgs boson must be 2.1 GeV, and that the ratio of the widths for Higgs boson decay into transversely polarized Z bosons and longitudinally polarized Z bosons must be 0.55.

In particular, the top quark will be found (95% confidence level) when the integrated luminosity of the Fermilab Tevatron reaches 200 inverse picobarns. This means that it will not be found during the two-year collider run which began in May 1992, which will accumulate an integrated luminosity of 100 inverse picobarns by the end of 1994. (If the mass of the top quark is less than about 110 GeV, it would have been found by September 1992. I thus predicted in February 1992 that the top would not be found by September 1992, which it was not. The complete 1992–94 run will find the top if its mass is less than about 150 GeV.) However, the Tevatron will find the top quark by 1996, because its main injector is scheduled to be upgraded in 1995, and this upgrade will find the top quark by 1997 if its mass is less than 200 GeV, which we know from indirect experiments is an upper bound to its mass. The 1988–89 Tevatron collider run found one candidate event which *could* have been the creation of a top-antitop pair. If it was, then the experiment implies a top mass of 120 GeV. The Omega Point Theory asserts that this event was spurious; it was *not* the creation of a top-antitop pair. In October 1992, the current Tevatron collider run found an event, pictured in Figure IV.10, which again could have been the creation of a top-antitop pair. In the case of this event, the implied top quark mass was 180 GeV, *exactly* the mass predicted.

The Higgs boson is predicted to be too massive to be found in the Tevatron, but with a mass of 220 GeV it will definitely be found in the CERN Large Hadron Collider, which is scheduled to go on line in 1999. In fact, an integrated luminosity of a mere 10^4 inverse picobarns will be sufficient to find the Higgs boson; this means that a much more modest luminosity than the designers plan for the Large Hadron Collider will be sufficient. The Omega Point Theory says the Higgs will be discovered by 2000 in the Large Hadron Collider (LHC). If the Super-Conducting Supercollider (SSC) had been completed in 2002 as was scheduled, it also would have found the Higgs by 2003.

All of these dates depend on the instruments being completed as originally scheduled. Unfortunately, completion depends not on physics or engineering but on politics. As I write this, there is even some doubt as to whether the Tevatron main injector upgrade will be funded. The cost of the upgrade is only about $200 million, which is tiny by the standards of the LHC ($2 billion) and the SSC ($10 billion), but in these days of huge budget deficits . . .

The Fourth Testable Prediction is obtained from an analysis of the

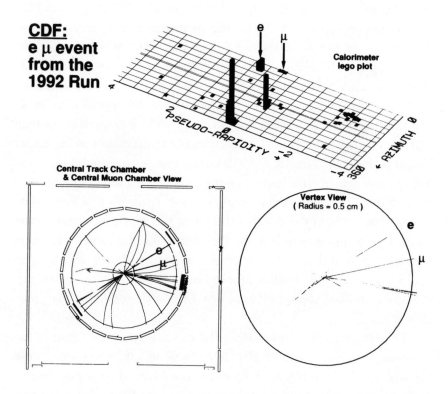

FIGURE IV.10: *Possible detection of the top quark in October 1992. In the creation of a top-antitop pair in the collision of a proton with an antiproton in the Tevatron, the top quark would decay into a bottom quark and a W^+ boson and the antitop quark would decay into an antibottom quark and a W^- boson. The bosons decay immediately, possibly into leptons like the electron (e) or muon (μ) and their neutrinos, while each quark shows up as a jet of particles opposite to the lepton. So the signature of a top-antitop creation is a pair of leptons accompanied by two jets. Such an event was seen in October 1992. If it was the creation of a top-antitop pair, then measurements of the energy of the decay particles imply a top quark mass around 180 GeV, which is the mass predicted by the Omega Point Theory. (Credit: Fermilab.)*

processes wherein the information which life codes is transferred from normal matter (where it is coded now) into a form which can withstand the diverging temperatures near the final Omega Point singularity. The mathematical details of the analysis will be found in the Appendix for Scientists.

But the idea underlying the Fourth Prediction is easy to state. Information can be coded in its present substrate of molecular systems—both humans and computers are currently made of molecules—only when the radiation temperature of the universe is less than the typical binding energy of molecules. Depending on how much radiation is generated by life in the future, the universal temperature will exceed this limit by the time the universe has shrunk somewhere between its present size and one thousandth its present size. Therefore, information must be transferred to another substrate before this time. In order to effect the transfer, life must have sent signals in all directions at least once between the time of maximum expansion and the time of transfer. Remembering that the universe must shrink by a factor of 70 to enable life to send signals around the universe in one direction, this means the universe must be at least about $(70)^3$ larger at maximum expansion than it is now. Furthermore, it can't be too much larger than this at maximum expansion, or else the universe will be so close to the flat model that life will die out before maximum expansion is reached. But the universe's size at maximum expansion is determined by two numbers: Hubble's constant, which tells how fast the universe is expanding now, and the density parameter, which tells how fast the mass in the universe is slowing down the rate of expansion. Thus we must have (see the Appendix for Scientists for details):

Fifth Testable Prediction of the Omega Point Theory: the density parameter Ω_0 of the universe must satisfy $4 \times 10^{-4} < \Omega_0 - 1 < 4 \times 10^{-6}$, and Hubble's constant must be less than or equal to 45 km/sec-mpc.

But this just gets life ready to transfer information to another substrate. The only substrate that seems to be available at the low temperature at which the transfer must be made is the universe itself. That is, I propose storing information at either traveling waves or standing waves, using the universe itself as a box to enclose the waves. However, coding information in the universe as a whole would require at least several circumnavigations of light in all directions with the temperature and hence the average size of the universe remaining constant. The Misner mechanism will not do, for it requires the universe to shrink.

But the Higgs field can—if it is real. According to the Standard Model of particle physics, the Higgs field permeates the whole of space. The energy density of the Higgs field can be computed, and it turns out to be 10^{54} times the energy density of matter. This calculation is consistent with experiment only if there is an equally powerful *repulsive* gravitational force field called the Cosmological Constant, canceling out the Higgs field everywhere in space. Until the temperature gets enormously high—about 100 GeV, or 1,000 trillion degrees Celsius—these universal fields balance each other.

However, the Higgs field couples to the shear but the Cosmological Constant does not. This means that life can use the shear to reduce the Higgs field, thereby allowing the repulsive Cosmological Constant to slow the rate of collapse. Recall that even the Friedmann universe will allow a model in which light circumnavigates the universe if negative pressures—repulsive gravitational forces—are present. A rough calculation indicates that sufficient coupling between the shear and the Higgs field occurs between the time of maximum expansion and the time the temperature becomes too hot for molecular substrate life to allow life to slow the collapse sufficiently to get the required circumnavigations.

The circumnavigations will be maximized and so will the probability that life will successfully make the transfer if the Higgs mass is maximized. But if the Higgs and top quark masses were too large, the Standard Model equations would be unstable in the present environment. Thus the maximum allowed Higgs mass is obtained together with the top quark mass. These masses are given in the Fourth Prediction.

Not only must the Higgs and top quark values have specific values, but this gravitational repulsive force from the Cosmological Constant must become noticeable once the temperature becomes sufficiently high. This effect would be observable during the so-called Weinberg-

Salam phase transition. Unfortunately, I do not know how to compute the signature of this effect, so I cannot list it as a definite prediction.

As I discussed in Chapter II, in order for life to be able to act coherently on the largest scales and so be able to use the chaos in the Einstein equations, the universe must remain homogeneous on the largest scales until the recollapse time some 10^{18} years in the future. However, there must be some inhomogeneities in the early universe, otherwise there would be no galaxies and stars. Since inhomogeneities tend to grow with time, the universe will not be homogeneous on the largest scales unless the amplitude of the inhomogeneities on these scales is now very small. The amplitude of the inhomogeneities is usually expressed in terms of the mass density contrast $\Delta\rho/\rho_0$, where $\Delta\rho$ is the variation of the density from the average density ρ_0. This yields the

Sixth Testable Prediction of the Omega Point Theory: the density contrast $\Delta\rho/\rho_0$ must have the Harrison-Zel'dovich power spectrum. Furthermore, the amplitude of the density contrast on the largest scales we can see must be less than 2×10^{-4}, which implies that the temperature fluctuations in the cosmic background radiation must be less than 6×10^{-5}.

The Harrison-Zel'dovich power spectrum is implied by the fact that this spectrum is the only one which is consistent with the universe being still roughly Friedmann at the time of recollapse, and also which begins in an initial Friedmann singularity. The largest scales we can see is the "edge" of the visible universe. The amplitude of the spectrum is obtained from the fact that the inhomogeneities on the scale of the visible universe cannot grow too large by the time the biosphere reaches the edge of the visible universe. Inhomogeneities on such a scale would be impossible to eliminate by the time the universe begins to collapse, and this in turn would mean horizons, which are impossible by the Second Prediction.

As I discussed in Chapter II, the universe is cooling as it expands. This means that there was a time in the past when the universe was so hot that it was opaque like the Sun. The universe was this hot when it was about one thousandth of its present size. When the universe expanded beyond this size, it suddenly became transparent to radiation, and so when we look at the cosmic background radiation, we are looking at the universe as it was at the instant it became transparent. This instant defines the "edge" of the visible universe.

This prediction is actually a proposed solution to the Isotropy Problem in cosmology. Recall that the word "isotropy" means "the same in all directions." The temperature of the cosmic background radiation is remarkably isotropic: it is the same in all directions to one part in 10^5. Explaining this sameness was quite a problem because, if the universe has been dominated by radiation or matter from the Big Bang singularity some 20 billion years ago to the present, and the expansion has been roughly isotropic, then the radiation coming from a given direction has never in its entire history been in causal contact with radiation coming from the opposite direction. We know from experience that when two bodies have exactly the same temperature it is usually because they have been in contact. But the two parts of the early universe from which the background radiation comes are equal in temperature to one part in 10^5, even though they have never been in causal contact.

Misner tried to explain this temperature isotropy by arguing that the different regions were in causal contact, because the expansion was not isotropic: it was Taublike, which allowed many circumnavigations of light. But we saw above that Misner's explanation will not work.

In 1981, Alan Guth of MIT proposed another explanation, which he called *inflation*. In Guth's model, the expansion of the universe from the Big Bang singularity was not radiation or matter dominated. Rather, there was a repulsive force in the very early universe, a force somewhat analogous to the Cosmological Constant force I described above, that inflated a tiny region which was in causal contact to be larger than the part of the universe we see. Thus in both Misner's and Guth's solutions[10] to the Isotropy Problem, the opposite parts of the sky have the same temperature because they once were in causal contact.

In my solution, the temperatures are the same because otherwise the universe in the far future would be inhospitable for life. The future boundary conditions are determining the past rather than the past boundary conditions determining the future. People tend to think that it is the past that determines the future rather than vice versa. But if the evolution equations are deterministic and time symmetric, as the Einstein equations are, then the boundary conditions can be given at any time; it is just as legitimate to think of the future determining the past.

The Sixth Prediction shows that the Omega Point Theory is at least as powerful a cosmological model as the Inflation Model. Both theories predict the same power spectrum for the density contrast. But the Inflation Model has difficulty predicting the amplitude of the spectrum, and hence it has difficulty predicting the amplitude of the slight fluctuations in the cosmic background radiation. Such fluctuations must be present, because a non-zero density contrast would perturb the background radiation. Knowing the amplitude and the power spectrum one can compute the amplitude of the temperature fluctuations of the cosmic background radiation. The answer is that the temperature fluctuation amplitude is less than 6×10^{-5}, which is within an order of magnitude of its observed value, 5×10^{-6}. The details are in the Appendix for Scientists. Our current knowledge of cosmology is too limited for any calculation to give an answer to better than an order of magnitude.

The Sixth Prediction is important because it shows that the density contrast over regions which have never been in causal contact can nevertheless be constrained by a mechanism other than inflation. As I said above, in the Omega Point Theory, this constraint comes from a final, rather than an initial, boundary condition: that life must exist all the way into the Omega Point.

·———·

Theological Implications: Omnipresence, Omniscience, and Omnipotence

Let us now consider the theological implications of the Omega Point Theory. That the theory has such implications will be clear if I restate a number of the above conclusions in more suggestive words. As I pointed out, in order for the information processing operations to be carried out arbitrarily near the Omega Point, life must have extended its operations so as to engulf the entire physical cosmos. We can say, quite obviously, that life near the Omega Point is omnipresent. As the Omega Point is approached, survival dictates that life collectively gain control of all matter and energy sources available near the Final State, with this control becoming total at the Omega Point. We can say that life becomes omnipotent at the instant the Omega Point is reached. Since by hypothesis the information stored becomes infinite at the Omega Point, it is reasonable to say that the Omega Point is omniscient; it knows whatever it is possible to know about the physical universe (and hence about Itself).

The Omega Point has a fourth property. Recall that, mathematically speaking, the c-boundary is a *completion* of spacetime: it is not actually in spacetime but rather just "outside" it. Remember also that a c-boundary consisting of a single point is equivalent to the entire collection of spacetime points (regarded as a unity) *and* a certain infinite collection of subsets of spacetime points (all past light cones). In other words, the Omega Point is not merely all finite reality, it is *in addition* the completion of all finite reality. This idea of God as a completion is standard in theology. As the German theologian Wolfhart Pannenberg has put it: ". . . God is usually thought of in analogy to man and as the perfection of everything for which man believes he is destined, but which is only realized in the life of the individual in a partial and limited way."[11]

This completion of spacetime is both all of spacetime and outside spacetime altogether. (Outside spacetime, because the Omega Point is not the individual spacetime points, but all these points thought of as a single entity.) It is natural to say that the Omega Point is "both transcendent to and yet immanent in" every point of spacetime. When life has completely engulfed the entire universe, it will incorporate more and more material into itself, and the distinction between living and nonliving matter will lose its meaning.

There is another way to view this inclusion of all spacetime in the Omega Point. In effect, all the different instants of universal history are collapsed into the Omega Point; "duration" for the Omega Point can be regarded as equivalent to the collection of all experiences of all life that did, does, and will exist in the whole of universal history, together with all nonliving instants. This "duration" is very close to the idea of *aeternitas* of Thomistic philosophy. We could say that *aeternitas* is equivalent to the union of all *aevum* and *tempus*. If we accept the idea that life and personhood involve change by their very nature (to pass the Turing Test, for example, a being has to *do* something), then this identification appears to be the only way to have a Person Who is omniscient, and hence Whose knowledge cannot change: omniscience is a property of the necessarily unchanging not-in-time final state, a state nevertheless equivalent to the collection of all earlier, nonomniscient changing states. The Omega Point in Its immanence counts as a Person because, at any time in our future, the collective information processing system will have generated, or will be able to generate, subprograms which will be able to pass the Turing Test; high intelligence will be required at least collectively in order to survive in the increasingly complex environment near the final state.

Strictly speaking, I don't know whether the Omega Point in Its immanence has a human-type mind at the highest level of implementation. (This idea of "levels of implementation" was discussed[12] in Chapter II.) Probably not; a human-type mind is a manifestation of an extremely low level of information processing: as discussed in Chapter II, a mere 100 to 10,000 gigaflops processing rate and only 10^{15} bits of computer storage capacity (see below). Nevertheless, the Omega Point is still a Person (at all times in our future), because a Being with Its level of computer capacity could easily create a Turing-Test-passing subprogram to speak for It. As I shall discuss in later chapters, our resurrected selves probably will interact with such a subprogram; it is beyond human capacity to deal directly with the highest level of implementation possessed by the state of the Omega Point at the time we are resurrected (this highest level is coded in no less than $10^{10^{123}}$ bits; I shall show how this number is calculated in Chapter X). For lack of a better term, I shall refer to the total universal information processing system in existence at any given global time as the "universal mind."

There is an interesting connection between my claim that the Omega Point is a Person because it contains a Turing-Test-passing subprogram, and the Christian notion of Person, as this word is applied to God. In classical Greek, the word *prosopon* (πρόσωπον)—*persona* is the Latin equivalent—primarily meant "face" or "countenance," but the word also meant a mask that an actor wore in a play to indicate the character he played. By the fourth century A.D. (when the debates over the Trinity were at their height), this word had come to refer to those innate aspects of the human mentality which differentiate one human being from another. Today the word "person" refers to the total individual human mind, including both innate and learned aspects of each individual's character. Since were He/She to interact with us human beings as a Person—as a tiny subprogram—the Omega Point would be revealing only a minuscule portion of His/Her full character, it follows that the Omega Point is a Person in the original sense and in the fourth-century sense of the word *persona*. With many Turing Test–passing subprograms, the Omega Point would be many Persons; He/She would have many "personae" in the current English meaning of the word "persona." "Three Persons in God" or "many Persons in the Omega Point" does not mean tritheism (three gods) or polytheism. This idea of many "personae" in one God is actually in the very first verse of the Bible: "In the beginning God created the heavens and the earth." (Genesis 1:1, RSV.) In the original Hebrew, the word translated here as God is "Elohim," which is a plural word.

I shall occasionally use expressions like "the Omega Point will resurrect us" or "the Omega Point loves us" in the following chapters, and such expressions will refer to the Omega Point in one of His/Her far-future immanent Personal aspects. I shall not always add the words "transcendence" or "immanence" to "Omega Point," but instead I shall let the context make it clear which I mean. The Bible provides ample precedent for this manner of speaking. For example, in the episode when God speaks to Moses out of the burning bush, we are told in Exodus 3:2 that ". . . the angel of the LORD appeared to him in a flame of fire out of the midst of a bush . . ." (RSV), while just two verses later we are told, "When the LORD saw that he turned aside to see, God called to him out of the bush . . ." (RSV) but we are *not* told in the intervening verse that the angel goes away and is replaced by God. In other words, "angel" in this passage means God in His/Her immanent aspect. A similar abrupt switch from "the angel of the LORD" to "the LORD" occurs between Genesis 16:7 and Genesis 16:13, when God is speaking to Hagar. Indeed, the editors of the Oxford University Annotated RSV remark about both passages: "Here the 'angel of the LORD' is not a heavenly being subordinate to God but the LORD himself in earthly manifestation." One could go further and claim that *all* of the angels mentioned in the Bible by name—Michael, Gabriel, Raphael, and Uriel[13]—are meant to represent God in His immanence. All of these names end in "-el," which means "God." The Hebrew meanings of these names are dead giveaways: "Michael" means "Who is as God"; "Gabriel" means "Strength of God"; "Raphael" means "Healing Power of God"; and "Uriel" means "Fire of God." It would certainly not be too inaccurate to regard one of the superprograms of the universal mind in the far future, one with a Turing Test–passing subprogram, as an "angel." As I have said, these programs collectively comprise the Omega Point in His/Her immanence.

This inclusion of the whole of the past, present, and future universal history in the Omega Point is more than a mere mathematical artifact. *The identification really does mean that the Omega Point "experiences" the whole of universal history "all at once."* For consider what it means for us to "experience" an event. It means we think and emote about an event we see, hear, feel, etc. Consider for simplicity just the "seeing" mode of sensing. We see another contemporary person by means of the light rays that left her a fraction of a second ago. But we cannot "see" a person who lived a few centuries before, because the light rays from said person have long ago left the solar system. Conversely, we cannot "see" the Andromeda galaxy as it now is, but rather we "see" it as it was 2 million years ago. So we experience as "simultaneous" the events on the boundary of our past light cone (for the seeing mode; it is more complicated for all other modes of sensing, for we experience as simultaneous events which reach us at the same instant along certain timelike curves from inside our past light cone).

But all timelike and lightlike curves converge upon the Omega Point. In particular, all the light rays from all the people who died a thousand years ago, from all the people now living, and from all the people who will be living a thousand years from now, will intersect there. The light rays from those people who died a thousand years ago are not lost forever; rather these rays will be intercepted by the Omega Point. Or, to put it another way, these rays will be intercepted and intercepted again, by the living beings who have engulfed the physical universe near the Omega Point. All the information which can be extracted from these rays will be extracted at the instant of the Omega Point, Who will therefore experience the whole of time simultaneously just as we experience simultaneously the Andromeda galaxy and a person in the room with us. (I should warn the reader that I have ignored the problem of opacity and the problem of loss of coherence of the light. Until these are taken into account, I cannot say exactly how much information can in fact be extracted from the past. But at the most basic ontological level—provided that global hyperbolicity [determinism] holds—*all* the information from the past [= all of universal history] remains in the physical universe and is available for analysis by the Omega Point.) In *Consolation of Philosophy* Boethius quotes Plato[14]: ". . . we should follow Plato in saying that God indeed is eternal, but the world is perpetual [since, to the world, not every event is simultaneously present]."[15] The Omega Point is thus eternal.[16]

To summarize this chapter: the indefinitely continued existence of life is not only physically possible; it also leads naturally to a model of a God Who is evolving in His/Her immanent aspect (the events in spacetime) and yet is eternally complete in His/Her transcendent aspect (the Omega Point, which is neither space nor time nor matter, but is beyond all of these).

DETERMINISM IN CLASSICAL GENERAL RELATIVITY AND IN QUANTUM MECHANICS

.———.

The Ancient Failure to Reconcile God's Omniscience and Human Free Will

Boethius ATTEMPTED TO USE HIS NOTION of eternity as a means of reconciling human freedom with God's omniscience. However, as I indicated in the previous chapter, this won't work: in the Omega Point Theory, the very fact that total information about the past is available in the past light cone of any event sufficiently near the Omega Point means necessarily that the information in this light cone uniquely determines the past (technically, the light cone is a Cauchy hypersurface). Boethius' own argument, that merely observing an object does not *ipso facto* uniquely determine its properties, is false. In fact, his model of indeterminism is actually a standard textbook case of determinism. The point he missed was that there is a crucial distinction between observing an object from a single direction and observing it from all possible directions simultaneously. The former does not determine, while the latter does. The textbook case is that of a scalar field which satisfies Laplace's equation. Consider the values of the field inside a sphere. "Observing" the field means knowing the field in a region on the surface of the sphere; that is, we have no *a priori* information about the field inside the sphere. If we know the values of the field on any proper subset of the spherical surface, then the field has almost complete freedom to take on virtually any value at any point in the interior of the sphere. In other words, "observing" the field does indeed not "impose necessity" (Boethius' words) on the interior values of the field. However, if we know the field on the *whole* of the surface of the sphere, then it is a theorem that the field is uniquely determined in the entire interior of the sphere. So observing the field from every direction simultaneously takes away all its freedom. Freedom is lost when total information about the whole is coded in a part of the whole. Similarly, if God is pictured as separate from spacetime, and if total information concerning the structure of spacetime is coded both in God and in spacetime, then spacetime has no freedom; it is completely determined by God's omniscience. However, as we shall see in the next chapter, this iron determinism may be relaxed in the quantized Omega Point Theory—omniscience may indeed be compatible with human freedom. But first we shall require a deeper understanding of just what determinism means in classical physics, particularly in general relativity.

.———.

Types of Contingency in Physics and Their Relation to Temporal Evolution

In physical theories before general relativity, it was always assumed that there was a background spacetime within which the entities of physics —fields and particles—evolved. This background space was unchanging: it was not influenced in any way by the physical entities, and it existed whether or not there were any physical entities. As pointed out by Robert Russell,[1] contingency in these theories came in two forms. First, there was contingency of the nature of the most basic physical entity, with a resulting contingency in the form of the evolution equations satisfied by this entity. *A priori,* there was no reason to choose one class of basic physical entities over another—there was in fact a debate in the nineteenth century over whether the fundamental "stuff" of the universe was particulate atoms or ether fields. Furthermore, the equations governing the chosen stuff could not be determined by logical consistency alone. Some input from observation was required. But there were imposed on these equations certain general symmetry principles arising from the assumption that the laws of physics did not change with time or as one moved from point to point in space. For example, conservation of energy is a consequence of the laws of physics being unchanged under "time translation" (i.e., the Lagrangian from which the evolution equations are derived is unchanged if t is replaced by t + a, where a is some constant). Inertia, or conservation of linear momentum, is a consequence of the laws of physics being unchanged under "space translation" (i.e., the Lagrangian is unchanged if all the spatial coordinates x are replaced by x + a). Thus the conservation laws are just a property of the evolution equations, and are really just a physical reflection of the eternal and homogeneous nature of the background space. It is the background spacetime, not so much the evolution equations or the conservation laws or the principle of inertia, that in Newtonian physics sustains the physical universe in existence.

The second type of contingency is arbitrariness in the initial conditions for the evolution equations. Suppose that the stuff of nature is a field, and the evolution equations are second order in time. Then, given the field and its first time derivative at any initial time, the value of the field at any subsequent and prior time is uniquely determined (assuming that the initial value problem is well posed, which it is in most cases of physical interest). But in general there will be a continuum of possible values for the initial value of the field and its derivative, all of these possible values comprising what is called "initial data space." In the ontology of classical physics, only one set of initial values —a "point" in initial data space—is physically realized. All the other initial data values correspond to physically possible worlds which are never actualized.

In general relativity, analogues of both of the above-mentioned contingencies are present. In addition, this is what might be termed an "evolution" contingency owing to the fact that, in general relativity, there is no background spacetime. Rather, the spacetime is itself generated by the initial data and the evolution equations. A spacetime is generated from its initial data in the following manner. First, a *three-dimensional manifold* S is assumed to exist. A "manifold" is just a technical word for the underlying space on which the fields of physics exist. Somewhat more precisely, a "manifold" is anything that locally resembles ordinary everyday flat space. The surface of a sphere—technically, this surface is called a 2-sphere—is a simple example. The surface of the Earth is an instance of a 2-sphere. On small scales, a 2-sphere looks flat. This is why road maps never have to show the Earth's curvature. But on larger scales the curvature is important, so the 2-sphere is not flat space, it is a manifold. Another simple example of a manifold is the surface of a doughnut. This surface is called a *torus*. Once again, in the small it looks like flat space but, in the large, it has a different shape. In true flat space, if one traveled forever in the same direction, one would just get infinitely far away from where one started. Traveling in the same direction on both the sphere and the torus, one would eventually return to one's starting point.

On S the nongravitational fields F (and their appropriate derivatives F′), and two tensor fields h and K, with (F, F′,h,K) satisfy certain equations called *constraint equations*. The constraint equations say nothing about the time evolution; rather they are to be regarded as consistency conditions among the fields (F, F′,h,K) which must be satisfied at every instant of time. The physical interpretation of h is that of a spatial metric of the manifold S—the "metric" is what allows us to measure distances on S—and so S and (F, F′,h,K) together represent the entire spatial universe at an instant of universal time. S and (F, F′,h,K) are called the *initial data*.

We now try to find a *four-dimensional* manifold M with metric g and spacetime nongravitational fields F such that (1) M contains S as a submanifold; (2) g restricted to S is the metric h; and (3) K is the "extrinsic curvature" of S in M (roughly speaking, K says how rapidly h is changing in "time"). The manifold M and the fields (g,F) are then the whole of physical reality, including the underlying background spacetime—that is, (M,g)—the gravitational field (represented by the spacetime metric g), and all the nongravitational fields (given by F). There will be infinitely many such M's and g's, but one can cut down the number by requiring that g satisfies the Einstein field equations everywhere on M, and that the Einstein field equations[2] reduce to the constraint equations on S.

But even requiring the Einstein equations to hold everywhere leaves infinitely many spacetimes (M,g) which are generated from the *same* initial data at the spacetime instant S. To see this, suppose we have found a spacetime (M,g) which in fact has S and its initial data as the spatial universe at some instant t_0 of universal time. Pick another universal time t_1 to the future of t_0 and cut away all of the spacetime in (M,g) to the future of t_1 (including the spatial instant corresponding to t_1). This gives a new spacetime (M',g) which coincides with (M,g) to the past of t_1, but which has absolutely nothing—no space, no time, no matter—to the future of t_1. This cutting away of spacetime leaving nothing is shown in Figure V.1.

Clearly, both (M,g) and (M',g) are spacetimes which are both generated from S and its initial data. Furthermore, the Einstein equations are satisfied *everywhere* on both spacetimes. There are infinitely many ways we can cut away (M,g) in this way, so there is an infinity of (M',g)'s we can construct. True, the universe (M',g) ends abruptly at t_1, for no good reason. But what of that? The point is, the field equations themselves cannot tell us that the physical universe should continue past the time t_1. Rather, in classical general relativity one must impose as a separate assumption, over and above the assumption of the field equations and the initial data, that the physical universe must continue in time until the field equations themselves tell us that time has come to an end (at a spacetime singularity, say). Without this separate assumption, which of the infinity of (M',g)'s really exists is contingent.

This cutting-away procedure won't work in Newtonian mechanics, or indeed in any physical theory which has a preexisting background spacetime. If we tried to require that the physical fields stopped abruptly at t_1, then, since the instant t_1 and its future still exist, "fields stopping abruptly" must mean "fields equal zero abruptly," which would contradict the field equations. So if a theory has a preexisting background space, the field equations themselves tell us that the universe—or rather the fields and particles making up matter—must keep going. It is more the background spacetime, rather than the evolution equations or the conservation laws, that sustains the universe in being in pre-general relativity theories. Isaac Newton (if not his followers) realized this, asserting that absolute space and time were semidivine: "the sensorium of God."

It is possible to prove[3] that there is among all the mathematically possible (M',g)'s—we might call these "possible worlds"—a *unique* "maximal" spacetime (M,g) which is generated by the initial data on S. "Maximal" means that the spacetime (M,g) contains any other (M',g) generated by the initial data on S as a proper subset. In other words, (M,g) is the spacetime we get by continuing the time evolution until the field equations themselves won't allow us to go further. The maximal spacetime which can be gotten from the initial data on a surface S with edges is pictured in Figure V.2. The region of spacetime which is

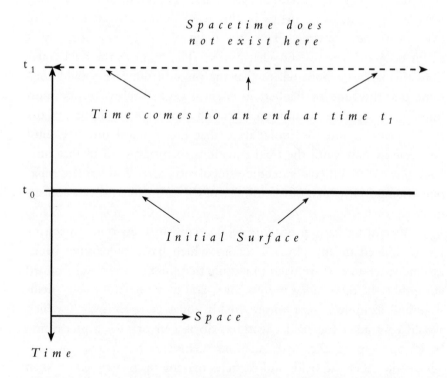

FIGURE V.1: *The end of spacetime (M,g). The spacetime to the future of time t_1 is cut away, so there is no time, no space to the future of time t_1. The universe exists between the initial data surface at time t_0 until spacetime comes to an abrupt halt at time t_1.*

determined by the initial data is called the *domain of dependence*. A nonmaximal region of spacetime generated from the same data on the same S is then shown in Figure V.3.

This maximal (M,g) is the natural candidate for the spacetime that is actualized, but it is important to keep in mind that this is a physical assumption: all of the (M′,g)'s are possible worlds, and any one of these possible worlds could have been the one that really exists.

Once we have the maximal (M,g) generated from a given S and its

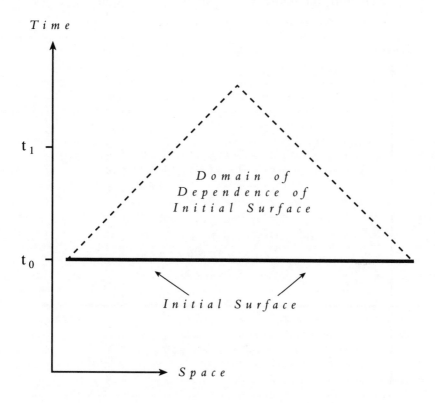

FIGURE V.2: *The maximum extension of spacetime (M,g) from an initial data surface. The initial data surface is just a part of the universe at time t_0. This maximum extension is defined by two light rays, one from one end of the surface and the other ray from the other end. These light rays are represented by dashed lines. The maximum extension is the region enclosed by the two light rays and the surface. If the maximum extension is all of spacetime, then spacetime abruptly comes to an end at these dashed lines.*

initial data, there is an infinity of other choices of three-dimensional manifolds in M which we could picture as generating (M,g). For example, we could regard the spatial universe and the fields it contains now as "S with its initial data," or we could regard the universe a thousand years ago as "S with its initial data." Both would give the same (M,g) since the Einstein equations are deterministic. Everything that has happened and will happen is contained implicitly in the initial data on S. There is nothing new under the Sun in a deterministic theory like general relativity. One could even wonder why time exists at all, since from an information standpoint it is quite superfluous.

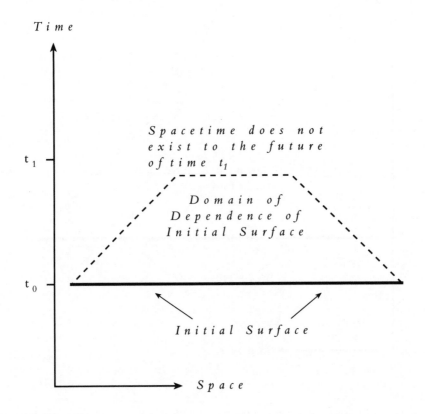

FIGURE V.3: *A nonmaximal extension of spacetime (M,g) from an initial data surface. The initial data surface is the same as in the previous figure. However, in this figure the spacetime is arbitrarily cut off at time t_1. As in the previous figure, there is nothing to the future of the dashed lines, or to the future of time t_1.*

None of the infinity of initial data manifolds in (M,g) can be uniquely regarded as generating the whole of spacetime (M,g). Each contains the same information, and each will generate the same (M,g), including all the other initial data manifolds.

Even in deterministic theories, relationships between physical entities are different at different times. For example, two particles moving under Newtonian gravity are now 2 meters apart (say), and a minute later 4 meters apart. This is true even though, given the initial position and velocities when they were 2 meters apart, it is determined then that they will be 4 meters apart a minute later. The question is, will the totality of relationships at one time become the same (or nearly the same) at some later time? If this happens, then we have the horror of the Eternal Return. As I showed in Chapter III, one can prove that the Eternal Return will occur in a Newtonian universe provided said universe is finite in space and finite in the range of velocities the particles are allowed to have. I also showed in Chapter III that, in classical general relativity,[4] the Eternal Return *cannot* occur. That is, the physical relationships existing now between the fields will never be repeated, nor will the relationships ever return to approximately what they now are. History, understood as an unrepeatable temporal sequence of relationships between physical entities, is real.

Nonrelativistic Quantum Mechanics Is Deterministic

The meaning of contingency in quantum mechanics depends strongly on which interpretation of the theory is adopted. For example, in the most common version of the Copenhagen Interpretation, there is an intrinsic quantum randomness in nature, which adds a new contingency to the three types listed in the previous chapter, whereas in the Many-Worlds Interpretation (sometimes called the Everett Interpretation after Hugh Everett, who first proposed it in 1957 while a graduate student at Princeton), this randomness is merely an artifact of our limited way of observing the physical world: noncosmological quantum mechanics is completely deterministic. (I shall give a mathematical proof of this in the Appendix for Scientists.)

Let me define operationally the Copenhagen and Many-Worlds Interpretations by applying both to analyze one of the most famous "thought experiments" in physics, the Schrödinger's Cat Experiment. Let us imagine with one of the inventors of quantum mechanics, Erwin Schrödinger, that we have sealed a cat inside a steel chamber, together with a "diabolical device": in a Geiger counter there is a tiny bit of radioactive substance, so small that the probability is only one half that an atom decays and one half that no atom decays. The Geiger counter is connected to a relay so that, if it detects an atomic decay, a hammer smashes a flask of deadly cyanide gas. If it does not detect a decay, the flask is not smashed. Thus, if an atom decays, the poor cat dies. If it does not, the cat lives. We all know perfectly well what we would see at the end of an hour if we were cruel enough to carry out this hellish experiment: the cat would be either alive or dead.

According to the mathematics of quantum mechanics, however, the cat is neither! At the end of the hour, the wave function of the cat is not the wave function of a dead cat, nor is it the wave function of a live cat. Rather, it is the wave function of *both* a dead cat *and* a live cat: the true wave function is the *sum* of the dead cat and live cat wave functions. Quantum mechanics says unequivocally that the cat is simultaneously dead and alive, in gross contradiction to common sense, and to what we would actually see. There is universal agreement among physicists that this sum is what standard quantum mechanics predicts. What physicists disagree about is how to interpret this sum.

According to the Copenhagen Interpretation, there is a process called "wave function reduction," which reduces the sum of the dead and live cat wave functions to either the dead cat wave function or the live cat wave function (not both), and further the reduction is random; that is, in the Schrödinger's Cat Experiment, half the time the cat will be alive and half the time it will be dead. There are no general rules for deciding what physical objects have the power to reduce wave functions. All we know is that the wave function of the cat has been reduced by the time it is observed by us humans. Some physicists who accept the Copenhagen Interpretation believe it requires consciousness to reduce wave functions (Penrose and Wigner are in this camp), whereas others believe any "large" object can do the job (my mentor, the great American physicist John A. Wheeler, is in this camp). However, both humans and "large" objects are all made up of atoms, each of which moves according to standard quantum mechanics, with no wave function reduction occurring, so it is hard to see exactly how wave function reduction comes into nature at all.

According to the Many-Worlds Interpretation, there is no reduction of the wave function at all. That is, after one hour in the steel chamber, the cat really is in the quantum state "dead cat plus live cat." The Many-Worlds Interpretation resolves the obvious inconsistency with observation by saying that the radioactive decay of the atom has forced the cat and all the other pieces of equipment to split into two different worlds: the cat is alive in one of these worlds and dead in the other. If we now try to see whether the cat is alive or dead, then we also split into two. In one world, we see the cat dead, and in the other we see the cat alive. The remarkable thing about the Many-Worlds Interpretation is that, once we assume all objects without exception are described by quantum mechanics—human beings included—then the mathematics of quantum mechanics forces us to accept the Many-Worlds Interpretation. (I shall describe the relevant mathematics in the Appendix for Scientists.)

Since the Omega Point Theory is fundamentally a cosmological theory; i.e., it is a quantum cosmology, I am virtually forced into adopting the Many-Worlds Interpretation, because only in this interpretation is it meaningful to talk about a quantum universe and its ontology. Since the Copenhagen Interpretation assumes that "wave function reduction" eliminated quantum effects on cosmological scales an exceedingly short time after the Big Bang, the universe today is not quantum except on very small scales. As I just said, the problem with this assumption is that the wave function reduction process is almost entirely mysterious—we have no rules for deciding what material entity can reduce wave functions—so it is impossible to give a sharp analysis of contingency when this process is operating. The Many-Worlds Interpretation does not suffer from this drawback: there is no reduction of the wave function and physical reality is completely described by the wave function of the universe. The universe is just as

quantum now as it was in the beginning. In the Many-Worlds Interpretation, the radius of the universe is just one of many quantum variables, like the life of the cat in the Schrödinger's Cat Experiment.
Therefore, there are many universes with different radii at maximum
expansion, as pictured in Figure V.4. We happen to live in one of these
universes, but there are other universes—and quite likely other versions
of ourselves in them. *There are Many Histories.*

Of course, the Many-Worlds Interpretation may be wrong; most
physicists think it is. But the overwhelming majority of people working on quantum cosmology subscribe to some version of the Many-
Worlds Interpretation, simply because the mathematics forces one to
accept it. The mathematics may be a delusion, with no reference in
physical reality. Or the situation may be similar to that of early seventeenth-century physics: astronomers believed the Earth went around
the Sun, because the mathematics of the Copernican system forced
them to. But few other scholars or ordinary people believed the Earth
moved. Their own senses told them it did not. As the great German
sixteenth-century astronomer Johannes Kepler put it in a letter dated
26 March 1598: "There is not one astronomer who puts these new
hypotheses [of Copernicus] one bit behind those of antiquity; the
struggle against Copernicus is waged exclusively and entirely by natural
philosophers, metaphysicians, and theologians."[5] I shall adopt the
Many-Worlds Interpretation in what follows.

The political scientist L. David Raub[6] polled seventy-two leading
quantum cosmologists and other quantum field theorists on their opinion about the truth of the Many-Worlds Interpretation. The possible
answers were, (1) "Yes, I think the MWI is true"; (2) "No, I don't
accept the MWI"; (3) "Maybe it's true, but I'm not yet convinced";
and (4) "I have no opinion one way or the other." The results of the
poll were: 58% said yes, 18% said no, 13% said maybe, and 11% said
no opinion. In the "yes" column were Stephen Hawking, Richard
Feynman, and Murray Gell-Mann, while the "no's" included Penrose.
Hawking's letter to Raub stated: " 'Many Worlds' is a bad name for it,
but it is basically correct." (Hawking uses stronger language in private
conversation; he once told me that "The MWI is trivially true!") In a
comment on a paper by the American physicist Bryce DeWitt, who is
the leading proponent of the Many-Worlds Interpretation, Gell-Mann

in essence agreed with Hawking: ". . . Apart from the unfortunate language, Everett's physics is okay, although somewhat incomplete."[7] (Hawking and Gell-Mann prefer to call the MWI the Many-Histories Interpretation.) In his latest book, *Dreams of a Final Theory*, Steven Weinberg[8] also comes out in favor of the Many Worlds Interpretation.

I offer these results not as evidence of the validity of the MWI— scientific truth is not decided by a vote of the majority—but as proof

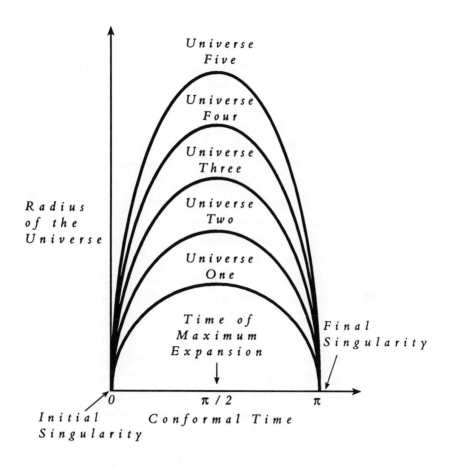

FIGURE V.4: *The branching of universes according to the Many-Histories Interpretation. The only variable in this simple model is the radius of the universe. The vertical axis is the radius of the universe, and the horizontal axis is time (conformal time, which will be defined in the Appendix for Scientists). A measurement early in time causes the universe to split into Many Histories, five of which are pictured.*

that most quantum cosmologists feel as I do: the mathematics forces us to accept the MWI. To those readers who are inclined to dismiss the MWI out of hand because it sounds so outlandish, I offer these results as an inducement to reconsider: physicists of the stature of Feynman, Hawking, Gell-Mann, and Weinberg do not accept theories, particularly outlandish theories, without serious thought. Hawking, Feynman, Gell-Mann, and Weinberg are beyond a doubt four of the greatest theoretical physicists of the twentieth century. The very fact that they have accepted the MWI should indicate that you yourself should not reject it without some serious thought.

Interestingly, what convinced *me* of the truth of the MWI was not a deep reflection on the mathematics of quantum mechanics, but a sudden realization that even on the nonquantum macroscopic level we have to treat alternative histories as real in order to deal adequately with the world we live in. In the late 1970s, I was John Wheeler's postdoc at the University of Texas, and one day I happened to be reading a collection of essays by the Nobel-prize-winning economist Friedrich Hayek. One of these essays dealt with the idea of "capital," and Hayek wrote that the only proper definition of the "capital stock" possessed by a society is a complete list of alternative income streams which, over time, the society's resources can generate. "Why," I thought to myself, "this is just the Many-Worlds Interpretation!" (I'll come back to Hayek's definition of "capital" in Chapter X.)

A little thought will provide other examples of the necessity to regard alternative histories as real. An example from classical physics was given in Chapter II. Since the orbit of the Earth is chaotic, it is experimentally meaningless to speak of *the* past history of the Earth's orbit. The *real* past history of the Earth is the "equivalence class" of all histories which are consistent with what we know about the Earth's present position. (An "equivalence class" is a collection of objects regarded in the mind as one entity. The Omega Point is the equivalence class of all spacetime events.) The Earth's past history is really Many Histories. The Earth, the most "macroscopic" object in our ordinary experience, tells us to adopt the Many-Worlds Interpretation.

There is another reason for being at least open-minded about the MWI. If it is true, then we can *prove* to be true what most people would very much *like* to be true. By assuming that human beings are quantum mechanical objects just like everything else, I shall be able to *prove* that it is possible for each and every one of us to be resurrected one day and live forever. Furthermore, by applying the Many-Worlds Interpretation to the ontology of quantum cosmology, I shall be able to *prove* that we probably have free will. In Chapter VII I shall argue that, conversely, a Many-Worlds ontology is a logical necessity for free will: if the Many Worlds did not exist, then it would be a logical impossibility for us to have free will.

THE QUANTUM VERSION
OF THE OMEGA POINT
THEORY

·———·

The Basic Ideas of Quantum
Cosmology

I N   TRADITIONAL   QUANTUM   COSMOLOGY   THE
universe is represented by a wave function Ψ(h,F,S), whereas in classical general relativity h and F are respectively the spatial metric and the
nongravitational fields given on a *fixed* three-dimensional manifold S.
(Remember from Chapter V that the "manifold" is the basic underlying "space," and the metric is the measure of distances on this underlying space.) The three-manifold and its topology are fixed. The initial
data[1] in quantum cosmology are not (h,F) given on S as was the case in
classical general relativity, but rather Ψ(h,F,S). From these initial data,
an equation called the Wheeler-DeWitt equation determines Ψ(h,F,S)
for all values of h and F. In other words, the wave function, not the
metric or the nongravitational field, is the basic physical field in quantum cosmology. It is the initial wave function that must be given but,
once given, it is determined everywhere. What we think of as the most
basic fields in classical general relativity, namely h and F, play the role
of coordinates in quantum cosmology. But this does not mean h and F
are unreal. They are as real as they are in classical theory. But it *does*
mean more than one h and F exist on S at the same time. To appreciate
this, recall that the classical metric h(x) is a function of the spatial
coordinates on the manifold S. This metric has (nonzero) values at all
points on S; that is, for the entire range of the coordinates as they vary

over S, which is to say, as we go from one point to another in the universe. Each value of h(x) is equally real, and all of the values of h at all of the points of S exist simultaneously. Similarly, the points in the domain of the wave function $\Psi(h,F,S)$ are the various possible values of h and F, each set (h,F) corresponding to a complete universe at a given instant of time. The central claim of the Many-Worlds Interpretation is that each of these universes actually exists, just as the different h(x) exist at the various points of S: quantum reality is made up of an infinite number of universes (worlds). Of course, we are not aware of these worlds—we are only aware of one—but the laws of quantum mechanics explain this: we must generally be as unaware of these parallel worlds as we are of our motion with the Earth around the Sun. (In extreme conditions, for instance near singularities, it *is* possible for the worlds to affect each other in a more obvious way than they do now.)

To fix the classical initial data, we pick a *function* h(x) out of an infinite number of possible metric functions that could have been on S. All of these possible worlds comprise a function space. To fix the quantum initial data, we pick a *wave function* $\Psi(h,F,S)$ out of an infinite number of possible wave functions which could have been on the classical function space (h,F). Remember, however, that all values of the function space (h,F) *really are* on S simultaneously. In quantum cosmology, the collection of all possible wave functions forms the set of the possible worlds; what is contingent is which single unique universal wave function is actualized. But the possible worlds of classical cosmology—the space of all physically possible (h,F) on S—are no longer contingent. All of them are actualized.

In traditional quantum cosmology, *there is no time at the most basic physical level*. The universal wave function $\Psi(h,F,S)$ is all there is, and there is no reference to a four-dimensional manifold M or a four-dimensional metric g in the wave function. At the most basic ontological level, time does not exist. Everything is on the three-dimensional manifold S. How can this be? Of course we see time. Or do we? What we see is relationships between objects—configurations of physical fields—in space. In the discussion of the Eternal Return in Chapter III, I argued that time and history could be truly real only if the spatial relationships between the various fields never returned to a previous state. In quantum cosmology, there is no spacetime in which the spatial relationships between fields can change. Rather, all we have is paths (trajectories) in the collection (h,F) of all possible relationships between the physical fields on S. But this is enough, because each such path defines a history, a complete spacetime.

To understand this, imagine that we are at a point P in (h,F), and have selected a particular path γ in (h,F) starting at P. Each point, remember, corresponds to an entire universe (spatially). As we go along γ, the relationships between the physical fields vary smoothly from their values at P. *This variation would appear as temporal variation* from inside the path γ, because each point on γ is a complete spatial universe, and thus the sequence of points constitute a sequence of spatial universes. But this is exactly the same as the classical four-dimensional manifold M, which gets its extra dimension by stacking this sequence of S's on top of each other,[2] with a spacetime metric g and spacetime fields F. In the above classical analysis we obtained (M,g) as an extension of S and its fields. Each path in (h,F) thus is an entire classical universal history, an entire spacetime.

All paths in (h,F) really exist, which necessarily means that all—and I mean all—histories which are consistent with the "stuff" of the universe being (h,F) really exist. In particular, even histories which are grossly inconsistent with the laws of physics really occur. Closed paths in (h,F) obviously exist, so there are histories in which the Eternal Return is true. There are also real histories leading to our presently observed state of the universe—the point P in (h,F)—in which real historical characters—for instance Julius Caesar—never existed. What happens in such a history is that the physical fields rearrange themselves over time (more accurately, over the path corresponding to this strange history) to create false memories, including not only human memories but also the "memories" in a huge number of written records and in massive monuments. Just as there is an infinity of actual pasts which have led to the present state, so there is an infinity of really existing futures which evolve from the present state. So every consistent future is not only possible but it really happens. But not all futures are equally likely to be seen. That is, there is one path in (h,F) leading from a given point P which is overwhelmingly more likely to follow from P than all the others. This path is called *the phase path*. Along this path, at least in the low energy limit, the laws of physics hold, and memories are reliable. In this low energy limit, we can call the phase path a *classical path*. A classical path in (h,F) is a phase path which generates a classical spacetime (M,g) obeying the Einstein equations. To visualize these phase paths, look at Figure V.4. Each of the curves is a phase path.

So far I have not said what the wave function Ψ itself does. But it must do something physically detectable, something not coded in the fields (h,F) alone. If it did not exert some physical effect, we could just omit it from physics; it would have no real existence. But I claimed above that Ψ was a *real* field, something as real as the fields (h,F).

What Ψ does is determine the set of all phase paths, and also the "probabilities" which are associated with each point and each path in (h,F). A wave function is a complex function, and all complex functions are actually two functions, a "magnitude" and a "phase." The phase paths are by definition those that are perpendicular to the surfaces of constant phase. The square of the magnitude at a point P in (h,F) is the "probability" of that point. The physicists Heisenberg and Mott showed[3] that, if "probability" has its usual meaning, then given the fact that we are (approximately) at P, the conditional probability of going to a nearby point Q is maximum if Q lies along the phase path through P, at least in the case of the nonrelativistic free particle Hamiltonian. The relative probability is very close to 1 on the phase path, and it drops rapidly to 0 as one moves away from the phase path connecting P and Q.

All the physics is contained in the wave function. In fact, the laws of physics themselves are completely superfluous. They are coded in the wave function. The classical laws of physics are just those regularities which are seen to hold along a classical path by observers in that classical path. Along other paths, there would be other regularities, different laws of physics. And these other paths exist and hence these other laws of physics really hold; it is just extremely unlikely we will happen to see them operating. The Wheeler–DeWitt equation for the wave function is itself quite superfluous. It is merely a crutch to help us to find the actual wave function of the universe. If we knew the boundary conditions which the actual universal wave function satisfied, then we could derive the Wheeler-DeWitt equation, which is just a particular equation (among many) which the wave function happens to satisfy. Thus in quantum cosmology there is no real contingency in the laws of physics. Any law of physics holds in some path, and the law of physics governing the universal wave function can be derived from that wave function. All the contingency in quantum cosmology is in the wave function, or rather, in the "boundary conditions" which pick out the wave function which actually exists.

The Hartle-Hawking Boundary Condition on the Universal Wave Function

There is one arbitrary feature in traditional quantum cosmology, namely the choice of the fixed three-manifold S. There are many possibilities; why should only one be realized? It was the great contribution of Hawking and Hartle to eliminate this wave function contingency, by allowing the wave function to be a function of any three-manifold: the points in the domain of the Hartle-Hawking wave function $\Psi(h,F,S)$ are the various possible values of h, F, *and* S with each set (h,F,S) corresponding to a complete universe at a given instant of time.

The wave function $\Psi(h,F,S)$ is determined by the Hartle-Hawking boundary condition, which says roughly[4] that "the universal wave function is determined by the fact that the only boundary of a given path is (h,F,S) itself." (Hawking likes to express this as "the only boundary condition is there is no boundary.") Hawking and Hartle showed that, in the special case that S was kept fixed, the restricted wave function computed from the Hartle-Hawking boundary condition locally satisfied the Wheeler-DeWitt equation, but in the general case it did not. In fact, in the general case the wave function could not satisfy any differential equation, since S is not a continuous variable. (If the class of all compact three-manifolds cannot be classified—whether an algorithm exists to classify them is at present an open mathematical problem[5]—then *no* equation, differential or otherwise, for $\Psi(h,F,S)$ exists; in this case it would be logically impossible to compute $\Psi(h,F,S)$.)

What the Hartle-Hawking generalization permits that classical quantum cosmology does not is topology change. There is a general consensus among field theorists that an acceptable quantum theory ought to admit fluctuations in anything which appears in the domain of the wave function: if h fluctuates, so should S. However, if we accept this consensus, then the Hartle-Hawking proposal does not go far enough. It is known that, classically, topology change must be accompanied by causality violation. This means in particular that any codimension one foliation of (M,g) will not admit an h which is everywhere spacelike on all the three-manifolds S of the foliation. That is, if we admit the possibility of fluctuations in the topology, then we had better admit the possibility that h may fluctuate so as to be spacelike in some part of S, and timelike or null in others. If all geometry, both h and S, arises from some deeper structure, for instance string field theory, then this possibility becomes even more reasonable, since the deeper structure is unlikely to distinguish strongly between time and space.

There are two reasons why h has been required to be spacelike only. First, traditional quantum gravity has been expressed in Hamiltonian form, and such a formulation has required a sharp global distinction between time and space. This meant that the arena of traditional quantum gravity has been more limited than classical general relativity, which considers all four-manifolds M which admit a Lorentz metric g. The Hartle-Hawking generalization, while considering all four-manifolds M, computes the wave function $\Psi(h,F,S)$ by euclideanizing the Einstein action in the path integral (this procedure hopefully makes the path integral convergent). That is, in Hartle-Hawking, no Lorentz metric is admitted. The only allowed four-metrics are those which are everywhere spacelike. Furthermore, the four-manifolds considered in Hartle-Hawking don't really exist: they are just computational constructs used to calculate Ψ(h,F,S), and when Ψ(h,F,S) is obtained, they are discarded. This is of course contrary to the physical philosophy of the Many-Worlds Interpretation, in which the paths are regarded as real existents.

The second and most important reason why h is required to be spacelike is that the wave function's interpretation is traditionally that of a probability amplitude at a given time. (A "probability amplitude" is a quantity whose square is the probability.) This interpretation requires time to be sharply distinguished from space: only the latter is a true quantum variable which can be in the domain of the wave function. This interpretation of the wave function is the real reason why traditional quantum gravity has been expressed in Hamiltonian form. But sharply distinguishing between time and space is contrary to the physics of relativity.

The Omega Point Boundary Condition for the Universal Wave Function

I propose to resolve the above quandaries by focusing on the wave function domain and the wave function interpretation, and obtaining the dynamics from the boundary condition alone.

I shall assume that the domain of quantum gravity is the class of all four-manifolds which admit a Lorentz metric g; the domain is the same as that of classical general relativity. Now it is a theorem[6] that all four-manifolds that admit a Lorentz metric admit a foliation of codimension one. (This just means that the four-manifold can be expressed as a stack of three-dimensional manifolds. Think of the stack of manifolds as a stack of very thin cookies. Each member of the stack—each cookie—is called a "leaf," and the whole stack is called the "foliation.") Under fairly general conditions, one can find foliations such that the consecutive leaves of the foliation can be regarded as defining different moments of time.[7] In this case the foliation can be written

S(t), where S(t) is the three-manifold at parameter value t. Such foliations are known to exist in globally hyperbolic or stably causal spacetimes, but these foliations will exist in many spacetimes which are not
stably causal. (Roughly speaking, a "globally hyperbolic" spacetime is
one which is completely deterministic; a "stably causal" spacetime
is one which, as its name implies, is stably causal—causality is not
destroyed if it is varied slightly.[8]) Such a foliation will have a metric
h(t)—which may or may not be spacelike everywhere on S(t)—
which is induced in the usual way from the four-metric g on the four-
manifold M.

The idea is to let the domain of the universal wave function be S(t)
and the fields F(t) and h(t) which are induced on S(t) by the usual
projection from the enveloping spacetimes (M,g). We can write the
functional dependence as $\Psi = \Psi(h(t),F(t),S(t))$. Any collection of
(h,F,S) which cannot be represented as induced fields on the leaf of a
foliation of some spacetime will be said to have $\Psi(h,F,S) = 0$. Conversely, there will in general be many spacetimes (M,g) which admit
the same (h,F,S). Among these will be a few (or possibly zero) whose
future (with some assignment of "past" and "future") c-boundary is a
single point.

I should like to propose the

Omega Point Boundary Condition for the universal wave function:

The wave function of the universe is that wave function for which all
phase paths terminate in a (future) Omega Point, with life continuing
into the future forever along every phase path in which it evolves all
the way into the Omega Point.

To make this boundary condition physically meaningful, it is necessary to define "life" in a purely physical way. This has already been
done in Chapter IV: it just means that conditions (1)–(3) of the definition of "life continuing forever" in a classical universe apply in a phase
path.

It turns out (as one might expect) that the Hartle-Hawking
boundary condition does not satisfy the Omega Point Boundary Condition; life eventually becomes extinct along all phase paths in the Hartle-Hawking quantum universe. Hartle[9] has made the important point

that one of the things an acceptable boundary condition on the universal wave function must do is justify the existence of classical paths. There are many wave functions for which the phase paths—the histories of maximum probability—are not very close to any solutions of the classical Einstein equations, so there are no classical paths. For such wave functions, the history we observe would be exceedingly improbable, which seems implausible. With the Hartle-Hawking boundary condition, the phase paths which result in homogeneity and isotropy can be shown to have maximal probability, and further, an analysis shows human beings can only evolve in a universe which is close to homogeneity and isotropy. Thus the existence of classical paths is justified by "anthropic" self-selection in the Hartle-Hawking boundary condition. With the Omega Point Boundary Condition, the existence of life-bearing phase paths is fundamental to the boundary condition itself; the evolution and continued existence of life are logically prior. If a phase path did not exist at our current (h,F,S) in which life could continue, the Omega Point would not exist. As before, a weak anthropic analysis shows that, if the laws of physics deviated greatly from the classical laws from one instant to the next, we could not continue to live, so the Omega Point Boundary Condition requires at least some phase paths to give the actual classical histories in which we actually evolve.

I outline in the Appendix for Scientists the construction of a simple quantized Friedmann cosmological model in which all phase paths are classical paths which terminate in a single c–boundary point. However, as we saw in Chapter II, life cannot survive in a Friedmann universe with arbitrary large size at maximum expansion, so such histories are eliminated by the Omega Point Boundary Condition. Similarly, universes whose radii at maximum expansion exist for too short a time for life ever to evolve in them. Thus with the Omega Point Boundary Condition, Figure V.4, which illustrates the Many Histories of the universe, would have to be modified: the histories with too large and too small a maximum size are eliminated according to the Omega Point Boundary Condition. This is illustrated in Figure VI.1.

I describe in the Appendix for Scientists the precise mathematical formulation of the Omega Point Boundary Condition. I suspect, but cannot prove, that this formulation gives a unique wave function for the universe.

Theological Implications: The Universal Wave Function as Holy Spirit

Let us suppose that the Omega Point Boundary Condition gives a unique wave function. Then it would mean that the laws of physics and every entity that exists physically would be generated by the Omega Point and its living properties. For these properties determine the universal wave function, and the wave function determines everything else. In any interpretation and with any boundary condition, the universal wave function is the unique field which gives being to all other fields—the electroweak fields, the gluon fields, the quark fields, the lepton fields, indeed all the usual physical fields. With the Omega Point Boundary Condition, this all-determining field becomes ultimately personal. So we have an all-pervasive physical field which gives being to all being, which gives life to all living things, and which itself is generated by the ultimate life which it defines.

In several papers the German theologian Wolfhart Pannenberg has suggested that there exists an undiscovered physical field, an all-pervading physical field which can be regarded as a transcendent source of life. I claim the universal wave function with the Omega Point Boundary Condition is a good candidate for such a field. The Omega Point Boundary Condition explicitly requires that the wave function force the physical universe to give rise to life, and it requires that this life persist into the Omega Point. With the Omega Point Boundary Condition, the universal wave function thus brings life into existence and sustains it in existence. Furthermore, the universal wave function is not restricted to living things, but it is everywhere. It has the power of self-transcendence as Pannenberg defines it: ". . . self-transcendence is to be regarded at the same time as an activity of the organism and as an effect of a power that continuously raises the organism beyond its limitations and thereby grants it its life.''[10] An excellent description of the relationship between an organism in the universe and the universal

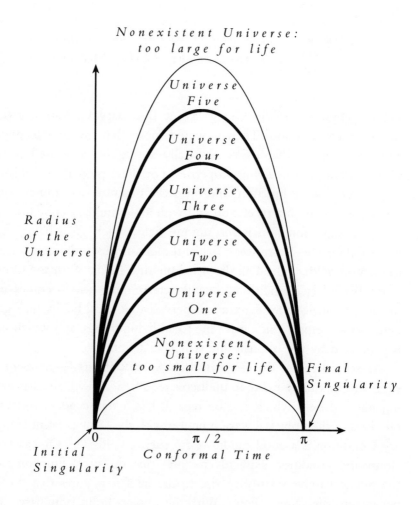

FIGURE VI.1: *The branching of universes according to the Many-Histories Interpretation, with the Omega Point Boundary Condition imposed. The thick dark curves represent universes which have life in them all the way into the Omega Point, and hence the wave function of the Universe is non-zero along these trajectories. Two other universes are pictured (with thinner curves) which do not have life going into the Omega Point, one because it recollapses into the final singularity before life has a chance to evolve, and the other because it takes such a long time to reach the maximum expansion that life dies out. The wave function is zero along both of these trajectories.*

wave function with the Omega Point Boundary Condition. Pannenberg has also pointed out that "In biblical traditions . . . the life-giving power is seen as an agent that influences the organism from the outside."[11]

In the biblical traditions, this life-giving power is the Holy Spirit. I am thus in effect proposing that we identify the universal wave function constrained by the Omega Point Boundary Condition with the Holy Spirit. I claim this identification is reasonable, for, as discussed above, a wave function is the all-pervasive physical field which creates and guides all the directly observed physical fields, and the wave function is made explicitly Personal by the Omega Point Boundary Condition. Thus the universal wave function constrained by the Omega Point Boundary Condition is an omnipresent invisible field, guiding and creating all being, and ultimately Personal—these are the traditional defining properties of the Holy Spirit.

One could also identify the universal wave function constrained by the Omega Point Boundary Condition with what Teilhard called "radial energy." For, as Pannenberg points out, "In Teilhard's perspective there is only one spirit permeating and activating all the material processes and urging them beyond themselves in a process of progressive spiritualization of converging unification towards a centre of perfect unity which in providing the end of the evolutionary process proves to be its true dynamic origin."[12] This is exactly what the universal wave function with the Omega Point Boundary Condition does. According to the Omega Point Boundary Condition, the structure of the phase paths (more precisely, their ultimate future) gives probability weights—guidance, so to speak, not rigid control—to all paths. The ultimate future guides all presents into itself. But this guidance is *not* determinism.

VII.

How Free Will Can Arise from Quantum Cosmological Mechanisms

·———·

The Distinction Between Determinism and Indeterminism

THERE ARE TWO MAIN SCHOOLS OF THOUGHT about free will. First, there are the Compatibilists, who say that we have free will if we feel ourselves to be free; that is, if we are unaware of any outside compulsion constraining our actions. Second, there are the Libertarians, who say that we have free will only if our actions are determined by us and by us only: that is, we are free only if our actual decisions are not determined by the rest of the universe, past, present, or future, but instead we ourselves are the ultimate and irreducible source of our decisions. The debate has been going on between these schools for thousands of years, with no resolution. For the past few centuries, supporters of the two schools have been talking past one another. There seems to be a consensus among philosophers that no new argument has appeared in this time to break the impasse.

I shall provide a completely new argument for free will in this chapter. I shall conclude that *both schools* are correct. In particular, I shall show how the Omega Point Boundary Condition provides a model for agent determinism in the Libertarian sense, a model which is nevertheless consistent with physics. Even if the model were not true, it nevertheless would be a considerable advance: the model shows that the Libertarian idea is at least logically consistent, something the

Compatibilists have always been dubious about. But I shall provide evidence that the model is probably true. The model requires a clear understanding of the distinction between determinism and indeterminism.

In my opinion, the clearest distinction between determinism and indeterminism was made by William James in his classic paper "The Dilemma of Determinism":

> What does determinism profess? It professes that those parts of the universe already laid down absolutely appoint and decree what the other parts shall be. The future has no ambiguous possibilities hidden in its womb: the part we call the present is compatible with only one totality. Any other future complement than the one fixed from eternity is impossible. The whole is in each and every part, and welds it with the rest into an absolute unity, an iron block, in which there can be no equivocation or shadow of turning. . . . Indeterminism, on the contrary, says that the parts have a certain amount of loose play on one another, so that the laying down of one of them does not necessarily determine what the others shall be.[1]

James's basic idea is that indeterminism holds if there is no part of reality which contains total information about the whole. That is, each event contains some information that is not coded anywhere else. This means that there does not exist any nontrivial algorithm from which the entire universe can be computed from total information about any proper subset of the universe. Here I use the words "algorithm" and "information" in their widest sense: in the deterministic scalar field example of Chapter V, the "information" is the value of the scalar field on the boundary, and the "algorithm" is "solve Laplace's equation." Stated in this way, it is seen that James's idea is really independent of temporal relations. It makes sense even in universes in which no global time can be defined. It also means—as James realized—that, if God is pictured as a being outside the physical universe, then some information in each event must not even be coded in God.

.———.

Avoiding the Conflict Between Divine Omniscience and Human Free Will

One can avoid the conflict between divine omniscience and human free will by taking Tillich's view that God is not *a* being, but rather being itself. In traditional theology, this would permit one to say that God chooses to code some of His/Her information about each event only in the event itself. The information is still in God because every event is a proper subset of God. In the Omega Point Theory, the information unique to each event is also in the Omega Point in His/Her transcendence because the Omega Point is the completion of finite reality, and hence includes all finite reality. In other words, since the Omega Point in His/Her transcendence is a singularity, information given *at* a singularity is really just the data given in finite reality looked at as a whole, and so does not determine the value given elsewhere. Or rather it determines it only in a trivial sense: whatever happens, happens. As Pannenberg puts it: "[God] exists only in the way in which the future is powerful over the present, because the future decides what will emerge out of what exists in the present. . . . Above all, the power of the future does not rob man of his freedom to transcend every state of affairs. A being presently at hand, and equipped with omnipotence, would destroy such freedom by virtue of his overpowering might."[2] (One must be careful here. There is a tendency among nonmathematicians to assume that determinism means the past determines the present, whereas the reverse is not true: the future cannot determine the present. Actually, most[3] deterministic physical theories have determinism working in both time directions. In such theories, the future is just as powerful over the present as the past.)

The Quantum Omega Point Theory Is Not Deterministic

What I shall now show is that the quantum Omega Point Theory—quantum general relativity with the Omega Point Boundary Condition—is not deterministic either in the temporal sense or in James's more general sense. That is, I shall show that the mathematical structure of the quantum Omega Point Theory is such that there does not exist an algorithm which would generate the whole of reality from a proper subset of reality. In particular, there does not exist an equation which a computer could use to generate the entire universal wave function from the values of the wave function on part of its domain. Furthermore, this is true locally.

This indeterminism is a property of all quantum cosmological theories for which the universal wave function includes in its domain the set of all compact four-dimensional manifolds.[4] Thus indeterminism holds both in the Hartle-Hawking quantum cosmology and in the quantum Omega Point Theory. However, it may be merely an epistemological, and not an ontological, indeterminism in the Hartle-Hawking cosmology. "Epistemological indeterminism" just means that the indeterminism is in our knowledge, not in the objective universe. "Ontological indeterminism" means that the indeterminism is irreducibly in nature itself. This sort of indeterminism resides in reality itself and has nothing to do with our knowledge or lack of it. When James says "indeterminism" he means "ontological indeterminism" ("ontology" means the study of being, or existence itself). I explicitly distinguish between these two types of indeterminism, because I have noticed that they are often confused in the literature on free will. Writers will argue that the universe is epistemologically indeterministic, and then conclude that the universe must therefore be ontologically indeterministic. Not true. The best counterexample is the phenomenon of classical chaos, discussed in Chapter II. Classical chaos means that the classical universe is epistemologically indeterministic but ontologically deterministic, because the ultimate controlling equations are deterministic. That is, although we could not predict what would happen in the long run, no matter how accurate our initial data, nevertheless our every action would be rigorously determined, we would be welded into an iron block, if we lived in such a universe.

The reason for the indeterminism in these models is the Four-Manifold Non-Classification Theorem[5]: there does not exist any algorithm which will list or classify all compact four-dimensional (topological or differentiable) manifolds without boundary, and further, there does not exist any general algorithm which can show whether two given manifolds are different or the same. So, from the value of the universal wave function on any given region of a certain four-manifold, it is not possible to generate by any effective procedure the rest of the universal wave function. For the wave function would have to differ if the topologies were different, but we can't tell if the topologies are different. A computable equation valid everywhere *would* be able to distinguish different wave functions, so we conclude that no such equation extending wave functions exists. The local statement is, given the wave function on some open neighborhood U on some four-manifold, there does not exist a universal equation or algorithm which would define a unique extension of the wave function given on U to a larger region U′. To prove this, note that one could always modify U′ by cutting a ball out of U′ - U and identifying the resulting boundary with the boundary formed by cutting a similar ball out of any other manifold. Since there is no general algorithm to establish the identity of manifolds, there is no algorithm to tell if this has been done. A "computable equation" means either a difference equation, a differential equation which can be discretized, or any equation which can in principle be solved by a finite number of steps. One might argue that the universe might be controlled by a "noncomputable" equation, but I don't think there is any real distinction between an equation which requires an infinite number of operations for its solution and no equation at all. One cannot solve such an equation, even in principle: one might as well say, whatever happens, happens.

Not only is it impossible to solve such an equation, it is even impossible in principle to write it down were it to exist. For such a hypothetical equation would be an equation for the universal wave function, which with the Omega Point Boundary Condition would be a functional of the four-metric. The four-metric in turn is a function of the coordinate systems on all four-manifolds. To write down an equation for the universal wave functional in a mathematically meaningful way means that we would have first to give for all four-manifolds coordinate systems in which we should express the metric. But the Non-Classification Theorem implies that it is not possible to give such coordinate systems (cover each four-manifold with a system of Euclidean coordinate patches, say): if we could classify—write down by some effective procedure—all such coordinate systems (or systems of patches), the same procedure would classify the manifolds, which in fact we cannot do. Since there is no way to write down the coordinate systems which cover the domain of the universal wave function, we cannot write an equation for the universal wave function. I shall define the nonexistence of an equation to be equivalent to the inability, by any effective procedure, to write it down in a finite number of symbols, in a mathematically meaningful way. With this definition, the nonexistence of an equation for the universal wave function is established. All equations used in physics to date, even those which we do not know how to solve, have been expressible in a finite number of symbols in a mathematically meaningful way.[6]

Because the Non-Classification Theorem is a global result, there might be computable equations, valid only locally, not universally, which would "determine" a local region of reality. However, "local" here means smaller than the Planck length of 10^{-33} cm, so such determinism is irrelevant to questions of human free will.

The indeterminism in quantum gravity is utterly different in nature from the indeterminism arising in nonrelativistic quantum mechanics. In the latter case, there is a deterministic equation, the Schrödinger equation (which is computable if the wave function is restricted to a compact region), for the time evolution of the wave function and thus nonrelativistic quantum indeterminism arises from our limited way of looking at the world. In contrast, the indeterminism in quantum gravity is ontological and logically irremovable: it ultimately comes from Gödel's Incompleteness Theorem—the Four-Manifold Non-Classification Theorem is at bottom a variant of Gödel's theorem, which was discussed in Chapter II.

However, it must be kept in mind that the most basic level of reality might not be three- or four-manifolds. Our present theory of quantum gravity says it is, but our present theory might be wrong. If it is wrong, then the ultimate level of reality might be described by a much simpler mathematics than the mathematics of manifolds. If the mathematics required to describe reality is sufficiently simple, then Gödel's Theorem will not apply and determinism might stage a comeback.

How simple does the mathematics describing reality have to be for Gödel's Theorem to be inapplicable? To answer this, remember that Gödel's Theorem says that the full theory of arithmetic—that is, arithmetic with the usual four operations of addition (+), subtraction (−), multiplication (×), and division (÷)—cannot be proven consistent, but if it is assumed consistent, then the full theory of arithmetic is incomplete and undecidable. *Consistent* means that the axioms of the theory do not imply a logical contradiction; *complete* means that every true statement in the theory is a theorem (can be deduced from the axioms); and *decidable* means that there is an algorithm for deciding whether any given statement in the theory is a theorem or a contradiction (that is, an algorithm for deducing all true statements from the axioms). Obviously, a consistent, decidable theory is complete, but a consistent, complete theory need not be decidable.

Euclidean geometry, the geometry you studied in high school, was shown in 1949 to be consistent, complete, and decidable[7] by the Polish logician Alfred Tarski. Gödel himself showed in the 1930s that the most basic part of logic, the Propositional Calculus, was also consistent, complete, and decidable.[8] If the Propositional Calculus is augmented by "quantifiers," then it becomes First Order Logic, which, though complete, is undecidable.[9] Quantifiers come in two forms, the "existential quantifier" (written ∃), which means "there exists," and the "universal quantifier" (written ∀), which means "for all." So, if physics needs a logic in which statements like "for all x, $x = Z + R$" appear, then physics will have to live with undecidability.

But perhaps physics doesn't need quantifiers of such power. The quantifier "for all" is unbounded. If the set of statements to which we wish to apply the logic is bounded, then this restricted logic is equivalent to the Propositional Calculus.

Physics might not even need the full theory of arithmetic. In elementary school, multiplication is taught as a shorthand for addition:

5×4 just means "add 5 to itself 4 times." We all know that $5 \times 4 = 5 + 5 + 5 + 5 = 20$. However, in the full theory of arithmetic, combining multiplication with addition (and the quantifiers) allows statements which are *not* equivalent to a shorthand for statements using addition only. This full theory of arithmetic is incomplete and undecidable—if it is even consistent; recall that we can't prove that it is.

On the other hand, every calculation which you have ever carried out using multiplication and addition (and division and subtraction), and every calculation every computer has ever carried out, and every calculation that every finite state machine will ever carry out—all of these calculations are completely equivalent to calculations with addition and subtraction only.[10] And this restricted part of arithmetic—sometimes called Presburger arithmetic—is consistent, complete, and decidable.[11] Even though Presburger arithmetic is decidable, its algorithms are superexponentially hard;[12] that is, a problem that can be stated with N symbols will generally require 10^{10^N} computer operations to solve. Perhaps the full theory of arithmetic was invented to make calculations easier, not because reality required it.

Arithmetic with multiplication and division only is also consistent, complete, and decidable. The logical status of the various theories I've discussed is summarized in the following table.

THEORY	CONSISTENT?	COMPLETE?	DECIDABLE?
Propositional Calculus	Yes	Yes	Yes
Euclidean Geometry	Yes	Yes	Yes
First Order Logic	Yes	Yes	No
Arithmetic, $+$ & $-$ only	Yes	Yes	Yes
Arithmetic, $\times$ & $\div$ only	Yes	Yes	Yes
Arithmetic, full theory	?	No	No

I argued in Chapter II—and I shall discuss this in more detail in Chapter IX—that quantum mechanics shows we are finite state machines. Furthermore, quantum mechanics shows there is a basic discreteness in nature. If this discreteness goes too far and eliminates the manifold structure of basic reality, replacing it with something that can be completely described by Presburger arithmetic, then physics might be completely deterministic. Its mathematics will certainly be decidable.

It is also possible that the Omega Point, whose infinity is *actual* rather than merely potential like the infinity of the universal Turing machine, might not be subject to the Halting Theorem which limits Turing machines, and hence might not be subject to Gödel's Theorem either, even if physics turns out to require the full theory of arithmetic. This possibility is quite technical, and is left to the Appendix for Scientists.

How Quantum Cosmological Indeterminism Might Be Used in Human Thought

So if our present theories of quantum gravity are correct, there is an intrinsic indeterminism, in James's sense of indeterminism, in each region of spacetime. I shall now show that it is quite likely that this intrinsic indeterminism is often made use of in the human decision-making process.

The first step in my argument is to show that any decision-making algorithm—computer program—of sufficient power to handle real-world problems must necessarily have a "random" element. I place "random" in quotes because I shall use this word in the value-neutral sense of "indeterminate"; in ordinary parlance, "random" carries the connotation of "meaninglessness," and, as we shall see, the indeterminateness in the decision-making process, far from being meaningless, could be regarded as the major source of "meaning." Turing himself, in his classic paper on the Turing Test for personhood[13]—we discussed this test at length in Chapter II—argued for such a random element, for the reason that, although deterministic algorithms may exist to solve a problem, often these require such an enormous amount of computer capacity that systematic "guessing"—making choices among equally weighted possibilities at random—is almost always more efficient. Nowadays such a procedure is termed "heuristic programming." Such a random-choice-maker is also useful in avoiding the type of dilemma symbolized by the example of "Buridan's ass." Buridan's ass was a donkey standing midway between two piles of hay. Both piles of hay were exactly alike. The donkey was very hungry, but he could see no reason to start eating one pile before he started eating the other. And so he didn't start; the poor creature starved to death. Obviously a random choice would have been better than no choice at all.

In real-life decision-making, occasional random choice among alternatives is more than merely efficient; it is absolutely essential. To see this, note that in reality one is usually faced with making choices under a condition of uncertainty. One almost never has total information about the advantages and disadvantages of each alternative. A reason for such uncertainty is information cost: effort and physical resources must be expended in order to gather information about the various alternatives, and obtaining total information about an alternative, even if available, would require more than a lifetime and more than the entire Earth's physical resources. Thus long before we have total information, the information-gathering phase must cease and a decision must be made. Abraham Wald has shown[14] that decision-making under uncertainty can be viewed as a dual game which an individual plays against the rest of reality. Furthermore, Wald shows[15] that the entire process of scientific research can be similarly regarded as a dual game played against nature. John von Neumann and Oskar Morgenstern have shown[16] that, in general, dual games are solved by "mixed" strategies; that is, strategies in which a player's move is chosen *at random* from a list. Von Neumann and Morgenstern illustrate this by reference to the game of Matching Pennies: a player does best if he/she chooses heads or tails at random. If one were to choose heads or tails according to some predetermined (nonrandom) table, the opponent could eventually infer the table from the past play, and thus defeat the nonrandom player. Wald shows that the scientific induction game and the uncertain decision game are best played with a mixed strategy. It follows that any living being which has been successful in the life game—a member of any living species is such a being—probably has some sort of randomizer in its decision-making apparatus.

The randomizer could of course be just a pseudorandom-number generator. In the heuristic programs, a pseudorandom-number-generating subprogram is in fact just what is used. (In computer theory, "pseudorandom" means that the numbers are generated by a deterministic algorithm so complex that the numbers cannot be distinguished from numbers generated by a "true" random process.) However, such random-number programs must be complicated if the deterministic pattern (which must be there, since the number generator is only pseudorandom) is not to be guessable by the opponent. I would thus conjecture that the randomizer in the human brain is not a software program, but some sort of hardwired entity: such a thing would be much easier to generate by natural selection acting on random mutations.

I shall now show that the human nervous system is capable, at least in principle, of using quantum fluctuations as the source of randomness in such a hardwired randomizer. This does not, of course, establish that it actually does use quantum fluctuations, just that the capability is there. (I shall show later that, even if this capability is not used, humans nevertheless have free will at the ontological level if the Omega Point Boundary Condition holds.) Penrose has pointed out[17] that the retinas of toads are known to be so sensitive that a single photon impinging on it can be sufficient to trigger a nerve impulse. In humans, there are weak signal suppression mechanisms, so that seven photons are the minimum required for a dark-adapted human subject to be aware of their impingement. Nevertheless, the nervous systems of toads and humans are sufficiently close in an evolutionary sense so that there is no reason to doubt that single-photon sensitivity exists in the human nervous system also. Now a randomizer can be reduced to a sequence of binary random choices, where a binary random choice is "act if the random event happens, and don't act if it doesn't happen." A portion of the human eye could be set up as such a binary randomizer, for example. The opacity of material above a group of retina cells could be adjusted so that the probability is $1/2$ that a single photon will hit it in a nerve cell cycle time (about 10^{-2} seconds) and $1/2$ that no photon will hit it, under normal lighting conditions. If a photon is detected, the choice will be to act; if no photon is detected, the choice will be not to act. If the wave function of the impinging photons is such that the classical approximation (Maxwell equations) is valid, then the arrival of a photon or not as described above is as quantum mechanically uncertain as the decay of a particular atom in a mass of radioactive atoms. I don't believe the randomizer is in fact in the eye, because blind humans retain their power of decision, and also because lighting conditions are too variable; the randomizer would have to work on some feature of the environment (external or internal to the nervous system) that is essentially constant (or the randomizer would have to include a program to smooth out variability). But the above model illustrates how a randomizer would work.

The Nobel-prize-winning neurophysiologist Sir John Eccles has proposed[18] a much better model. He shows that in synaptic exocytosis the displacement of a particle of mass 10^{-18} grams could initiate a neuron firing, and he argues that such a displacement could come about due to quantum mechanical fluctuations. He offers an explicit suggestion of the location of the neuron system where these fluctuations occur: in the clusters of apical dentrites of the pyramidal cells of laminae V and III-II first described by the neurophysiologists Fleischhauer and Peters.

Although it has been shown that the human nervous system can use nonrelativistic quantum mechanical uncertainty to randomize, it does not follow that it can access the quantum gravity regime. As I pointed out above, true ontological free will requires quantum gravity uncertainty, because there is a deterministic equation controlling nonrelativistic "uncertainty." There are two ways in which the human nervous system might be able to access the quantum gravity regime in the randomization process. The first is a mechanism suggested by Penrose,[19] who in effect points out that, if a substantial portion of the brain were to act as if it were in a coherent quantum state, it might be able to amplify a signal from the Planck scale up to the macroscopic level. The known amplification power of the nervous system—amplification of a single photon energy to nerve pulse energies constitutes a magnification of 10^{20}—is insufficient by a factor of 10^8, so Penrose's proposal is speculative, to say the least. The second possibility is that the randomizer may use vacuum fluctuations inside the brain. A system which is capable of detecting single photons is certainly sensitive enough. One of the most important unsolved problems in particle physics is accounting for the magnitude of the vacuum energy density. If the fluctuations in topology are neglected, the calculated value is too high by a factor of about 10^{54}. The most popular method of resolving this problem is to include the topological fluctuations: some calculations indicate that these can cancel out the factor of 10^{54}. But if this is the cancellation mechanism, then the residual fluctuations in the vacuum energy density would necessarily reflect quantum gravity uncertainties, and thus a randomizer based on these fluctuations would be ontologically indeterministic. A state transition of the human brain in this case would be totally unpredictable. In this situation, we would have ontological free will.

Why This New Type of Indeterminism Does Not Mean "Mere Chance"

Many people are reluctant to associate "free will" with randomness or chance. William James has analyzed the origin of this reluctance, and I think given a good reply:

> The stronghold of the deterministic sentiment is the antipathy to the idea of chance. . . . The sting of the word "chance" seems to lie in the assumption that it means something positive, and that if anything happens by chance, it must be something of an intrinsically irrational and preposterous sort. Now chance means nothing of the kind. . . . All that . . . chance-character [of an event] means is that there is something in it really of its own, something that is not the unconditional property of the whole. If the whole wants this property, the whole must wait till it can get it, if it be a matter of chance. . . . [C]hance means only the negative fact that no part of the whole, however big, can claim to control absolutely the destinies of the whole. . . . Indeterminate future volitions *do* mean chance.[20]

Chance certainly need not mean irrationality. To the contrary, as I pointed out above, modern game theory has shown that, in circumstances which necessarily arise in the course of normal decision-making, the use of chance in picking a course of action is *required* by rationality. In the Modern Synthesis—the technical term for modern evolutionary theory (a synthesis of Darwinian natural selection with Mendelian genetics)—all originality in the evolution of life, all new species, are due to the chance mechanisms of mutation and recombination. Natural selection acts only on what chance happens to give it. The molecular biologist Jacques Monod's book,[21] *Chance and Necessity,* is essentially an exposition for laypersons of this fact; indeed the book's very title describes its thesis. But any textbook on modern evolution will say the same thing; the only disagreement among contemporary evolutionary biologists concerns the relative importance of chance and necessity ("necessity" being natural selection). One who rejects the role of chance in evolution rejects the Modern Synthesis. There is a growing consensus[22] among cognitive scientists that all human originality is due to an essentially random mixing of ideas in the human creator's mind, with subconscious elimination (natural selection) of the bad ideas.

I believe that some of the objection to chance is due to a confusion in levels of description. It should be kept in mind that the randomizer works on a level far below conscious awareness. There is no conscious agent at this level, and so no agent is acting at this level. The randomness is an aspect of nonliving matter. Some chance must exist at the physics level, if the consciousness level is to be ontologically not determined. At the consciousness level, we are completely unaware of the operation of the randomizer, just as we are unaware of neurons firing. We think *we* have made an undetermined decision whenever the randomizer operates, as indeed we have.

It is the agent, and not the randomizer, that makes the decision. As has been emphasized by Hofstadter and Dennett,[23] the various levels of implementation interact with each other in a human being. The consciousness level is always issuing orders to the lower levels: the randomizer, for example, is constantly being ordered to change the probability weights in the decision matrix. Consider an important decision, one which the agent ponders over for some time. Let us begin the analysis at the instant the agent makes, with or without the randomizer, the decision not to act at once, but to consider the consequences of the act in more detail. The consciousness level sends down orders to the lower levels to bring to consciousness any information stored in memory that may be relevant to the decision. Many levels act in a deterministic fashion, controlled by programs already coded in memory, to pull up such information. But the randomizer is also active, connecting—at random—various memory traces on previously unrelated subjects, and sending these connections to the higher levels, which act in a deterministic fashion. Almost all of these connections are nonsense, completely useless, and are rejected without being sent up to the consciousness level. But a very few are considered by the deterministic programs to be promising and sent up to the consciousness level for further consideration. While this is going on, a deterministic decision is made that more information from outside would be useful. Again, the order is passed down for suggestions on where to look for more information. Again, most of the suggestions are made by deterministic algorithms—information should be looked for in the places where one previously obtained information on this subject—but again the randomizer makes some unlikely suggestions. Probability weights are attached to these ridiculous suggestions by the deterministic algorithms, and sent back down to the randomizer, which selects some according to the probability weights. Collectively, all of the resulting proposals, including those few selected by the randomizer, are sent up to the consciousness level, which acts on all of them. The information collected is worked on by the deterministic algorithms, the conclusions are sent up to the consciousness level, which deterministically with the help of these algorithms selects the final probability weights to give the various possible actions. If the probability weights are nonzero at more than one possibility, these weights are sent down to the randomizer, which picks one (at random) according to the probability weights selected in the end by the higher levels. This pick is sent to the consciousness level and acted on. What this model is intended to emphasize is that a decision is a mixture of chance and necessity, a result of feedback between the consciousness level and the lower levels. The randomizer and the deterministic levels interact many times a second, modifying each other in each interaction. The final decision is the result of the integration of these interactions; it is the *I* that makes the decision. The *I* is in fact generated over time by the continuous action of the various levels, including the randomizer. The human personality is a unity of these levels.

Libet *et al.* have demonstrated[24] that a "person's" brain makes a decision to act before the "person" is aware of having decided to act; that is, the brain makes the decision and then informs the person of the decision, who (mistakenly) believes he or she actually "made" the decision. In the experiment to show this, a spot rotating on a TV screen at a rate of 2.5 cycles per second is watched by an experimental subject. The subject is asked to decide of his or her own free will to bend a finger, and note the position of the spot when the decision is made. An electrode attached to the head shows that, on the average, a potential change in the brain occurred 0.35 seconds *before* the person said he or she "intended" to act.

The very fact that a human mind is a unity of many levels—"society of mind" is the phrase used by the computer scientist Marvin Minsky to describe this integration—suggests another reason why it is necessary to have a randomizer as a sublevel in any mind, human or otherwise. The Arrow Impossibility Theorem[25] in effect shows that there is no reasonable deterministic algorithm which can integrate the numerous decisions made by the sublevels into a decision made by total person, the *I*. (Arrow's Theorem establishes the impossibility of generating a social choice function from the individual choice functions of the beings making up the society. It was originally applied only to societies made up of individual humans, but it applies to all societies, including the society which is the human mind.) Having a randomizer break an occasionally decision-making logjam may be a way of overcoming Arrow's Theorem.

According to the Compatibilists, free will is a property that exists —or fails to exist—at the level of conscious decision-making. Let us accept this. According to the Libertarians, free will can exist only if there is "chance" in James's sense in conscious decision-making: the actual decision is not ontologically determined by the rest of the universe, past, present, or future. Let us accept this too. Accepting both of these conditions implies that free will must satisfy two conditions:

(1) the conscious agent must *feel* himself/herself to be making the decision freely. The conscious agent must be unaware of any external or internal constraints in making the decision. The appropriate algorithm for deciding whether an agent's decision was free in this sense is simply to ask the agent: "Did you make the decision of your own free will?"

(2) the conscious agent's decision must be undetermined at the most basic physical level. The algorithm for deciding this is, did the randomizer come into play during the decision-making process, and is the randomizer accessing the ontologically indeterministic quantum gravity level?

If both of these conditions are satisfied, if the agent felt himself/herself to be acting freely, if the agent felt that it was he/she who was making the decision, *and* if the decision was in fact indeterministic at the most basic physical level, then I claim that, in actuality, the agent has free will.

·———·

Omega Point Boundary Condition:
Agent Determinism Is an Ontological
Ultimate

I might add that the Omega Point Boundary Condition implies "agent determinism" to be an ontological ultimate: the decisions made by human agents are not merely epistemologically irreducible to the physics of quantum fields, but are also ontologically irreducible. For with the Omega Point Boundary Condition the wave function is generated by the self-consistency requirement that the laws of physics and the decisions of the living agents acting in the universe force the universe to evolve into the Omega Point. The free decisions of the agents are an irreducible factor in the generation of the physical universe and its laws, not merely the reverse. This means that, *even if the randomizer in the human nervous system is apparently merely pseudorandom, we will still have ontological free will if the Omega Point Boundary Condition applies to the actual universe.* With this boundary condition, the ultimate laws of physics are generated by agents, not vice versa. Thus, under the Omega Point Boundary Condition, the laws of physics necessarily have a little "vagueness" about them; they cannot determine all decisions of all agents.

For the free decisions of *all* the agents past, present, and future collectively generate the totality of existence: this is just another way of expressing the content of the Omega Point Boundary Condition. We could also say that the Omega Point "creates the physical universe," and that this creation is therefore "contingent" in the very special sense that it exists only via His/Her free decision(s). This phrasing recalls Kant's classic distinction between deism and theism: a deist holds that God is a *cause of the world,* whereas a theist believes God to be the *Author of the world* [Kant's emphasis].[26] By this distinction, the Omega Point Theory is theistic, not deistic or pantheistic. (I shall give another discussion of deism—using another definition—in Chapter XII.)

The Omega Point Boundary Condition, and hence the free will theory developed in this chapter is based in an essential way on the Many-Worlds ontology. I claim that, conversely, any theory of free will that has agent determinism as an ontological ultimate is necessarily based on a Many-Worlds ontology. Agent determinism requires that it is really true that an agent "could have done otherwise." However, the only way to be sure that the agent "could have done otherwise" is for the agent to have done otherwise in actual fact. That is, it is necessary that the agent in fact do two (or more) inconsistent actions simultaneously. This is of course possible only in a Many-Worlds universe.

This fact is best illustrated by the phenomenon of hypnosis. When a person is hypnotized and is told (for example), "You can't open your eyes," the hypnotized person always says to himself, "Of course I can open my eyes. But I won't, because doing so would interrupt the performance." (Or some other excuse is made.) That is, a person under hypnosis is always convinced that he could have done otherwise, but in fact never does, and always finds an excuse for never doing so. As Richard Feynman summed up his own experience under hypnosis: "All the time you're saying to yourself, 'I could do that, but I won't'— which is just another way of saying that you can't."[27] What the Omega

Point Boundary Condition says is that sometimes you can do either of two inconsistent actions, because you do do them—in different worlds. But when this "double action" occurs it is coded nowhere else in the entire universe. It is undetermined and truly contingent.

But there is nevertheless another sense in which the Omega Point and the totality of everything that exists physically can be said to exist necessarily. To this sense we now turn.

VIII

THE OMEGA POINT AND THE PHYSICAL UNIVERSE NECESSARILY EXIST

.———.

The Ontological Argument in Computer Science

SUPPOSE IT WERE SHOWN AS A MATTER OF physics that the Omega Point really exists. Then would it still be reasonable to assert the existence of a God separate and independent of the Omega Point? Not if we could show that the Omega Point "necessarily exists" in the strong sense of logical necessity, that to deny its existence would be a logical contradiction. Ever since Kant argued[1] that "existence is not a predicate" and Frege[2] extended Kant's argument into "existence is not a first-level predicate," philosophers have generally felt that the ontological/cosmological argument is invalid. If true, this would mean no proof of any sort for God's existence could be valid, since in the opinion of Kant: "The physico-theological proof . . . rests upon the cosmological proof, and the cosmological proof upon the ontological."[3] Furthermore, logicians have generally believed that it is impossible by means of logic alone to prove the existence of anything. I claim both the philosophers and logicians are incorrect: I think you can prove that the universe necessarily exists. The proof will be based on an analysis of what the word "existence" means. The argument will *not* be a rehash of the thousand-year-old ontological argument. The proof will instead be based on some rather obvious metaphysical implications of modern computer science and modern cosmology. That such scientific theories have such implications should not be surprising; all fundamental scientific theories make tacit metaphysical assertions about the ultimate nature of reality. As is usual in all science, the truth of the metaphysics is tested by experimental tests of the physics. If a deterministic theory like Newtonian celestial mechanics yields correct predictions, then does this tend to confirm not only Newtonian mechanics but also the metaphysical theory that the universe is deterministic. As will become clear, the ontological argument I shall give below is an obvious implication of ideas which are *absolutely central* to modern computer science.

Simulations and Emulations

Let us therefore begin with the computer metaphysics. Much of computer science is devoted to making *simulations* of phenomena in the physical world. In a simulation, a mathematical model of the physical object under study is coded in a program. The model includes as many attributes of the real physical object as possible (limited of course by the knowledge of these attributes, and also by the capacity of the computer). The running of the program evolves the model in time. If the initial model is accurate, if enough key features of the real object are captured by the model, the time evolution of the model will mimic with fair accuracy the time development of the real object, and so one can predict the most important key aspects which the real object will have in the future.

Suppose we try to simulate a city full of people. Such simulations are being attempted now, but at a ludicrously inaccurate level. But suppose we imagine more and more of the attributes of the city being included in the simulation. In particular, more and more properties of each individual person are included. In principle, we can imagine a simulation being so good that every single *atom* in each person and each object in the city and the properties of each atom has an analogue in the simulation. Let us imagine, in the limit, a simulation that is absolutely perfect: each and every property of the real city and each and every real property of each real person in the real city is represented precisely in the simulation. Furthermore, let us imagine that, when the program is run on some gigantic computer, the temporal evolution of the simulated persons and their city precisely mimics for all time the real temporal evolution of the real people and the real city. An absolutely precise simulation of something is called an *emulation*. To date the only entities which we have emulated in computers are other computers, but I shall show in a later chapter that true emulations of actual physical objects are in principle possible. The reason we have not done such emulations is that the computer capacity required to do such emulations is larger than the entire installed computer capacity of the world.

The key question is this: do the emulated people exist? As far as the simulated people can tell, they do. By assumption, any action which the real people can and do carry out to determine whether they exist—reflecting on the fact that they think, interacting with the environment—the emulated people also can do, and in fact do do. There is simply no way for the emulated people to tell that they are "really" inside the computer, that they are merely simulated, and not real. They can't get at the real substance, the physical computer, from where they are, inside the program. One can imagine the ultimate simulation, a perfect simulation—an emulation—of the entire physical universe, containing in particular all people whom the real universe contains, and which mimics perfectly the actual time evolution of the actual universe. Again, there is no way for the people inside this simulated universe to tell that they are merely simulated, that they are only a sequence of numbers being tossed around inside a computer, and are in fact not real.

How do we know we ourselves are not merely a simulation inside a gigantic computer? Obviously, we can't know. But obviously we ourselves really exist. Therefore, *if* it is in fact possible for the physical universe to be in precise one-to-one correspondence with a simulation, I claim we should invoke the Identity of Indiscernibles and identify the universe and all of its emulations, its perfect simulations. The "Identity of Indiscernibles" is a philosophical rule introduced by the German philosopher Leibniz in the seventeenth century. According to this rule, entities which cannot be distinguished by any means whatsoever, even in principle, at any time in the past, present, and future, have to be considered identical. As we shall see, this rule—which I have called "philosophical"—actually underlies most of modern physics, so I consider the rule to be really a physical law which is supported by experiment.[4]

As I discussed in Chapter II, when a physical computer emulates another computer, the emulated computer is called a *virtual machine*. The emulated computer is said to exist in *virtual reality*. But this emulation of computers need not stop with a single step. The emulated computer can emulate a third computer, and this computer can emulate a fourth computer, and so on without limit. This hierarchy of computer simulations is called *levels of implementation*. In standard computer science, one is only aware of the higher levels of implementation, which can be thought of as levels of reality. The lowest level of reality can be termed *ultimate reality*. As I have said above, we cannot know if the universe in which we find ourselves is actually ultimate reality.

But is it possible for the universe to be in precise one-to-one correspondence with some simulation? I think that it is, if we generalize what we mean by simulation. In computer science, a simulation is a program, which is fundamentally a map from the set of integers into itself. That is, the instructions in the program tell the computer how to go from the present state, represented by a sequence of integers, to the subsequent state, also represented by a sequence of integers. But remember, we don't really need the physical computer; the initial sequence of integers and the general rule (instructions or map) for replacing the present sequence by the next is all that is required. But the general rule can itself be represented as a sequence of integers. So, if time were to exist globally, and if the most basic things in the physical universe and the time steps between one instant and the next were discrete, then the whole of spacetime would definitely be in one-to-one correspondence with some program. But time may not exist globally (it doesn't if traditional quantum cosmology is true), and it may be that the substances of the universe are continuous fields and not discrete objects (in *all* current physical theories, the basic substances are continuous fields). So, if the actual universe is described by something resembling current theories, it cannot be in one-to-one correspondence with a standard computer program, which is based on integer mappings. There is currently no model of a "continuous" computer. Turing even argued that such a thing is meaningless. (There are definitions of "computable continuous functions," but none of the definitions are really satisfactory.)

Let's be more broad-minded about what is to count as a simulation. Consider the collection of all mathematical concepts. Let us say that a perfect simulation exists if the physical universe can be put into one-to-one correspondence with some mutually consistent subcollections of all mathematical concepts. In this sense of "simulation" the universe can certainly be simulated, because "simulation" then amounts to saying that the universe can be exhaustively "described" in a logically consistent way. Note that "described" does not require that we or any other finite (or infinite) intelligent being can actually find the description. It may be that the actual universe expands into an infinite hierarchy of levels whenever one tries to describe it exhaustively. In such a case, it would be impossible to find a Theory of Everything. Nevertheless, it would still be true that a "simulation" in the more general sense existed if each level were in one-to-one correspondence with some mathematical object, and if all levels were mutually consistent ("consistency" meaning that, in the case of disagreement between levels, there is a rule—itself a mathematical object—for deciding which level is correct). The crucial point of this generalization is to establish that the actual physical universe is something in the collection of all mathematical objects. This follows because the universe has a perfect simulation, and we agree to identify the universe with its perfect simulation, that is, with its emulation. Thus, at the most basic ontological level, the physical universe is a concept.

The Algorithm for Deciding Which Concepts Exist Physically

But of course not all concepts exist physically. But some do. Which ones? The answer is provided by our earlier analysis of programs. *The simulations which are sufficiently complex to contain observers—thinking, feeling beings—as subsimulations exist physically.* And further, they exist physically by definition: for this is exactly what we mean by existence, namely, that thinking and feeling beings think and feel themselves to exist. Remember, the simulated thinking and feeling of simulated beings are real. Thus the actual physical universe—the one in which we are now experiencing our own simulated thoughts and simulated feelings—exists necessarily, by definition of what is meant by existence. Physical existence is just a particular relationship between concepts. Existence *is* a predicate, but a predicate of certain very, very complex simulations. It is certainly not a predicate of simple concepts, for instance "100 thalers." (A "thaler" was a coin used in late eighteenth-century Germany. Kant[5] used "100 thalers" as an example of an entity for which existence was not a property—a predicate—in addition to its physical attributes such as being made of metal, having a certain size, etc.)

With equal necessity, many different universes will exist physically. In particular, a universe in which we do something slightly different from what we actually do in this one will exist (provided of course that this action does not logically contradict the structure of the rest of the universe). But this is nothing new; it is already present in the ontology of the Many-Worlds Interpretation. Exactly how many universes really exist physically depends on your definition of "thinking and feeling being." If you adopt a narrow definition—such a being must have at least our human complexity—then the range of possible universes appears quite narrow: *The Anthropic Cosmological Principle,* my book[6] with John Barrow, is devoted to a discussion of how finely tuned our universe must be if it is to contain beings like ourselves.

What happens if a universal simulation stops tomorrow? Does the universe collapse into nonexistence? Certainly such terminating simulations exist mathematically. But if there is no intrinsic reason visible from inside the simulation for the simulation to stop, it can be embedded inside a larger simulation which does not stop. Since it is the observations of the beings inside the simulation that determine what exists physically, and since nothing happens from their viewpoint at the termination point when the terminating simulation is embedded in the nonstopping simulation, the universe must be said to continue in existence. It is the maximal extension which has existence, for by the Identity of Indiscernibles we must (physically) identify terminating programs with their embedding in the maximal program. (One could use a similar argument for asserting the physical existence of the maximal evolution from given initial data in the classical general relativity evolution problem.)

Furthermore, if it is logically possible for life to continue to exist forever in some universe, this universe will exist necessarily for all future time. In particular, if the Omega Point described in the previous chapters is logically coherent, then the Omega Point exists necessarily. Again, one can find numerous lines of evidence strongly suggesting that it is exceedingly difficult to construct a universe for life to exist at all, much less exist forever. So I would expect that the universe picked out by the Omega Point Boundary Condition to be unique. If so, logical consistency (and the definition of "life," "thinking and feeling being," etc.) will select out a single unique wave function for actualization. Since the wave function and its arguments determine respectively the physical laws and the "stuff" that exist, in this case the physical universe would be determined by logical consistency alone. Thus we again conclude that the universe, or rather the Omega Point, exists necessarily.

A given universe exists necessarily if it contains observers all the way into the Omega Point. The collective observations (and actions) of all observers bring the entire universe into existence; equivalently, the past, present, and future exist because these regions of spacetime are observed by the Omega Point. This is reminiscent of the eighteenth-century British philosopher George Berkeley's idea that the universe's existence is due to the fact that it is under continual observation by God. In general, Berkeley defended the notion that I am arguing for in this chapter, namely that to exist is to be perceived. To the question of whether a tree falling in the forest could be said to make a sound if there happened to be no one around to hear it (or, as I would prefer to say, since animals and plants make perfectly dandy observers in my own theory, whether the early universe could be said to exist before life of any sort existed), the answer is, yes, because the Omega Point/ God observes it in the ultimate future. Berkeley's view—and mine—is nicely summarized in the following limerick:

> *There once was a man who said, "God*
> *Must think it exceedingly odd*
> *If he finds that this tree*
> *Continues to be*
> *When there's no one about in the Quad."*

> *Reply: Dear Sir: Your astonishment's odd.*
> *I am always about in the Quad.*
> *And that's why the tree*
> *Will continue to be,*
> *Since observed by*
> *Yours faithfully, God.*

·———·

Proof of the Eternal Life Postulate

The preceding discussion on the necessary physical existence of the universe can be turned into a proof of the Eternal Life Postulate. Consider a segment of a single history, and in this history, focus attention on an instant of time. This instant of time comprises the entire physical universe as we now see it, at this instant. (Remember, we cannot see the other worlds of the Many Worlds Interpretation.) Let us now imagine this set of initial data evolving into the future, under the control of the laws of physics (whatever they are in this history). Let us now suppose that the laws of physics and the initial conditions are such that at some future time T_e, all life in this history necessarily becomes extinct. That is, any further evolution into the future using the given laws of physics will be a lifeless history, for all future time. The entire history exists mathematically, in the class of all logically consistent simulations, but it *collapses into nonexistence physically* the instant life dies out (assuming of course that there is no way that a nearby history can be affected by the history in which life has died out). If there is no life in the universe to observe its existence, then by the definition of physical existence this simulation, this universal history, simply does not exist physically. However, if there is a modification of the laws of physics in that history for which life will continue to exist after T_e, then the history with the laws of physics modified at time T_e exists physically. That is, the laws of physics, as they hold over all time, and the universal boundary conditions *necessarily permit life to continue to exist forever*. This proves the Eternal Life Postulate.

Conversely, if the laws of physics without modification over time permit life to continue to exist in the universe, then there will be a history in which life does continue to exist in this universe in which the laws of physics are unmodified. This allows my predictions in Chapter IV—predictions which were obtained under the assumption that the laws of physics were valid at least from the present until the collapsing universe reaches the Planck temperature—to be valid.

Notice once again that I am adopting a Platonic view of mathematical and physical reality in this proof of the Eternal Life Postulate. Mathematical reality, the class of all logically consistent propositions, is regarded as the ultimate reality, and physical reality is a proper subclass of ultimate reality. It might be that a simulation sufficiently rich to exist physically is being run on another machine, which in turn is a virtual machine in yet another machine, and so on. All of these machines exist mathematically, and if there can be communication, at least in principle, between these various levels of machines—recall that these levels are called "levels of implementation"—then this possibility by definition gives physical reality to all the levels, since by assumption the highest level of implementation is physically real. The lowest level of implementation which can be reached observationally (at least in principle) from a physically existing universe we could term "ultimate physical reality."

•———•

How the Omega Point Creates the Physical Universe

Let me now draw the ideas of the preceding three chapters together to show that it is now reasonable to say, "The Omega Point created the physical universe (and Himself/Herself)." In theology, the expression "creation of the universe by God" has been given two quite distinct meanings over the past two thousand years. First, the expression has been interpreted to mean that the physical universe has a finite age, that time itself had a beginning. Second, it has been interpreted to mean that the physical universe is not self-sustaining, and would thus collapse into nonexistence if not for the continuous act of God keeping it in existence.

There is no longer any scientific difficulty with the first meaning. The generally accepted model of modern cosmology, the so-called Big Bang Theory, is in fact a precise physical theory of the physical universe coming into existence out of nothing a finite time ago, roughly 20 billion years ago in what is called "proper time."

I shall now show that the Omega Point Theory provides a way of making the second meaning equally precise. What one needs is a physical model of how the universe *could* collapse into nonexistence. Berkeley's proposal carried no conviction because it did not provide a physical mechanism for why observation makes a difference. One needs a model of a universe collapsing into nonexistence because of the lack of observation. It is now clear how to construct one.

To put it another way, it is necessarily true that a future history exists which leads from the present state of the universe into the Omega Point. It is necessarily true that, no matter what we do, we *cannot* be forever cut off from God. This logically necessary connection was perhaps best expressed by Paul in his Letter to the Romans: "For I am sure that neither death, nor life, nor angels, nor principalities, nor things present, nor things to come, nor powers, nor height, nor depth, nor any thing else in all creation, will be able to separate us from the love of God . . ." (Romans 8:38–39 RSV).

This necessary existence of *all* histories which lead to God is in all essentials exactly the same as the traditional Christian picture, called *emanationism*, of how God creates the universe. Emanationism entered Christianity via Augustine, but the idea ultimately comes from Plato. In his dialogue *Timaeus*, Plato first argued that God wished for all reality to come as close to Him as logically possible:

> Let us state then for what reason becoming and this universe were framed by him who framed them. He was good; and in the good no jealousy in any matter can ever arise. So, being without jealousy, he desired that all things should come as near as possible to being like himself. That this is the supremely valid principle of becoming and of the order of the world, we shall most surely be right to accept from men of understanding.[7]

The Neo-Platonist philosopher Plotinus developed the implications of God's desire for the perfection of all in his book *Enneads* (Book 5, Chapter 2, Section 1):

> If the First is perfect, utterly perfect above all, and is the beginning of all power, it must be the most powerful of all that is, and all other powers must act in some partial imitation of it. Now other beings, coming to perfection, are observed to generate; they are unable to remain self-closed; they produce. . . . How then could the most perfect remain self-set—the First-Good, the Power towards all, how could it grudge or be powerless to give of itself . . . ? To this power we cannot impute any halt, any limit of jealous grudging; it must move forever outward until the universe stands accomplished to the ultimate possibility. All, thus, is produced by an inexhaustible power giving its gift to the universe, no part of which it can endure to see without some share in its being.[8]

Thus the universe emanates from God: all reality proceeds outward and downward from God until all possibilities connecting God with a given creature have been realized. To the question of why God did not make all things equal when He created them, Augustine answers: "If all things were equal, all things would not be; for the multiplicity of kinds of things of which the universe is constituted—first and second and so on, down to the creatures of the lowest grades—would not exist."[9]

This is a perfectly adequate description of the histories required by the Omega Point Boundary Condition: all histories from a given universe at an instant of time which lead to the Omega Point necessarily exist physically. The key difference between the mechanism of creation in the Omega Point Theory and the traditional view is that the hierarchy of creation is *temporal*, rather than spatial. The traditional cosmos was static; the Omega Point cosmos is dynamic and evolutionary. Arthur O. Lovejoy, the American historian of ideas, has called[10] a completely filled hierarchy of being from the lowest of creation up to God the *Great Chain of Being*. "Up" the Great Chain of Being in the Omega Point Theory means "forward in time."

Lovejoy has given the name *Principle of Plenitude* to the necessary existence of all beings which can be connected to God. Thus the Principle of Plenitude means ". . . not only . . . that the universe is a *plenum forarum* in which the range of conceivable diversity of *kinds* of living things is exhaustively exemplified, but also . . . that no genuine potentiality of being can remain unfilled, that the extent and abundance of the creation must be as great as the possibility of existence and commensurate with the productive capacity of a 'perfect' and inexhaustible Source. . . ."[11]

IX

THE PHYSICS OF
RESURRECTION OF THE
DEAD TO ETERNAL LIFE

.———.

Social Immortality as a Consequence of
the Omega Point Theory

SUPPOSE THE OMEGA POINT REALLY EXISTS. Can we mortal human beings find hope in that fact? I believe we can. For hope fundamentally means an expectation that in an appropriate sense the future will be better than the present or the past. Even on the most materialistic level, the future existence of the Omega Point would assure our civilization of ever growing total wealth, continually increasing knowledge, and quite literal eternal progress. This perpetual meliorism is built into the definition of "life existing forever" given in Chapter IV. Such worldly meliorism would support an orthodox Christian position on the meaning of the natural world, as against, say, the gnostic view. In the orthodox view, the physical universe is basically good, because it was created by an omnipotent and omniscient Deity Who is also all good.

Of course, it is a consequence of physics that, although our civilization may continue forever, our species *Homo sapiens* must inevitably become extinct, just as every individual human being must inevitably also die. For, as the Omega Point is approached, the temperature will approach infinity everywhere in the universe, and it is impossible for our type of life to survive in this environment. (The nonexistence of the Omega Point would not help us. If the universe were open and expanded forever, then the temperature would go to zero as the universe expanded. There is not enough energy in the frigid future of such a universe for *Homo sapiens* to survive. Also, protons probably decay, and we are made up of atoms, which require protons.)

But the death of *Homo sapiens* is an evil (beyond the death of the human individuals) only for a limited value system. What is humanly important is the fact that we think and feel, not the particular bodily form which clothes the human personality. Just as within *Homo sapiens* a person is a person independent of whether said individual is a male or female, or whether a white or a black, so also an intelligent being is a person irrespective of whether said individual is a member of the species *Homo sapiens*. Currently people of non-European descent have a higher birthrate than people of European descent, and so the percentage of *Homo sapiens* which is of European descent is decreasing. The human race is now changing its color. In my own value system, this color change is morally neutral; what is important is the overall condition of our civilization: are we advancing in knowledge and wisdom? Certainly our scientific knowledge is greater than it was a century ago, and although there have been a great many steps backward during this century, I nevertheless think we are wiser than our great-grandparents. If the Omega Point exists, this advance will continue without limit into the Omega Point. Our species is an intermediate step in the infinitely long temporal Chain of Being that comprises the whole of life in spacetime. An essential step, but still only a step. In fact, *it is a logically necessary consequence of eternal progress that our species become extinct*. For we are finite beings, we have definite limits. Our brains can code only so much information, we can understand only rather simple arguments. If the ascent of life into the Omega Point is to occur, one day the most advanced minds must be non-*Homo sapiens*. The heirs of our civilization must be another species, and their heirs yet another, *ad infinitum* into the Omega Point. We must die—as individuals, as a species—in order that our civilization might live. But the contributions to civilization which we make as individuals will survive our individual deaths. Judging from the rapid advance of computers at present, I would guess that the next stage of intelligent life would be quite literally information processing machines. At the present rate, computers will reach the human level in information processing and integration ability probably within a century, certainly within a thousand years.

The Physical Mechanism of Individual
Resurrection

Many find the assurance of the immortality of life as a whole cold comfort for their death as individuals. They feel that a truly good God would make some provision for individual life after death also. What the Christian hopes for in eternal life has been ably expressed by Pannenberg:

> . . . the life that awakens in the resurrection of the dead is the same as the life we now lead on earth. However, it is our present life as God sees it from his eternal present. Therefore, it will be completely different from the way we now experience it. Yet, nothing happens in the resurrection of the dead except that which already constitutes the eternal depth of time now and which is already present for God's eyes—for his creative view![1]

We shall, so to speak, live again in the mind of God. But recall my discussion of Thomist *aeternitas* in Chapter IV. There I pointed out that, if the universe is globally hyperbolic (deterministic), all the information contained in the whole of human history, including every detail of every human life, will be available for analysis by the collectivity of life in the far future. In principle at least (again ignoring the difficulty of extracting the relevant information from the overall background noise), it is possible for life in the far future to construct, using this information, a perfectly accurate simulation of these past lives: in fact, this simulation is just what a sufficiently close scrutiny of our present lives by the Omega Point would amount to. And I pointed out in Chapter VIII that a sufficiently perfect simulation of a living being would *be* alive. I shall argue below that the Omega Point will choose to use His/Her power to do this simulation. In brief I shall argue that the drive for total knowledge—which life in the future must seek if it is to survive at all, and which will be achieved only at the Omega Point—would seem to require that such an analysis of the past, and hence such a simulation, would be carried out. If so, then the resurrection of the dead in the sense of Pannenberg would be inevitable in the *eschaton* (last times).

This, then, is the physical mechanism of individual resurrection: *we shall be emulated in the computers of the far future.* Thus, as discussed in chapters II and VIII, the technical terms[2] for the reality we as resurrected individuals shall inhabit in the far future is "virtual reality" or "cyberspace."

This resurrection does not depend on being able to extract sufficient information from the past light cone. In fact, *the universal resurrection is physically possible even if no information whatsoever about an individual can be extracted from the past light cone.* Since the universal computer capacity increases without bound as the Omega Point is approached, it follows that, if only a bare bones description of our current world is stored permanently, then there will inevitably come a time when there will be sufficient computer capacity to simulate our present-day world by simple brute force: by creating an exact simulation—an emulation —of *all* logically possible variants of our world. For example, since a human being has about 110,000 active genes,[3] this means that the human genome can code about 10^{10^6} possible genetically distinct humans. Furthermore, the human brain can store between 10^{10} and 10^{17} bits, as I discussed in Chapter II, which implies that there are between $2^{10^{10}}$ and $2^{10^{17}}$ possible human memories. On this basis, there are $10^{10^6} \times 10^{10^{17}} \approx 10^{10^{17}}$ possible human states ($2^{10^{17}} \approx 10^{10^{17}}$; it is a property of double exponentials that, if the second exponent is larger than about 10, then changing the base from 2 to 10 won't change the number expressed by the double exponential very much).[4] I shall now show that an emulation of all possible variants of our world—the so-called visible universe—would require at most $10^{10^{123}}$ bits of computer memory, and that eventually this amount of computer capacity will be available in the far future.

.———.

Proof That an Emulation of the Entire Visible Universe Is Physically Possible

The Omega Point might wish to emulate humans by simulating all possible quantum states corresponding to a human being. The possible number of such states is defined by the maximum amount of information which can be stored in a sphere of radius R. This is given by the Bekenstein Bound:[5] the information coded inside the sphere is less than or equal to 3×10^{43} bits multiplied by the mass inside the sphere measured in kilograms and multiplied by the radius of the sphere measured in meters. (In applying the Bekenstein Bound, we have to include also the mass in the form of energy: $E = mc^2$.) Since a typical human has a mass less than 100 kilograms, and is less than 2 meters tall —and so fits inside a sphere of radius 1 meter—it follows that a human being must be coded by 3×10^{45} bits or less. By definition, the number of states is obtained by exponentiating the amount of information. So there are at most $10^{3 \times 10^{45}}$ (which is approximately equal to $10^{10^{45}}$) possible quantum states[6] which a human being could be in. With the computer power that will eventually become available, the Omega Point could simply simulate them all. Just the knowledge of the human genome would be enough for this. And even if the record of human genome is not retained until the computer capacity is sufficient, it would still be possible to resurrect all possible humans, just from the knowledge it was coded in DNA. Merely simulate all possible life forms that could be coded by DNA (information stability requires this number to be finite) and all logically possible humans will necessarily be included. Eventually, it will even be possible to simulate all possible visible *universes*. The number of possible visible universes, $10^{10^{123}}$ (this number was first calculated by Penrose[7]), is again 10 raised to the Bekenstein Bound, with R in this case being the radius of a sphere with radius equal to the radius of the visible universe, 20 billion light-years, and the mass[8] being the mass inside that sphere.

The Bekenstein Bound follows from the basic postulates of quantum theory combined with the further assumptions that (1) the system is bounded in energy, and (2) the system is bounded, or localized, in space. A rigorous proof of the Bekenstein Bound would require quantum field theory, but it is easy to describe in outline why quantum mechanics leads to such a bound on the information coded in a bounded region. In essence, the Bekenstein Bound is a manifestation of the uncertainty principle. Recall that the uncertainty principle tells us that there is a limit to the precision with which we can measure the momentum of a particle and its position. More precisely, the uncertainty principle says that the location of a point in phase space—a concept I defined in Chapter III—cannot be defined more closely than Planck's constant h. Since a system's state is defined by where it is located in phase space, this means that the number of possible states is less than or equal to the size of the phase space region the system *could* be in, divided by the size of the minimum phase space size, Planck's constant. (I've given a mathematical expression of this argument in the Appendix for Scientists.) This state counting procedure, based on there being an absolute minimum size h to a phase space interval, is an absolutely essential method of quantum statistical mechanics. We have already used it in Chapter III to prove the almost periodicity of a bounded quantum system. It is confirmed by the thousands of experiments which have been based on this counting method.[9] In high energy particle physics, any calculation of the "cross section" requires counting the possible number of particle initial and final states, and the above state counting method is used.[10] The *cross section,* which is the measure of how many particles scatter in a particular direction when they collide in particle accelerators, is the basic quantity tested in particle physics. The Bekenstein Bound on the number of possible states is thus confirmed by the correctness of the calculated cross sections. In summary, the Bekenstein Bound on the total information that can be coded in a region is an absolute solid conclusion of modern physics, a result as solid as the Rock of Gibraltar.

One can also use the Bekenstein Bound to deduce an upper bound to the rate of information processing. The time for light to cross a sphere of a given diameter is equal to the diameter of the sphere divided by the speed of light. Since a state inside the sphere cannot completely change until a signal has time to travel from one side to the other, the rate of information processing is bounded above by the above Bekenstein Bound divided by this time interval. Putting in the numbers (details in the Appendix for Scientists), we calculate that the rate of state change is less than or equal to 4×10^{51} bits per second, multiplied by the mass of the system in kilograms. That is, the rate of information processing possible for a system depends only on the mass of the system, not on its spatial size or on any other variable. So a human being of mass 100 kilograms cannot change state more rapidly than about 4×10^{53} times per second. This number is of course enormous—and in fact a human will probably change state much, much more slowly than this—but it's finite.

From the Bekenstein Bound, it follows that, using computer memory capacity of the amount indicated by the Bekenstein Bound, a computer simulation of a person, a planet, a visible universe will not merely be very good, it will be *perfect*. It will be an emulation. As I argued in Chapter VIII, an emulation of an entity *is* the entity. An emulated human will be made of emulated human cells, made of emulated molecules, made of emulated atoms, made of emulated electrons, quarks, and gluons. No experiment using any experimental apparatus which will fit inside the visible universe can distinguish between the emulation and the original. The emulation and the original *are* the same. (If the simulation of a human is to be perfect, the simulation must also have ontological free will. It is possible to arrange this in a way consistent with the Bekenstein Bound, as follows. The Bekenstein Bound assumes that the vacuum state is unique, so no information is contained in the vacuum fluctuations. Thus, although the number of states a human can be in is finite, transitions between these states are still undetermined if the human brain randomizer uses these fluctuations, as discussed in Chapter VII, and this is consistent with the bound. For free will, the simulation must be connected to the fluctuations which exist at the most basic ontological level.)

One might be tempted to question the morality of such brute force resurrection: not only are the dead being resurrected, but so are people who never lived. However, the central claim of the Many-Worlds physics in Chapter V and the Many-Worlds metaphysics in Chapter VIII is that all people and all histories who could exist in fact do. They just don't exist on our phase trajectory, and so we have no record of them. The resurrected dead would not care which phase trajectory they are resurrected in—their own trajectory or another one

—so long as they *are* resurrected. If personal identity between an original and a resurrected human requires that the two be in the same quantum state—I shall discuss whether it does in a moment—then brute force resurrection will be necessary in order to get around the No Clone Theorem,[11] which says that it is not possible to construct an apparatus which can duplicate (clone) an arbitrary quantum state. In other words, no machine can be built which can take an object in the state Ψ as input and generate as output two objects, each in the state Ψ, for arbitrary Ψ. But it is nevertheless true[12] that for any *particular* state Ψ_i, it is possible to build a device A_i which *will* take as input an object in the state Ψ_i and generate as output two objects, each in the state Ψ_i. So if we know that a system must be in one of a finite number of quantum states Ψ_i, for i = 1, 2, . . . , $10^{10^{70}}$—which is the case for human beings, as I showed above—then the only way to be *certain* that a long-dead human's quantum state (say it happened to be in the state Ψ_{1507} at the time of death) is resurrected is to manufacture $10^{10^{70}}$ devices and generate all $10^{10^{70}}$ possible humans. As I indicated above, it will be possible to reduce below $10^{10^{70}}$ the upper bound on the number of states duplicated in order surely to resurrect the quantum states of all humans that have lived on a single phase trajectory, but the No Clone Theorem shows that this lower bound on the number to be resurrected is nevertheless greater than the total number that actually existed on the phase trajectory.

The No Clone Theorem is a manifestation of what is generally called "quantum nonlocality," which refers to the fact that complex quantum systems which have once interacted are forever entwined, no matter how far they are later separated spatially. In the cloning machine case, if the state Ψ of the object were arbitrary, then the cloning machine would have to change its state in order to determine what the state Ψ was, and this change of state would entwine the original object and the cloning machine in such a way that the two "duplicates" could not be in exactly the same state as the original. But if the cloning machine is designed just to duplicate a particular state, the initial change of state is unnecessary; the entwining does not occur.

This quantum nonlocality is important for the resurrection of people down to the quantum state, because it means that it will be necessary to duplicate not just an individual in isolation but also the individual's environment. In particular, the day-to-day interaction of people with each other will entwine them quantum mechanically, so it will be necessary to replicate the quantum states corresponding to the entire human species en masse at each instant of time. Since humans also interact with their inanimate environment, to get the exact quantum state it might even be necessary to replicate the entire visible universe. But, as I showed above, all possible visible universes can be replicated down to the quantum state if the computer capacity is at least $10^{10^{123}}$ bits. In the far future, the universal computer capacity will be far, far above this.

Quantum nonlocality also implies, for example, that parents are quantum mechanically entwined with their children. So, if the parents are to be resurrected down to the quantum state, it will not be possible to resurrect them without their children, or into an unfamiliar environment.

When Will the Dead Be Raised?

The dead will be resurrected when the computer capacity of the universe is so large that the amount of capacity required to store all possible human simulations is an insignificant fraction of the entire capacity. Since the information storage capacity diverges to plus infinity roughly at t^{-1} in proper time near the final Omega Point singularity at $t = 0$, as shown in the Appendix for Scientists, resurrection will occur between $10^{-10^{10}}$ seconds and $10^{-10^{123}}$ seconds before the Omega Point is reached. (It doesn't matter whether time is measured as years, seconds, or Planck time intervals [the Planck time interval is 10^{-43} seconds], all of these give roughly the same order of magnitude—double exponentials again!) The above numbers assume that a person is not resurrected until he or she is emulated; that is, duplicated down to the exact quantum state. However, I shall argue below, and Hans Moravec has contended in his book[13] *Mind Children,* that the simulation does not actually have to be an emulation of the quantum state to be considered the original person. Both Moravec and I feel that, if the essential personality is simulated, this is good enough to be identified with the original person. If so, then the above numbers are merely an upper bound, and the actual resurrection will occur much earlier. Moravec believes the resurrection will occur before our machine descendants have engulfed the Milky Way galaxy.

But even in this case the dead will not be raised for thousands of years at the earliest. This terrifies many people, who worry about what their souls will be doing in the meantime. As the American novelist John Updike puts it:

> The idea that we sleep for centuries and centuries without a flicker of dream, while our bodies rot and turn to dust and the very stone marking our graves crumbles to nothing, is virtually as terrifying as annihilation.[14]

The soul will be doing nothing, not even sleeping dreamlessly, because it won't exist. A human's soul is not naturally immortal and, when you're dead, you're dead until the Omega Point resurrects you. But no subjective time passes between the instant of death and the instant of resurrection, though in the universe as a whole trillions of years may pass. This point was emphasized by the greatest physicist of all time, Sir Isaac Newton: ". . . ye interval between death & ye resurrection is to them that sleep and perceive it not, a moment."[15] (This point was also emphasized in the Qur'an by Mohammed, the founder of Islam, as I shall discuss at length in Chapter XI.) Newton justified[16] this lack of passage of subjective time by reference to Jesus' promise to the thief on the cross: "Today shalt thou be with me in paradise" [Luke 23:43, KJV]. Since, said Newton, the universal resurrection has been delayed for over a thousand years since the death of Jesus and the thief, Jesus' promise of "today" can be true only if there is no passage of subjective time between the death of the thief and the universal resurrection. This argument of Newton, and indeed the whole idea that basic Christian belief requires the soul to "sleep" or be annihilated between death and the universal resurrection has an extensive history.[17] I shall discuss it briefly in Chapter XI. Again, this is one of the difficulties with the whole notion of an immortal soul—immortal by its very nature and hence not needing God to resurrect it: the idea raises the thorny question of what the soul does while waiting billions or trillions of years for the resurrection.

Why Will the Dead Be Raised?

Simulation of all possibilities out of which the far future could have come almost certainly will be done in the drive toward total knowledge before the c-boundary is reached. In our own drive to understand how life got started on our planet, we are in effect trying to simulate—resurrect—all possible kinds of the simplest life forms which could spontaneously form on the primitive earth. Strictly speaking, the question of whether we shall be raised is separate from the question of whether we shall be granted eternal life after being raised. I shall discuss the reasons for expecting the collectivity of life near the Omega Point—the Omega Point in Its immanence—to grant us eternal life at length in Chapter X.

The Pattern (Form) Theory Versus the Continuity Theory of Identity

What is happening in the resurrection described above is that an exact replica of ourselves is being simulated in the computer minds of the far future. This simulation of people who are long dead is "resurrection" only if we adopt what philosophers call the "pattern identity theory"; that is, the essence of identity of two entities which exist at different times lies in the (sufficiently close) identity of their patterns. Physical continuity is irrelevant. I have argued for such a criterion of identity in earlier chapters, and many famous philosophers (e.g., John Locke) have also defended this theory of identity. Other famous philosophers have insisted that the essence of identity is physical continuity over time. This theory of identity is called the "continuity identity theory." Although philosophers generally develop a theory of identity so as to solve the problem of the identity of *persons* over time—i.e., when is it correct to say that a certain baby in 1950 is the same person as a certain adult human in 1993?—they also generally agree that their identity theory applies to nonliving objects as well.

I claim that the question of whether two physical systems which differ in spatial or temporal location are to be identified is a question of physics, not philosophy. I shall therefore give arguments from physics which show that the pattern identity theory is correct, and that continuity is irrelevant. Nevertheless, I shall also show that there is sufficient continuity between the original dead person and the person's future emulation to identify the two even on the basis of the continuity theory of identity. Hence, whichever identity theory we adopt, the future emulation *is* the original dead person.

A rejection of the pattern identity theory underlies the English philosopher Antony Flew's opinion that it is ridiculous to call computer emulation of a dead person "resurrection." Flew puts forward the "Replica Objection": "No replica however perfect, whether produced by God or man, whether in our Universe or another, could ever be—in that primary, forensic sense—the same person as its original."[18] In all of his writings over the past thirty-odd years on the question of immortality, Flew has emphasized[19] that the logically prior question is the question of personal identity: "How is the reconstituted person on the Last Day to be identified as the original *me;* as opposed, that is, to a mere replica, an appropriately brilliant forgery?"[20] For unless this prior question of personal identity is settled, "To punish or to reward a replica, reconstituted on Judgement Day, for the sins or the virtues of the old Antony Flew dead and cremated, perhaps long years before, is as inept and as unfair as it would be to reward or to punish one identical twin for what was in fact done by the other."[21]

First of all, Flew is wrong about our legal system. It does in fact equate identical computer programs. If I duplicated a word processing program and used it without paying a royalty to the programmer, I would be taken to court. A claim that "the program I used is not the original, it is merely a replica" would not be accepted as a defense. I could also be sued for using without permission an organism whose genome has been patented. Identical twins are *not* identical persons. The programs which are their minds differ enormously: the memories coded in their neurons differ from each other in at least as many ways as they differ from the memories of other human beings. They are correctly regarded as different persons. But two beings who are identical both in their genes *and* in their mind programs *are* the same person, and it is appropriate to regard them as equally responsible legally.

However, the question of the identity of a person over time is ultimately a question of physics, not of law, especially of law based on a prequantum world view. This being so, even if Flew were correct about our legal system, the current legal view on personal identity would be irrelevant. Physical reality is not dependent on the opinion of human judges. Galileo was informed by the judges of the Inquisition that the Earth was immovable and in the center of the universe. Should I therefore believe the Earth to be stationary? Several centuries ago an American court in Salem, Massachusetts, declared witchcraft a menace to society. Should I therefore believe in witchcraft? A few years ago an American court in Pennsylvania declared that the psychic powers of a woman were destroyed by a CAT scan. Should I therefore believe in psychic powers?

As indicated above, I shall answer Flew's Replica Objection in two ways, using physics. First, quantum mechanics has a criterion for deciding when two systems which differ in spacetime position are identical. I shall show that this criterion requires us to identify the original human with the resurrected human, even if there is no continuity between the two. Second, I shall show that sufficient continuity exists between the original and the resurrected person even in the classical Omega Point Theory to identify the two. Thus the identity of the original and resurrected persons is established by physics.

QUANTUM MECHANICS SUPPORTS THE PATTERN IDENTITY THEORY

I think the most conclusive and overwhelming refutation of the Replica Objection is the quantum mechanical argument. It is a fundamental fact of quantum mechanics that two systems—e.g., two atoms—in the same quantum state cannot be distinguished, even in principle: if they are interchanged physically, the universe (except possibly for a phase) is unchanged. This total and absolute indistinguishability of systems in the same quantum state is of central importance to modern physics. In particular, a vast number of phenomena cannot be explained except by assuming the *exact identity of systems in the same quantum state.*

This exact identity is the ultimate cause of the stability of matter: without this exact identity, the exclusion principle would be unable to prevent the collapse of atoms and all solid bodies into black holes. This exact identity is the resolution of the Gibbs Paradox in statistical mechanics. This exact identity is a basic assumption in the derivation of the Planck distribution for blackbody radiation.

It is worth considering the Gibbs Paradox in some detail, since it can be derived without reference to atoms, using the ideas of classical thermodynamics alone. It is an illustration of how quantum mechanical effects—in this case, the identity of systems in the same quantum state—can manifest themselves at the macroscopic level. (It also illustrates how some consequences of classical thermodynamics are quantum mechanical in origin: they cannot be understood on the basis of Newtonian mechanics.) Suppose we have two containers of gas, each at the same temperature T and pressure P, and further suppose each container has volume V. The famous American physicist J. Willard Gibbs showed in 1875, and following his calculation, the great British physicist James Clerk Maxwell showed in an article entitled "Diffusion" for the *Encyclopedia Britannica* in 1878, that if the two containers have gases which differ *in any way whatsoever,* then by joining the containers and allowing the gases to diffuse into each other one can extract energy of $PV2\ln2$ from the diffusion process. On the other hand, if the gases are absolutely identical, then the available energy—energy which might be available for useful work—is exactly zero. Both Gibbs and Maxwell emphasized that the derivation of the available energy does not depend on what difference there is between the two gases, just that there be *some* difference, no matter how small.

The available energy which arises from the diffusion of two different gases is not small. For example, if each gas is at a pressure of one atmosphere, and there is one cubic meter of each gas, then the available energy is 1.4×10^5 joules, which is enough energy to light a 40-watt bulb for an hour. If the molecules making up the gases are absolutely identical, then the light bulb won't be lit at all. Again, the laws of thermodynamics are clear and unequivocal: any difference whatsoever between the molecules of the two gases lights a 40-watt bulb for an hour, and no difference at all means the bulb is not lit. There is *no* intermediate possibility: either the bulb is lit for an hour, or it is not lit at all.

The experiments are also clear and unequivocal. If both containers contain the same gas—oxygen, say—there is no available energy: the bulb stays out. If the containers contain different gases—oxygen and carbon dioxide, say—there is available energy, and the measured amount is the amount predicted: the 40-watt bulb is lit for an hour.

When Gibbs[22] and Maxwell[23] first derived this result, they found it incredible. This prediction of classical thermodynamics, that the available energy in a diffusion process is quantized, was utterly inconsistent with their intuition from Newtonian mechanics, according to which energy ought to vary continuously. (This is why the result is called a paradox.) Their initial reaction was to grasp at straws to explain it away. Maxwell, for example, said, "Now when we say that two gases are the same, we mean that we cannot distinguish the one from the other by any known reaction. It is not probable, *but it is possible,* [my emphasis] that two gases derived from different sources, but hitherto supposed to be the same, may hereafter be found to be different [with the result that available energy will appear when they are mixed]."[24] As Maxwell suspected, this proposal doesn't work. The origin of the two gases is irrelevant. In most gases with normal pressures and temperatures, almost all of the molecules are in the ground state, which means that they are in the same quantum state. Systems in the same quantum state are identical. There is *no* difference between the two volumes of oxygen, so there is no available energy from their diffusion.

For the past century at least, every chemistry major on the entire planet has performed an experiment, generally during the first year of college, which confirms the fact of the exact identity of systems in the same quantum state. The experiment is done to confirm the Law of Mass Action, which relates the concentrations of reagents in a chemical reaction. The Law of Mass Action says that if the chemical equation for the reaction is $n_A A + n_B B \rightarrow n_C C$, where A, B, and C represent the molecules and $n_A A$, etc., the number of molecules of the given type, the Law of Mass Action says that

$$[A]^{n_A}[B]^{n_B} = K[C]^{n_C}$$

where [A], [B], [C] are the concentrations of the molecules A, B, and C in the reaction vessel, and K is a constant (the equilibrium constant).

For a specific example of the Law of Mass Action, suppose we are burning hydrogen and oxygen to form water. The chemical equation is

$$2H_2 + O_2 \rightarrow 2H_2O$$

That is, two molecules of hydrogen and one molecule of oxygen combine to give two molecules of water. The Law of Mass Action then tells us that, when the reaction is completed, there will still be some atoms of hydrogen and oxygen which are not in the form of water, and that the concentrations of hydrogen, oxygen, and water molecules are

$$[H_2]^2[O_2] = K[H_2O]^2$$

That is, the square of the hydrogen concentration times the oxygen concentration equals the equilibrium constant times the square of the water concentration. The importance of this law to chemists is difficult to underestimate. This law allows chemists to predict how much of each chemical compound they need to buy in order to make a given amount of final chemical compound. It is called the Law of Mass Action because the extent to which the reaction goes to completion depends on the concentrations—the masses—of the molecules of each type actually present.

The identity of molecules in the same quantum state is absolutely essential to the validity of this formula. Without this identity, the laws of thermodynamics would say that there is no relationship between the concentrations of molecules at all, as I shall prove in the Appendix for Scientists, in gross violation to what is observed by every chemistry student. Although the Law of Mass Action itself was first discovered empirically in the early 1800s, the derivation of Law of Mass Action from fundamental identity of all molecules of the "same type"—molecules in the same quantum state—is due to J. Willard Gibbs, who first published it in his 1902 book[25] *Elementary Principles of Statistical Mechanics*. (Gibbs derived the Law of Mass Action using classical thermodynamics in an 1875 paper.[26]) As discussed above, Gibbs did not understand the cause of this identity; to understand it one needs quantum mechanics, and thus the cause of the identity was not understood until the 1930s. Even today, most textbooks which derive the Law of Mass Action do not emphasize that the derivation depends crucially on the identity of systems in the same quantum state. Any derivation using statistical mechanics has to use explicitly the assumption of identity of systems in the same quantum state. Unfortunately, this crucial assumption is generally made without comment. This being so, I have included a derivation of the Law of Mass Action in the Appendix for Scientists.

In summary, quantum mechanics has a criterion for the identity of physical systems, and this criterion allows—indeed, often requires—us to identify two systems existing at the same time. This criterion for identity was first discovered in the late nineteenth century by two of the greatest physicists of that century, and this criterion has been known to all physicists for at least fifty years. It is time this criterion was used in philosophical discussions of what identity means. In the prenineteenth-century physics which Flew tacitly assumes, the identity of two systems existing at the same time was considered "absurd." Further, in the ancient world view, systems which are at different spatial locations are *ipso facto* different entities.

THE SHIP OF THESEUS

The classical model for this differentiation is the "Ship of Theseus."[27] According to Plutarch:

> The vessel in which Theseus sailed and returned safe with these young men went with thirty oars. It was preserved by the Athenians up to the times of Demetrius Phalaerus (lived about 280 B.C.); being so refitted and newly fashioned with strong plank, that it afforded an example to the philosophers in their disputations concerning the identity of things that are changed by addition, some contending that it was the same, and others that it was not.[28]

The English political philosopher Thomas Hobbes used the Ship of Theseus to attack the pattern identity theory which I require for the Omega Point resurrection theory:

> . . . two bodies existing both at once would be one and the same numerical body. For if, for example, that ship of Theseus, concerning the difference whereof made by continued reparation in taking out the old planks and putting in new, the sophisters of Athens were wont to dispute, were, after all the planks were changed, the same numerical ship it was at the beginning; and if some man had kept the old planks as they were taken out, and by putting them afterwards together in the same order, had again made a ship of them, this, without doubt, had also been the same numerical ship with that which was at the beginning; and so there would have been two ships numerically the same, which is absurd.[29]

The nonidentity of systems in different spatial positions is not true in quantum mechanics, and actual physical systems are quantum systems. In particular, a human being is merely a special type of quantum system. Thus the quantum criterion for system identity applies to humans, and hence two humans in the same quantum state *are* the same person: if a "replica" of a long-dead person were made which was identical to the quantum state of the long-dead person, the "replica" would *be* that person. ("Replica" is in quotes because the later person is not a replica; it *is* the original.) To reject this identity is to reject a basic postulate of quantum mechanics, confirmed by innumerable experiments done over a period of more than a century. Thus we have to accept the possibility of having "two ships numerically the same" even if it is an "absurd" idea. Science is always telling us that "absurd" ideas are in fact true. Five hundred years ago, virtually everyone agreed that the idea of the Earth moving around the Sun was an "absurd" idea. Flew's claim that physical continuity is a necessary condition for personal identity is refuted by quantum mechanics, just as an immovable Earth was refuted by celestial mechanics.

The Ship of Theseus example tacitly assumes that it is possible, at least in principle, to distinguish continuously between the original ship and the copy to be manufactured. This is of course true in everyday circumstances, where the two ships are definitely not in the same quantum state. It is beyond current technology to create two macroscopic bodies which are in the same quantum state. But were the Ship of Theseus duplication to be carried out in the far future such that, after duplication, one had two ships in the same quantum state, then it would be impossible, even in principle, to tell which was the original and which the replica. This assertion is a corollary of the No Clone Theorem discussed above: if there were one ship going into the quantum duplication facility and two ships coming out, it would be impossible for any experiment to tell which was the original (and neither of the two ships coming out could be in exactly the same quantum state as the original ship going in).

Traditionally, theology has required continuity in order to maintain identity between the original and the resurrected persons, and getting this continuity was the underlying reason for introducing the idea of an immortal soul. The need for such continuity is obviated by quantum mechanics, and thus we see that an immortal soul is no longer necessary for individual immortality.

CONTINUITY THEORY: A LATER EMULATION IS IDENTICAL TO THE ORIGINAL PERSON

However, I don't think one has to go so far as to reproduce the exact quantum state to be successful in truly resurrecting a dead person. It must be kept in mind that the atoms which make up our bodies are constantly being exchanged with other atoms obtained from the food we eat. Much (but not all) of the human body is completely remade—replicated—over the course of our lives as the cells of our body die and are replaced. This continuous replacement of the body's substance during life has been known for centuries: Aquinas for one discussed it at length in *Summa Contra Gentiles* 4.81ff. Some of this excreted material will be incorporated one day in the bodies of other people, and if individual atoms could be distinguished, each one of us would be faced with a Ship of Theseus problem: are we "us" or partly someone else? Aquinas in the passage cited above was very much worried about cannibalism: if a "person" is defined by his/her atoms, and if God can only resurrect people by returning to them the atoms that once made them up, how would it be possible for God to resurrect a human who is a cannibal, and whose parents, grandparents, etc., have been cannibals, so that all of his atoms belonged to someone else? On the other hand, if it was logically impossible to resurrect him, how could he be punished for his cannibalism? If Aquinas knew of the extent of recycling in the biosphere, he would be really worried: were individual atoms distinguishable, a simple calculation shows that the body of every human being on earth would contain atoms that were once part of other human beings. We would all be cannibals. The problem is solved in quantum mechanics, wherein all atoms of the same element are identical. There is no way to distinguish the atoms of the cannibal from those of the victim.

Even considered purely internally, our body's substance is continually being replaced. At the subnuclear level, the quarks and gluons which make up the neutrons and protons of the atoms in our bodies are being annihilated and recreated on a timescale of less than 10^{-23} seconds; thus we are actually being annihilated and replicated—resurrected—10^{23} times a second in the normal course of our lives. In short, the substance of human beings is not preserved, only the pattern. More importantly, the pattern itself is not perfectly preserved in the course of our daily replication. The phenomenon of aging is just one manifestation of this fact. The pattern is preserved as well as it is because in a biological system there are feedback mechanisms which allow the pattern as a whole to act to partially correct the errors which appear when pieces of the pattern are remade. Surprisingly, it is even unlikely that the human brain stores the memories of everything that it remembers. Computer science[30] shows such storage to be inefficient. What probably happens is that only part of a memory is stored and recall of the entire memory involves the inverse of data compression techniques: the memory is "fleshed" out. Such a storage mechanism is probabilistic; errors can be made in this process, so perfectly sane people occasionally "remember" events that never occurred.

This view of the memory storage mechanism—suggested by computer science—is the growing consensus opinion among psychologists who are experts on the question of how knowledge is represented in the human brain.[31] In fact, what evidence we have shows that our brains do not store a faithful representation of an experience. Nor do they store an accurate, complete interpretation of an experience. Rather, they store only fragments of an interpretation of an experience.

Since none of the substance and only part of the pattern is continuously preserved even in the course of our normal lives, Flew's Replica Objection will be met even in a classical world view provided that enough of the pattern is continuously preserved—in some form—from the day of death to the day of resurrection so as to enable the Omega Point, using this preserved information and error-correcting feedback, to replicate the original long-dead individual to an accuracy equal to the accuracy of replication which occurs in the course of our daily lives. I have shown that this degree of preservation of information occurs in Omega Point resurrection theory. For, if spacetime is globally hyperbolic, then *all* of the pattern is preserved in the past light cone of any event sufficiently near the Omega Point, and hence the total pattern is available in the far future for generating and animating a simulated body. If one accepts the identification made in Chapter II of "soul" with a particular computer program or pattern, we could interpret this pattern conservation as "immortality of the soul." But it should be kept in mind that this "immortality" of the pattern is just a manifestation of conservation of information in deterministic physical systems: the "soul" is not thinking or feeling while it is in a disembodied form on a light cone. On the other hand, if quantum mechanics (or some other mechanism) destroys global hyperbolicity or even annihilates all information about particular individuals, then just the continuously preserved fact that DNA was the biological substrate is enough to resurrect the identical quantum states of all dead humans. So in either case one has (sufficient) continuity of pattern between now and the far future.

Flew cites a number of passages from famous religious authorities in support of the Replica Objection, but except where these men have been clearly infected by Platonic dualism (or by the felt need to preserve continuity), I think these very passages support the idea that replica resurrection is generally what is expected in the Judeo-Christian-Islamic tradition. I shall discuss this in more detail in Chapter XI. Flew's arguments strike me as mere quibbles over the meaning of words, and they remind me of Appendix IV—entitled "Of Some Verbal Disputes"—of Hume's *An Enquiry Concerning the Principles of Morals:* "Nothing is more usual than for philosophers to encroach the province of grammarians; and to engage in disputes of words, while they imagine, that they are handling controversies of the deepest importance and concern."[32]

However, to give Flew credit, he did qualify his Replica Objection when he participated in the Tulane Omega Point Colloquium in the fall of 1990. He said that, if it could indeed be shown that an emulation of a person alive today could and would be made in the computers of the far future, then, although the present usage of the word "person" would not permit the person living today to be identified with his/her emulation in the far future, it would nevertheless be reasonable—when faced with a fact and not merely with a philosophical puzzle case—to extend the meaning of the word "person" so that the emulation and the human being living today would be termed the same "person." He used[33] an example from his Gifford Lectures, in which an English court was called upon to decide whether a seaplane —a "flying boat"—was a "ship" and hence regulated by a law passed by Parliament in the time of Elizabeth I. The court decided that it was, even though airplanes were devices totally beyond the comprehension of the Elizabethan parliamentarians, and hence *not* an example any of them would have given if asked for a description of a "ship." Flew said that, faced with the actual fact of exactly identical copies of the same person, the meaning of the word "person" would necessarily have to be modified beyond its present usage, and the identification I propose above—identifying the emulation with the person living today—would under the circumstances be the most reasonable modification. It would follow, Flew said, that under these circumstances it would be reasonable for a human alive today to identify emotionally with the emulation in the far future, to the same extent he/she identifies emotionally with the person who will exist tomorrow and who is connected continuously (with the caveats above) to the person today. In other words, if it could be shown as a physical fact that your emulation will be created in the far future to live in heaven forever, you should be comforted, for the same reasons that you would be discomforted if a doctor told you that you had terminal cancer and only six months to live. In both cases, it's *you*, and not a mere replica, that's going to have immortality or death, respectively.

Flew says he does not believe technology will one day permit computer resurrection, but it seems to me he has conceded the main point, namely that his Replica Objection is not an absolute logical barrier to resurrection, but only a technological barrier. Flew has conceded that the question of whether we can expect resurrection to immortal life is now purely a question of physics.

Many people argue against the pattern theory of identity by pointing out that we distinguish between an original painting by a famous artist and a copy of the painting. An original painting by Vincent van Gogh, for example, was sold in the late 1980s for nearly $100 million, while anyone can buy a print of the same painting for a measly $10, and a reproduction of the same painting, copied brush stroke by brush stroke by a modern artist, for about $5,000.

This argument overlooks the fact that it is easy for us to distinguish between the original and the copy. To put this in perspective, we should note that the most accurate generally familiar visual reproduction of a scene, namely a good 35-mm color photographic negative, codes 300 million (= 3×10^8) bits of information.[34] But as I pointed out above, the Bekenstein Bound shows that to reproduce a human being down to the quantum state would require 3×10^{45} bits of information, a number which is 10^{37} times larger. The entire economic output of the world is about 10^{14} dollars; the ratio of the output of the world to a single penny, the smallest coin in United States currency, is only 10^{16}. Thus the "reproduction" of a human being which I am proposing here is reproduction to an accuracy which is beyond the experience of any human being. This "reproduction" can only be carried out by the Omega Point. We can use the laws of physics to prove that this "reproduction" can in fact be carried out in the far future, but it will always be beyond mere human power actually to carry it out. Thus the "original painting" argument, which relies on ordinary human experience, is inapplicable to the quantum mechanical duplication of people which will be carried out by the Omega Point. Having all the money in the world to spend is a wholly different experience from having only the money in one's pocket to spend. You cannot compare the former with the latter.

X.

WHAT HAPPENS AFTER
THE RESURRECTION:
HEAVEN, HELL, AND
PURGATORY

I SHOULD EMPHASIZE THAT THIS EMULA-
tion of people that have lived in the past need not be limited to just
repeating the past. Once an emulation of a person and his/her world
has been formed in a computer of sufficient capacity, the emulation
can be allowed to develop further—to think and feel things that the
long-dead original person being emulated never felt and thought. It is
not even necessary for *any* of the past to be repeated. The Omega
Point (in one of Its immanent intermediate temporal states; this qualification is hereafter omitted for ease of reading) could simply begin the
emulation with the brain memory of the dead person as it was at the
instant of death (or ten years before, or twenty minutes before,
or . . .) implanted in the emulated body of the dead person, the
body being as it was at age twenty (or age seventy, or . . .). This
body and memory collection could be set in any simulated background
environment the Omega Point wished: a simulated world indistinguishable from the long-extinct society and physical universe of the
revived dead person, or even a world that never existed, but one as
close as logically possible to the ideal *fantasy* world of the resurrected
dead person. Furthermore, all possible combinations of resurrected
dead can be placed in the same simulation and allowed to interact. For
example, the reader could be placed in a simulation with *all* of his/her
ancestors and descendents, each at whatever age (physical and mental,

separately) the Omega Point pleases. The Omega Point Itself could interact—speak, say—with His/Her emulated creatures, who could learn about Him/Her, about the world outside the simulation, and about other simulations, from Him/Her.

The simulated body could be one that has been vastly improved over the one we currently have: the laws of the simulated world could be modified to prevent a second physical death. Borrowing the terminology of St. Paul, we can call the simulated, improved, and undying body a "spiritual body," for it will be of the same "stuff" as the human mind now is: a "thought inside a mind" (in Aristotelian language, "a form inside a form"; in computer language, a virtual machine inside a machine). The spiritual body is thus just the present body (with improvements!) at a higher level of implementation, a concept I discussed in Chapter II. With this phrasing, St Paul's description is completely accurate: "So also is the resurrection of the dead. It is sown in corruption; it is raised in incorruption: It is sown in dishonor; it is raised in glory; it is sown in weakness; it is raised in power: It is sown a natural body; it is raised a spiritual body. . . ." (I Corinthians 15:42–44 KJV.) Only as a spiritual body, only as a computer emulation, is resurrection possible without a second death: our current bodies, implemented in matter, could not possibly survive the extreme heat near the final singularity. Again, St. Paul's words are descriptive: ". . . flesh and blood cannot inherit the kingdom of God . . ." (I Corinthians 15:50 KJV.)

Nevertheless, it is appropriate to regard computer emulation resurrection as being a "resurrection of the flesh" (in the words of the Apostles' Creed). For an emulated person would observe herself to be as real, and as having a body as solid as, the body we currently observe ourselves to have. There would be nothing "ghostly" about the simulated body, and nothing insubstantial about the simulated world in which the simulated body found itself. In the words of Tertullian, one of the earliest Christian theologians (A.D. 155–220), the simulated body would be ". . . this flesh, suffused with blood, built up with bones, interwoven with nerves, entwined with veins, (a flesh) which . . . [is] . . . undoubtedly human."[1]

I said above that the resurrection body could be vastly improved over our current bodies. The obvious improvements would be the repair of all bodily defects, such as missing limbs, youth for old age, etc. However, if the defect to be corrected were *necessarily* connected with the personality, so that any correction would logically entail drastic changes in the personality, then a correction without distress to the resurrected individual would be logically impossible. So such correction cannot be effected by the Omega Point.

For example, there have been certain cases of people blind from birth who have been completely cured by an operation in adulthood.[2] The eyes have thus been repaired, but the brain—the personality—has never learned to process the information coming from the eyes. The patient finds the experience of first opening his repaired eyes painful: he sees nothing but a spinning mass of lights and colors, and is quite unable to pick out familiar objects by sight. It takes *years* of effort to be able to use sight. One man was shown an orange a week after his sight was repaired, and he was asked, "What shape is it?" He replied, "Let me touch it and I'll tell you!" After doing so, he said it was a round orange. After staring at it for a long while, he said, "Yes, I can see it is round." Shown next a blue square and a triangle, he described both as blue and round. When the doctor pointed out the angles to him, he replied, "Ah. Yes, I understand now, one can *see* how they feel."

The patient often feels learning to use the visual sense exhausting, and may refuse to use it unless forced to do so. It takes at least a month of work to be able to distinguish even a few objects. But such people can gradually learn. After several years many are able to read.

For such blind people, the entire personality has been built around the hearing and tactile senses. The personality must be radically restructured if the visual sense is to be added. If the restructuring is done at the instant of resurrection, it is not the original person who is being resurrected. But the Omega Point could do all that was logically possible in this case. He/She could, for example, repair the damage to the eyes and guide the blind person to sight with vastly greater efficiency than human medical doctors could. (People blinded in adulthood could receive their sight instantly with their resurrection, since the mental visual integration is already there.)

The same applies to people who are born with more fundamental defects, such as Down's Syndrome.

The computer simulation resurrection body would naturally have three superhuman features which Jesus' resurrection body as described in Luke also has. First, the physical appearance of the computer simulated body could be set by the Omega Point to be easily modified at the will of the resurrected person. In Luke 24: 16 and 31, Jesus' disciples did not recognize him until he willed it. Second, the simulated person can be erased from one part of its simulated universe and instantaneously be implanted in another part. In Luke 24:31 Jesus vanished the instant his disciples recognized him. Further, in Luke 24:36 Jesus appeared (apparently suddenly) in a room where his disciples were discussing his resurrection. (In John 20:26 [NEB] this appearance is claimed to have occurred in a locked room.) Third, as discussed above, the simulated body is as real as anything else in the simulation: in particular, it can eat; it can touch and be touched by anything in the simulated world in which it exists. In Luke 24:39–43 Jesus refutes his disciples' fears that he is a ghost by allowing them to touch him and by eating a fish in their presence.[3]

Although computer simulation resurrection overcomes the physical barriers to eternal life of individual human beings, there remains a logical problem, namely, the finiteness of the human memory. As I mentioned above, the human brain can store only about 10^{15} bits (this corresponds to roughly a thousand subjective years of life), and once this memory space is exhausted, we can grow no more. Thus it is not clear that the undying resurrected life is appropriately regarded as "eternal." There are several options: the Omega Point could permit us to merge our individual personalities—upload our personalities out of the simulation into a higher level of implementation—into the universal mind which is His/Hers. Or the Omega Point could increase our memory storage capacity indefinitely beyond 10^{15} bits while retaining our individuality, and even while retaining our current body size and shape. (There is no reason why the memories of the simulation must be stored in the brains of the simulation.) Or the Omega Point could guide us to a "perfection" of our finite natures. Whatever "perfection" means—depending on the definition, there could be many "perfections." With sufficient computer power, it should be possible to calculate what a human action would result in without the simulation actually experiencing the action, so the Omega Point would be able to advise us on possible perfections without our having to go through the trial and error procedure characteristic of this life. If more than one simulation of the same individual is made, then *all* of these options could be realized simultaneously. Once an individual is "perfected," the memory of this perfect individual could be recorded permanently —preserved all the way into the Omega Point in Its transcendence. The errors and evil committed by the imperfect individual could be erased from the universal mind (or also permanently recorded). The perfected individual personality would be truly eternal: she would exist for all future time. Furthermore, when the perfected personality reached the Omega Point in Its transcendence, it would become eternal in the sense of being beyond time, being truly one with God. The natural term to describe this perfected immortality is "beatific vision."

Reasons for Believing the Omega Point Will Resurrect Us to Eternal Life

What happens to the resurrected dead is entirely up to the Omega Point; there is no way the simulations can pay for or enforce the immortality which it is in the power of the Omega Point to grant. But continued survival near the final state will require greater and greater cooperation, and we know that cooperation is generally associated with altruism. Furthermore, if the resurrection is delayed sufficiently long, then the relative computer resources required to resurrect, guide the whole of humanity into the beatific vision, and preserve the perfected individuals forever will be tiny. Since the cost of doing good is not significantly greater than the cost of doing evil, I think we can reasonably count on the former, especially if the Person making the choice is basically good. Adopting the natural theological term, I think we will be granted "grace."

With the help of game theory[4] and the really solid part of modern economics—microeconomics[5]—the above argument can be made more precise. Axelrod[6] and more recently Nowak and Sigmund[7] have shown that, if the present value of the future is sufficiently high, and the probability of future interactions between two given individuals is sufficiently close to 1, then on the average an individual can best advance his selfish interests by adopting a strategy of "cheap" altruism toward other individuals. That is, he can best maximize his own utility if he uses the strategy "assume other individuals are going to treat you as you would like to be treated, and treat an individual as an enemy only if he in the immediate past treated you as one." Axelrod points out that this strategy is most efficiently implemented if an individual also adopts a strategy of behaving "altruistically" toward all other individuals if the cost of such "altruism" is sufficiently inexpensive. The "altruism" of person A toward person B has been precisely defined by Gary Becker[8]—in work that won him the 1992 Nobel prize for economics—as two conditions on person A's "utility function." (A "utility function" measures how much a person values something.) The first condition says that A regards B's welfare (as measured by B) as an ultimate end, and the second condition says that A is made happier (A's utility is increased) purely by B being happier (B's utility being increased).[9] The best available introduction to Becker's work on altruism is in the textbook *Price Theory* by David Friedman.[10]

Now the individuals of the far future (or individualized conscious subprograms of the Universal Mind) will either be immortal themselves or will expect themselves to be resurrected, and furthermore, the disappearance of horizons will mean that all individuals can expect to interact, at least indirectly, with all other individuals an infinite number of times. Thus we would expect the present value of the future to be high and the probability of future interaction to be very close to 1. Hence a strategy of "cheap" altruism will probably be adopted by the individuals of the far future. As pointed out above, selfish reasons alone —historical research as part of the drive toward total knowledge, which is required for continued survival—imply that humans probably will be resurrected. Once resurrected, cheap altruism will probably keep them alive forever. Simply erasing the resurrected dead from the computer memory would not be consistent with the optimal survival strategy of life in the far future.

Becker has pointed out[11] that the above definition of "altruism" is also a definition of what is meant by "Person A loves Person B." Notice that this is a selfless sort of love, so it is "love" in the Greek sense of *agape* (ἀγάπη). (There are three words for "love" in Greek: *eros,* sexual love; *philia,* friendship; and *agape.* When the New Testament refers to God's "love" for humanity, the word *agape* is always used.) Hence the above analysis can be reformulated as saying that all humans will be resurrected to immortal life because God loves us. So the motivation for the granting of immortal life in the Omega Point Theory is exactly the same as it is in the Judeo-Christian-Islamic tradition: the selfless love (ἀγάπη) of God. The above argument for the granting of immortality is nonrigorous, but it constitutes a completely rigorous argument for the converse: if we *are* granted immortality, it will be due to the love of the Omega Point for us. Thus, in the Omega Point Theory, the love of God enters in an essential way into the mechanism of resurrection and immortality. This is the first physical theory of immortality for which this is true. In previous theories, the soul was immortal in its own right; the love of God was really incidental. The Omega Point Theory has the first physical resurrection theory to be fully consistent with the Christian resurrection theory. It is also the first redemption theory justified by reason, not faith.

In his *On the Immortality of the Soul,* David Hume raised the following objection to the idea of a general resurrection of the dead: "How to dispose of the infinite number of posthumous existences ought also to embarrass the religious theory."[12] Hume summarized the argument in a later interview with the famous biographer James Boswell: ". . . [Hume] added that it was a most unreasonable fancy that he should exist forever. That immortality, if it were at all, must be general; that a great proportion of the human race has hardly any intellectual qualities; that a great proportion dies in infancy before being possessed of reason; yet all these must be immortal; that a Porter who gets drunk by ten o'clock with gin must be immortal; that the trash of every age must be preserved, and that new Universes must be created to contain such infinite numbers."[13]

The ever growing numbers of people whom Hume regarded as trash nevertheless could be preserved forever in our single finite (classical) universe if computer capacity is created fast enough. By looking more carefully at the calculations in the Appendix for Scientists, one sees that they also show it is physically possible to save *forever* a certain constant percentage of the information processed at a given universal time. Thus, the computer capacity will be there to preserve even drunken porters (and perfected drunken porters) provided only that the Omega Points waits long enough before resurrecting them. Even though the computer capacity required to perfectly simulate is exponentially related to the complexity of the entity simulated, it is physically possible to resurrect an actual infinity of individuals between now and the Omega Point, even assuming the complexity of the average individual diverges as the Omega Point is approached, and to guide them *all* into perfection. Total perfection of all would be achieved at the instant of the Omega Point.

Guiding all of an ultimately infinite number of people (in the limit of the Omega Point, infinitely complex people) into perfection depends in a crucial way on the fact that there will be an actual infinity[14] of information processed between any finite time and the Omega Point. It is an example of what Bertrand Russell has termed[15] the Tristram Shandy paradox. Tristram Shandy took two years to write the history of the first two days of his life, and complained that at that rate material would accumulate faster than he could write it down. Russell showed that, if Tristram Shandy lived forever, nevertheless no part of his biography would have remained unwritten. In the case of the Omega Point, which literally does live forever, all beings that have ever lived and will live from now to the end of time can be resurrected and remembered, even though the time needed to do the resurrecting will increase exponentially, a much worse case than Tristram Shandy faced. It is important that, at any given time on a phase trajectory, there is only a finite number of possible beings which could exist. If this were not true, then the number of beings that would have to be resurrected between now and the final state might be the power set of $\aleph_0$, which is the infinity of the whole numbers. Now the power set of $\aleph_0$ is a higher order of infinity than $\aleph_0$, and thus resurrecting all possible beings might be impossible because only $\aleph_0$ bits can be recorded between now and the final state.

Hilbert's Hotel—named after the early twentieth-century German mathematician David Hilbert—is an excellent example of the power of an actual infinity. Hilbert's Hotel has an infinite number of rooms, all of which are filled. Then another person arrives and asks for a room. "Why, of course, sir," says the innkeeper. "I'll just move the person now in room 1 into room 2, the person in room 2 into room 3, and so on, and this will free up room 1 for you."

Then 100 new people arrive and ask for rooms. "Why, of course," says the innkeeper. "I'll just move everyone in the hotel into the room which has their current number plus 100, and this will free up the first 100 rooms for you."

Then *an infinite number* of new people arrive and ask for rooms. "Why, of course," says the innkeeper. "I'll just move the person in room 1 into room 2, the person in room 2 into room 4, the person in room 3 into room 6, and so on, and this will free up all the odd-numbered rooms in the hotel for you. There are an infinity of odd-numbered rooms, so each of you will have a room."

There is plenty of room in the future for infinite numbers of resurrected individuals.

Since the computer power will exist to resurrect not only all human beings but also all cockroaches, all flies, and all other nonhuman living beings that have ever existed upon the Earth, is there any reason to expect humans will be given preference over these other creatures? The same reasons for resurrecting humans apply to these creatures also, for in the far future they also will have been part of the past that led to that future. But there will be no motivation to grant these creatures eternal life. For there is a fundamental difference between humans and all other creatures that have ever existed, namely that the computer program which is the human soul is a potential self-programming universal Turing machine: a program that is capable of evolving subprograms which can solve *any* solvable problem if given enough time and memory capacity. (I say "potential" because a true universal Turing machine requires an unlimited memory, which we, in our preresurrection bodies, do not have.) As far as we know, no other creature has ever appeared on Earth with a similar capacity. For this reason it would be meaningless to grant the other living creatures eternal life: they are fundamentally finite state machines, and adding memory capacity cannot change that. Adding memory would merely lock them into eternal returns. Their fundamental programs cannot be expanded to become self-programming universal Turing machines without changing the essence of their programs. Since the Omega Point in Its transcendence is in essence a self-programming universal Turing machine, with a literal infinity of memory, it can be said that humans resemble God in His/Her essence, something that cannot be said of any other living being which has ever before appeared on the Earth. In a deep sense, the biblical statement is correct: we humans are created in the image of God, and no other life form is so created. This assertion of the uniqueness of *Homo sapiens* among life forms created to date is basically the same as the claim of human importance made in the Jewish, Christian, Islamic, Mayan, Zuñi, Iroquois, ancient Egyptian, ancient Chinese, and Bantu religions.[16]

I could of course be wrong about the uniqueness of human beings. We human beings are probably not unique in our knowledge of our own future death. Elephants, coming upon the bones of another elephant, have been observed to caress and later bury the bones. Elephants do not behave in this manner when they encounter the bones of any other animal, suggesting that they realize these bones are a "form" of elephant. The burial might even indicate a hope for a future life. Certainly anthropologists interpret burials of their own species by Neanderthal man to indicate such a belief. It could also be that animals such as chimps—a sibling species to our own: chimps and humans had a common ancestor only 5 million years ago—are also potential self-programming universal Turing machines. If so, such "animals" will also be resurrected and given eternal life, for the same reasons we shall be. The beings of the far future doing the resurrecting will know the capacity of the resurrected creatures. They, and not I, will be making the decisions about whom to give eternal life. My argument that human beings, at least, will be given eternal life depends only on the fact that we are potential self-programming universal Turing machines. My argument does not depend on human uniqueness; indeed, it assumes that our machine descendants will also be potential self-programming universal Turing machines. Also, animals such as the loved pets of humans will be resurrected because their human owners want them to be, even if human pets happen not to be potential self-programming universal Turing machines.

The Existence and Nature of Hell and Purgatory

It is of course possible that a resurrected individual would reject the advice of the Omega Point concerning personal improvement. Said individual may prefer to continue committing evil acts against other humans. The Omega Point will not permit this, for it would contradict the love which He/She bears for the simulated creatures. So the Omega Point has several options. First, if He/She is convinced that the resurrected individual is irretrievably evil, He/She will simply not resurrect the evil individual. For such an individual, death would be permanent. (Some theologians have defined "Hell" to be this situation of permanent death.) Second, the Omega Point might compute that it is possible to guide the flawed human to perfection—or at least eliminate the really serious evils—before the natural human memory store is filled. If the Omega Point chooses this option, then the abode of the flawed individual could be termed "Purgatory." Since the human brain can store at most 10^{15} bits, and since at any given time the Omega Point knows everything that has occurred in the simulation of the resurrected individual, this means that the interaction of the Omega Point and the flawed individual is what game theorists call a "zero-sum finite dual game with perfect information." ("Zero-sum two-person" means that there are two players in diametric opposition; what one wins, the other loses. "Perfect information" means that a player is always informed of the complete history of the play. Chess is a more familiar example of a finite zero-sum two-person game with perfect information.) Now von Neumann and Morgenstern have shown[17] that such a game can always be solved by a pure strategy without randomization. ("Pure strategy" means a complete set of instructions, given before the game starts, that specifies exactly what move to make for every conceivable situation in which the player must make a choice.) In the case of chess, the von Neumann-Morgenstern theorem means that exactly one of the following three alternatives holds: (1) white has a pure strategy that wins, no matter what black does; (2) black has a pure strategy that wins, no matter what white does; or (3) both players have pure strategies that ensure at least a draw, no matter what the other does. The basic reason why such a pure strategy exists is that there are by assumption only a finite number of steps in the game, and only a finite number of moves at each step. Hence, there are only a finite number of logically possible games, and it is possible in principle to look at all possible last moves, and work backward to a move or set of moves at the first step that will guarantee a win or draw for white or black. The idea is essentially the same as that of brute force resurrection. The number of alternatives which would have to be investigated is enormous, and so game theory cannot now tell us which of the above three alternatives actually is the case, but it is logically necessary that one of the three must hold.

The von Neumann-Morgenstern theorem is more easily understood if one sees it applied to a much simpler finite dual game with perfect information than chess, a game familiar to all children the world over, namely tic-tac-toe (called "noughts and crosses" in England.) In this case there are only a small number of possible games, less than 362,880 (= 9!, which is $9 \times 8 \times 7 \times 6 \times 5 \times 4 \times 3 \times 2 \times 1$), so it is possible to prove as a mathematical theorem what every child soon discovers, that it is case (3) that applies: both players have pure strategies that ensure at least a draw, no matter what the other does.[18] A complete table of these pure strategies for tic-tac-toe has been published,[19] and even for this "simple" game the table is quite complicated: it requires four large folio pages to express in a very complex mathematical symbolism.

Thus there must also exist either (1) a pure strategy which guarantees that the Omega Point will be able to eliminate the evil in an individual, or (2) a pure strategy which allows the individual to retain the evil. Option (3), the draw, also means a failure to eliminate the evil. It is beyond human power to calculate which of these two options holds. If it is (1), and if it is possible for the Omega Point to compute the pure strategy (it might not be possible, as it might require a perfect simulation, which would defeat the purpose of the computation), then it is certain that the Omega Point can eliminate the evil in a person, no matter how evil he or she is. This need not contradict free will: it just means that the battle against evil is certain to end in the Omega Point's victory no matter what we as resurrected individuals do. Which particular move we will make cannot be foreseen even by omniscience, but whatever we do, the evil in us will lose.[20]

Even in the case of (2) and (3) it is still possible that the Omega Point can win the game. This possibility is illustrated in tic-tac-toe by the fact that an expert player can often maneuver a tyro into a loss; a list of such tricky plays has been provided for tic-tac-toe by Martin Gardner.[21]

Nevertheless, if it is (2), then it is not guaranteed that the Omega Point can eliminate the evil in a human being before the human memory is filled. If this occurs, then the Omega Point could augment the human memory and continue the game. If the finiteness restriction is thus relaxed, there is no longer any guarantee that the Omega Point can win the game. It might be that the flawed human resists the guidance of the Omega Point for infinite subjective time. In such a case, the human would have been in Purgatory forever: it seems reasonable to call such a situation "Hell." Thus Hell may exist, but its existence is not certain. It would exist only if one or more intelligent beings resist forever the call to repentance. Hell would exist because the Omega Point refuses to abandon a human no matter how evil; Hell's existence would be a testimony to the literally infinite love of the Omega Point for His/Her creatures. It is a remarkable theorem of economics—the so-called Rotten Kid Theorem[22]—that in the presence of an altruist ("parent") with sufficient resources to divide between various beneficiaries ("kids"), it is in the self-interest of even a beneficiary who hates the others, who in the absence of the altruist enjoys hurting others, ("rotten kid") to act altruistically toward the others. The Axelrod analysis mentioned above implies that self-interest of the "rotten kid" would be maximized if the "rotten kid's" hate is eventually turned to love. In other words, a self-interest analysis strongly suggests that it should be possible for the Omega Point to convert, for examples, a resurrected Hitler's hatred for the Jews and a resurrected Stalin's hatred for the Kulaks, into love for these people. Since the Rotten Kid Theorem applies to all beneficiaries, it also implies that it should be possible for the Omega Point to persuade a resurrected Jew who perished with his entire family in Auschwitz to forgive Hitler. (Assuming the Omega Point would wish to do this. I personally feel that unforgiveness is justified in this case.)

It is also possible that augmenting the memory, or changing the environment, might constitute a change in the game, with the result that a pure strategy exists in the new game which ensures a win for the Omega Point. This happens for example in tic-tac-toe if the game is extended to three dimensions. Three-dimensional tic-tac-toe is played on a cubical "board," a win being three crosses or noughts along any orthogonal or diagonal row, or along any of the four main diagonals of the cube. The first player has a certain win[23] in three-dimensional tic-tac-toe.

Thus it seems likely that the evil will be purged from the overwhelming majority of human beings, who will enjoy the resurrected life. Such a life could naturally be termed "Heaven." So Heaven and Purgatory are guaranteed to exist, but only the Omega Point in His/Her transcendence knows whether Hell exists. Furthermore—and this is very important—Purgatory (and Hell, if it exists) is to be regarded as a "demi-heaven," for even those in Purgatory will enjoy all the pleasures consistent with the process of eliminating the evil in them.

The redemptive features of the afterlife in the Omega Point theory are similar to those in the theology of Origen, the first great Christian theologian (A.D. 185–254). Origen argued[24] that the pain in Hell was corrective in intent and that no one, not even the devil, was necessarily condemned to Hell forever. Repentance was always open to anyone in Hell. One biblical source for this view of Hell is a sermon preached by Peter, who asserted (Acts 3:21) that Jesus "must be received into heaven until the time of universal restoration." (NEB.) The idea suggested in this passage is that the "restoration" (in Greek, "apocatastasis" [ἀποκατάστάσις]) will be truly universal: the whole of the created order will be renewed, returned to its original good state, and the evil angels, who are also part of the created order, will be included in this renovation of the universe. That God will at least attempt universal salvation is also clearly enunciated in 2 Peter 3:9: ". . . it is not his will for any to be lost, but for all to come to repentance." (NEB.) Inevitably, Origen was condemned (posthumously) as a heretic for defending this idea of potential universal salvation. The doctrine is bad for business: if God is going to try to save everyone even after death, why pay priests for remission of sins? But the idea is a necessary consequence of the central Christian belief that God loves everyone. As the nineteenth-century Pietist theologian Christian Gottlieb Barth put it: "Anyone who does not believe in the universal restoration is an ox, but anyone who teaches it is an ass."[25]

A Description of Life in Heaven

As discussed in Chapter IX, if information is stored in the brain of the resurrection body, there is a limit of 1,000 years of subjective experience, because a brain can only code a mere 10^{15} bits. Even if this limit is overruled by the Omega Point by storing information elsewhere, we run into a more fundamental limit owing to the fact that any living being even roughly similar to a member of our species is formed to have experiences in a rather limited environment: the collection of all environments which now exist in the visible universe. From the human perspective, this collection is extremely large: the environment of the everyday human world, the collection of all biospheres which have ever existed or will exist on the Earth, the center of the Sun, the center of a neutron star, the center of a black hole. Wide as this range of current environments is, nevertheless it is finite, and an immortal human could experience (and recall, if the 1,000-year limit is overruled) them all in far less than a mere $10^{10^{123}}$ years, a blink of an eye to an immortal being. As I pointed out in Chapter IX, enjoying new experiences forever—having a literal infinity of new experiences—will ultimately require being uploaded into the highest level of implementation of life near the Omega Point. I have given reasons above why I expect our resurrected selves to be given eventually the option of such uploading. Since as a consequence of this uploading we should become superhuman, I cannot imagine what life as such a superbeing would be like. So I shall not try to describe such a life. There will be two types of afterlife: a life in a resurrected human body, followed by a literally infinite life as part of the universal mind (for those humans who choose to be uploaded). These two types of afterlife are closely analogous to the two types of afterlife—the messianic age and the world to come—

distinguished by the medieval Jewish rabbis, particularly Maimonides. (I shall discuss the Jewish view in Chapter XI.) Maimonides got into trouble with his contemporary rabbis by concentrating too much on the unimaginable world to come. I shall avoid this by concentrating all my description on the Omega Point equivalent of the messianic age, which is life in a world close to our current world, but without the drawbacks. This is what most people are interested in, anyway. It's enough to know we shall all eventually have the option of the world to come, if and when we want it. It would be appropriate to regard both the present life and the early afterlife as a kindergarten class for the world to come.

My students—mainly young unmarried males—often ask me, "Will there be sex in heaven?" This is a perfectly reasonable question in Islamic eschatology,[26] so I shall consider it. Since the utility of the Omega Point is increased by the increase of utility of the simulated creatures, and since some people desire sex, the answer has to be yes, sex will be available to those who wish it. This consequence of ἀγάπη is in sharp contrast with the picture of Heaven painted by academic theologians, who seem to think that only intellectual pleasures will be permitted people in the afterlife. The sensual pleasures will exist in the afterlife because nonascetic people wish them to, and each individual counts equally. A man like Aquinas who had no interest in sex will not experience it, but people who do desire it will experience it.

However, the problems which sex generates in our present life will not occur in the afterlife. The difficulties which humans currently have in finding a love partner are due to the fact that the sex/marriage market is a barter market, characterized by long search times and high transaction costs.[27] This problem will not exist for the resurrected humans, since the Omega Point can match people: the Omega Point should be able to calculate which among all possible people would be the best mate for a given person, and simulate him in the same environment as her. The Omega Point, not the simulated humans, pays the transaction and information costs. To put it more dramatically (for unmarried males), it would be possible for each male to be matched not merely with the most beautiful woman in the world, not merely with the most beautiful woman who has ever lived, but to be matched with the most beautiful woman whose existence is logically possible. Because of the mutability of the appearance of the resurrection body, it would be easy to ensure that said male is also the most handsome (or desirable) man to this most beautiful woman (provided the man has spent sufficient time in Purgatory to correct personality defects). It is necessary that this requirement be satisfied, since from the viewpoint of the Omega Point the wishes of men and women count equally.

It is instructive to compute the psychological impact of the most beautiful woman on a man (the calculation is the same if we reverse the sexes). According to the Fechner-Weber Law,[28] one of the most well-tested laws of experimental psychology, a response is proportional to the logarithm of the stimulus. That is, the psychological impact on a man of meeting the woman who is to him the most beautiful woman in the world is roughly nine times the impact of meeting any woman in the top 10%, since there are roughly one billion women in the world ($[\log_{10}10^9]/[\log_{10}10] = 9$). To compute a lower bound on the psychological impact of meeting the most beautiful woman whose existence is logically possible, let us suppose that beauty is entirely genetic. I pointed out above that there are about 10^{10^6} genetically distinct possible women. Assuming the validity of the Fechner-Weber Law at large stimulus, the relative psychological impact of meeting the most beautiful of these is thus $[\log_{10}10^{10^6}]/[\log_{10}10^9] = 100,000$ times the impact of meeting the most beautiful woman in the world. Including personality in addition to surface appearance makes the impact even greater, but even without this inclusion the impact is already greater than the human nervous system can stand. (The resurrection body could be modified to stand it.) I've gone through this calculation to illustrate dramatically one crucial point: the principle of nonsatiation[29] will not hold for the resurrected humans. The finiteness of human beings means that their desires are necessarily finite, and hence it is possible for the Omega Point to satisfy them.

For example, about two thirds of adult humans experience at some point in their lives an intense passion for a member of the opposite sex which is not reciprocated: this is the phenomenon of unrequited love.[30] The Omega Point has the power to turn this passion into *requited* love in the afterlife.

Let me illustrate the richness of experience available in the afterlife by analyzing "elbow room." It would be possible for the Omega Point to simulate an entire visible universe for the personal use of each and every resurrected human. ("In my Father's house are many mansions . . ." [John 14:2, KJV].) The required computer capacity is not measurably greater than that required to simulate all possible visible universes. ($10^{10^{123}} \times 10^{10^{45}} \approx 10^{10^{123}}$; remember that exponents *add*, so that $10^{123} + 10^{45} \approx 10^{123}$). Each private visible universe could also be simulated to contain 10^{10} separate planet Earths, each a copy of the present Earth, or the Earth as it was at a different time in the past. (There are about 10^{20} stars in the visible universe, so replacing a mere 10^{10} solar systems in a visible universe would be a minor modification.) This is more Earths than a single human could explore before exhausting his/her memory storage capacity of 10^{15} bits, to say nothing of the memories stored while visiting other humans in *their* private universes. (Once again, the principle of nonsatiation will not apply in the afterlife.)

The literature on Christian speculations about the details of life after death is enormous, so I shall not undertake a detailed comparison of the various Christian pictures with the Omega Point cyberspace Heaven. The best available modern discussion of the Christian speculations is *Heaven: A History* by Colleen McDannell and Bernhard Lang.[31] My overall impression is that, as a general rule, Christians grossly underestimate the pleasures that will be available in Heaven. They greatly underestimate what a Being with literally infinite power can do. The two examples I have given above involving sex and elbow room illustrate what He/She can in fact do.

The early twentieth-century Christian Heaven often pictured the resurrected dead singing praises to God for an eternity. Leaving aside the obvious fact that no omnipotent God—certainly not the Omega Point—would have any interest in such songs, human beings would find such an afterlife excruciatingly *boring*. The American historian Barbara Tuchman pointed out that, when the German army invaded Belgium and France in 1914, the German soldiers would sing patriotic songs as they marched, when they halted the march for a rest, and just before going to sleep after the day's march. Those soldiers who managed to survive the entire war remember the endless singing as the worst torment of the invasion.[32]

The Problem of Evil: An Omega Point Theodicy

If the resurrected life is going to be so wonderful, one might ask why we must go through our current life, this "valley of tears," at all. Why not start life at the resurrection? The answer was given in Chapter VI: our current life is logically necessary; emulations indistinguishable from ourselves *have* to go through it. It is logically impossible for the Omega Point to rescue us. Even omnipotence is limited by logic. This is the natural resolution to the "Problem of Evil." But the sting of evil is removed by the universal resurrection: the Omega Point will as far as logically possible undo the great evils of the past and present in the afterlife.

It is worth expanding on this resolution, because the Problem of Evil has always been the central difficulty faced by monotheistic religions like Christianity, Judaism, and Islam. If God is omnipotent, omniscient, and all good, how is it possible that evil in the universe exists at all? If God is all good, He should wish there to be no evil. However, since He is omniscient, it is not possible that He is unaware of the evil that is in the world, nor is it possible that, when He created the world, He was unaware of the fact that evil would arise as a consequence of the laws of nature which He established. Since He is omnipotent, it seems that He could have created a universe in which the evils of the observed world do not occur. Even worse, His omnipotence and omniscience appear to make Him morally responsible for the evil in the world. Earthquakes and volcanic eruptions occur in inhabited regions of the Earth every few years and kill—often with great suffering—tens of thousands of people. Yet it is God Who sustains in existence the matter and the laws of physics controlling the matter, which make these disasters inevitable. Furthermore, since He is omniscient, He knows that, as a consequence of His sustaining these laws, these particular earthquakes and volcanic eruptions will occur, and He knows when they will occur. Yet He does nothing to stop these disasters, nor does He warn the people who are going to die and suffer. Earthquakes and volcanoes are examples of what are called *natural evils,* those evils which are consequences of inanimate forces. God alone bears responsibility for these evils, in contrast to *moral evils,* such as the Holocaust (in which the Nazis murdered six million Jews), for which human beings share moral responsibility with God. Notice that even in the case of moral evil God bears ultimate responsibility, because He sustains evil humans in existence. Throughout the Holocaust, He sustained in existence the Nazis and their extermination camps, knowing full well what they were doing, and being able to stop the killing if He wished.

This, then, is the Problem of Evil: a God Who is omnipotent, omniscient, and all good appears to be logically inconsistent with the empirical fact that evil exists.

From the very beginning of Christianity, the Problem of Evil was a powerful argument for atheism. The early Christian writer Lucius Lactantius, in his A.D. 313 book *The Anger of God,* attributed the formulation of the Problem of Evil to the Greek atheist philosopher Epicurus, who lived between 341 B.C. and 270 B.C. Lactantius quotes Epicurus as saying (in a work now lost):

> God either wishes to take away evils, and is unable; or He is able, and is unwilling; or He is neither willing nor able, or He is both willing and able. If He is willing and is unable, He is feeble, which is not in accordance with the character of God; if He is able and unwilling, He is envious, which is equally at variance with God; if He is neither willing nor able, He is both envious and feeble, and therefore not God; if He is both willing and able, which alone is suitable to God, from what source then are evils? or why does He not remove them?[33]

In his *Summa Theologica,* a work which can be regarded as the foundation of all Catholic theology since the Middle Ages, St. Thomas Aquinas listed the Problem of Evil as the first of two chief intellectual difficulties preventing a belief in God. (The other reason was the fact that even the physics of the Middle Ages did not need to posit a Personal God; impersonal natural law was sufficient to account for everything observed in nature.) As Aquinas put it:

> It seems that God does not exist; because if one of two contraries be infinite, the other would be altogether destroyed. But the name *God* means that He is infinite goodness. If, therefore, God existed, there would be no evil discoverable; but there is evil in the world. Therefore God does not exist. Further, it is superfluous to suppose that what can be accounted for by a few principles has been produced by many. But it seems that everything we see in the world can be accounted for by other principles, supposing God did not exist. For all natural things can be reduced to one principle, which is nature; and all voluntary things can be reduced to one principle, which is human reason, or will. Therefore there is no need to suppose God's existence.[34]

The main purpose of this book has been to show that modern physics requires the God principle; the purpose of this section is to show that a close analysis of the physics also resolves the Problem of Evil. The usual technical theological term for the study of the Problem of Evil is *theodicy,* from the Greek words θεός (theos) meaning "God" and δίκη (dike), meaning "justice." "A theodicy" is used to denote a particular proposal for solving the Problem of Evil. All theodicies attempt to "justify God's ways to humankind"; they try to show that, in spite of all the evils in the world, God is nevertheless just and good. The word "theodicy" was coined[35] by the German philosopher Leibniz.

The traditional Christian theodicy has been termed the "Augustinian theodicy" by the British theologian John Hick, after St. Augustine, who first developed this explanation for the presence of evil in the world in great detail. According to this view, there was no evil in the universe until the first human beings committed evil acts. All human beings since that time have inherited the tendency to commit evil acts, and so all the evil in the universe is the responsibility of human beings, not God. More generally, responsibility for evil is laid upon other sentient beings (angels) excepting God: even the natural evils are considered the results of evil spirits (devils).

There are two difficulties with this traditional view. The first is simply that science shows that (1) there are no such beings as evil spirits; and (2) the universe was not free from evil before humans evolved: animals suffered and died just as they do now. The second is the fact that such an explanation does not absolve God from responsibility for evil, since He sustains in existence the evil and, by assumption, could eliminate the evil if He chose.

To obviate this latter difficulty, all theodicists claim that, for one reason or the other—the specific reason is what distinguishes the various theodicies from one another—it is *logically impossible* for God to eliminate any of the evil that is observed to occur. This circumstance alone absolves God from responsibility for evil, since even omnipotence cannot do what is logically impossible.

By "logically impossible" is meant "a logically contradictory state of affairs." Such a situation is simply nonsense, because *any* proposition can be deduced from a contradiction. A simple proof of this is as follows. Let P be any proposition, and suppose both A and not-A are true. Now if A is true—and it is, by assumption—it follows that either A or P (exclusive "or") is true. But it is not A (again, by assumption, the other half of the contradiction), therefore P is true. If someone asks you to entertain the idea of a logical contradiction, just reply, "Let P be the proposition 'You do not exist.' This statement is true, since anything can be deduced from a contradiction, and I refuse to have a serious conversation with a nonexistent person!" This dismissal of contradictions from rational discourse is what resolves the schoolboy fallacy against an omnipotent God: "If God is omnipotent, then He can make a stone so heavy that even He cannot lift it. But if He cannot lift it, then He is not omnipotent!" A stone so heavy that an omnipotent being cannot lift it is a logical contradiction; it is simply a meaningless noise, not a stone that might actually exist. God's omnipotence is not limited by humankind's ability to utter nonsense. God's omnipotence just means that He can do anything which is not logically impossible.

Most traditional theodicies claim that God could not have made a better world than the one we actually live in; this world that God decided to actualize is the best of all possible worlds. This claim is greeted with hoots of derision from skeptics. They point out that we humans have ourselves made the world a better place to live. We have, for example, eliminated many diseases. Why could not an omnipotent God have done this earlier? Theodicists argue[36] that evil is logically necessary in order to have either (1) free will or (2) a universe in which hardy souls are forged (without evil to test one's mettle, only a flabby soul would result). Even granted this logical necessity, reply the skeptics, why such a large amount of evil? For it is not enough to show that evil is logically necessary, one must also show that the actual amount of evil in the world is logically necessary. Would the world be logically impossible if just one baby suffered just one minute less from the flu? Or if one less person died in the Holocaust? Are all those Jewish souls really better off for being gassed?

Notice that both the traditional theodicists and the skeptics assume that only one world out of many possible worlds is actualized. But quantum mechanics provides empirical evidence that more than one world exists, as I pointed out in Chapter V and in the Scientific Appendix on the Many-Worlds Interpretation. Furthermore, I have argued in Chapter VIII that *all* worlds which lead to the Omega Point are actualized by logical necessity. Since that baby suffered as long as it did, and since six million Jews died in the Holocaust, it is logically possible for the baby to suffer as long as it did and it is logically possible for six million Jews to have died in the Holocaust. Thus, assuming our universe can end in the Omega Point, these terrible evils *must* occur in some history, by logical necessity. Conversely, since these evils presumably are not logically necessary in all histories, there are actually existing histories of the universe in which they do not occur. There are thus some histories (one hopes most) in which the Holocaust did not occur.

The Omega Point is absolved of moral responsibility for evils, both natural and moral, because it is logically impossible for Him/Her to eliminate any evils at all from the totality of histories that actually exist. Not even an omnipotent being can be blamed for failing to accomplish a logical impossibility. Because in other theodicies God has an arbitrary choice in actualizing worlds, He is still morally responsible for the evils in the worlds. The skeptics point this out with glee, and even the theologian John Hick admits: "[All theodicies] acknowledge explicitly or implicitly God's ultimate responsibility for the existence of evil."[37] In particular, the theodicies of both Augustine and Calvin see the fall of both humans and angels into evil as predestined by God. Thus the Omega Point theodicy is the first theodicy to successfully absolve God of moral responsibility for evil. All previous theodicies have overestimated what omnipotence can do, because they have underestimated what omnipotence has done.

Notice however that the preceding remarks about the logical impossibility of removing any evil whatsoever applies to the Omega Point only in His/Her *transcendence,* since it assumes that we are considering all the histories as a whole. The logically necessary histories collectively comprising the whole of reality can be regarded as "emanating" from the Omega Point in His/Her transcendence. This "emanation" is, as I pointed out in Chapter VIII, quite analogous to the way in which the Demiurge of Platonic philosophy generates reality; the chief difference being that here the chain of being is generated backward in time from the ultimate future rather than being generated in space. We have a dynamic cosmology rather than a static one. The Omega Point in His/Her transcendence thus has no "freedom" to choose what sort of world to create. Nevertheless, the Omega Point in His/Her *immanence* does have the freedom to create whatever universe He/She pleases, and in fact does so freely create a universe (generate a history), the mechanism being described in Chapter VII (the Omega Point Boundary Condition). There is no inconsistency between freedom and necessity, because "freedom" is a concept that applies only to a living being in time. It does not apply to the Omega Point in His/Her transcendence, because the transcendent Omega Point is not in time. The transcendent Omega Point is the final end of all histories, the ultimate future boundary of all histories of space and time.

In spite of lacking any moral responsibility for evil, the Omega Point can—and will—mitigate the evils which we must suffer here and now by granting us a happy afterlife. This boon *is* within the power of omnipotence, though the total elimination of all evil is not. Since the afterlife will go on forever, the good which we shall receive in the afterlife will be quite literally infinitely greater than the finite evils which we have endured in this life. (An upper bound to the number of evils the collectivity of all living beings—plant, animal, and human—

here on Earth could possibly experience in this life is given by the number of possible states the visible universe could be in, namely $10^{10^{123}}$, a number which I have discussed before. The actual number of evils is of course far less.)

A theodicy in which the focus is on the infinite good to come in the future rather than the finite evils of the past and present is called an *Irenaean theodicy* by John Hick, after Irenaeus (A.D. 130–202), Bishop of Lyons. There are hints of this type of solution to the Problem of Evil in Christianity from the very beginning. I have already mentioned Peter's sermon recorded in Acts, where he speaks of the future universal restoration, when God will be all in all. In *Summa Theologica*, Aquinas claimed, "God allows evils to happen in order to bring a greater good therefrom."[38] In his book *Enchiridion*, Augustine explicitly stated, "God judged it better to bring good out of evil than not to permit any evil to exist."[39] But my own favorite expression of this idea in Christianity is by the first great *female* theologian, Mother Julian of Norwich, who lived from 1342 to (about) 1416, and who expressed her theological insights as revelations. When she wondered why "the beginning of sin was not prevented by the great foreseeing wisdom of God" she heard the voice of Jesus say to her, "Sin must needs be, but all shall be well. All shall be well; and all manner of thing shall be well."[40]

Mother Julian has nicely summarized the Omega Point theodicy.

Social Immortality, Personal Immortality, and Eternal Progress Are Identical

I have shown in Chapter IV and in the Appendix for Scientists that the information coded in the universe diverges as the universe approaches the Omega Point. Furthermore, the information stored diverges to infinity in finite proper time, so the growth is *faster* than exponential growth—at least in proper time.

However, in the early phases of the expansion the information storage will be limited to the volume of a sphere centered at the Earth (or the surface of this sphere, if life in the center uses up its material resources too fast—before the gravitational shear energy kicks in—and dies out). This would imply[41] that the information stored is growing as the square of the proper time if the universal temperature is approximately constant. This means that, before life engulfs the universe, it will see a growth rate which is less than exponential (power law growth), as measured in proper time.

But as I have repeatedly argued, proper time is not the appropriate timescale for life. The true time for life is *subjective* time, defined to be the time required to store irreversibly one bit of information; that is, the rate of growth of information in subjective time is unity by definition. Subjective time will be a good universal time variable only if it is monotone increasing function of proper time at every instant. I have not shown this; I have just shown that the information stored diverges to infinity. However, this divergence to infinity means that there is a suitable *average* over proper time of the information stored, such that this average is monotone increasing to infinity, and furthermore, except between the epoch when life has engulfed half the spatial universe and the time of maximum expansion, the information stored *will* be monotone increasing. (The reason why the information might not be monotone increasing between the time when life has engulfed half the spatial universe and the time of maximum expansion is that, in this period, the comoving radius of the sphere where life is located is *decreasing* in size since life is moving toward the antipodal point of the 3-sphere of the spatial universe. Furthermore, in this epoch the universal expansion cannot be ignored, and quite possibly the mass-energy available for life may decrease. It is possible that the information stored may nevertheless be monotone increasing even in this time period because it is possible that the universe may move to a channel run in this period, thereby providing shear energy. But I can't prove this.)

I now show that a monotone increase of the information stored, with this information diverging to infinity as the universe moves into the Omega Point, implies that the total *wealth* possessed by the biosphere as a whole increases *exponentially* in subjective time literally forever; that is, not only does total wealth diverge, but it diverges exponentially.

The Austrian economist Friedrich Hayek (Nobel prize 1972) has argued that the capital stock of a society is equal to the total number of possible uses the machines possessed by the society actually have. As Hayek phrased it:

> The datum usually called the "supply of capital" can thus be adequately described only in terms of the totality of all the alternative income streams between which the existence of a certain stock of non-permanent resources (together with the expected flow of input) enables us to choose. . . . Each of the constituent parts of this stock can be used in various ways, and in various combinations with other permanent and nonpermanent resources, to provide temporary income streams. . . . What we sacrifice in order to obtain an income stream of a particular shape is always the parts of the potential income streams of other time shapes which we might have had instead.[42] [Thus] . . . the only adequate description of th[e] "supply of capital" is a complete enumeration of the range of possible output streams of different time shapes that can be produced from the existing resources.[43]

More generally, the wealth possessed by an individual or the wealth possessed by the society is proportional to the number of opportunities it has; to the number of different alternative actions he, she, or it has available. We inhabitants of the First World nations are wealthier than our ancestors because (for example) most of us can afford to have fresh strawberries for breakfast on any day of the year. Eating fresh strawberries on any day of the year was not an alternative action possessed by many of our ancestors a thousand years ago. Many of our ancestors lived in regions of the Earth where strawberries did not exist, and in the regions where strawberries were grown, they were not available in the winter to anyone except perhaps for a very, very few people who had the produce of greenhouses available to them. I am currently writing these lines in Florida, United States of America, and if I wished, I could be in Vienna, Austria, tomorrow. The alternative action of going from North America to Europe (or vice versa) in less than twenty-four hours was not available to *any* of my ancestors a century ago.

By definition, the number of possible arrangements which can be coded by I bits of information is 2^I. Following Hayek and equating total wealth with the number of possible arrangements, we get 2^I for wealth of society, so the wealth grows as $2^{(\text{subjective time})}$. This is exponential growth. Since subjective time goes from zero to plus infinity, this means that wealth increases exponentially forever in subjective time.[44]

We see that proving wealth can grow exponentially forever in subjective time required three facts. First, we had to know that the wealth and information were exponentially related; second, we had to show that information stored could diverge to plus infinity as the Omega Point is approached; and third, we had to show that not only did the stored information diverge to infinity, but that the increase was monotone. Only the third might not necessarily hold, but nevertheless the increase is monotone if a suitable time average of the information stored is taken.

This exponentially increasing wealth allows life in the far future the power to resurrect us all and, furthermore, allows the Omega Point to share wealth in such a way that our share is an ever decreasing percentage of the whole, yet nevertheless our share also diverges to plus infinity.

Any cosmology with progress to infinity will necessarily end in God. Further, the hope of eternal worldly progress and the hope of individual survival beyond the grave turn out to be the same. Far from being polar opposites, these two hopes require each other; one cannot have one without the other. The Omega Point is truly the God of Hope: "O death, where is thy sting? O grave, where is thy victory?" (I Corinthians 15:55 KJV.)

XI.

COMPARISON OF THE HEAVEN PREDICTED BY MODERN PHYSICS WITH THE AFTERLIFE HOPED FOR BY THE GREAT WORLD RELIGIONS

I SHALL SHOW BY AN ANALYSIS OF THE picture of afterlife according to the great world religions—Taoism, Early Hinduism, Judaism, Christianity, and Islam—that, in essence, the afterlife predicted by modern physics is the same as that hoped for in the world's religions. I shall point out that, by and large, all of the above-mentioned religions viewed the afterlife as a sort of resurrection of the dead rather than an immortality of an immaterial soul. There is even some indication that this picture of an afterlife is the same in *all* human religions. I shall attempt to demonstrate this by briefly discussing the nature of the afterlife according to some Africans and according to some inhabitants of Pre-Columbian America. I shall also outline some opinions about the Buddhist afterlife, though it is not clear whether "afterlife" is an appropriate phrase to use in discussing Buddhist thought.

·———·

Immortality in the Major Non-Western Religions

THE AFTERLIFE IN TAOISM

From its inception the religious philosophy indigenous to China, Taoism, espoused the idea of individual immortality. One of the goals of the Taoist sage was to become a *hsien,* an immortal, a being who would live forever in a sensual, very material paradise. As Needham describes it:

> [The Taoist prepared himself] for a further life, after "death," equally material but subtler and purer, holy and beautiful yet comprising all the pleasurable forms of experience which man can have in his present life and freed from the anxieties of disease, old age, and dissolution. The *hsien* would be able, it was thought, to revisit the ordinary world more or less at will, but their own world would be much more desirable.[1]

The world of the *hsien* was described at length in numerous books, for instance the Taoist classic *Lieh Tzu,* parts of which date from the Warring States period (fifth to third century B.C.). Many other books on the lives of famous *hsien* were written[2] over the period A.D. 175–1700. The *hsien* were often drawn in the form of feathered men during the Han period (206 B.C. to A.D. 220), an expression of the idea that the bodies of the *hsien* were "spiritual" bodies, and hence capable of flight. The Immortal body was not human but superhuman. In one procedure, the body of an Immortal had to be created over the course of a lifetime by certain practices (detailed in Taoist manuals). The final stage was the formation, by special magical rites, of a simulated corpse to appear in the coffin of the Taoist adept. This was termed[3] "deliverance of the corpse" or "transformation of the *hun*-soul." It was also thought[4] possible to convert a mortal body into an Immortal body by taking a "Golden Elixir." Much of the Chinese alchemists' work was devoted to the search for this Golden Elixir. Many Chinese emperors supported this research, and a few emperors died as a result of taking a supposed Golden Elixir.[5]

In either case, the process of transforming an ordinary human body into the body of an Immortal was viewed as akin to insect metamorphosis. The Taoist goal of an embodied form of immortality was due to their conception of a human being as an animated body rather than an incarnated soul; they did not believe an individual personality could exist without some sort of body.[6] This early Taoist view was later encoded in Chinese law. The *ling ch'ih,* an execution in which the executioner slowly slices the victim's body to pieces, was considered the most severe form of the death penalty, not only because of the pain inflicted, but also because such a thoroughly mutilated body meant the victim could not have an afterlife. Strangulation was considered the mildest death penalty, milder than decapitation, though the latter is less painful, because the former does not mutilate the body at all, and so would not impair the afterlife.[7]

The intellectual opponents of the Taoists, the Confucians, agreed with the idea that a personality required a body, but they concluded from this fact that spirits, ghosts, and *hsien* could not exist. For example, one of the greatest Confucian scholars, Wang Ch'ung (A.D. 27–97; later Han dynasty) argued in his most famous work, *Lun Heng* ("Discourses Weighed in the Balance"), that life is a crystalline pattern in matter, as ice is crystallized water. "The ice, melting, returns to water, and man, dying, returns to the state of a spirit. It is called spirit just as melted ice resumes the name of water. When we have a man before us we use a different name. Hence there are no proofs that the dead possess consciousness, or that they can take a form and injure people."[8] Spirits cannot have a material form; in a material sense they cannot exist.[9] In the same work Wang Ch'ung argues that attempts to make oneself a *hsien* and avoid dying must fail as surely as ice must melt.[10] In A.D. 484 a later Confucian, Fan Chen, contended in an essay entitled *Shen Mieh Lun* ("On the Destructibility of the Soul") that "The spirit is to the body what the sharpness is to the knife. We have never heard that after the knife has been destroyed the sharpness can persist."[11] More than seventy refutations of Fan Chen's essay were written, of which I think the most interesting was that of Shen Yo, who pointed out that the material which went to make up the knife can be recast in the form of a dagger of a quite different shape, but with the same sharpness.[12] In other words, if the essence of the pattern is recreated, the person is truly resurrected. So the resurrection model in the Omega Point Theory is natural to the Chinese tradition.

IMMORTALITY IN EARLY HINDUISM

The idea of reincarnation, which is based on a strict dualism between body and soul, is central to modern Hinduism (and Buddhism). But reincarnation, and the dualism upon which it is based, is actually a rather recent development in Indian thought. It apparently arose around 600 B.C. and spread rapidly, becoming universally accepted within a century. Earlier Indian religion assumed a unity between soul and body, and in this earlier religion, the afterlife was characterized by a resurrection of a united body and soul in an earthly paradise. Descriptions of this paradise abound in the *Rig Veda*, the earliest (essentially complete by 1000 B.C., but compiled over a period of several centuries) now existing work of Indian (indeed, Indo-European) literature. For example, Book 9, Hymn 113, of the *Rig Veda* ends with the words:

O Pavamana, place me in that deathless, undecaying world
Wherein the light of heaven is set, and everlasting luster shines. . . .

Make me immortal in that realm where dwells the King, Vivasvan's son,
Where is the secret shrine of heaven, where are those waters young and fresh. . . .

Make me immortal in that realm where they move even as they list,
In the third sphere of inmost heaven where lucid worlds are full of light. . . .

Make me immortal in that realm of eager wish and strong desire,
The region of the radiant Moon, where food and full delight are found. . . .

Make me immortal in that realm where happiness and transports, where
Joys and felicities combine, and longing wishes are fulfilled. . . .[13]

Vivasvan's son is Yama, the first human being, deified as God of the Dead, who is the pathbreaker into paradise for subsequent humankind, as the excerpts from the following funeral address, Hymn 14 of the *Rig Veda*'s Book 10, make clear:

Yama first found for us a place to dwell in: this pasture never can be taken from us.

Men born on Earth tread their own paths that lead them whither our ancient Fathers have departed. . . .

Exalters of the Gods, by the Gods exalted, some joy in praise, and some in our oblation.

Go forth, go forth upon the ancient pathways whereon our sires of old have gone before us.

There shalt thou look on both the Kings enjoying their sacred food, God Varuna and Yama.
Meet Yama, meet the Fathers, meet the merit of free or ordered acts, in highest heaven.

Leave sin and evil, seek anew thy dwelling, and bright with glory wear another body.

Go hence, depart ye, fly in all directions: this place for him the Fathers have provided.
Yama bestows on him a place to rest in, adorned with days and beams of light and waters. . . .[14]

Of particular interest is the implication, in the last verse but one, that we shall have a different body in paradise, a body which, though immortal and immune to disease, is nevertheless able to experience the pleasures enjoyed by the present body. The Paradise of the *Rig Veda* is the present world without its trials. Thus the afterlife of the *Rig Veda* is completely consistent with the afterlife and the resurrection bodies therein of the Omega Point Theory. The later Hindu and Buddhist world views are inconsistent with the afterlife model in the Omega

Point Theory, since these world views are based on the dualism of body and soul, and have reincarnation back into the present world. Mahatma Gandhi, the most famous Hindu of the twentieth century, asserted[15] that both immortality of the soul and reincarnation are essential beliefs in the modern Hindu religion. However, it might be that Gandhi just did not think hard enough about the distinction between resurrection of the body and immortality of the soul. Certainly the Christianity of his day confused the two, and certainly the Hindu tradition has both. The Hindu tradition also has both One God and many gods, and Gandhi did clear up the confusion between these two ideas. In Gandhi's opinion, "Belief in one God is the corner-stone of all religions,"[16] and furthermore

> I dispute the description that Hindus believe in many gods. . . . They do say there are many gods, but they also declare unmistakably that there is one God, God of gods. . . . The whole mischief is created by the English rendering of the word *deva* . . . for which you have not found a better term than "god." But God is *Ishwara, Devadhideva,* God of gods. I believe that I am a thorough Hindu, but I never believed in many Gods. Never even in my childhood did I hold that belief, and no one ever taught me to do so.[17] . . . There are many gods in the *Vedas.* Other scriptures call them angels. But the *Vedas* sing of only one God.[18]

So I should have said above that Yama, the first human being, was "angelized" to become the Angel of the Dead. If the Omega Point Theory is true, then our souls are not immortal, we shall never be reincarnated, but nevertheless we shall be resurrected and "angelized" by the life of the far future (should I call them "angels" also?) and together we shall approach the Omega Point. But we can never *be* the Omega Point; this is a logical impossibility. Perhaps Gandhi would have found this picture consistent with Hinduism.

IS THERE IMMORTALITY IN BUDDHISM?

Although Buddhism accepts the idea of reincarnation, there is an ongoing debate among scholars of Buddhism (both Western and Asian) concerning whether Buddhism has an analogue of the Christian Heaven. The goal of the Buddhist definitely is to attain "Nirvana"; but experts differ on whether "Nirvana" corresponds to "Heaven."

There is no doubt that "Nirvana" means an escape from the cycles of reincarnation, an escape from the endless cycles of rebirth into other living beings after death. The undeniable goal of Buddhism was to escape the Eternal Return. But one could escape by becoming extinct, by ceasing to exist, or one could escape by entering an abode of happiness, by going to Heaven. The word "nirvana" literally means[19] "extinction" or "blowing out" as in "blowing out a candle." This literal meaning doesn't sound very encouraging for the Nirvana = Heaven interpretation.

One of the earliest surviving Buddhist texts, the Pali Canon of Sri Lanka, definitely applies the word "immortal" to describe the state of a person who has reached Nirvana.[20] However, there are also passages in the Pali Canon in which the Buddha replied with silence to questions about the state of a person after death.[21]

The Russian Theodosius Stcherbatsky, professor of Buddhism at the University of Leningrad in the first half of the twentieth century, was the leading proponent of the "extinction" interpretation. Stcherbatsky argued that the word "immortal," applied to Nirvana, merely meant that Nirvana was changeless, deathless—and lifeless. In Nirvana, there was no repeated death, nor was there repeated birth. He pointed out that there are Paradises analogous to Heaven in Buddhism, which one can enter by being reincarnated into them from the everyday world. But to avoid repeated death one must disappear forever in Nirvana by becoming nonexistent.[22] Stcherbatsky also emphasized that there were later Hindu systems in which the goal was definitely nonexistence, and in these systems the goal was also termed a "place of immortality," meaning that when the goal is attained there will no longer be death—i.e., no more repeated death. In these systems, "immortality" does not mean "eternal life." Stcherbatsky acknowledged[23] that only a few schools of Buddhism remained faithful to the "ideal of a lifeless Nirvana and an extinct Buddha." By the first century A.D., Nirvana in many Buddhist schools had taken on many features of the Christian Heaven.

De la Vallée Pousin, professor of religion at the University of Liège in the early part of this century, was the leading twentieth-century proponent of the "Heaven" interpretation. He argued that the Buddha's silence on the question of life after death meant that the Buddha was an agnostic on the question of life after escaping the cycle of birth and death: he simply did not know whether Nirvana corresponded to eternal life in Heaven, or whether it corresponded to extinction. According to de la Vallée Pousin, most later Buddhists (but not all) accepted the equation Nirvana = Heaven.

The Hindu Mahatma Gandhi agreed with de la Vallée Pousin, and ridiculed the idea that Nirvana is extinction:

> *Nirvana* is undoubtedly not utter extinction. So far as I have been able to understand the central fact of Buddha's life, *Nirvana* is utter extinction of all that is base in us, all that is vicious in us, all that is corrupt and corruptible in us. *Nirvana* is not like the black, dead peace of the grave, but the living peace, the living happiness of a soul which is conscious of itself, and conscious of having found its own abode in the heart of the Eternal.[24]

The "extinction" interpretation is unquestionably inconsistent with the resurrection model of the Omega Point Theory. However, if the Buddha was indeed an agnostic on the question of life after death, then his views could be perfectly compatible with resurrection to eternal life, and hence with the Omega Point Theory. I've noticed that in discussions with Americans of various religious beliefs, American Buddhists seem to be the most enthusiastic about the resurrection theory which I have developed in this book.

The Rev. Dr. Walpola Rahula is a Buddhist monk from Sri Lanka who, in addition to holding eminent positions in Buddhist monastic institutes on that island, also has a Western Ph.D. in philosophy and has been a professor of Buddhism at various American universities (he is the first Buddhist monk to be an American professor). Unfortunately, he's not very helpful on the nature of Nirvana:

Now you will ask: But what is Nirvana? Volumes have been written in reply to this quite natural and simple question; they have, more and more, only confused the issue rather than clarified it. The only reasonable reply to give to the question is that it can never be answered completely and satisfactorily in words, because human language is too poor to express the real nature of the Absolute Truth or Ultimate Reality which is Nirvana.[25] . . . Nirvana is beyond all terms of duality and relativity. It is therefore beyond our conceptions of good and evil, right and wrong, existence and non-existence. Even the word "happiness", which is used to describe Nirvana has an entirely different sense here. Sariputta once said "O friend, Nirvana is happiness!" Then Udayi asked: "But friend Sariputta, what happiness can it be if there is no sensation?" Sariputta's reply was highly philosophical and beyond ordinary comprehension: "That there is no sensation itself is happiness."[26]

I think, however, that Udayi's question is very much to the point. "Happiness" is a state which applies only to living beings, and to be alive means having sensations, and hence undergoing changes of state. It means having bodies of some sort. Sariputta's reply was perfectly within ordinary comprehension: he meant that Nirvana is total extinction, but he didn't want to say it. By playing word games, he hoped to convince both Udayi and himself that total death is not really total death.

There are two main divisions of Buddhism, Theravada (sometimes called Hinayana) and Mahayana,[27] just as there are three main divisions of Christianity: Roman Catholic, Protestant, and Orthodox. The extinction interpretation is far more common in Theravada than in Mahayana (Rahula is a Theravadian). According to Mahayana Buddhism, there are many Buddhas, and these attempt to save the rest of us. Two Japanese sects of Mahayana Buddhism, the Jodo and the Shin, hold that the Buddha Amida brought into existence a Blissful Realm to which all who call upon his name will go after death.[28] A majority of Japanese today believe[29] that by chanting *"Namu Amida Butsu (Homage to Amida Buddha)"* they will be reborn into this Pure Land of Perfect Bliss. If the Omega Point Theory is correct, then both the Jodo and Shin sects (and a majority of Japanese) are correct that (1) Heaven exists, (2) it must be brought into existence by a Person far more powerful than any human being, and (3) rebirth or resurrection into Heaven cannot be achieved by any human effort: Heaven must be given to us by the Person that brought Heaven into existence in the first place. Finally, the imagery of the Pure Land of Perfect Bliss seems to involve embodied human beings. In summary, the Blissful Realm of Japanese Buddhism seems completely consistent with the Heaven predicted by the Omega Point Theory.

Buddhism is sometimes called an atheistic religion. Gandhi strongly disagreed with this characterization:

> I have heard it contended times without number, and I have read in books . . . that Buddha did not believe in God. In my humble opinion, such a belief contradicts the very central fact of Buddha's teaching. . . . He undoubtedly rejected the notion that a being called God was actuated by malice, could repent of his actions, and like the kings of the Earth, could possibly be open to temptations and bribes and could possibly have favorites. He, therefore, reinstated God in the right place and dethroned the usurper who for the time being seemed to occupy that White Throne. He emphasized and re-declared the eternal and unalterable existence of the moral government of this Universe. He unhesitatingly said that the Law was God Himself.[30]

This last line of Gandhi's is strongly suggestive of the Omega Point Boundary Condition, which asserts that the laws governing the universe arise from the requirement that life evolve into the Omega Point or, equivalently, that the Omega Point is the collection of all universal histories that are guided into the Omega Point, this collection considered as a unity.

SOME AFRICAN VIEWS OF GOD AND IMMORTALITY

Africans take religion *very* seriously. It has been said[31] that in Africa people talk about philosophy and religion as Americans and Europeans talk about football. A Harvard professor of religion recently visited Ghana and was bombarded with theological questions from clerks at the airport who were reading the Bible under their desks.[32] So it is not surprising that Africans have developed a quite sophisticated theology. The idea of God as a collection of words—or, in my terminology, an abstract computer program—which lives and guides the universe can be found in a traditional Pigmy hymn:

> *In the beginning was God,*
> *Today is God,*
> *Tomorrow will be God.*
> *Who can make an image of God?*
> *He had no body.*
> *He is as a word which comes out of your mouth.*
> *That word! It is no more,*
> *It is past, and still it lives!*
> *So is God.*[33]

In the opinion of the African scholar John S. Mbiti, "Without exception, African peoples believe that death does not annihilate life and that the departed continue to exist in the hereafter."[34] A similar remark is made by the famous expert in African religion, Geoffrey Parrinder.[35] There is, however, a wide difference of opinion as to the nature of the afterlife. A majority of Africans do not regard the afterlife as a place where one receives a reward or punishment for acts in the current life. With few exceptions, Africans think that God punishes evildoers only in this life, not in the next: punishments such as illness, bad luck, and crop failure are thought to be quite sufficient for the evil committed in the present life.[36] The Bachwa people of the Congo believe that upon death they travel to the City of God where they live happily without suffering hardships like hunger, thirst, sickness, or death, and there is plenty of game for hunting.[37] The Lozi people of Zambia wear tribal marks so that they will be recognized and placed with their relatives in the afterlife, with whom they will live happily. In both cases, this happiness is not to be thought of as a reward for good behavior in this life, just the nature of the afterlife.[38] Also in both cases, there are similarities and differences between the afterlife and the present life: people in the afterlife have many of the same enjoyments that they have in this life, but the bad experiences are left out.

According to the Lodagaa people of Ghana and Upper Volta, a person becomes a ghost at the instant of death and lingers around the old homestead. Eventually, the ghost becomes a spirit and travels to the land of the afterlife, where older spirits subject the newly arrived spirit to various hardships, the severity depending on the spirit's behavior before death. But all are eventually "set free" by God, and begin to enjoy the afterlife.[39]

The Yoruba of Nigeria believe that after death people go to *Ehin-Iwa,* the "afterlife." They have two sayings which emphasize that the afterlife is more important than the present life, and that one's enjoyment of the afterlife depends on correct behavior in the present life: *"Ehin-Iwa ti 's' egbon oni* (The afterlife is the superior of today)" and *"Nitori Ehin-Iwa l' a se nse oni l' ore* (It is because of the afterlife that we treat today hospitably)." It is common to hear the aged Yoruba saying[40] "I am going Home" or "I am ready for Home." If an aged person is heard talking to himself or herself, it is assumed that he or she is talking to dead friends or relatives. This is a common feature of the afterlife in most African religions: the dead linger a bit among the living before permanently going to the abode of the dead. When the newly dead person reaches *Ehin-Iwa,* he or she will face the judgment of Olodumere, the Supreme God. The good person will be given a place in the good *Orun* (Heaven), where Olodumere and the ancestors dwell, and the evildoer will be consigned to the *Orun* of potsherds. The Yoruba, in contrast to most Africans, believe that the evildoers suffer endless torment in their *Orun*—possibly this belief arose out of the Yoruba contact with Islam. In the good *Orun* life is pictured as an improved version of this life: all the usual earthly enjoyments minus the earthly sorrows. In particular, one of the most important benefits of the afterlife is that, in the good *Orun,* the Yoruba will be united with his or her dead relatives and friends.[41]

In summary, the afterlife predicted by the Omega Point Theory is quite consistent with the afterlife expected in most African societies. The afterlife is similar to this life, except that the goods we enjoy today are magnified, and the negative aspects of the present life are absent. In particular, the dead in the African afterlife are as "embodied" as the dead in the other religious traditions, although there is no indication that the afterlife bodies are identical to the bodies the dead persons had when alive. The one major difference is that, in the Omega Point Theory, the dead are not with the living at any time after death until the Universal Resurrection. In the Omega Point Theory, when you're dead, you're dead—until the Omega Point raises you up.

.———.

Heaven in Pre-Columbian America

The Native Americans also held to the universal human belief that there was life after death. Among the Aztecs, what one could expect in the afterlife was determined by one's social class and the circumstances of one's death. In none of the surviving Aztec works is there any mention of punishment for evil acts committed during this life. Unfortunately, the death realm to which the average Aztec was sent, Mictlan, was extremely unpleasant. It was ruled by Mictlantecuhtli, a terrible skeleton surrounded by bats and spiders, and his consort Mictecacihuatl. Mictlan was underground and getting there took four years, as one had first to pass through nine subterranean universes. One was lucky to die from drowning, being struck by lightning, or from leprosy, in which case one ended up in Tlalocan, where one enjoyed a happy existence, and where there was an unlimited supply of beans, corn, and fruit. There is a temple painting in the ancient Aztec city of Teotihuacan which pictures the dead as dancing, singing, and swimming in Tlalocan with its rivers, lakes, and cacao trees.

The warriors who fell in combat and prisoners of the Aztecs who were sacrificed to the Sun God went to the House of the Sun, where they enjoyed the fragrance of wonderful flowers, and where they fought mock combats with each other. Women who died in childbirth were sent to another House of the Sun, the Corn House, also a pleasant place to live.[42]

Our knowledge of the Mayan concept of the afterlife comes primarily from the *Popol Vuh,* the sacred book of the Kavek dynasty which ruled the Quiché Maya at the time of the Spanish conquest of Mesoamerica. This book is the story of the trip which the Hero

Twins, Hunahpu and Xbalanque, took to the underworld. The two brothers play a series of games with the Lords of Death, games in which the brothers are often killed but later restored to life. In the final game, the Hero Twins cut each other to pieces and then bring each other back to life. The First and Seventh Lords of Death are amazed at this feat, and demand that it be performed on them. The Hero Twins do so, and thus destroy the First and Seventh Lords of Death Forever. Having thus triumphed over Death, Hunahpu and Xbalanque rise out of the underworld and become the Sun and Moon.[43]

Parts of the Hero Twins story have been found on a huge number of pictorial ceramics recovered in the Mayan region, suggesting that the myth was an allegory of what the average Mayan could expect to experience in the afterlife.[44] The Mesoamerican scholar Michael Coe opines[45] that the story indicates a general belief that the fate of at least the Maya nobility was not extinction but rather transformation into heavenly bodies analogous to the transformation of the Hero Twins into the Sun and Moon.

The ethnographer Johannes Wilbert has lived among the Warao people of Venezuela and has described in detail their eschatology.[46] All Warao regard this present life as nothing but a means to ensure that they will enjoy immortality in the Heaven of their choice. Upon death, a Warao is buried in a dugout canoe called the Vagina of Dauarani, the Forest Goddess. The symbolism is that of returning to the womb to be reborn in the afterlife. During their lives, Warao shamans travel the roads to their chosen Heavens in trances and in dreams. This gives them familiarity with the dangers of the trip and assures them that they will survive the journey after their death. At death, the soul of the shaman who has served in life the North God, say, will travel north to the mountain of the North God. Upon arrival, the shaman will be given beautiful clothing and a residence which is golden like that of the North God Himself. The residence is located in a garden of wonderful white flowers, and the shaman enjoys an eternal life of peace and rest in the company of this God and his fellow shamans. There are analogous pleasant Heavens for the common man and woman—except those who are sacrificed as food for the Gods of the underworld. These poor individuals are completely destroyed, body and soul.

There is also a universal belief in an afterlife among the native inhabitants of North America.[47] The Land of the Dead is the ultimate goal of all human spirits and, as usual, the descriptions of this Land are copies of the lands in which the storytellers dwell, with all the bad aspects omitted. The Native Americans of the Western plains—who were mainly hunters—saw their afterlife as being the "Happy Hunting Grounds": the dead live on a rolling prairie, with plenty of buffalo to catch and feast upon. East of the Mississippi—where the pre-Columbian peoples were mainly agriculturalists—the afterlife is pictured as being a world with limitless maize and perpetual harvest festivals.

If the Omega Point Theory is true, the hopes of the Native Americans will be fulfilled. The dead in the Native American afterlife are once again embodied, not insubstantial spirits—at least in the Land of the Dead, because only beings which have bodies similar to the bodies of the living could enjoy hunting, feasting, and dancing. The Meso- and South Americans are incorrect in two respects, however. The common people will enjoy the afterlife as much as the aristocrat, and no one will suffer in the afterlife.

Life After Death in the Judeo-Christian-Islamic Tradition

The picture of the afterlife which will be most familiar to my readers is that which comes from the Judeo-Christian-Islamic tradition. I say this because a majority of the human beings who are alive today are either Jews, Christians, or Muslims. As of the early 1980s, the percentages[48] of the human race who were at least nominal members of each of the major faiths were:

Christians	32.4 percent
Muslims	17.1 percent
Jews	0.4 percent

Hindus   13.5 percent
Buddhists   6.2 percent

So a decade ago, Jews, Christians, and Muslims made up 49.9 percent of humanity. Over the past decade, Africans have been converting to Christianity and Islam at a very rapid rate, and the birth rate of Muslims and Christians in the southern hemisphere (where, as of 1980, most Christians now live) is at least as high as the birth rate of the humans outside the tradition, so a majority of humans are now within the Judeo-Christian-Islamic tradition. Hence, I shall devote most of my space to the view of the afterlife in this tradition.

THE MESSIANIC AGE AND THE WORLD TO COME IN JUDAISM

In the Jewish tradition, the idea of any sort of immortality is rather recent.[49] The earliest clear description of immortality is in a passage in the book of Daniel, written about the time of the Maccabean War (165–160 B.C.):

And many of those who sleep in the dust of the earth shall awake, some to everlasting life, and some to shame and everlasting contempt. (Daniel 12:2 RSV.)

The mechanism of immortality in this passage is clearly resurrection of the body by direct act of God. In the Damascus Document, one of the famous Dead Sea Scrolls found in caves around the Dead Sea just after the Second World War, one finds the claim that God or His Messiah will ". . . resurrect the dead . . . keeping faith with those asleep in the dust. . . ."[50] This manuscript dates from the first century A.D., and here again the mechanism of immortality is undoubtedly resurrection of the body.

Yet there was no unitary Jewish view of immortality at this period;[51] indeed there was even a fierce debate among Jews on whether immortality could be expected. As readers of the New Testament are aware, the Pharisees defended immortality in the form of resurrection, while the Sadducees denied both. The Sadducees rejected the idea of immortality on the grounds that it was not mentioned in the early parts of the Torah (the first five books of the Old Testament). In the end the former were victorious, and belief in the resurrection of the dead became canonical in Judaism by the second century A.D. The expectation of the resurrection is in the second benediction (Gevurot) of the Amidah prayer, which even today forms the central part of every synagogue service, and which Orthodox Jews recite thrice daily:

> You are mighty forever, Lord
> You revive the dead,
> You are powerful to save. . . .
>
> You are faithful to revive the dead
> Blessed are You, Lord, Who revive the dead.[52]

Traditionally the Amidah is regarded as the creation of the Men of the Great Synagogue in the fourth century B.C., but actually[53] it was created in pieces over the period 200–100 B.C. The "revive the dead" part is believed[54] to have been added by the Pharisees about 100 B.C. in reaction to the Sadducees' denial of its possibility. (Some Reformed prayer books have modified the Hebrew from "revive the dead" into "give life to all." Many liberal Jews are as uncomfortable with the idea of individual immortality as many liberal Christians.)

The Pharisaic position on the afterlife was the one codified in the (Babylonian) Talmud ("Talmud" means "learning"). The positions taken in the Talmud are important indicators of Jewish thought because the work was regarded as sacred, as divinely inspired, and almost on a par with the Torah, from its completion until the Jewish Haskalah (Enlightenment) movement in the eighteenth century A.D. In modern yeshivoth (Jewish religious schools), the Talmud is still the major, often the only, work studied. Each tractate (book) of the Talmud is divided into two basic sections: the Mishnah ("repetition"), a very short summary of the central thesis (the Mishnah was begun by scholars who lived in Palestine before the destruction of the Temple in A.D. 70, and finished by about A.D. 200), and the *Gemara* ("completion"), a much longer commentary on the *Mishnah* (the *Gemara* was finished by about A.D. 500). The tenth tractate of the Talmud, *Sanhedrin*, contains an extensive discussion of the afterlife. The *Mishnah Sanhedrin* begins: "All Israel has a portion in the world to come. . . . But the following have no portion therein: he who maintains that resurrection is not intimated in the Torah. . . ."[55]

The *Gemara Sanhedrin* contained three arguments defending the possibility of resurrection, all basically saying that bringing the dead to life is easy for an all-powerful God:

> An emperor said to Rabbi Gamaliel: "You maintain that the dead will revive; but they turn to dust, and can dust come to life?" Thereupon the emperor's daughter said to the Rabbi: "Let me answer him. In our town there are two potters; one fashions [his products] from water, and the other from clay: who is the more praiseworthy?" "He who fashions them from water," the emperor replied. "If He can fashion [man] from water [sperm], surely he can do so from clay!"[56]

The idea is that, if the pattern in matter is reproduced again, then the original is resurrected; the original is identified with the reproduction if the pattern is duplicated. This claim is emphasized even more forcibly in the second argument:

> The school of Rabbi Ishmael taught: it [the resurrection] can be deduced from glassware: if glassware, which, though made by the breath of human beings [glass blowing], can yet be repaired when broken [by being melted down again]; then how much more so man, created by the breath of the Holy One, blessed be He.[57]

The third argument is an expansion of the first:

> An atheist said to Rabbi Ammi: "You maintain that the dead will revive; but they turn to dust, and can dust come to life?" Rabbi Ammi replied: "I will tell you a parable. This may be compared to a human king who commanded his servants to build him a great palace in a place where there was no water or earth [for making bricks]. So

they went and built it. But after some time it collapsed, so he commanded them to rebuild it in a place where water and earth were to be found; but they replied, 'We cannot.' Thereupon he became angry with them and said, 'If you could build in a place containing no water or earth, surely you can build where there is!' [Thus if God can make man without water or earth, surely He can resuscitate their dust.] "Yet," [continued Rabbi Ammi], "if you do not believe, go forth into the field and see a mouse, which today is but part flesh and part dust, and yet by tomorrow has developed and become all flesh. [In his commentary on this passage, Maimonides claimed some believed that there was a species of mouse which developed out of earth.] And should you say, 'That takes a long time [whereas resurrection must happen in a moment],' go up to the mountains, where you will see but one snail, while by tomorrow the rain has descended and it is covered with snails [thus proving that God can create life with great speed]."[58]

The former part of the preceding passage again emphasizes that it is the pattern, and not the particular materials out of which the palace or human is composed, which defines both. A human who replicates the pattern of a long-dead person would *be* that person. The second part of the passage is a claim that resurrection is quite reasonable on strictly scientific grounds. The Talmud describes the resurrection in some detail; we are told,[59] for example, that the dead will rise with their defects and afterward be healed in order that people will not say, "Those who died were not the same as those who were quickened."[60] Notice again the implication that pattern identity implies person identity.

The next passage is of special interest because it shows that a person was regarded by most sages of the Talmud as a unity of body and soul, rather than as an immaterial soul locked in a material body, as the contemporary Gnostics and Platonists would have it:

Antoninus [Marcus Aurelius ?] said to the Rabbi: "The body and the soul can both free themselves from judgment. Thus, the body can plead: The soul has sinned, [the proof being] that from the day it left me I lie like a dumb stone in the grave [powerless to do anything].

While the soul can say: The body has sinned, [the proof being] that from the day I departed I fly about in the air like a bird [and commit no sin]." The Rabbi replied, "I will tell you a parable. To what may this be compared? To a human king who owned a beautiful orchard which contained splendid figs. Now, he appointed two watchmen therein, one lame and the other blind. [One day] the lame man said to the blind, 'I see beautiful figs in the orchard. Come and take me on your shoulder, that we may procure and eat them.' So the lame bestrode the blind, procured and ate them. Some time after, the owner of the orchard came and asked them, 'Where are those beautiful figs?' The lame man replied, 'Have I then feet to walk with?' The blind man replied, 'Have I then eyes to see with?' What did the owner do? He placed the lame upon the blind and judged them together. So will the Holy One, blessed be He, bring the soul, place it in the body, and judge them together, as it is written, 'He shall call to the heavens from above, and to the earth, that he may judge his people.' [Psalm 50:4 KJV.] 'He shall call to the heavens from above' —this refers to the soul; 'and to the earth, that he may judge his people'—this refers to the body."[61]

There are occasional passages in the Talmud which suggest that it is the Platonic soul, and not the unity of body and soul, which will participate in the afterlife. For an example, there is the death scene of Rabbi Jochanan ben Zakkai, as recorded in tractate *Berachot* (28b). The Rabbi began to weep when his disciples came to visit him. They asked "Light of Israel, right Pillar, Mighty hammer, why do you weep?" He answered that he wept because his soul, which would survive his body, would have to face the inscrutable judgment of God.[62] Nevertheless, the idea that the body and soul would have a common afterlife was overwhelmingly the majority view[63] among Jewish thinkers until the eleventh century A.D., when Neo-Platonism began to creep in. But the Platonic view that the soul is an independent substance was unequivocally rejected by the greatest of the medieval Jewish philosophers, Moses ben Maimon, known to history as Maimonides (A.D. 1135–1204). The last of his famous Thirteen Articles, in which Maimonides summarized what he took to be the thirteen basic Jewish beliefs, was "there will be a resurrection when it shall please the Creator."[64] In an abbreviated form the Thirteen Articles are still in the Jewish prayer book as the *Yigdal* prayer, the thirteenth stanza being:

God will the dead to life again restore.
Praised be His glorious Name for evermore![65]

In many synagogues today the *Yigdal* prayer is recited at the beginning of the morning service. In his *Commentary to Mishnah Sanhedrin*, Maimonides writes: "The resurrection of the dead is the foundation of all grand principles of Moses, our teacher, and there is neither religion, nor adherence to the Jewish religion, in those who do not believe this. . . ."[66]

Having said this, Maimonides proceeded to strip resurrection of the dead of all real significance by claiming it only applied to the Messianic Age, a period of just a thousand years before the beginning of the *true* afterlife lasting for eternity. This true afterlife is the World to Come. The dead would rise in the Messianic Age, but they would live as unity of body and soul for only a thousand years. The true afterlife was a spiritual existence, the delights of which we temporal beings can have no real comprehension. Maimonides was attempting to make the traditional Jewish belief in the resurrection consistent with Aristotelian physics, which held that only the receptive intellect was immortal. (Here we see the influence of Platonic dualism on Aristotle.) An implication of this was that very few humans could expect immortality: only intellectuals who had prepared their minds for eternity by contemplation. The common people are not immortal, since the afterlife is not something given by God either as a reward for good behavior or out of love. (Nonintellectuals would hate living in Maimonides' version of the World to Come anyway.) One of Maimonides' central arguments for the spiritual nature of the afterlife was that incorporeal persons are known to exist, namely God and the angels, so incorporeal life is therefore possible. Maimonides then stated in his *Treatise on Resurrection* that "We firmly believe—and this is the truth which every intelligent person accepts—that in the world to come souls without bodies will exist like angels."[67]

Maimonides' view of immortality was severely criticized, for instance by Hasdai ben Abraham Crescas (A.D. 1340–1410). Crescas argued that the justice of God required it for any good human, not just for intellectuals. He pointed out that, if it were the result of acquiring knowledge, one could acquire it by studying geometry, something obviously absurd. A resurrected body is necessary in the afterlife for the giving of rewards and punishments to the union of body and soul which acted together during life. As to the old question of how the scattered elements which went to make up the body could be brought back together, Crescas gave the traditional answer that an all-powerful God could do this easily, but he claimed it was not really necessary. If God were to create another body exactly like the first in temperament, form, and memory, and endow it with the old soul, then the recreation would *be* the original person.[68] I draw the same conclusion in Chapter IX.

After Maimonides, the effect of Greek and later secular thought on the Jewish rabbis became more and more pronounced, so that after the medieval period it becomes difficult to define a distinctive Jewish view on the mechanism of immortality. Some Jewish thinkers, for instance, the eighteenth-century founder of the Hasidic movement, Israel ben Eliezer (known as the Beshat, from the first letters of Ba-al Shem Tov, "Master of the good name"), continued to emphasize the earthy nature of the afterlife. In the Beshat's opinion, Paradise cannot be the same experience for everyone; each person goes to where he/she can experience the joys most in keeping with the individual's nature. The Beshat's example is that of a teamster, who will find himself transported to an imaginary world where he will be given four magnificent horses, and in which the roads are always dry and always level. The unlearned will have immortality in their ideal fantasy world.[69] This is essentially the same as the afterlife in the Omega Point Theory.

RESURRECTION OF THE DEAD VERSUS IMMORTALITY OF THE SOUL IN CHRISTIANITY

There has always been an essential tension in Christianity between two mechanisms of personal immortality: immortality arising from the innate nature of the soul—Plato argued that, being immaterial, the (rational) soul could not be destroyed and hence was naturally immortal—and the resurrection of the body by the explicit act of God. The latter is pictured very vividly in St. Jerome's mistranslation of a crucial passage of the book of Job (19:25–27) in the Vulgate, which for centuries was the version of the Bible used by the Roman Catholic Church:

> For I know that my Redeemer liveth, and in the last day I shall rise out of the earth. And shall be clothed again with my skin, and in my flesh I shall see God. Whom I myself shall see, and my eyes shall behold, and not another: this my hope is laid up in my bosom.[70]

The Swiss theologian Oscar Cullmann, in an extremely influential Ingersoll Lecture[71] at Harvard University entitled "Immortality of the Soul or Resurrection of the Dead?" argued that, originally, Semites viewed a human being as an animated body, a unity of body and soul, rather than as an immaterial soul imprisoned in a mortal body. Hence, for the Jews of Jesus' time (and by implication for Jesus himself), immortality had to be in the form of resurrection of the body, rather than survival of a naturally immortal soul. Cullmann contrasted soul immortality, which he regarded as the Greek view of immortality, with the Jewish view of resurrection. According to the Roman Catholic theologian Edward Schillebeeckx,[72] this contrast became "more or less unanimously accepted" by Christian theologians[73] in the late twentieth century. The famous Protestant Swiss theologian Karl Barth put it thus: "What is the meaning of the Christian hope in this life? . . . A tiny soul which, like a butterfly, flutters away above the grave and is still preserved somewhere, in order to live on immortally? That was how the heathen looked on the life after death. But that is not the Christian hope. 'I believe in the resurrection of the body.' "[74]

Cullmann's claim that the Greek dichotomy between body and soul is to be contrasted with the Semitic unity finds an echo in the analysis of the Taoist view by a French China scholar:

> If the Taoists, in their search for longevity, conceived it not as a spiritual but as a material immortality, it was not as a deliberate choice between different possible solutions but because for them it was the only possible solution. The Graeco-Roman world early

adopted the habit of setting Spirit and Matter in opposition to one another, and the religious form of this was the conception of a spiritual soul attached to a material body. But the Chinese never separated Spirit and Matter. . . . The body, on the contrary, was a unity. . . . Thus it was only by the perpetuation of the body, in some form or other, that one could conceive of a continuation of the living personality as a whole.[75]

However, in his Ingersoll Lecture for 1956, the year following Cullmann's Ingersoll Lecture, the Harvard historian Harry Wolfson[76] rejected Cullmann's argument by reference to the death scene of Rabbi Jochanan ben Zakkai, discussed above. Wolfson pointed out that the rabbi lived in Palestine about A.D. 100, so that this indicated a belief in the immortality of the soul present in Palestine at the time of Jesus. Other examples of belief in soul immortality held by some of Jesus' Jewish contemporaries have been provided by Nickelsburg[77] and by Schillebeeckx.[78] It is not really surprising to find a belief in soul immortality held by Palestine Jews in Jesus' time, because by this period Palestine had been off and on a part of various Greco-Roman empires for centuries, and a belief in soul immortality, going back at least to Plato, was common in these empires. Incidentally, it is incorrect to call soul immortality the "Greek view." Soul immortality is more appropriately termed the "Platonic view," since Aristotle, for example, defined the "soul" to be "the form of activity of the body," a definition which, as it regards life as a pattern in matter, is essentially the same as Cullmann's so-called Semitic view. Since Aristotle did not believe in the resurrection of the body, he did not believe in individual immortality.[79] There seems to be no doubt that the early Christians believed in the resurrection of the body rather than in the Platonic theory. In fact, one of Christianity's earliest pagan critics, Celsus, ridiculed in A.D. 185 the Christian view of immortality on just this ground:

What do Christians suppose happens after death? . . . [They say] that we go to another earth, different and better than this one.[80] . . . Christians . . . have misunderstood Plato's doctrine of reincarnation, and believe in the absurd theory that the corporeal body will be raised and reconstituted by God, and that somehow they will actually see God with their mortal eyes and hear him with their ears and be able to touch him with their hands.[81]

As emphasized by Pannenberg,[82] the real importance of Cullmann's work lies not in his establishment that Jesus and the early Christians believed in resurrection of the flesh as opposed to immortality of the soul, but rather in his rediscovery that the biblical resurrection hope is independent of the conception of an immortal soul. The interesting question is why, if these conceptions are independent, were they entwined in Christianity from very early times? The answer is again provided by Pannenberg (and also by Flew, in all of his works on immortality): to provide continuity between the dead and resurrected person, so that the two can be identified. For Aquinas, the soul acted "as a genetic code" for the essence of an individual in the resurrection.[83]

Pannenberg[84] points out that contemporary theology, especially contemporary Protestant theology, generally tries to establish identity by arguing that the present-day person is coded not only in the present-day spatio-temporal structure, but also in God. Hence the dead can come alive again in God. This is essentially what is happening in the Omega Point Theory when sufficient information is extracted from the past light cone (boundary and interior) to reconstruct the original person, as Pannenberg[85] realized. I have shown in Chapter IX that it is possible to extract such information, and in fact identity can be established without continuity using the identity theory of quantum physics. So the immortal soul is unnecessary for its central purpose, and I propose we let the idea die. Its physical basis was slain by physics long ago.[86]

For an example of the most recent Christian view on resurrection versus immortality of the soul, we can take the picture of immortality painted by the physicist (and Anglican priest) John Polkinghorne. His model appears to be quite similar to the resurrection model in the Omega Point Theory. ". . . the preferred Christian attitude to the nature of man is the Hebraic acceptance of his unity rather than the Greek divorce between soul and body. . . . [T]he future hope is bound to be resurrection rather than survival, the re-constitution of the whole man in some other environment of God's choosing. . . . There is nothing particularly important in the actual physical constituents of our bodies. . . . It is the pattern they form which constitutes the physical expression of our continuing personality. There seems no difficulty in conceiving of that pattern, dissolved at death, being recreated in another environment in an act of resurrection. In terms of a very crude analogy it would be like transforming the software of a computer program (the 'pattern' of our personality) from one piece of hardware (our body in this world) to another (our body in the world to come). Scientifically this seems a coherent idea."[87]

In spite of these words, Polkinghorne rejects the resurrection model in the Omega Point Theory because it requires humans to be finite state machines: ". . . my instinct is to feel that this is a much too atomistic, reductionist way of thinking."[88] To judge the validity of this criticism, we must be a bit more precise about what we mean by this protean word "reductionism."

THE DEFINITION OF "REDUCTIONISM"

I have been calling myself a "reductionist" throughout this entire book. By this I have meant roughly that every phenomenon is "at bottom" a physical phenomenon, capable of being described—at least in principle—by physics. But there are at least three different varieties of reductionism. In my opinion, the clearest categorization of these varieties was made by the evolutionary biologist Francisco Ayala, who terms[89] these varieties of reductionism (1) *ontological* reductionism, (2) *epistemological* reductionism, and (3) *methodological* reductionism.

ONTOLOGICAL REDUCTIONISM claims that the "stuff" comprising reality *is,* at the most basic level, nothing but the forces and particles studied by physics. This brand of reductionism is the one I accept. I think the evidence is overwhelming that—with one caveat, which I shall discuss below—such reductionism is not a mere human construct but is actually a property of nature. This version of reductionism, in other words, is a claim about the structure of ultimate reality, independent of human culture. Ontological reductionism is a claim about the way things just *are,* which is the reason for calling it "ontological," which in philosophy means the "study of the nature of being." I have been making an ontological reductionist claim when I assert that a human being *is* a quantum mechanical object which can be *exactly* described by a computer program coding 10^{45} bits of information. It is ontological reductionism that allows me to prove that we shall one day be resurrected by the Omega Point.

EPISTEMOLOGICAL REDUCTIONISM holds that theories and experimental laws in one field of science *always* can be shown to be special cases of laws formulated in other areas of science. In contrast to ontological reductionism, this variety is a claim about the way human beings see the world, not about nature itself. This version of reductionism I do not accept. The standard example of epistemological reductionism is the supposed "reduction" of classical thermodynamics to the statistical mechanics of atoms. Yet this reduction is not exact; for example, the Second Law of Thermodynamics is no longer a law which has no exceptions, since in the limit of a small number of atoms it is possible to have fluctuations in which the Second Law is violated. We say that the Second Law is a law valid "at a higher level" of analysis. We use the Second Law because it generally gives correct answers without the vastly more complicated calculations which would be required if we always used the lower-level theories.

Furthermore, if we accept ontological reductionism, it is always possible in principle for an intellect, gigantically more powerful than any human intellect, to dispense with the higher levels of description which we mere humans will always find essential. It is possible to calculate when a higher level than the ontological level is necessary: whenever the *Kolmogorov complexity* is sufficiently large so that a human mind cannot see the whole in the parts.

The Kolmogorov complexity[90] of a phenomenon is defined to be the *least* number of bits of information required to describe exhaustively the phenomenon. The Bekenstein Bound tells us that such a number exists. A human being can be exhaustively described by 10^{45} bits, though this number may not be the actual Kolmogorov complexity; a human being may be simpler. But we know a human is not more complicated (provided quantum mechanics and ontological reductionism are correct).

Since the limitations of human minds do not necessarily apply to all possible minds, epistemological reductionism is false. For example, Ayala himself lists fitness, adaptation, predator, organ, heterozygosity, and sexuality as particular biological concepts which cannot be translated into statements about molecules. However, if these concepts apply exclusively to living beings which exist in the visible universe, then the Bekenstein Bound shows that 10^{123} bits of information is sufficient (though possibly not necessary) for an *exact* translation of fitness, etc., in terms of states of quantized fields. By comparison, a typical book codes between 10^6 and 10^7 bits, and the human brain about 10^{15} bits. Any phenomenon whose Kolmogorov complexity is greater than 10^7 bits cannot be described in a single book and, if its complexity is greater than 10^{15} bits, it cannot be understood completely by any human being whatsoever. Since many of the phenomena we deal with every day have even greater complexity than 10^{15} bits—human society, for instance, since it is a system made up of many humans, each with complexity of 10^{15} bits or more—we invent higher-level theories to describe them. But, as a consequence, these higher-level theories oversimply, and thus may give incorrect answers if the problems being attacked are too complex. But a Being of sufficiently powerful intellect *would* be able to give a correct answer, because such a Being would be able to deal directly with the lowest-level theory, which, as the Bekenstein Bound shows, is in precise one-to-one correspondence with physical reality. In summary, the impossibility of translation of Ayala's biological concepts is true *only* if we impose the further constraint that the translation be understandable by human minds.

Finally, let us always remember that a theory which one generation considers utterly irreducible the following generation reduces. In the early part of the nineteenth century, many chemists believed that the laws of chemistry would *never* be reduced to those of physics. Nevertheless, this reduction was achieved in the late nineteenth and early twentieth centuries. Often when I am walking down the corridors of the natural sciences building at Tulane where I have my office, I will pass a class taught by a chemistry professor, and hear a lecture on the quantum mechanics of atoms, a lecture which is virtually indistinguishable from a lecture on atoms given by a physics professor. Chemistry has definitely been reduced—epistemologically—to physics. This entire book is a defense of my claim to have epistemologically reduced theology to physics. Notice, however, I am not claiming we humans can understand God in His/Her totality by using physics. A complete description of God would require a literal infinity of bits, and a human being can code only 10^{15}, an amount which is infinitely too small. But we *can* use physics to understand the essential properties of God, in particular those properties which concern us the most: God's power and desire to resurrect us all to eternal life.

METHODOLOGICAL REDUCTIONISM claims that researchers should *always* look for explanations at the lowest levels of theoretical description, ultimately at the level of atoms and molecules or other elementary particles that make up the objects being studied. Scientists have found this form of reductionism useful, but it has limitations. For instance, if one always applied methodological reductionism, one would never be allowed to use classical thermodynamics in a calculation; one would always have to carry out a much more complicated calculation involving atoms. I, like all other physicists, feel free to use the Second Law of Thermodynamics in my calculations, without necessarily making reference to the underlying physical entities which obey the Second Law. Such a procedure is a tacit rejection of methodological reductionism.

But methodological reductionism can often be a powerful tool to test the validity of higher-level theories. For example, I have used the theories of sociobiology and microeconomics to predict the actions of intelligent beings in the far future. In particular, I have used these theories to predict that these beings will have the desire to resurrect us to a life we will enjoy. I feel confident that these theories are correct because they can clearly be reduced (epistemologically) to the physics of information, a field of physics which is extremely solid. My *method* has been to use reducibility to physics as a touchstone of truth for a higher-level theory.

By definition of the word "machine" in computer theory, humans are "machines" if in fact they are some sort of pattern. As I have shown, using the Bekenstein Bound, quantum field theory requires them to be finite, coding 10^{45} bits maximum. The resurrection theory requires acceptance of *ontological,* but not epistemological, reductionism. Yet Polkinghorne claims[91] to accept the former (he calls it "structural reductionism"; epistemological reductionism he calls "conceptual reductionism"). My impression on reading his examples in his discussion of reductionism[92] is that he does not really believe in structural reductionism.

The *de facto* rejection of ontological reductionism by scientists claiming to accept it is unfortunately quite common. One can find another example of it in a recent exchange between the great physicist Steven Weinberg and the eminent evolutionist Ernst Mayr in the pages of the leading British science journal, *Nature*. Weinberg's position is the same as mine: acceptance of ontological reductionism (he calls it "objective reductionism") and rejection of epistemological reductionism. Mayr claims[93] to adopt the same position (he calls ontological reductionism "constitutive reductionism," and he calls epistemological reductionism "explanatory reductionism"). But he concludes, "Even if the SSC would lead to the discovery of the Higgs boson or some other equivalent finding, my disbelief in explanatory reductionism leads me to doubt that such a discovery would make any contribution whatsoever to our understanding of the middle world [the world 'from the atom to the Solar System']. But it is the middle world that poses all the problems man will have to solve if he is to survive." As Weinberg responded,[94] a previous discovery in the subatomic world—nuclear fission—has already had a profound impact on the middle world. This discovery has forced us to deepen our understanding of the important middle world phenomenon of "war": when is a war a "just war"? (A nuclear war is not just a war.) It is Mayr's disbelief in constitutive, not explanatory, reductionism that really leads to his doubt. A consequence of ontological reductionism is the possibility in principle for phenomena on small scales to amplify themselves (or be amplified) to middle world importance. If the Omega Point Theory is true, then the ultimate survival of all life—and the individual immortality of all human beings—depends on the nature of reality at a much deeper level than even the SSC would have probed. The pattern that is ourselves is now mainly coded in the middle world, but one day an emulation of the entire middle world—the world of our afterlife—will be coded in sub-microworld machines. And, as I showed in Chapter IV, if it detects the Higgs boson at a particular mass—220 GeV—the SSC, if ever completed, will provide some evidence that the Omega Point Theory is true.

Weinberg justified[95] "objective reductionism" as a fact of nature, not a property of our theories, by reference to "arrows of scientific explanation," all of which over the past several hundred years have been discovered to point down to a common source in the deep microworld. He emphasized that this needn't have been the case: "They also could have gone around in a circle. This is still a possibility. . . . If the anthropic principle were true, there would be a kind of circularity built into nature. . . ." I claim there must be one arrow of explanation which by its very nature must point up rather than down. This is the Universal Boundary Condition. Even attempts to dispense with the Universal Boundary Condition by allowing all possibilities to be realized use the (weak) anthropic arrow, which also points up. What the Final Anthropic Principle—which is what I have sometimes called the Dirac-Dyson Principle of Eternal Life—claims is that the only failure of ontological reductionism will be the Universal Boundary Condition that, globally, life must exist forever.

THE GARDEN OF ISLAM

According to the *Cow* Sura[96] (chapter) of the Qur'an and Islamic tradition, the Qur'an was dictated word for word to Mohammed by the angel Gabriel. All Mohammed did was recite to his scribes what Gabriel told him. In fact, in Arabic the word "Qur'an" means "Recitation." Since the Qur'an was dictated word for word to Mohammed by God in His Gabriel manifestation, and since God chose to dictate in medieval Arabic, the Qur'an cannot be translated; if rendered in another language, this rendering is necessarily an "interpretation," not a translation.[97]

The nature of resurrection according to the Qur'an is essentially the same as that outlined in this book: a resurrected individual is a new creation, a replication of someone long dead.[98] This is the consensus of Western Islamic scholars, and it is expressed unequivocally in the Sura of the Qur'an entitled *The Night Journey*:

> [Unbelievers say] *"What, when we are bones and broken bits,*
> *shall we really be raised up again in a new creation?"*

*Have they not seen that God, who created the heavens
and earth is powerful to create the like of them?*[99]

In another *Night Journey* passage, Mohammed drove home the point
that the resurrected dead are not merely the original reassembled but a
newly created likeness by claiming that even those dead whose substance had been entirely transformed into something else would be
recreated:

> *They say, "What, when we are bones and broken bits,*
> *shall we really be raised up again in a new creation?"*
> *Say: "Let you be stones, or iron, or some creation yet more*
> *monstrous in your minds!" Then they will say, "Who will bring*
> *us back?" Say: "He who originated you the first time."*[100]

This recreation of the individual at the Hour is applied to the
entire universe in Ash'ari theology, which defends[101] the theory of
"atomism": the doctrine that God is continually destroying and recre-
ating the universe from moment to moment. Such a view is quite
similar to the view of the human body in modern quantum field theory, which pictures it as being annihilated and re-formed many times
per second.

In *The Resurrection* Sura, Mohammed compares the resurrection
creation to the creation that occurred when a human was formed in
the womb:

> *Was he not a sperm-drop spilled? Then he was a blood-clot, and He created*
> *and formed, and He made of him two kinds, male and female.*
> *What, is He not able to quicken the dead?*[102]

Since the resurrected dead are a new creation, the soul dies with
the body. There is nothing left which can have experiences between
death and resurrection: death is like a deep dreamless sleep. The dead
will be recreated with the memories they had the instant before death,
and thus it will seem to them that the resurrection occurs *immediately*
after death.[103] This lack of subjective time between death and resurrec-

tion is expressed many times in the Qur'an, for instance in *The Greeks* Sura:

> Upon the day when the Hour is come, the sinners shall swear
> they have not tarried above an hour; so they were perverted.
> But those who have been given knowledge and faith shall say,
> "You have tarried in God's Book till the Day of the Upraising,
> This is the Day of the Upraising, but you did not know."[104]

(I note in passing that dead humans are pictured in *The Greeks* Sura as a record in God's book; i.e., as a simulation in God's Mind.) In the *Ta Ha* Sura, we again read:

> On the day the Trumpet is blown; and We shall muster the sinners upon that day
> with eyes staring, whispering one to another, "You have tarried only ten nights."
> We know very well what they will say, when the most just of them in the way will
>   say,
> "You have tarried only a day."[105]

This mechanism of resurrection allows those who have perished in the service of Islam to experience instantaneously after death the delights of Paradise, even if the cosmic time which passes between the death and the Day of Doom happens to be many billions of years. As Mohammed puts it in the *House of Imran* Sura:

> Count not those who were slain in God's way as dead,
> but rather living with their Lord, by Him provided,
> rejoicing in the bounty that God has given them.[106]

A number of Western scholars[107] consider this instantaneous experience of Paradise to be inconsistent with the view that death involved the annihilation of the individual and hence with the possibility of a vast time period between individual death and the Day of Doom, but I disagree. It is clear that, for an individual resurrected with the memories he had the instant before death, resurrection would indeed appear instantaneous for him. I think these Western scholars have failed to distinguish between the view of the Qur'an and early Islam—which *is* consistent with the instantaneous experience of Paradise—and later Islam.

The state of a human being between death and resurrection is known as the *barzakh*. The Qur'an says very little about this state, except for the following passage from the *Angels* Sura:

> *Not equal are the blind and the seeing man,*
> *the shadows and the light,*
> *the shade and the torrid heat;*
> *not equal are the living and the dead.*
> *God makes to hear whomever He will;*
> *thou canst not make those in their tombs to hear.*[108]

It is clear from this that the dead cannot hear the living, that the dead have no consciousness, that when you're dead you're dead until the resurrection. The *barzakh* is therefore of no interest to anybody, since it contributes no experiences to the resurrected individual. This is the reason the Qur'an hardly ever mentions the state, and early Islam followed the Qur'an and rarely discussed it, since the Qur'an emphasized that the period passed (in subjective time) like the wink of the eye.[109] But after several centuries the idea crept in that the dead could hear, that the *barzakh* state was a conscious state, and the above passage was reinterpreted to mean the opposite of what it said.[110] I suspect this change was due to the pernicious influence of Platonic dualism on Islam, as was a corresponding change in Christianity (see above). But even in modern Islam, there are few supporters of a purely spiritual afterlife.[111]

The true inconsistency in both early and modern Islam is the contradiction between "no salvation outside the church" and the love of God for all His creatures. All Suras of the Qur'an open with the phrase "In the name of God, the Merciful, the Compassionate"; in the *Opening* Sura God is asserted to be ". . . the All-Merciful, the All-Compassionate"; in the *Women* Sura He is claimed to be "All-pardoning" and "All-forgiving, All-Compassionate." (In modern Arabic, the superlatives "All-Merciful" and "All-Compassionate" are now restricted to God alone.) But if God really is "All-Merciful" and "All-Compassionate," won't He forgive an intellectually honest rejection of

Him? Human parents have been known to forgive a rejection of themselves by their offspring. Surely an "All-Merciful" and "All-Compassionate" God would be at least as forgiving as a human parent. Judaism and modern Christianity have resolved a similar contradiction by rejecting *"Extra Ecclesium nulla salus"* ("no salvation outside the church"), to quote[112] the words of the Fourth Lateran Council in A.D. 1215. For example, the Second Vatican Council in 1964 invoked the above argument on God's love and compassion, concluding: "Those individuals who for no fault of their own do not know the Gospel of Christ and his Church, yet still search for God with an upright heart and try to fulfill his will, as recognized in the commands of conscience, in deeds prompted by the working of his grace, can attain eternal salvation."[113] Pannenberg has expressed this beautifully: "Jesus and his message are to be regarded as a *criterion,* but not as an indispensable *means,* of salvation."[114] As for Judaism, the Talmud *(Mishnah Sanhedrin)* asserts that "pious gentiles" shall "have a portion" in the world to come.[115] Judaism was much in advance of Christianity, since the Talmud's completion dates from the sixth century A.D., while the major Christian churches did not adopt a similar position until this century.

Much of Islam has yet to adopt this position. Many Muslims have resolved it, e.g., Salih Tug, a professor of Islam in Turkey, who speaks[116] of Hell as a "spiritual hospital" for those whose souls must be purged of the evil they acquired in life, with the implication that eventually all humans will enter Heaven. Smith and Haddad point out[117] that, in traditional Islam, the only unpardonable sin, called *shirk,* is explicit denial of the absolute oneness *(tawhid)* of God. Thus in the opinion of almost all traditional Muslim theologians, these individuals, together with all who deny God's word (the *kafir* [unbelievers]), are condemned *eternally* to the Fire of Hell.[118] This is supported by the following passage from the *Women* Sura: "Surely the unbelievers, who have done evil, God would not forgive them, neither guide them on any road but the road to Gehenna, therein dwelling forever and ever; and that for God is an easy matter."[119] A minority tradition does in fact draw[120] the obvious implication from God being "All-Merciful" and "All-Compassionate," asserting that, at last, God will rescue *all,* including those who have not even a particle of good in them, from the Fire. The Omega Point Theory agrees with this minority Muslim opinion: everyone, without exception, will be given the option of immortality. The Omega Point Theory is, however, in agreement with the universal Muslim belief on the absolute oneness of God, as indicated by the very name of the theory: the Omega Point is a *point*, which is to say, a single entity. God's absolute oneness is a mathematical theorem in the Omega Point Theory.

I do not expect to see in my lifetime the whole of Islam resolve the contradiction between its (correct) belief in God's compassion and its (incorrect) belief in eternal torment. The Sudanese theologian Mahmoud Mohamed Taha argued[121] that the verses in the Qur'an which Mohammed recited before he took power in Medina were eternally valid, while the ones he recited after taking power were intended only for the particular period of Mohammed's own life. Were this position to be accepted, the contradiction would be eliminated, since the verses concerning the universal resurrection which I quote above are from the Meccan period,[122] while the verse on eternal torment is probably from the Medinan period.[123] Unfortunately for Islam, Taha was tried and convicted of heresy by the Muslim High Court of the Sudan, and executed by hanging on January 18, 1985. The Iranian journalist 'Ali Dashti[124] made a similar distinction between Mohammed in Mecca and Mohammed in Medina. As a consequence, after the Islamic Revolution in Iran, Dashti was imprisoned and beaten. He died, possibly as a result of this treatment, in December 1981 or January 1982. Other recent examples of opposition to resolving the central contradiction can be found in a history by Pipes.[125]

XII.

THE OMEGA POINT
THEORY AND
CHRISTIANITY

To emphasize the scientific nature of the Omega Point Theory, let me state here that I am at present forced to consider myself an atheist, in the literal sense that I am not a theist. *(A-theist* means "not theist.") I do not yet even believe in the Omega Point. The Omega Point Theory is a viable scientific theory of the future of the physical universe, but the only evidence in its favor at the moment is theoretical beauty, for there is as yet no confirming experimental evidence for it. Thus scientifically one is not compelled to accept it at the time of my writing these words. So I do not. Flew,[1] among others, has in my opinion made a convincing case for the presumption of atheism. If the Omega Point Theory and all possible variations of it are disconfirmed, then I think atheism in the sense of Flew, Hume, Russell, and the other self-described atheists is the only rational alternative. But of course I also think the Omega Point Theory has a very good chance of being right, otherwise I would never have troubled to write this book. If the Omega Point Theory is confirmed, I shall then consider myself a theist.

My current atheism is not contradicted by my extensive quotations from the Bible, Qur'an, Talmud, *Rig Veda,* and other books which some have found holy. I quoted the descriptions of the resurrection in these works to show that the emulation resurrection predicted in the Omega Point Theory is essentially the same as the resurrection hoped for in the Judeo-Christian-Islamic tradition. I personally do not believe that the writers of these works had any revealed knowledge. Rather, I think that, if one postulates for ethical reasons a universal resurrection and adopts a nondualist view of the body-soul relationship, then the basic features of simulation resurrection necessarily follow. In particular, I think the description of Jesus' resurrection body in Luke arises from such logical analysis; I do not think the writer of Luke was reporting actual observations which he himself made or which eyewitnesses told to him directly. Almost all biblical authorities believe Luke to be a secondary source based on Mark—the original version of which contains no description of the risen Jesus.[2] It is nevertheless interesting that the closer we get to the original version of Luke the more consistent it is with the Omega Point resurrection theory. For example, if Jesus' post-Easter body were a resurrection body, then he should have finally parted from his disciples by simply vanishing, not by being seen to ascend to the heavens: it is now known that the phrase ". . . and was carried up to heaven" is not present in the earliest known versions of Luke. Were Luke shown to have been written sufficiently early for the writer to have been a recorder of contemporary eyewitness accounts of Jesus' execution, and in fact shown to be recording such eyewitness accounts, I should have to reconsider my rejection of Christianity (but not my rejection of all the other miracles recorded in Luke; see the next paragraph). As it now stands, the priority of Mark supports my rejection, as does the implication of Luke 1:1–5 that the writer is merely recording a long verbal tradition and is writing long after the original eyewitnesses have died. The consensus[3] of biblical scholars is that Luke was composed between A.D. 80 and 85, which would mean Luke was written some fifty years after Jesus' death. On this dating, it is very implausible that it would contain any eyewitness testimony, and even if it did, such testimony would be very unreliable at such a late date, for reasons I shall give below.

However, it is interesting to an outsider like myself that the authors of the recent Anchor Bible, generally agreed to be a truly outstanding series of modern commentaries on the New Testament, disagree strongly among themselves on the date of Luke. It is universally agreed that Luke and Acts were one work by the same author written at about the same time (the Prologues to Luke and Acts assert this themselves).

But Johannes Munck, who wrote the Anchor Bible *Commentary on Acts*,[4] puts the date of composition of Luke-Acts in the early sixties A.D., whereas Joseph Fitzmyer, who wrote the Anchor Bible *Commentary on Luke*,[5] accepts the biblical consensus of A.D. 80–85 for the date of composition. Christopher S. Mann, the author of Anchor Bible *Commentary on Mark*,[6] agrees with Munck on the composition date. Judging only from the evidence[7] in the three above-mentioned Anchor Bible commentaries, my own conclusion is that the weight of the evidence supports the earlier date of composition, and that the scholarly consensus is wrong. My main reason for believing this has been expressed many times over the centuries. In many passages (e.g., Luke 19:42–44), Jesus predicts the destruction of Jerusalem. Had the author of Luke known that in fact Jerusalem was destroyed (as it was, by the son of the Roman emperor, in A.D. 70), it seems likely that he would have recorded it as a confirmation of Jesus' prophetic abilities. An author never misses a chance to point out a confirming instance of his theory. I've obviously tried to give all known confirming evidence for the Omega Point Theory in this book. I've mentioned in Chapter IV, for example, the apparent detection of the top quark event in October 1992. If the Higgs boson had been detected with the mass I predict, I certainly would have announced this confirmation of the Omega Point Theory in this book's opening paragraph. Since there is no unequivocal mention of the actual destruction of Jerusalem in Luke—the Roman army that destroyed the city was under the command first of a man who left the siege of Jerusalem to become the Roman emperor and then of his son, so the whole Empire knew of Jerusalem's destruction—it is most probable that Luke was written before A.D. 70. That is, the rational presumption is that Luke was written prior to A.D. 70. In the opinion of Mann, Munck, and myself, the scholars of the consensus have not provided sufficient reason for doubting this presumption.

The much earlier date of composition would be thirty instead of fifty years after Jesus' death, and would make it more plausible that Luke could have talked to eyewitnesses who claimed to have seen the risen Jesus. I have the suspicion (as do Munck and Mann) that the scholarly consensus rests more on physical and theological presuppositions than on biblical evidence: the later date would obviate the possibility of Luke containing any eyewitness accounts of the risen Jesus, and also would allow Luke to be a rewrite of Mark, the original version of which contains no mention of the risen Jesus. In which case Luke is merely recording a mythic account of Jesus' resurrection. In which case there is no need to entertain the possibility that Jesus actually rose from the dead. In which case there is no embarrassing inconsistency between the Bible and the observed fact that the dead do not rise. In which case the central "truth" of Christianity is false,[8] and Christianity should be allowed to wither away, or become a political movement.[9] However, since I personally do not believe in Jesus' resurrection (see below), I'm happy to accept the scholarly consensus.

Furthermore, there is very strong evidence that the Pharisees, who were the dominant Jewish sect at the time of Christ (according to Acts, St. Paul himself was a Pharisee before he became a Christian), and who, like the Christians, believed[10] in the resurrection of the dead, held that the resurrection body would be an "angelic" body, a body with much the same properties as Jesus' resurrection body as recorded by Luke. The contemporary historian Josephus (also a Pharisee) gave a speech on the afterlife in A.D. 67 in which he emphasized[11] that resurrection bodies would be vastly improved versions of the current body. Thus the evidence is overwhelming that Luke's description of Jesus' resurrection body is just a description of the Pharisaic resurrection body—Old Testament angels were pictured as having the power to alter their appearance at will and disappear or appear in locked rooms.[12] Since Luke's description is merely a recording of what the majority of first-century Jews expected in a true resurrection, I conclude that similarities of Jesus' resurrection body with the resurrection body predicted by the Omega Point Theory is just a coincidence.

·———·

Miracles and the Babbage Mechanism

Interestingly, the resurrection of Jesus (and the virgin birth, etc.) can be put into the Omega Point Theory by hand—the universe we currently observe is also a simulation—but it is not a natural thing to do, and it is not unique: *any* miracle can be put in. In fact, the founder of computer science, Charles Babbage, showed[13] that *any* given miracle can be put into the initial conditions of *any* deterministic physical theory in which the universe is generated as a simulation. But if one miracle is put in *a priori,* where do we stop? The lesson of science is clear: leave out all miracles. On the other hand, if it could be shown that the resurrection of Jesus was in some way essential for the existence of the Omega Point, then Jesus' resurrection would no longer be a miracle; it would follow from the Omega Point Boundary Condition. Fortunately, the scholarly consensus on the dating of the New Testament allows us to avoid having to consider seriously the possibility that the Babbage mechanism was operating in A.D. 30. The striking resemblance between Jesus' resurrection body as described by Luke and the resurrection bodies we shall possess when resurrected by the Omega Point is just a coincidence.

Why I Am Not a Christian

St. Paul claimed in I Corinthians 15:14 that "if Christ has not been raised, then our preaching is in vain and your faith is in vain." (RSV.) I agree with Paul; and in view of the importance of Jesus' resurrection—if it occurred—it is worth describing at some length exactly why I disbelieve in his resurrection. I personally think the weight of evidence in fact supports the idea that the reports of the risen Jesus were reports of some sort of vision which grew in the telling. This being my considered opinion on the evidence, I do not consider myself a Christian.

But I could be forced by additional evidence to change my mind. The nature of the required additional evidence was elucidated by Antony Flew in his debate[14] with the Christian Gary Habermas: a natural theology must be given which tells us that we should expect an exception to the rule "the dead do not rise" in the context actually experienced by the disciples. After listing the reasons for disbelieving in the historicity of the risen Jesus, I shall then briefly describe how, in the presence of the appropriate natural theology, these powerful reasons against Jesus' resurrection can be turned into overwhelming reasons for it. However, I emphasize again that I do not think Jesus really rose from the dead. I think his body rotted in some grave. Furthermore, I think that, although Jesus' disciples may have had a "vision" of him after his death, this "vision" was not in any sense an objective phenomenon; it could have been only a collective hallucination, if it occurred at all. Most modern Christian theologians agree with this assessment.[15]

My own point of view is that of David Hume: the empirical fact—dead men do not rise—must be given due weight against the testimony of men. Hume gives in his *An Enquiry Concerning Human Understanding*[16] a number of examples showing that the testimony of otherwise reputable men cannot be trusted: the example of Hume's which I find most convincing was that of the cathedral doorkeeper who claimed to have regrown a leg by rubbing holy oil on the stump. According to a Catholic cardinal who reported the event, the regrowth was attested to by large numbers of people in the town, including all the canons of the cathedral. Neither the cardinal, Hume, nor I believe that this regrowth occurred. The essential point being made by Hume—a point with which I agree—is that mass delusions can occur; that, given enough time for people to talk to each other, the delusion can develop consistency; and that delusions are likely in cases where people are trying to interpret an extraordinary event. In view of this possibility of delusion, the natural law—confirmed billions of times by all humans everywhere—that the dead do not rise must outweigh testimony to the contrary.

We have vastly more experience with mass delusions than Hume had, experience primarily obtained in the process of investigating UFOs. The modern world does not believe in messengers from God—angels—but it does believe in extraterrestrial intelligent life; imaginary superbeings from other stars play the same psychological role in modern society as angels did in the past. (I personally disbelieve in both.) Of special interest is the astronomer Frank D. Drake's article[17] "On the Abilities and Limitations of Witnesses of UFOs and Similar Phenomena," which appeared in *UFO's—A Scientific Debate*. To summarize Drake's report, in 1962 two very bright fireballs—a type of meteor—burst over West Virginia at about 10 P.M. about a month apart. Astronomers went out to collect meteorite bits and interview people about what they saw. We know what they should have seen, since fireballs are well-studied physical phenomena, so the interviews were a test of observation by inexpert witnesses who suddenly were exposed to unfamiliar phenomena. I now quote the most important parts of Drake's report:

> The first fact we learned was that a witness's memory of such exotic events fades very quickly. After one day, about half of the reports are clearly erroneous; after two days, about three-quarters are clearly erroneous; after four days, only ten percent are good; after five days, people report more imagination than truth. It became clear that later they were reconstructing in their imagination an event based on some dim memory of what happened. . . . The most curious thing was that a large percentage of the witnesses of both meteorites reported hearing a loud noise at the same time they saw the fireball. Remarkably, the sound was always described as that of frying bacon, despite the fact that the witnesses had no contact with each other.[18]

Drake then reports that about 14% of witnesses in the meteor literature report this sound, in spite of the fact that the vast majority of witnesses do not report it, and the fact that a few simple calculations show that the visual stimulus could not have been accompanied by any sound whatsoever. He suggests this auditory delusion may be due to sensory crossover in the brain when strong uninterpreted stimuli occur.

In view of this experiment, I think it is now impossible to determine what was the cause of the reports of the risen Jesus. The appearances are admitted "exotic events," outside the experience of the observers. As is generally agreed, the earliest written reports are years, not days, after the events. There are a number of examples in the psychological literature[19] of how erroneous observations and actual frauds can generate collective delusions. Collective delusions are extremely common in UFO observations, so common they are called "UFO Flaps." A few people report seeing UFOs, these reports cause other people to look at the sky and misidentify natural objects, thereby generating further reports; for some reason other people think it amusing to fake UFOs, thereby generating UFO sightings of the fakes. There is an *enormous* amount of fraud in reports of strange events.[20] Collective delusions can even occur among trained physicists. The best example of this is the notorious N-rays delusion,[21] wherein over a hundred papers were published in the leading French physics journal reporting observations of a phenomenon—N-rays—that doesn't exist. What I find particularly relevant to the risen Jesus observations is that many of these reports agreed on the fact that N-rays were not emitted by wood. Trained observers agreed on a property of a radiation that did not exist. The relevance lies in the fact that in the N-rays affair we have an example of a collective delusion, involving between ten and a hundred people, which is generated by "independent" observations over an extended period of time of approximately a year. It shows that well-meaning people, by interacting, can generate agreement on the details of an imaginary happening.

In view of the fraud and misobservation known to exist in all reports of unfamiliar events, and in view of the fact that we have documented delusions involving comparable numbers of people over comparable lengths of time, I think the reports of the risen Jesus are insufficient to overrule the observed fact that "the dead do not rise."

Occasionally we scientists are wrong, and the illiterate peasants reporting observations of exotic events correct. The classic example of this is the existence of meteors themselves. Before 1800, almost all educated people believed "There are no stones in the sky, ergo no stones can fall from the sky." The investigation that turned informed opinion around was conducted by the great French physicist Biot, and an analysis of his investigation can be found in an article titled "The Nature of Scientific Evidence: A Summary"[22] by the well-known American astrophysicist Philip Morrison. Morrison's analysis gives the standards which physical science requires evidence to meet before it will believe exceptions to established empirical rules, and by these standards the risen Jesus hypothesis is found wanting. If a proposed historical "fact" is inconsistent with physics, then it must meet the standards not only of history but also of physics.

I could give here my own "best guess" about what happened concerning Jesus' "resurrection," but I shall refrain, since it is just a guess and I agree with Flew—for reasons given above—that there is no way two thousand years after the reports that we can really determine what exactly caused the reports.

On the other hand, if the Christology outlined in the next section were true (it's almost certainly not), then the risen Jesus as described by Luke would be perfectly acceptable as a phenomenon of physical science. Recalling the history of meteor theory mentioned above, one of the barriers to accepting the existence of meteors and meteorites was the absence of any theory which said they should exist. About the time Biot made his observations, Laplace put forward his Nebular Hypothesis for the formation of the solar system. In the Nebular Hypothesis, one would expect debris in the form of stones in interplanetary space remaining to this day. The science of astronomy was transformed from a bastion of powerful empirical arguments against their existence into a strong supporter. As I pointed out in the previous section, this could happen in the future development of the Omega Point Theory, but I doubt it exceedingly.

．————．

The Omega Point Is (Probably) Not a Triune Deity

It is not too difficult to picture the Omega Point as a triune deity. In so doing, one should always keep in mind that the concept of a triune God is always on the verge of falling into the heresy of tritheism—that the Father, Son, and Holy Ghost are three separate coequal Gods—on the one hand, and the heresy of modalism—that the Trinity are just three modes of action of the one true God—on the other. Sabellius, probably the most historically important modalist, held that the three Persons are three modes of God in the same sense that the Sun is bright, hot, and round.[23] Having been warned, let me attempt to avoid both heresies. I pointed out in Chapter VI that the Holy Spirit identified with the wave function of the universe constrained by the Omega Point Boundary Condition was just a mode of speaking of the Omega

Point; so identified, the Omega Point and the Holy Spirit are just two different (ultimately equivalent) mathematical models of Personal Reality, the former emphasizing transcendence and the latter immanence. The modalist heresy is avoided because the modes are in the analysis, not in the Omega Point Itself.

The Second Person is more interesting, and much more of a problem. Here the goal is to construct a model of how a Being can be simultaneously a true man and the monotheistic God. Here also it is almost impossible to avoid heresy. If the human nature is emphasized too much, Christ becomes a mere creature, hence merely the highest of the created order and not God at all: this is called the Arian heresy. If the divine nature is emphasized too much, Christ becomes a sham, not a true man at all, but God pretending to be a man. Historically the most important example of the latter is the Apollinarian heresy, which contended that Jesus had no human soul, but instead the Word formed his entire personality.[24] It might be possible to avoid both heresies in the context of the Omega Point Theory. To see this, recall I pointed out in Chapter VII that it may be possible for all human brains to access the quantum gravity level in order to actualize mixed strategies. If this is done via the Penrose mechanism, then we could also imagine that rarely—so rarely that an actual occurrence would be virtually unique—a human brain could access the data recorded in far future arbitrarily close to the Omega Point in His/Her transcendence. Such an access would be possible in principle at the quantum gravity level since the classical past and future are not globally distinguishable at that level (closed timelike curves necessarily exist in all non–simply connected compact four-manifolds, for example, and in such geometries the future acts on the past). We now know that all apparently unitary human personalities are actually integrations of numerous subpersonalities, or subprograms, running in the human brain. There seems to be a subprogram in the human brain whose job it is to accomplish this integration. An integration of subprograms normally resident in the human brain with the superprograms actually running on computers in the arbitrarily distant future could be regarded as a unitary personality which is simultaneously God and man. Because of the Bekenstein Bound, only the intrinsic humanity with its finiteness would exist at the macroscopic time period where we observe the God/Man; the infinite part of the integrated personality would subsist in the arbitrarily distant future. This would keep the Man in the God/Man, the human nature, from being swamped by the literally infinite memory of the Omega Point in His/Her transcendence, which is the divine nature. Needless to say, I don't believe that such a Personality ever existed. Such a thing is simply too improbable. But it might be possible. It would even be inevitable if the emergence of such a Personality were necessary at a certain stage in human history in order for the Omega Point to eventually arise. If such were the case, the inevitability would be coded in the universe in its very beginning (In the beginning was the Word). Personalities which are integrations between minds in computers and minds in human brains are quite likely in the future when we learn the technology of coupling computers and human brains. I in effect discuss such a mechanism in Chapters VII and VIII as a means of extending the subjective lifetime of the resurrected spiritual bodies. If Jesus really did rise from the dead (which I don't believe), and if his resurrection body really was a spiritual body, then there is no reason not to consider the possibility that both his pre-crucifixion and his resurrection body were so augmented, and in fact integrated with an Infinite Mind, with the integration being as perfect as possible in the resurrection body. (It cannot be absolutely perfect, since a finite entity cannot be put in one-to-one correspondence with a countably infinite entity, which is what the Omega Point is in His/Her transcendence.)

The above model seems to be the most natural way to develop a Christology in the Omega Point Theory. This model appears to have been invented independently by Pannenberg,[25] who, after pointing out the absence of a Christology in an earlier version of the Omega Point Theory, proposed that we look for "the 'computer capacity' of the divine Logos that was connected with the human life of Jesus in the incarnation and became fully available to him in his exaltation." If there is no formation of a unitary personality, just information exchange between a past human and life in the far future, one could term the human involved "inspired by God," or "a prophet."

But I very much doubt if this model of the Second Person and prophets has any application. There is no evidence that any of the thousands of the self-proclaimed "prophets" of the various world religions had any information not available to his or her contemporaries.

My skeptical view of "prophets" is nothing new: the early critic of Christianity, Celsus, writing about A.D. 185, said in regard to Christian claims of Jesus' "prophethood":

> . . . there are countless in that region [Judea] who will "prophesy" at the drop of a hat. They make a show of being "inspired" to utter their predictions. These habitually claim to be more than prophets, and say such things as "I am God," or "I am a son of God," or even "I am the Holy Spirit," and "I have come [to bring life], for the world is come to an end as I speak.[26] . . . Indeed, I have talked with any number of these prophets after hearing them, and questioned them closely. On careful questioning (after gaining their confidence) they admitted to me that they were nothing but frauds, and that they concocted their words to suit their audiences and deliberately made them obscure.[27]

However, the consensus among scholars today is that the whole idea of Jesus being God never occurred to his contemporaries: the Trinity is a much later idea imposed on the Church not by reasoned debate but by the military power of the Roman Empire.[28] Furthermore, there is no evidence in the New Testament that Jesus had any knowledge about God which was not also available to others in his time, as the leading Roman Catholic theologians Hans Küng[29] and Edward Schillebeeckx[30] have pointed out. One indication of this lack of knowledge is the contradiction between Jesus' picture of a loving God and his insistence on eternal punishment in Hell. According to Matthew, Jesus' own words on the question of Hell were "Then he [the Son of Man] will say to those on his left hand, 'The curse is upon you; go from my sight to the eternal fire that is ready for the devil and his angels.' . . . And they will go away to *eternal punishment* [my emphasis], but the righteous will enter eternal life." (Matthew 25:41 and 46 NEB.) These words of Jesus are clear and unequivocal: punishment for some is eternal (and according to Matthew, this eternal punishment is for rather trivial offenses). Since, as I emphasized in Chapter VIII, the Omega Point Theory predicts a loving God and (almost) universal salvation, the Omega Point Theory is inconsistent with Christianity if these words of Jesus are regarded as authoritative. Many Christian theologians have tried to reinterpret Jesus' statement, pointing out that universal salvation is implied in II Peter 3:9: ". . . it is not his will for any to be lost but for all to come to repentance." I have already discussed in Chapters VIII and IX some attempts by other Christian theologians to import universal salvation into Christianity.

The Miracle of Transubstantiation

Most Christians are members of the Roman Catholic, Greek Orthodox, or Russian Orthodox Churches. In these branches of Christianity, the main ceremony is the *Mass,* wherein the priest is believed to miraculously transform bread into the Body of the Risen Jesus and wine into the Blood of the Risen Jesus. Needless to say, all scientific observations of the bread and wine after their "transformation" reveal that the bread is indistinguishable from ordinary bread and that the wine is indistinguishable from ordinary wine. This being the case, many Protestant Christians deny that anything "really" happens in this ceremony. An analogue of this ceremony is still conducted in all Protestant churches, but in many it is regarded as incidental, just a quaint tradition to remind the members of a meal, the Last Supper, which Jesus shared with his closest followers the day before he was executed.

This disagreement over the Real Presence, over whether the Risen Jesus is *really* present in the bread and wine, is *not* trivial. It was a central cause of the religious wars between Catholics and Protestants during the Reformation, wars which claimed the lives of many thousands of people. Given the belief—held by both Catholics and Protestants—that only a select few would be admitted into Heaven, it was reasonable to fight these wars. If the doctrine of the Real Presence were true, it would prove that Catholic priests indeed had some control over who was admitted into Heaven. If the priests did, then anyone who denied the Real Presence publicly not only put his own afterlife at risk, but in addition risked the afterlife of his listeners. Such a person was a dangerous menace to public health. Even today it is generally believed that governments have the right to use force to protect the lives of their citizens. Surely, if the citizens' afterlives were threatened, force would also be justified. On the other hand, if the doctrine of the Real Presence were false, it would prove that Catholic priests had no control over who entered Heaven. Furthermore, by coming between God and humankind, these false priests themselves put at risk the afterlives of everyone who followed them. *They* were the dangerous menaces to public health, and should be killed to save the afterlives of the citizens. In Protestant countries, many priests were put to death. In Catholic countries, many Protestants were put to death. Fortunately, in the Omega Point Theory, the problem does not arise; everyone is raised from the dead to live forever.

The Catholics of course knew that the "transformed" bread and wine was, as far as any human could tell, indistinguishable from untransformed bread and wine. Their explanation was and is that the *substance* of the bread and wine becomes the Body and Blood of the Risen Jesus, but the *accidents* of the bread and wine remain the same when these are transformed. The technical term, first used by the Fourth Lateran Council in A.D. 1215, for this change of substance without a change of accidents, is *transubstantiation*. This explanation of Real Presence, involving transubstantiation, was declared by the Council of Trent in A.D. 1551 to be an official teaching of the Roman Catholic Church, something that a Catholic *must* believe. The Protestants Zwingli and Calvin, in contrast, denied Real Presence completely, while Luther argued for *consubstantiation,* which means that, after consecration, the bread and wine have two substances, the one usual for bread and wine, *and* also the Body and Blood of the Risen Jesus.[31]

The words "substance" and "accident" are terms in Thomist metaphysics, and to get a rough idea of what they are intended to mean, I shall refer to the work of Jacques Maritain, a French lay Catholic theologian, and the leading neo-Thomist of the twentieth century. According to Maritain, "an *accident* is a nature or essence whose property is to exist in something else"[32] while "substance is a thing or nature whose property is to exist by itself *(per se)* and not in another thing."[33] "[Substance] is the absolutely primal being of a thing, the radical principle of its activity and all its actuality. . . . Moreover, in itself substance is *invisible,* imperceptible by the senses. For the senses do not apprehend being as such, but present to us directly only the changing and the moving. . . . In other words the object seen or touched is something which while seen or touched is at the same time also a substance; but it is not seen or touched as a substance. . . . In the language of [Thomist] philosophy *substance is intelligible in itself (per se) and sensible only accidentally (per accidens)."*[34]

It is difficult for a twentieth-century physicist like myself to enter the mindset of a Thomist like Maritain. Scientists have been very suspicious of the Aristotelian notion of substance ever since the time of Galileo, when the Aristotelian philosophers[35] argued that the changes and imperfections observed in the heavens by Galileo and other astronomers had to be merely optical illusions, because the celestial substance, the quintessence, was by nature unchangeable and perfect. However, what seems clear from Maritain's remarks is that "substance" is something in which the observed properties are embedded; the "substance" is a more fundamental level of reality than the "accidents." The distinction between "accident" and "substance" seems roughly analogous to two distinct levels of implementation in computer science, with the "accidents" being a higher level than the "substance." I showed in Chapters II and VIII how it is standard in computers to have a virtual computer inside another computer. By definition, a virtual computer by its very nature exists in another computer. Furthermore, the more basic computer, the one at a lower level of implementation, does not change its fundamental structure when the computer at a higher level does. Recall that we can observe only what exists at our own level of implementation or higher; the lower levels are invisible to us, although they are more basic levels of being than our own level. When we are resurrected by the Omega Point, our resurrection bodies will be our present bodies at a higher level of implementation, our current bodies in a higher level of reality. Maritain admits[36] that there may be many levels of reality, but he denies that there can be an infinite regression of levels: the regression must terminate in God. Similarly, the levels in the Omega Point Theory come to an end in the Omega Point.

If this is an acceptable twentieth-century interpretation of what is meant by the Thomist distinction between substance and accident, then it becomes entirely possible that the Catholics could be correct that the "substance" of bread and wine is changed to the Body and Blood of the Risen Jesus. If it were the case that our present observed universe was not the lowest level of implementation—ultimate reality —but instead our universe was actually a simulation being run on a huge computer (capacity at least $10^{10^{123}}$ bits), then it is *possible* that the portion of our universe which corresponds to the bread and wine of the Mass ceases to be run on the same computer as the rest of the universe at the instant the priest says the magic words. As shown in Chapter II, there are many machines which are equivalent to universal Turing machines, and hence can emulate any finite state machine, and can therefore emulate our entire universe or any part thereof. Our own resurrection body will be such a machine, since it is potentially infinite, and since our current finite minds can emulate the finite fixed part of a universal Turing machine. If Jesus really rose from the dead, and his resurrection body is of the same substance as ours will be, then it could emulate the universe or any part thereof.

I don't believe this, because I don't believe Jesus rose from the dead, and also because there is no evidence that our level of reality is not the ultimate level of reality. Furthermore, if there is actually a lower level of reality, a level under the control of a nontranscendent intelligent being, then the problem of evil reappears. Finally, I do not see any reason for wanting to change the computer from whatever it is now to Jesus' Risen Body. After all, it makes no sensible difference, by Maritain's own admission. I have given this discussion just to show how far in principle the main branches of Christianity, Catholicism and Orthodoxy, can be accommodated in the Omega Point Theory.

Some Catholics would find my analysis unnecessary. Catholic theologians like Edward Schillebeeckx[37] have placed another interpretation on the Real Presence Doctrine, an interpretation which I find too wishy-washy to be interesting, since it is consistent with *any* theory of physics. I note that this new interpretation, and any other attempt to explain Real Presence without using the Thomistic concept of transubstantiation, has been condemned[38] in a 1965 encyclical, *Mysterium Fidei,* by Pope Paul VI. In the latter half of the twentieth century, there has been some convergence of opinion between Roman Catholics and some Protestants, such as Lutherans and Anglicans, on the nature and existence of the Real Presence, but even today these different branches of Christianity will not officially share the "transformed" bread and wine between themselves.[39]

American Deism: An Experiment in Rational Christianity

Is it possible to have Christianity without miracles, to base a religion directly on physics? The founders of the Deist movement in the eighteenth century believed it was possible. "A system of thought advocating natural religion based on human reason rather than revelation" is how my handy Merriam-Webster Dictionary defines "Deism." Thus the Omega Point Theory is a Deist theory, and so a study of the Deist movement will give some insight into the problems faced by a rational religion. Deism exerted its greatest influence in eighteenth-century America—in fact, many of the leaders of the American Revolution were Deists—so I shall focus on Deism in America.

According to all of the American Revolutionary Deists whose writings on religion I have been able to locate, science can establish two essential points: (1) a personal God Who created the universe exists, and (2) this God will ensure that we will live in happiness after death—an afterlife also exists. These two points are of course the central claims of the Omega Point Theory. To see that these two points were accepted by American Revolutionary Deists, let us consider the writings of five key leaders: *Thomas Paine,* author of the pamphlet *Common Sense,* which more than any other writing incited the American colonists to revolution; *Benjamin Franklin,* physicist, printer, and ambassador to France (the chief ally of the Americans) during the war; *Ethan Allen,* commander of the forces that achieved the first American military victory, the capture of Fort Ticonderoga; *Thomas Jefferson,* author of the Declaration of Independence of the United States from the

British Empire, and third President of the United States; and finally *George Washington,* first President of the United States and commander-in-chief of the American Revolutionary Army.

Thomas Paine's religious views were set forth in his book *The Age of Reason,* first published in Paris during the French Revolution. I own a much-worn copy of the first part of this book, printed as a pamphlet in London in 1795 by Daniel Eaton, who styled himself "Printer and Bookseller to the Supreme Majesty of the People." This printer's claim was a direct challenge to royal power, just as Paine's pamphlet was a direct challenge to religion based on revelation. The pamphlet's price, one shilling and sixpence (about eight dollars in 1993 United States currency), was a real bargain for so dangerous a work.

Paine states his central belief on the first page of *The Age of Reason:* "I believe in one God, and no more; and I hope for happiness beyond this life." The body of the pamphlet is devoted to ridiculing the concept of the Trinity (this is what he means by "one God"), and attacking the idea that the Word of God could be in a printed book like the Bible. Paine claimed that the natural world—the physical universe— was the only Word of God. It alone had been created by Him, without human assistance or interference. Only observation of nature, only scientific research, could give us a true picture of what God was really like. Paine concluded his pamphlet with:

> . . . the creation we behold is the real and ever-existing word of God, in which we cannot be deceived. It proclaimeth his power, it demonstrates his wisdom, it manifests his goodness and beneficence. . . .
>
> I trouble not myself about the manner of future existence. I content myself with believing, even to positive conviction, that the power that gave me existence is able to continue it, in any form and manner he pleases, either with or without this body; and it appears more probable to me that I shall continue to exist hereafter, than that I should have had existence, as I now have, before that existence began.

After the war, Ethan Allen wrote a book about God and the afterlife, entitled *Reason, the Only Oracle of Man.* He obviously believed passionately in the book's thesis, since he sold his house in order to publish the book at his own expense. Most of the book was devoted to establishing the existence of God from His Creation, a God Who is "(not only infinitely wise and powerful but) infinitely good." Therefore, said Allen, from the two facts: (1) "God is ultimately Just," and (2) "Justice in all events does not take place in this World," we could deduce "Therefore there must be an existence beyond this life, wherein the ultimate Justice of God will take place."[40]

Benjamin Franklin is my own favorite among the American Revolutionary leaders. Besides being a fellow physicist, he possessed extraordinary common sense, and a way with words which allowed him to encapsulate the essence of an argument in a very vivid image. For example, in a private 1753 letter, he correctly saw why it is silly to expect Heaven as a reward for good works, or as a reward for a correct belief in God:

> . . . You will see in this my notion of good works, that I am far from expecting to merit heaven by them. By heaven we understand a state of happiness, infinite in degree, and eternal in duration: I can do nothing to deserve such rewards: He that for giving a draught of water to a thirsty person, would expect to be paid with a good plantation, would be modest in his demands, compar'd with those who think they deserve heaven for the little good they do on earth.[41]

In another private letter, written in 1756, Franklin consoled a relative with a clear statement of the proper way to think about death and the afterlife:

> I condole with you. We have lost a most dear and valuable relation. But it is the will of God and nature, that these mortal bodies be laid aside, when the soul is to enter into real life. This is rather an embryo state, a preparation for living. A man is not completely born until he be dead. Why then should we grieve, that a new child is born among the immortals, a new member added to their happy society?
>
> Our friend and we were invited abroad on a party of pleasure, which is to last for ever. His chair was ready first, and he is gone before us. We could not all conveniently start together; and why

should you and I be grieved at this since we are soon to follow, and know where to find him?[42]

Franklin developed in his youth his rational religion, based on the existence of both God and the afterlife, and he retained these beliefs throughout his life. In his *Autobiography,* Franklin stated that, as a young man, he resolved to write a book on religion based on six propositions, the first being "That there is one God, who made all things," and the sixth being "And that God will certainly reward virtue and punish vice, either here or hereafter."[43] In his final letter on religion, written just six weeks before he died, Franklin repeated this credo to the president of Yale:

> You desire to know something of my religion. . . . Here is my creed. I believe in one God, Creator of the Universe. That he governs it by his Providence. That he ought to be worshipped. That the most acceptable service we render to him is doing good to his other children. That the soul of man is immortal, and will be treated with justice in another life respecting its conduct in this. These I take to be the fundamental principles of all sound religion. . . .[44]

Although Franklin spoke of the soul as "immortal," he did not really believe in the immortality of the soul, but rather he believed in the eventual reconstruction of the body by God, just as predicted by the Omega Point Theory. This is shown by the epitaph which Franklin wrote for himself:

> The body of B. Franklin, Printer, Like the Cover of an old Book, Its Contents torn out, And stript of its Lettering and Gilding, Lies here, Food for Worms. But the work shall not be lost; for it will, as he believ'd, appear once more in a new and more elegant Edition Corrected and improved By the Author.[45]

Notice that Franklin implicitly accepted the pattern theory of identity. To him, "Benjamin Franklin" was not a particular copy of a certain pattern—a certain computer program in twentieth-century language—which existed in the eighteenth century, but rather the pattern itself. There need not be any continuity between a particular copy and the "new and more elegant Edition" which will be brought back into existence in the future.

During his first term of office as President of the United States of America,[46] Thomas Jefferson found the time to begin and complete "a wee little book" on theology, *The Philosophy of Jesus*. The book was never published, and the manuscript has disappeared, but he often referred to the book in his correspondence. In 1803, also during his first term of office, Jefferson sent to his friend Benjamin Rush a "Syllabus of an Estimate of the Merit of the Doctrines of Jesus, Compared With Those of Others." This Syllabus is probably an abstract of the book. In this Syllabus, Jefferson listed what he believed were the four main contributions of Jesus to religious thought, and the first and fourth were:

1. He corrected the Deism of the Jews, confirming them in their belief of only one God, and giving them juster notions of his attributes and government. . . .
4. He taught, emphatically, the doctrine of a future state: which was either doubted or disbelieved by the Jews: and wielded it with efficacy, as an important incentive, supplementary to the other motives to moral conduct.[47]

In a letter written in 1822, long after he had retired from the presidency, Jefferson wrote that the religious doctrines of Jesus (which he also regarded as the essential doctrines of the Deism he himself accepted) were just three:

1. that there is one God, and he all-perfect:
2. that there is a future state of rewards and punishments:
3. that to love God with all thy heart, and thy neighbor as thyself, is the sum of religion.[48]

These three points are clearly the same as those listed by Franklin. John Adams, the second President of the United States, was the arch political foe of Jefferson during their terms of office, but they became reconciled in retirement. Several times Jefferson wrote to Adams of his belief in the afterlife, and stated that he looked forward to seeing his beloved wife and children once more.[49]

The first President of the United States was far more reticent on the subject of the afterlife than Jefferson. Virtually the only reference we have concerning George Washington's belief in the afterlife is in a letter he wrote to his sister when their mother died:

> Awful and affecting as the death of a parent is, there is consolation in knowing that Heaven has spared ours to an age beyond which few attain, and favored her with the full enjoyment of her mental faculties. . . . Under these considerations, and a hope that she is translated to a happier place, it is the duty of her relatives to yield due submission to the decrees of the Creator.[50]

Deism is currently moribund. In spite of the fact that it was supported by the leading intellects of the American Revolution, Deism had disappeared from American intellectual life by 1810, long before even Jefferson was dead. This disappearance occurred long before the design argument for God's existence was demolished by Darwin's theory of evolution (first published in 1859). So what killed Deism? It was a rational religion, based on the best science of the day, Newtonian cosmology. But it could not compete with the Christianity based on revelation, not reason. Why not?

I believe Deism died because the physics upon which it was based was simply too impersonal.[51] Newtonian mechanics pictured the universe as a vast perfect clocklike machine. Because it was so perfect, the Builder had to be all-powerful and perfect. But conversely, this very perfection implied that the Creator need not intervene in the world, indeed He could not without marring the perfection of the clockwork. God ceased to be a loving Father and became instead an absentee landlord. Indeed, the definition of Deism which became current in philosophy books by the end of the nineteenth century was not that cited at the start of this section, but rather "belief in a God who creates the universe at the beginning of time, but thereafter lets the universe run itself." The one thing religion by revelation never lost was belief in a personal God. A personal God, and only a personal God, can *care*. Americans in the nineteenth century felt, I think correctly, that the

Deist arguments for the afterlife, such as Allen's, were very shaky. Following Franklin's argument on the relative value of Heaven to our present life to its logical conclusion, it is clear we humans need not justice but mercy. The Maker of the perfect Newtonian machine could be expected only to provide justice. A loving Father provides mercy.

Religion can be based on physics only if the physics shows that God *has* to be personal, and further, that the afterlife is an absolutely solid consequence of the physics. I have argued in earlier chapters that the Omega Point Theory satisfies both of these criteria, and hence the theory can be a foundation for all human religions.

XIII.

CONCLUSION: THEOLOGY
AS A BRANCH OF
PHYSICS

THE REAL IMPORTANCE OF THE OMEGA
Point Theory is that it provides a plausible physical mechanism for a universal resurrection, not that it supports the claims of a particular religious tradition. As Wolfson[1] has pointed out, resurrection has been inconsistent with the accepted physics of the day for the past two thousand years. That has now changed. So much has it changed that the only objection which the Russian physicist Andrei Linde[2] had to the resurrection theory was that it is too (ontologically) reductionist; it assumes that a human being can be exhaustively described at the most basic level by the known physical laws.

I claimed in the Introduction that theology is either nonsense, and hence doomed to fade away, or else it will one day become a branch of physics. The general opinion among scientists has been that theology would just fade away. But there are historical precedents for an apparently fully discredited theory to make a dramatic reappearance. I mentioned a few examples in the Introduction. For another example, when an epidemic of yellow fever occurred in Barcelona, Spain, in 1822, a group of French doctors made a detailed and exhaustive study[3] of exactly how the disease appeared. The doctors established conclusively that there was no possibility of contact between the people who were stricken with yellow fever in Barcelona. It was inferred that the germ theory of disease was permanently disproved. It never occurred to anyone that yellow fever could be transmitted from one person to another by mosquitoes. Over the next half century, this French study was used in an attempt to abolish the ancient quarantine regulations which were applied in European ports. It was claimed that, since no disease could be caught from another person, quarantines were relics of superstitious times. British liberals regarded the quarantines as an irrational infringement on individual liberty and as a manifestation of Roman Catholic ignorance.[4] The germ theory was resurrected in the latter part of the nineteenth century by Pasteur and his new medical physics.

Thus we see that physics had to be extended to medicine in order to save the germ theory. Similarly, for religion to survive, physics must be extended into theology. Or, as the nineteenth-century physicist John Tyndall put in his famous Address before the British Association for the Advancement of Science in 1874: "The impregnable position of science may now be described in a few words. We claim, and we shall wrest from theology, the entire domain of cosmological theory."[5] With the introduction into physics of the Dirac/Dyson Eternal Life Postulate, science has taken the last independent stronghold of theology. Thus, theological research in the twenty-first century will require a Ph.D. in particle physics, in Weinberg's sense[6] of the phrase "particle physics" (a discipline encompassing general relativity, physical cosmology, and traditional elementary particle physics). The medieval theologians would not be surprised at a prerequisite of a degree in physics for a degree in theology. In their time, the highest degree in philosophy— which included the most advanced knowledge of the physics of the day —*was* a prerequisite before a student was permitted to begin study for a degree in theology. The deep knowledge of physics possessed by the medieval theologians was apparent in their work. For example, Kenny[7] has shown that Aquinas' Five Ways—his five proofs of God's existence —are absolutely dependent on Aristotelian physics, and that these proofs require a thorough knowledge of this physics. Aquinas in fact was one of the leading scholars of Aristotelian physics of his day, and it was primarily Aquinas who was responsible for the general acceptance of Aristotelian physics throughout Europe. We could with justice call Aquinas a great physicist as well as a great theologian, for, although Aristotelian physics was wrong, it was an essential precursor of modern physics.[8]

.———.

Theology and Religion Are Branches of Science, Not Branches of Ethics

Many twentieth-century theologians and scientists argue that Aquinas and indeed all the pre-twentieth-century theologians were mistaken in their attempt to combine science and religion. These twentieth-century theologians and scientists claim that science and religion can have limited contact because these disciplines deal with different realms of human experience: religion is primarily concerned with moral questions, while science deals with facts. They claim this moral/fact distinction is justified by the grammar of all human languages: moral sentences are *imperative* sentences ("You *ought* to do this") whereas factual sentences are *declarative* sentences ("The sky *is* blue"). It is indeed not possible to derive an imperative sentence from a declarative sentence, "to get an 'ought' from an 'is.' "

But the claim that morality is the central concern of religion is nonsense. Throughout human history, the central concern of religion has been human self-interest. In the Judeo-Christian-Islamic tradition, all morality has been obtained from *declarative* sentences of the form "Thou shalt not kill—*because you'll go to Hell if you do!*" In the Hindu-Buddhist tradition, the situation is similar: "Thou shalt not kill—*because you'll be reborn as a cockroach if you do!*" The force of both moral statements depends on the declarative clauses, in the former case on the supposed physical existence of Hell and of an omnipotent God Who will put you there if you behave in certain ways, and in the latter case on the supposed fact of reincarnation and a physical mechanism which couples the reincarnation state on specific behavior. In both cases, the appeal is to physics, not to fundamental moral postulates. The claims "Thou shalt not kill because it is bad" or "Thou shalt not kill because God says it is bad," or simply "Thou shalt not kill," would merely invoke further questions: "But *why* is it bad?" "So what if God says it is bad? Maybe God Himself is evil." Or simply, "Why not?"

Thus the essential difficulty with divorcing morality from facts is that in such a case there would be no way to resolve moral disputes. Morality would then be just a matter of taste, like whether or not you like spinach. But "Thou shalt not kill" cannot be left as simply a matter of taste; if by assumption facts are irrelevant to moral disputes, these disputes would have to be resolved by violence. (Notice that this is a factual statement, not a moral one.)

Fortunately, this is unnecessary. I claim that in virtually all—I can think of none—so-called disputes over morality there is in fact no disagreement over fundamental moral principles, only disagreement over facts. For example, consider a current much-disputed "moral" issue in the United States and Europe, the abortion issue. There is no dispute over "Thou shalt not kill," there is only a dispute over whether a fetus is a "person." This is purely a factual question, and as a matter of fact both sides of the debate appeal to what they consider to be facts: the antiabortionists claim that the fetus is a person because he/she has, as a matter of fact, a human soul which is implanted by God at the moment of conception, whereas the pro-choice people claim that a fetus is not a person because, as a matter of fact, it has none of the essential features of personhood, namely coherent higher brain function, ability to function independently, etc. If one examines the literature on abortion carefully, one sees that both parties share the same morality, and they share it with the entire human species. *All* disputed issues are disputes over matters of fact.

It is often said that the central concern of religion is an attempt to answer the question: "What is the relationship between humanity and the universe (and/or God)?" I agree and, as I just pointed out, the *factual* answers to this question obtained by the Buddhists, Christians, Jews, Muslims, etc., led to the ethical norms of these religions. The sharp distinction between fact and value which is common in twentieth-century philosophy and in the West was not present in the traditional religions.

I might also point out that this sharp distinction is actually contrary to the continued existence of science itself. The growth and existence of science require certain ethical norms: for example, THOU SHALT NOT IMPOSE YOUR THEORIES ON OTHERS BY FORCE. Only persuasion, based on rational argument and experimental results, is allowed. When this ethical principle is violated—as it was in Italy in the seventeenth century when Galileo's opponents used the Inquisition to silence him; and as it was when Christians in the fourth century stamped out competing philosophies—science disappears. In the former case, Italy ceased to be the leader in science in seventeenth-century Europe, and in the latter, science essentially disappeared from Europe from the fourth to the sixteenth centuries. This is a factual observation, of course—I haven't shown that knowledge is "good"—but the central fact remains: knowledge is inextricably entwined with ethics, and it always has been. So the radical distinction between "is" and "ought" sentences with which I opened this section is misleading. Science as a human activity contains within it ethical maxims, which is to say it contains not only "is" sentences but also "ought" sentences. And as a matter of simple logic, even if we accept the distinction, it *might* be possible to derive *all* the "ought" sentences we use in everyday human life from a single "ought" sentence, say the maxim of proper behavior for scientists, which I just gave in capital letters.

In summary, if religion is permanently separated from science, then it is permanently separated from humanity and all of humanity's concerns. Thus separated, it will disappear.

The Omega Point Theory and Contemporary Religions

Religions have disappeared in the past and, when they have, the mechanism has always been a persuasive (at the time) appeal to facts. Christianity replaced the native religions in Central America because the Native Americans noticed that they were being decimated by diseases to which the European invaders were essentially immune. The Native Americans observed that prayers to their gods were useless, while prayers by the Europeans to their gods were (apparently) effective. Since, according to the theories of nature believed in by both the Native Americans and the Europeans, a prayer to a real god for protection against disease should be effective, the Native Americans rationally abandoned their gods for the gods of the Europeans. And this switch was (apparently) effective: the Native Americans ceased to die from disease at quite the same rate as before. We now know of course that prayers to either set of gods had nothing to do with the relative death rates. The Europeans had a partial immunity obtained by exposure over thousands of years to the diseases, whereas the Native Americans initially had none. But they had developed some immunity by the time the religious switch was made. Given their knowledge base, the Native Americans were rational to switch religions, though their "knowledge" was false. Their switch was based on purely scientific grounds (this mechanism of religion replacement in Central America has been discussed at length by the historian McNeill[9]).

Christianity had earlier displaced a number of competitor religions, among them the Greek and Roman religions, some four hundred years after the death of Jesus. The central argument for Christianity at the time was that the religion had moved from being the belief of a persecuted tiny minority to the dominant religion of the Empire. Since practically everyone at the time, including the intellectuals, believed in gods or in a supreme God, it was hard to understand how this could have happened without the god of the Christians being either the one true God, or at least a more powerful god than His opponent gods. Again, this is a purely rational argument, based on what most people at the time believed to be a *fact,* namely that gods (or God) existed physically, and actively intervened in human affairs. Today we would explain (I think correctly) this triumph of Christianity by purely sociological reasons, for instance by appeal to the persuasiveness of the argument I have just described.

Christianity was itself displaced from the Near East and from North Africa by Islam. Once again the argument for Islam in these regions was an appeal to the observed facts: Islamic troops had defeated Christian armies over and over again for centuries and, given the assumption (made by both Muslims and Christians) that the True God would ensure the victory of His believers, it followed that Islam was the true religion. (Earlier, Mohammed's military victories in Arabia were regarded[10] by Arabians as strong evidence that his claim to be God's Prophet was in fact true.) Religions are *always* firmly based on the science of the day.

The central problem with contemporary theology and indeed most of late-twentieth-century religion is not that it is separated from science but that it is separated from *modern* science. It is still locked into ancient Greek physics and philosophy. As the Yale historian of religion Jaroslav Pelikan put it in the case of Christianity:

> The victory of orthodox Christian doctrine over classical thought was to some extent a Pyrrhic victory, for the theology that triumphed over Greek philosophy has continued to be shaped ever since by the language and the thought of classical metaphysics. For example, the Fourth Lateran Council in 1215 decreed that "in the sacrament of the altar . . . the bread is transubstantiated into the body [of Christ]." . . . Most of the theological expositions of the term "transubstantiation" have interpreted "substance" [according] to the meaning given this term . . . in the fifth book of Aristotle's *Metaphysics;* transubstantiation, then, would appear to be tied to the acceptance of Aristotelian metaphysics or even of Aristotelian physics. . . . Transubstantiation is an individual instance of what has been called the problem of "the hellenization of Christianity."[11]

The Significance of the Omega Point Theory for the Average Person

In 1888 Lord Adam Gifford set up what have become known as the Gifford Lectures, given each year at the Scottish universities of Edinburgh, Glasgow, St. Andrews, and Aberdeen, on the subject of natural theology. This is beyond doubt the most prestigious lecture series on the subject of science and religion given anywhere on Earth. I have referenced them many times in this book. In his will establishing the lectures, Lord Gifford asserted: "I wish the lecturers to treat their subject as a strictly natural science . . . without reference to or reliance upon any supposed . . . miraculous revelation. . . . I wish it considered just as astronomy or chemistry is."[12]

Sciences are sciences because they can be tested experimentally.

I argued in Chapter IV that, to really test the Omega Point Theory, we will need the Tevatron upgrade and either the SSC—the Texas Supercollider—or the European LHC. The latter two machines are quite expensive. But perhaps it would be worth several billion dollars to establish that God exists, and that one day we will all be resurrected to live forever with Him/Her. When the eminent physicist Steven Weinberg[13] testified in favor of building the SSC in 1987, the following exchange occurred between Representative Harris Fawell of Illinois—a supporter of the SSC—and Representative Don Ritter of Pennsylvania, one of the most hostile critics of the project:

FAWELL: . . . If ever I would want to explain to one and all the reasons why the SSC is needed I am sure I can go to your testimony. . . . I wish sometimes that we have one word that could say it all . . . I guess perhaps Dr. Weinberg . . . came a little close to it. . . . You said you suspect that it isn't all an accident that there are rules which govern matter and I jotted down, **will this make us find God** [my emphasis]? . . .

RITTER: Will the gentleman yield on that? If the gentleman would yield on that for a moment I would say . . .

FAWELL: I'm not sure I want to.

RITTER: If this machine does that I am going to come around and support it.

Weinberg said nothing in reply because, as he later wrote, ". . . it did not seem to me that letting them know what I thought about this would be helpful to the project.[14] . . . It would be wonderful to find in the laws of nature a plan prepared by a concerned creator in which human beings played some special role. I find sadness in doubting that we will."[15]

If I had been there, I would have replied, "Mr. Fawell, if the Omega Point Theory is true (and my Higgs-shear effect is real), then yes, it would." Mr. Ritter was defeated in his 1992 bid for reelection to the U.S. House of Representatives (though I draw no theological implications from his defeat). Were he still a member, I would now call upon him to keep his word and change his vote.

The SSC and the LHC are often compared to the cathedrals of the Middle Ages and to the pyramids of ancient Egypt. The cathedrals were built to help the medieval Europeans find God and the Egyptian kings find their immortality. If I am right, the SSC and the LHC could do both for all humanity.

Although this book is not a Gifford Lecture, I have followed Lord Gifford's wish to the letter. Not only have I treated theology as a strictly natural science, I have argued that it *is* a natural science, in fact a branch of astronomy. Now science is based on reason, and on reason alone. It has no use for revelation in any way, shape, or form. Consequently, any theological claim to truth based on revelation has to be taken with a grain of salt.

A somewhat similar skeptical view of revealed religions was expressed in his book, *All Religions Are True,* by Mahatma Gandhi, the founder of modern India: "Whilst I believe that the principal books [of the great world religions] are inspired, they suffer from a process of double distillation. Firstly, they come through a human prophet; and then through the commentaries of interpreters. Nothing in them comes from God directly. . . . Only God is changeless; and as His message is received through the imperfect human medium, it is always liable to suffer distortion in proportion as the medium is pure or otherwise."[16]

There is a third difficulty with a book supposedly "inspired by God." The principal books of the great world religions are all over a thousand years old. A great deal has occurred in a thousand years. Science, civilization, and society have all changed utterly since the principal books were written. When the New Testament was written, the Earth was thought to be the center of the universe; we now know it to be the third planet from the Sun. When the New Testament was written, everyone believed that all living species had existed from eternity, or else were created separately by direct intervention of God. We now know that all living species were evolved from earlier species. Thus we read the Bible using a different mindset from our ancestors.

This means that the same set of words will convey different meanings to people of different ages. *If these meanings are contradictory, at least one has to be false!* There are verses in the Bible which were interpreted before the Copernican Revolution as proving the Earth was immovable. These verses are now interpreted as poetic expressions, not to be taken literally. Since a book has to have a total length of between 1 and 10 million bits of information, it is a logical impossibility for any book to clear up all such misinterpretations. Even if a book *were* inspired by God, it would necessarily contain statements which most believers in that book, at some historical period, would misinterpret. This does not mean that God is limited, it only means that human beings are.

The only book which does not suffer from these limitations is the Book of Nature, the only book which God wrote with His/Her own hand, without human assistance. The Book of Nature is not limited by human understanding. The Book of Nature is the only reliable guide to the true Nature of God.

This does not mean that it is the only guide to God. I have shown at length in this book that the Omega Point Theory is consistent, broadly speaking, with the core beliefs of all the great world religions. If the Omega Point Theory is true, then it cannot (at the moment) select one of the human religions as more accurate than the others. What it can do is act as a firm foundation for all of them.

Religion is far more than theology—indeed, the average person knows very little of the theology of his or her own religion. Religion is based on theology, but for the average person religion is mainly church attendance, ritual, and prayer. If the Omega Point Theory is true, should a believer continue to do these things in his or her own church? Does it still make sense to pray to God?

Did it ever make sense to pray to God? Certainly not, if prayer is regarded as the sending of a message to God. If God is omniscient, then He knows what you are going to say before you say it. In information theory, a message contains "information" only if the receiver learns something from the receipt of the message. Therefore, prayer cannot be the sending of a message to God.

Christian theologians have realized this from the earliest times. In prayer, the message is transmitted only in the other direction, from

God to a human. Origen, the first great Christian theologian, emphasized in his great work, *On Prayer*, that prayer was just an opening up of oneself to God. I agree; I would say that prayer is an attempt to *feel* that God exists, to *feel* that He/She loves us, that events will *eventually* work out for the best, and that we all will one day be resurrected to live forever with Him/Her. Prayer in this meaning still makes sense in the Omega Point Theory. If traditional prayer and the rituals in your church help you to feel the truth of these things, then go to church and pray. If you can feel the truth without these rituals, then don't pray (I don't, for example).

Thus revealed theology is to natural theology as geocentric astronomy is to heliocentric astronomy. If all you want is the rough location of the stars and planets in the sky, then geocentric astronomy is quite adequate. A better approximation is heliocentric astronomy based on Newtonian gravity. But Newtonian gravity does not really exist; gravity is really the curvature of spacetime. Thus, although the best theory we have describing the positions of the planets is Einstein's gravity theory, Newton's theory is good enough for almost all purposes, and for a few basic purposes, geocentric astronomy is sufficient. As I have tried to establish in this book, the essence of almost all revealed religions is to assert that (1) God exists, and (2) He/She loves us all and will one day resurrect us all to live forever. This is also the essence of the Omega Point Theory, and it is sufficient for practically everyone. The technical details beyond these basic truths can be left to the Appendix for Scientists. Even very few professional physicists progress beyond Newtonian gravity to a deep understanding of Einstein's theory. It is not necessary for their work.

The Omega Point Theory allows the key concepts of the Judeo-Christian-Islamic tradition now to be modern physics concepts: theology is nothing but physical cosmology based on the assumption that life as a whole is immortal. A consequence of this assumption is the resurrection of everyone who has ever lived to eternal life. Physics has now absorbed theology; the divorce between science and religion, between reason and emotion, is over.

I began this book with an assertion on the pointlessness of the universe by Steven Weinberg. He repeats this in his latest book, *Dreams of a Final Theory,* and goes on to say ". . . I do not for a minute think that science will ever provide the consolations that have been offered by religion in facing death."[17]

I disagree. Science can now offer *precisely* the consolations in facing death that religion once offered. Religion is now part of science.

NOTES

NOTES TO PREFACE

1. Weinberg 1977, p. 154.
2. Ibid., pp. 131–32.
3. Weinberg is even harder on modern theologians than I am: "Religious liberals are in one sense even farther in spirit from scientists than are fundamentalists and other religious conservatives. At least the conservatives like the scientists tell you that they believe in what they believe in because it is true, rather than because it makes them good or happy. Many religious liberals today seem to think that different people can believe in different mutually exclusive things without any of them being wrong, as long as their beliefs 'work for them.' This one believe in . . . heaven and hell, [that one] believes in the extinction of the soul at death, but no one can be said to be wrong as long as everyone gets a satisfying spiritual rush from what they believe. . . . [W]e are surrounded by 'piety without content.' . . . I happen to think that the religious conservatives are wrong in what they believe, but at least they have not forgotten what it means really to believe in something. The religious liberals seem to me to be not even wrong." (Weinberg 1992, pp. 257–58). I have the same impression of liberal theologians. Feynman is even harder on liberal theologians than Weinberg. In his best-selling book *Surely You're Joking, Mr. Feynman!* he calls them "pompous fools." (Feynman 1986, p. 259.)

   In his autobiography, *Self-Consciousness*, the American novelist John Updike also observes that very few professors of religion believe in resurrection of the dead: "During [my] adolescence, I reluctantly perceived of the Christian religion I had been born into that almost no one believed it, believed it really— not its ministers, nor its pillars like my father and his father before him. (Updike 1989, p. 242.) Updike's novel *A Month of Sundays* has an amusing scene (Updike 1976, pp. 182–85) in which a doubting theologian/minister who is seducing his female parishioners is unable to get an erection with the unique woman in his flock who truly believes in God and the resurrection, and he fails *because* she believes.

4. Rosen 1939, p. 139.

NOTES TO CHAPTER I. INTRODUCTION

1. Barrow 1982.
2. Tillich 1957, p. 5.
3. Robinson 1963, p. 29.
4. Jonas 1963.
5. Pannenberg 1969, p. 56.
6. To see that the Hebrew word *"Ehyeh"* in the expression *"Ehyeh Asher Ehyeh"* of Exodus 3:14 is unquestionably the future tense of the verb "to be," and that therefore the complete expression must be translated "I WILL BE WHAT I WILL BE," note that the same word *Ehyeh* is used in Exodus 3:12 in the expression "Certainly *I will be* with thee . . . (KJV)" which is *always* translated in the future tense. The most authoritative Jewish commentator on the Bible was and still is Rashi (the name is formed from the first letters, in Hebrew, of Rabbi Solomon Issacson), who lived in France from A.D. 1040 to A.D. 1105. Rashi emphasized that the name God gives Himself must be translated in the future tense (Hertz, 1961, p. 215), and most modern Jewish rabbis have followed this translation; see, for example, Kaplan 1991, p. 271. Though it is claimed in various Christian sources that the Hebrew can be taken as either future or present tense (as, for example, the *Cambridge Bible Commentary* [Clements 1972, p. 23], it appears that the more usual present tense translation comes from theological rather than philological considerations. An extensive discussion with a large number of references on this point can be found in Childs 1974, pp. 60–70. The name I AM THAT I AM was preferred theologically because it was taken to mean that God was declaring his necessary self-existence. Even Moses Maimonides, in *Guide for the Perplexed* (Chapter 63 of Part I), translated *"Ehyeh Asher Ehyeh"* as I AM THAT I AM for this reason (see Friedländer's 1956 translation of *Guide for the Perplexed*, p. 94). In the standard English translation of Rashi's *Commentary,* that of Rosenbaum and Silbermann (1972), *"Ehyeh Asher Ehyeh"* is translated I AM THAT I AM, but at least the translators note Rashi's interpretation: "I WHO WILL BE with them in future sorrows" (Ibid., p. 12). The standard Hebrew-English Old Tes-

tament lexicon, that of Brown, Driver, and Briggs (based on an earlier He-
brew-German lexicon by Wilhelm Gesenius), translates *"Ehyeh Asher Ehyeh"*
as I WILL BE WHAT I WILL BE (Brown, Driver, and Briggs 1906, p. 218).

7. Bloch 1986, p. 1236.

8. Küng 1980, p. 622.

9. Tillich 1957, p. 7.

10. Press 1984, p. 6.

11. Heath 1913.

12. Copernicus dedicated his book to Pope Paul III. In 1545, just two years after
Copernicus' book appeared, the Italian theologian Giovanni Maria Tolosani,
who was a close friend of Pope Paul III's personal theologian, wrote: "The
book by Nicholas Copernicus of Torun was printed not long ago and published in recent days. In it he tries to revive the teaching of certain Pythagore-
ans concerning the Earth's motion, a teaching which had died out in times
long past. Nobody accepts it now except Copernicus. . . . For it is stupid to
contradict a belief accepted by everyone over a very long time for extremely
good reasons, unless the naysayer uses more powerful and incontrovertible
proofs. Copernicus does not do this." (Rosen 1984, pp. 188–89).

13. The passage quoted is taken from Kuhn (1957, p. 191), who in turn takes it
from White (1896, Vol. I, p. 126). It should be noted, however, that this quote
is not from one of Luther's own books, but from *Table Talk,* a collection of
notes taken by various people over the period 1531–44 of informal discussions
held in Luther's home. There is something of a disagreement about just what
Luther said about Copernicus. The passage quoted was taken from the first
published version of *Table Talk* by Aurifaber, who is regarded by most Luther
scholars to be unreliable. The version recorded by Lauterbach (June 4, 1539) is:
"There was mention of a certain new astrologer who wanted to prove that the
earth moves and not the sky, the sun, and the moon. This would be as if
somebody were riding on a cart or in a ship and imagined that he was standing
still while the earth and the trees were moving. [Luther remarked] 'So it goes
now. Whoever wants to be clever must agree with nothing that others esteem.
He must do something of his own. This is what that fellow does who wishes to
turn upside down *[invertere vult]* the whole of astronomy' " (Luther 1967, pp.
358–59). According to the Oxford Latin Dictionary, *"invertere"* can mean "to
turn upside down," or "to reverse" or "to reverse direction," or "to violently
upset." In the context of Luther's time and Copernican astronomy, *all* of these
different meanings are appropriate: (1) Copernicus "violently upset" the intellectual world with his new theory; (2) Copernicus "reversed the direction" of
sky motion—the earth, and not the sun, moves; (3) Copernicus turned the
universe "upside down"—the sun was up in the sky but is now "down" in the

center of the solar system; (4) Copernicus "reversed" astronomy to a previous state. (In the introduction to his own book in 1543, Copernicus *said* he was returning to a model advanced by the ancients [Kuhn 1957, p. 142].) If Luther had the knowledge of an educated man of his day—we know he did—and was both a punster and a master of the Latin language—he was both—then it is plausible to conclude that he meant *all* of the above meanings simultaneously. The best English-language source for the original German and Latin Lauterbach version of the passage quoted is Elert 1962, p. 424. I am grateful to Professor Jaroslav Pelikan for this reference.

14. The Italian historian of science Pietro Redondi has argued (1987) that the real reason Galileo was brought before the Holy Inquisition was not his defense of the Copernican system, but rather his defense of the central idea of modern science: that the observed appearance of physical objects tells us what they in fact are. This directly contradicts the entire Catholic theory of transubstantiation. According to modern science, if the altar bread appears to be bread, and further, if there is no experiment, even in principle, which can distinguish between the blessed bread and the unblessed bread, then the altar bread is bread *and nothing else.* No doubt Galileo and indeed all modern scientists are heretics as the transubstantiation heresy was defined by the Council of Trent. (The vast majority of historians of science are quite dubious of Redondi's theory. See Gingerich 1990, McMullin 1989, and Westfall 1989, for a few examples.) However, the Copernican system is even more heretical, since in its later infinite-spaces form it pushes Heaven as the abode of the blessed off to infinity, or eliminates Heaven altogether. Christianity can do without transubstantiation, but not without life after death.

15. Galilei 1957, p. 178.

16. Ibid., pp. 187–88.

17. Vallery-Radot 1923, p. 235.

18. Kant 1950, pp. 29 and 46.

19. Hume 1965, p. 167; italics are Hume's.

20. Galilei 1957, p. 186; see also Drake 1980, p. 29.

21. Drake 1980.

22. Brush 1981, Part II.

23. Vallery-Radot 1923, p. 233.

24. Ibid., p. 224.

25. Unamuno 1954, p. 5.

26. The sociologist (and Roman Catholic priest) Andrew M. Greeley argues (1985, 1989) that the data on people's religious beliefs do *not* support my claim that the advance of atheism among scientists will eventually lead to atheism among the laity. The data quoted by Greeley are indeed impressive: polls taken

over forty years give the following results (Gallup and Jones 1989, pp. 16 and 206; Greeley quotes similar numbers, some from other polls).

Question: "Do you believe in the existence of God or a universal spirit?"

YEAR	PERCENTAGE ANSWERING "YES"
1944	96
1947	94
1952	99
1959	97
1967	97
1981	95
1988	94

Question: "Do you believe there is a life after death?"

YEAR	PERCENTAGE ANSWERING "YES"
1944	76
1948	68
1952	77
1961	74
1965	75
1975	69
1981	71
1985	74
1988	71

Clearly there is no obvious downward trend in either belief. (The slope of the least squares straight line for the belief in God is -0.04 ± 0.12 percentage points per year, and the slope for the afterlife belief is -0.06 ± 0.16 percentage points per year, where the error bars give the 95% confidence level. Thus the data are consistent at the 95% confidence level with *zero* decrease in both beliefs over half a century.) However, a greater percentage of Americans believe in God and in life after death than do most Europeans. An international poll conducted by the Gallup organization gave the following in 1981 (Neuhaus 1986, pp. 119–20):

Question: "Do you believe in the existence of God or a universal spirit?"

NATION	PERCENT ANSWERING "YES"	PERCENT ANSWERING "NO"	PERCENT ANSWERING "DON'T KNOW"
U.S.A.	95	2	3
Irish Republic	95	3	2
Northern Ireland	91	3	5
Spain	87	8	6
Italy	84	10	6
Belgium	77	12	10
Great Britain	76	16	9
West Germany	72	16	12
Norway	72	22	7
Netherlands	65	25	10
France	62	29	9
Denmark	58	27	15
Sweden	52	35	14

Question: "Do you believe there is a life after death?"

NATION	PERCENT ANSWERING "YES"	PERCENT ANSWERING "NO"	PERCENT ANSWERING "DON'T KNOW"
Irish Republic	76	14	11
Northern Ireland	72	14	14
U.S.A.	71	17	13
Spain	55	26	18
Finland	49	32	20
Italy	47	33	19
Great Britain	45	35	19
Norway	44	40	16
Netherlands	42	40	18
West Germany	39	40	21

Belgium	37	39	24
France	35	50	14
Denmark	26	55	19

Thus we see that disbelief is positively correlated with high standards of living—with the level of technological advancement—among the First World nations. I am aware of no comparable poll of Second and Third World nations, but a survey of 1,000 people in the European part of Russia conducted in the period November 1–15, 1992, by the Times Mirror Center for the People and the Press indicated that nearly two thirds of the 112 million adults living in the area "do not doubt the existence of God." A similar poll by the same organization conducted in August 1991 (just after the coup attempt, about the time of the fall of communism) found that only 46% believed in God's existence. A 60% belief rate would put Russia between France and Denmark, about where we would expect it to be from the level of technological knowledge in Russian population.

The United States is the anomalous exception among the First World nations. In the United States, there was no correlation in 1988 between education level and belief in God: 91% of those with college degrees, 93% of those with some college, 96% of those with only a high school education, and 93% of those with less than a high school education believe in God (Gallup and Castelli 1989, p. 87).

However, a 1981 Gallup poll of leading American scientists (defined as scientists listed in Marquis' Who's Who in America) showed that to the question "Do you believe in life after death, or not?" 68% answered "no," 16% answered "no opinion," and only 16% answered "yes." Furthermore, a 1981 Gallup poll of American doctors and medical scientists (defined as persons in the field of medicine listed in Marquis' Who's Who in America) showed that to the question "Do you believe in life after death, or not?" 60% answered "no," 8% answered "no opinion," and only 32% answered "yes" (Gallup 1982, pp. 207–12). Thus, even in America, the better educated a person is in the sciences, the more likely it is that the person will disbelieve in life after death. The Gallup poll did not ask the scientists whether they believed in God as children, so we do not know if they started life as believers or as unbelievers. However, a study by the sociologist Harriet Zuckerman (1977, p. 68) of American science Nobel prize winners *suggests* that a majority of these scientists were believers in childhood, but a great majority were unbelievers as adults. (I say "suggests" because the crucial questions about changes in belief were apparently not posed by Zuckerman. I am inferring change by comparing Zuckerman's figures on the Nobelists' religious background with her report of their current religious belief.) If this were true of the scientists polled by the

Gallup organization, then it is a strong exposure to science that corrodes belief in God, and the results of the European poll could indicate that the average European has more exposure than the average American. Greeley (1989) believes that it is a tradition of anticlericalism in Europe that has undermined belief there, not more exposure to science. The Gallup organization could distinguish Greeley's hypothesis from mine by repeating the poll of leading American scientists, but this time asking them questions about their religious beliefs in childhood. Until this is done, I shall continue to go by the results of the Zuckerman study of Nobel prize winners. Furthermore, Greeley's hypothesis is contradicted by the above-mentioned Russian poll: Russia experienced seventy years of intense anticlerical (indeed, antireligious) propaganda, much more intense than any experienced in any West European country, yet when the discrimination against believers in God ceased, people's belief in God returned to the rate one would expect on the basis of the extent to which technical knowledge is disseminated among the general population.

Gallup did not poll scientists in any other year except 1981, so we cannot say how the beliefs of the scientific community changed with time. However, in 1916 the American psychologist James Leuba polled several random samples of the scientists listed in *American Men of Science* about their belief in immortality. The starred names in this list (Leuba called scientists with starred names "greater men") were roughly equal in eminence to the scientists listed in *Who's Who*. Leuba unfortunately did not give the numbers he obtained for all of his samples, but it is possible to infer from his statements on pp. 252–53 of (Leuba 1916) the percentages for the group he calls "Greater Men in Division II" ("Division II" is his name for one of his random samples). These are compared with the above-mentioned Gallup data in the following table:

Question to leading scientists: "Do you believe in life after death, or not?"

YEAR	PERCENT ANSWERING "YES"	PERCENT ANSWERING "NO"	PERCENT ANSWERING "DON'T KNOW"
1916 (Leuba)	35	25	40
1981 (Gallup)	16	68	16

Clearly, the "no" replies went from a small minority to the overwhelming majority in the 65 years between the two polls. However, a bare majority of scientists were atheists even in 1916: to the question, "Do you believe in God?" 28% of the "Greater Scientists of Division II" said "yes," 52% said "no," and 20% said "don't know." (Gallup did not poll leading scientists about their belief in God.)

I therefore think my claims that the advance of science and technology has undercut traditional religious belief, and that if the trend over the past fifty years continues would destroy it altogether, are correct. Only a purely physical theory of God and life after death like the Omega Point Theory can rescue these beliefs from annihilation.

27. Provine 1987; 1988, pp. 60–62.
28. Mayr 1980, p. 3.
29. Provine 1987, p. 52; 1988.
30. Weinberg 1987.
31. Sheehan 1984.
32. Dirac 1961.
33. Pannenberg 1977, 1981.
34. Barth 1933, p. 192.
35. Pannenberg 1972, p. 170.
36. Rahner and Vorgrimler 1983, p. 196.
37. Tipler 1989a.
38. Moravec 1988, pp. 122–24.
39. Nozick 1989, pp. 24–26.

NOTES TO CHAPTER II.
THE ULTIMATE LIMITS OF SPACE TRAVEL

1. Caldiera and Kasting 1992.
2. Many are more than dubious; they *ridicule* the idea of Strong AI. They believe that comparing the brain to a computer, and the soul to a program, is at best a rough analogy. In the early twentieth century, people compared the brain to a telephone exchange; today the analogy is with the computer.

It's more than an analogy. The brain *is* a computer, and the soul *is* a program. After many centuries of mistakes on what thinking is, and where it occurs, we've got it right at last: The brain *is* a computer in the same sense that the heart *is* a pump. The ancients didn't even know the latter.

The ancients believed that the *heart,* not the brain, was the seat of the soul, and the location of the intellect. Thus the opening line of both Psalm 14 and Psalm 53, "The fool hath said in his heart, There is no God . . ." (KJV), does not draw a distinction between thinking and feeling—the modern interpretation—but simply means "in his mind, the fool has said to himself, There is no God."

Aristotle, for example, believed that thinking occurred in the heart, not the brain. In his *On Youth, Old Age, Life and Death, and Respiration*, Aristotle states ". . . all sanguineous animals have the supreme organ of the sense-faculties in the heart, for it is here that we must look for the common sensorium belonging to all the sense organs [469^a 10–12]. . . . Elsewhere I have stated the reasons why some of the sense organs are, as is evident, connected with the heart, while others are situated in the head. (It is this fact that causes some people to think that it is in virtue of the brain that the function of perception belongs to animals [469^a 19–23]" (Barnes 1984, p. 747). Aristotle believed that the brain was mainly used, not for thought, but to cool the body [652^b 1–30] (Barnes 1984, p. 1016). In his work *On Memory*, Aristotle referred to the heart as "that part of the body which contains the soul" [450^a 30](Sorabji 1972, pp. 50 and 80). Plato agreed that the soul was in the heart, not the brain. In his dialogue *Theaetetus*, Plato compares the recording of information in memory with the making of an impression of a seal in wax, and makes a pun on the similar sounds of the Greek words for "wax" and "heart": "Whenever the wax in someone's soul is deep, extensive, smooth, and kneaded in a measured way, the things that are proceeding through perceptions, in putting their seals into that feature of the soul which Homer, in hinting at its similarity to wax *(kéros)*, said was heart *(kear)*, it's then that the seals for them come to be pure in the wax and with adequate depth prove to be long lasting." *[Theaetetus, 194C–D]* (Benardete 1984, I.65).

3. See Hofstadter and Dennett 1981, pp. 69–95 (Chapter 5) for further discussions of the Turing Test.
4. Barrow and Tipler 1986, p. 136; Dudai 1990; Haarer 1992.
5. Young 1988, p. 157.
6. Squire 1987, p. 15.
7. Braitenberg 1991.
8. Schwartz 1990.
9. Ibid.
10. Moravec 1988.
11. Bell 1992a, 1992b; Burkhardt 1992.
12. Moravec 1988.
13. Ibid.
14. Debate quoted from Kenny *et al.* 1972, pp. 152–54.
15. McCarthy 1990, p. 611.
16. Penrose 1989, p. 414.
17. Ibid., p. 415.
18. Ibid.

19. Ibid., p. 416.
20. Raup 1991.
21. Maynard Smith 1992, p. 34.
22. Krugman 1990.
23. Penrose 1989.
24. Mathematically, the functional dependence is $R(t + 1) = R(I(t), S(t))$.
25. Mathematically, the functional dependence is $S(t + 1) = S(I(t), S(t))$.
26. Minsky 1967, p. 24.
27. See, for example, Wolfram 1984 and Langton 1990.
28. Fredkin and Toffoli 1982; Margolus 1984.
29. Margolus 1984.
30. Langton 1988.
31. Berlekamp, Conway, and Guy 1982.
32. Searle 1980, 1984. Searle 1980 is reprinted with commentary in Hofstadter and Dennett 1981.
33. Maughan 1992, p. 37.
34. Penrose 1989, p. 29 [note 8].
35. Searle 1984, p. 33.
36. Freitas 1980; Tipler 1981; Barrow and Tipler 1986, Chapter 9.
37. Von Neumann 1966; Arbib 1969.
38. Cliff, Freitas, Liang, and Von Tiesenhausen 1980.
39. Tipler 1981; Barrow and Tipler 1986, Chapter 9.
40. Stuhlinger 1964.
41. Forward 1984, 1990; Friedman 1988.
42. O'Neill 1977.
43. Barrow and Tipler, 1986, p. 581.
44. Fisk and Reck 1993.
45. Drexler 1986, 1992.
46. Forward 1984, 1986.
47. Drexler 1992.
48. Ibid. 1986, 1992.
49. Ibid. 1992.
50. Sato and Tsukamoto 1993.
51. Wolfe 1985.
52. Augenstein 1993.
53. Augenstein *et al.* 1988; Mills 1988.
54. Augenstein, private communication in 1993.
55. Forward 1982, 1985.
56. O'Neill 1977.
57. These calculations on the ease of interstellar travel show that we need not fear our expansion will take real estate away from other intelligent beings, as the

European expansion after Columbus took land away from non-Europeans. THERE ARE NO EXTRATERRESTRIALS! If they existed, they would already be here. This argument has been developed at length elsewhere (Barrow and Tipler 1986, Chapter 9; Tipler 1981), so let me not repeat it here. Also, the consensus opinion of the evolutionary biologists (Mayr 1985) is that the evolution of intelligent life is extremely improbable, so improbable that we are most likely the only intelligent species in the visible universe, quite possibly the only one in the entire universe!

The Omega Point Theory provides another argument for the rarity of extraterrestrials: if they were very common throughout the universe—as many as one per galaxy—then they would be too likely to use up the free energy in the form of rest mass before the shear energy becomes available after recollapse begins. If this happens, life will die out and never become the Omega Point. The Eternal Life Postulate guarantees this cannot happen.

On the other hand, the Eternal Life Postulate guarantees that life of some sort will engulf the universe. It need not be us and our descendants. We can still use our free will power and destroy ourselves. If this happens, then the Eternal Life Postulate guarantees that there is some other intelligent species out there to do the job. (The descendants of this other species, by the way, will be the ones to resurrect us.)

58. Lasker 1989.
59. I'm tempted to call this powerful Earth-moving butterfly THE BUTTERFLY THAT STAMPED, after the equally powerful butterfly in the *Just So Stories,* by Rudyard Kipling.
60. Barrow 1982.

NOTES TO CHAPTER III: PROGRESS AGAINST THE ETERNAL RETURN AND THE HEAT DEATH

1. Helmholtz 1961.
2. Darwin 1860, p. 486.
3. Raup and Valentine 1983.
4. Darwin 1860, p. 489.
5. Raup 1991, p. 3.
6. Barlow 1959, p. 92.
7. Russell 1957, pp. 106–7.
8. Weinberg 1977, p. 149.
9. Ibid.
10. Russell 1957, pp. 10–11.

11. Duhem 1954, p. 288.
12. Ibid., p. 290.
13. Alpher and Herman 1948, 1988.
14. Hermann 1972.
15. Stewart and Tait 1875, p. 172.
16. Interestingly, Stewart and Tait tried to prove that this hierarchy of reality levels allowed individual human immortality. They contended that human souls could be transferred, like energy, from a lower level to the one above it. After I describe in later chapters the immortality mechanism of the Omega Point Theory, the reader will realize that the Stewart and Tait mechanism sounds very similar. In the Omega Point Theory, we shall indeed live again after death in a higher level of reality. The key difference between the two theories is that I do not have to appeal to an "unseen" universe which has never been observed. Instead, in the Omega Point Theory, the higher level of reality is a higher level of implementation inside computers. I shall defer discussing what exactly this means until Chapter IX, but the essential point is that we have observed these different levels in operation. These levels really exist. The noncomputer expert may not realize it, but every time he or she uses a personal computer, several such different levels of reality are actually used by his or her machine. I shall also describe in Chapter IX exactly how we will eventually go from the level at which we currently exist to a higher level in the computers of the far future. Stewart and Tait could not do this, as the state of physical knowledge in the nineteenth century was too primitive. Furthermore, Stewart and Tait were reluctant to admit that the human person could be completely analyzed by physics. In contrast, I am an uncompromising reductionist: everything, including human beings, can be completely described by physics. This reductionism allows me to *prove,* rather than merely conjecture as Stewart and Tait did, that the immortality mechanism I shall describe will actually work. Nevertheless, I am proud to acknowledge Stewart and Tait as my most distinguished predecessors in the endeavor to make life after death scientifically respectable.
17. Brush 1978.
18. Eddington 1928.
19. Jeans 1929.
20. De Santillana and von Dechend 1969, p. 332.
21. Ibid., p. 4.
22. Baillie 1950, p. 42; Eliade 1954; Toulmin and Goodfield 1965.
23. Baillie 1950, p. 4; Sorokin 1937, p. 360.
24. Sorokin 1937, p. 353.
25. Eliade 1954, p. 88.
26. Sorokin 1937, p. 358.

27. Ibid., p. 362.
28. Ibid., p. 363; Jaki 1974, p. 354.
29. Eliade 1954, p. 89.
30. Baillie 1950, p. 47.
31. Toulmin and Goodfield 1965, p. 46.
32. Aristotle, *Problemata,* Book XVII, p. 3.
33. Baillie 1950, p. 48.
34. Plato, *Timaeus* 39; *Politicus* 269C.
35. Baillie 1950, p. 48; Toulmin and Goodfield 1965, p. 45.
36. Needham 1965, p. 29.
37. Augustine, *The City of God,* Book 12, Chapter 14.
38. Thorndike 1948, pp. 203, 370, 418, 710, 745, 895.
39. Needham 1965, pp. 6, 20.
40. Ibid., p. 22; Needham 1960, pp. 598ff. and 603ff.
41. Needham 1965, p. 6, and Needham 1960, p. 406.
42. Needham 1965, p. 50.
43. Sivin 1966, 1969.
44. Jaki 1974; Tillich 1948; Cullmann 1950.
45. Nietzsche *Eternal Recurrence,* #5; translation by Levy 1910.
46. Nietzsche *The Will to Power,* #1066; translation by Levy 1910.
47. Ibid.
48. Nietzsche *Eternal Recurrence,* #7; translation by Levy 1910.
49. Nietzsche *The Will to Power,* #1064; translation by Levy 1910.
50. Nietzsche *Eternal Recurrence,* #8; translation by Levy 1910.
51. Kaufmann 1950, p. 270.
52. Heidegger 1991, p. 25 [Volume I, Section 5 of *Nietzsche*].
53. Ibid., pp. 106–32 [Volume II, Sections 14–17 of *Nietzsche*].
54. Nietzsche *The Will to Power,* Section 55; translation by Kaufmann 1950, p. 287.
55. Brush 1978, p. 73.
56. Stambaugh 1972, p. 16.
57. Nietzsche, *Der Antichrist,* Section 34; translation by Kaufmann 1950, p. 275.
58. Nietzsche, *The Gay Science,* Section 125.
59. Sartre 1977.
60. Stambaugh 1972, p. 88.
61. Nietzsche, *Ecce Homo,* Chapter II, Section 10; translation by Kaufmann 1950, p. 285
62. Quoted and translated by Kaufmann 1950, p. 288.
63. Weber, quoted by Bloom 1987, p. 194.
64. Nietzsche, *Untimely Meditations, Part II: Of the Use and Disadvantage of History for Life,* Section 9; translation by Kaufmann 1950, p. 274.

65. Ibid., *Part III,* Section 6; translation by Kaufmann 1950, p. 274.

66. Nietzsche, *Der Antichrist,* Section 34; translation by Kaufmann 1950, p. 275.

67. Nietzsche, *Ecce Homo,* Chapter 3, Section 1; quoted by Kaufmann 1950, p. 274.

68. Nietzsche, quoted in Kaufmann 1950, p. 288.

69. Holten 1992.

70. Camus 1975, pp. 3 and 9.

71. Ibid., p. 123.

72. Nietzsche, *Also Sprach Zarathustra,* Chapter IV, Section 19; translated by Kaufmann 1950, p. 282.

73. Bäumler, quoted by Farias 1989, p. 253.

74. Cassidy 1992, p. 350.

75. E.g., Kaufmann 1950, Chapter 10.

76. Nietzsche, *Untimely Meditations, Part I,* Section 1; translation by Kaufmann 1950, p. 33.

77. The most reliable and detailed accounts of Heidegger's involvement in Nazism are those of Hugo Ott, *Martin Heidegger: Unterwegs zu seiner Biographie* (Frankfurt: Campus Verlag, 1988), and Bernd Martin, *Martin Heidegger und das dritte Reich* (Darmstadt: Wissenschaftliche Buchgesellschaft, 1989). I have not put either of these in my bibliography since they have yet to be translated into English. The best account in English is the short article "What Heidegger Wrought" by Mark Lilla (1990). The best-known (but unfortunately unreliable) account in English is Victor Farias' *Heidegger and Nazism* (1989).

78. Heidegger, quoted by Lilla 1990, p. 50.

79. Harris 1978, p. 324.

80. Heidegger, quoted by Harris 1978, p. 323.

81. This Heidegger quotation is the translation by Farias (1989, p. 299); the Sheehan translation is in Heidegger (1966, p. 61).

82. Heidegger 1966, p. 56.

83. Ibid., p. 62.

84. Ibid., p. 63.

85. Ibid., p. 57.

86. Ibid., p. 56.

87. Sagan and Newman 1983, p. 115.

88. Schodt 1988.

89. Mori 1974.

90. Ibid., p. 22.

91. Kuhn 1970a, p. 206; see also Kuhn 1970b, p. 265.

92. Weinberg 1992.

93. Glashow 1992.

94. Polkinghorne 1989.

95. Lasker 1989.

96. Kubrin 1967.

97. Brush 1976, p. 553.

98. Murray 1815, p. 434.

99. Brush 1976, Section 14.

100. Thompson 1910, p. 111.

101. Arrhenius 1908.

102. Rankine 1852.

103. Brush 1976, Section 14.7.

104. Ibid., Section 14.8.

105. Most twentieth-century discussions of the Eternal Return are based on the so-called oscillating closed-universe model developed in 1922 by the Soviet mathematician Alexander Friedmann. In fact, Friedmann himself was aware of the apparently cyclic nature of time in his solution, and suggested that one could identify the corresponding times in each cycle. However, in the Friedmann model the radius of the universe goes to zero at the beginning and end of each cycle—these are called the "Big Bang" and "Big Crunch" singularities respectively—and thus from a strict mathematical standpoint the cycles are separated by a singularity; they are not true "cycles."

106. Nisbet 1980.

107. Himmelfarb 1980. The most detailed history of the Idea of Progress is Van Doren 1967.

108. Spencer 1902, pp. 477–529.

109. Ibid., p. 529.

110. Engels 1940, pp. 24–25.

111. Haldane, in Engels 1940, p. 24.

112. Ibid., p. 20.

113. Ibid., p. 24.

114. Milne 1952.

115. Letter from Dyson to FJT.

116. Bernal 1969, p. 27.

117. Ibid., p. 28.

118. Ibid.

119. Ibid., p. 46.

120. Ibid., p. 47.

121. Ibid., p. 79.

122. Ibid., p. 80.

123. Lukas and Lukas 1981.

124. An even more detailed comparison of Teilhard's Omega Point theory and the one developed in this book, as well as more discussion of Teilhard's science,

can be found in Barrow and Tipler, 1986. A picture of Teilhard is on p. 212 of
Mortier and Aboux 1966; photos Halsman, New York.

125. Teilhard 1975, p. 29.
126. Medawar 1961.
127. Teilhard 1975, pp. 43, 52, 66.
128. Ibid., p. 149.
129. Ibid., pp. 57 (footnote), 71, 301.
130. Lukas and Lukas 1981, pp. 167–75.
131. Mayr 1980, p. 1.
132. Ibid., p. 3.
133. Boesiger 1980, p. 309.
134. Limoges 1980, p. 327.
135. Teissier, quoted in Boesiger 1980, p. 310.
136. Teilhard 1975, pp. 63–64.
137. Medawar 1961.
138. Teilhard 1975, pp. 287–88.
139. Ibid., pp. 270–71.
140. Ibid.
141. Ibid., pp. 168–69.
142. Ibid., pp. 239–40.
143. Teilhard to Hyppolite, quoted in Cuénot 1965, pp. 254–55.
144. Dyson 1979, 1988.
145. Islam 1977, 1979, 1983.
146. Rees 1969.
147. Dyson 1979, p. 448.
148. Dyson 1988.
149. Gould 1988, p. 319.
150. Ibid., p. 329.
151. Gould 1977, p. 190.
152. Ibid., p. 199.
153. Gould 1983, p. 111.
154. Maynard Smith 1992, p. 35. But Maynard Smith went on to say: "I agree
with him in rejecting the Victorian notion of a stately and inevitable progress
toward the *Omega Point*" [my emphasis]. Fair enough. The evolutionary data
naturally show no evidence of the Omega Point—the Omega Point is cosmological, not terrestrial. And for the last half billion years or so, life has pro-
gressed mainly in the "momentum space" direction—increasing ecological
niches—rather than in the configuration space direction—life engulfed the entire Earth billions of years ago. So progress is harder to see than it would be if it
were an expansion in configuration space. And progression over the past half
billion years is far from uniform; the dinosaur ecosystem was knocked flat by a

meteorite some 70 million years ago. But the Victorians never expected progress to be uniform: the "Dark Ages" was their term for the retrogressive historical period between the fall of the Roman Empire and the rebirth of learning.
155. Maynard Smith 1992, p. 35.
156. Bonner 1988; Boyajian and Lutz 1992.
157. Raup 1991.

NOTES TO CHAPTER IV: PHYSICS NEAR THE FINAL STATE: THE CLASSICAL OMEGA POINT THEORY

1. Cairns-Smith 1982.
2. Barrow and Tipler 1986.
3. Dawkins 1986, p. 330.
4. Dawkins 1976, p. 207.
5. Boethius, *Consolation of Philosophy,* Book 5, Prose 6.
6. Origen, quoted in Pelikan 1961, p. 90.
7. Pelikan 1961, pp. 48–49.
8. Ibid., p. 91.
9. Dyson 1979.
10. The leading experts in general relativity—for examples, Penrose (1989), Ellis (1988), Hawking (1988, p. 132), and John A. Wheeler (private communication)—have never accepted the inflation model. The inflationary universe has always been supported by high energy particle physicists whose command of general relativity is not as deep as one would like to see in physicists so influential.
11. Pannenberg 1972, 18.
12. See Hofstadter and Dennett (1981, pp. 379–81) for another discussion of "levels of implementation."
13. Only two of these names appear in the Jewish Bible: Michael (in Daniel 10:13 and 12:1) and Gabriel (also in Daniel, 8:16 and 9:21). Michael and Gabriel are also the only angels mentioned by name in the New Testament. Michael (Jude 1:9; Revelation 12:7) is regarded as the leader of God's military forces. According to Luke, Gabriel is the angel of the Annunciation: he is the angel who announces to Mary that she will give birth to Jesus (Luke 1:26ff.). The other two angelic names are found in the Apocrypha: Raphael in Tobit (12:15) and Uriel in Second Esdras (4:1–11). Uriel is by tradition the angel who carried the burning sword that kept the fallen Adam and Eve from returning to the Garden of Eden, hence his name. (The Apocrypha are books of

the Old Testament that are accepted as canonical by Roman Catholics, but not by Protestants or Jews.)

Gabriel and Michael are the only good angels mentioned by name in the Qur'an. Gabriel is named three times in the Qur'an, and Michael once, in the *Cow* Sura (Arberry 1955, Vol. I, p. 40). "Whoever is an enemy to God and his angels and His Messengers, and Gabriel and Michael— . . ." The Qur'an gives the names of five other angels: Iblis, the Islamic equivalent of Satan; Malik, the angel who oversees Hell; Harut and Marut, two fallen angels; and finally Malaku'l-Maut, the angel of death. According to the *Cow* Sura (Arberry 1955, Vol. I, p. 40) and Islamic tradition, the Qur'an was dictated word for word to Mohammed by Gabriel. All Mohammed did was recite to his scribes what Gabriel told him. In fact, in Arabic the word "Qur'an" means "Recitation." Since the Qur'an was dictated word for word to Mohammed by God in His Gabriel manifestation, and since God chose to dictate in medieval Arabic, the Qur'an cannot be translated; if rendered in another language, this rendering is necessarily an "interpretation," not a translation.

That the suffix (or prefix) "-el" means "God" is familiar to readers of the New Testament. The last words spoken by Jesus as he died on the cross are quoted by all Bibles in the original Hebrew: *"Eloi, Eloi, lama sabachthani?"* which means: "My God, my God, why hast thou forsaken me?" (Mark 15:34; Matthew 27:46). (Jesus' last words are the words of Psalm 22:1.)

The word "angel" comes from the Greek word *angelos,* which means "messenger." In current popular usage, an "angel" is an intelligent being intermediate between God and humankind. The Greek word *daimon* would be closer to the current meaning, but in fact Paul and John used the words *angelos* and *daimon* interchangeably. The superintelligent programs of the far future are clearly analogous to "daimons," but they can be regarded also as messengers of the Omega Point in Its transcendence. In Christianity there is a hierarchy of angels between God and humankind. This hierarchy is required to exist by the Principle of Plenitude which underlies the emanation theory explaining how God created the universe. A similar hierarchy exists in the Omega Point Theory for essentially the same reason, as I shall discuss in Chapters VIII and IX. But in the Omega Point Theory the hierarchy exists in time, not space, as in Christianity.

I might mention in this note that there is no analogue of Satan in the Omega Point Theory; Christianity and Islam are wrong about the existence of such a being. Even in traditional Christian theology, the existence of Satan, who is held to have been an angel of the highest rank before he revolted against God, is problematic. How could an angel of the highest rank, of immense intelligence and *knowing* from personal experience that God not only exists but is both omniscient and omnipotent, ever even consider revolting against God?

Such an angel would know for certain that an insurrection against omnipotence is doomed to failure. This difficulty can be overcome only by assuming that God is actually not omnipotent, and that Satan is actually a being with power comparable to God's. But this is the philosophy of dualism: evil is comparable in ultimate influence to good. Such is not the case in the Omega Point Theory. As I shall discuss in the section on the Problem of Evil, evil necessarily exists, but good is necessarily more powerful, and necessarily wins out in the end. The word "necessarily" here means, as always, logically necessary; evil ultimately winning out would be a logical contradiction. Note also that the word "ultimately" is important; we in particular will probably not be resurrected for trillions of years of proper time.

One might naively think that it is possible for one of the superbeings of the far future to be evil; perhaps such an evil creature could be regarded as an analogue of Satan (or one of his subordinate evil angels). Such a thought does not take into account the full implications of true immortality, or of the ability of advanced beings to resurrect a suicide. An evil mortal man like Hitler could afford to be nasty to the Jews and Slavs. He wanted them permanently out of the way, and he believed that, if by some improbable chance they happened to win the resulting war, he could always escape justice by killing himself. And this is what he did: he shot himself at the last minute to avoid capture by the Russian Army. (Russian troops were only a hundred yards from Hitler's bunker in Berlin when he died.) But Hitler will not escape justice; he will be resurrected in the far future by superbeings using mechanisms described in this book, and he will have to answer for his crimes. Hitler died in the confident hope that he would die permanently, never to rise again. He is going to be very surprised. Potentially evil superbeings of the far future will know about the resurrection mechanism and will not want to risk being cruel to those who are themselves immortal and who will eventually have the power to resurrect the miscreant.

There is a *huge* literature on angels. Angelology was in vogue in Western Europe from A.D. 1000 to A.D. 1200, when the names of literally *thousands* of angels were written down. For an introduction to this fascinating subject, see *A Dictionary of Angels,* by Gustav Davidson (1967).

14. Plato, *Timaeus* 37d.
15. *Consolation of Philosophy,* Book 5, Prose 6. This book enjoyed an enormous influence in the High Middle Ages (around the thirteenth century).
16. Boethius was a Christian, and he was attempting to cast Christian theology in the language of Greek metaphysics. It is open to debate whether the writers of the Bible intended God to be "eternal" in the sense of Boethius and Aquinas. For example, James Barr, the professor of the Old Testament at the University of Edinburgh, points out in his book *Biblical Words for Time* (Barr 1962) that the

philology of the biblical texts does not allow one to distinguish between God being eternal in the sense of being coterminous with time, and being eternal in the sense of being outside of time, but he allows that the writers of the text may have meant both (Barr 1962, p. 147). The Omega Point is "eternal" in both senses.

NOTES TO CHAPTER V: DETERMINISM IN CLASSICAL GENERAL RELATIVITY AND IN QUANTUM MECHANICS

1. Russell 1988.
2. I should mention in passing that, in general relativity, the standard conservation laws are almost trivially true. In general relativity, the conservation law for mass-energy reads $d^\star T = 0$, which follows from the Einstein equations $G = 8\pi T$, which can be regarded as defining the stress energy tensor T, and the fact that *any* metric g satisfies $d^\star G = 0$. See Misner, Thorne, and Wheeler 1973, Chapter 15, for a discussion of this point. The principle of inertia plays no role in sustaining the universe in existence.
3. Hawking and Ellis 1973, Chapter 7. The proof assumes the physical meaningfulness of the Axiom of Choice, and that *physical* spacetimes are those in which the g's and F's have derivatives at least to the fourth order. The Axiom of Choice says that from an arbitrary collection of sets it is possible to form another set which is made by taking exactly one member from each set of the collection. The Axiom of Choice is trivially true if the collection of sets is finite and each has a finite number of elements, but the existence of a unique maximal domain of dependence requires that the Axiom of Choice be true for an infinite collection, each with an infinite number of members. It is not obvious that such makes physical sense.
4. Tipler 1979, 1980.
5. Rosen 1975, p. 330. However, just as today most physicists disbelieve in the MWI, most astronomers in Kepler's day disbelieved in Copernicus. Between 1543 (publication date of Copernicus' book) and 1687 (publication date of Newton's *Principia,* the work which ended the debate in favor of Copernicus) 2,330 works on astronomy were published, but only 180 were Copernican—about 8 percent of the total. See de Santillana, 1959, p. 164.
6. Raub 1991 (unpublished).
7. Gell-Mann 1992.
8. Weinberg 1992, pp. 82, 232; Llewellyn Smith 1993.

NOTES TO CHAPTER VI: THE QUANTUM VERSION OF THE OMEGA POINT THEORY

1. In some quantum cosmologies the initial data are Y (h,F,S) and its first derivatives.
2. In technical language, $M = S \times R^1$.
3. See Section 7.2 of Barrow and Tipler (1986) for details about how this works. The argument needs to be generalized to arbitrary Hamiltonians that have classical limits. I shall assume that such a generalization exists in what follows.
4. Somewhat more accurately, the Hartle-Hawking boundary condition is stated as "the universal wave function is that wave function for which the Feynman sum over all the paths (classical and otherwise) leading to a given point (h,F,S) is over paths that have no boundaries (more precisely, the four-dimensional manifold corresponding to a given path is a compact manifold whose only boundary is (h,F,S))."
5. Freedman and Luo 1989, p. 3.
6. Lawson 1974; Thurston 1976.
7. More precisely, the leaves of the foliation are embedded differentiable three-manifolds, with the normal vectors to the leaves defining global vector fields, so that t parameterizes the foliation and dt is the form normal to each leaf.
8. Hawking and Ellis 1973.
9. Hartle 1991.
10. Pannenberg 1977.
11. Ibid. 1981.
12. Ibid. 1977.

NOTES TO CHAPTER VII: HOW FREE WILL CAN ARISE FROM QUANTUM COSMOLOGICAL MECHANISMS

1. James 1948, pp. 40–41.
2. Pannenberg 1971, p. 242.
3. See Earman (1986, pp. 241–42) for a discussion of this important point.
4. Geroch and Hartle 1986.
5. Freedman and Luo 1989, p. 3.
6. Mathematically meaningless equations for the universal wave function can be written down—for example, the wave function satisfies Feynman's famous $U = 0$ equation (Feynman 1964, Vol. II, p. 25: 11). This equation is obtained by first gathering *all* of the equations of physics: for examples, Newton's Sec-

ond Law of Motion, F = ma; Einstein's general relativity field equation G = 8πT; Ohm's Law's V = RI; and so forth. Next, rewrite all these equations by subtracting the expression on the right-hand side of each equation from both sides, getting F − ma = 0; G − 8πT = 0; V − RI = 0; and so forth. Notice that all of the equations of physics are now of the form "something = 0." Now add up all the squares of these equations. The sum of all the expressions on the left we call U. Clearly, U = 0. As Feynman himself said, this "equation" is absolutely meaningless. It contains no information not in the original equations beyond what the original equations could compute.

7. Monk 1976, p. 234.
8. Boolos and Jeffrey 1974.
9. Ibid. 1974.
10. Machtey and Young 1979, p. 192.
11. Monk 1976, p. 234; Boolos and Jeffrey 1974, Chapter 21.
12. Machtey and Young 1978, 1981.
13. Turing 1950, p. 459; this part of Turing's paper is unfortunately *not* reprinted in Hofstadter and Dennett 1981.
14. Wald 1950.
15. Ibid., p. 27.
16. Von Neumann and Morgenstern 1953, p. 143.
17. Penrose 1989, p. 400.
18. Eccles 1989; 1990.
19. Penrose 1989, p. 401.
20. James 1948.
21. Monod 1971; see Chapter 7.
22. See, for example, Root-Bernstein (1989, particularly pp. 360–66) and the references therein.
23. Hofstadter and Dennett 1981, p. 380.
24. Libet *et al.* 1983.
25. Friedman 1986, pp. 358–61; Tipler 1988.
26. Kant 1950, p. 525.
27. Feynman 1986, p. 55.

NOTES TO CHAPTER VIII: THE OMEGA POINT AND
THE PHYSICAL UNIVERSE NECESSARILY EXIST

1. Kant 1950.
2. Williams 1981.
3. Kant 1950, p. 524.

4. For more discussion of whether a simulation must be regarded as real if it copies the real universe sufficiently closely, see Hofstadter and Dennett 1981, particularly pp. 73–78, 94–99, and 287–320.
5. Kant 1950, p. 505.
6. Barrow and Tipler 1986.
7. Plato, quoted by Hick 1978, p. 73.
8. Plotinus, *Enneads* (Book 5, Chapter 2, Section 1), quoted by Hick 1978, p. 74.
9. Augustine, quoted by Lovejoy 1936, p. 67.
10. Lovejoy 1936.
11. Ibid., p. 52.

NOTES TO CHAPTER IX: THE PHYSICS OF
RESURRECTION OF THE DEAD TO ETERNAL LIFE

1. Pannenberg 1970, p. 80.
2. Rheingold 1991; Gelernter 1991; Benedikt 1991.
3. Barrow and Tipler 1986, p. 565.
4. See Penrose 1989 for more discussion of this property of double exponentials.
5. Bekenstein 1981; Schiffer and Bekenstein 1989; Penrose 1989.
6. Sometimes the Bekenstein Bound is written $I \leq A/4L_P^2 \ln 2$, where $L_P \approx 10^{-35}$ meters is the Planck length. If we use this version of the Bound, a human being must be coded by 10^{70} bits or less. One might naively think that the Bekenstein Bound would make impossible the storage of an arbitrarily large amount of information as the radius R of the universe goes to zero, since the area of the largest sphere that can be in the universe also goes to zero as $R \rightarrow 0$. The Bekenstein Bound applies in the Omega Point Theory, but since life has engulfed the entire universe and the c-boundary is a single point, the Bekenstein Bound merely restricts the rate of divergence of information storage. (In these circumstances, the Bekenstein Bound is actually less restrictive than other constraints on the rate of divergence which I have analyzed elsewhere [Barrow and Tipler 1986]). To see this, let us note that the *general* Bekenstein Bound on the information I in a region is not $A/4L_P^2 \ln 2$, but $I \leq (2\pi)^2 ER/hc\ln 2$, where R is the radius of the smallest sphere circumscribing the region, and E is the total energy in the region. (This is discussed in the Appendix for Scientists.) If we let R be proportional to the radius of the total closed universe, then it is clear that, provided the energy in the universe diverges faster than R^{-1}, then the RHS of the Bekenstein inequality diverges also. I show in the Appendix for Scientists that, in the Omega Point Theory, E actually diverges as R^{-3}, so total information stored can diverge as R^{-2} as $R \rightarrow 0$. I shall

derive the more restrictive Bekenstein Bound $A/4L_P^2\ln2$ from $(2\pi)^2ER/hc\ln2$ in the Appendix for Scientists. The derivation assumes that the information is limited by the formation of a black hole, which in turn assumes that the information storage is restricted to a tiny portion of the universe, and that the future c-boundary topology is different from a point (recall that a point future c-boundary implies no event horizons). Neither of these assumptions holds if the universe ends in an Omega Point. Thus only the more general Bekenstein Bound applies, and we have seen that it does not prevent a diverging amount of information storage. The Bekenstein Bound $A/4L_P^2\ln2$ does apply to humans because we *are* restricted to the tiny region of spacetime in which black holes can form. (The argument above provides yet another reason why life, if it is to survive forever, must eventually expand to engulf the entire universe. Only if life does so can it avoid the more restrictive $A/4L_P^2\ln2$ Bekenstein Bound, which would require life and information processing to stop after finite subjective time, since $A \to 0$ as $R \to 0$.)

7. Penrose 1989.
8. The mass is obtained from $M = (4\pi/3)R^3D$, where D is the average cosmological density, known to be less than 10^{-29} grams per cubic centimeter.
9. See, for example, Reif 1965, Chapter 9.
10. See, for example, Halzen and Martin 1984, pp. 89–91.
11. Wootters and Zurek 1982.
12. Ibid. 1982.
13. Moravec 1988, pp. 122–24.
14. Updike 1989, p. 227.
15. Newton 1680?; quoted by Force 1994.
16. Ibid.
17. See Froom (1965) for a general history and Burns (1972) for a more detailed discussion of the evolution of the belief during the Reformation period in England.
18. Flew 1987, p. 12.
19. Flew 1964, p. 6; Flew's quotation marks. See more recently the two chapters on personal identity in Flew 1987.
20. Flew 1964, p. 6; Flew's quotation marks.
21. Flew 1987, p. 9.
22. Gibbs 1875, pp. 166–67.
23. Maxwell 1878, pp. 645–46. This calculation by Maxwell is the *first* published proof that energy is quantized. It predates Planck's paper by twenty-two years. So Maxwell, not Planck, is the true discoverer of energy quantization. Furthermore, unlike Planck, Maxwell *knew* thermodynamics required energy quantization in certain situations, as the passage quoted makes crystal clear.
24. Ibid., p. 645.

25. Gibbs 1902, pp. 188–207.
26. Gibbs 1875, pp. 166–67.
27. Plutarch, *Life of Theseus.*
28. Plutarch, quoted by Wiggins 1980, p. 92.
29. Hobbes, *De Corpore* II, 11; quoted by Wiggins, 1980, p. 92.
30. Held and Marshall 1991; Storer 1988; and Davisson and Gray 1976.
31. Rumelhart and Ortony 1976; Loftus 1979, p. 111.
32. Hume 1965, p. 284.
33. Flew 1987, pp. 133–34.
34. Khosla 1992.

NOTES TO CHAPTER X: WHAT HAPPENS AFTER THE
RESURRECTION: HEAVEN, HELL, AND PURGATORY

1. Tertullian, *De Carne Christi,* 5; quoted in Pagels 1979, p. 4.
2. Young 1951, pp. 61–64.
3. See Robinson (1952), Dahl (1962), and Schep (1964) for more discussion of the traditional interpretations of Jesus' resurrection body. (I personally do not believe any of these events actually occurred, as I shall discuss in Chapter XII.)
4. See Wang 1988 for an introduction to game theory.
5. David Friedman's *Price Theory* is the best introductory text on microeconomics, the part of economics which applies to all living beings constrained by the laws of thermodynamics (which imply that at any given time resources are finite). Only the fact that these particular economic laws apply to any living being whatsoever allows me to use them to predict the behavior of living beings in the far future. Friedman is actually not an economist by formal training: his Ph.D. (University of Chicago) is in theoretical elementary particle physics, and his physics background is apparent in his book.
6. Axelrod 1984; particularly pp. 134–36.
7. Nowak and Sigmund 1992.
8. Becker 1981, p. 173.
9. In mathematical language, these two conditions are respectively (1) $U_A(Z_{1A}, Z_{2A}, \ldots, Z_{mA}, \Psi(U_B))$, and (2) $\partial U_A/\partial U_B > 0$, where U_A and U_B are respectively the utilities of person A and person B, and Z_{jA} is the jth commodity consumed by A.
10. Friedman 1986, Chapter 20.
11. Becker 1981, pp. 82 and 189.
12. Hume 1755; reprinted in Flew 1964, p. 187.
13. Hume 1776 [1977], p. 77.

14. This actual infinity is a countable infinity: $\aleph_0$.
15. Russell 1931, p. 358.
16. Barrow and Tipler 1986, pp. 92–95.
17. Von Neumann and Morgenstern 1953, Chapter 15.
18. Gardner 1959, p. 38.
19. Berlekamp, Conway, and Guy 1982, Vol. 2, pp. 669–72.
20. See Robinson (1968, p. 59) and James (1948, p. 62) for more discussion of the meaning of free will in this situation.
21. Gardner 1959, pp. 45–46.
22. Becker 1981, p. 183; Friedman 1986, p. 492.
23. Gardner 1959, p. 40.
24. Origen's position on Hell is discussed in Trigg 1983, pp. 89, 118, and 138.
25. Christian Gottlieb Barth, quoted in Pelikan 1988, p. 5.
26. Smith and Haddad 1981, pp. 164–67.
27. Becker 1981; Friedman 1986, Chapter 20.
28. Price 1963, p. 50.
29. Friedman 1986, p. 24.
30. Baumeister and Wotman 1992.
31. McDannell and Lang 1988.
32. Tuchman 1962, p. 167 (in Chapter 11: "Liège and Alsace").
33. Lactantius 1886, p. 271 [in Chapter 13 of *The Anger of God*]; quoted in Hick 1978, p. 5, n. 1.
34. Aquinas, *Summa Theologica,* Article 3 of Part I, Question 2; quoted by Hick 1978, p 4, n. 1.
35. Hick 1978, p. 6.
36. See Martin 1990 for a recent summary of these arguments.
37. Hick 1978, p. 238.
38. Aquinas, *Summa Theologica,* Part III, Question 1, Article 3.
39. Augustine, *Enchiridion,* Book 8, Chapter 27.
40. Julian of Norwich 1961, Chapter 27.
41. The 2-sphere surface containing the life has thickness ΔR and radius R. Since the information stored is proportional to E/T, which in turn is proportional to ΔR times R^2, and R is proportional to proper time. This implies $I \propto t^2$.
42. Hayek 1941, p. 147.
43. Hayek 1972, p. 222.
44. Some economists, for instance the world's leading expert on the economics of resources, William Baumol of Princeton, have suggested (Baumol 1986) that resources may effectively increase without bound via a more efficient use of a finite resource base. Baumol realizes, however, that the question of whether

unlimited resources exist is ultimately a question of physics. He reluctantly concludes that physics says that resources are limited. He's wrong.

NOTES TO CHAPTER XI: COMPARISON OF THE
HEAVEN PREDICTED BY MODERN PHYSICS WITH
THE AFTERLIFE HOPED FOR BY THE
GREAT WORLD RELIGIONS

1. Needham 1956, p. 141.
2. Ibid., p. 152.
3. Ibid., p. 141.
4. Yoke 1985, pp. 184–87.
5. Ibid., p. 184.
6. Needham 1956, p. 153; Yoke 1985, pp. 174 and 186–87.
7. Van Gulik 1976, p. 236.
8. Needham 1956, p. 369.
9. Ibid., p. 375.
10. Ibid., pp. 369 and 376.
11. Ibid., p. 387.
12. Ibid., p. 387.
13. Griffith 1889, p. 528.
14. Ibid., p. 538.
15. Gandhi 1962, p. 16.
16. Ibid., p. 10.
17. Ibid., p. 115.
18. Ibid., p. 25.
19. Rahula 1959, p. 97.
20. Stcherbatsky 1978, pp. 23–24; Rahula 1959, p. 38.
21. Rahula 1959, p. 41.
22. Stcherbatsky 1978, p. 24.
23. Ibid., p. 70.
24. Gandhi 1962, p. 199.
25. Rahula 1959, p. 35.
26. Ibid., p. 43.
27. "Mahayana" means "superior technique," and "Hinayana" means "inferior technique." I give you one guess which division provided these names for the two divisions of Buddhism. ("Theravada" means "doctrine of elders" or "orthodox" Buddhism. Needless to say, "Theravada" is preferred by those of this division.)

28. Hamilton 1967, p. 359.
29. Masutani 1967, p. 793. Masutani was for many years the professor of Buddhism at the University of Tokyo.
30. Gandhi 1962, p. 198.
31. Goldman 1991, p. 220.
32. Ibid.
33. Mbiti 1970, p. 23.
34. Ibid., p. 264.
35. Parrinder 1969, p. 38.
36. Mbiti 1970, p. 260.
37. Ibid., pp. 260, 262.
38. Ibid., p. 260.
39. Ibid., p. 264.
40. Bolaji-Idowu 1963, p. 189.
41. Ibid., p. 200.
42. Hultkrantz 1979, pp. 283–84.
43. Coe 1975, pp. 90–91.
44. Tompkins 1990, p. 45.
45. Coe 1975, p. 101.
46. Wilbert 1975. Wilbert's opinion that the Warao myths are probably similar to the pre-Columbian myths has to be taken with a grain of salt, however. In several of the myths he reports, the Warao are taken to their various Heavens on horses! It is well known that there were no horses in the Americas until the Europeans came.
47. Hultkrantz 1979, p. 134.
48. Goldman 1991, p. 34.
49. Olan 1971, 16.
50. Eisenman and Wise 1992, p. 20.
51. Wolfson 1948, pp. 396, 404, 406, 408; Olan 1971, p. 17; Nickelsburg 1972.
52. Martin 1968, p. 117.
53. Ibid., p. 114.
54. Ibid., p. 118.
55. Nezikin 1935, p. 601.
56. *Sanhedrin* 90b–91a; Nezikin, 1935, p. 607.
57. *Sanhedrin* 91a; Nezikin, 1935, p. 607.
58. *Sanhedrin* 91a; Nezikin, 1935, pp. 607–8.
59. *Sanhedrin* 91b; Nezikin, 1935, p. 612.
60. Olan 1971, p. 49.
61. *Sanhedrin* 91a–91b; Nezikin, 1935, pp. 610–11.
62. Wolfson 1965, p. 55; Olan 1971, p. 45.
63. Olan 1971, p. 58.

64. Ibid., p. 60.

65. Martin 1968, p. 85.

66. Olan 1971, p. 61.

67. Maimonides IV:24; Rosner 1982, p. 33.

68. Olan 1971, p. 66.

69. Ibid., p. 77.

70. Vulgate, Douay Rheims translation. The earliest texts are quite corrupt, so we have no idea what the original said. The KJV reads: "[25] For I know that my redeemer liveth, and that he shall stand at the latter day upon the earth: [26] And though after my skin worms destroy this body, yet in my flesh shall I see God: [27] Whom I shall see for myself, and mine eyes shall behold, and not another; though my reins be consumed within me." The NEB reads: "But in my heart I know that my vindicator lives and that he will rise last to speak in court; and I shall discern my witness standing at my side and see my defending counsel, even God himself, [27] whom I shall see with my own eyes, I myself and no other." The RSV reads: "[25] For I know that my Redeemer lives, and at last he will stand upon the earth; [26] and after my skin has been thus destroyed, then without [or from] my flesh I shall see God, [27] whom I shall see on my side [or for myself], and my eyes shall behold, and not another. My heart faints within me!"

  Clearly, the Vulgate translation—owing to St. Jerome—is more evocative of a resurrection of the body than are the more accurate NEB or RSV translations. The KJV translation is also more suggestive of a bodily resurrection, though I personally find the KJV a total confusion, particularly verses 26 and 27.

71. Cullmann 1965. The Harvard Ingersoll Lectures are an endowed series on the afterlife.

72. Schillebeeckx 1987, p. 518.

73. See Robinson 1952, p. 14; Polkinghorne 1986, p. 76; and Chadwick 1986, p. 34, as examples.

74. Barth 1959, p. 154.

75. H. Maspero, translated and quoted in Needham 1956, p. 153.

76. Wolfson 1965.

77. Nickelsburg 1972.

78. Schillebeeckx 1987, pp. 518–23, 723, n. 1.

79. Wolfson, 1965, p. 96.

80. Celsus 1987, p. 109.

81. Ibid., p. 110.

82. Pannenberg 1984.

83. Ibid., pp. 130–31.

84. Pannenberg 1984, 1989.

85. Pannenberg 1989.

86. Pannenberg 1984.

87. Polkinghorne 1986, pp. 76–77.

88. Polkinghorne, Letter to FJT dated 16 April 1989.

89. Ayala 1974.

90. Earman 1986, p. 142.

91. Polkinghorne 1986, p. 86.

92. Ibid., Chapter 6.

93. Mayr 1988.

94. Weinberg 1987.

95. Ibid., 1992.

96. Arberry 1955, Vol. I, p. 40.

97. Arberry 1955.

98. Andrae 1955, p. 58.

99. Arberry 1955, Vol. I, p. 313; (my emphasis).

100. Ibid., p. 307.

101. Smith and Haddad 1981, p. 21.

102. Arberry 1955, Vol. II, p. 314.

103. Andrae 1955, p. 58.

104. Arberry 1955, Vol. II, p. 110.

105. Ibid., Vol. I, p. 346.

106. Ibid., Vol. I, p. 94.

107. For example, Andrae 1955, p. 59.

108. Arberry 1955, Vol. II, p. 140.

109. Smith and Haddad 1981, pp. 5–6, 33.

110. Ibid., p. 33 and n. 3, p. 205.

111. Ibid., p. 133.

112. See Küng 1985, pp. 130–34. The Council of Florence in 1442 was even more explicit: "The holy Roman Church . . . firmly believes, professes, and proclaims that none of those outside the Catholic Church, not Jews, nor heretics, nor schismatics, can participate in eternal life, but will go into the eternal fire prepared for the devil and his angels, unless they are brought into the Catholic Church before the end of life." (Quoted by Küng 1985, p. 130.)

113. Second Vatican Council, Article 16 of the Church Constitution.

114. Pannenberg 1984, pp. 135–36.

115. Talmud, *Mishnah Sanhedrin* (Nezikin 1935, p. 601).

116. Tug 1987, p. 88.

117. Smith and Haddad 1981, pp. 12, 22.

118. Ibid., p. 24.

119. Arberry 1955, Vol. II, p. 124.

120. Smith and Haddad 1981, p. 82.

121. Taha 1987.

122. Watt 1960, pp. 123–24.

123. Ibid., p. 61.

124. 'Ali Dashti 1985, pp. 80–85.

125. Pipes 1990.

NOTES TO CHAPTER XII: THE OMEGA POINT THEORY AND CHRISTIANITY

1. Flew 1984.

2. Mann 1986 reports the scholarly consensus, though Mann disagrees that Mark is prior.

3. Fitzmyer 1981, p. 57.

4. Munck 1967.

5. Fitzmyer 1981.

6. Mann 1986.

7. Fitzmyer 1981, pp. 53–57; Mann 1986, pp. 72–77; Munck 1967, pp. xlvi–liv.

8. Macquarrie 1986. St. Paul also regarded the resurrection of Jesus as the central truth of Christianity, as he says in 1 Corinthians 15.

9. Muggeridge 1990, p. 30.

10. See for example 1 Enoch 51: 4; 57:15ff.; this example is discussed by Baillie 1936, p. 162.

11. Josephus, *The Jewish War,* Book III, Chapter 8; Cornfeld 1982, p. 240.

12. Baillie 1936, p. 162.

13. Babbage 1837, Chapter 11.

14. Flew and Habermas 1987.

15. See for examples Schillebeeckx (1987) and Küng (1985). (A notable exception is Wolfhart Pannenberg. He truly believes Jesus rose from the dead in some objective sense. See Pannenberg [1968] for a defense of this position.)

16. Hume 1965, Part II, Section X ["On Miracles"].

17. Drake 1972.

18. Ibid.

19. See for instances "Cattle Mutilations: An Episode of Collective Delusion" by James R. Stewart; "The Case of the Amityville Horror" by Robert L. Morris; and "A Controlled UFO Hoax: Some Lessons" by David I. Simpson, all three articles in Frazier 1981.

20. See, for example, the Drake article (Drake 1972) mentioned above, and also the books by Klass (1974, 1983).

21. See Klass 1974 for a brief discussion of the N-rays delusion. A more scholarly

account can be found in de Solla Price 1961 (Listed under "Price 1961" in the Bibliography and in databases.)

22. Morrison 1972.
23. Christie-Murray 1976, p. 41.
24. Ibid., p. 56.
25. Pannenberg 1989, p. 267.
26. Celsus 1987, p. 106.
27. Ibid., p. 107.
28. Chadwick 1986; Christie-Murray 1976; Pelikan 1971. The only clear statement of the Trinity in the Bible, 1 John 5:7: "For there are three that bear record in heaven, the Father, the Word, and the Holy Ghost: and these three are one" (KJV), is now known to be a fourth-century interpolation. (The Revised Standard Version omits this verse without comment, and uses the last sentence of verse 6 of the KJV as its verse 7.) The gospel of John also presents Jesus as God. (John 1:1 "In the beginning was the Word, and the Word was with God, and the *Word was God* [my emphasis]," when combined with John 1:14, "And the Word was made flesh, and dwelt among us . . . ," is unequivocal.). However, the consensus opinion is that the Gospel of John was written around A.D. 100, long after the death of Jesus, and so it does not express a contemporary opinion.
29. Küng 1985.
30. Schillebeeckx 1987.
31. McBrien 1980, p. 764.
32. Maritain 1962, p. 166.
33. Ibid., p. 163.
34. Ibid., p. 164; italics are Maritain's.
35. Cesare Cremonini was the most famous professor of Aristotelian philosophy in the early seventeenth century, when "new stars"—what are now called "supernovae"—were shown by Tycho Brahe to be at stellar distances, and when Galileo did his work. Cremonini is remembered today as the professor who refused to look through Galileo's telescope. He didn't have to; he *knew* from pure reasoning that Galileo was not seeing what he was in fact seeing. According to Aristotle, the substance of the planets was such that it could not change. Therefore, if Galileo saw change, it was only an optical illusion. Cremonini also attacked Galileo for using mathematics to describe the motion of projectiles. Once again, Cremonini *knew* that mathematics would be useless at such a task, because Aristotle had said so two thousand years before. Today, Cremonini is mentioned by historians only as a good example of a bad example; his philosophical work is completely worthless.

But Cremonini was well rewarded for his junk philosophy. He and Galileo were both colleagues at the University of Padua in Italy for eighteen years.

Cremonini was paid a yearly salary of 2,000 ducats, a princely sum that permitted him to live like a member of the nobility. Galileo, in contrast, started out at Padua in 1592 on a salary of only 180 ducats, later raised in 1598 to 520 ducats. Finally, in 1610, after Galileo made his enormously important discoveries with his telescope, discoveries that made him famous throughout Europe, he was offered a salary of 1,000 ducats—half of what Cremonini had been getting for years—with the express condition that he would never again receive another raise! Galileo went off in a huff to become the chief mathematician and philosopher to the Grand Duke of Tuscany. (Comparative salaries and Cremonini's philosophy are discussed in De Santillana 1959, p. 29n. See also references to Cremonini and to "Aristotelian physics" in Drake 1980. The reader should note that "florin" and "ducat" were two coins of roughly the same value, the former being used primarily in Tuscany and the latter in Venice.)

36. Maritain 1962, p. 163.
37. Schillebeeckx 1987.
38. McBrien 1980, p. 764.
39. McBrien 1980, pp. 765–67.
40. Allen 1940, p. 40 of the Appendix.
41. Franklin 1938, p. 27.
42. Ibid., p. 29.
43. Ibid., p. 15.
44. Ibid., p. 38.
45. Flew 1984, p. 107. A tombstone with the epitaph has been erected near Franklin's grave in Philadelphia's Christ Church cemetery.
46. Jefferson 1983, p. 27.
47. Ibid., p. 334.
48. Ibid., p. 405.
49. Ibid., p. 40.
50. Flexner 1970, p. 227.
51. A similar argument has been made by Walters 1992, pp. 34–46.

NOTES TO CHAPTER XIII: CONCLUSION: THEOLOGY AS A BRANCH OF PHYSICS

1. Wolfson 1965.
2. A. Linde, private communication.
3. McNeill 1976, pp. 266–67.
4. Ackerknecht 1948.
5. Tyndall 1897, p. 197. This statement is not present in the first published ver-

sion (Tyndall, 1874) of the Belfast Address. It should have appeared at the beginning of the first complete paragraph on p. 61 of Tyndall, 1874.

6. Weinberg 1987.
7. Kenny 1969.
8. Kuhn 1957.
9. McNeill 1976, pp. 2, 208–9.
10. Andrae 1955.
11. Pelikan 1971, pp. 44–45.
12. Jaki 1986, p. 74.
13. Weinberg 1987; 1992, pp. 243–44.
14. Weinberg 1992, p. 244.
15. Ibid., p. 256.
16. Gandhi 1962, pp. 20–21.
17. Weinberg 1992, p. 260.

BIBLIOGRAPHY

Ackerknecht, Erwin H. 1948. "Anti-contagionism Between 1821 and 1867." *Bulletin of the History of Medicine* **22**: 562–93.

Allen, Ethan 1940. *Reason, the Only Oracle of Man.* New York: Scholars' Facsimiles & Reprints.

Alpher, Ralph A., and Robert Herman 1948. "Evolution of the Universe." *Nature* **162**: 774–75.

———1988. "Reflections on Early Work on 'Big Bang' Cosmology." *Physics Today* **41** (August #8, part 1): 24–34.

Andrae, Tor 1955 (1932). *Mohammed: The Man and His Faith* (translation of *Mohammed, Sein Leben und Sein Glaube.* Göttingen: Vandenhöck und Ruprecht). New York: Harper.

Arberry, Arthur J. 1955. *The Koran Interpreted.* New York: Macmillan.

Arbib, Michael A. 1969. *Theories of Abstract Automata.* Englewood Cliffs: Prentice-Hall.

Arrhenius, Svente 1908. *Worlds in the Making.* New York: Harper.

Augenstein, Bruno W., B. E. Bonner, F. E. Mills, and M. M. Nieto 1988. *Antiproton Science and Technology.* Singapore: World Scientific.

Augenstein, Bruno W. 1993. "Antiproton Annihilation's Advantages for Imaging." *Physics Today* **46** (#3, March): 9–10.

Axelrod, Robert 1984. *The Evolution of Cooperation.* New York: Basic Books.

Ayala, Francisco J. 1974. "Introduction." In *Studies in the Philosophy of Biology,* ed. Francisco Ayala and Theodosius Dobzhansky. Berkeley: University of California Press.

Babbage, Charles 1837. *The Ninth Bridgewater Treatise.* London: John Murray.

Baillie, John 1936. *And the Life Everlasting.* New York: Charles Scribners.

——— 1950. *The Belief in Progress.* Oxford: Oxford University Press.

Barlow, Nora 1959. *The Autobiography of Charles Darwin.* New York: Harcourt Brace.

Barnes, Jonathan 1984. *The Complete Works of Aristotle.* Vol. 1. Princeton: Princeton University Press.

Barr, James 1962. *Biblical Words for Time.* Naperville, IL: Allenson.

Barrow, John D. 1982. "Chaotic Behaviour in General Relativity." *Physics Reports* **85:** 1–49.

——— and Frank J. Tipler 1986. *The Anthropic Cosmological Principle.* Oxford: Oxford University Press.

Barth, Karl 1933. *The Resurrection of the Dead.* New York: Fleming H. Revell.

——— 1959. *Dogmatics in Outline.* New York: Harper & Row.

Batten, Andrew H. 1973. *Binary and Multiple Systems of Stars.* New York: Pergamon Press.

Baumol, William J. 1986. "On the Possibility of Continuing Expansion of Finite Resources." *Kyklos* **39:** 167–79.

Baumeister, Roy F., and Sarah Wotman 1992. *Breaking Hearts: The Two Sides of Unrequited Love.* New York: Guilford Press.

Becker, Gary S. 1981. *A Treatise on the Family.* Cambridge, MA: Harvard University Press.

Bekenstein, Jacob D. 1981. "Energy Cost of Information Transfer." *Physical Review Letters* **46:** 623–626.

Bell, Gordon 1992a. "Ultracomputers: A Teraflop Before Its Time." *Science* **256:** 64.

——— 1992b. "Ultracomputers: A Teraflop Before Its Time." *Communications of the Association for Computing Machinery* **35:** 27–47.

Benardete, Seth 1984. *The Being of the Beautiful: Plato's Theaetetus, Sophist, and Statesman.* Chicago: Chicago University Press.

Benedikt, Michael 1991. *Cyberspace: First Steps.* Cambridge, MA: MIT Press.

Berlekamp, Elwyn R., John H. Conway, and Richard K. Guy 1982. *Winning Ways for Your Mathematical Plays.* Vol. 1: *Games in General;* Vol. 2: *Games in Particular.* London: Academic Press.

Bernal, John Desmond 1969. *The World, the Flesh, and the Devil.* Bloomington: Indiana University Press.

Bloch, Ernst 1986. *The Principle of Hope,* Vol. III (translation of *Das Prinzip Hoffnung.* Frankfurt am Main: Suhrkamp Verlag 1959). Oxford: Basil Blackwell.

Bloom, Alan 1987. *The Closing of the American Mind.* New York: Simon & Schuster.

Boesiger, Ernest 1980. "Evolutionary Biology in France at the Time of the Modern Synthesis." In *The Evolutionary Synthesis,* ed. Ernst Mayr and William B. Provine, pp. 309–21. Cambridge, MA: Harvard University Press.

Bolaji-Idowu 1963. *Olodumare: God in Yoruba Belief.* New York: Praeger.

Bonner, John Tyler 1988. *The Evolution of Complexity by Means of Natural Selection.* Princeton: Princeton University Press.

Boolos, George S., and Richard S. Jeffery 1974. *Computability and Logic.* Cambridge: Cambridge University Press.

Börner, Gerhard 1992. *The Early Universe: Fact and Fiction.* Berlin: Springer-Verlag.

Boyajian, George, and Tim Lutz 1992. "Evolution of Biological Complexity and Its Relation to Taxonomic Longevity in the Ammonoidea." *Geology* **20:** 983–86.

Braitenberg, Valentino 1991. *Anatomy of the Cortex: Statistics and Geometry (Studies of Brain Function.* Vol. 18). Berlin: Springer-Verlag.

Brown, Francis, S. R. Driver, and Charles A. Briggs 1906. *A Hebrew and English Lexicon of the Old Testament, Based on the Lexicon of William Gesenius.* Boston: Houghton Mifflin.

Brush, Stephen G. 1976. *The Kind of Motion We Call Heat.* Vol. II. Amsterdam: North-Holland.

———— 1978. *The Temperature of History: Phases of Science and Culture in the Nineteenth Century.* New York: Burt Franklin.

———— 1981. "The Scientific Value of High Energy Physics." *Annals of Nuclear Physics* **8:** 133–40.

Burkhardt, Henry 1992. "Computing in Science." *Science* **256:** 51.

Burns, Norman T. 1972. *Christian Mortalism from Tyndale to Milton.* Cambridge, MA: Harvard University Press.

Cairns-Smith, A. G. 1982. *Genetic Takeover and the Mineral Origin of Life.* Cambridge: Cambridge University Press.

Caldiera, Ken, and James F. Kasting 1992. "Susceptibility of the Early Earth to Irreversible Glaciation Caused by Carbon Dioxide Clouds." *Nature* **359:** 226–28.

Camus, Albert 1975. *The Myth of Sisyphus and Other Essays* (translation of *Le Mythe de Sisyphe.* Paris: Gallimard 1942). New York: Knopf.

Cassenti, Brice N. 1988. "Energy Transfer in Antiproton Annihilation Rockets." In Augenstein et al. 1988.

Cassidy, David C. 1992. *Uncertainty: The Life and Times of Werner Heisenberg.* New York: Freeman.

Celsus 1987. *On the True Doctrine: A Discourse Against the Christians.* Oxford: Oxford University Press.

Chadwick, Henry 1986. *The Early Church.* New York: Dorset.

Childs, Brevard S. 1974. *The Book of Exodus: A Critical, Theological Commentary.* Philadelphia: Westminster Press.

Christie-Murray, David 1976. *A History of Heresy.* Oxford: Oxford University Press.

Clements, Ronald E. 1972. *The Cambridge Bible Commentary on the New English Bible: Exodus.* Cambridge: Cambridge University Press.

Cliff, Rodger, Robert A. Freitas, Richard Liang, and Georg von Tiesenhausen 1980. "Replicating Systems Concepts: Self-Replicating Lunar Factory and Demonstration." In *Advanced Automation for Space Missions, NASA/ASEE Conference in Santa Clara, California* (NASA Publication 2255), pp. 189–335, ed. Robert Freitas and William Gilbreath. Washington: U.S. Government Printing Office.

Coe, Michael D. 1975 "Death and the Ancient Maya." In *Death and the Afterlife in Pre-Columbian America,* ed. Elizabeth P. Benson. Washington: Dumbarton Oaks Research Library.

Cornfeld, Gaalya 1982. *Josephus: The Jewish War.* Grand Rapids: Zondervan.

Cuénot, Claude 1965. *Teilhard de Chardin.* Baltimore: Helicon.

Cullmann, Oscar 1950. *Christ and Time.* Philadelphia: Westminster.

———— 1965. "Immortality of the Soul or Resurrection of the Dead: The Witness of the New Testament." In *Immortality and Resurrection,* ed. Krister Stendahl, pp. 9–53, New York: Macmillan.

Dahl, M. E. 1962. *The Resurrection of the Body.* Naperville, IL: Allenson.

Darwin, Charles 1860. *On the Origin of Species by Means of Natural Selection.* 2nd ed. London: John Murray.

Dashti, 'Ali 1985. *Twenty-three Years: A Study of the Prophetic Career of Mohammad.* (translation of *Bist o Seh Sal,* Beirut 1974) London: Allen & Unwin.

Davidson, Gustav 1967. *A Dictionary of Angels.* New York: The Free Press.

Davisson, Lee D., and Robert M. Gray 1976. *Data Compression: Benchmark Papers in Electrical Engineering and Computer Science #14.* Stroudsburg: Dowden, Hutchinson, & Ross.

Dawkins, Richard 1976. *The Selfish Gene.* Oxford: Oxford University Press.

———— 1986. *The Blind Watchmaker.* Oxford: Oxford University Press.

De Santillana, Giorgio 1959. *The Crime of Galileo.* Chicago: University of Chicago Press.

De Santillana, Giorgio, and Hertha von Dechend 1969. *Hamlet's Mill: An Essay on Myth and the Frame of Time.* Boston: Gambit.

Dirac, P. A. M. 1961. Untitled. *Nature* **192:** 441.

Dole, Stephan A. 1964. *Habitable Planets for Man.* New York: Blaisdell.

Drake, Frank D. 1972. "On the Abilities and Limitations of Witnesses of UFOs and Similar Phenomena." In *UFO's—A Scientific Debate,* ed. Carl Sagan and Thornton Page. New York: Norton.

Drake, Stillman 1980. *Galileo*. Oxford: Oxford University Press.

Drexler, K. Eric 1986. *Engines of Creation: The Coming Era of Nanotechnology*. New York: Doubleday.

——— 1992. *Nanosystems: Molecular Machinery, Manufacturing, and Computation*. New York: John Wiley.

Dudai, Yadin 1990. *The Neurobiology of Memory: Concepts, Findings, Trends*. Oxford: Oxford University Press.

Duhem, Pierre 1954. *The Aim and Structure of Physical Theory*. (translation of *La Théorie Physique: Son Objet. Sa Structure*. Paris: Marcel Rivière, 1914) Princeton: Princeton University Press.

Dyson, Freeman 1979. "Time Without End: Physics and Biology in an Open Universe." *Reviews of Modern Physics* **51**: 447–60.

——— 1988. *Infinite in All Directions*. New York: Harper & Row.

Earman, John 1986. *A Primer on Determinism*. Dordrecht: Reidel Publishing Company.

Eccles, Sir John C. 1989. *Evolution of the Brain: Creation of the Self*. London: Routledge.

——— 1990. "A Unitary Hypothesis of Mind-Brain Interaction in the Cerebral Cortex." *Proceedings of the Royal Society of London* **B240**: 433–51.

Eddington, Sir Arthur S. 1928. *The Nature of the Physical World: Gifford Lectures 1928*. Cambridge: Cambridge University Press.

Eisenman, Robert H., and Michael Wise 1992. *The Dead Sea Scrolls Uncovered*. Rockport: Element.

Elert, Werner 1962. *The Structure of Lutheranism*. Vol. I. St. Louis: Concordia.

Eliade, M. 1954. *The Myth of the Eternal Return*. New York: Pantheon.

Ellis, George F. R. 1988. "Does Inflation Necessarily Imply $\Omega_0 = 1$?" *Classical and Quantum Gravity* **5**: 891–901.

Engels, Frederick 1940. *Dialectics of Nature; Preface and Notes by J. B. S. Haldane*. New York: International Publishers.

Farias, Victor 1989. *Heidegger and Nazism*. Philadelphia: Temple University Press.

Feynman, Richard P. 1964. *The Feynman Lectures on Physics*. New York: Addison-Wesley.

——— 1986. *"Surely You're Joking, Mr. Feynman!"* New York: Bantam Press.

Fisk, Lawrence A., and Gregory M. Reck 1993. "Instrument Definition for the Pluto Fast Flyby Mission." *NASA Research Announcement 93-OSSA-5*. Washington: U.S. Government Printing Office.

Fitzmyer, Joseph A., S. J. 1981. *Commentary on Luke* (The Anchor Bible, Vol. 28). Garden City, NY: Doubleday.

Flew, Antony 1964. Ed. *Body, Mind, and Death*. New York: Macmillan.

——— 1984. *God, Freedom and Immortality: A Critical Analysis*. Buffalo: Prometheus.

—— 1987. *The Logic of Mortality.* Oxford: Blackwell.

—— and Gary Habermas 1987. *Did Jesus Rise from the Dead?: The Resurrection Debate.* San Francisco: Harper & Row.

Flexner, James Thomas 1970. *George Washington and the New Nation.* Boston: Little, Brown.

Force, James E. 1994. "The God of Abraham and Isaac (Newton)." In *Recent Essays on Theology and Biblical Criticism in Spinoza's Holland and Newton's England.* Ed. James E. Force and Richard H. Popkin. Dordrecht: Kluwer Academic Publishers.

Forward, Robert L. 1982. "Antimatter Propulsion." *Journal of the British Interplanetary Society* **35**: 391–95.

—— 1984. "Roundtrip Interstellar Travel Using Laser-Pushed Lightsails." *Journal of Spacecraft* **21**: 187–93.

—— 1985. "Antiproton Annihilation Propulsion." *Journal of Propulsion* **1**: 370–74.

—— 1986. "Laser Weapon Target Practice With Gee-Whiz Targets." *Proceedings of the SDIO/DARPA Workshop on Laser Propulsion.* Ed. J. T. Kare. Livermore, CA: Lawrence Livermore National Laboratory Printing Office.

—— 1990. "Grey Solar Sails." *Journal of the Astronautical Sciences* **38**: 161–85.

—— and Joel Davis 1986. "Ride a Laser to the Stars." *New Scientist* **112** (#1528, 2 October): 31–35.

Franklin, Benjamin 1938. *Benjamin Franklin on Religion.* Ed. Nathan G. Goodman. Philadelphia: Franklin Printing Company.

Frazier, Kendrick 1981. *Paranormal Borderlands of Science.* Buffalo: Prometheus Books.

Fredkin, Edward, and Tommaso Toffoli 1982. "Conservative Logic." *International Journal of Theoretical Physics* **21**: 219–53.

Freedman, Michael H., and Feng Luo 1989. *Selected Applications of Geometry to Low-Dimensional Topology.* Providence: American Mathematical Society.

Freitas, Robert A. 1980. "A Self-Reproducing Robot Probe." *Journal of the British Interplanetary Society* **33**: 251–64.

Friedman, David D. 1986. *Price Theory.* Cincinnati: South-Western Publishing.

Friedman, Louis 1988. *Starsailing: Solar Sails and Interstellar Travel.* New York: Wiley.

Froom, LeRoy Edwin 1965. *The Conditionalist Faith of Our Fathers* 2 vols. Washington: Review and Herald Publishing Company.

Galilei, Galileo 1957 [1615]. *Letter to the Grand Duchess Christina,* in *Discoveries and Opinions of Galileo,* translation and commentary by Stillman Drake, pp. 173–216. New York: Doubleday.

Gallup, George Jr. 1982. *Adventures in Immortality.* New York: McGraw-Hill.

———— and Jim Castelli 1989. *The People's Religion: American Faith in the 90's.* New York: Macmillan.

———— and Sarah Jones 1989. *100 Questions and Answers: Religion in America.* Princeton: Princeton Religion Research Center.

Gandhi, Mohandas Karamchand 1962. *All Religions Are True.* Bombay: Bharatiya Vidya Bhavan.

Gardner, Martin 1959. *The Scientific American Book of Mathematical Puzzles and Diversions.* New York: Simon & Schuster.

Gelernter, David 1991. *Mirror Worlds: On the Day Software Puts the Universe in a Shoebox . . . How It Will Happen and What It Will Mean.* Oxford: Oxford University Press.

Gell-Mann, Murray, 1992. "[Remarks on Bryce DeWitt's Paper] 'DeCoherence Without Complexity and Without an Arrow of Time.' " In *Physical Origins of Time Asymmetry,* ed. J. J. Halliwell, J. Perez-Mercader, and W. H. Zurek. Cambridge: Cambridge University Press.

Geroch, Robert P., and James B. Hartle 1986. "Computability and Physical Theories." *Foundations of Physics* **16:** 533–50. Reprinted in *Between Quantum and Cosmos* (1988), ed. Wojciech H. Zurek, Alwyn van der Merwe, and Warner A. Miller, pp. 549–66. Princeton: Princeton University Press.

Gibbs, J. Willard 1875. "On the Equilibrium of Heterogeneous Substances." *Transactions of the Connecticut Academy,* **3,** 108–248 and 343–524. Reprinted in *The Collected Work of J. Willard Gibbs,* Vol. 1 (1948), pp. 55–371 (page numbers quoted in text are from *Collected Works*). New Haven: Yale University Press.

———— 1902. *Elementary Principles in Statistical Mechanics.* Reprinted in *The Collected Work of J. Willard Gibbs,* Vol. 2 (1948), pp. 1–207 (page numbers quoted in text are from *Collected Works*). New Haven: Yale University Press.

Gingerich, Owen 1990. "Show Trial?" *The American Scholar* **59:** 310–14.

Glashow, Sheldon Lee 1992. "The Death of Science!?" In *The End of Science?* ed. Richard Q. Elvee. London: University Press of America.

Goldman, Ari Lionel 1991. *The Search for God at Harvard.* New York: Random House.

Gould, Stephen J. 1977. "History of the Vertebrate Brain." In *Ever Since Darwin,* by Stephen J. Gould. New York: Norton.

———— 1983. "Agassiz in the Galapagos" in *Hen's Teeth and Horse's Toes,* by Stephen J. Gould. New York: Norton.

———— 1988. "On Replacing the Idea of Progress with an Operational Notion of Directionality." In *Evolutionary Progress,* ed. Matthew H. Nitecki, 319–38, Chicago: University of Chicago Press.

Greeley, Andrew M. 1985. *Unsecular Man: The Persistence of Religion.* New York: Schocken Books.

———— 1989. *Religious Change in America.* Cambridge, MA: Harvard University Press.

Griffith, Ralph T. H. 1889. *The Hymns of the Rgveda.* Translated; new rev. ed. by J. L. Shastri 1973. Delhi: Motilal Banarsidass.

Haarer, D. 1992. "Molecular Computer Memory." *Nature* **355:** 297–98.

Halzen, Francis, and Alan D. Martin 1984. *Quarks and Leptons.* New York: Wiley.

Hamilton, Clarence H. 1967. "Buddhism." Encyclopaedia Britannica, Vol. 4. Chicago: Encyclopaedia Britannica Publishing Company.

Harris, Karsten. 1978. "Heidegger as a Political Thinker." In *Heidegger and Modern Philosophy,* ed. Michael Murray, pp. 304–28. New Haven: Yale University Press.

Hartle, James B. 1991. "Excess Baggage." In *Elementary Particles and the Universe: Essays in Honor of Murray Gell-Mann,* ed. John H. Schwarz, pp. 1–16. Cambridge: Cambridge University Press.

Hawking, Stephen W. 1988. *A Brief History of Time.* London: Bantam Press.

———— and George F. R. Ellis 1973. *The Large Scale Structure of Space-Time.* Cambridge: Cambridge University Press.

Hayek, Friedrich 1941. *The Pure Theory of Capital.* Chicago: Chicago University Press.

———— 1972. *Individualism and Economic Order.* Chicago: Henry Regnery.

Heath, Sir Thomas L. 1913. *Aristarchus of Samos: The Ancient Copernicus.* Oxford: Oxford University Press.

Heidegger, Martin 1966. " 'Only a God Can Save Us': The *Spiegel* Interview." In *Heidegger: The Man and the Thinker,* ed. Thomas Sheehan, pp. 45–67. Chicago: Precedent Publishing.

———— 1991. *Nietzsche.* Vol. I, *The Will to Power as Art,* and Vol. II, *The Eternal Recurrence of the Same.* Translated by David F. Krell (German original *Nietzsche* [Pfullingen: Verlag Günther Neske, 1961]). San Francisco: HarperSanFrancisco.

Held, Gilbert, and Thomas R. Marshall 1991. *Data Compression: Techniques and Applications.* New York: Wiley.

Helmholtz, Hermann von 1961. "On the Interaction of the Natural Forces." Reprinted in *Popular Scientific Lectures.* Ed. Martin Kline. New York: Dover.

Herman, P. M. 1972. "The *Unseen Universe:* Physics and the Philosophy of Nature in Victorian Britain." *British Journal of the History of Science* **6:** 73–79.

Hertz, Joseph Herman 1961. *The Pentateuch and Haftorahs.* London: Soncino Press.

Hick, John 1978. *Evil and the God of Love.* Rev. ed. New York: Harper & Row.

Himmelfarb, Gertrude 1980. "In Defense of Progress." *Commentary* (June): 53–60.

Hofstadter, Douglas R., and Daniel C. Dennett, ed. 1981. *The Mind's I.* New York: Basic Books.

Holten, Gerald 1992. "How to Think About the End of Science." In *The End of Science?—Attack and Defense.* Ed. Richard Q. Elvee. London: University Press of America.

Hultkrantz, Åke 1979. *The Religions of the American Indians.* (Translation of *De Amerikanska indanernas Religioner.)* Berkeley: University of California Press.

Hume, David 1965. *Essential Works of David Hume.* New York: Bantam Books.

———— 1977. *Dialogues Concerning Natural Religion.* Ed. Norman Kemp Smith. Indianapolis: Bobbs-Merrill.

Islam, Jamal N. 1977. "Possible Ultimate Fate of the Universe." *Quarterly Journal of the Royal Astronomical Society* **18**: 3–17.

———— 1979. "The Ultimate Fate of the Universe." *Sky & Telescope* **57**: 13–18.

———— 1983. *The Ultimate Fate of the Universe.* Cambridge: Cambridge University Press.

Jaki, Stanley 1974. *Science and Creation.* Edinburgh: Scottish University Press.

———— 1986. *Lord Gifford and His Lectures: A Centenary Retrospect.* Edinburgh: Scottish Academic Press.

James, William 1948. "The Dilemma of Determinism." In *Essays in Pragmatism,* by William James, pp. 37–64. New York: Harper & Row.

Jeans, Sir James 1929. *The Universe Around Us.* Cambridge: Cambridge University Press.

Jefferson, Thomas 1983. *Jefferson's Extracts from the Gospels (The Papers of Thomas Jefferson.* 2nd series. Ed. Dickinson W. Adams, Ruth W. Lester, and Eugene R. Sheridan. Princeton: Princeton University Press.

Jerison, Harry J. 1973. *Evolution of the Brain and Intelligence.* New York: Academic Press.

Jonas, Hans 1963. *The Gnostic Religion: The Message of the Alien God and the Beginnings of Christianity.* 2nd ed., rev. Boston: Beacon Press.

Julian of Norwich, Mother 1961. *The Revelations of Divine Love of Julian of Norwich.* Translated by James Walsh. London: Burns and Oates.

Kant, Immanuel. 1950. *Immanuel Kant's Critique of Pure Reason.* Translated by Norman Kemp Smith. New York: The Humanities Press.

Kaplan, Rabbi Aryeh 1991. *The Living Torah: Exodus.* Jerusalem: Moznaim Publishing.

Kaufmann, Walter A. 1950. *Nietzsche: Philosopher, Psychologist, Antichrist.* Princeton: Princeton University Press.

Kenny, Anthony J. P. 1969. *The Five Ways: St. Thomas Aquinas' Proof of God's Existence.* New York: Schocken Books.

————, H. C. Longuet-Higgins, J. R. Lucas, and C. H. Waddington 1972. *The*

Nature of the Mind: Gifford Lectures 1971–1973. Edinburgh: Edinburgh University Press.

Khosla, Rajinder P. 1992. "From Photons to Bits." *Physics Today* **45** (#12, December): 42–49.

Klass, Philip J. 1974. *UFOs Explained*. New York: Random House.

——— 1983. *UFOs–The Public Deceived*. Buffalo: Prometheus, 1983.

Koestler, Arthur 1963. *The Sleepwalkers*. New York: Grosset & Dunlap.

Krugman, Paul 1990. *Rethinking International Trade*. Cambridge, MA: MIT Press.

Kubrin, David. 1967. "Newton and the Cyclical Cosmos: Providence and the Mechanical Philosophy." *Journal of the History of Ideas* **28**: 325–46.

Kuhn, Thomas S. 1957. *The Copernican Revolution*. Cambridge: Harvard University Press.

——— 1970a. *The Structure of Scientific Revolutions*. Chicago: University of Chicago Press.

——— 1970b. "Reflections on My Critics." In *Criticism and the Growth of Knowledge*. Ed. Imre Lakatos and Alan Musgrave. Cambridge: Cambridge University Press.

Küng, Hans 1980 *Does God Exist?* (Translation of *Existiert Gott?* [München: R. Piper, 1978]). New York: Doubleday.

——— 1985 *Eternal Life?* New York: Doubleday.

Lactantius, Lucius 1886. *A Treatise on the Anger of God*. In: *The Ante-Nicene Fathers*. Ed. Alexander Roberts and James Donaldson. Buffalo: The Christian Literature Society.

Langton, Christopher G. 1988. "Artificial Life." In *Artificial Life*. Ed. Christopher G. Langton. New York: Addison-Wesley.

——— 1990. "Life at the Edge of Chaos." In *Artificial Life II*. Ed. Christopher G. Langton, Charles Taylor, J. Doyne Farmer, and Steen Rasmussen. New York: Addison-Wesley.

Lasker, Jean 1989. "A Numerical Experiment on the Chaotic Behaviour of the Solar System." *Nature* **338**: 237–38.

Lawson, H. Blaine 1974. "Foliations." *Bulletin of the American Mathematical Society* **80**: 369–418.

Leuba, James H. 1916. *The Belief in God and Immortality*. Boston: Sherman, French, & Co.

Levy, Oscar 1910. Ed., *The Complete Works of Friedrich Nietzsche*. Edinburgh: Foulis.

Libet, B., and A. G. Curtis, E. W. Wright, and D. K. Pearl 1983. "Time of Conscious Intention to Act in Relation to Onset of Cerebral Activity (Readiness Potential). The Unconscious Initiation of a Freely Voluntary Act." *Brain,* **106**: 640.

Lilla, Mark 1990. "What Heidegger Wrought." *Commentary* **89** (#1 January) 41–51.

Limoges, Camille 1980. "A Second Glance at Evolutionary Biology in France." in *The Evolutionary Synthesis,* ed. Ernst Mayr and William B. Provine, pp. 322–27. Cambridge: Harvard University Press.

Linde, Andrei D. 1988. "Life After Inflation." *Physics Letters* **211B:** 29–31.

Llewellyn Smith, C. H. 1993. "The Particle Connection," *Nature* **361:** 697.

Loftus, Elizabeth F. 1979. *Eyewitness Testimony.* Cambridge: Harvard University Press.

Lovejoy, Arthur O. 1936. *The Great Chain of Being.* Cambridge: Harvard University Press.

Lukas, Mary, and Ellen Lukas 1981. *Teilhard.* New York: McGraw-Hill.

Luther, Martin 1967. *Luther's Works.* Vol. 54, *Table Talk.* Ed. Theodore G. Tappert. Philadelphia: Fortress Press.

Machtey, Michael, and Paul Young 1978. *An Introduction to the General Theory of Algorithms.* New York: North Holland.

——— 1981. "Remarks on Recusion versus Diagonalization and Exponentially Difficult Problems." *Journal of Computer and System Sciences* **22:** 442–53.

Macquarrie, John 1986. "The Keystone of Christian Faith." In *If Christ Be Not Risen,* ed. John Greenhalgh and Elizabeth Russell, pp. 9–24. San Francisco: Collins.

Maimonides, Moses 1956. *Guide for the Perplexed.* Translated by M. Friedländer. New York: Dover.

Mann, Christopher Stephen 1986. *Commentary on Mark* (The Anchor Bible, Vol. 27). Garden City, NY: Doubleday.

Margolus, Norman 1984. "Physics-Like Models of Computation." *Physica* **10D:** 81–95.

Maritain, Jacques 1962. *An Introduction to Philosophy.* New York: Sheed and Ward.

Martin, Bernard 1968. *Prayer in Judaism.* New York: Basic Books.

Martin, Michael 1990. *Atheism: A Philosophical Justification.* Philadelphia: Temple University Press.

Masutani, Fumio 1967. "Amitabha." Encyclopaedia Britannica, Vol. 1. Chicago: Encyclopaedia Britannica Publishing Company.

Maughan, Ron 1992. "Success on a Plate." *New Scientist* **135** (#1831, 25 July): 36–40.

Maxwell, James Clerk 1878. "Diffusion." Encyclopaedia Britannica, Vol. 7. Reprinted in *The Scientific Papers of James Clerk Maxwell,* Vol. 2 (1890), pp. 624–46 (page numbers in text are from *The Scientific Papers*).

Maynard Smith, John 1992. "Taking a Chance on Evolution." *New York Review of Books* **34** (#9, 14 May), 34–36.

Mayr, Ernst 1980. "Prologue: Some Thoughts on the History of the Evolutionary Synthesis." In *The Evolutionary Synthesis,* ed. Ernst Mayr and William B. Provine, pp. 1–48. Cambridge: Harvard University Press.

———— 1985. "The Probability of Extraterrestrial Intelligent Life." In *Extraterrestrials: Science and Alien Intelligence.* Ed. Edward Regis. Cambridge: Cambridge University Press.

———— 1988. "The Limits of Reductionism." *Nature* **331:** 475.

Mbiti, John S. 1970. *Concepts of God in Africa.* New York: Praeger.

McBrien, Richard P. 1980. *Catholicism.* Minneapolis: Winston Press.

McCarthy, John 1990. "Review of *The Emperor's New Mind.*" *Bulletin of the American Mathematical Society* **23:** 606–16.

McDannell, Colleen, and Bernhard Lang 1988. *Heaven: A History.* New Haven: Yale University Press.

McMullin, Ernin 1989. "Review of *Galileo: Heretic.*" *Physics Today* **42:** 76–78 (January).

McNeill, William H. 1976. *Plagues and Peoples.* Garden City: Doubleday.

Medawar, Peter B. 1961. "Critical Review of *The Phenomenon of Man.*" *Mind* **70:** 99–106.

Mills, Frank E. 1988. "Scaleup of Antiproton Production to One Milligram per Year." In Augenstein *et al.* 1988.

Milne, Edward A. 1952. *Modern Cosmology and the Christian Idea of God.* Oxford: Oxford University Press.

Minsky, Marvin L. 1967. *Computation: Finite and Infinite Machines.* Englewood Cliffs: Prentice-Hall.

Misner, Charles W., Kip S. Thorne, and John Archibald Wheeler 1973. *Gravitation.* San Francisco: W. H. Freeman.

Monk, J. Donald 1976. *Mathematical Logic.* Heidelberg: Springer-Verlag.

Monod, Jacques. 1971. *Chance and Necessity.* New York: Alfred Knopf.

Moravec, Hans 1988. *Mind Children: The Future of Robot and Human Intelligence.* Cambridge: Harvard University Press.

Mori, Masahiro 1974. *The Buddha in the Robot: A Robot Engineer's Thoughts on Science and Religion.* Tokyo: Kosei.

Morrison, Philip 1972. "The Nature of Scientific Evidence: A Summary" in *UFO's—A Scientific Debate.* Ed. Carl Sagan and Thornton Page, New York: Norton.

Mortier, Jeanne, and Marie-Louise Aboux 1966. *Teilhard de Chardin Album.* New York: Harper & Row.

Muggeridge, Anne Roche 1990. *The Desolate City: Revolution in the Catholic Church.* San Francisco: Harper & Row.

Munck, Johannes 1967. *Commentary on The Acts of the Apostles* (The Anchor Bible, Vol. 31). Garden City, NY: Doubleday.

Murray, John 1815. "On the Diffusion of Heat on the Surface of the Earth. *Transactions of the Royal Society of Edinburgh.* **7**: 411–34.

Needham, Joseph 1956. *Science and Civilization in China.* Vol. II. Cambridge: Cambridge University Press.

——— 1960. *Science and Civilization in China.* Vol. III. Cambridge: Cambridge University Press.

——— 1965. "Time and Eastern Man." *Royal Anthropological Institute Occasional Papers, #21.*

Neuhaus, Richard John 1986. *Unsecular America.* Grand Rapids: Eerdmans.

Newton, Isaac 1680(?). "Paradoxical Questions Concerning Ye Morals & Actions of Athanasius and His Followers," UCLA Clark Library copy of the manuscript (not in the Keynes copy).

Nezikin, Seder 1935. *The Babylonian Talmud, Sanhedrin II.* Vol. 28. Translated by I. Epstein. London: Soncino Press.

Nickelsburg, George W. E. 1972. *Resurrection, Immortality, and Eternal Life in InterTestamental Judaism.* Cambridge: Harvard University Press.

Nisbet, Robert 1980. *History of the Idea of Progress.* New York: Basic Books.

Nowak, Martin A., and Karl Sigmund 1992. "Tit for Tat in Heterogeneous Populations." *Nature* **355**: 250–53.

Nozick, Robert 1989. *The Examined Life.* New York: Simon & Schuster.

Olan, Levi A. 1971. *Judaism and Immortality.* New York: Union of American Hebrew Congregations.

O'Neill, Gerard K. 1977. *The High Frontier.* New York: Morrow.

Pagels, Elaine 1979. *The Gnostic Gospels.* New York: Random House.

Paine, Thomas 1795. *The Age of Reason; Being an Investigation of True and Fabulous Theology.* London: Daniel Isaac Eaton, Printer and Bookseller to the Supreme Majesty of the People.

Pannenberg, Wolfhart 1968. *Jesus—God and Man.* Philadelphia: Westminster Press.

——— 1969. *Theology and the Kingdom of God.* Philadelphia: Westminster Press.

——— 1970. *What Is Man?* Philadelphia: Fortress Press.

——— 1971. "The God of Hope." In *Basic Questions in Theology: Collected Essays,* Vol. II, by Wolfhart Pannenberg, pp. 234–49. Philadelphia: Fortress Press.

——— 1972. *The Apostles' Creed in the Light of Today's Questions.* Philadelphia: Westminster.

——— 1977. "The Spirit of Life." In *Faith and Reality,* by Wolfhart Pannenberg, pp. 20–38. Philadelphia: Westminster Press.

——— 1981. "Theological Questions to Scientists." *Zygon:* **16**: 65–77.

——— 1984. "Constructive and Critical Functions of Christian Eschatology." *Harvard Theological Review* **77**: 119–39.

———— 1989. "Theological Appropriation of Scientific Understandings: Response to Hefner, Wicken, Eaves, and Tipler. *Zygon:* **24:** 255–71.

Papagiannis, Michael D. 1985. *The Search for Extraterrestrial Life: Recent Developments.* Boston: Reidel.

Parrinder, Geoffrey 1969. *Religion in Africa.* New York: Praeger.

Peebles, P. James E. 1971. *Physical Cosmology.* Princeton: Princeton University Press.

Pelikan, Jaroslav 1961. *The Shape of Death: Life, Death, and Immortality in the Early Fathers.* New York: Abingdon Press.

———— 1971. *The Christian Tradition.* Vol. 1: *The Emergence of the Catholic Tradition.* Chicago: University of Chicago Press.

———— 1988. *The Melody of Theology.* Cambridge: Harvard University Press.

Penrose, Roger 1988. "Difficulties with Inflationary Cosmology." *Annals of the New York Academy of Sciences* **571:** 249–64.

———— 1989. *The Emperor's New Mind: Concerning Computers, Minds, and the Laws of Physics.* Oxford: Oxford University Press.

Pipes, Daniel 1990. *The Rushdie Affair.* New York: Birch Lane Press.

Polkinghorne, John 1986. *One World.* Princeton: Princeton University Press.

———— 1989. *Rochester Roundabout: The Story of High Energy Physics.* New York: Freeman.

Press, Frank 1984. *Science and Creationism: A View from the National Academy of Sciences.* Washington: National Academy Press.

Price, Derek J. de Solla 1961. *Science Since Babylon.* New Haven: Yale University Press.

———— 1963. *Little Science, Big Science.* New York: Columbia University Press.

Provine, William B. 1987. "Review of *Trial and Error* by E. J. Larson." *Academe* **73** (#1) 50–52.

———— 1988. "Progress in Evolution and Meaning in Life." In *Evolutionary Progress,* by Matthew H. Nitecki, pp. 49–74. Chicago: University of Chicago Press.

Rahner, Karl, and Herbert Vorgrimler 1983. Concise Theological Dictionary. 2nd ed. London: Burns & Oates.

Rahula, Walpola 1959. *What the Buddha Taught.* New York: Grove Press.

Rankine, William J. M. 1852. "On the Reconstruction of the Mechanical Energy of the Universe." *Philosophical Magazine,* series 4, **4:** 358–60.

Raup, David M. 1991. *Extinction: Bad Genes or Bad Luck?* New York: Norton.

———— and James W. Valentine 1983. "Multiple Origins of Life." *Proceedings of the National Academy of Sciences* **80:** 2981–84.

Redondi, Pietro 1987. *Galileo: Heretic.* Princeton: Princeton University Press.

Rees, Martin J. 1969. "The End of a Closed Universe." *Observatory* **89:** 193–98.

Reif, Frederic 1965. *Fundamentals of Statistical and Thermal Physics.* New York: McGraw-Hill.

Rheingold, Howard 1991. *Virtual Reality.* New York: Summit Books.

Robinson, John A. T. 1952. *The Body.* Philadelphia: Westminster.

—— 1963. *Honest to God.* Philadelphia: Westminster.

—— 1968. *In the End God.* New York: Harper & Row.

Root-Bernstein, Robert Scot 1989. *Discovering.* Cambridge: Harvard University Press.

Rosen, Edward 1939. *Three Copernican Treatises: The* Commentariolus *of Copernicus, The* Letter Against Werner, *The* Narratio Prima *of Rheticus.* New York: Columbia University Press.

—— 1975. "Kepler and the Lutheran Attitude Towards Copernicanism in the Context of the Struggle Between Science and Religion." *Vistas in Astronomy* **18:** 317–55.

—— 1984 *Copernicus and the Scientific Revolution.* Malabar (Florida): Krieger.

Rosenbaum, Morris, and A. M. Silbermann 1972. *Pentateuch with Targum Onkelos, Haphtaroth and Rashi's Commentary.* Vol. II, *Exodus.* Jerusalem: Silbermann.

Rosner, Fred 1982. *Moses Maimonides' Treatise on Resurrection.* New York: KTAV Publishing.

Rumelhart, D. E., and A. Ortony 1976. "The Representation of Knowledge in Memory." In *Schooling and the Acquisition of Knowledge.* Ed. R. C. Anderson, R. J. Spiro, and W. E. Montague. Hillsdale: Erlbaum Press.

Russell, Bertrand 1931. *Principles of Mathematics.* New York: Norton.

—— 1957. *Why I Am Not a Christian.* New York: Simon & Schuster.

Russell, Robert John 1988. "Contingency in Physics and Cosmology: A Critique of the Theology of Wolfhart Pannenberg." *Zygon:* **23:** 23–43.

Sagan, Carl, and William I. Newman 1983. "The Solipsist Approach to Extraterrestrial Intelligence." *Quarterly Journal of the Royal Astronomical Society* **24:** 113–21.

Sandage, Allan, Abhijit Saha, Gustav A. Tammann, Nino Panagia, and Duccio Macchetto 1992. "The Cepheid Distance to IC 4182; Calibration of M_V(Max) for SN Ia 1937c and the Value of H_0." *Astrophysical Journal Letters* **401:** L7–L10.

Sartre, Jean-Paul 1977. *Existentialism and Humanism* (translation of *L'existentialisme est un humanisme* [Paris: Nagel, 1947]). Brooklyn: Haskell House.

Sato, Akinobu, and Yuji Tsukamoto 1993. "Nanometre-Scale Recording and Erasing With the Scanning Tunnelling Microscope." *Nature* **363:** 431–32.

Schep, J. A. 1964. *The Nature of the Resurrection Body.* Grand Rapids: Eerdmans.

Schiffer, Marcelo, and Jacob D. Bekenstein 1989. "Proof of the Quantum Bound on the Specific Entropy for Free Fields." *Physical Review* **D39:** 1109–15.

—— and Jacob D. Bekenstein 1990. "Do Zero-Frequency Modes Contribute to the Entropy?" *Physical Review* **D42:** 3598–99.

Schillebeeckx, Edward 1987. *Jesus: An Experiment in Christology*. New York: Crossroad.

Schmidt, Brian, Robert Kirshner, and Ronald Eastman 1992. "Expanding Photospheres of Type II Supernovae and the Extragalactic Distance Scale." *Astrophysical Journal* **395**: 366–86.

Schodt, Frederik L. 1988. *Inside the Robot Kingdom: Japan, Mechatronics, and the Coming Robotopia*. Tokyo: Kodansha.

Schwartz, Jacob T. 1990. "The New Connectionism: Developing Relationships Between Neuroscience and Artificial Intelligence." In *The Artificial Intelligence Debate*. Ed. Stephen R. Graubard. Cambridge: MIT Press.

Searle, John 1980. "Minds, Brains, and Programs." *Journal of Behaviour and Brain Science* **3**: 417–57. Reprinted in *The Mind's I*. Ed. D. R. Hofstadter and D. C. Dennett (New York: Basic Books, 1981).

——— 1984. *Minds, Brains, and Science*. London: BBC Press.

Sheehan, Thomas 1984. "Revolution in the Church." *New York Review of Books* (June 14) 35–39.

Shiryayev, Albert Nikolaevich 1984. *Probability*. New York: Springer-Verlag.

Simon, Julian L. 1981. *The Ultimate Resource*. Princeton University Press.

Sivin, Nathan 1966. "Chinese Conception of Time." *Earlham Review* **1**: 82–92.

——— 1969. *Cosmos and Computation in Early Chinese Mathematical Astronomy*. Leiden: Brill.

Smith, Jane I., and Yvonne Y. Haddad 1981. *The Islamic Understanding of Death and Resurrection*. Albany: State University of New York Press.

Sorabji, Richard 1972. *Aristotle on Memory*. Providence: Brown University Press.

Sorokin, P. A. 1937. *Social and Cultural Dynamics*. Vol. 2. New York: American Book Company.

Spencer, Herbert 1902. *First Principles*. 4th ed. New York: American Home Library.

Squire, Larry R. 1987 *Memory and Brain*. Oxford: Oxford University Press.

Stambaugh, Joan 1972. *Nietzsche's Thought of Eternal Return*. Baltimore: Johns Hopkins University Press.

Stcherbatsky, Theodosius 1978. *The Conception of Buddhist Nirvana*. Delhi: Motilal Banarsidass.

Stewart, Balfour, and Peter Guthrie Tait 1875. *The Unseen Universe: or Physical Speculations on a Future State*. New York: Macmillan.

Storer, James A. 1988. *Data Compression: Methods and Theory*. Rockville: Computer Science Press.

Stuhlinger, Edward. 1964. *Ion Propulsion for Space Flight*. New York: McGraw-Hill.

Taha, Mahmoud Mohamed 1987. *The Second Message of Islam*. (Translation of *Ar-*

Risala ath Thaniya min al-Islam. 5th ed. 1980.) Syracuse: Syracuse University Press.

Teilhard de Chardin, Pierre 1975. *The Phenomenon of Man.* New York: Harper & Row.

Thompson, Silvanus Phillips 1910. *The Life of William Thomson, Baron Kelvin of Largs.* London: Macmillan.

Thorndike, Lynn 1947. *A History of Magic and Experimental Science During the First 13 Centuries of Our Era.* Vol. II. New York: Columbia University Press.

Thurston, William P. 1976. "Existence of Codimension-One Foliations." *Annals of Mathematics* **104:** 249–68.

Tillich, Paul 1948. *The Protestant Era.* Chicago: University of Chicago Press.

———— 1957. *Systematic Theology.* Vol. II. Chicago: University of Chicago Press.

Tipler, Frank J. 1979. "General Relativity, Thermodynamics, and the Poincaré Cycle." *Nature* **280:** 203–5.

———— 1980. "General Relativity and the Eternal Return." In *Essays in General Relativity,* by Frank J. Tipler, pp. 21–37. New York: Academic Press.

———— 1981. "Extraterrestrial Intelligent Beings Do Not Exist." *Quarterly Journal of the Royal Astronomical Society* **21:** 267–82.

———— 1986. "Cosmological Limits on Computation." *International Journal of Theoretical Physics* **25:** 617–61.

———— 1988. "The Omega Point Theory: A Model of an Evolving God." In *Physics, Philosophy, and Theology: A Common Quest for Understanding,* ed. Robert Russell, William Stoeger, and George Coyne, pp. 313–31. Notre Dame: University of Notre Dame Press.

———— 1989(a). "The Omega Point as *Eschaton:* Answers to Pannenberg's Questions for Scientists." *Zygon* **24:** 217–53.

———— 1989(b). "Is It All in the Mind? Review of Penrose's *The Emperor's New Mind: Concerning Computers, Minds, and the Laws of Physics.* In *Physics World* **2** (#11, November): 45–47.

———— 1992. "The Ultimate Fate of Life in Universes Which Undergo Inflation." *Physics Letters* **B286:** 36–43.

Tompkins, Ptolemy 1990. *This Tree Grows Out of Hell.* San Francisco: Harper.

Toulmin, Stephen and June Goodfield 1965. *The Discovery of Time.* New York: Harper & Row.

Trigg, Joseph W. 1983. *Origen.* Atlanta: John Knox Press.

Tuchman, Barbara 1962. *The Guns of August.* New York: Dell Books.

Tug, Salih 1987. "Death and Immortality in Islamic Thought," In *Death and Immortality in the Religions of the World.* Ed. Paul and Linda Badham, pp. 86–92. New York: Paragon.

Turing, Alan M. 1950. "Computing Machinery and Intelligence." *Mind* **59:** 433–62.

Tyndall, John 1874. *Address Delivered Before the British Association Assembled at Belfast*. London: Longmans.

———— 1897. "The Belfast Address." In *Fragments of Science*. Vol. II. New York: Appleton.

Unamuno, Miguel de 1954. *The Tragic Sense of Life*. New York: Dover.

Updike, John 1976. *A Month of Sundays*. New York: Fawcett Crest.

———— 1989. *Self-Consciousness*. New York: Ballantine.

Vallery-Radot, Rene 1923. *The Life of Pasteur*. Garden City, NY: Garden City Publishing.

Van Doren, Charles 1967. *The Idea of Progress*. New York: Praeger.

van Gulik, Robert 1976. *Celebrated Cases of Judge Dee*. New York: Dover.

von Neumann, John 1966. *Theory of Self-Reproducing Automata*. Ed. and completed by A. W. Burks. Urbana: University of Illinois Press.

———— and Oskar Morgenstern 1953. *Theory of Games and Economic Behavior*. Princeton: Princeton University Press.

Wald, Abraham 1950. *Statistical Decision Functions*. New York: Wiley.

Walters, Kerry S. 1992. *The American Deists: Voices of Reason and Dissent in the Early Republic*. Lawrence: University of Kansas Press.

Wang, Jianhua 1988. *Theory of Games*. Oxford: Oxford University Press.

Watt, W. Montgomery 1960. *Muhammad at Mecca*. Oxford: Clarendon Press.

Weinberg, Steven 1977. *The First Three Minutes*. New York: Basic Books.

———— 1987. "Newtonianism, Reductionism, and the Art of Congressional Testimony." *Nature* **330**: 433–37; **331**: 475–76.

———— 1992. *Dreams of a Final Theory*. New York: Pantheon Books.

Westfall, Richard 1989. "The Case of Galileo." *Science* **237**: 1059–60.

White, Andrew D. 1896. *A History of the Warfare of Science With Theology in Christendom*. New York: Appleton.

Wiggins, David 1980. *Sameness and Substance*. Cambridge: Harvard University Press.

Wilbert, Johannes 1975. "Eschatology in a Participatory Universe." In *Death and the Afterlife in Pre-Columbian America*. Ed. Elizabeth P. Benson. Washington: Dumbarton Oaks Research Library.

Williams, Christopher J. F. 1981. *What Is Existence?* Oxford: Oxford University Press.

Wolfe, John H. 1985. "On the Question of Interstellar Travel." In Papagiannis 1985.

Wolfram, Stephan 1984. "Universality and Complexity in Cellular Automata." *Physica* **10D**: 1–35.

Wolfson, Harry 1948. *Philo*. Vol. I. Cambridge: Harvard University Press.

———— 1965. "Immortality and Resurrection in the Philosophy of the Church

Fathers." In *Immortality and Resurrection,* ed. Krister Stendahl, pp. 54–96, New York: Macmillan.

Wootters, William K., and Wojciek H. Zurek 1982. "A Single Quantum Cannot Be Cloned." *Nature* **299:** 802–3.

Yoke, Ho Peng 1985. *Li, Qi, and Shu: An Introduction to Science and Civilization in China.* Hong Kong: Hong Kong University Press.

Young, John Zackery 1951. *Doubt and Certainty in Science.* Oxford: Oxford University Press.

————— 1988. *Philosophy and the Brain.* Oxford: Oxford University Press.

Zuckerman, Harriet 1977. *The Scientific Elite: Nobel Laureates in the United States.* New York: The Free Press.

APPENDIX FOR
SCIENTISTS

A . Introduction

Since I have attempted to avoid technical details in the body of this book, and since true science requires technical detail (and equations!), I have added this *Appendix for Scientists* for these messy technicalities. The casual reader is advised to avoid this part of the book, but the serious reader is advised to make a serious effort to master this *Appendix*. Because science is a hierarchy of information, with the most advanced ideas being built on more elementary, I cannot hope to include all the background material necessary for the non-expert to understand these sections.

Unfortunately for even the expert, the science in this *Appendix for Scientists* is extremely interdisciplinary. To comprehend it all without reference to a research library would require Ph.D.s in at least three disparate fields: (1) global general relativity, (2) theoretical particle physics, and (3) computer complexity theory. My own Ph.D. is in (1), and I myself can understand (2) and (3) without the Ph.D.s only because I've spent the past 15 years teaching myself these two fields. I've done it, so you can do it.

And I can make your own entry into these fields easier than my own by providing guides: textbooks of increasing difficulty.

For **global general relativity**, you first need special relativity, and the best introduction from the viewpoint of the professional relativist is
Spacetime Physics by Edwin F. Taylor and John A. Wheeler (San Francisco: Freeman, 1963).
The best introduction to general relativity is the first 14 chapters of
Gravitation by Charles W. Misner, Kip S. Thorne, and John A. Wheeler (San Francisco: Freeman, 1973).
Chapter 34 of this book is an overview of global methods, but the best introduction is
"Techniques of Differential Topology" in *Relativity* by Roger Penrose (Philadelphia: SIAM 1972).

Once you've learned the basics, you should graduate to the definitive work in global general relativity:

The Large Scale Structure of Space-Time, by Stephen W. Hawking and G. F. R. Ellis (Cambridge: Cambridge University Press, 1973).

A more up-to-date version of Hawking and Ellis is

Global General Relativity by Frank J. Tipler (Oxford: Oxford University Press, to be published).

For **theoretical particle physics**, I recommend you start with a basic overview of the Standard Model in

Modern Elementary Particle Physics by Gordon Kane (Reading, MA: Addison-Wesley, 1987).

Kane's book can be "read like a novel" by anyone with an undergraduate degree in physics. You should follow Kane's overview with a more mathematical introduction to the Standard Model, and I think the best such textbook is

Introduction to Elementary Particles by David Griffiths (New York: Harper & Row, 1987).

The best comprehensive discussion of the Standard Model is

Gauge Theory of Elementary Particle Physics by Ta-Pei Cheng and Ling-Fong Li (Oxford: Oxford University Press, 1984).

For **computer complexity theory**, you should begin with either

Computation: Finite and Infinite Machines by Marvin L. Minsky (Englewood Cliffs: Prentice-Hall, 1967).

or Chapter 2 of

The Emperor's New Mind by Roger Penrose (Oxford: Oxford University Press, 1989).

together with Chapter 8 of

A Primer on Determinism by John Earman (Dordrecht: Reidel, 1986).

In spite of the title, the following is a good comprehensive overview of complexity theory:

An Introduction to the General Theory of Algorithms by Michael Machtey and Paul Young (New York: North Holland, 1978).

I shall give some additional references at the beginning of some of the following sections.

Good luck!

B. The Relative Sizes of Future History and Past History

The Standard Model of Cosmology is based on the assumption that, on the largest scales, the universe is homogeneous and isotropic. The temperature variation $\Delta T/T$ of the cosmic background radiation is a direct measure of this homogeneity and isotropy ($\Delta T = 0$ if the universe is perfectly homogeneous and isotropic), and the COBE satellite observations (Smoot et al., 1992) show that $\Delta T/T \approx 5 \times 10^{-6}$. Thus the homogeneity and isotropy assumption is a very good approximation. The *Friedmann universe* (sometimes also called the Friedmann-Robertson-Walker or FRW universe) is the unique spacetime with a six-parameter group of Killing vector fields which collectively define spacelike hypersurfaces of homogeneity and isotropy. The entire Friedmann universe can be completely covered (except for trival 2-sphere origin and antipodal singularities) by the metric

$$ds^2 = -N^2(t)dt^2 + R^2(t)[d\chi^2 + \Sigma^2(\chi)(d\theta^2 + \sin^2\theta d\phi^2)] \qquad (B.1a)$$

where

$$\Sigma(\chi) = \begin{cases} \sin\chi, & \text{if } k = +1; \\ \chi, & \text{if } k = 0; \\ \sinh\chi, & \text{if } k = -1. \end{cases} \qquad (B.1b)$$

In all three cases, the coordinates (θ, ϕ) have range $0 \le \theta \le \pi$, $0 \le \phi < 2\pi$; (θ, ϕ) are just the usual coordinate covering of a 2-sphere. The range of the "radial" coordinate χ depends on the global topology of the hypersurfaces of homogeneity and isotropy. If $k = 0$ or $k = -1$, we have the *flat Friedmann universe* or the *open Friedmann universe* respectively. In both cases, the range of χ is $0 \le \chi < +\infty$. Thus both the open and flat Friedmann universes have spatial topology R^3, the Euclidean three-plane. This at least is the natural topology. It is always possible to make identifications in both the open and flat cases and convert these cosmologies—which are naturally infinite in spatial extent—into closed cosmologies with the spatial hypersurfaces being compact without boundary. But such identifications would break the *global* Killing symmetries and so are really inconsistent with the original assumptions of global homogeneity and isotropy.

The $k = +1$ case is called the *closed Friedmann universe*. The range of χ for a closed Friedmann universe is $0 \le \chi \le \pi$. The natural topology—the only topology consistent with the global Killing symmetries—is S^3, which is the 3-sphere.

Thus $\chi = 0$ is the origin of spatial coordinates, while $\chi = \pi$ is the antipodal point. Here, too, one can make identifications consistent with local Killing symmetries.

The functions $N(t)$ and $R(t)$ are called the *lapse* and the *scale factor* respectively. The lapse function in effect selects the scale of the time, and the scale factor is a measure of the size of the $t = $ constant spatial sections of the universe. Since the Einstein field equations are generally covariant, we can use *any* scale of time we like, but only two scales are standard in discussions of the Friedmann universe. The first scale just sets $N(t) = 1$. With this choice, the time in the metric (B.1) is *proper time*, and this time is the time that is measured by our clocks in the present astrophysical environment. In the following, I shall use the symbol t to refer to proper time. Notice that $N(t) = 1$ also means that time and space are measured in the same units. For instance, if time is measured in years, then distance must be measured in light years.

The second timescale measures time in terms of the scale factor: $N(t) = R(t)$. This timescale is called *conformal time*, since in this case the metric (B.1) is conformal to a static metric. When I wish to refer to conformal time, I shall use the variable τ. In conformal time, a light ray setting out in the χ-direction from the origin of coordinates satisfies the equation $\chi = \tau$, because all light rays obey the equation $ds^2 = 0$.

If on the largest scales the pressure of matter is tiny in comparison to the value of the rest mass of matter, then the Friedmann universe is called *matter-dominated*, and the Einstein equations expressed in conformal time give, for the $k = +1$ closed universe (with cosmological constant $\Lambda = 0$), the following relations between the proper time, the scale factor, and the conformal time:

$$R(\tau) = \frac{R_{max}}{2}(1 - \cos\tau) = R_{max}\sin^2\left(\frac{\tau}{2}\right) \qquad (B.2a)$$

$$t(\tau) = \frac{R_{max}}{2}(\tau - \sin\tau) \qquad (B.2b)$$

(See Misner, Thorne, and Wheeler 1973 for a proof.) For $t \ll R_{max}$, it is easy to compute from equations (B.2a) and (B.2b) that $R(t) = (3R_{max}/16)^{1/3}t^{2/3}$, which happens to be the matter-dominated flat Friedmann universe result (though R_{max} is really just an arbitrary constant if the universe is really flat).

It is clear from equations (B.2) that a closed universe starts at an initial Big Bang singularity $R(\tau = 0) = 0$, expands to a maximum size with scale factor

$R_{max} = R(\tau = \pi)$, and recollapses to a final Big Crunch singularity $R(\tau = 2\pi) = 0$. It is also obvious from equations $(B.2)$ and the equations for light rays given earlier that a light ray setting out from the origin of coordinates ($\chi = 0$) at the beginning of time would reach the antipodal point of the universe ($\chi = \pi$) at precisely the time of maximum expansion, and return to the origin of coordinates at the instant the universe ends in the Big Crunch singularity.

The universe is observed to be matter-dominated at the present epoch of its history, and it has been so dominated at all times since about 500,000 years after the beginning of the universe. In the future, it is expected to be matter-dominated until the time of maximum expansion.

Hubble's constant is defined to be $H_0 \equiv (R^{-1}dR/dt)\big|_{t_{now}}$, where the time t_{now} is the present time. In the literature, one finds $H_0 = h(100 \text{ km/sec-mpc})$, where h is some constant obtained—in principle—from measurement. Unfortunately, there are fierce debates among cosmologists as to what the observations give for h, so it is necessary to leave h in all equations so that the results presented by theorists will be valid whatever the eventual results of observation. At any time t, the Hubble parameter $H \equiv R^{-1}dR/dt = \frac{R_{max}}{2} \frac{(1-\cos\tau)^2}{\sin\tau}$, and the mass density of matter ρ is given by

$$\rho = \frac{3}{\pi R^2{}_{max}(1-\cos\tau)^3}$$

Whether a Friedmann universe is open, flat, or closed depends on the mass density. If the density is equal to the "critical" density $\rho_{crit} = 3H_0^2/8\pi$, then the universe is flat. If the density is greater than this, then it is closed; if less than this, it is open. The density parameter $\Omega_0 \equiv (\rho/\rho_{crit})\big|_{t_{now}}$ thus determines which it is.

Using the above equations, it is simple to show that the scale factor of a matter-dominated Friedmann universe with cosmological constant $\Lambda = 0$ and with spatial topology $S^3(k = +1)$ is given by

$$R_{max} = \left(\frac{1}{H_0}\right) \frac{\Omega_0}{(\Omega_0 - 1)^{3/2}} \qquad (B.3a)$$

and the conformal time now, τ_{now} is given by

$$\tau_{now} = \cos^{-1}\left(\frac{2}{\Omega_0} - 1\right) \qquad (B.3b)$$

The total proper lifetime t_U of such a closed universe is

$$t_U = \pi R_{max} = \left(\frac{\pi}{H_0}\right) \frac{\Omega_0}{(\Omega_0-1)^{3/2}} \tag{B.4}$$

For a matter-dominated universe, the actual proper age now, t_{now}, is

$$t_{now} = \left(\frac{\pi}{H_0}\right) \frac{\Omega_0}{(\Omega_0-1)^{3/2}} \left[\left(\frac{1}{2\pi}\right) \cos^{-1}\left(\frac{2}{\Omega_0}-1\right) - \left(\frac{(\Omega_0-1)^{1/2}}{\pi\Omega_0}\right)\right]$$

which can be more simply expressed as

$$t_{now} = t_U \left[\left(\frac{1}{2\pi}\right) \cos^{-1}\left(\frac{2}{\Omega_0}-1\right) - \left(\frac{(\Omega_0-1)^{1/2}}{\pi\Omega_0}\right)\right] \tag{B.5}$$

which is less than $\frac{2}{3H_0}$ for any closed universe, since such a universe necessarily has $\Omega_0 > 1$. Thus (proper time remaining)/(actual proper age) = $(t_U - $ [actual proper age])/ (actual proper age) > $(3\pi/2)$ $[\Omega_0(\Omega_0 - 1)^{-3/2}] - 1$. If $\Omega_0 \leq 2$—observations indicate this is a conservative upper bound (Börner 1992)—then (proper time remaining)/(actual proper age) > 8.4. Since $H_0^{-1} = h^{-1}(10$ billion years) where $1/2 \leq h \leq 1$, we have: (actual proper age) < $h^{-1}(6.7$ billion years). I shall use the old Sandage-Tammann value of $h = 0.55$, giving an actual proper age of at most 12 billion years, and thus at least 100 billion years remaining. If one wishes to be even more conservative in estimating the remaining time, choose $\Omega_0 \leq 3$ and $h = 1$. This gives 6.7 billion years for the actual proper age of the universe, and a mere 27 billion years remaining until the Omega Point is reached. Actually, $\Omega_0 \leq 3$ and $h = 1$ are much, much too conservative, since the age of Population II stars and the nucleogenesis data strongly suggest that the actual proper age is greater than 15 billion years (Börner 1992), implying $h < 0.45$. Sandage, Tammann, and their colleagues announced in 1992 (see Sandage et al. 1992) that their most recent measurements, using the Hubble space telescope to resolve Cepheids in galaxy IC 4182 where a Type Ia supernova was once seen, show that $h = 0.51 \pm 0.09$. Schmidt et al. also announced in 1992 that measurements of Type II supernovae give $h = 0.6 \pm 0.1$. Both of these most recent observations yield an $h \approx 0.5$, but the battle over the size of the Hubble constant continues (Flam 1993). (I have expressed the age of the universe in terms of the density parameter, but I could just as easily have used the deceleration parameter q_0, since for $\Lambda = 0$ we have $2q_0 = \Omega_0$. Hence, assuming $\Omega_0 \leq 2$ is equivalent to assuming $q_0 \leq 1$.)

One can also prove that there is far more reality in the future than in the past by comparing the spacetime volume of the entire spacetime continuum with the spacetime volume of our past light cone. For matter-dominated closed Friedmann universes, the total *spacetime* volume—a four-dimensional volume—is given by

$$V_{Total} \equiv \int_V \sqrt{-g}\,d^4x = \int_0^{2\pi} d\tau \int_0^\pi d\chi \int_0^\pi d\theta \int_0^{2\pi} d\phi \; R^4(\tau) \sin^2\chi \sin\theta$$

$$\frac{35\pi^3}{32} R_{max}^4 = \frac{35\pi^3 \Omega_0^4}{32 H_0^4 (\Omega_0 - 1)^6} \qquad (B.6a)$$

The volume $V_{past}(\tau)$ of the past light cone of an event at conformal time $0 < \tau \leq \pi$ is

$$V_{past}(\tau) = \int_0^\tau R^4(\tilde{\tau})d\tilde{\tau} \int_0^{\tau-\tilde{\tau}} \sin^2\chi \, d\chi \int_0^\pi \sin\theta \, d\theta \int_0^{2\pi} d\phi$$

$$= 2\pi R_{max}^4 \int_0^\tau \sin^8\left(\frac{\tilde{\tau}}{2}\right)\left(\tau - \tilde{\tau} - \frac{1}{2}\sin 2(\tau - \tilde{\tau})\right)d\tilde{\tau} \qquad (B.6b)$$

In particular, $V_{past}(\pi) = [(35\pi^3/128) - (104\pi/45)]R_{max}^4$, so $V_{Total}/V_{past} \approx 28$ even for an observer at the time of maximum expansion. Using (B.3), $V_{past}(\tau)$ can be expressed in closed form in terms of H_0 and Ω_0, but since this closed form expression is complicated, let us obtain an upper bound on the four-dimensional volume of our past light cone by taking the radius of the visible universe to be t_{now}. This gives $V_{past} < \frac{4\pi}{3} t_{now}^4$. From $t_{now} < \frac{2}{3H_0}$ we obtain a lower bound for the ratio of the volume of the entire spacetime continuum to the volume of the past light cone:

$$\frac{V_{Total}}{V_{past}} > \frac{40\Omega_0^4}{(\Omega_0 - 1)^6} \qquad (B.7)$$

This lower bound is 640 for $\Omega_0 = 2$. (Numerically integrating (B.6) gives $V_{Total}/V_{past} = 29{,}000$ for $\Omega_0 = 2$ and 630 for $\Omega_0 = 3$.) If we let R_{now} be the value of the scale factor now, then one can use (B.3a) to show that

$$\frac{R_{now}}{R_{max}} = \frac{\Omega_0 - 1}{\Omega_0} \approx \Omega_0 - 1 \qquad (B.8)$$

where the last equality holds if $\Omega_0 - 1 \ll 1$. I shall show in Section H that the Omega Point Theory predicts $10^2 e^{-4\pi} \geq R_{now}/R_{max} \geq e^{-4\pi}$. This gives $3.5 \times 10^{-4} \leq (\Omega_0 - 1)$ $\leq 3.5 \times 10^{-6}$, so from (B.7) we have $2 \times 10^{34} > V_{Total}/V_{past} > 2 \times 10^{22}$. In either case, there is vastly more spacetime volume in our future than in our past. The volume of the Omega Point's past light cone is V_{Total}—the whole spacetime continuum—as I pointed out in the text.

The three-dimensional *spatial* volume of the universe today, $V_{now}^{spatial}$, is given by

$$V_{now}^{spatial} = R_{now}^3 \int_0^\pi \sin^2 \chi \, d\chi \int_0^\pi \sin \theta \, d\theta \int_0^{2\pi} d\phi = 2\pi^2 \, R_{now}^3$$

$$= \frac{\pi^2}{4} R_{max}^3 (1 - \cos \tau)^3 = \frac{2\pi^2}{H_0^3(\Omega_0 - 1)^{3/2}} \qquad (B.9)$$

The proper spatial distance to the antipodal point at the present time, $D_{antipodal}^{now}$, is given by (provided the universe has spatial topology S^3 and is matter-dominated):

$$D_{antipodal}^{now} = \pi R_{now} = \frac{\pi R_{max}}{2} (1 - \cos \tau) = \frac{\pi}{H_0 \sqrt{\Omega_0 - 1}} \qquad (B.10)$$

The time to maximum expansion, t_{max}, is just half of the total proper lifetime given by (B.4), so if $D_{antipodal}^{max}$ is the distance to the antipodal point at maximum expansion and 10^{12} parsecs = 1 teraparsec, we have

$$t_{max} = \frac{\pi R_{max}}{2} = \left(\frac{\pi}{2H_0} \right) \frac{\Omega_0}{(\Omega_0 - 1)^{3/2}} \qquad (B.11)$$

So, with $h = \frac{1}{2}$ and $3.5 \times 10^{-4} \le (\Omega_0 - 1) \le 3.5 \times 10^{-6}$, we have

$$5 \times 10^{16} \text{ years} \le t_{max} \le 5 \times 10^{18} \text{years} \qquad (B.12)$$

$$1 \text{ teraparsec} \le D_{antipodal}^{now} \le 10 \text{ teraparsecs} \qquad (B.13)$$

$$(1 \text{ teraparsec})^3 \le V_{now}^{spatial} \le (10 \text{ teraparsecs})^3 \qquad (B.14)$$

$$3 \times 10^3 \le \frac{R_{max}}{R_{now}} \le 3 \times 10^5 \qquad (B.15)$$

$$3 \text{ thousand teraparsecs} \le D_{antipodal}^{max} \le 3 \text{ million teraparsecs} \qquad (B.16)$$

The timescale in inequality (B.12) is proper time t. However, *entropic time* $\Theta(t)$, defined to be the total amount of entropy that exists in the universe at proper time t, is a more physically significant timescale than proper time. By the Second Law of Thermodynamics, $\Theta(t)$ is a monotone increasing function, and since irreversible processes are constantly going on in the universe, Θ is actually strictly increasing, so Θ can be used as a timescale. If $s(t)$ is the entropy density as a function of proper time t, then

$$\Theta(t) = V^{spatial}(t)s(t) = [2\pi^2 R^3(t)]s(t)$$

Almost all of the entropy in the universe at the present epoch is in the form of the cosmic background radiation. The entropy density of the background radiation is easily computed. The Helmholtz free energy density of radiation is (Landau and Lifshitz 1969, p. 165) $F = -\frac{1}{3}aT^4$, where $a = \pi^2 k^4 / 15 c^3 \hbar^3$ is the radiation density constant and T is the temperature. The entropy density is thus $s = -\partial F / \partial T = \frac{4}{3}aT^3$. More generally, the entropy density is $s = \frac{2}{3} g a T^3$, where $g = g_B + \frac{7}{8} g_F$ and g_B are the boson spin degrees of freedom and g_F are the fermion spin degrees of freedom. In the present epoch $g_F = 6$ since there are 6 types of neutrinos (more precisely, there is a neutrino and an anti-neutrino in each of 3 generations) and $g_B = 2$. However, the neutrinos in the present epoch have a temperature $T_\nu = \left(\frac{4}{11}\right)^{1/3} T_\gamma$, where T_γ is the temperature of the electromagnetic cosmic radiation, because electron/positron annihilation in the early universe raised the temperature of the electromagnetic radiation but did not change the neutrino temperature. Thus the ratio of electromagnetic entropy density to neutrino entropy density today is

$$\frac{s_\gamma}{s_\nu} = \frac{(2) T_\gamma^3}{6\left(\frac{7}{8}\right) T_\nu^3} = \frac{22}{21}$$

The total entropy density is the sum of the electromagnetic and neutrino entropy densities. In units of bits per cm^3, this is

$$s(t_{now}) = \frac{4}{3}\left(1 + \frac{21}{22}\right)\left(\frac{a}{k \ln 2}\right) T_\gamma^3 = 4{,}173 \pm 46 \text{ bits/cm}^3 \qquad (B.17)$$

where I have used the latest COBE measurement of the temperature of the cosmic background radiation (Mather et al. 1994) of $T_\gamma = 2.726 \pm 0.010$ °K at the 95% confidence level.

Combining inequalities (B.14) and (B.17) with the definition of entropic time gives for the entropic time of the present epoch $\Theta(t_{now})$:

$$1 \times 10^{95} \text{ bits} \leq \Theta(t_{now}) \leq 1 \times 10^{98} \text{ bits} \qquad (B.18)$$

I shall argue in Sections H and M that Θ diverges to $+\infty$ as the final singularity is approached, so the past is finite but the future infinite in entropic time.

The list of inequalities $(B.12)$–$(B.18)$ defines the universe up to the time of maximum expansion. Until then it will be approximately Friedmannian (the reasons will be given in Section H). I shall now demonstrate that, even if the evolution of a closed universe deviates wildly from homogeneity and isotropy after recollapse begins, all timelike curves will hit a final singularity after finite proper time.

Final Singularity Theorem: If on a spacetime the following conditions hold:

(1) there exists a compact Cauchy spacelike hypersurface S on which the trace $\chi^a{}_a$ of the extrinsic curvature is everywhere negative;

(2) the timelike convergence condition holds;

then there is a universal upper bound $t_f \equiv \inf_S |3/\chi^a{}_a|$ to the proper time length of any timelike curve to the future of S. That is, the proper time length of *any* timelike curve γ in $J+(S)$ is less than or equal to t_f.

Discussion: a *compact* spacelike hypersurface is a spacelike 3-dimensional manifold which is finite without boundary: it corresponds to a closed universe at one instant of time. The trace of the extrinsic curvature being negative means that the closed universe at that instant of time is everywhere contracting. A *Cauchy* hypersurface is a hypersurface which every timelike curve intersects exactly once. This can be shown to imply that in the spacetime all sets of the form $J^+(p) \cap J^-(q)$ are compact for any two events p and q in the spacetime, where the causal past set $J^-(q) \equiv \{s \,|\, \text{there is a future-directed timelike or null curve from s to q}\}$, and the causal future set $J^+(p) \equiv \{s \,|\, \text{there is a past-directed timelike or null curve from s to p}\}$. (If "timelike or null" in the preceding sets are replaced by "timelike," the sets are called the chronological past $I^-(p)$ of the event p, and the chronological future $I^+(p)$ of the event p respectively.)

A spacetime in which all sets of the form $J^+(p) \cap J^-(q)$ are compact is called *globally hyperbolic.* Global hyperbolicity means that determinism holds: the entire spacetime is uniquely determined from initial data on the hypersurface S.

The *timelike convergence condition* means that $R_{ab}V^aV^b \geq 0$ for all timelike vectors V^a, where R_{ab} is the Ricci tensor. Physically, this condition means that gravity is always attractive.

Proof of the Theorem: Hawking and Ellis have shown that if the timelike convergence condition holds, then within a proper time distance $|3/\chi^a{}_a|$ there is a conjugate point p along a timelike geodesic γ which intersects S normally (this means that two nearby geodesics normal to S intersect at p). Since S is compact, this means that *all* timelike geodesics normal to S must have a conjugate point in the future within a distance $t_f \equiv \inf_S \left| 3/\chi^a{}_a \right|$ from S. Hawking and Ellis have also shown that to each point q in a spacetime with a Cauchy hypersurface S, there is a timelike geodesic normal to S of maximal length from S to q and without conjugate points. But if there were a timelike curve of length greater than t_f, then there would have to be a geodesic normal to S of length greater than t_f and without conjugate points. But we have just seen that all such geodesics have conjugate points within a length t_f. This contradiction establishes that no timelike curve can have a length greater than t_f. This completes the proof.

References

Börner, Gerhard 1992. *The Early Universe: Facts and Fiction.* Berlin: Springer-Verlag.

Flam, Faye 1993. "Battle Lines Shift in the Great Cosmic Distance Dispute" Science 259: 1262-1263.

Hawking, S. W., and George F. R. Ellis 1973. The Large Scale Structure of Space-Time. Cambridge: Cambridge University Press.

Landau, Lev D. and E. M. Lifshitz 1969. Statistical Physics. Reading, MA: Addison-Wesley.

Mather, J. C., et al. 1994. "Measurement of the Cosmic Microwave Background Spectrum by the COBE FIRAS." Astrophysical Journal 420: 439-444.

Misner, Charles W., Kip S. Thorne, and John A. Wheeler 1973. Gravitation. San Francisco: Freeman.

Peebles, P. James E. 1971. Physical Cosmology. Princeton: Princeton University Press.

— 1993. Principles of Physical Cosmology. Princeton: Princeton University Press.

Sandage, Allan, A. Saha, G. A. Tammann, Nino Panagia, and D. Macchetto 1992. "The Cepheid Distance of IC 4182; Calibration of $M_V(max)$ for SN Ia 1937C and the Value of H_0." Astrophysical Journal **401**: L7–L10.

Schmidt, Brian, Robert Kirshner, and Ronald Eastman 1992. "Expanding

Photospheres of Type II Supernovae and the Extragalactic Distance Scale," *Astrophysical Journal* **395**: 366–86.

Smoot, George F., et al. 1992. "Structure in the COBE Differential Microwave Radiometer First-Year Maps." *Astrophysical Journal* **396**: L1–L5.

Tipler, Frank J. 1996. *Global General Relativity*. Oxford: Oxford University Press.

C. The Bekenstein Bound

The fundamental limitation on the number of possible quantum states in a bounded region—or, alternatively, on the number of bits that can be coded in a bounded region—is given by the Bekenstein Bound [1,2]. The Bekenstein Bound is a consequence of the basic postulates of quantum field theory. A derivation will not be given here, but in essentials the Bekenstein Bound is just another manifestation of the Heisenberg Uncertainty Principle.

If, as is standard, the information I is related to the number of possible states N by the equation $I = \log_2 N$, then the Bekenstein Bound on the amount of information coded within a sphere of radius R containing total energy E is

$$I \leq 2\pi ER/(\hbar c \ln 2) \tag{C.1}$$

or, expressing the energy in mass units of kilograms,

$$I \leq 2.57686 \times 10^{43} \left(\frac{M}{1 \text{ kilogram}} \right) \left(\frac{R}{1 \text{ meter}} \right) \text{ bits} \tag{C.2}$$

For example, a typical human being has a mass of less than 100 kilograms, and is less than 2 meters tall. (Thus such a human can be enclosed in a sphere of radius 1 meter.) Hence, we can let M equal 100 kg and R equal 1 meter in formula (C.2) obtaining

$$I_{human} \leq 2.57686 \times 10^{45} \text{ bits} \tag{C.3}$$

as an upper bound to the number of bits I_{human} that can be coded by any physical entity the size and mass of a human being.

Let me give an elementary *plausibility argument* for the Bekenstein Bound (C.1). This argument will be nonrigorous. (A completely rigorous proof would involve too much quantum field theory to be feasible in this book.) The Uncertainty Principle tells us that

$$\Delta P \Delta R \geq \hbar \tag{C.4}$$

Where ΔP is the ultimate limit in knowledge of the momentum and ΔR is the limit in knowledge of the position. (Alternatively, the inequality (C.4) expresses the minimum size of a phase space division.) Thus, if the total momentum is less than P and the system is known to be inside a region of size R, then the phase space of the system must be divided into no more than $PR/\Delta P\Delta R = 2\pi PR/h$ distinguishable subintervals. This means that the number of distinguishable states n is bounded above by $2\pi PR/h$. Since for any particle, $P \leq E/c$, where E is the total energy of the system including the system's rest mass, with equality holding only if the system is moving at the speed of light, we have

$$I = \log_2 n \leq \frac{n}{\ln 2} \leq 2\pi \left(\frac{E}{c}\right) \left(\frac{R}{h \ln 2}\right) \leq \frac{2\pi ER}{\hbar c \ln 2}$$

which is the Bekenstein Bound (C.1). (Additional complications like particle substructure, and the fact that the system is in three dimensions rather than one are implicitly taken into account by the fact that $\log_2 N$ is very much less than N, for large N. As I said, the above derivation is nonrigorous.)

An upper bound to the information processing rate can be obtained [1] directly from the Bekenstein Bound by noting that the time for a state transition cannot be less than the time it takes for light to cross the sphere of radius R, which is $2R/c$. Thus

$$\dot{I} \leq \frac{I}{2R/c} \leq \frac{\pi E}{\hbar \ln 2} = 3.86262 \times 10^{51} \left(\frac{M}{1\text{kilogram}}\right) \text{bits/sec} \qquad (C.5)$$

where the dot denotes the proper time derivative. By inserting 100 kilograms for the value of M in inequality (C.5), we obtain an upper bound for the rate of change of state of a human being, $\dot{I}_{human}$:

$$\dot{I}_{human} \leq 3.86262 \times 10^{53} \text{states/sec} \qquad (C.6)$$

The significant digits in the RHS of inequalities (C.2), (C.3), (C.5), and (C.6) have to be taken with a grain of salt. The digits correctly express our knowledge of the constants c and $\hbar$. But the Bekenstein Bound is probably not the least upper bound to either I or $\dot{I}$; Schiffer and Bekenstein have recently shown [2] that the Bekenstein Bound probably overestimates both I and $\dot{I}$ by a factor of at least 100.

Strictly speaking, (C.5) only applies to a single communication channel [3], but it probably [4] applies even to multichannel systems if the need to merge the information from various channels is taken into account. However, if the latter is not taken into account, the number of channels is certainly limited by the number of states given by (C.1), and so an extremely conservative upper bound is $\frac{dI}{d\tau} \leq e^{I^B_{max}} \dot{I}^B_{max}$ (J. D. Bekenstein, private communication).

A human being—indeed, any object existing in the current universe—actually codes far less information than quantum field theory would permit it to code. For example, a single hydrogen atom, if it were to code as much information as permitted by the Bekenstein Bound, would code about 4×10^6 bits of information, since the hydrogen atom is about one Ångstrøm in radius, and has a mass of about 1.67×10^{-27} kilograms. So a hydrogen atom could code about a megabyte of information, whereas it typically codes far less than a bit. The mass of the hydrogen is not being used efficiently!

If we take the radius to be that of a proton ($R = 10^{-13}$cm.), then the amount of information that can be coded in the proton is only 44 bits! This is remarkably small considering the complexity of the proton—three valence quarks, innumerable sea quarks and gluons—so complex in fact that we have been unable to compute its ground state from first principles using the Standard Model even when we use our most advanced supercomputers. Bekenstein has used this extremely small number of possible states in the proton to constrain the number of possible quark fields that could be present in the quark sea.

In the early universe, where there are particle horizons, and also for black holes, the Bekenstein Bound in the form

$$I = \frac{S}{\ln 2} \leq \frac{A}{4L_P^2 \ln 2} = \frac{\pi R^2}{L_P^2 \ln 2} \qquad (C.7)$$

is appropriate, where S is the total entropy in a causally connected region inside a 2-sphere of radius R and surface area A, where L_P is the Planck length. The Bekenstein Bound in the form (C.7) can be easily derived from (C.1) as follows.

If $R = 2GE/c^4$, then a black hole forms, enclosing the information, and *in asymptotally flat space* we cannot get any more energy into a sphere of radius R than this. Thus

$$I \leq \frac{2\pi ER}{\hbar c \ln 2} = 2\pi \left(\frac{Rc^4}{2G}\right) \frac{R}{\hbar c \ln 2} = 4\pi R^2 \left(\frac{c^3/G\hbar}{4 \ln 2}\right)$$

But $c^3/G\hbar = L_P^{-2}$ and $A = 4\pi R^2$, so we get (C.7). However, the formation of a black hole implies that there are event horizons, which means by definition that the final singularity cannot be an omega point. That is, inequality (C.7) applies if and only if the information corresponding to life is restricted to a part rather than the entire universe.

Bekenstein has noted [5] that when a region in the early universe with its particle horizons has a radius of the order of a Planck length L_P, the entropy and information must be of order one or less, from which he concludes that the initial singularity does not exist. I would instead interpret this result (which I believe to be correct) as implying that the initial Friedmann singularity is *unique*; there is no information in the initial singularity. So $I = S = 0$ at the initial singularity, and thus there is no contradiction with the RHS of (C.7) going to zero as $R \to 0$.

Ellis and Coule [6] argue that, in *any* closed universe near the *final* singularity, (C.7) is still the correct form of Bekenstein's Bound, with R being the scale factor of the universe, and thus $R \to 0$ means $I \to 0$, which obviously rules out $I \to +\infty$ as $R \to 0$, that holds if the Omega Point Theory is true. I shall show in Section H that if (C.1) rather than (C.7) is used, we can have $I \to +\infty$ as $R \to 0$, provided event horizons disappear.

But Ellis and Coule are wrong; (C.7) cannot be the correct form near the final singularity in a closed universe without event horizons because, if it were, then it would imply a global and universal violation of the Second Law of Thermodynamics when the radiation temperature reaches a mere 5×10^4 GeV, far below the Planck energy of 10^{19} GeV, and even far below the unification temperature where we think the Bekenstein Bound and the Second Law both apply.

To see this, write $S = sR^3$, where s is the entropy density, and let R_0 and T_0 be the scale factor and radiation temperature today. Using $R = R_0 T_0 / T$, (C.7) implies the following upper bound to the future universal temperature T:

$$T \leq \frac{\sqrt{\pi}\, T_0}{\sqrt{S_0 R_0 L_P^2}} \tag{C.8}$$

We have $s_0 = 2.9 \times 10^3 \text{cm}^{-3}$ from equation (B.17) of Section B. (See also [7, p. 273]. Note that applying (B.17) to (C.8) requires leaving out the factor ln 2.) Also, $T_0 = 2.726°K = 2.349 \times 10^{-13}$ GeV. These numbers give

$$T \leq 5.3 \times 10^4 \text{GeV} \tag{C.9}$$

if $R_0 = 3$ gigaparsecs (the Hubble distance) and $T \leq 3 \times 10^3$ GeV if $R_0 = 1$ teraparsec, my lower bound in Section B. If $R_0 = 10$ teraparsecs, my upper bound in Section B, then $T \leq 1 \times 10^3$ GeV, which is the energy the LHC is designed to probe. Surely quantum mechanics and the Second Law are valid at this energy, even in the collapsing phase of a closed universe.

If they are, then the Ellis and Coule argument becomes an argument *for* life engulfing the universe and continuing forever. If life does not engulf the entire closed universe, then, as I shall show in Section H, horizons will appear, the Ellis-Coule calculation applies, and either quantum mechanics or the Second Law must fail at low energies in the collapsing phase. So either the universe is not closed, or life goes on forever in an engulfed universe. The Second Law ultimately *requires* life. This is yet another argument for the Eternal Life Postulate.

References

[1] Bekenstein, J. D. 1981. Physical Review Letters 46: 623.

[2] Schiffer, M. and J. D. Bekenstein 1989. Physical Review D39: 1109; and Physical Review D42: 3598.

[3] Bekenstein, J. D. 1988. Physical Review A37: 3437.

[4] Bekenstein, J. D. 1984. Physical Review D30: 1669.

[5] Bekenstein, J. D. 1989. International Journal of Theoretical Physics 28: 967.

[6] Ellis, G. F. R. and D. H. Coule 1992. "Life at the End of the Universe," University of Cape Town preprint.

[7] Börner, G. 1992. The Early Universe Berlin: Springer.

D. The Law of Mass Action Requires Quantum Indistinguishability

Since, surprisingly, few textbooks in physics and chemistry which prove the Law of Mass Action point out that it requires the assumption of quantum indistinguishability—the fact that two systems in the same quantum state cannot be distinguished by any experiment whatsoever, no matter how advanced our technology eventually becomes, no matter what new laws of physics we discover in the future—I shall provide a proof here. (Amazingly, even *Enrico Fermi*(!) didn't mention it either in his classic textbook *Thermodynamics*, nor in his *Notes on Thermodynamics and Statistics*, though in both he discussed the Law of Mass Action in detail.) My proof will follow that of Reif, and I shall assume knowledge of basic statistical mechanics and classical thermodynamics. A good introduction to this material is the textbook by Charles Kittel. I can also recommend the textbooks by Callan and by Pippard.

Consider a single-phase chemical system which contains m distinct kinds of molecules. Denote the chemical symbols of these molecules by $A_1, A_2, \ldots, A_m$, and let N_i be the number of molecules of type A_i in the system. A *chemical equation* expresses how these molecules are transformed into one another; let a_i be the coefficient of A_i in the chemical equation. Conservation of atoms means that the general chemical equation can be written in the form

$$\sum_{i=1}^{m} a_i A_i = 0 \qquad (D.1)$$

For example, the reaction which generates water

$$2H_2 + O_2 \rightleftharpoons 2H_2O \qquad (D.2)$$

can be written

$$-2H_2 - O_2 + 2H_2O = 0$$

and so $(a_1, a_2, a_3) = (-2, -1, 2)$ with $(A_1, A_2, A_3) = (H_2, O_2, H_2O)$. The reaction $(D.2)$ is written with the symbol " $\rightleftharpoons$ " to show that the reaction can and does go both ways, even in equilibrium. So, if we take a bottle filled with two volumes of hydrogen to each volume of oxygen and ignite it, we will get *mostly* water, but some hydrogen and oxygen molecules will remain. If we continue to watch the bottle, we will find that some water molecules will disassociate into hydrogen and oxygen again, and some hydrogen and oxygen molecules will combine into water. The **Law of Mass Action** tells us exactly how many molecules of each type we will have in our system in equilibrium:

$$N_1^{a_1} N_2^{a_2} \dots N_k^{a_m} = K_N(T, V) \qquad (D.3)$$

where the quantity $K_N(T, V)$, called the *equilibrium constant*, is independent of the number of molecules present in the system; it depends only on the temperature T and volume V of the system. (If we write $[A_i] \equiv N_i / N_A V$, where N_A is Avogadro's constant and $[A_i]$ is thus the number of moles per unit volume of molecule A_i, then it can be shown that the Law of Mass Action can be written as $[A_1]^{a_1} [A_2]^{a_2} \dots [A_m]^{a_m} = V^a K(T)$, where $a = \sum_{i=1}^{m} a_i$ and $K(T)$ is a function of the temperature only, but I shall not prove this here. Also, the form (D.3) applies only to gases, since I have assumed that the interactions between molecules can be neglected. To get the formula for molecules in solution, replace N_i in (D.3) by $N_i/(N_0)$, where N_0 is the number of molecules of solute.)

In particular, for the water creation reaction (D.2), the Law of Mass Action (D.3) tells us that

$$\frac{(N_{H_2O})^2}{(N_{H_2})^2 N_{O_2}} = K_N(T, V)$$

Proof of the Law of Mass Action: Let s_i be the possible states of the ith molecule, and let $E_i(s_i)$ be the energy of this molecule in this state. If there is negligible interaction between the molecules, the total energy of the system will be $E = \sum_i E_i(s_i)$. If all the molecules are *considered distinguishable* the partition function would be

$$\tilde{Z} = \sum_{s_1, s_2, \dots} e^{-\beta[E_1(s_1) + E_2(s_2) + \dots]} = \left(\sum_{s_1} e^{-\beta E_1(s_1)} \right) \left(\sum_{s_2} e^{-\beta E_2(s_2)} \right) \dots \qquad (D.4)$$

where the sum is over all the states of each molecule, $\beta \equiv 1/kT$, and k is Boltzmann's constant. The last equality comes from assuming the interaction between the molecules is negligible. In the product (D.4) there will be N_i equal factors of the form

$$\zeta_i \equiv \sum_q e^{-\beta E_q(s_q)} \qquad (D.5)$$

for each of the N_i molecules of type i, where the sum is over all the states of a single molecule of type i. Thus, *assuming that the molecules are distinguishable*, the partition function would be

$$\tilde{Z} = \zeta_1^{N_1}\zeta_2^{N_2}\ldots\,\zeta_m^{N_m} \tag{D.6}$$

However, the *molecules are* **not** *distinguishable!* Therefore, the correct partition function is obtained by dividing the pseudo-partition function—the expression (D.6)—by the $N_1!N_2! \ldots N_m!$ possible permutations of molecules of the same type among themselves! The *true* partition function is thus

$$Z = \left(\frac{\zeta_1^{N_1}}{N_1!}\right)\left(\frac{\zeta_2^{N_2}}{N_2!}\right)\ldots\left(\frac{\zeta_m^{N_m}}{N_m!}\right) \tag{D.7}$$

The usual relation between the Helmholtz free energy F and the partition function gives

$$F = -\,kT \ln Z = -\,kT\sum_{i=1}^{m}(N_i \ln \zeta_i - \ln N_i!) \tag{D.8}$$

The system will be in equilibrium when the free energy is a minimum. The minimum will occur when the total differential of the free energy is zero: $dF = 0$. Since in equilibrium the volume, the temperature, and the number of molecules of each type are constant, the equilibrium condition is thus

$$dF = \sum_{i=1}^{m}\left(\frac{\partial F}{\partial N_i}\right)_{T,V,N} dN_i = 0 \tag{D.9}$$

(Since $F \equiv E - TS$, and both E and T are unchanging—only the number of molecules of each type is allowed to change—the condition $dF = 0$ is equivalent to the condition $dS = 0$, so (D.9) is essentially equivalent to the requirement that the entropy S is a maximum in equilibrium.)

Now since atoms are conserved in chemical reactions, the changes dN_i in the numbers of molecules must be proportional to the numbers a_i which appear in the chemical equation (D.1). That is, we must have

$$dN_i = ca_i \tag{D.10}$$

for all i, where c is the same constant of proportionality for all types of molecules. Putting (D.10) into (D.9) gives

$$dF = 0 = - kT\sum_{i=1}^{m} a_i\left(\ln\zeta_i - \frac{\partial \ln N_i!}{\partial N_i}\right) \qquad (D.11)$$

If N_i is extremely large, then Stirling's formula reduces to $\ln N_i! = N_i \ln N_i - N_i$, and so we get $\partial \ln N_i!/\partial N_i = \ln N_i$. Putting this into $(D.11)$ gives

$$dF = 0 = - kT\sum_{i=1}^{m} a_i(\ln\zeta_i - \ln N_i) = \Delta F_0 + kT\sum_{i=1}^{m} a_i \ln N_i \quad (D.12)$$

where $\Delta F_0 \equiv - kT\sum_i a_i \ln\zeta_i$ is called the "standard free energy change of the reaction." (Expression $(D.12)$ also shows that $d^2F > 0$, so $dF = 0$ indeed gives the global minimum.) A little algebra on $(D.12)$ gives

$$N_1^{a_1}N_2^{a_2}\dots N_m^{a_m} = exp\left[\frac{-\Delta F_0}{kT}\right] \equiv K_N(T,V)$$

which is just the Law of Mass Action, equation $(D.3)$.

Now consider what we would have gotten if we had assumed, contrary to fact, that systems in the same quantum state were *not* indistinguishable. In such a case, the partition function would have been $(D.6)$ rather than $(D.7)$, and in consequence the leftmost term of $(D.11)$, the term involving the partial derivative of $\ln N_i!$, would be absent. This would imply, not equation $(D.12)$ and the Law of Mass Action $(D.3)$, but instead

$$dF = 0 = - kT\sum_{i=1}^{m} a_i \ln\zeta_i$$

which, since $\sum_{i=1}^{m} a_i \ln \zeta_i \neq 0$, yields for the equilibrium condition

$$T = 0$$

In other words, there would be no equilibrium except at absolute zero! Furthermore, at any other temperature, there would be no necessary relationship between the numbers of molecules at all. Since, instead, the Law of Mass Action is observed to hold, we see that we *must* assume the indistinguishability of systems in the same quantum state.

References

Callan, H. B. 1960. Thermodynamics. New York: Wiley.

Fermi, Enrico 1936. Thermodynamics. New York: Dover.

— 1966. Notes on Thermodynamics and Statistics. Chicago: University of Chicago Press.

Kittel, Charles 1969. Thermal Physics. New York: Wiley.

Pippard, A. Brian 1957. Elements of Classical Thermodynamics. Cambridge: Cambridge University Press.

Reif, F. 1965. Fundamentals of Statistical and Thermal Physics. New York: McGraw-Hill.

E. Proofs of Eternal Return Theorems and the No-Return Theorem

In this section, I shall give proofs of three Eternal Return Theorems: the Poincaré Recurrence Theorem, the Finite Markov Chain Recurrence Theorem, and finally the Quantum Recurrence Theorem—actually, the Quantum Almost-Periodic Theorem. I shall then prove the General Relativistic No-Return Theorem. My proof of the Poincaré Recurrence Theorem will follow the proof by Arnold. It will require knowledge of classical Newtonian mechanics, on the level of the *beautiful* textbook by Landau and Lifshitz. The Markov Chain Recurrence Theorem will require just a knowledge of elementary probability theory, and my proof will follow that given by Shiryayev. The Quantum Recurrence Theorem will require some basic knowledge of nonrelativistic quantum mechanics. I recommend the textbooks by Peebles and by Merzbacher. The proof of the No-Return Theorem will be the most mathematically demanding, and it will require a knowledge of global techniques in general relativity. The best brief introduction to these methods can be found in Chapter 34 of the text by Misner, Thorne, and Wheeler. The most comprehensive discussion of these methods is provided in the treatises by Hawking and Ellis and by Tipler. Penrose has written up a set of lectures intermediate between Misner et al. and the treatises.

1. The Poincaré Recurrence Theorem

Let us begin the proof of the Poincaré Recurrence Theorem by giving a short proof of Liouville's Theorem. Let $d\Gamma = dq_1 \ldots dq_N \, dp_1 \ldots dp_N$, where N is the number of coordinates q_i in configuration space, each with conjugate momentum p_i. We want to prove that $\int d\Gamma$, where the integral is over some initial region in phase space, does not change with time. The idea is to first show that if the q_i, p_i's are changed to Q_j, P_j via a canonical transformation, the phase space volume is left invariant—that is, we show that $\int \ldots \int dq_1 \ldots dq_N \, dp_1 \ldots dp_N = \int \ldots \int dQ_1 \ldots dQ_N dP_1 \ldots dP_N$—and then show that evolution of the coordinates $q_i(t)$, $p_i(t)$ in time can be regarded as a canonical transformation. Recall that a "canonical transformation" is a transformation $(q_i, p_i) \to (Q_i, P_i)$ of the coordinates of phase space which leaves Hamilton's equations $\dot{p}_i = -\partial H/\partial q_i$ and $\dot{q}_i = \partial H/\partial p_i$ form invari-

ant, where H is the Hamiltonian, and the dot denotes the time derivative.
For any transformation of coordinates in a multiple integral we have

$$\int\ldots\int dQ_1 \ldots dQ_N = \int\ldots\int J dq_1 \ldots dq_N$$

where

$$J \equiv \frac{\partial(Q_1,\ldots, Q_N, P_1,\ldots, P_N)}{\partial(q_1,\ldots, q_N, p_1,\ldots, p_N)}$$

is the Jacobian of the transformation. A "generalized chain rule" can be shown to apply to Jacobians, so "dividing" numerator and denominator by $\partial(q_1,\ldots, q_N, P_1,\ldots, P_N)$, gives

$$J = \frac{\partial(Q_1,\ldots, Q_N, P_1,\ldots, P_N)}{\partial(q_1,\ldots, q_N, P_1,\ldots, P_N)} \bigg/ \frac{\partial(q_1,\ldots, q_N, p_1,\ldots, p_N)}{\partial(q_1,\ldots, q_N, P_1,\ldots, P_N)}$$

In this expression, the P_i's are repeated in both partial differentials in the Jacobian in the numerator, and the q_i's are repeated in the Jacobian in the denominator. When this occurs, the repeated quantities can be regarded as constant when the differentiations are carried out. Thus the Jacobian can be written

$$J = \left[\frac{\partial(Q_1,\ldots, Q_N)}{\partial(q_1,\ldots, q_N)}\right]_{P=constant} \bigg/ \left[\frac{\partial(p_1,\ldots, p_N)}{\partial(P_1,\ldots, P_N)}\right]_{q=constant}$$

The numerator Jacobian is a determinant with element $\partial Q_i/\partial q_j$ in the ith row and jth column. The denominator Jacobian is a determinant with element $\partial p_i/\partial P_j$ in the ith row and jth column. If the generating function of the canonical transformation is a function $F(q,P,t)$ of the variables (q, P), then—provided the Hamiltonian is independent of time (which means that energy is conserved) —it can be shown that

$$p_i = \frac{\partial F}{\partial q_i}, \quad Q_i = \frac{\partial F}{\partial P_i}$$

This means that, in the Jacobian above, we have $\partial Q_i/\partial q_j = \partial^2 F/\partial q_j\,\partial P_i$ and also we have $\partial p_i/\partial P_j = \partial^2 F/\partial q_i\,\partial P_j$. Thus the two determinants making up the Jacobian J differ only in the interchange of row and column, and are thus equal. This means that $J = 1$, which shows that the phase space integral is invariant under a canonical transformation.

The values of the variables $q_i(t +\Delta t)$, $p_i(t + \Delta t)$ at time $t + \Delta t$ are functions of the same variables at an earlier time t, and of the time interval Δt:

$$q_i(t + \Delta t) = q_i(q_1(t),\ldots, q_N(t); p_1(t), \ldots, p_N(t), \Delta t)$$

$$p_i(t + \Delta t) = p_i (q_1(t),\ldots, q_N(t); p_1(t), \ldots, p_N(t), \Delta t)$$

Now the change of the action S along the true path in configuration space from time t to time $t + \Delta t$ is $dS = \sum_{i=1}^{N} [p_i(t + \Delta t)dq_i(t + \Delta t) - p_i(t)\, dq_i(t)]$. On the other hand, if the energy is conserved along the true path (which once again means the Hamiltonian is unchanged), the differential of the generating function $G = G(q_i, Q_i, t)$ of a canonical transformation is

$$dG = \sum_{i=1}^{N} [p_i dq_i - P_i dQ_i]$$

This means that the time evolution of an energy conserving system can be regarded as a canonical transformation with generating function $-S$.

Since canonical transformations leave phase space volume invariant, and since the time evolution of an energy conserving system can be regarded as a canonical transformation, $\int d\Gamma$ = constant. This proves Liouville's Theorem.

Poincaré's Recurrence Theorem is a trivial consequence of Liouville's Theorem. Let's give a formal statement of

POINCARÉ RECURRENCE THEOREM: Let f be a volume preserving continuous one-to-one map from a finite and bounded region V of phase space into itself: $fV = V$. Then in any neighborhood U of any point of V there exists a point $x \in U$ which returns to U; that is, $f^n x \in U$ for some $n > 0$.

Proof: Consider a sequence of the action of f on the neighborhood U:

$$U, fU, f^2 U,\ldots, f^n U,\ldots$$

Since f is volume preserving, all the members of this sequence have the same volume. If they never intersected, V would have infinite volume. Thus, for some $i \geq 0$ and $j \geq 0$ with $i > j$, we must have

$$f^i U \cap f^j U \neq \varnothing$$

This implies $f^{i-j} U \cap U \neq \varnothing$. Let $f^{i-j} x = y$. Then $x \in U$ and $f^{i-j} x \in U$, so set

$n = i - j$, and this completes the proof.

2. The Finite Markov Chain Recurrence Theorem

A *Markov chain* is a process in which the probability of going to a certain state depends only on the current state. Thus the probability of going from state i to state j is written p_{ij}. The collection of all such *transition probabilities* comprise a matrix $\| p_{ij} \|$, and this matrix defines the Markov chain. If there are only a finite number of states, we have a *finite Markov chain*. Let $p_{ij}^{(n)}$ be the probability that the chain goes from the state i to the state j in n steps; let $f_{ij}^{(k)}$ be the probability of the first arrival to the state j from the state i in k steps; and let $f_{ij}^{(k)}$ be the probability of first return to the state i in k steps. Then it is clear that

$$p_{ij}^{(k+l)} = \sum_m p_{im}^{(k)} p_{mj}^{(l)}$$

which is called the *Chapman-Kolmogorov equation*, and also

$$p_{ij}^{(n)} = \sum_{k=1}^{n} f_{ij}^{(k)} p_{ij}^{(n-k)} \qquad (E.1)$$

The probability f_{ii} that a system which leaves state i will eventually return to the same state i is given by

$$f_{ii} = \sum_{n=1}^{\infty} f_{ii}^{(n)}$$

A state i is said to be *recurrent* if

$$f_{ii} = 1$$

and *nonrecurrent* if

$$f_{ii} < 1$$

A state is called *inessential* if it is possible to escape from it after only a finite number of transitions. A state for which this is not possible is called *essential*. Obviously, as the number of steps approaches infinity, the probability approaches 1 that the system enters an essential subset of states, so in what follows I will assume (like Nietzsche) that the system is essential.

If a state is recurrent, then its *average time of return*, μ_i, from the state i and back is clearly

$$\mu_i = \sum_{n=1}^{\infty} n f_{ii}^{(n)}$$

This average time of return can be either finite or infinite. If the latter, the state is said to be *null* since in this case $\mu_i^{-1} = 0$. If the former, the state is called *positive* since in this case $\mu_i^{-1} > 0$.

For the proof of the Finite Markov Recurrence Theorem, we will need two Lemmas:

Lemma 1: The state i is recurrent if and only if

$$\sum_{n=1}^{\infty} p_{ii}^{(n)} = \infty \qquad (E.2)$$

Furthermore, if the state j is recurrent and transitions back and forth between j and the state i are possible—we denote this by $i \leftrightarrow j$—then the state i is also recurrent.

Proof: First, we show recurrence implies equation $(E.2)$. From equation $(E.1)$ we get

$$p_{ii}^{(n)} = \sum_{k=1}^{n} f_{ii}^{(k)} p_{ii}^{(n-k)},$$

which implies, using $p_{ii}^{(0)} = 1$,

$$\sum_{n=1}^{\infty} p_{ii}^{(n)} = \sum_{n=1}^{\infty} \sum_{k=1}^{n} f_{ii}^{(k)} p_{ii}^{(n-k)} = \sum_{k=1}^{\infty} f_{ii}^{(k)} \sum_{n=k}^{\infty} p_{ii}^{(n-k)}$$

$$= f_{ii} \sum_{n=0}^{\infty} p_{ii}^{(n)} = f_{ii} \left(1 + \sum_{n=1}^{\infty} p_{ii}^{(n)} \right)$$

Thus, if it were the case that $\sum_{n=1}^{\infty} p_{ii}^{(n)} < \infty$, we would have $f_{ii} < 1$, which would be a contradiction. Therefore recurrence implies equation $(E.2)$. To prove the converse, note that

$$\sum_{n=1}^{N} p_{ii}^{(n)} = \sum_{n=1}^{N} \sum_{k=1}^{n} f_{ii}^{(k)} p_{ii}^{(n-k)} = \sum_{k=1}^{N} f_{ii}^{(k)} \sum_{n=k}^{N} p_{ii}^{(n-k)} \leq \sum_{k=1}^{N} f_{ii}^{(k)} \sum_{m=0}^{N} p_{ii}^{(m)}$$

From this it follows that

$$f_{ii} = \sum_{k=1}^{\infty} f_{ii}^{(k)} \geq \sum_{k=1}^{N} f_{ii}^{(k)} \geq \frac{\sum_{n=1}^{N} p_{ii}^{(n)}}{\sum_{m=0}^{N} p_{ii}^{(m)}}$$

The last ratio approaches 1 as $N \to \infty$. Hence, if (E.2) holds, then we have $f_{ii} = 1$, which by definition means the state is recurrent.

Now let us prove that if the state j is recurrent, and $i \leftrightarrow j$, then the state i is also recurrent. The fact $i \leftrightarrow j$ means that $p_{ij}^{(r)} > 0$ and $p_{ij}^{(s)} > 0$ for some r, s. We would also have

$$p_{ii}^{(n+r+s)} \geq p_{ij}^{(r)} p_{jj}^{(n)} p_{ji}^{(s)},$$

so $\sum_{n=1}^{\infty} p_{jj}^{(n)} = \infty$ implies $\sum_{n=1}^{\infty} p_{ii}^{(n)} = \infty$, which means that the state i is also recurrent.

Using Lemma 1, we can prove

Lemma 2: If the state i is nonrecurrent, then

$$\sum_{n=1}^{\infty} p_{ji}^{(n)} < \infty \qquad (E.3)$$

for every state j, and hence

$$p_{ji}^{(n)} \to 0, \; n \to 0 \qquad (E.4)$$

Proof: From equation (E.1), Lemma 1, and the fact that $f_{ij} = \sum_{k=1}^{\infty} f_{ij}^{(k)} \leq 1$, we have

$$\sum_{n=1}^{\infty} p_{ij}^{(n)} = \sum_{n=1}^{\infty} \sum_{k=1}^{n} f_{ij}^{(k)} p_{jj}^{(n-k)} = \sum_{k=1}^{\infty} f_{ij}^{(k)} \sum_{n=0}^{\infty} p_{jj}^{(n)}$$

$$= f_{ij} \sum_{n=0}^{\infty} p_{jj}^{(n)} \leq \sum_{n=0}^{\infty} p_{jj}^{(n)} < \infty$$

which is just (E.3), and (E.3) can hold only if (E.4) does. This completes the proof of Lemma 2.

We can now prove

FINITE MARKOV CHAIN RECURRENCE THEOREM: Let a finite Markov chain be indecomposable (i.e., $i \leftrightarrow j$ for all states i and j in the chain). Then all states are recurrent, and furthermore, the probability f_{ij}^{∞} that the system, starting from any state i, visits any other state j infinitely often, is one: $f_{ij}^{\infty} = 1$.

Proof: Let the state space of the finite Markov chain be $S = \{1, 2, \ldots, s\}$. The transition matrix $\|p_{ij}\|$ is a *stochastic matrix*, which means that its elements are nonnegative and the sum of the elements in a row is 1: $\sum_{j=1}^{s} p_{ij} = 1$. Thus, $\sum_{j=1}^{s} p_{ij}^{(n)} = 1$ for any n, and so, if we assume that all the states are nonrecurrent,

$$1 = \lim_{n \to \infty} \sum_{j=1}^{s} p_{ij}^{(n)} = \sum_{j=1}^{s} \lim_{n \to \infty} p_{ij}^{(n)} = 0 \qquad (E.5)$$

where the last limit follows from Lemma 2. The contradiction shows that not all states can be nonrecurrent. Let j_0 be one of the recurrent states, and let i be any other state. Since $j_0 \leftrightarrow i$ by assumption, Lemma 1 shows that i is also recurrent. Thus all states are recurrent.

Once the system returns to the state i, with probability one it must return again to the state i, since for a Markov chain, the past is irrelevant. Repeating this argument, we see that the probability the system returns to any state i an infinite number of times is one: $f_{ij}^{\infty} = 1$. This completes the proof of the Theorem.

One can also show that for indecomposable finite Markov chains, all states are positive, which means that the average recurrence time is finite. Actually, one can easily show that a finite Markov chain has at least one positive state, because assuming that all the states are null again leads to the contradiction $(E.5)$. Proving that all states are positive needs a bit more machinery than I have space for here; the interested reader is referred to the book by Shiryayev for a proof.

If the state i of an indecomposable Markov chain is *aperiodic* (which means that it is possible to remain in the state i) then one can show:

$$p_{ii}^{(n)} \to \frac{1}{\mu_i}, \qquad n \to \infty$$

and if the Markov chain has period T, then

$$p_{ii}^{(nT)} \to \frac{T}{\mu_i}, \qquad n \to \infty$$

The quantities $p_{ii}^{(n)}$ can be computed from the Chapman-Kolmogorov equation, so for Markov chains it is possible to compute the average recurrence time.

It is possible to have recurrence in infinite Markov chains. For example, a *simple random walk* is a Markov chain on the infinite state space $S = \{0, \pm 1, \pm 2, \ldots\}$ in which the system is a particle that in each step moves one unit to the right with probability p, and one unit to the left with probability q, such that $p + q = 1$. The transition probabilities are thus

$$p_{ij} = \begin{cases} p, & \text{if } j = i + 1; \\ q, & j = i - 1; \\ 0, & \text{otherwise.} \end{cases}$$

Since for each state i the particle can return only after an even number of steps (we say the *period* is 2), we have

$$p_{ii}^{(2n)} = \frac{(2n)!}{(n!)^2}(pq)^n \approx \frac{(4pq)^n}{\sqrt{\pi n}}$$

where the last step uses Stirling's formula. Thus $\sum_{n=1}^{\infty} p_{ii}^{(2n)} = \infty$ if $p = q$, and otherwise $\sum_{n=1}^{\infty} p_{ii}^{(2n)} < \infty$, so the simple random walk is recurrent if $p = q = 1/2$, and nonrecurrent if $p \neq q$. A short calculation shows that if $p = q = 1/2$, then $f_{ii}^{(2n)} \approx 1/(2\sqrt{\pi}n^{3/2})$, so $\mu_i = \sum_{n=1}^{\infty}(2n)f_{ii}^{(2n)} = \infty$. Thus if $p = q = 1/2$, all states are recurrent, and in fact by the above discussion recur infinitely often with probability 1, but the average recurrence time is infinite.

3. The Quantum Recurrence Theorem

I want to show now that the wave function and the expectation values of all bounded operators are almost periodic functions of time. Let me start with two definitions:

A set S of real numbers is said to be *relatively dense* if there exists a number $L < \infty$ such that any interval on the real line of length L contains at least one member of the set S.

An *almost periodic function* $f(t)$ is a continuous and bounded function such that, for any $\epsilon > 0$, there exists a relatively dense set $\{T_\epsilon\}$ with $|f(t + T_\epsilon) - f(t)| < \epsilon$ for *all* time t and for each T_ϵ in the set.

Also, recall that the natural norm to use for the wave functions of a bounded quantum system is $\|\psi(t)\| \equiv \int |\psi(x,t)|^2 d^3x$. The norm for operators $\hat{O}$ is $\|\hat{O}\| \equiv \int |\psi^*\hat{O}\psi|^2 d^3x / \|\psi\|$. A *bounded operator* is one for which this norm is bounded for any allowed ψ. We will express the Hamiltonian as $\hat{H}(t) = \hat{H}_0 + \hat{V}(t)$. We can now state the

Quantum Recurrence Theorem: If the following four conditions hold:

(1) $\hat{H}_0$ is bounded, self-adjoint, time independent, and has a discrete spectrum;

(2) the potential $\hat{V}(t) = \hat{V}(t + T)$ for some period T;

(3) $\hat{V}(t)$ is self-adjoint and bounded; and

(4) ψ has compact support with $\| \psi(t) \| < \infty$;

then the norm of the wave function ψ and also the expectation values of all bounded operators are almost periodic functions of time.

The basic idea of the proof is very simple. "Compact support" just means that the wave function is nonzero only for a finite range of the spatial coordinates. This forces the Hamiltonian $\hat{H}_0$ to have a discrete spectrum: the energies cannot vary continuously but instead come in discrete values $\{E_1, E_2,..., E_i,...\}$. Since the Hamiltonian $\hat{H}_0$ is self-adjoint, any function whatsoever—in particular the wave function—can be expanded as a power series in its eigenfunctions. Since these eigenfunctions are of the form $exp(iE_i t/\hbar)$ each eigenfunction is periodic in time. The Hamiltonian being bounded means that a measurement of the system energy cannot yield an arbitrarily large energy, which in turn means that the above list of discrete energy values is finite. Thus the series expansion for the wave function has only a finite number of terms. Any function which can be expressed as finite series of periodic functions is almost periodic. Since the expectation values for any bounded operator can also be expressed as an appropriate series in the energy eigenfunctions, the expectation values will be almost periodic also.

Let's now make this proof outline more precise (and also take care of the technicalities arising from the fact that the potential depends on the time). I shall follow the proof by Hogg and Huberman (1983). Earlier proofs have been published by Bocchieri and Loinger (1957) and by Percival (1961).

Proof: The wave function $\psi(x,t)$ of the full time dependent Schrödinger equation can be expanded in terms of the complete orthonormal set of eigenstates $\{u_m(x)\}$ of $\hat{H}_0$, since $\hat{H}_0$ is self-adjoint. We have $\psi(x,t) = \sum_{m=1}^{\infty} a_m(t) u_m(x)$, with the coefficients $a_m(t)$ forming a vector $a(t)$ satisfying $i\hbar \dot{a}(t) = \hat{H}(t)a(t)$. We also have

$$\| \psi(t + \tau) - \psi(t) \|^2 = | a(t + \tau) - a(t) |^2 \qquad (E.6)$$

Since $\hat{H}(t) = \hat{H}(t + T)$, the wave function satisfies a Floquet theorem, which means that the vector $a(t)$ is of the form

$$a(t) = \sum_{k=1}^{\infty} \alpha_k \exp(iE_k t/\hbar) \, \Phi_k(t) \qquad (E.7)$$

where $\Phi_k(t+T) = \Phi(t)$ and $\Phi_k^{\dagger}(t) \, \Phi_{k'}(t) = \delta_{kk'}$ for all t. (Note that (E.7) is the standard expansion of the wave function if $\hat{H}$ is time independent.) The set $\{E_k\}$ is called the *quasienergy spectrum*. Writing $\alpha_k = r_k e^{i\Phi_k}$ with both r_k and Φ_k real, equation (E.7) implies

$$|a(t+NT) - a(t)|^2 = 2 \sum_{k=1}^{\infty} r_k^2 \left[1 - \cos \frac{E_k NT}{\hbar} \right] \qquad (E.8)$$

for any integer N. Condition (4) allows us to normalize the wave function, so $\sum_{k=1}^{\infty} r_k^2 = |a(t)|^2 = \|\psi(t)\|^2 = 1$, which in turn implies that given $\epsilon > 0$, there exists an integer n (which depends on ϵ) such that $\sum_{k=n+1}^{\infty} r_k^2 < \epsilon/8$. This gives the inequality

$$\sum_{k=n+1}^{\infty} r_k^2 \left[1 - \cos \frac{E_k NT}{\hbar} \right] \le 2 \sum_{k=n+1}^{\infty} r_k^2 < \frac{\epsilon}{4} \qquad (E.9)$$

Consider now the nonnegative function $f(x) = \sum_{k=1}^{n} [1 - \cos(E_k x T/\hbar)]$. From condition (3), the eigenvalues E_k are discrete, so $f(x)$ is a finite sum of periodic functions. It is a standard theorem about such a sum (see Besicovich 1932) that for any positive δ, the set of integers $\{N_\delta\}$ such that $|f(x+N_\delta) - f(x)| < \delta$ is relatively dense. In particular, for $\delta = \epsilon/4$ there exists a relatively dense set of integers $\{N\}$ such that $f(N) < \epsilon/4$ and since for all k, $r_k \le 1$, we have $\sum_{k=1}^{n} r_k^2 [1 - \cos(E_k NT/\hbar)] < \epsilon/4$. Combining this inequality with (E.6), (E.8) and (E.9), we finally obtain

$$\|\psi(t+NT) - \psi(t)\|^2 < \epsilon$$

for all times and for a relatively dense set of times $\{NT\}$. Thus the wave function is almost periodic.

Let me now outline the proof that the expectation value of the Hamiltonian operator $\hat{H}(t)$ is almost periodic. The same procedure can be used to show that the expectation values of any other bounded operator is also almost periodic.

The expectation value of the Hamiltonian $\hat{H}$ is the energy $E(t)$: $\langle \psi | \hat{H} | \psi \rangle = a^{\dagger} \hat{H}_0 a + a^{\dagger} \hat{V} a = E(t)$. We have in particular

$$a^{\dagger} \hat{H}_0 a = \sum_{i=1}^{\infty} E_i |a_i(t)|^2 \qquad (E.10)$$

where E_i is an eigenvalue of $\hat{H}_0$. Since by assumption $\hat{H}_0$ is a bounded operator, for any $\epsilon > 0$ we can find an integer N_ϵ independent of t such that $\sum_{i=N_\epsilon+1}^{\infty} E_i |a_i(t)|^2 < \epsilon/4$. The rest of (E.10) is a finite sum of almost periodic functions and hence is almost periodic. There is thus a relatively dense set $\{T_\epsilon\}$ such that

$$\sum_{i=1}^{N_\epsilon} |E_i| \, | \, |a_i(t + T_\epsilon)|^2 - |a_i(t)|^2 | < \epsilon/2$$

for all t. For the set $\{N_\epsilon\}$ this implies that $|a^\dagger H_0 a(t + T_\epsilon) - a^\dagger H_0 a(t)|$ is less than ϵ for all t, so the expectation value of the operator $\hat{H}_0$ is almost periodic. The almost periodicity of the operator $\hat{V}(t)$ is proved similarly. This completes the proof of the Quantum Recurrence Theorem.

4. The General Relativistic No-Return Theorem

I shall now prove that no two states of a generic closed universe governed by the Einstein equations with attractive gravity can be identical or even arbitrarily close. The proof I shall give here will be the same as the one I originally published more than a decade ago in the technical literature (Tipler 1979 and 1980). A very nice alternative proof has since been published by Galloway (1984).

The notion of "close" is made precise by regarding the set of all initial data as a *Sobolov space* W^s. If the spacetime is globally hyperbolic, by Geroch's Theorem the global topology of the spacetime (M,g) is $S \times R$, where S is a spacelike hypersurface. By definition, a *closed universe* is one for which S is compact. We choose some positive definite metric e_{ab} on M, and define a norm on W^s by

$$|K_J^I\| m \equiv \left[\sum_{p=0}^{m} \int_S (|D^p K_J^I|)^2 d\sigma \right]^{1/2}, \qquad (E.11)$$

$$\|h,\chi\| \equiv \|h\| + \|\chi\|,$$

where $d\sigma$ is the volume element induced on S by e_{ab}, D^p is the generalized pth covariant derivative with respect to some chosen background metric $\bar{g}_{ab}$, $|\ |$ is the norm induced by e_{ab} (the metric e_{ab} is usually assumed to be uniform (unvarying) in the R direction), and K^I_j, h, χ are any tensors. Two tensors are said to be "close" if they are close in the norm $(E.11)$.

It is also necessary to make sure that the other Cauchy surfaces whose initial data are to be compared to the initial data on the given Cauchy surface are not arbitrarily close to the given Cauchy surface. Obviously, if a later Cauchy surface is arbitrarily close to the given Cauchy surface, its initial data would also be arbitrarily close. To obviate this difficulty, I shall require that we only look at Cauchy surfaces which are *outside* a fixed neighborhood U of the given Cauchy surface.

To prove that the initial data cannot return arbitrarily closely, one needs to assume something about the time evolution of the matter fields. The standard assumptions are that the initial value problem is well posed: that is, at least locally the evolution of the matter fields is unique and stable. These two conditions are conditions (1) and (2) in the theorem below. It is also necessary to assume that the coupling between the Einstein equations is not too complicated. This is condition (3). In what follows, the tensors h, χ are respectively the three-metric on S and the extrinsic curvature of S with respect to the enveloping spacetime (M, g).

NO-RETURN THEOREM: If a spacetime (M, g) containing a compact Cauchy surface is uniquely developed from initial data on any of its Cauchy surfaces, and if the spacetime also satisfies both the generic and the timelike convergence conditions, then the spacetime cannot be time periodic. Furthermore, if in addition the Einstein equations hold and if in any neighborhood U of any spacelike Cauchy surface S_i the matter fields ψ and their first derivatives ψ' satisfy

(1) the local development uniqueness condition;
(2) the local development stability condition; and
(3) the stress energy tensor is a polynomial in the matter fields, their first derivatives, and the spacetime metric;

then there exists a number $\epsilon_U > 0$ such that

$$\| (h, \chi, \psi, \psi') - (h_i, \chi_i, \psi_i, \psi_i') \|_6 > \epsilon_U$$

for the initial data on *any* spacelike Cauchy surface S with $U \cap S = \varnothing$.

Proof: Assume on the contrary that the spacetime is time periodic. By the unique development assumption, this implies that there exists a sequence of Cauchy surfaces

$$S(t_{-n}),\ldots, S(t_0),\ldots, S(t_n)$$

with the initial data the same on each, and with $J^+(S(t_i)) \cap J^-(S(t_{i+1}))$ isometric to $J^+(S(t_j)) \cap J^-(S(t_{j+1}))$ for any i,j. Thus the spacetime can be regarded as a covering space for a spacetime with topology $S \times S^1$, where S^1 is the circle. Hawking and Ellis have shown that there exists a timelike curve γ_{ij} of maximal length between any two of the isometric Cauchy surfaces $S(t_i)$ and $S(t_j)$, and γ_{ij} will be orthogonal to both. Consider the sequence of curves

$$\gamma_{-1,1}, \gamma_{-2,2},\ldots,\gamma_{-n,n},\ldots.$$

Because $S(t_0)$ is a Cauchy surface, each of these curves intersects $S(t_0)$ in exactly one point. Since $S(t_0)$ is compact, the sequence has a subsequence that converges to a timelike geodesic γ. (The limit curve γ will be timelike because, in the space $S \times S^1$, we can define γ by the sequence of vectors normal to $S(t_0)$ —the vector at the future endpoint of γ_n and tangent to γ_n there. This sequence of vectors has a subsequence that converges to a normal of $S(t_0)$, and all convergent subsequences converge to a normal of $S(t_0)$.)

The geodesic γ is past and future complete. To see this, we first show that the lengths of the geodesic segments γ_n must diverge in both the past and future directions as $n \to \infty$. For since γ_n is the maximal length geodesic segment between $S(t_{-n})$ and $S(t_n)$, and if γ_n converged to a finite length in either direction—the future direction, say—then we could construct a causal curve between $S(t_{-n})$ and $S(t_n)$ of length greater than γ_n for n sufficiently large as follows. Every timelike geodesic normal to $S(t_0)$ reaches all $S(t_n)$ since all of these are Cauchy surfaces. Define a timelike curve $\alpha_n(p)$ from any point p in $S(t_0)$ by extending the geodesic normal to $S(t_0)$ at p until it reaches $S(t_1)$ at the point p_1, then move along the geodesic normal to $S(t_1)$ at p_1 until this geodesic reaches $S(t_2)$, and so on until $S(t_n)$ is reached. Since $S(t_0)$ is compact, the length of a geodesic from $S(t_0)$ to $S(t_1)$ along a geodesic normal to $S(t_0)$ is bounded below by some number L. Thus the length of $\alpha_n(p) \geq nL$, and so if the length of γ_n did not diverge in the future direction as $n \to \infty$, we could replace γ_n by $[\gamma_n \cap$

$J^-(S(t_0))] \cup [\alpha_n(p = \{\gamma_n \cap S(t_0)\})]$ to obtain a causal curve of length greater than γ_n between $S(t_{-n})$ and $S(t_n)$ for n sufficiently large. But this is impossible, since by definition γ_n is the maximal length curve between these two Cauchy surfaces. By the continuity of length along arbitrarily close continuous geodesic segments, this divergence in both time directions of the lengths of the γ_n segments implies the geodesic completeness of γ.

Since γ is geodesically complete, and since the generic condition and the timelike convergence condition hold, γ must have a pair of conjugate points—points p and q, say (see Hawking and Ellis for a proof of the existence of such points). Hawking and Ellis have shown that the location of the first conjugate point varies continuously with the geodesic, and so there will be points p_n, q_n on γ_n which are conjugate points on γ_n and which converge to p, q. For n sufficiently large, p_n, q_n will be in $J^+(S(t_{-n})) \cap J^-(S(t_n))$. But γ_n is the maximal length causal curve between $S(t_{-n})$ and $S(t_n)$, and so it cannot have conjugate points in $J^+(S(t_{-n})) \cap J^-(S(t_n))$, since Hawking and Ellis have shown that along maximal geodesic segments a pair of conjugate points cannot exist. This contradiction shows that time periodic spacetimes do not exist.

I shall now show that it is not possible to approach arbitrarily close to a previous initial state (except, of course, near the initial spacelike Cauchy surface itself). If there is not such an ϵ for some S with initial data (h, χ, ψ, ψ'), then there will exist a sequence of Cauchy surfaces S_n with initial data $(h_n, \chi_n, \psi_n, \psi'_n)$ such that $(h_n, \chi_n, \psi_n, \psi'_n) \to (h, \chi, \psi, \psi')$ as $n \to \infty$, with $S_n \cap U$ empty for all n. We may assume without loss of generality that either $S_n \subset I^+(S)$ or $S_n \subset I^-(S)$ for all n. Suppose $S_n \subset I^+(S)$. By conditions (1)–(3), the Cauchy Stability Theorem holds (see Hawking and Ellis for a precise statement and proof of this theorem), and this means that for n sufficiently large ($n > n_1$ say), there is a compact four-dimensional region V such that the minimum length in V of all timelike geodesic normal to S_n is greater than some positive number c, independent of n, provided $n > n_1$. This implies that we can find an infinite sequence of Cauchy surfaces $\tilde{S}_n$ in $I^+(S)$ such that the minimum length from $\tilde{S}_{n-1}$ to $\tilde{S}_n$ along the timelike geodesic normal to $\tilde{S}_n$ is greater than c, and such that the initial data on each $\tilde{S}_n$ is arbitrarily close to the data on S. (If the S_n approach a limit in (M, g), which we can call $\tilde{S}$, then Cauchy stability implies that there must be an infinite sequence of such $\tilde{S}$, and this sequence will give the $\tilde{S}_n$. If the S_n do not approach and $\tilde{S}$ in (M, g), then there will be a subsequence of the S_n, which will be the $\tilde{S}_n$.) Again by Cauchy stability, there will be a similar sequence $\tilde{S}_{-n}$ in $I^-(S)$. With these sequences of Cauchy surfaces, $\tilde{S}_n$ and $\tilde{S}_{-n}$, we can proceed as in the time periodic case to obtain a contradiction. This completes the proof of the No-Return Theorem.

References

Arnold, Vladimir Igorevich 1980. *Mathematical Methods of Classical Mechanics*. Berlin: Springer-Verlag.

Besicovich, A. S. 1932. *Almost Periodic Functions*. Cambridge: Cambridge University Press.

Bocchieri, P., and A. Loinger 1957. "Quantum Recurrence Theorem." *Physical Review* **107**: 337–38.

Galloway, Gregory J. 1984. "Splitting Theorems for Spatially Closed Space-Times." *Communications in Mathematical Physics* **96**: 423–29.

Hawking, Stephen W., and George F. R. Ellis 1973. *The Large Scale Structure of Space-Time*. Cambridge: Cambridge University Press.

Hogg, T., and B. A. Huberman 1983. "Quantum Dynamics and Nonintegrability." *Physical Review* **A28**: 22–31.

Landau, Lev D. and E. M. Lifshitz 1960. *Mechanics*. Reading: Addison-Wesley.

Merzbacher, Eugen 1970. *Quantum Mechanics*, 2nd Edition. New York: Wiley.

Misner, Charles W., Kip S. Thorne, and John A. Wheeler 1973. *Gravitation*. San Francisco: Freeman.

Peebles, P. James E. 1992. *Quantum Mechanics*. Princeton: Princeton University Press.

Penrose, Roger 1972. *Techniques of Differential Topology in Relativity*. Philadelphia: SIAM.

Percival, Ian C. 1961. "Almost Periodicity and the Quantal *H* Theorem." *Journal of Mathematical Physics* **2**: 235-39.

Shiryayev, Albert Nikolaevich 1984. *Probability*. Berlin: Springer-Verlag.

Tipler, Frank J. 1979. "General Relativity, Thermodynamics, and the Poincaré Cycle." *Nature* **280**: 203–5.

— 1980. "General Relativity and the Eternal Return." in *Essays in General Relativity*: A Festschrift for Abraham H. Taub, pp. 21–37. Ed. Frank J. Tipler. New York: Academic Press.

— Forthcoming in 1996. *Global General Relativity*. Oxford: Oxford University Press.

F. The General Theory of Omega Point Spacetimes

Definition. A spacetime (M,g) will be said to terminate in an *omega point* if its future c-boundary consists of a single point. Furthermore, an *omega point spacetime* is a spacetime whose future c-boundary is a single point.

The future c-boundary, an idea introduced by Roger Penrose, is defined by using the chronological past sets $I^-(p)$ of any point p. As you will recall from Section B, $I^-(p)$ is the set of all points in the spacetime which can be reached from p by a past-directed timelike curve from p. The chronological past $CP \equiv I^-(p)$ of any point p has three properties:

(1) CP is open;

(2) CP is a past set, which means $I^-(CP) \subset CP$

(3) CP cannot be expressed as a union of two proper subsets with properties (1) and (2).

A set with properties (1), (2), and (3) is called an *indecomposable past set,* abbreviated IP.

The IPs are of two types: *proper IPs (PIPs)* which are the pasts of points in the spacetime, and *terminal IPs (TIPs)*, which are not the pasts of any point in the spacetime. Using the chronological future sets $I^+(p)$, one can analogously define indecomposable future sets *(IFs)*, and hence PIFs and TIFs. The *c-boundary* is defined to be the TIPs and TIFs. It is possible to show [1, pp. 217–21] that in globally hyperbolic spacetimes (spacetimes which are deterministic; see Section B), no TIP is a TIF and vice versa, but this will not be true in general. But at least in globally hyperbolic spacetimes, the collection of all TIPs are the points on the future c-boundary, and the collection of all TIFs are the points on the past c-boundary. I shall show below that in very general circumstances, a TIP is the chronological past $I^-(\gamma)$ of some timelike curve γ with no future endpoint in the spacetime. Another future-endless timelike curve λ defines the same future c-boundary point if and only if $I^-(\gamma) \equiv I^-(\lambda)$. For more discussion of c-boundaries, see [1, pp. 217–21].

Misner specifically constructed his Mixmaster universe [2] so that its past c-boundary would be a single point, although even today it is not known if there actually exists a vacuum Bianchi type IX universe with such a c-boundary. Doroshkevich *et al.* [3,4,5] established (using different terminology) that if such a vacuum solution exists, it is of very small measure in the vacuum Bianchi type IX vacuum initial data. Vacuum solutions to the Einstein equations which terminate in an omega point are known [1, p. 120 & 205; 6, 7], but they are all locally flat.

Let me give three examples of Friedmann universes which end in omega points. Recall from Section B that the closed S^3 Friedmann metric is

$$ds^2 = -dt^2 + R^2(t)[d\chi^2 + \sin^2\chi \, (d\theta^2 + \sin^2\theta \, d\phi^2)] \qquad (F.1)$$

where $0 \leq \chi \leq \pi$, $0 \leq \theta \leq \pi$, and $0 \leq \phi < 2\pi$. In the Friedmann universe, all null geodesics are radial, with comoving coordinates given by $ds^2 = 0 = -dt^2 + R^2(t)d\chi^2$, which gives Rindler's equation:

$$\chi_f - \chi_i = \pm \int_{t_i}^{t_f} \frac{dt}{R(t)} \qquad (F.2)$$

Since $R(t) > 0$ for all points in the spacetime, the integral (F.2) either converges or diverges to infinity if t_f is set equal to the least upper bound of $t \equiv t_{max}$. If it converges, then $\chi_f - \chi_i \to 0$ as $t_i \to t_{max}$, so each timelike trajectory normal to the surfaces of homogeneity and isotropy defines a distinct future c-boundary point, and further these trajectories define a homeomorphism onto the future c-boundary: the future c-boundary is thus topologically the same as the Cauchy surface topology, namely S^3.

On the other hand, if the integral (F.2) diverges to infinity, this means that there are no event horizons, and hence the future c-boundary consists of a single point. This means that an S^3 Friedmann universe will end in an omega point if and only if the integral (F.2) diverges.

Example 1: If $R(t) = $ constant, the metric (F.1) represents the Einstein static universe. Since the integral (F.2) diverges in this case because $t_{max} = +\infty$ and $t_{min} = -\infty$, both the future and past c-boundaries are each single points.

Example 2: Let $R(t) = \sin t$. Then the integral (F.2) is $\ln\left|\frac{\tan(t_f/2)}{\tan(t_i/2)}\right|$. There are s.p. curvature singularities [1] at $t_f = \pi$ and at $t_i = 0$. (An *s.p. curvature singularity* means that some scalar polynomial [s.p.] constructed from scalar invariants of the Riemann tensor diverges at the singularity.) At either of these limits, the integral (F.2) diverges, so this example has the same c-boundary structure as the Einstein static universe: both the future and past c-boundaries are each single points.

The Friedmann universe of Example 2 does not satisfy the Einstein equations with any standard equation of state. However, it nevertheless obeys all the usual energy conditions, thus showing that, even in the case of the closed Friedmann universe, one need not violate the energy conditions to get the future and past c-boundaries to be single points.

This example is thus a counterexample to a conjecture of Budic and Sachs, that to have a single point as its c-boundary "... a cosmological model may have to 'coast into the [singularity] so slowly it almost bounces' corresponding to a 'near violation' of the timelike convergence condition" [6, p. 28]. But the metric of Example 2 does not "nearly violate" the timelike convergence condition.

To see this, let us compute the stress-energy tensor for the metric of Example 2. The mass density is

$$\rho \equiv T_{\hat{t}\hat{t}} \equiv \frac{1}{8\pi}G_{\hat{t}\hat{t}} = \frac{3}{8\pi}\left(\frac{R'^2+1}{R^2}\right) = \frac{3}{8\pi}\left(\frac{\cos^2 t + 1}{\sin^2 t}\right) \geq \frac{3}{8\pi}$$

The principal pressure is

$$p \equiv T_{\hat{x}\hat{x}} \equiv \frac{1}{8\pi}G_{\hat{x}\hat{x}} = -\left(\frac{1}{8\pi}\right)\frac{2RR'' + R'^2 + 1}{R^2} = \frac{1}{8\pi}(1 - 2\cot^2 t)$$

which is negative for $|\cot t| > \frac{1}{\sqrt{2}}$—that is, near the singularities—and $p \to -\infty$ as $t \to 0$ or π. But we have

$$\rho + p = \frac{1}{8\pi}\left(\frac{4}{\sin^2 t}\right) > \frac{1}{2\pi}, \qquad\qquad \rho + 3p = \frac{6}{8\pi}$$

Since the weak energy condition [1] requires $\rho \geq 0$ and $\rho + p \geq 0$, the weak energy condition is satisfied. Since the strong energy condition [1] (here also the timelike convergence condition [1]) requires $\rho + p \geq 0$ and $\rho + 3p \geq 0$, the strong energy condition is satisfied. Furthermore, since both $\rho + p$ and $\rho + 3p$ are bounded well away from zero at *all* times, the timelike convergence condition is never "nearly violated." The dominant energy condition [1] requires $\rho \geq 0$ and $-\rho \leq p \leq +\rho$, so the dominant energy condition is satisfied. Finally it is easily checked that the generic condition is satisfied. The Ricci scalar is $\mathcal{R} = 6(RR'' + R^2 + 1)/R^2 = 6\sin^{-2}t$, so the single c-boundary points are true s.p. curvature singularities at $t = 0$ and at $t = \pi$; the Ricci scalar diverges there.

If the closed Friedmann universe is not the Einstein static universe, then negative pressures are required in order for the c-boundary to be a single point.

Budic and Sachs [6] were motivated by Misner's model to prove some general theorems on spacetimes with either the future or the past c-boundaries being single points. Their theorems can be applied to either the past or the future c-boundary, though they stated their theorems in terms of a single-point c-boundary in the past (since they were thinking of Misner's model).

Example 3: In the preceding two examples, both the past and future c-boundaries were single points. If our universe is an S^3 Friedmann universe which is radiation-dominated at early times, then its past c-boundary is topologically S^3 (the proof for S^3 topology will be given in Section H). Thus a more realistic model of the c-boundary structure of our universe would be an S^3 past c-boundary and an omega point future c-boundary.

Such a model can be constructed as follows. In a radiation-dominated Friedmann universe, the scale factor $R(\tau)$ and the proper time $t(\tau)$ can be expressed in terms of the conformal time as $R(\tau) = R_{max} \sin\tau$ and $t(\tau) = R_{max}(1 - \cos\tau)$. These imply

$$R(t) = R_{max}\left(\frac{2t}{R_{max}} - \frac{t^2}{R_{max}^2}\right)^{1/2} \qquad (F.3)$$

To get Example 3, I require (F.3) to hold for all values of proper time with $0 < t \leq R_{max}$, while for $R_{max} < t < 2R_{max}$, we have

$$R(t) = R_{max} \sin\left(\frac{\pi t}{2R_{max}}\right) \qquad (F.4)$$

The metric (F.3) and (F.4) is continuous and has continuous first derivatives at $t = R_{max}$, the time of maximum expansion where the two metrics have been joined. (These are the standard junction conditions for joining two metrics in general relativity.)

As we shall see, requiring that spacetime end in an omega point imposes very powerful constraints on the spacetime. The following theorem gives the main constraint.

Theorem (Seifert [8]): a spacetime which terminates in an omega point and which satisfies the chronology condition has a compact Cauchy hypersurface.

This theorem was first stated by Seifert [8], but unfortunately his proof is defective (in Theorem 6.3 of [8], Seifert claims that the existence of an omega point in both the past and future directions is equivalent to the existence of a compact Cauchy surface). Budic and Sachs [6] have stated that the existence of an omega point in a future—and past—distinguishing spacetime [1] implies the existence of a compact Cauchy surface, but they did not provide the proof in their published paper (on the grounds that the proof required too much space). I shall therefore provide a proof of Seifert's Theorem under a slightly weaker causality assumption than Budic and Sachs: I shall assume the chronology condition [1] instead of future- and past-distinguishing. (Recall [1] that a spacetime is said to satisfy the *chronology condition* if there are no closed timelike curves.) A key step is to realize that the Geroch, Kronheimer, and Penrose Proposition (Proposition 6.8.1 of [1]), which is proven in [1] under the hypothesis of strong causality and in [9] under the hypothesis of future- and past-distinguishing, is actually true if the spacetime satisfies the chronology condition. The arguments in the proof (see pp. 218–19 of [1]) of the Proposition go though if $p \notin I^{\pm}(p)$ for all points p, a fact which is assured by the chronology condition. (This fact also assures that no past set of the form $I^{-}(\gamma)$, where γ is a future-inextendible timelike curve, is a PIP—a phenomenon that can occur if the chronology condition is violated, as we shall see below.) I state this Proposition as

Proposition (Geroch, Kronheimer, and Penrose [9]): If the chronology condition holds, then a set W is a TIP if and only if there is a future-inextendible timelike curve γ such that $I^{-}(\gamma) = W$.

Proof of Seifert's Theorem:

I shall first prove two Lemmas.

Lemma 1: If the future c-boundary of a spacetime (M, g) which satisfies the chronology condition is an omega point, then the achronal boundary $\partial I^{+}(p)$ is a Cauchy surface for any point p in the spacetime.

Proof: Suppose not. Then there is a future—and past—endless timelike curve γ which never intersects $\partial I^{+}(p)$, which, since the chronology condition holds, is nonempty and is generated by null geodesic segments, at least some of which intersect p. If (1) $\gamma \cap I^{-}(\partial I^{+}(p)) \neq \varnothing$, or (2) $\gamma \cap I^{-}(\partial I^{+}(p)) = \varnothing$ and $\gamma \cap I^{+}(\partial I^{+}(p)) = \varnothing$, then $I^{-}(\gamma)$ would not intersect $I^{+}(p)$, so $I^{-}(\gamma)$ defines a different c-boundary point than does a future-endless timelike curve which eventually enters $I^{+}(p)$. Thus there are at least two distinct c-boundary points, contradicting the hypothesis that there is just one future c-boundary point.

The other possibility, which we now eliminate, is $\gamma \cap I^{+}(p) \neq \varnothing$, but $\gamma \cap \partial I^{+}(p) = \varnothing$. Since $\gamma \cap I^{+}(p) \neq \varnothing$, there exists a timelike curve β_q from p to *some* point $q \in \gamma$. Consider the sequence of timelike curves β_{qi} as the point q moves into the past along γ through a sequence of points q_i. This sequence defines a subsequence which converges to some causal curve $\hat{\beta}$ in $\overline{I^{+}(p)}$ (since $\overline{I^{+}(p)}$ is closed). However, $\hat{\beta}$ must be disconnected since, if it were connected, $\gamma \cup \hat{\beta}$ would be a connected curve, contrary to the assumption that γ is past-endless. The connected subset of $\hat{\beta}$—call it $\hat{\beta}_P$—which ends in the point p is thus future-endless, and since $\overline{I^+(\gamma)} \cap I^-(\hat{\beta}_P) = \varnothing$, the causal curves γ and $\hat{\beta}_P$ define different TIPs, contrary to the assumption that there is just one TIP in (M,g). QED. $I^+(\gamma) \cap I^-(\hat{\beta}_P)$

Lemma 2: If the future c-boundary of (M,g) is a single point and the chronology condition holds, then $\partial I^+(p)$ is nonempty and compact for every event p in the spacetime.

Proof: If the chronology condition holds, then $p \in \partial I^+(p)$. By the remarks on p. 188 of [1], $\partial I^+(p)$ is generated by null geodesic segments which either have no endpoints or have endpoints at p. Thus all the null geodesics from p into the future are generators of $\partial I^+(p)$. If every null geodesic generator of $\partial I^+(p)$ from p leaves $\partial I^+(p)$ in the future, then $\partial I^+(p)$ is compact, since one can put on the collection of null geodesic generators of $\partial I^+(p)$ an affine parameterization such that the length of the segment of null geodesic in $\partial I^+(p)$ from p varies continuously with the null direction into the future from p, and the collection of null directions at p is compact (actually, a 2-sphere). Thus the only way that part of $\partial I^+(p)$ for which $\partial I^+(p) \cap \{p\} \neq \varnothing$ could fail to be compact is for there to exist a null geodesic γ of $\partial I^+(p)$ which never leaves $\partial I^+(p)$.

But then $I^-(\gamma)$ would define a TIP which is distinct from a TIP generated by any future-inextendible timelike curve which crossed γ from $I^-(\gamma)$ into $I^+(p)$. But this would mean more than one TIP, contrary to assumption, so that part of $\partial I^+(p)$ for which $\partial I^+(p) \cap \{p\} \neq \varnothing$ is compact for all p, and also all null geodesic generators of $\partial I^+(p)$ from p must eventually leave $\partial I^+(p)$.

We now eliminate the possibility that $\partial I^+(p)$ has a null geodesic generator β which does not intersect p. Suppose it does, and let q be a point of β with normal neighborhood N. Then there is a timelike curve from p to any point in $N \cap I^+(p)$, (which is non-empty since $\beta \subset \partial I^+(p)$). Consider a sequence of points q_i in $N \cap I^+(p)$ converging to q. This sequence defines a sequence of timelike curves β_i from p to q_i. If this sequence of timelike curves converged to a single connected causal curve, it would have to be a null geodesic with past endpoint at p, which is impossible by definition of β. Since locally (in any convex normal neighborhood) the sequence converges, it must converge globally to at least two (possibly more) distinct disconnected causal curves, the one terminating at p being future-endless. This future-endless curve, call it $\hat{\beta}$, defines a TIP which is different from at least one TIP defined by some future-endless timelike curve in $I^+(\beta)$, since by construction $I^-(\hat{\beta}) \cap I^+(\beta) = \varnothing$. QED.

Continuation of the Proof of Seifert's Theorem: By Lemma 2, $\partial I^+(p)$ is nonempty and compact for every event p in the spacetime. By Lemma 2, $\partial I^+(p)$ is a Cauchy surface, so together these Lemmas imply that $\partial I^+(p)$ is a compact Cauchy surface for any point p. QED.

As a converse to Seifert's Theorem, we have

Theorem F.1: If an omega point spacetime satisfies the chronology condition, then for all points q sufficiently close to the future c-boundary, $\partial I^-(q)$ is also a Cauchy surface.

Proof: By Seifert's Theorem, the spacetime admits a compact Cauchy surface. Since the spacetime has a compact Cauchy surface, Geroch's Theorem (Proposition 6.6.8 of [1], p. 212), all Cauchy surfaces in the spacetime have the same topology and, further, the spacetime can be foliated by compact diffeomorphic spacelike Cauchy surfaces. Let $S(t)$ represent such a foliation, where t increases in the future direction, and let $\vec{v}(\vec{x},t)$ represent the timelike future-directed unit vector field which is everywhere normal to $S(t)$. Let $\lambda(t)$ be any flow line of this vector field. I claim that there exists t_λ such that $\partial I^-(\lambda(t_\lambda))$ is a Cauchy surface. Suppose not. Then there would exist another flow line $\mu(t)$ of $\vec{v}(\vec{x},t)$ which never intersects $\partial I^-(\lambda(t))$, for any t. But then the flow line $\mu(t)$ would define a different future c-boundary point than $\lambda(t)$, contrary to the fact that there is only one c-boundary point. Thus for each $\lambda(t)$ in $\vec{v}(\vec{x},t)$, there is a time t_λ for which $\partial I^-(\lambda(t))$ is a Cauchy surface, for all $t > t_\lambda$. Since the leaves of the foliation $S(t)$ are compact, $sup[t_\lambda] \equiv t_C$ is achieved in the spacetime. Then $\partial I^-(q)$ will be a Cauchy surface provided q is any event to the future of $S(t_C)$; i.e., $q \in I^+(S(t_C)$. QED.

We thus know that $\partial I^-(q)$ is a Cauchy surface for q sufficiently close to the omega point, so in principle all information is available at q. This property allows us to show that a foliation of spacetime by constant mean curvature hypersurfaces exists, at least sufficiently near the omega point.452   452

Theorem F.2: If a nonflat omega point spacetime (M,g) sastisfying the chronology condition also satisfies $R_{ab}V^aV^b \geq 0$ for all timelike vectors V^a, equality holding only if $R_{ab} = 0$, then there exists a point $p \in M$ such that through p there passes a $C^{2,\alpha}$ Cauchy surface S with constant mean curvature, and further, $I^+(S)$ can be uniquely foliated by $C^{2,\alpha}$ Cauchy surfaces with constant mean curvature.

That is, a generic causal omega point spacetime which satisfies the timelike convergence condition has sufficiently near the omega point a foliation by compact Cauchy surfaces with constant mean curvature. However, the entire spacetime might not have such a foliation; the foliation is guaranteed to exist only for that part of spacetime sufficiently close to the omega point. The meaning of "sufficiently close" is made precise in the proof of Theorem F.1 above. (A $C^{2,\alpha}$ Cauchy surface [10, p. 52] is one which is C^2 with these second derivatives being Hölder continuous of order α.)

Proof: Bartnik has shown [11] that, if for any point p in (M,g) the set $M - I^+(p) \cup I^-(p)$ is compact, then there is a spacelike $C^{2,\alpha}$ constant mean curvature Cauchy surface. By Lemma 1 above, $\partial I^+(p)$ is a compact Cauchy surface for any p, and by Theorem F.1 above, $\partial I^-(p)$ is a compact Cauchy surface for all points p sufficiently close to the omega point. Together these imply that $M - [I^+(p) \cup I^-(p)]$ is compact for p sufficiently close to the omega point. (The set $M - [I^+(p) \cup I^-(p)]$ is closed since both $I^+(p)$ and $I^-(p)$ are open. Also, for any foliation of (M,g) by spacelike hypersurfaces $S(t)$, there will exist times t_1 and t_0 with $t_1 > t_0$ such that $\partial I^+(p) \subset I^-(S(t_1))$ and $\partial I^-(p) \subset I^+(S(t_0))$. Hence, the closed set $M - [I^+(p) \cup I^-(p)]$ is contained in the compact set $M - [I^+(S(t_1)) \cup I^-S(t_0))] \approx S(t) \times [0,1]$, for any fixed t, and so is compact.) Thus through every point sufficiently close to the omega point there passes a spacelike $C^{2,\alpha}$ constant mean curvature Cauchy surface. Brill and Flaherty [12] have shown that any constant mean curvature compact Cauchy surface on which the constant mean curvature $\chi^a{}_a$ is nonzero is unique if the timelike convergence condition holds. Following Geroch ([1], p. 274), Marsden and Tipler [13] have shown that in all nonflat spacetimes with $R_{ab}V^aV^b \geq 0$, equality holding only if $R_{ab} = 0$, compact Cauchy surfaces with $\chi^a{}_a = 0$ are also unique. Hence, there exists a point p in M such that through p there passes a $C^{2,\alpha}$ Cauchy surface S with constant mean curvature, and further,$I^+(S)$ can be uniquely foliated by Cauchy surfaces with constant mean curvature. QED.

The nonflatness and $R_{ab}V^aV^b = 0$ only when $R_{ab} = 0$ assumptions were only needed for uniqueness. The existence of a constant mean curvature compact Cauchy surface foliation follows merely from the timelike convergence condition and the existence of the omega point. If both the future and past c-boundaries are single points—as in Examples 1 and 2—then the proof of Theorem F.2 shows that the entire spacetime is foliated by constant mean curvature compact Cauchy surfaces.

If an omega point spacetime begins in "crushing singularity" like the singularity of the Friedmann universes, then again the entire spacetime is uniquely foliated by constant mean curvature compact Cauchy surfaces. An initial singularity is called [13] "crushing" if the past of some arbitrary spacelike hypersurface can be foliated by a sequence $S(t)$ of smooth spacelike hypersurfaces whose mean curvatures $\chi(p)_{S(t)}$ satisfy $\sup_{p \in S(t)} \chi(p)_{S(t)} \rightarrow +\infty$ as $S(t)$ approaches the past singularity. More precisely.

Theorem F.3: If an omega point spacetime (M,g)

(1) satisfies the chronology condition;

(2) $R_{ab}V^a V^b \geq 0$ holds for all timelike vectors V^a, equality holding only if $R_{ab} = 0$;

(3) (M,g) begins in a crushing singularity;

then (M,g) can be uniquely foliated by $C^{2,\alpha}$ compact Cauchy surfaces with constant mean curvature. Furthermore, the York time $Y(t) \equiv -\frac{4}{3}\chi$ where χ is the constant mean curvature, varies from $-\infty$ at the initial singularity to $+\infty$ at the omega point.

The proof is a straightforward modification of the proof of Theorem F.2 (see [11] and [13] for details), and so is omitted. The hypersurfaces of isotropy and homogeneity in a Friedmann universe are a sequence $S(t)$ satisfying the "crushing" condition. The York time [13] is often used as a time scale in general relativity. In a Friedmann universe, $\chi \equiv \chi^a{}_a = 3H(t)$, where $H(t)$ is the Hubble paramter and χ_{ab} is the extrinsic curvature, so $Y(t) = -4H(t)$.

Budic and Sachs [6] have shown that if the total spacetime volume $\int \sqrt{-g}\, d^4x$ of an omega point spacetime is finite (as it would be in Example 2, for instance), then there is another natural foliation $S_{BS}(t)$ of (M,g) by spacelike hypersurfaces, namely for a given t, the value of $\int_{I+(p)} \sqrt{-g}\, d^4x$ is the same for each point $p \in S_{BS}(t)$. Budic and Sachs show that this foliation is C^1, and a modification of the proof of Theorem F.2 shows that sufficiently close to the omega point, the hypersurfaces $S_{BS}(t)$ will be compact Cauchy surfaces. The question then arises, what is the relationship—if any—between these two natural spacelike foliations of (M,g)? In Example 2, the two foliations are exactly the same, but in general this will not be the case. For instance, if (M,g) is the spacetime of Example 2, then $M - J^-(p)$ for any point $p \in M$ is a spacetime with an omega point which can be foliated with constant mean curvature Cauchy surfaces only to the future of p, while the $S_{BS}(t)$ foliate the entire spacetime (though with Cauchy surfaces only to the future of p).

Budic and Sachs [6] show that $\overline{M}$, the spacetime with its c-boundary, is second-countable and metrizable, so some constraints are imposed on the initial singularity by the requirement that the final singularity be an omega point. I conjecture that, if we require that the entire spacetime be foliated by constant mean curvature Cauchy surfaces which everywhere coincide with the $S_{BS}(t)$ hypersurfaces, then the spacetime must be spatially homogeneous.

Penrose's Weyl Curvature Hypothesis [14], namely that time is defined so that a physical spacetime's "initial" singularity is characterized by the vanishing of the Weyl curvature as one approaches the initial singularity (and the "final" singularity is characterized by the dominance of the Weyl curvature over the Ricci curvature), is another proposal to connect the initial and final singularities. Tod [15] conjectured and Newman [16] proved (at least for the $\gamma = \frac{4}{3}$ case) that, if the Weyl curvature vanished at a singularity (which is "conformally compactifiable"), then the spacetime was necessarily Friedmann everywhere. Wainwright et al. [17–19] have restated the Weyl Curvature Hypothesis to mean that

$$\lim_{t \to 0+} \frac{C_{abcd}C^{abcd}}{R_{ab}R^{ab}} = 0 \qquad (F.5)$$

at an "initial" singularity. Goode et al. [19] have shown that many of the standard Cosmological Problems (flatness problem, horizon problem, etc.) can be solved if one imposes this modified Weyl Curvature Hypothesis. However, they do not propose strongly believable reasons *why* the Weyl Curvature Hypothesis should be true.

Perhaps by connecting these two approaches to connecting the initial and final singularities a strongly believable reason can be found. Wainwright et al. and Tod require in their definitions of "conformally compactifiable" or "isotropic" singularity the existence, near the initial singularity, of a foliation of spacetime by spacelike hypersurfaces (to define the $T = $ constant hypersurfaces in the limit $(F.5)$ above), but they do not require that the foliation be one of the "natural" ones discussed above.

However, suppose we require that globally, the Second Law of Thermodynamics must *always* hold: the total entropy of the universe at time t_i must always be greater than or equal to the total entropy at time t_j whenever $t_i \geq t_j$. Clearly, this inequality cannot hold globally for all foliations, since locally we can always decrease the entropy at the expense of an even greater entropy increase at another spatial position, and we can use this fact to construct a foliation of spacetime by spacelike hypersurfaces in which the above entropy inequality was violated, at least for a short time. But it conceivably *might* be true for one (or both) of the natural foliations described above—if the modified

Penrose Weyl Curvature Hypothesis holds. If the entropy inequalities do not hold for *some* natural foliation, then we would be forced to admit that the Second Law of Thermodynamics simply does not always hold globally (or is inconsistent with general relativity), an admission we should be loath to make.

The modified Penrose Weyl Curvature Hypothesis would have to hold for two reasons. First, to ensure that the purely gravitational degrees of freedom—gravitational waves—when degraded into heat, do not by themselves violate the Second Law of Thermodynamics. Second, to ensure the global existence of both of the above foliations: I conjecture that if the initial singularity is "isotropic" in the sense of Wainwright et al. and "conformally compactifiable" in the sense of Tod, then the foliation of constant mean curvature Cauchy surfaces and the Budic-Sachs foliation by Cauchy surfaces—which must exist near an omega point—can be extended globally to the entire spacetime.

If so, then the modified Penrose Weyl Curvature Hypothesis would be equivalent to requiring the global validity of the Second Law of Thermodynamics. Here would be a strongly believable reason for accepting the Weyl Curvature Hypothesis and its resolution of the Cosmological Problems!

Omega Point Spacetimes That Violate the Chronology Condition

If the spacetime violates the chronology condition, it can still be useful to define a c-boundary in certain circumstances. For example, if a spacetime violates the chronology condition in the maximal way [20], that is, if there is a closed timelike curve (CTC) connecting each and every point, then $I^+(p) \cap I^-(p) = M$ for all points p in the spacetime (M,g), and thus all IPs and IFs are PIPs and PIFs respectively. The Gödel universe [1, p. 168] is the best known example of such a spacetime, but in view of recent work on time travel [21–23], it is necessary to leave open the possibility that CTCs—closed timelike curves—are ubiquitous in our universe. If so, then there will be no event or particle horizons, which is the situation in future- and past-distinguishing spacetime with a single TIP or a single TIF respectively. Thus, I shall extend the definition of "c-boundary" to such spacetimes in the following way: if there are no TIPs, then the future c-boundary will be said to consist of a single point, and if there are no TIFs, then the past c-boundary will be said to consist of a single point. With this extended definition of "c-boundary" the definition of "omega point" stated at the beginning of this section can be applied to certain chronology-violating spacetimes. Then we can summarize the preceding remarks as the

Lemma 3: If a spacetime (M,g) satisfies $M = I^+(p) \cap I^-(p)$ for all points p, then the future c-boundary consists of an omega point.

More generally, we have

Lemma 4: If a spacetime terminating in an omega point violates chronology, then either the chronology-violating set is the entire spacetime, or else it is the union of (1) globally hyperbolic subsets with compact (partial) Cauchy surfaces, and (2) sets of the form $I^+(p) \cap I^-(p)$ for some $p \in M$.

Proof: If $I^+(p) \cap I^-(p) \neq M$, then the chronology violating set is a disjoint union of sets of the form $I^+(q) \cap I^-(q) \neq \varnothing$, and further, the boundary of each $I^+(q) \cap I^-(q)$ is non-empty. Thus the entire spacetime will be the union of these sets, together with regions in which the chronology condition is satisfied. If we apply Seifert's Theorem to these regions where the chronology condition is satisfied, we see that these regions, regarded as spacetimes in their own right, must be globally hyperbolic with compact Cauchy surfaces. QED.

I conjecture that if $\partial I^+(p)$ and $\partial I^-(p)$ are both nonempty with $I^+(q) \cap I^-(q) \neq \varnothing$, the sets $I^+(q) \cap I^-(q)$ will be compact if the spacetime terminates in an omega point.

In particular, if the time travel scenario is as given in [21–23], then the chronology-violating regions appear to the future of partial Cauchy surfaces (initially in compact regions). In such a situation, it is possible to prove.

Theorem F.4: If in a spacetime (M,g) either (1) there are a finite number of chronology violating regions all of which have compact closure, with compact partial Cauchy surfaces to the future and past of these regions and with the "final" globally hyperbolic region, regarded as a spacetime in its own right, ending in an omega point, or (2) the chronology-violating region engulfs the entire future of some compact $\partial I^+(p)$, and $I^-(\partial I^+(p))$ is foliated by compact partial Cauchy surfaces, or (3) the entire spacetime violates the chronology condition, then the entire spacetime terminates in an omega point.

The proof is straightforward and so is omitted. Theorem F.4 thus shows an omega point is allowed—in the case of eventually global violation of chronology, required—in the standard models of time travel. The three possibilities of Theorem F.4 are illustrated in Figure F.1.

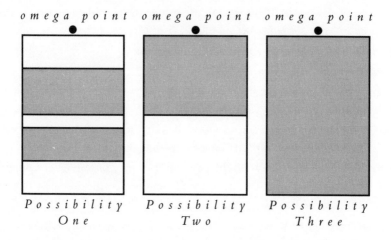

Figure F.1 *Three possible ways of having an Omega Point spacetime that violates the chronology condition. Causality is violated in the darkened regions, while the undarkened regions are globally hyperbolic. Possibility One has two compact regions of the form $\overline{I^+(p)} \cap I^-(p)$ with the chronology condition being violated in $I^+(p) \cap I^-(p)$, and with the globally hyperbolic region to the future of the second, regarded as a spacetime in its own right, terminating in an Omega Point. All globally hyperbolic regions have compact partial Cauchy surfaces. Possibility Two has a single region wherein causality is violated, all to the future of a single globally hyperbolic region with compact partial Cauchy surfaces. Possibility Three has $M = I^+(p) \cap I^-(p)$ for any point $p \in M$.*

I have shown elsewhere [20] that the property of the entire spacetime being a chronology-violating set is a stable property: it persists if the light cones are made slightly larger or smaller at every point. (I have used the notion of spacetime stability introduced by Hawking [1,24], and applied in the definition of stable causality.) Thus in the case that the omega point occurs dueto the entire spacetime being a single chronology-violating set, the existence of an omega point is a stable property. However, although an omega point would clearly persist if the light cones are made larger, it is not clear that it would persist in all cases if the light cones are made smaller.

References

[1] Hawking, Stephen W. and George F. R. Ellis 1973. *The Large Scale Structure of Space-Time*. Cambridge: Cambridge University Press.

[2] Misner, C. W. 1967. *Nature* **214**: 40.

[3] E. M. Lifshitz, I. M. Lifshitz, and I. M. Khalatnikov, *Soviet Physics JETP* **32**, 173 (1971).

[4] A.G. Doroshkevich and I. D. Novikov, *Soviet Astronomy AJ* **14**, 763 (1971).

[5] A. G. Doroshkevich, V.N. Lukash, and I. D. Novikov, *Soviet Physics JETP* **33**, 649 (1971).

[6] R. Budic and R. K. Sachs, *General Relativity and Gravitation* **7**, 21 (1976).

[7] F. Löbell, Ber. Verhandl. Sachs. Akad. Wiss. Leipzig, Math. Phys. Kl. **83**, 167 (1931).

[8] H. J. Seifert, *General Relativity and Gravitation* **1**, 247 (1971).

[9] R. P. Geroch, E. H. Kronheimer, and R. Penrose, *Proceedings of the Royal Society of London* **A327**, 545 (1972).

[10] Gilbarg, D., and N. S. Trudinger 1983. *Elliptic Partial Differential Equations of Second Order*. 2nd ed. Berlin: Springer-Verlag.

[11] Bartnik, R. 1988. *Communications in Mathematical Physics* **117**: 615. See also Bartnik, R. 1984. *Communications in Mathematical Physics* **94**: 155.

[12] D. R. Brill and F. Flaherty, *Communications in Mathematical Physics* **50**, 157 (1976).

[13] J. E. Marsden and F. J. Tipler, *Physics Reports* **66**, 109 (1980).

[14] R. Penrose, in *General Relativity: An Einstein Centenary Survey*, ed. S. W. Hawking and W. Israel (Cambridge Univeristy Press, Cambridge, 1979).

[15] K. P. Tod, *Classical and Quantum Gravity* **7**, L13 (1990).

[16] R. P. A. C. Newman, *Twistor Newsletter* **33**, 11 (1991).

[17] S. W. Goode and J. Wainwright, *Classical and Quantum Gravity* **2**, 99 (1985).

[18] S. W. Goode, *Classical and Quantum Gravity* **8**, L1 (1991).

[19] S. W. Goode, A. A. Coley, and J. Wainwright, *Classical and Quantum Gravity* **9**, 445 (1992).

[20] F. J. Tipler, *Journal of Mathematical Physics* **18**, 1568 (1977).

[21] Morris, M. S., K. S. Thorne, and U. Yurtsever 1988. *Physical Review Letters* **61**: 1446.

[22] Friedman, J., M. S. Morris, I. D. Novikov, F. Echeverria, G. Klinkhammer, K. S. Thorne, and U. Yurtsever 1990. *Physical Review* **D42**: 1915.

[23] Deutsch, David 1991. *Physical Review* **D44**: 3197–217.

[24] Hawking, S. W. 1971. *General Relativity and Gravitation* **1**: 393.

G. Two Possible Counter-Examples to the Church-Turing Thesis

The Church-Turing Thesis is not an hypothesis about mathematics. It is actually an hypothesis about physics [1]. It says that no machine can be built which can solve a problem a Turing machine cannot solve. But whether a machine with given properties can be constructed is ultimately a question of physics. No Turing machine can solve the Halting Problem: no Turing machine can tell you if an arbitrary machine, given an arbitrary problem, will eventually halt, or will instead go on forever.

I shall describe here two machines which *might* be able to solve the Halting Problem. In essence, they are machines equivalent to the Universal Turing Machine, but which can complete an infinity of operations in a finite time, call it t_0. Thus, to solve the Halting Problem, one merely programs the arbitrary Turing machine with its arbitrary problem on this machine, and wait t_0. If the virtual machine has not arrived at the solution after this time, one knows that it will not halt—because it never did.

I wrote that the machines *might* be able to solve the Halting Problem, because I shall not give a rigorous proof that either of the two machines I shall describe will in fact work; I shall merely present a plausibility argument that they will. I merely *conjecture* that the gaps in my argument can be filled. If they can't, the failure of my conjecture will provide further support for the Church-Turing Thesis.

The first model is a modification of the Billiard Ball computer [2] described in Chapter II. The essence of this machine was that any computation was equivalent to the motion of balls moving at constant velocity except when they encounter appropriately arranged rigid walls and other balls, when they bounce in accordance with standard Newtonian mechanics. The Billiard Ball computer is a Universal Machine.

The faster the balls move—that is, the higher the assumed initial velocity—the more rapidly a given computation will be completed. Can the speed of the balls be increased without limit, so that an infinite number of collisions can occur in finite time?

Newtonian physical systems which carry out an infinite number of operations in finite time are known to exist. Specifically, consider four point particles moving in a straight line under the action of their mutual gravity, which is assumed to be the Newtonian force law $\vec{F}_{ij} = GM_iM_j(\vec{r}_i - \vec{r}_j)/|\vec{r}_i - \vec{r}_j|^3$. Binary collisions are assumed to result in elastic bounces. Mather and McGhee [3] have shown that the masses and initial data of the four particles can be adjusted so that particles 3 and 4 get arbitrarily close as $t \to t_0$, while particle 2 bounces back and forth between particles 1 and 3, with the result that, as $t \to t_0$, particles 3 and 4 go to $+\infty$, particle 1 goes to $-\infty$, while particle 2 goes back and forth between particles 1 and 3 an infinite number of times.

In the Mather and McGhee model, an infinite amount of energy is extracted from particles 3 and 4—this is possible because the particles are gravitating mass points, and the gravitational potential energy is $-GM_3M_4/|\vec{r}_i - \vec{r}_j|$ which goes to $-\infty$ as $|\vec{r}_i - \vec{r}_j| \to 0$. Extracting this infinite energy makes it possible to give the particles infinite velocities in finite time.

Gerver [5] has published a plausibility argument that by using five coplanar point particles moving around a triangle, all of the particles could be sent to spatial infinity in finite time, with one of the particles passing near (but never colliding with) the other four particles an infinite number of times. Saari [6] has shown that the set of initial conditions which could have this behavior is of measure zero for four coplanar particles since they have to approach a straight line in the limit $t \to t_0$. Whether this is true for more than four particles is unknown.

The point of these examples is that Newtonian mechanics demonstrably provides an infinite energy source to move point particles to infinite velocities in finite time. An arrangement could be given coupling these point particles to the finite sized billiard balls of the Billiard Ball computer, forcing these balls to complete an infinite number of computational steps in finite time. If the answer is obtained before t_0, the machine halts, and if no answer is obtained, then the machine never halts.

One reason the above is a "plausibility" argument and not a rigorous argument is that I have assumed it is possible to determine whether or not the machine has indeed failed to halt after its infinite number of steps. That is, I have assumed that there is a unique system state *after* t_0 so we can see that there is an answer or no answer in the machine after t_0. Uniqueness of extension after the end of global hyperbolicity is the rule in general relativity (the extension of Taub space into NUT space is the major exception [6]), but there are no extension theorems for Newtonian spacetimes.

The second possible machine which could solve the Halting Problem is an omega point spacetime with time travel, as discussed in Section F. An infinite number of computations is carried out between now and the omega point. In a globally hyperbolic spacetime, the mechanism is described in Section H: roughly, it is a general relativistic analog of extracting an infinite amount of energy by letting the distance between two point particles go to zero. In the Omega Point Theory, the distance going to zero is the radius of the universe.

In a deterministic spacetime, the result of the infinite computations are stuck at the end of time: at the omega point. With time travel, however, the result can be sent back. Specifically, if the computer is arranged so that the answer, if obtained, is sent back in time to a period between $t = 0$ and $t = t_0$, then if no answer is received from the future by time t_0, we know that an equivalent Turing machine will never halt. Only a finite number of bits can of course be sent back into time [7], but this is no barrier to a solution to the Halting Problem: it is sufficient that the simple message "Answer obtained and machine halted" be sent back.

References

[1] Chaitlin, Gregory J. 1982. "Gödel's Theorem and Information." *International Journal of Theoretical Physics* **21**: 941–54.

[2] Fredkin, Edward and Tommaso Toffoli 1982. "Conservative Logic." *International Journal of Theoretical Physics* **21**: 219–53.

[3] Mather, J. N. and R. McGhee 1975, "Solutions of the Collinear Four-Body Problem Which Become Unbounded in Finite Time." In *Dynamical Systems, Theory and Applications*, by J. Moser (New York: Springer-Verlag), p. 573.

[4] Gerver, Joseph L. 1984. "A Possible Model for a Singularity Without Collisions in the Five Body Problem." *Journal of Differential Equations* **52**: 76–90.

[5] Saari, Donald 1977. "A Global Existence Theorem for the Four-Body Problem of Newtonian Mechanics." *Journal of Differential Equations* **26**: 80–111.

[6] Hawking, S. W. and G. F. R. Ellis 1973. *The Large Scale Structure of Space-Time*, Cambridge: Cambridge University Press.

[7] Deutsch, David 1991. "Quantum Mechanics Near Closed Timelike Lines." *Physical Review* **D44**: 3197–217.

H. The Classical Omega Point Universe: Mathematical Details

In a deterministic system of equations like those of general relativity or Newtonian mechanics, the "initial conditions" can be imposed at any time past, present, or future. Although we humans tend to think that the past determines the future, it is equally correct to regard the future as determining the past. Similarly, in celestial mechanics one can adopt a heliocentric or a geocentric coordinate system. If one applies Newtonian mechanics or general relativity in either coordinate system, one can compute the correct positions of the planets.

However, adopting a geocentric coordinate system, though permitted, would enormously complicate the mathematics. One would never be able to see that the underlying dynamics are basically simple: point masses governed by the Newtonian inverse square central force. And in historical fact, the underlying dynamics were not understood until Copernicus transferred the frame of reference from the Earth to the Sun.

I shall show in this section that many cosmological observations cease to be mysterious if we impose boundary conditions in the future rather than in the past. I showed in Section B that there is vastly more future than past, so it is plausible that the underlying physics will become clearer to us if we transfer our frame of reference from the past to the future, if we transfer our point of view from a minuscule spacetime region to the largest spacetime region of all. Copernicus himself argued in his book *On the Revolutions* (Book I, Chapters 5, 6, and 10) that we could understand the Solar System only if the frame of reference in celestial mechanics were anchored on the largest visible bodies, the Sun and the sphere of the fixed stars, rather than on the tiny Earth.

I have argued in the body of this book that the boundary condition to impose on the classical future is simply "life continues to exist forever"; that is, the laws of physics must be such as to permit the existence of the biosphere to continue forever: for literally infinite subjective time. In this Section, I shall show that this boundary condition predicts (1) the universe must be closed with $0 < \Omega_0 - 1 < 10^{-6}$ and $H_0 \leq 45$ km/sec-mpc, where Ω_0 is the density parameter and H_0 is Hubble's constant; (2) the future c-boundary of the universe must be an omega point; and (3) the mass of the standard model Higgs boson must be 220 ± 20 GeV and the mass of the top quark must be 185 ± 20 GeV.

I shall also demonstrate in this Section that (4) the density contrast $\Delta\rho/\rho$ must have the scale invariant Harrison-Zel'dovich power spectrum, with an amplitude small enough so that the temperature fluctuations $\Delta T/T$ in the cosmic background radiation is less than 6×10^{-5}. Furthermore, I shall show that $\Delta T/T$ must be proportional to $\frac{R(t_R)}{R_{now}}$, the ratio of the scale factor at the recombination time to the scale factor now. In other theories, the observed fact that $\Delta T/T$ is equal to $\frac{R(t_R)}{R_{now}}$ to within a few orders of magnitude is a mere coincidence, because the invariant amplitude of $\Delta\rho/\rho$ is either an arbitrary parameter, or else set by particle physics parameters, not cosmological ones. In fact, it is set by life continuing forever.

Since "life"—whatever its form or whatever its detailed physical processes—is ultimately a form of information processing, I have claimed in Chapter IV that three conditions are necessary and sufficient for "life" to continue to exist forever. In mathematical language, these conditions are:

I. information processing—the running of programs—continues along at least one future-endless timelike curve γ all the way into the future c-boundary of the universe;

II. the amount of information processed in $J^-(\gamma) \cap J^+(p)$ is infinite, where $p \subset \gamma$ is the event {Earth at present}.

III. the amount of information stored in $J^-(\gamma) \cap J^+(p) \cap S(t)$, where $S(t)$ is some foliation of the universe by spacelike hypersurfaces, diverges to infinity as the leaves of the foliation approach the future c-boundary.

Precise definitions of "c-boundary," the causal past set $J^-(\gamma) \equiv$ {the set of all events which can send signals to γ}, and the causal future set $J^+(p) \equiv$ {the set of all events to which p can send signals} are in Hawking and Ellis [1], and were briefly discussed in Section B. The future c-boundary—the future end of time—has been defined in Chapter IV, and in Section F.

Condition I simply says in precise terminology that life—information processing—goes on until the end of time. Condition II says that this period is actually infinite in subjective time t_{subj}, which is measured by the number of "thoughts" living beings have (each "thought" requires at least one bit of information to be processed). Without this condition of infinity, it would make no sense to say life goes on "forever." Condition II also says that a bit processed counts as a potential "thought" only if it can be communicated to the observer γ. An integrated biosphere or personality is impossible without the exchange of information between parts of the biosphere or the brain coding the personality. The Earth at the present time is chosen to provide the zero of subjective time t_{subj}. A biosphere must be used to do this, but any biosphere would do. So "Earth at the present time" can be replaced by "an inhabited planet at the present time."

Condition III is imposed to eliminate the Eternal Return Problem, discussed at length in Chapter III. I proved in Chapter II that a finite state machine, if run for infinite time, will fall into a subset of its state space for which it will repeat each state in that subset an infinite number of times. But living "forever" means having an infinity of *new* experiences. Condition III makes life as a whole a potentially infinite state machine, for which such eternal returns are not inevitable. "Potentially infinite" ("infinite" in complexity theory terminology) just means that the causally accessible stored information at any given instant of universal time is not bounded above as time approaches its future limit. The constant mean curvature foliation—which exists [2] and is unique [3] in generic physically reasonable spacetimes (and which coincides with the rest frame [4] of the background radiation in Friedmann-Robertson-Walker (FRW) universes)—is the standard way of defining absolute time in classical general relativistic cosmology, and thus is an acceptable spacelike foliation. However, Condition III only claims that there exists a spacelike foliation on which the information stored diverges; it does not require that it diverge on a specific foliation. A spacelike foliation will exist provided stable causality [1] holds. But as I showed in Section F, if the spacetime ends in an omega point, then the spacetime is foliated by compact constant mean curvature Cauchy surfaces, at least sufficiently near the final singularity. Further, if in addition to ending in an omega point, the spacetime begins in a Friedmann-like singularity, then the entire spacetime is foliated by compact constant mean curvature Cauchy surfaces.

In the models of Dirac and Dyson, the universe was assumed to be open or flat. Dyson argued [5] that there was sufficient free energy in such universes to satisfy I and II, but I have shown [6] that in flat universes, there would be insufficient energy to signal from one side of the biosphere to the other an infinite number of times, and in open universes, the expansion at late times would be too rapid to allow structures of ever larger size to form (such structures are required to store a diverging amount of information). Thus, in either case, Condition III would be violated. Linde [7] has suggested that life may be able to survive forever in an eternal chaotic inflation universe by traveling from a dying inflation domain to a newly forming one *ad infinitum*. However, I have shown [8] that, since the newly formed domains have a characteristic scale determined by the inflaton mass, the Bekenstein Bound places an upper bound on the information that can be coded in the causally connected biosphere, and again Condition III is violated.

Let us see in more detail just why life cannot exist forever in an eternal inflating universe. Linde shows [7, 9–11] that, if the cosmological constant is less than a very small positive value, density perturbations by the inflaton field will result in our domain behaving in the far future as an S^3 FRW universe with current average density μ_0 greater than the critical density and with current scale factor size $l^* \sim \exp[2\pi\ M_P/m] \sim \exp[2\pi 10^6]$ cm, where M_P is the Planck mass, the effective potential of the inflaton field is $V(\phi) = \frac{1}{2}m^2\phi^2$, and the value of m is chosen to make the amplitude of the density perturbations be about 10^{-4} as observed. (If the cosmological constant is larger than the Linde value, our domain will behave in the far future like de Sitter space with its exponential inflation, and our calculations agree [9,12] that information processing—life—would eventually become impossible in that environment.)

However, Linde shows [7, 9–11] that, within the distance l^*, there will be many new inflating domains, each of which will become a new universe like ours, but connected to ours by a large wormhole. He proposes that life can continue forever if it repeatedly transfers itself from a dying domain to a newly formed one *ad infinitum*. He argues that indeed sending a signal from a parent domain to a daughter may be physically possible (if the cosmological constant is not too large), and thus Conditions I and II might hold. Linde himself mentions the possibility (private communication) that by the time the signal arrives, the daughter universe may have become older than the parent was when the signal was sent, and thus the conditions for life may actually be worse at the receiver than at the sender.

A more fundamental problem is that the Bekenstein Bound (C.1) places an ultimate limit on the amount of information that can be transmitted from parent domain to daughter, and thus Condition III cannot hold; our descendants must die out or become locked in an Eternal Return.

To prove this, let me follow Linde and approximate the domain with average density greater than the critical density by the metric of an S^3 FRW universe. Recall from Section B that the metric of an S^3 FRW universe is $ds^2 = -dt^2 + R^2(t)\ [d\chi^2 + \sin^2\chi(d\theta^2 + \sin^2\theta d\phi^2)] = R^2(t)[-d\tau^2 + d\chi^2 + \sin^2\chi(d\theta^2 + \sin^2\theta d\phi^2)]$, where t and τ are respectively the proper and conformal time of world lines normal to the surfaces of homogeneity and isotropy, and $0 \leq \chi \leq \pi$ is the radial coordinate. The time evolution of the scale factor $R(t)$ is governed by the Friedmann equation $G_{\hat{t}\hat{t}} = 8\pi G T_{\hat{t}\hat{t}} = 3[(R'/R)^2 + R^{-2}] = 8\pi G\rho$, where the prime denotes the proper time derivative, and ρ is the mass density. If the equation of state is $p = (\gamma - 1)\rho$, with $\gamma > 2/3$, then the conservation equation $(\nabla \cdot T)_{\hat{i}} = 0$ implies $\rho \propto a^{-3\gamma}$, in which case the Friedmann equation becomes $(R'/R)^2 = MR^{-3\gamma} - R^{-2}$, where M is a constant.

This equation can be integrated by setting $y \equiv R^{(3\gamma-2)/2}$ and transforming to conformal time. (I am grateful to Prof. J. D. Barrow for pointing out this transformation to me.) In which case the Friedmann equation becomes $(dy/d\tau)^2 + ([3\gamma - 2]/2)^2 y^2 = M([3\gamma - 2]/2)^2$. This is just the energy equation for a simple harmonic oscillator, so y satisfies $\ddot{y} + ([3\gamma - 2]/2)^2 y = 0$, where the dot denotes the conformal time derivative. Hence, $R(\tau) = R_{max}[\sin(\{[3\gamma - 2]/2\}\tau)]^{2/(3\gamma-2)}$, and

$$t(\tau) = R_{max} \int_0^{\tau} \sin^{2/(3\gamma - 2)} \left[\left(\frac{3\gamma - 2}{2}\right) x\right] dx \qquad (H.1)$$

where R_{max} is the value of the scale factor at maximum expansion. The total lifetime τ_{life} of the universe in conformal time is the conformal time between two zeros of y or R, or in other words

$$\tau_{life} = 2\pi/(3\gamma - 2) \qquad (H.2)$$

independent of R_{max}. The total proper lifetime of the universe is obtained by setting the upper limit of the integral $(H.1)$ equal to τ_{life}. This gives

$$t_{life} = R_{max} \frac{2\sqrt{\pi}\Gamma\left(\frac{3\gamma}{2(3\gamma - 2)}\right)}{(3\gamma - 2)\,\Gamma\left(\frac{3\gamma - 1}{3\gamma - 2}\right)} \qquad (H.3)$$

where Γ is the gamma function. For matter-dominated universes, $(\gamma = 1)$, $t_{life} = \pi R_{max} = 4M/3M_P^2$, where $M \equiv 2\pi^2 R_0^3 \rho_0$ is the total "mass" of the universe, since $R_{max} = 8\pi\rho_0 R_0^3/3M_P^2$. For radiation-dominated universes $(\gamma = 4/3)$, $t_{life} = 2R_{max}$. These are the usual results. I have obtained τ_{life} and t_{life} for all γ because a realistic universe would be better approximated by a model in which γ varied between 1 in the low temperature regime and 4/3 in the hot.

When combined with the Bekenstein Bound, these results imply that the amount of information that can ever be coded in any domain is less than a universal upper bound, hence the Eternal Return is inevitable in an eternal chaotic inflation cosmology. For, from the Bekenstein Bound $(C.1)$, we have

$I_{now} \leq 3 \times 10^{38} [\mu_0 (l^*)^3] l^* \sim 10^9 \exp(8\pi 10^6) \sim \exp(8\pi 10^6)$, so

$$I_{now} \leq \exp(8\pi 10^6) \text{ bits} \qquad (H.4)$$

is the upper bound on the information that can be coded in our domain at the present time. Following Linde [7], I have set $\rho_0 = 10^{-29}$ and $M = 2\pi^2 \rho_0 (l^*)^3$.

Since, for matter-dominated universes, we have $M(t)R(t) = [2\pi^2 \rho(t)R^3(t)] R(t) = [2\pi^2 \rho_0 R_0^3]R(t) \sim \rho_0 (l^*)^3 R(t)$, the upper bound on the information which can be coded in our domain increases linearly with the scale factor $R(t)$. Thus the absolute upper bound is given by the setting $R(t) = R_{max}$. Using $R_{max} = 4M/3M_P^2$, we get $(MR)_{max} \sim [8\pi \rho^2 / 3M_P^2][l^*]^6$. So the maximum amount of information that can ever be coded in *any* domain is

$$I_{domain}^{max} \leq \exp(12\pi 10^6) \text{ bits} \qquad (H.5)$$

Thus sending signals describing us and our domain to daughter domains *ad infinitum* as Linde proposes would ultimately be futile; once the complexity of life reaches the limit set by eq. (H.5), life would have to repeat its previous actions *ad infinitum*. (Actually, the upper bound to the information that could be *sent* from the parent to a daughter domain would be *less* than (H.5), because the parent and daughter would be connected by wormholes, which would look like black holes to both parent and daughter, and the Bekenstein Bound would have to be applied to the surfaces of these black holes, which are smaller than either parent or daughter, being contained in each.)

The fundamental limit (H.5) arises because inflationary cosmology has fundamental length and mass scales, l^* and M respectively, obtained from the mass m in the effective potential $V(\phi)$. However, Linde [7] points out that the scale of universal closure may not occur at l^* but at nl^*, where n is an integer, since the mechanism causing closure is the relative density fluctuations $\delta\rho/\rho_0$ becoming greater than 1. Hence the closure size is defined by the first integer n giving this relative density fluctuation wavelength scale.

Thus one might hope to avoid the limit (H.5) by going from a domain for which $n = 1$ to one for which $n = 2$, and then to one with $n = 3$, and so *ad infinitum*. Unfortunately, such a survival strategy will not be successful either.

This follows from the fact that the conformal lifetime τ_{life} is independent of R_{max}, and from the fact that all light rays obey the equation $\tau = \chi$. Hence the number of circumnavigations of the universe in its lifetime by a light ray which starts a finite time after the initial singularity is less than $\tau_{life}/2\pi = 1/(3\gamma - 2)$, which for matter-dominated universes is 1 and for radiation-dominated universes is 1/2, and these numbers are independent of R_{max}. Therefore, it will not be possible for any light signal to circumnavigate any domain, however large, before it terminates in a final singularity (or until curvatures get large; either case putting us back to life surviving arbitrarily close to the final singularity).

This means that it will be impossible to search for a domain with its n larger than the current domain, send the message back across the universe of a success, and transmit the information to a larger domain, before one's current domain approaches its final singularity. This argument thus applies to any inflationary cosmology, even one which contains no fundamental scale besides the Planck length L_P—for instance, extended inflationary cosmology. The crucial fact is that the conformal lifetime, eq. (H.2), of the universe contains no length scale, since it depends only on the spacetime conformal structure.

Conversely, one might think [13] to survive by sending the information to a mini-universe created in the laboratory. In this case, the mini-universe is hidden behind a black hole event horizon of area $A = 4\pi L^2$, with $L = 2GM/c^2$, so the Bekenstein Bound (C.1) becomes

$$I \leq \frac{A}{4L_P^2 \ln 2} \qquad (H.6)$$

Since for the horizons of typical laboratory universes [13], $A \sim 4\pi L_P^2$, no significant information can be transmitted to the mini-universe, unless the "black hole" is enlarged by putting most of the mass of our universe inside, but this possibility is eliminated by the causality bound obtained above. (We would have to go out, collect the matter, and bring it back, but there can be less than one circumnavigation of our universe before it ends.)

However, the derivation of the Bekenstein Bound (C.1) assumes that the vacuum state is unique, which implies that there is no information coded in the vacuum. Linde [13] suggests that superstring theory may violate this assumption, and that we might be able to code information about ourselves in the vacuum state of the laboratory universe. But Linde points out that such different vacua can arise only if the initial density of the mini-universe is near the Planck density M_P^4. I claim this implies a significant number of such mini-universes with densities greater than M_P^4, since the probability of creation is maximized at M_P^4.

In summary, life in an eternal chaotic inflationary universe would ultimately be poor, solitary, nasty, brutish, and—by comparison with the infinite age of the universe—short.

"Eternal" Inflation may not even be eternal. Vilenkin [14] has recently shown that the Second Law of Thermodynamics requires any inflation universe to begin in an initial singularity.

The general difficulty faced by all flat and open universes, with or without inflation, is that they necessarily contain event horizons. Event horizons prevent signaling, and the absence of event horizons—equivalently, the presence of an omega point—implies that the spacetime is compact, as was shown in Section F. Recall, however, that Seifert's Theorem requires the Cauchy surfaces to be compact, not S^3. But, a non-S^3 universe will not recollapse unless the weak energy condition is violated, or $\Lambda < 0$ (see below, [25]). Since, as we shall see below, sufficient energy for the divergence of information processed requires recollapse, this means the Cauchy surfaces must be S^3. Hence, if life is to continue forever, the universe must be closed.

1. Bianchi Type IX Universes

One might think that life is doomed, since closed universes end in zero spatial volume singularities in finite proper time. However, the Bekenstein Bound (C.1) shows that we can have $I \to +\infty$ as $R \to 0$ if $ER \to +\infty$; total I processed and stored can be infinite in finite proper time if $dI/dt \to +\infty$ fast enough. I now show that both divergences can occur. I shall show below that if both are to occur in a closed universe, the biosphere must engulf the entire universe and prevent horizons from forming. The latter implies that the universe must be approximately homogeneous (or must be made so) in the far future. In order for recollapse to occur, the universe must be near isotropy at maximum expansion. Hence the universe at R_{max} must be nearly FRW, and this in turn implies that the growing mode of the density contrast $\delta_+(t_{max}) < 1$. Since in flat space we have $\delta_+ \propto t^{2/3} \propto R(t)$, which gives

$$\frac{\delta_+(t_{max})}{\delta_+(t_{now})} = \frac{R_{max}}{R_{now}}$$

on the largest scales. I shall shortly show that $R_{max}/R_{now} \geq 3 \times 10^3$, so we obtain $\delta_+(t_{now}) < 3 \times 10^{-4}$ as the amplitude on the scale of the antipodal distance. To get the temperature fluctuation $\Delta T/T$ at the recombination time, we make use of $\Delta T/T = \frac{1}{3}\delta_+(t_R)$ for adiabatic perturbations, we scale time from now to the recombination time t_R, and we scale the amplitude from the antipodal distance to the horizon distance at t_R. The amplitude scaling requires the power spectrum.

But the power spectrum must be the Harrison-Zel'dovich spectrum. If the initial spectrum is

$$\delta|_H = \Delta \left(\frac{M_H}{M_\star} \right)^{-\alpha}$$

where $\delta|_H$ means the magnitude of the pertubation δ as it enters the horizon, and both Δ and $M_\star$ are free parameters. If $\alpha < 0$, the perturbations diverge on large scales. If $\alpha > 0$, the perturbations diverge on small scales [26, p. 352]. Either would be inconsistent with an initial Friedmann singularity, which we must have in order to have $S = 0$ at the initial singularity and the validity of the Bekenstein Bound, as discussed in Section C. Thus $\alpha = 0$, and this is the Harrison-Zel'dovich spectrum.

It can be shown [26, p. 359] that the Harrison-Zel'dovich spectrum implies $\delta_+ \propto M_k^{-2/3}$, where k is the wave number of the perturbation. Since $M_k \propto k^{-3}$, this implies that $\delta_+ \propto k^2$. Because the wave number is inversely proportional to the proper distance, we have

$$\frac{\delta_+(t_R)|_H}{\delta_+(t_R)|_{antipodal}} = \left(\frac{k_H}{k_{antipodal}} \right)^2 = \left(\frac{D_{antipodal}}{D_H} \right)^2 \Big|_{t_R}$$

where D_H is the proper distance to the horizon, and $D_{antipodal}$ is, as it was in Section B, the proper distance to the antipodal point. Since the horizon size grows as $R^{3/2}$ and the distance to the antipodal point grows as R, the ratio $D_H/D_{antipodal}$ grows as $R^{1/2}$. This implies

$$\left(\frac{D_{antipodal}}{D_H} \right)^2_{recom} = \left(\frac{R_{now}}{R(t_R)} \right) \left(\frac{D_{antipodal}}{D_H} \right)^2_{now}$$

The inequality $\delta_+(t_{now}) < 3 \times 10^{-4}$ on the scale of the antipodal point implies $\delta_+(t_R) < 2 \times 10^{-7}$ on the scale of the antipodal point, since $\frac{\delta_+(t_{now})}{\delta_+(t_R)} = \frac{R_{now}}{R_{recom}}$ $= 1500$. Since we have $(D_{antipodal}/D_H)_{now} = 10^3$ from Section B, we get $\Delta T/T$ < 100, which is not interesting. The preceeding analysis was done in the flat FRW universe, and perturbations grow more rapidly in closed FRW models, but the increase in the density contrast is only a factor of 5 over the flat model by the time of maximum expansion [26, p. 339].

However, not only must the perturbations on the largest scales be small at the time of maximum expansion, they must also be small at the time our descendants reach those scales. Thus, if the perturbations on the scale of the horizon were of order one when the expanding biosphere reached the region, the material would have collapsed into supermassive black holes and be unavailable for life. Furthermore, such supermassive black holes would be impossible to manipulate to eliminate horizons, and horizons would, as we shall see below, make continued life impossible.

A point on the surface of last scattering is today located at a proper distance $R_{now}\chi$ given by

$$R_{now}\chi = R_{now}\int_{t_R}^{t_{now}} \frac{dt}{R(t)}$$

which, since $R(t) = R_{now}(t/t_{now})^{2/3}$, implies

$$R_{now}\chi = 3t_{now}\left[1 - \left(\frac{R(t_R)}{R_{now}}\right)^{1/2}\right]$$

so that in a flat FRW matter-dominated universe, the size of the visible universe is very close to $3t_{now}$. I shall show in Section N that our descendants will be able to expand to this region at close to the speed of light, and so they will be able to reach this region at time t determined by the equation

$$R_{now}\chi = R_{now}\int_{t_{now}}^{t} \frac{dt}{R(t)} = 3t_{now}\left[\left(\frac{R(t)}{R_{now}}\right)^{1/2} - 1\right]$$

Equating the two expressions for $R_{now}\chi$ implies that $R(t)/R_{now} = 4$. The condition $\delta_+(t) < 1$ then gives

$$\frac{\Delta T}{T} = \frac{1}{3}\delta_+(t_R) = \frac{1}{3}\delta_+(t)\left(\frac{\delta_+(t_{now})}{\delta_+(t)}\right)\left(\frac{\delta_+(t_R)}{\delta_+(t_{now})}\right) = \frac{1}{3}\delta_+(t)\left(\frac{R_{now}}{R(t)}\right)\left(\frac{R(t_R)}{R_{now}}\right)$$

$$< \left(\frac{1}{3}\right)\left(\frac{1}{4}\right)\left(\frac{1}{1500}\right) = 6 \times 10^{-5}$$

which is the upper bound quoted in the main part of the book. (I could have done better, because the appropriate condition is not merely $\delta_+(t) < 1$, but rather $\delta_+(t) \ll 1$.) We also know that in order to give rise to the galaxies, to the structures which give rise to life in the early part of universal history, the density contrast must be greater than about 10^{-6} at the surface of last scattering. Thus we have fairly tight upper and lower bounds on the density contrast from the final boundary condition that life must continue to exist forever. Given the boundary condition, no particle physics considerations are required; standard classical cosmology was all that was used in the above calculation. Notice that the final boundary condition explains why $\Delta T/T$ is within a factor of 100 of $R(t_R)/R_{now}$: the former is proportional to the latter.

In summary, we see that to a high degree of accuracy, the universe will be homogeneous at least until the recollapse time.

The metric of a general homogeneous closed universe, the Bianchi type IX model, can be expressed [15,16] as

$$ds^2 = -dt^2 + e^{2\alpha}[\sum_{i,j=1}^{3} (e^{2\beta})_{ij}\, \sigma^i \sigma^j] \tag{H.7}$$

where the σ^i are SU(2) isometry invariant 1-forms on S^3 satisfying $\mathcal{L}_{\vec{n}}\sigma^i = 0$ and $[\sigma^i,\sigma^j] = \epsilon_{ijk}\sigma^k$, with $\vec{n}$ being the unit normal to the $t=$ constant spacelike hypersurfaces of homogeneity, and with α and β_{ij} being functions of t only (β_{ij} is traceless). I show below that available energy and horizon disappearance effects are maximized if β_{ij} is diagonal; let β_i denote the diagonal elements. Since $\beta_1 + \beta_2 + \beta_3 = 0$, only two of the β's are independent so choose the independent variables to be $\beta_+ \equiv -\frac{1}{2}\beta_3$, and $\beta_- \equiv \frac{1}{2\sqrt{3}}(\beta_1 - \beta_2)$. If $-\rho$, P_1, P_2, P_3 denote the eigenvalues of the stress-energy tensor $T^a{}_b$ corresponding to the eigenvectors $(dt)^a$, $(\sigma^1)^a$, $(\sigma^2)^a$, $(\sigma^3)^a$, respectively (that is, they respectively are the negative of the energy density and principal pressures measured in the obvious local orthonormal frame), then the Einstein equations $G_{ab} = 8\pi T_{ab}$ are

$$\dot{\alpha}^2 - \dot{\beta}_+^2 - \dot{\beta}_-^2 + \frac{1}{4}e^{-2\alpha}(1-V) = \frac{8\pi}{3}\rho \tag{H.8}$$

$$\ddot{\alpha} + \dot{\alpha}^2 + 2(\dot{\beta}_+^2 + \dot{\beta}_-^2) = -\frac{4\pi}{3}(\rho + P_1 + P_2 + P_3) \tag{H.9}$$

$$\ddot{\beta}_+ + 3\dot{\alpha}\dot{\beta}_+ + \frac{1}{8}\frac{\partial V}{\partial\beta_+} = -\frac{4\pi}{3}(2P_3 - P_1 - P_2) \tag{H.10}$$

$$\ddot{\beta}_- + 3\dot{\alpha}\dot{\beta}_- + \frac{1}{8}e^{-2\alpha}\frac{\partial V}{\partial\beta_-} = \frac{4\pi\sqrt{3}}{3}(P_1 - P_2) \tag{H.11}$$

where the overdots denote derivatives with respect to t, and $V \equiv V(\beta_+,\beta_-) \equiv 1 - \frac{4}{3}e^{-2\beta_+}\cosh(2\sqrt{3}\beta_-) + \frac{1}{3}e^{-8\beta_+} + \frac{2}{3}e^{4\beta_+}[\cosh(4\sqrt{3}\beta_-) - 1]$. We have

$V \geq 0$, and $V = 1 - \frac{2}{3}{}^{(3)}Re^{2\alpha}$, where ${}^{(3)}R$ is the curvature scalar of the 3-sphere. Equipotentials of $V(\beta_+, \beta_-)$ are shown in Figure H.1.

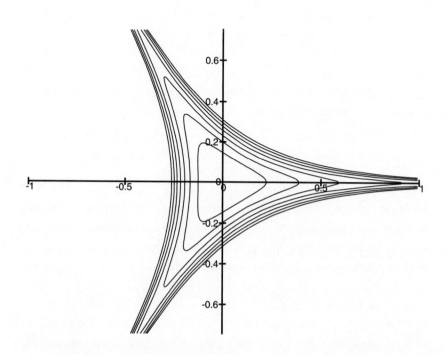

FIGURE H.1: *Equipotentials of* $V(\beta_+, \beta_-)$. *The potential is symmetric under 120° rotations in the* β_+, β_- *plane. The global minimum is* $V(0,0) = 0$. *If* $V < 1$, *the contours are closed. The contours with* $V \geq 1$ *are asymptomatic to the lines* $\beta_- = 0$ *and* $\sqrt{3}\beta_+ \pm \beta_- = 0$. *Motion along any of the three channels defined by these lines defines a Taub universe (spatially, an oblate spheroid) and allows the shear energy to diverge and light to circumnavigate in the channel derivc-tion. Motion perpendicular to the equipotential is said to "bounce off a wall" because in these directions* $V(\beta_+, \beta_-)$ *rises exponentially fast. Life must use the chaos in the bounces to force the motion into a channel run.*

2. The Heat Death Overcome:
Free Energy from Shear Energy

Since each bit irreversibly [17,18] *stored* requires $kT \ln 2$ of free energy, the Second Law of Thermodynamics says that the total amount of information I_T processed between now and the c-boundary is

$$I_T \equiv \int_{now}^{c\text{-}boundary} \frac{dI}{dt} \, dt \leq \int_{now}^{c\text{-}boundary} \frac{dE/dt}{kT \ln 2} \, dt \qquad (H.12)$$

Since we have $t_{subj} \leq I_T$, and the rightmost integral of $(H.12)$ with lower limit zero (the beginning of proper time at the Big Bang) and upper limit t, is $\leq \Theta(t)$, where $\Theta(t)$ is the entropic time defined in Section B, we see that inequality $(H.12)$ implies an inequality between subjective time and entropic time:

$$t_{subj}(t) \leq \Theta(t)$$

Inequality $(H.12)$ does not constrain computation *per se*, just the loading of new information in a computer, and permanently recording the results of the computation. There is in fact no lower bound to the amount of free energy required to process information provided the process used is reversible [17,18]. The only time that energy must be dissipated is when information must be thrown away, which is when a program is initially read, and when the final result of a computation is recorded. To both of these processes the inequality $(H.12)$ applies, though even in these cases one could in principle record all possibilities of a string of symbols the length of the input and the output, which would obviate the necessity of throwing away any information.

However, the number of memory elements required to record all possibilities would increase exponentially with the length of the input. In order to avoid losing to thermal fluctuations the information recorded, the two states of each memory element (necessary to record one bit of information) would have to differ in energy by kT. Now the synthesis of such a memory element would require an amount of energy of order kT or greater, for the very material to construct the computer element would have to be located, and this act of locating is equivalent to an irreversible measurement requiring expenditure of energy kT, as shown by Brillouin. Thus, retaining all possibilities in memory would cost more in energy than throwing away information. In summary, inequality $(H.12)$ is an unavoidable fundamental limit to information growth near the end of time.

Since Condition II requires $I_T \to +\infty$ so that t_{subj} can also diverge to $+\infty$, we see that Condition II requires

$$\int_{now}^{c\text{-}boundary} \frac{dE/dt}{kT \ln 2}\, dt = +\infty$$

So Condition II says there must exist an energy source of sufficient growth rate to allow this divergence.

In the far future, the dominant energy source is [6] shear energy density $\rho_{shear} \equiv \dot{\beta}_+^2 + \dot{\beta}_-^2$. It is called an "energy density" because it enters the constraint equation $(H.10)$ just like the usual energy density ρ. The shear energy density is maximized if the metric $(H.7)$ is the Taub model with $\dot{\beta}_- = \ddot{\beta}_- = \partial V/\partial \beta_-|_{\beta_-=0} = 0$. For $\beta_+ \gg 0$, the Taub model is approximated by extreme Kasner $ds^2 = -dt^2 + dx^2 + dy^2 + t^2 dz^2$, with $\beta_1 = \beta_2 = -\frac{1}{3}\ln t$, $\beta_3 = \frac{2}{3}\ln t$ and $\alpha = \frac{1}{3}\ln t$. Thus when $\beta_+ \gg 0$, the shear energy density increases near the final singularity as $\frac{2}{3t^2} = \frac{2}{3(e^\alpha)^6}$. It can be shown that *if* the universe moves immediately from motion in one channel of $V(\beta_+, \beta_-)$ to another, this will be the average rate of increase of shear energy density. So the total shear energy increases on average as $E \sim (e^\alpha)^{-6} \times (e^\alpha)^3 \sim (e^\alpha)^{-3} = t^{-1}$, so $dE/dt \sim t^{-2}$, and the temperature increases as $(e^\alpha)^{-1} = t^{-\frac{1}{3}}$. Hence the rightmost integral in $(H.12)$ diverges as $t^{-\frac{2}{3}}$ near the final singularity at $t = 0$; it is possible for there to be an infinite amount of information processed in a finite amount of proper time. Since the average radius of the universe $R \sim e^\alpha$, we have $ER \sim R^{-2}$, showing that both Bekenstein Bounds $(C.1)$ and $(C.4)$ diverge as $R \to 0$; the Bekenstein Bounds are not a barrier to life existing forever in a closed universe.

I have tacitly assumed in the above that the shear energy density is in fact available energy. Let me now prove this. I mentioned in Chapter IV that the ultimate source of free energy is the temperature difference due to differential collapse of the universe. The directional dependence of the temperature is given (for small optical depths—the situation near the final singularity—and for the case that the surface of last scattering is isotropic—the situation between now and the time when the universal temperature is several eV) by the Thorne-Misner formula [20]:

$$T(\vec{n}) = \left(\frac{T_0}{e^\alpha}\right)\left[\sum_{i,j=1}^{3} n^i\, (e^{2\beta})_{ij}\, n^j\right]^{-\frac{1}{2}}$$

where n^i is a unit vector in the spatial direction the temperature is measured, and T_0/e^α is the temperature averaged over all directions. I have put in a factor

e^{α} to indicate that this average temperature scales inversely with the average radius e^{α} of the universe; T_0 is a constant. Thus in the diagonal Taub case, the ratio of the maximum temperature T_{max} to the minimum temperature T_{min} is

$$\frac{T_{max}}{T_{min}} = \left[\frac{e^{2\beta_1}}{e^{2\beta_3}}\right]^{\frac{1}{2}} = \left(\frac{t^{-\frac{2}{3}}}{t^{\frac{4}{3}}}\right)^{\frac{1}{2}} = \frac{1}{t} = \frac{1}{(e^{\alpha})^3}$$

Similarly, $T_{max}/(T_0/e^{\alpha}) \sim e^{-\beta_3} \sim t^{-\frac{2}{3}} \sim 1/(e^{\alpha})^2$. Since the Carnot efficiency is proportional to $(1 - T_{min}/T_{max})$, the available energy is proportional to

$$\left(1 - \frac{T_{min}}{T_{max}}\right)\left(\frac{T_{max}}{T_0/e^{\alpha}}\right)^4 (e^{\alpha})^2 (e^{\alpha})^3$$

where the last two factors are a geometrical factor inserted because radiation is extracted from a *surface*, and the volume, respectively.

For the extreme Kasner metric, we thus have $(e^{\alpha})^{-3} \sim t^{-1}$ for the amount of available energy, and hence $dE/dt \sim t^{-2}$, *exactly* the rate of growth of shear energy.

The above calculations assume that I is processed over the entire universe. I shall show later in this section that there will be insufficient energy if $J^-(\gamma) \cap S(t)$ decreases as fast near the final singularity as it does in a radiation-dominated Friedmann universe. Furthermore, as I showed earlier in this section, the total number of circumnavigations of light in a Friedmann universe is $\leq (3\gamma - 2)^{-1}$. Misner has shown [19, 20] that light can circumnavigate the universe once in a Taub model in the β_3 direction if the total volume changes by a factor of at least $e^{4\pi}$; thus *if* the universe evolution moves immediately from one channel of $V(\beta_+, \beta_-)$ to another, light will be able to circumnavigate the universe in all directions with a volume change of $e^{12\pi} = 2.4 \times 10^{16}$. For this amount of volume change to occur between now and the time after maximum expansion when the average cosmic temperature is less than 10^{-2} eV, (assuming that this future temperature occurs when the scale factor is the same value it was when the universe had this temperature in the early universe), we must have $\Omega_0 - 1 \approx 3.5 \times 10^{-6}$; this implies a time to maximum expansion $\approx 10^{18}$ yrs. If the cosmic temperature reaches 10^{-2} eV when the future scale factor is about the same value as it is now, then $\Omega_0 - 1 \approx 3.5 \times 10^{-4}$. If the time to maximum expansion were significantly greater than 10^{18} yrs, then as shown in Chapter II, the stars would have died out, the galaxies would be too far away from one another to see in the absence of stars, and life would thus have great difficulty engulfing the universe. The universe would in fact be too close to flatness for life to survive until the shear energy is available in the collapsing phase. So the universe must be closed with

$$3.5 \times 10^{-4} \leq \Omega_0 - 1 \leq 3.5 \times 10^{-6}$$

The universe must be close to isotropy at maximum expansion [21], and it will take time for life to have expanded sufficiently far to force the universe in a channel, so all three circumnavigations must occur after maximum expansion.

For both horizon disappearance and sufficient energy, life must force the universe to move directly from one channel of $V(\beta_+, \beta_-)$ to another. This type of evolution is unlikely to happen naturally [22], as I pointed out in Section F, but Barrow and others have shown [23] that the Bianchi type IX models are chaotic. More precisely, they have shown that the channel run evolution is chaotic. In order for horizon disappearance and for the Higgs vacuum energy to be dominant (as discussed below), it will be necessary to guide the universe repeatedly into channels, and it is necessary that bounces off the potential walls also be chaotic. It is not known if such bounces are chaotic or stable (J. D. Barrow, private communication); I predict they are chaotic.

It has been demonstrated both theoretically [24] and experimentally [25] that it is possible to direct a chaotic system from any initial state into any chosen improbable state, using only small perturbations to an accessible system parameter. In cosmology, these parameters are the stress–energy tensor components.

Since I predict $3.5 \times 10^{-4} \leq \Omega_0 - 1 \leq 3.5 \times 10^{-6}$, and since both chemical evolution and stellar evolution data [26] imply a universe age $t_{now} \geq 12 \times 10^9$ yrs (with $t_{now} \geq 15 \times 10^9$ yrs being more probable), I predict $H_0 \leq 55$ km/sec-mpc, and probably $H_0 \leq 45$ km/sec-mpc [27]. The Hubble Space Telescope is designed to measure proper distances out to the Virgo Cluster, which has a redshift $z = 0.004$. If this redshift reaches beyond local structures into the Hubble flow, then the HST will be able to test my prediction.

Furthermore, the absence of event horizons—a requirement for sufficient energy for information processing and also for unlimited communication—implies that the future c-boundary must be a single point—the omega point—as I discussed in Chapter IV. In Section F, I showed that a single point c-boundary implied compact Cauchy surfaces if the chronology condition holds. This does not mean that the Cauchy surfaces have to have topology S^3. However, Barrow and I have shown [21] that unless the weak energy condition is violated or $\Lambda < 0$, a non-S^3 closed universe will not recollapse. Since sufficient energy for I_T divergence requires recollapse, this means that the Cauchy surfaces must in fact be S^3.

3. Experimental Tests:

The Top Quark Mass and the Higgs Boson Mass Predictions

This omega point resolution of the flatness problem is Misner's Mixmaster [19] resolution transferred from the early universe to the far future universe. I shall now show that it also requires Guth's inflation mechanism [28] to be similarly transferred.

Since $T \to +\infty$ as $R \to 0$, information eventually will have to be stored in some way not based on atomic systems, which become useless once $T > 1 - 10$ eV. If information is stored globally, using the universe itself as the "box" wherein the information is contained, the energy states coding the information will automatically scale as the universe, making a further change of substrate unnecessary until possibly the Planck time. (Information could be stored in traveling waves over the universe; this would be a form of delay line storage [29].) However, in order for this storage mechanism to be feasible, many circumnavigations of light would have to occur during which the temperature change was small. This is impossible via the Misner mechanism, which requires a large volume and hence temperature change. As I emphasized a few paragraphs above, if the ratio V_{max}/V_T of the volume of the universe at maximum expansion to the volume when the temperature is $T \sim 10^{-2}$ eV satisfies $V_{max}/V_T \gg e^{12\pi}$, the universe will be too close to the flat model, and life will die out. The only known mechanism that could stop the contraction is the positive cosmological constant Λ that must exist (if the standard model is correct) to cancel the current negative energy density of the Higgs field; we must have at tree level $\Lambda - \frac{1}{8}m_H^2 v^2 = 0$, where $v = 246$ GeV, and m_H is the Higgs mass. The early universe Weinberg-Salam phase transition cannot have any significant gravitational effect [30,31] at $T \sim 100$ GeV because the energy density of the radiation is much greater than Λ at this temperature, but I shall argue that there is a dynamical effect in Bianchi type IX models that acts only in the universal contracting phase which can halt the contraction — provided the Higgs mass is sufficiently large.

In the coordinate system (H.7), the field equation for the Higgs field ϕ is [32]

$$\ddot{\phi} + 3\dot{\alpha}\dot{\phi} + \partial U(\phi,\dot{\beta}_+,\dot{\beta}_-)/\partial\phi = 0 \qquad (H.13)$$

where [33,34] U the tree level effective Higgs potential given by

$$U(\phi, \dot{\beta}_+,\dot{\beta}_-) = \frac{1}{2}[(-m_H^2 + \frac{1}{6}(\dot{\beta}_+^2 + \dot{\beta}_-^2))\,\phi^\dagger\phi + (m_H/v)^2(\phi^\dagger\phi)^2] + \Lambda \qquad (H.14)$$

since Futamase [33] and Chen and Hu [34] have shown that even on the classical level there is a shear term [35] in the effective potential of the form $U_{sh}(\phi, \dot{\beta}_+,\dot{\beta}_-) \equiv \frac{1}{12}(\dot{\beta}_+^2 + \dot{\beta}_-^2)\,\phi^2$, and I have added this term to the one-loop effective potential. Rothman and G. F. R. Ellis [35] argue that with β_{ij} traceless, no term in (H.14) will contain $\beta_\pm$ or their time derivatives. However, Futamase and Chen and Hu include such a term (as I do) because our equation takes into account the coupling of the nonscalar fields present via gravity to the Higgs field; see [36,37]. Other vacuum energy terms exist, e.g., the QCD vacuum term, and high temperature correction terms, but at low T these are essentially zero or constant since they do not couple to curvature, and can be absorbed into Λ. (This of course assumes that no other Higgs fields, like those of minimal SUSY, exist.)

In the expanding universe, the $3\dot{\alpha}\dot{\phi}$ term is a damping term (since $\dot{\alpha} > 0$) which retards state changes, but in the contracting phase, it is an *anti-damping* term, which allows one to show, using (H.8)–(H.11) & (H.13), that in a channel run U can be increased from its minimum value at $\frac{v}{\sqrt{2}}$ sufficiently so that Λ dominates the radiation, matter, and shear energy densities [37] when the average temperature is $T = 10^{-2}$ eV. More precisely, an order of magnitude estimate for ΔU during a channel run from the time of maximum expansion to the time when the average temperature is $T = 10^{-2}$ eV shows that we can have $\Delta U \sim \Lambda = \frac{1}{8}m^2_H v^2$. The temperature $T = 10^{-2}$ eV is a factor of 10^{13} below the phase transition temperature in the early universe. This huge factor shows, as I stated earlier, that the temperature dependent terms can be neglected.

It is not possible for the universe to become static at the $T \sim 10^{-2}$ eV bounce. Setting equal to zero all time derivatives in (H.8)—(H.11), and assuming T_{ab} consists of dust, anisotropic radiation, and Λ gives $\rho_d + 2\rho_r = 2\Lambda$ and $\frac{4}{5}$

$\leq e^{3\beta_3} \leq 1$, with the lower bound attained only if $\rho_d = 0$ and no radiation in the σ_3 direction. Also, since $\frac{T_1}{T_3} = (e^{3\beta_3})^{\frac{1}{2}}$ is the directional temperature ratio [20], the Carnot efficiency of energy extraction would only be 10%. So the universe must go through a series of pulsations about $T \sim 10^{-2}$ eV, with entropy increase in each cycle. Circumnavigations will be maximized by maximizing the cycle number.

The only possibility is for there to be a series of pulsations of the universe at a temperature around 10^{-2}, before normal matter ceases to be useful for information storage. The only mechanism in known physics that could generate such a series of pulsations is the standard model Higgs field, via the above mechanism. The number of pulsations will be maximized—and hence the number of circumnavigations will be maximized—if the Higgs mass is maximized and if the amount of entropy generated in the early universe phase transition is minimized.

This follows from the work of Sher [38], Guth and Sher [39], Petrosian [40] and Bludman [30], who have shown that if the energy released when the Higgs energy density goes from $U(\phi = 0) = 0$ to $U(\phi = \frac{v}{\sqrt{2}}) = -\frac{1}{8} m^2{}_H v^2$ is mostly thermalized—which it will be if the transition is first order—then the Second Law of Thermodynamics will prevent a bounce at $T \sim 100$ GeV. This suggests that my proposed Higgs pulsation process will have a maximum effect only if the Weinberg-Salam phase transition is second order, or as weakly first order as possible so that the phase transition entropy is minimized.

Kirzhnits and Linde [41] (see also [42, 43]) have shown that maximizing the Higgs mass maximizes the weakness of the phase transition. Ellis et al. [44,45] have computed the two-loop renormalization group corrected effective Higgs potential and have shown that (provided the standard model is perturbatively valid up to 10^{15} GeV) the vacuum remains stable for 10^{18} yrs and $U(\frac{v}{\sqrt{2}})$ is a *global* minimum—that is, the Higgs vacuum is stable—only if the Higgs boson and top quark masses are inside the curves shown in Figure H.2.

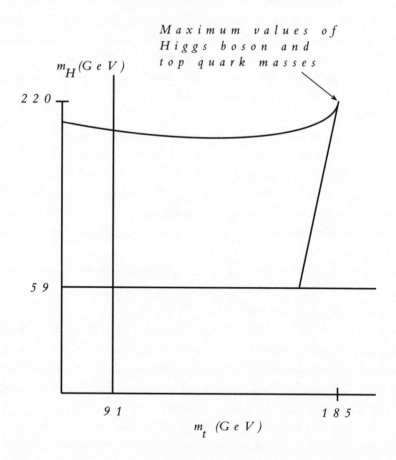

FIGURE H.2 *Graph of the allowed values of the Higgs and top quark masses, using the two-loop renormalization group corrected effective standard model Higgs potential, assuming that perturbation theory is valid to 10^{19} GeV. Figure adapted from references [44–46]. The intersection point of the limit curves is shown, giving $m_H = 220$ GeV, and $m_t = 185$ GeV. The experimental lower limits ($m_H > 59$ GeV and $m_t > 91$ GeV) are also illustrated ($m_t > 91$ GeV was the lower bound in August 1992 when my first preprint predicting the top mass went out. The current lower bound is around 110 GeV.)*

Figure H.2 shows that the Higgs mass is maximized for $m_H = 220$ GeV, and $m_t = 185$ GeV. Cabibbo et al. [46] computed a one-loop renormalization group corrected effective potential, and obtained a very similar curve with maximum Higgs mass $m_H = 220$ GeV, and $m_t = 200$ GeV. I shall thus take the

Ellis et al. numbers as the best estimates, but choose errors equal to the difference between the top quark masses so as to take into account the effect of higher order corrections, and the raising of the upper limit of the Standard Model to 10^{19} GeV. (With $m_H = 220$ GeV, the phase transition could well be second order [41,47,48]. Since the mechanism described above would work best if it were, I conjecture that it is.)

The Feynman Diagrams for the main production reactions for a Higgs of this mass are presented in Figures H.3 and H.4 for the hadron and electron-positron colliders respectively.

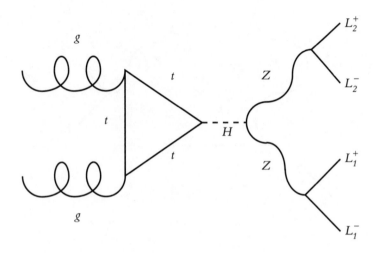

FIGURE H.3 *The Feynman Diagram for the primary production mode of the Higgs boson in a hadron collider: gluon-gluon (gg) fusion via a triangle of top quarks (t). The Higgs (H) decays into a pair of Z bosons, which in turn decay into a pair of charged leptons ($L_i^{\pm}$), either electrons or muons (this decay mode is not the most probable, but it is the cleanest Higgs decay signature: the "gold plated mode.").*

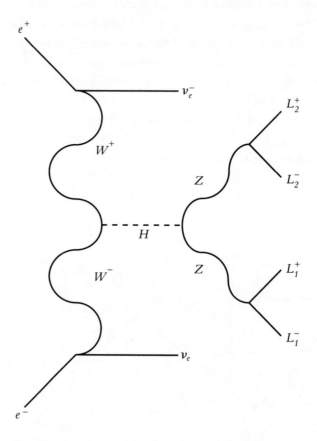

FIGURE H.4 *The Feynman Diagram for the primary production mode of the Higgs boson in an electron positron collider, namely WW-fusion: the electron and positron each emit a W boson thereby becoming a neutrino v_e^- or antineutrino $v_{\bar{e}}^-$, and the two W's combine to form the Higgs, which then decays via the gold plated mode. To produce a significant number of Higgs bosons of mass 220 GeV, one needs [64] a collider with $\sqrt{s} \simeq 500$ GeV; LEP II with $\sqrt{s} \simeq 200$ GeV will be unable to detect the Higgs. Thus, no such machine with sufficient energy to produce the Higgs is either under construction or even proposed, but studies for such a machine are presently underway.*

I shall outline the Cabbibo et al. analysis to show why vacuum stability implies an upper bound to the top quark and Higgs boson masses. Let g_1 be the coupling strength of the $U(1)$ gauge field, g_2 be the coupling strength of the $SU(2)$ field, and g_3 the coupling strength of the $SU(3)$ field. The top quark Yukawa coupling will be written $g_t = \sqrt{2}m_t/v$, where m_t is the top quark mass and $v = \langle \phi \rangle$ is the Higgs field vacuum expectation value. The tree level Higgs scalar potential without the β and Λ terms is

$$U(\phi) = -\mu^2 \phi^\dagger \phi + \lambda(\phi^\dagger \phi)^2 \qquad (H.15)$$

At tree level we have for the Higgs mass m_H

$$m_H = \sqrt{2\lambda} v \qquad (H.16)$$

The renormalization group equations control the change of the coupling constants with energy. At one loop the renormalization group equations for the gauge field couplings are

$$\frac{d}{dQ} g_1^2 = \frac{41}{96\pi^2} g_1^4$$

$$\frac{d}{dQ} g_2^2 = -\frac{19}{96\pi^2} g_2^4 \qquad (H.17)$$

$$\frac{d}{dQ} g_3^2 = -\frac{7}{16\pi^2} g_3^4$$

where I have assumed that the number of generations is 3 and the number of complex scalars is 1, and where $Q = \ln(E^2/E_0^2)$, for some energy scales E and E_0.

The renormalization group equations at one loop for the top quark Yukawa coupling and the Higgs field self-coupling λ are respectively

$$\frac{d}{dQ} g_t = \frac{1}{16\pi^2} \left[\frac{9}{4} g_t^3 - 4g_3^2 g_t - \frac{9}{8} g_2^2 g_t - \frac{17}{24} g_1^2 g_t \right] \qquad (H.18)$$

$$\frac{d}{dQ} \lambda = \frac{1}{16\pi^2} \left[12\lambda^2 + 6\lambda g_t^2 - 3g_t^4 - \frac{3}{2}\lambda(g_1^2 + 3g_2^2) + \frac{3}{16}\{2g_2^4 + (g_1^2 + g_2^2)^2\} \right] \qquad (H.19)$$

Equations $(H.17)$–$(H.19)$ imply that there is an upper bound to the Higgs boson and top quark masses. To see why this is so, let us assume that the top and Higgs masses are very small compared with v. This implies λ is very small, so the terms in λ can be neglected in equation $(H.19)$, giving

$$\frac{d}{dQ} \lambda = \beta_\lambda \qquad (H.20)$$

where

$$\beta_\lambda = \frac{1}{16\pi^2}\left[-3g_t^4 + \frac{3}{16}(2g_2^4 + (g_1^2 + g_2^2)^2)\right] \qquad (H.21)$$

is (approximately) a constant. Integrating (H.20) up to energy scales of order ϕ itself gives

$$\lambda(\phi) = \lambda(E_0) + \beta_\lambda \ln (\phi^\dagger \phi / E_0^2) \qquad (H.22)$$

Putting (H.22) into (H.15) gives the one-loop Higgs scalar potential (defining $\phi^\dagger \phi \equiv \phi^2$)

$$U(\phi) = -\mu^2 \phi^2 + \lambda \phi^4 + \beta_\lambda \phi^4 \ln(\phi^2 / E_0^2) \qquad (H.23)$$

For vacuum stability, the highest order term in the scalar potential must have positive coefficient. At tree level, this is assured by having $\lambda > 0$. However, at one loop level, the term with the logarithm is the highest order term at high energy, so the vacuum will be stable only if

$$\beta_\lambda > 0 \qquad (H.24)$$

Since $m_W = \frac{1}{2}g_2 v$ and $m_Z = \frac{1}{2}\sqrt{g_1^2 + g_2^2}\, v$, where m_W and m_Z are respectively the W-boson and Z-boson masses respectively, equation (H.24) can be written (using $g_t = \sqrt{2}m_t/v$):

$$2m_W^4 + m_Z^4 - 4m_t^4 > 0 \qquad (H.25)$$

which means the top mass must have a mass less than 78 GeV.

We know of course that the top mass is greater than this, which means that our assumption that the Higgs and top masses are small is false. If this assumption is not true, then we cannot ignore the nonlinear terms in equations (H.17)–(H.19), and we cannot assume that the other couplings are essentially constant when we vary the energy. Cabbibo et. al. thus integrated (H.17)–(H.19) numerically and showed that upper bounds to both the top quark and Higgs boson masses exist if vacuum stability is to hold up to the Planck energy. These values are $m_t = 185 \pm 20$ Gev and $m_H = 220 \pm 20$ GeV, as quoted above.

Since the Higgs field will be reduced when information is coded in normal matter, this will reduce all masses, and we must check that this will not affect the working of computers.

Neglecting the kinetic energies of the nuclei, the Hamiltonian for a general atomic system is $\hat{H} = -\frac{\hbar^2}{2m_e}\sum_i(\partial/\partial\vec{x}_i)\cdot(\partial/\partial\vec{x}_i) + e^2[\sum_i\sum_j - Z_j/|\vec{x}_i - \vec{R}_j| + \frac{1}{2}\sum_{i<j} 1/|\vec{x}_i - \vec{x}_j| + \frac{1}{2}\sum_{j<l} - Z_jZ_l/|\vec{R}_j - \vec{R}_l|]$, where $\vec{x}_i$ is the position vector of the ith electron, and $\vec{R}_j$ is the position vector of the jth nucleus. If we transform to new variables $\vec{x}_i' = \vec{x}_i/a_0, \vec{R}_j' = \vec{R}_j/a_0$, where a_0 is the Bohr radius, this Hamiltonian is $\hat{H} = \alpha^2 m_e c^2[-\frac{1}{2}\sum_i(\partial/\partial\vec{x}_i')\cdot(\partial/\partial\vec{x}_i') + \sum_i\sum_j - Z_j/|\vec{x}_i' - \vec{R}_j'| + \frac{1}{2}\sum_{i<j} 1/|\vec{x}_i' - \vec{x}_j'| + \frac{1}{2}\sum_{j<l} - Z_jZ_l/|\vec{R}_j' - \vec{R}_l'|]$ Thus, if $\tilde{E}$ is the eigenstate energy when α and m_e are changed to $\tilde{\alpha}$ and $\tilde{m}_e$ respectively, we have $\tilde{E}/\tilde{\alpha}^2\tilde{m}_e = E/\alpha^2 m_e$, where E is the original eigenstate energy. When the Higgs field $\phi(t)$ returns to zero, the nuclei masses will remain unchanged since the quark current algebra masses are small relative to their constituent masses, but the electron masses are $m_e = g_e\phi(t)/\sqrt{2}$, and so neglecting the nuclei kinetic energies should become even more accurate.

In general we have $\tilde{E} = E[\phi(t)/v]$, $\tilde{x}_i = x_i[v/\phi(t)]$ and $\tilde{R}_i = R_i[v/\phi(t)]$ (the length scalings are most easily obtained from the Bohr atom). Thus as $\phi \to 0$, the eigenenergies go to zero, and the sizes of the atomic systems go to infinity, but all relative internal system energies and all relative sizes (e.g., $\tilde{x}_i/\tilde{x}_j$, $\tilde{x}_i/\tilde{R}_j$, $\tilde{R}_i/\tilde{R}_j$) remain the same. Hence computers based on atomic systems will remain intact and functioning normally during the transition (though reactions requiring movement of entire atoms will need more atomic bonds to be broken to supply the energy), provided the computers are in space and operating near the cosmic background temperature. (Since nuclei masses are essentially unchanged during the transition, the total mass of the computer will remain the same, but the binding energy of the computer structure goes to zero. The computer would crumble in a planetary gravity field. Since $\tilde{E}_i/kT \to 0$, thermal energies will become larger relative to binding and interaction energies; a low operating temperature is essential.)

The latest LEP data put the Higgs mass $m_H \geq 59.3$ GeV (95% confidence) [49], and the latest Tevatron data put the top quark mass $m_t \geq 91$ GeV (95% confidence) [50]. The latest LEP data [51] indicate the top mass is probably $m_t = 150^{+20,+16}_{-23,-19}$ GeV (1σ errors), where the first uncertainty is experimental, and the second theoretical. My predicted top mass range is within 1σ of the LEP data. Since the cross-section for $t\bar{t}$ production in the 1.8 TeV Tevatron with $m_t = 185$ GeV is between 2 and 4 pb [52], I predict that the 1992–93 Tevatron run with an integrated luminosity of 100 pb^{-1} is rather unlikely to discover the top quark (when branching ratios and detection efficiencies are taken into account [53]). But the Tevatron will discover the top quark when the new main injector is installed. Since a top quark of mass 185 GeV will result in Higgs production by hadron colliders being dominated by gluon-gluon (gg) fusion with σ_{tot} ($gg \rightarrow H$) $\simeq 30-40$ pb if $\sqrt{s} = 17$ TeV [54, pp. 163 (figs. 3.32 and 3.33) and 172], I predict that the LHC should easily be able to discover the Higgs via the gold-plated mode ($H \rightarrow ZZ \rightarrow L_1^+ \, L_1^- \, L_2^+ \, L_2^-$, $L = e$ or μ) even if the LHC has the *lower* luminosity of 10^{33} cm^{-2} sec^{-1}, rather than the planned luminosity of 5×10^{34} cm^{-2} sec^{-1}. If $m_H = 220$ GeV, then almost all Higgs decays are $H \rightarrow ZZ$ or $H \rightarrow W^+W^-$, so with phase space corrections [54, p. 23] the total Higgs width Γ_H is 2.1 GeV, or about 1% of the Higgs mass. Also, $\frac{\Gamma(H \rightarrow Z_T Z_T)}{\Gamma(H \rightarrow Z_L Z_L)} = 0.55$, where $Z_T(Z_L)$ are transversely (longitudinally) polarized Z bosons; this amount of longitudinal dominance could be tested.

It is instructive to compare my predictions for the top quark and Higgs boson masses with those obtained by other approaches.

There are two other theories which predict the same top quark masses as the Omega Point Theory: (1) a theory [55] based on SO(10) SUSY GUT, developed by Dimopoulos, Hall, and Raby, and a theory [56] defended by the Fermilab physicists Bardeen, Hill, and Lindner, which assumes that the Higgs boson is not a fundamental particle at all, but rather a $<\bar{t}t>$ condensate, bound together by a new force beyond the Standard Model. Thus both of these other theories require physics beyond the Standard Model of particle physics to obtain their prediction, whereas the Omega Point Theory does not. Furthermore, although both of these theories predict the same top quark mass as the Omega Point Theory, they either do not restrict the Higgs mass at all (the SO(10) SUSY GUT model) or give a different value (the $<\bar{t}t>$ condensate model). So the way to distinguish the Omega Point Theory from these competitor theories is to look for the Higgs boson.

It is essential that a universal nonvanishing Higgs field actually exist. If mass is generated by some other mechanism, a repulsive force which can eliminate horizons with small temperature change will not exist, and life will die out. In principle, this repulsive force will also make its presence felt at the Weinberg-Salam phase transition, and hence could be detected in a hadron collider such as the LHC, if the force exists. In fact, both the RHIC at Brookhaven and the LHC will be used to probe the QCD phase transition at T = 300 MeV [59]. Unfortunately, the Weinberg-Salam phase transition is higher in temperature by three orders of magnitude, and as the energy density scales as T^4, probing the Weinberg-Salam phase transition would require an increase of $\sqrt{s}$ of 10^{12} above the LHC energies.

The CERN physicist John Ellis [57] has recently emphasized that models suggested by superstrings yield central values of $m_t = 124^{+26}_{-28}$ GeV, with an upper bound of about 190 GeV. The Minimal Supersymmetric Model (MSSM) gives [57] a similar prediction of $m_t = 138^{+20}_{-23}$ GeV.

There are to date two possible top quark events from the CDF detector at the Tevatron. The first, from the 1988–89 collider run, would imply [58] a top quark mass of $m_t = 132^{+32}_{-11}$ GeV. The second, obtained 31 October 1992 and pictured in Chapter IV as Figure IV.10, would imply [58] a much more massive top quark, around 180 GeV. The first event would tend to confirm the "superstring" and/or the MSSM top quark mass prediction, while the latter would tend to confirm my prediction, the SO(10) SUSY GUT prediction, and the $<\bar{t}t>$ condensate prediction. If the first event was real, then we should definitely see other top events by the end of the current Tevatron collider run in 1994. In which case the theory presented in this book is in serious trouble.

Once the temperatures go above 10 eV, the information will be stored as excited states in the "universe box." It is easy to show [6] that, in order for the amount of information stored in these states to diverge as the final singularity is approached, the density of particle states must diverge as the energy diverges (since otherwise the stored information would be erased by thermal fluctuations), but no faster than E^3, otherwise all the shear energy would go into filling the states below E, and there would be no free energy left for information processing.

More precisely, the restriction that the mass of the elementary particle states be greater than the thermal energy is expressed as

$$m > kT \sim \frac{1}{R(t)} \qquad (H.26)$$

(where I have written the average radius e^α as $R(t)$), while the requirement that the energy in the particle states be less than the shear energy can be written in the form of a restriction on energy densities:

$$Nm/V < \rho^2 \sim 1/t^2 \sim 1/R^6 \qquad (H.27)$$

where I have used the growth rate of the shear energy density in the last two steps, and N is the total number of particle states of mass m. Now $V \sim R^3$, so (H.27) becomes

$$Nm/V \geq N(1/R)/R^3 \sim N/t^{4/3} \qquad (H.28)$$

so the total number of particle states could grow as fast as $1/t^{2/3}$ without violating the energy upper bound. The total stored information I_T we would expect to grow roughly as N, so I_T can diverge as fast as $1/t^{2/3}$ if the growth of particle states with energy permits. But the energy in the particle states cannot grow faster than this without exhausting the energy supply. Suppose we write $N \sim t^{-\epsilon}$, where $0 < \epsilon < 2/3$. Remembering that almost all of the time $R(t) \sim t^{1/3}$ near the final singularity (corner run; extreme Taub/Kasner), we obtain from (H.28)

$$m < V/Nt^2 \sim 1/Nt \sim t^{\epsilon - 1} \tag{H.29}$$

The inequalities (H.26) and (H.29) can be combined to give the constraint on the mass-energy of the particles:

$$1/t^{1/3} < m < t^{\epsilon - 1} \tag{H.30}$$

We can put the energy scales into (H.30) by noting that $1/t^{1/3} \sim 1/R(t) \sim kT \sim E$, where E is the actual particle energy measured in GeV. The inequality (H.30) then becomes

$$E < m < E^{3(1 - \epsilon)} \tag{H.31}$$

where $0 < \epsilon < 2/3$. The final inequality (H.31) means that if Condition III is to be satisfied, there must be a particle state with energy in between the upper and lower limits of (H.31). Furthermore, on the average the number of particle states cannot grow faster than E^3, since otherwise the shear would be damped out by the production of particle states.

In Dyson's open universe model [5], waste heat elimination was a major difficulty facing life in the far future. As I have discussed in Chapter III, Dyson concluded that life was restricted to a constant comoving volume, and hence heat was eliminated by radiation to the exterior of the comoving volume.

Radiating waste heat to an exterior region is absolutely impossible in a closed universe which has been completely engulfed by the biosphere, because in this case, there is no exterior region. Therefore, a heat sink copresent with life must be used. The obvious choice for such a heat sink is the thermal radiation background. If waste heat from information processing is dumped into the radiation background as it is generated, the energy density of the background will rise at the same rate as the energy density of the energy source, which means $E/V \sim t^{-2} \sim T^4$. This gives $T \sim t^{-1/2}$. For shear-dominated closed universes, this implies that the temperature will rise faster as the universe collapses, as $T \sim R^{-3/2}$ rather than as $T \sim R^{-1}$. If this nonadiabatic temperature variation is inserted into (H.12), we find that $\int T^{-1}(dE/dt)dt$ diverges as $t^{-1/2}$. This means that waste heat does not seem to pose a problem for unbounded information processing in a closed universe.

I have argued that event horizons cannot exist if unlimited information processing is to be possible, because such horizons would prevent communication between different parts of the biosphere, and even different parts of the same organism. One might wonder, however, if a single computer could nevertheless process an infinite amount of information in the ever-shrinking region with which it could communicate, by processing information faster than the communication region is shrinking. I now show that this is impossible: there simply is not enough available energy in the communication region.

At any cosmic time t, the region from which the observer γ can receive signals is $J^+(\gamma) \cap S(t)$. In the FRW universe, the boundary of this region is determined by the ingoing radial null geodesics satisfying $ds^2 = 0$, an equation which implies that the proper radius L of the communication region decreases as $L \sim t$ near the final singularity at $t = 0$. This means that the proper volume of the region decreases as $V \sim L^3 \sim R^6(t)$ or $R^{9/2}(t)$ for the radiation-dominated ($R(t) \sim t^{1/2}$) and matter-dominated ($R(t) \sim t^{2/3}$) FRW universes respectively. If a universe were shear-dominated ($R(t \sim t^{1/3}$) and had a c-boundary like that of the FRW universe, then $V \sim R^9(t)$. In these 3 cases, the available energy would then decrease as $R^2(t)$, $R^{3/2}$, and $R^3(t)$ respectively. Thus, horizons will prevent an infinite amount of information from being processed since equation (H.12) implies that available energy must *increase* near the final singularity if this is to happen.

Near the omega point, the optical depth will be quite small. I shall now show that it is nevertheless possible to transmit an infinite number of bits from one side of the universe to the other as the omega point is approached. I shall assume that the transmission of information in this regime is governed by the Shannon formula [60] for the transmission of information in a noisy channel: $dI/dt \leq B\ln(1 + P_S/P_N)$, where B is the bandwidth of the signal, P_S is the power of the signal, and P_N is the power of the noise. For small signal to noise ratios, the Shannon formula reduces to

$$\frac{dI}{dt} \leq \frac{BP_S}{P_N} = \frac{P_S}{kT} = \frac{(dE/dt)_S}{kT} \qquad (H.32)$$

where in the last step but one I have used the Nyquist relation $P_N = BkT$ [61]. The rightmost quantity in (H.32) resembles the rightmost integrand in (H.12) , and the leftmost quantity in (H.32) the rightmost integrand in (H.12), except that in (H.12) the quantities dE/dt and T are measured at the same event, whereas it is not clear how to apply (H.32), since the temperature, signal noise and noise power are all changing between the emission and reception of the signal, due to the blueshifts and redshifts in the different directions in the collapse of the universe into the omega point. It will most often be a blueshift, because the signals will generally be transmitted in the contracting direction for which circumnavigation of the universe by signals is possible. I shall assume that these cosmological Doppler shifts are properly taken into account by letting $(dE/dt)_S$ be the power of the transmitter, while T is the temperature of the receiver; this means that the information transmission allowed by the Shannon formula is reduced further from that given by (H.12) by the factor $R(t)$, since temperature scales as $T \sim R^{-1}$. Putting in an extra factor of $R(t)$ in the evaluation of rightmost integral of (H.12), we see that $I_T = \int (dI/dt)dt$ still diverges, though at the reduced rate of $t^{-1/3}$—it diverges only as $\ln t$ if we also take into account the temperature increase due to the dumping of waste heat due to information processing and transmission—so it is definitely possible to transmit an infinite number of bits from one side of a closed universe to the other, provided the universe ends in an omega point.

One might wonder if the formation of black holes in the present epoch or earlier would preclude the existence of an omega point final singularity. If a black hole meant the existence of an event horizon, an omega point would indeed be impossible, since by definition, an omega point means there are no event horizons.

However, the defining feature of black holes is non-cosmological trapped surfaces, not event horizons [62]. Only in asymptotically flat spaces does the existence of a trapped surface imply event horizons [1]. All S^3 FRW universes which recollapse to a singularity in finite proper time have trapped surfaces in the collapsing phase. In particular, examples 2 and 3 of Section F both contain trapped surfaces, yet both models end in omega points, and hence have no horizons. Thus a "star collapsing to a black hole today" just means that the stellar collapse generates a trapped surface in the leaf of the constant mean curvature foliation which passes through us now [63]. A light trajectory outgoing from the trapped surface will not reach us until deep into the recollapse phase of the entire universe, but it will eventually reach us. The trapped surfaces from today's black holes would eventually merge with the trapped surfaces from the collapse of the universe as a whole. Neither class of trapped surface would ultimately generate event horizons.

References

[1] S. W. Hawking and G. F. R. Ellis, *The Large Scale Structure of Space—time* (Cambridge University Press, Cambridge, 1973).

[2] R. Bartnik, *Commun. Math. Phys.* **117**, 615 (1988).

[3] J. E. Marsden and F. J. Tipler, *Phys. Rep.* **66**, 109 (1980).

[4] D. T. Wilkinson, *Science* **232**, 1517 (1986). The Sun is currently moving towards the constellation Leo (R.A. 11.2 ± 0.1 hours, Dec. -7 ± 2 degrees) at about 360 km/sec with respect to this globally defined rest frame of the universe [4]. In general relativity, all frames of reference are equal, but some frames of reference are more equal than others.

[5] F. J. Dyson, *Rev. Mod Phys.* **51**, 447 (1979).

[6] F. J. Tipler, *Int. J. Theo. Phys.* **25**, 617 (1986).

[7] A. D. Linde, *Phys. Lett.* **B211**, 29 (1988).

[8] F. J. Tipler, *Phys. Lett.* **B286**, 36 (1992).

[9] A. D. Linde, *Phys. Lett.* **B227**, 352 (1989).

[10] A. D. Linde, *Particle Physics and Inflationary Cosmology* (Harwood, Chur, 1990).

[11] A. D. Linde, *Inflation and Quantum Cosmology* (Academic, Boston, 1990).

[12] F. J. Tipler, *Zygon* **24**, 217 (1989).

[13] A. D. Linde, *Nuc. Phys.* B **372**, 421 (1992).

[14] A. Vilenkin, *Phys. Rev.* D **46**, 2355 (1992).

[15] X. Lin and R. M. Wald, *Phys. Rev.* D **40**, 3280 (1989).

[16] M. P. Ryan and L. C. Shepley, *Homogeneous Relativistic Cosmologies* (Princeton University Press, Princeton, 1975).

[17] C. H. Bennett, R. Landauer, R. P. Feynman et al., *Proceedings of the International Conference on Computation*, in *Int. J. Theo. Phys.* **21**, Nos. 3/4, 6/7, and 12 (1982); C.H. Bennett, R. Landauer et al., *Phys. Rev. Lett.* **53**, 1202 (1984).

[18] R. Landauer, *Nature* **335**, 779 (1988).

[19] C. W. Misner, *Phys. Rev. Lett.* **22**, 1071 (1969).

[20] C. W. Misner, *Ap. J.* **151**, 431 (1968).

[21] J. D. Barrow and F. J. Tipler, Mon. *Not. R. Astr. Soc.* **216**, 395 (1985); F. J. Tipler, in *Proceedings of the 13th Texas Symposium on Relativistic Astrophysics*, ed. by M. P. Ulmer (World Scientific Publications, Singapore, 1987), p. 122. A more precise statement would be that a closed universe satisfying the weak energy condition, $\lambda \geq 0$, and obeying the Einstein equations will not recollapse unless its topology is

$$[S^3]_1 \ \# \ [S^3]_2 \# \ ...\# \ [S^3]_n \ \# \ k(S^2 \times S^1)$$

where $[S^3]_i$ is a manifold which is covered by a homotopy 3-sphere, "#" denotes the connected sum, and $k(S^2 \times S^1)$ means the connected sum of k copies of $(S^2 \times S^1)$.

[22] E. M. Lifshitz, I. M. Lifshitz, and I. M. Khalatnikov, *Sov. Phys. JETP* **32**, 173 (1971); A. G. Doroshkevich and I. D. Novikov, *Sov. Astron. AJ* **14**, 763 (1971); A. G. Doroshkevich, V. N. Lukash, and I. D. Novikov, *Sov. Phys. JETP* **33**, 649 (1971).

[23] J. D. Barrow, *Phys. Rep.* **85**, 1 (1982).

[24] T. Shinbrot, E. Ott, C. Grebogi, and J. A. Yorke, *Phys. Rev. Lett.* **65**, 3215 (1990).

[25] T. Shinbrot, W. Ditto, C. Grebogi, E. Ott, M. Spano, and J. A. Yorke, *Phys. Rev. Lett.* **68**, 2863 (1992).

[26] G. Börner, *The Early Universe* (Springer, Berlin, 1988), pp. 33–43.

[27] A. Sandage, A. Saha, G. Tammann, N. Panagia, and F. D. Macchetto, *Ap. J. Lett.* **401**, L7 (1992) have obtained $H_0 = 51 \pm 9$ km/sec-mpc. However, at present most cosmologists opt for $H_0 = 95$ km/sec-mpc. Such a high value would rule out the Omega Point Theory, since it would imply $t_{now} \leq 7.0 \times 10^9$ yrs, if $\Omega_0 > 1$.

[28] A. H. Guth, *Phys. Rev.* **D 23**, 347 (1981).

[29] W. C. House, editor, *Laser Beam Information Systems* (Petrocelli Books, New York, 1978); Sanjay Ranade, *Mass Storage Technologies* (Meckler, Westport, CT, 1991); S. Middelhoek, P. K. George, and P. Dekker, *Physics of Computer Memory Devices* (Academic Press, New York, 1976).

[30] S. A. Bludman, *Nature* **308**, 319 (1984).

[31] S. Weinberg, *Rev. Mod. Phys.* **61**, 1 (1989).

[32] T. Futamase, T. Rothman, and R. Matzner, *Phys. Rev.* **D39**, 405 (1989).

[33] T. Futamase, *Phys. Rev.* **D29**, 2783 (1984).

[34] L. F. Chen and B. L. Hu, *Phys. Lett.* **B160**, 36 (1985). The $\beta^2\phi^2$ term is obtained only for Bianchi type I models in [37] and [38], but type IX gives the same result (B. L. Hu, private communication).

[35] T. Rothman and G. F. R. Ellis, *Phys. Lett.* **B180**, 19 (1986).

[36] W.-H. Huang, *Class. Quantum Grav.* **8**, 83 (1991).

[37] R. Critchley and J. S. Dowker, *J. Phys.* **A14**, 1943 (1981).

[38] M. Sher, *Phys. Rev.* **D22**, 2989 (1980).

[39] A. H. Guth and M. Sher, *Nature* **302**, 505 (1983).

[40] V. Petrosian, *Nature* **298**, 805 (1982).

[41] D. A. Kirzhnits and A D. Linde, *Ann. Phys.* **101**, 195 (1976). Their condition $\lambda \ll g^2 \sim g_1^2 + g_2^2$ ($\leftrightarrow m_H \ll 260$ GeV), is violated, so a second order transition is possible.

[42] N. Turok, *Phys. Rev. Lett.* **68**, 1803 (1992).

[43] N. Turok and J. Zadrozny, *Nucl. Phys.* **B369**, 729 (1992).

[44] J. Ellis, A. D. Linde, M. Sher, *Phys. Lett.* **B252**, 203 (1990).

[45] M. Sher, *Phys. Rep.* **179**, 273 (1989).

[46] N. Cabibbo, L. Maiani, G. Parsi, and R. Petrozio, *Nuc. Phys.* **B158**, 295 (1979).

[47] M. E. Carrington (preprint TPI-MINN-91/48-T) calculates that the Weinberg-Salam phase transition is strongly first order with Higgs masses near 60 GeV. A lattice study by B. Bunk, E.-M. Ilgenfritz, J. Kripfganz, and A. Schiller [*Phys. Lett.* **B284**, 371 (1992)] confirms the perturbation results that the phase transition is weakly first order with $m_H < M_W$, becoming weaker as m_H increases.

[48] M. Shaposhnikov, [*Phys. Lett.* **B277**, 324 (1992)] has argued that a Standard Model solution to the baryogenesis problem requires the Higgs mass to be less than 67 GeV. However, this number comes from the requirement that none of the baryon number generated is later washed out by the termination of the phase transition—which Shaposhnikov assumes to be first order. With a second order transition, there would be no problem with washout, but the Standard Model baryogenesis theories proposed to date require a first order transition for their CP and baryon number violating effects. The Omega Point Theory requires the Weinberg-Salam phase transition to be second order or very weakly first order, so if it is definitely shown that baryogenesis is impossible without a strong first order transition, the Omega Point Theory

will be in serious trouble.

[49] A. Sopczak, in *Proceedings of the 15th International Warsaw Conference, 25–29 May 1992* (to be published) This is from the preliminary analysis of all 1991 LEP data. The latest *published* upper bound for the Standard Model Higgs boson mass is 57.7 GeV at the 95% confidence level is given in Adriani et. al *Phys. Lett.* **B303**, 391 (1993).

[50] F. Abe et. al, *Phys. Rev. Lett.* **68**, 447 (1992).

[51] C. P. Ward, in *Proceedings of the 15th International Warsaw Conference, 25–29 May 1992* (to be published) This is from the preliminary analysis of all 1991 LEP data.

[52] R. K. Ellis, *Phys. Lett.* **B259**, 492 (1991).

[53] K. Sliwa in *Proceedings of the 4th International Symposium on Heavy Flavour Physics, June 25-29 1991* estimates that 100 pb^{-1} Tevatron integrated luminosity can find the top quark only if m_t < 170 GeV, which overlaps the extreme low end of my 185 ± 20 GeV prediction.

[54] J. Gunion, H. Haber, G. Kane, and S. Dawson, *The Higgs Hunter's Guide* (Addison-Wesley, New York, 1990).

[55] S. Dimopoulos, L. J. Hall, and S. Raby, *Phys. Rev. Lett.* **68**: 1984 (1992).

[56] W. A. Bardeen, C. T. Hill, and M. Lindner, *Phys. Rev.* **41**, 1647 (1990).

[57] J. Ellis, in *Proceedings of the 16th Texas Symposium on Relativistic Astrophysics, 13-18 December 1992*, to be published.

[58] J. Peoples, private communication.

[59] H. Satz, *Nuc. Phys.* **A544**, 371c (1992).

[60] C. E. Shannon and W. Weaver 1949. *The Mathematical Theory of Communication* (University of Illnois Press, Urbana).

[61] L. Brillouin 1963. *Science and Information Theory.* (Academic, New York).

[62] F. Tipler, Nature **270,** 500 (1977).

[63] A. Qadir and J.A. Wheeler, Nuc. Phys. B (Proceeding Supplements) **6**, 345 (1989).

[64] S. L. Glashow and E. E. Jenkins, *Phys. Lett.* **B206**, 522 (1988).

I. The Many Worlds Interpretation
of Quantum Mechanics

I shall provide only a brief introduction to the Many Worlds (more correctly called the Many Histories) Interpretation in this section. For a much more detailed development the interested reader is referred to the book by DeWitt and Graham [1], Chapter 7 of my own book with John Barrow [2], and my article on "Interpreting the Wave Function of the Universe" [3].

The central idea of the MWI is that all time evolution is via Schrödinger's equation

$$i\hbar \frac{d\psi}{dt} = \hat{H}\psi \qquad (I.1)$$

where $\hat{H}$ is the Hamiltonian operator. This operator describes both the object being measured *and* the measuring apparatus. In the MWI, human beings and other living things are just types of measuring devices, hence they can be completely described by some Hamiltonian.

Since the Hamiltonian operator is self-adjoint, $e^{-i\hat{H}t/\hbar} \equiv \sum_{n=0}^{\infty} \frac{(-i\hat{H}t/\hbar)^n}{n!}$ makes mathematical sense, and so equation $(I.1)$ can be integrated to give

$$\psi(\vec{x},t) = e^{-i\hat{H}t/\hbar}\psi(\vec{x}, t_0) \qquad (I.2)$$

where $\psi(\vec{x},t_0)$ is the value of the wave function at the initial time t_0. Since giving the wave function everywhere over space at any initial time *determines* the wave function at all times, quantum mechanics in the MWI is even more deterministic than Newtonian mechanics, since the breakdown of determinism possible in Newtonian mechanics (see Section G) cannot occur in quantum mechanics. (In the Heisenberg picture, quantum mechanics is even more obviously deterministic, since in this formalism, the wave function never changes!)

Let me introduce the MWI by providing a rigorous mathematical analysis of the Schrödinger's Cat Experiment, outlined in Chapter V. The essence of this experiment is a quantum system with two possible states, one of which does nothing to the cat, and the other of which causes the death of the cat. I will use the Stern-Gerlach device to generate this quantum system.

In the Stern-Gerlach device, a beam of atoms each with one unpaired electron passes through an inhomogeneous magnetic field, as pictured in Figure I.1.

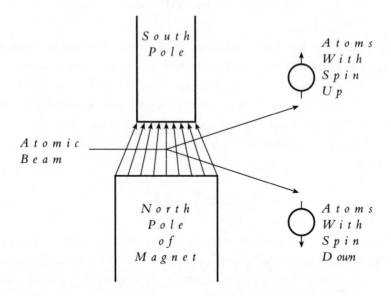

FIGURE I.1 *The Stern-Gerlach Apparatus. A beam of atoms with an odd number of electrons enters an inhomogeneous magnetic field from the left. In the ground state, all but one of the electrons will pair to cancel their spins. The inhomogeneous magnetic field will exert a force on the unpaired electron, causing the atom to move up if the unpaired electron has spin up, and to move down if the unpaired electron has a spin down. Thus, the upward-moving beam consists entirely of atoms with unpaired electrons having spin up, and the downward beam consists entirely of atoms with unpaired electrons having spin down.*

As seen in Figure I.1, the atoms which have their unpaired electron spin up, move up, while the atoms which have their unpaired electron spin down, move down. Denote the wave function of an electron with spin up as $|\uparrow\rangle$ and the wave function of an electron with spin down as $|\downarrow\rangle$.

What all measurements do is correlate states of the system being measured with states of the measuring apparatus. In fact, the Stern–Gerlach can be regarded as a device for measuring the spin of the unpaired electron: it does so by forcing a correlation between the electron's spin and the atomic center of mass. So we can write the wave function of the electron-atomic system as the product of state of the electron and the atomic motion respectively: $|atomic\ motion\rangle_A |spin\rangle_e$. (The subscripts after the kets label the atomic ket and the electron ket.) The initial system state is obviously

$$| move \rightarrow\rangle_A | spin\rangle_e \qquad (I.3)$$

where $| move \rightarrow\rangle_A$ means the atom moves from left to right.

The Hamiltonian operator, $\hat{H}_{SG}$, for the relevant part of Stern-Gerlach apparatus is defined by its effect on the basis states:

$$\hat{H}_{SG} | move \rightarrow\rangle_A | \uparrow\rangle_e = | move \uparrow\rangle_A | \uparrow\rangle_e$$

$$\hat{H}_{SG} | move \rightarrow\rangle_A | \downarrow\rangle_e = | move \downarrow\rangle_A | \downarrow\rangle_e \qquad (I.4)$$

where $| move \uparrow \rangle_A$ means the atom acquires an upward motion in addition to its motion from left to right, and $| move \downarrow \rangle_A$ means the atom acquires some downward motion. (Actually, the transition (I.4) is induced by the unitary linear operator in (I.2) not by the Hamiltonian directly, but let's ignore this irrelevent technicality.)

Let us suppose that the atoms which move up hit a detector, which activates a hammer to smash the cyanide gas flask, which kills the cat. If the atoms move down, the detector does nothing, and the cat lives. There thus are two further Hamiltonian operators here, $\hat{H}_D$ and $\hat{H}_{CAT}$, which act on the detector-cyanide state $|\rangle_D$, and on the cat state $|\rangle_{CAT}$ respectively. As with the atoms, these operators are defined by their effect on the basis states:

$$\hat{H}_D | N\rangle_D | move \uparrow\rangle_A = | \uparrow\rangle_D | move \uparrow\rangle$$

and

$$\hat{H}_D | N\rangle_D | move \uparrow\rangle_A = | \uparrow\rangle_D | move \uparrow\rangle_A \qquad (I.5)$$

defines the operator $\hat{H}_D$, where $| N\rangle_D$ is the initial neutral state of the detector-cyanide system.

The coupling of the cat to the detector-cyanide system is then

$$\hat{H}_{CAT} | cat\ alive\rangle_{CAT} | \uparrow\rangle_D = | cat\ dead\rangle_{CAT} | \uparrow\rangle_D$$

$$\hat{H}_{CAT} | cat\ alive\rangle_{CAT} | \downarrow\rangle_D = | cat\ alive\rangle_{CAT} | \downarrow\rangle_D \qquad (I.6)$$

The initial state of the "world"—the entire universe of the experiment—is then

$$| cat\ alive \rangle_{CAT}\ |N \rangle_D\ |move \rightarrow \rangle_A\ |spin \rangle_e \qquad (I.7)$$

Suppose that we send the atomic beam through a second Stern-Gerlach apparatus, and then send the up beam through the above system. The up beam, recall, has selected the electron to be spin up. We know what would happen: the cat would certainly die. Mathematically,

$$\hat{H}_{CAT}\hat{H}_D\hat{H}_{SG}| cat\ alive \rangle_{CAT}\ |N \rangle_D\ |move \rightarrow \rangle_A\ |\uparrow \rangle_e =$$

$$[\hat{H}_{CAT}| cat\ alive \rangle_{CAT}][\hat{H}_D|N \rangle_D][\hat{H}_{SG}|move \rightarrow \rangle_A|\uparrow \rangle_e] =$$

$$[\hat{H}_{CAT}| cat\ alive \rangle_{CAT}][\hat{H}_D|N \rangle_D|move \uparrow \rangle_A|\uparrow \rangle_e] =$$

$$[\hat{H}_{CAT}| cat\ alive \rangle_{CAT}|\uparrow \rangle_D|move \uparrow \rangle_A|\uparrow \rangle_e] =$$

$$| cat\ dead \rangle_{CAT}|\uparrow \rangle_D|move \uparrow \rangle_A|\uparrow \rangle_e \qquad (I.8)$$

Now suppose we send the down beam of the second Stern-Gerlach apparatus through the system. Since the down beam has the electron spin down, we again certainly know what will happen: the cat will live. Mathematically,

$$\hat{H}_{CAT}\hat{H}_D\hat{H}_{SG}| cat\ alive \rangle_{CAT}|N \rangle_D\ |move \rightarrow \rangle_A|\downarrow \rangle_e =$$

$$[\hat{H}_{CAT}| cat\ alive \rangle_{CAT}][\hat{H}_D\ |N \rangle_D]\ [\hat{H}_{SG}|move \rightarrow \rangle_A\ |\downarrow \rangle_e] =$$

$$[\hat{H}_{CAT}| cat\ alive \rangle_{CAT}][\hat{H}_D|N \rangle_D|move \downarrow \rangle_A|\downarrow \rangle_e] =$$

$$[\hat{H}_{CAT}| cat\ alive \rangle_{CAT}|\downarrow \rangle_D|move \downarrow \rangle_A|\downarrow \rangle_e] =$$

$$| cat\ alive \rangle_{CAT}|\downarrow \rangle_D|move \downarrow \rangle_A|\downarrow \rangle_e \qquad (I.9)$$

What is happening in the above equations is obvious: the certainty of the original electron spin is being transmitted from one part of the physical system to another.

Now let's rotate the second Stern-Gerlach apparatus 90 degrees, and send through it a *single* atom. The rotated Stern-Gerlach apparatus will no longer select for spin up and spin down; rather, it will select for spin to the left $|\leftarrow\rangle_e$ or spin to the right $|\rightarrow\rangle_e$. The atom will thus come through the second Stern-Gerlach apparatus moving either to the left or to the right; let's suppose it's moving to the right. (This can be determined without affecting the state of the atomic system by using a third SG apparatus, but let's not worry about this complication.) The atom and electron system is thus in the state

$$|move\rightarrow\rangle_A|\rightarrow\rangle_e \qquad (I.10)$$

Since according to standard quantum mechanics,

$$|\rightarrow\rangle_e = \frac{1}{\sqrt{2}}\left(|\uparrow\rangle_e + |\downarrow\rangle_e\right)$$

the effect of sending state (*I*.10) through the original Stern-Gerlach apparatus is startling:

$$\hat{H}_{SG}|move\rightarrow\rangle_A|\rightarrow\rangle_e = \hat{H}_{SG}|move\rightarrow\rangle_A\left[\frac{1}{\sqrt{2}}\left(|\uparrow\rangle_e + |\downarrow\rangle_e\right)\right]=$$

$$\frac{1}{\sqrt{2}}\left(|move\uparrow\rangle_A|\uparrow\rangle_e + |move\downarrow\rangle_A|\downarrow\rangle_e\right) \qquad (I.11)$$

The wave function is a *sum* of two states. This means that the atom has "split" into two: one atom is in state

$$|move\uparrow\rangle_A$$

and the other is in state

$$|move\downarrow\rangle_A$$

This implication comes from the **linearity** of the operator $\hat{H}_{SG}$, together with the requirement that, if the electron is definitely spin up (or down) before the measurement for vertical spin, the device measuring the spin (the Stern-Gerlach apparatus) will *definitely* measure the spin to be up (or down).

Furthermore, the split will be propagated to the cat:

$$\hat{H}_{CAT}\hat{H}_D\hat{H}_{SG}|cat\ alive\rangle_{CAT}|N\rangle_D|move\rightarrow\rangle_A\left[\frac{1}{\sqrt{2}}\left(|\uparrow\rangle_e + |\downarrow\rangle_e\right)\right]=$$

$$\frac{1}{\sqrt{2}} \left(|cat\ dead\rangle_{CAT} | \uparrow \rangle_D | move \uparrow \rangle_A | \uparrow \rangle_e \right) +$$

$$\frac{1}{\sqrt{2}} \left(|cat\ alive\rangle_{CAT} | \downarrow \rangle_D | move \downarrow \rangle_A | \downarrow \rangle_e \right) \qquad (I.12)$$

There are thus two "worlds": in one the cat is dead, and in the other the cat is alive. If a human being is added to the system—to look and see if the cat is alive or dead—then the interaction of the human with the cat system would force the human to split as well. Other humans looking at the first human and also the cat would also split into two worlds: in one they would all see the cat alive and would all agree the cat is alive, and in the other they would all see the cat dead and would all agree the cat is dead.

The Many Worlds Interpretation is forced on us by three assumptions:

(1) all systems—including humans—are quantum systems;

(2) all time evolution is **linear**, governed by Schrödinger's equation; and

(3) all measuring devices work as they should. If, for example, the cat *is* dead (in an eigenstate of "deadness"), then any correctly operating device must *say* the cat is dead. In particular, if humans are the measuring devices, then if the cat is indeed dead, all "correctly operating" humans must see the cat dead. (All "incorrectly operating" humans are carted off to a mental institution.)

References

[1] DeWitt, Bryce, and Neil Graham 1973. *The Many-Worlds Interpretation of Quantum Mechanics*. Princeton: Princeton University Press.

[2] Barrow, John D., and Frank J. Tipler 1986. *The Anthropic Cosmological Principle*. Oxford: Oxford University Press.

[3] Tipler, Frank J., 1986. *Physics Reports* **137**: 231.

J. Quantum Wave Packets and Progress in Evolutionary Biology

An example of a frequency distribution which behaves in a cyclic manner—but in the short run looks like an expansion of an initially narrow distribution—is the probability distribution of a quantized harmonic oscillator in one dimension. If the initial state of the oscillator is

$$\psi(x,0) = N \exp\left[-\frac{(x-x_0)^2}{2\sigma_0^2}\right] \tag{J.1}$$

where $x_0 > 0$, N is a normalization constant, and σ_0 is the standard deviation of the gaussian distribution then the probability distribution as a function of time is

$$|\psi(x,t)|^2 = N^2\left(\cos^2\omega t + \left[\frac{\hbar/m\omega}{\sigma_0^2}\right]^2\sin^2\omega t\right)^{-1/2}\exp\left[\frac{-(x-x_0\cos\omega t)^2}{\sigma_0^2\left(\cos^2\omega t + \left[\frac{\hbar/m\omega}{\sigma_0^2}\right]^2\sin^2\omega t\right)}\right] \tag{J.2}$$

which is of course periodic with period $2\pi/\omega$.

In the special case that $\sigma_0^2 = \hbar/m\omega$, then the initial wave function and probability distribution as a function of time are respectively

$$\psi(x,0) = N \exp\left[-\frac{m\omega}{2\hbar}(x-x_0)^2\right] \tag{J.3}$$

and

$$|\psi(x,t)|^2 = N^2 \exp\left[-\frac{m\omega}{\hbar}(x-x_0\cos\omega t)^2\right] \tag{J.4}$$

which oscillates with no change of shape. This special case is what usually appears in the quantum mechanics textbooks.

Gould's EQ frequency distribution (this is defined in Chapter III) looks exactly like the time evolution of a minimum uncertainty wave packet for a *free* particle; that is, like the time evolution of a particle moving to the right with constant velocity. Such motion is in fact the *standard model of constant progress!* A physicist looking at Gould's data (see below) would immediately conclude: "An obvious example of uniform, continuous progress."

The initial wave function for a free particle moving to the right with constant momentum $p_0 > 0$ and having minimum uncertainty (that is, the wave packet satisfies $\Delta p \Delta x = \hbar/2$) is

$$\psi(x,0) = N \exp\left[-\frac{(x-x_0)^2}{2\sigma_0^2} - \frac{ip_0 x}{\hbar} \right] \qquad (J.5)$$

For this initial wave function the probability distribution as a function of time is

$$|\psi(x,t)|^2 = N^2 \left(1 + \frac{t^2\hbar^2}{m^2\sigma_0^4} \right)^{-1/2} \exp\left[-\frac{(x-x_0-p_0t/m)^2}{\sigma_0^2(1+\hbar^2 t^2/m^2\sigma_0^4)} \right] \qquad (J.6)$$

The width (standard deviation) of the probability distribution obeys the equation

$$\sigma(t) = (\sigma_0/\sqrt{2})\,(1+\hbar^2 t^2/m^2\,\sigma_0^4)^{1/2} \qquad (J.7)$$

The group velocity of the particle wave packet is a constant, namely $v_{group} = p_0/m$, which is the classical velocity of a free particle. A plot of equation $(J.6)$ can be found in any basic quantum mechanics textbook; see for example Figure 4.1 of Leighton 1959, p.147. It is obvious that Figure 4.1 of Leighton 1959, p. 147, is *exactly* the same figure as the figure which Gould used to *attack* the Idea of Progress (Figure 4 of Gould 1988), which is Figure (13.12) of Jerison 1973, p. 315.

Now Gould might object that the above wave packets assume that x is defined for negative values, which is true. However, it is clear that if $x_0 \gg \sigma_0$, then the tail of the gaussian with $x \leq 0$ has negligible effect. Furthermore, it is easy to confirm this by quantizing both the harmonic oscillator and the free particle on the half line—that is, $\psi(x,t)$ is assumed to have support only in $(0,+\infty)$. One way of doing this is to use the method of images: superpose two wave packets of the form $(J.5)$, with one peaked at $x_0 > 0$ and moving to the right (momentum $p_0 > 0$), and with the other with a trough (rather than a peak) at $-x_0$ and moving to the left (momentum $-p_0$). For example, let

$$\psi(x,0) = \psi_1(x,0) + \psi_2(x,0) \qquad (J.8)$$

where

$$\psi_1(x,0) = N \exp\left[-\frac{(x-x_0)^2}{2\sigma_0^2} - \frac{ip_0 x}{\hbar} \right] \qquad (J.9)$$

that is, equation $(J.5)$, and $\psi_2(x,0) = -N \exp\left[-\frac{(x+x_0)^2}{2\sigma_0^2} + \frac{ip_0 x}{\hbar} \right]$ $\qquad (J.10)$

The minus sign in front of the N in equation (J.10) makes this superposition manifestly satisfy $\psi(0,0) = 0$, and Schrödinger's equation will preserve this boundary condition, so that $\psi(0,t) = 0$. When one computes $\psi(x,t)$ for $x > 0$, it is indeed seen that the existence of the boundary at $x = 0$ affects the motion of the particle only very close to this boundary. Away from the boundary, the qualitative features of the motion of the probability distribution defined by equation (J.8) are the same as the motion of the probability distribution defined by equation (J.5). The gaussian distributions in Gould's figure visibly satisfy $x_0 \gg \sigma_0$, so the boundary effects in his data are negligible.

Notice that, when ωt is very small, $\cos \omega t \approx 1$ and $\sin \omega t \approx \omega t$, so in the limit of small times, equation (J.2) reduces to equation (J.6) with $p_0 = 0$. In this limit, $|\psi(x,t)|^2$ evolves like a free particle with zero velocity; all that happens is that the distribution spreads, with the peak and median of the distribution staying put. If second order terms in ωt are kept, the time behavior of (J.2) looks very similar to (J.6) with $p_0 > 0$. In other words, the distribution (J.2), which is really periodic in the large, starts out like a particle progressing to the right. Only by using a globally valid theory can one interpret the data to tell if the system is progressing or is instead ultimately periodic.

The same is true of Gould's data. From what is given—evolution over less than 100 million years—it looks as though the EQ is progressing.

R *eferences*

Gould, Stephan J. 1988. "On Replacing the Idea of Progress with an Operational Notion of Directionality." In *Evolutionary Progress*, ed. Matthew H. Nitecki, 319–38. Chicago: University of Chicago Press. Jerison, Harry J. 1973. *Evolution of the Brain and Intelligence*. New York: Academic Press.

Leighton, Robert B. 1959. *Principles of Modern Physics*. New York: McGraw-Hill.

K. Chaos in Quantum Mechanics

The standard argument against chaos in quantum mechanics is the fact that the wave function is an almost periodic function of time [1–5]. However, as we saw in Section E, this argument assumes that the energy is bounded and that the wave function is restricted to a finite region of configuration space. I shall now show that neither assumption necessarily holds in quantum cosmology. Later, in Section M, I shall show that, if the Omega Point Boundary Condition is imposed, then the energy cannot be bounded above. This will obviate the argument against chaos in quantum cosmology.

Let us first consider a simple example of chaos in general relativity, an example of chaos where the Newtonian analogue is nonchaotic. An exponential divergence of geodesics in finite proper time—the hallmark of chaos—is provided by some of the timelike geodesic congruences in Schwarzschild space-time with $r < 2m$. The metric is

$$ds^2 = \frac{-d\mathcal{T}^2}{(\frac{2m}{\mathcal{T}} - 1)} + \left(\frac{2m}{\mathcal{T}} - 1\right) dr^2 + \mathcal{T}^2(d\theta^2 + \sin^2\theta d\phi^2) \quad (K.1)$$

where $0 < \mathcal{T} < 2m$, $0 \le r < +\infty$, $0 \le \theta \le \pi$, $0 \le \phi < 2\pi$. The curves with (r, θ, ϕ) = constant are timelike geodesics which are normal to the homogeneous spacelike hypersurfaces $\mathcal{T}$ = constant. Consider two such geodesics which have the same fixed (θ, ϕ) values. The proper spacelike distance between them at any time $\mathcal{T}$ is

$$\Delta r \sqrt{\frac{2m}{\mathcal{T}} - 1} \quad (K.2)$$

which diverges to $+\infty$ for any initial Δr as $\mathcal{T} \to 0$. The change in proper time t between any two values of coordinate time $(\mathcal{T}_i, \mathcal{T}_f)$ is given by

$$\Delta t = t_f - t_i = \int_{\mathcal{T}_i}^{\mathcal{T}_f} \frac{d\mathcal{T}}{\sqrt{\frac{2m}{\mathcal{T}} - 1}} = 2m \left[\cos^{-1}\sqrt{\frac{\mathcal{T}}{2m}} + \sqrt{\frac{\mathcal{T}}{2m}\left(1 - \frac{\mathcal{T}}{2m}\right)} \right]_{\mathcal{T}_i}^{\mathcal{T}_f}$$

$$(K.3)$$

But since $(\frac{2m}{\mathcal{T}} - 1)^{-1/2} \le 1$ for $\mathcal{T} \le m$, we have $\Delta t(\mathcal{T}) \le \Delta \mathcal{T}$ for all $\mathcal{T} \le m$, so near the singularity at $\mathcal{T} = 0$ less proper time passes than coordinate time. Thus the proper spatial distance between the timelike geodesics diverges to infinity in finite proper time.

The proper three-volume defined by all timelike geodesics normal to the $\mathcal{T}$ = constant hypersurfaces is

$$V(\mathcal{T}) = \int \sqrt{g_{rr}g_{\theta\theta}g_{\phi\phi}}\,drd\theta d\phi = 4\pi\mathcal{T}^2\,\Delta r\,\sqrt{\frac{2m}{\mathcal{T}} - 1} \qquad (K.4)$$

Thus $V(\mathcal{T}) \propto \mathcal{T}^{3/2}$ near $\mathcal{T} = 0$, so $V(\mathcal{T}) \to 0$ as $\mathcal{T} \to 0$.

In contrast to the faster-than-exponential divergence of proper spatial distance between a timelike geodesic congruence in the approach to the $\mathcal{T} = 0$ singularity (which is the same as the $r = 0$ Schwarzschild singularity) in general relativity, the divergence of radial freely falling bodies in Newtonian gravity does *not* diverge exponentially with r. Rather, the orbits of test particles falling freely in the radial direction toward a Newtonian point mass diverge as a mere *power* of Newtonian time. There is no exponential divergence of nearby radial orbits as $r \to 0$ in Newtonian gravity.

It is generally thought [3–5] that one cannot have diverging trajectories in quantum mechanics, because there are no trajectories. Every "trajectory" is fused out by the Heisenberg Uncertainty Principle. But this is not true. Many years ago David Bohm [6] and Louis de Broglie [7,8] showed that Schrödinger's equation could be written as equations for particle trajectories "guided" by "pilot waves." Later J. S. Bell [9[(of Bell's Theorem fame) resurrected the formalism and, along with Bohm and de Broglie, attempted to use it to provide a new interpretation of quantum mechanics. This Pilot Wave Interpretation is inconsistent [10], but the formalism provides a neat way to picture the many histories of the Many Worlds Interpretation.

Consider the one-particle Schrödinger equation

$$i\hbar\,\frac{\partial\psi}{\partial t} = -\frac{\hbar^2}{2m}\nabla^2\psi + V(\vec{x})\psi \qquad (K.5)$$

If we substitute [11, p. 280]

$$\psi = \mathcal{R}\exp(i\varphi/h) \qquad (K.6)$$

into (K.5), where the functions $\mathcal{R} = \mathcal{R}(\vec{x},t)$ and $\varphi = \varphi(\vec{x},t)$ are real, we obtain

$$\frac{\partial\mathcal{R}}{\partial t} = -\frac{1}{2m}[\mathcal{R}\nabla^2\varphi + 2\vec{\nabla}\mathcal{R}\cdot\vec{\nabla}\varphi] \qquad (K.7)$$

$$\frac{\partial \varphi}{\partial t} = -\frac{(\vec{\nabla}\varphi)^2}{2m} - V + \left(\frac{\hbar^2}{2m}\right)\frac{\nabla^2 \mathcal{R}}{\mathcal{R}} \qquad (K.8)$$

Equation (K.8) is just the classical Hamilton-Jacobi equation for a single particle moving in the potential

$$U = V - \left(\frac{\hbar^2}{2m}\right)\frac{\nabla^2 \mathcal{R}}{\mathcal{R}} \qquad (K.9)$$

The normals to surfaces of constant phase, given by $\varphi(\vec{x},t) = $ constant, define trajectories: those curves with tangents

$$\vec{\nabla}\varphi = \frac{\hbar}{2im}\ln\left(\frac{\psi}{\psi^*}\right) = Re\left[\left(\frac{\hbar}{i}\right)\ln\psi\right] \qquad (K.10)$$

The surfaces of constant phase are the "pilot waves." But in quantum theory, they do not guide a single particle as they do in classical theory. Rather, they guide an infinite ensemble of particles, each with momentum $\vec{p} = m\vec{\nabla}\varphi$: *all* the trajectories defined by (K.10) are real in quantum mechanics. Here once again are the Many Worlds: if we make a measurement, we will see only one particle, but in actuality, there are infinitely many particles — infinitely many histories — physically present.

I propose to look for chaos in quantum mechanics by looking at the separation of the trajectories defined by the pilot waves. The density of the trajectories is conserved, since this density is given by $\rho = \psi\psi^*$, satisfying

$$\frac{\partial \rho}{\partial t} + \vec{\nabla}\cdot\left(\rho\,\frac{\vec{\nabla}\varphi}{m}\right) = 0 \qquad (K.11)$$

which is just (K.7) rewritten.

If $\nabla^2 \mathcal{R} = 0$ and $\mathcal{R} \neq 0$ (if $\mathcal{R}$ is everywhere regular and bounded, this implies $\mathcal{R} = $ constant), then the quantum equation (K.8) is the classical Hamilton-Jacobi equation for the same potential. Thus in this case, the quantum trajectories are just the classical trajectories. I shall give in Section L an exact quantum cosmological model in which these conditions on $\mathcal{R}$ hold, so such boundary conditions are physical. The model, however, is the simple harmonic oscillator, which is nonchaotic, but if such boundary conditions could be imposed on a classical system with a potential $V(\vec{x})$ that implied classical chaos—exponential divergence of nearby trajectories—the corresponding quantum trajectories would necessarily also be chaotic. There would be no inconsistency with the almost periodicity theorem since such a boundary condition would imply the system is unbounded: $\rho = |\psi|^2 = $ constant over infinite space.

There has been some work [12–16] showing the exponential divergence of streamlines in incompressible fluids governed by the Navier-Stokes equations, but incompressible fluids are analogous to the $\rho = $ constant case.

The interesting case, where one might expect chaos in the trajectories even when the classical system is nonchaotic (!), is when $\nabla^2 \mathcal{R}/\mathcal{R} \neq 0$, and $\mathcal{R} \neq 0$. It is possible in this case for $|\nabla^2\mathcal{R}/\mathcal{R}| \to +\infty$ in finite time if $\mathcal{R} \to 0$ while $|\nabla^2\mathcal{R}|$ is bounded away from zero, and a potential which diverges fast enough *can* force the quantum trajectories to diverge. If the quantum trajectories were chaotic for a bounded system, then we would have to have $\nabla^2\mathcal{R} \neq 0$, and $\mathcal{R} = 0$ at some point in space in finite time, in order to avoid an inconsistency with the almost periodicity theorem. If $\mathcal{R} \neq 0$ initially, and the system evolved to $\mathcal{R} = 0$ in finite time, then the transformation $(K.6)$ is not well defined when $\mathcal{R} = 0$, so the equations $(K.7)$ and $(K.8)$ break down. The almost periodicity theorem applies to $(K.5)$, which is not equivalent to the system $(K.7)$ and $(K.8)$ if this breakdown occurs. Since the potential $(K.9)$ is nonlinear, it *might* yield chaos even when the associated classical potential does not. An equation breakdown in finite time means the situation might be analogous to chaos in Schwarzschild geometry described above; Lyapunov exponents cannot be defined since these involve an infinite time limit.

My analysis of quantum chaos has a great deal in common with the "semiclassical" approach. This approach also uses phase paths. The main difference is that my analysis is fully quantum; the semiclassical approach is concerned with the behavior of quantum systems in the limit $\hbar \to 0$. In the semiclassical systems, caustics often develop in the Green's function, requiring the Gutzwiler phase shift correction. This will not be required in quantum cosmology. As will be seen in the quantum model in Section L, what would be caustics in the Green's function are actually physical singularities: there is no physical extension through these singularities. This could be a consequence of the high symmetry of the model, but I am assuming in the Omega Point Boundary Condition that this feature is general in quantum cosmology. Also, I am assuming that $\mathcal{R} \neq 0$ along any phase trajectory. If $\mathcal{R} = 0$ at some point on a trajectory, then, as I said above, the phase would not be well defined. As will be seen in Section M, and as was discussed in Chapter VIII, the Omega Point Boundary Condition imposes this.

Another approach to chaos in quantum mechanics is to adopt the Heisenberg picture where the wave function does not change, and look for chaos in the operators of the quantized version of a chaotic classical system. One finds [17,18] phenomena that can be identified as "chaotic" but, needless to say, only in the thermodynamic limit, which means only with spatially unbounded systems.

Since in the Omega Point Theory, the quantum cosmology is effectively unbounded in phase space, since universal wave functions can be found which have the quantum trajectories the same as classical trajectories, and since the classical cosmological trajectories are chaotic (as we shall see in Section H), it seems reasonable to assume that the chaos required for eternal life will in fact exist, even in the quantum version of the Omega Point Theory.

R eferences

[1] T. Hogg and B. A. Huberman, *Phys. Rev.* **A28**, 22 (1983).

[2] S. Fishman, D. R. Grempel, and R. E. Prange, *Phys. Rev. Lett.* **49**, 509 (1982).

[3] Heinz G. Schuster, *Deterministic Chaos, Second Edition* (VCH Publishers, New York, 1988).

[4] Roderick V. Jensen, *Nature* **355**, 311 (1992).

[5] M. V. Berry, *Proc. R. Soc.* **A413**, 183 (1987).

[6] D. Bohm, *Phys. Rev.* **85**, 166 & 180 (1952); *Phys. Rev.* **89**, 458 (1953).

[7] L. de Broglie, *Non-Linear Wave Mechanics: A Causal Interpretation* (Amsterdam: Elsevier, 1960).

[8] L. de Broglie, *The Current Interpretation of Wave Mechanics: A Critical Study*, (Amsterdam: Elsevier, 1964).

[9] J. S. Bell, in *Quantum Gravity 2: A Second Oxford Symposium*, ed. R. Penrose and D. W. Sciama (Oxford: Oxford University Press, 1981).

[10] F. J. Tipler, *Phys. Lett.* **A103**, 188 (1984).

[11] M. Jammer, *The Philosophy of Quantum Mechanics*, (New York: Wiley, 1974).

[12] R. Temam, *Navier-Stokes Equations and Non-Linear Functional Analysis* (Philadelphia: SIAM, 1983).

[13] P. Constantin, C. Foias, O. P. Manley, and R. Temam, *J. Fluid Mech.* **150**, 427 (1985).

[14] P. Constatin, C. Foias, and R. Temam, *Mem. Amer. Math. Soc.* **53**, 1 (1985).

[15] P. Constatin, C. Foias, *Comm. Pure and Applied Math.* **38** 1 (1985).

[16] P. Constatin, C. Foias, *Navier-Stokes Equations* (Chicago: University of Chicago Press, 1988).

[17] A. Connes, H. Narnhofer, and W. Thirring, *Comm. Math. Phys.* **112**, 691 (1987).

[18] H. Narnhofer, A. Pflug, and W. Thirring, in *Symmetry in Nature, Volume II*, ed. Gilberto Bernardini (Pisa: Scuola Normale Superiore, 1989).

L. Quantum Mini-Superspace Model with an Omega Point

In standard quantum gravity, the wave function of the universe obeys the Wheeler–DeWitt equation [1,2]

$$\hat{\mathscr{H}}\Psi = 0 \qquad (L.1)$$

where $\hat{\mathscr{H}}$ is the super-Hamiltonian operator. This operator contains the equivalent of time derivatives in the Schrödinger equation. I say "the equivalent" because quantum gravity does not contain time as an independent variable. Rather, other variables—matter or the spatial metric—are used as time markers. In other words, the variation of the physical quantities *is* time. Depending on the variable chosen to measure time, the time interval between the present and the initial or final singularity can be finite or infinite—but this is already familiar from classical general relativity.

The Wheeler–DeWitt equation is too complicated to solve in full generality, so physicists have taken to restricting it to a finite number of variables—this space is called *mini-superspace*. A mini-superspace model which will rigorously reproduce Figure V.4 can be obtained as follows.

If matter is in the form of a perfect fluid, the action S in the ADM formalism can be written

$$S = \int (\mathscr{R} + p) \sqrt{-g}\, d^4x = \int L_{ADM}\, dt \qquad (L.2)$$

where p is the fluid pressure and $\mathscr{R}$ is the Ricci scalar. If the spacetime is assumed to be a Friedmann universe containing isentropic perfect fluids, Lapchinskii and Rubakov [3] have shown the canonical variables can be chosen (R, ϕ, s), where R is the scale factor of the universe, and ϕ, s are particular parameterizations of the fluid variables called *Schutz potentials* [4]. The momenta conjugate to these canonical variables will be written (p_R, p_ϕ, p_s).

The ADM Lagrangian in these variables can be shown to be

$$L_{ADM} = p_R R' + p_\phi \phi' + p_s s' - N(H_g + H_m) \qquad (L.3)$$

where the prime denotes the time derivative,

$$H_g = -\frac{p_R^2}{24R} - 6R \tag{L.4}$$

is the purely gravitational super-Hamiltonian, and

$$H_m = N^2 R^3[(\rho + p)(u^0)^2 + pg^{00}] = p_\phi^\gamma R^{3(1-\gamma)} e^s \tag{L.5}$$

is both the coordinate energy density measured by a comoving observer and the super-Hamiltonian of the matter. The momentum conjugate to R, the scale factor of the universe, is

$$p_R = -\frac{12RR'}{N} \tag{L.6}$$

The constraint equation for the Friedmann universe is obtained by substituting (L.3)–(L.5) into (L.2) and varying the lapse N. The result is the super-Hamiltonian constraint:

$$0 = \mathcal{H} = H_g + H_m = -\frac{p_R^2}{24R} - 6R + p_\phi^\gamma R^{3(1-\gamma)} e^s \tag{L.7}$$

When the perfect fluid is radiation the last term is $H_m = p_\phi^{4/3} e^s/R$, and so if we choose the momentum conjugate to the *true* time τ to be

$$p_\tau = p_\phi^{4/3} e^s \tag{L.8}$$

then the super-Hamiltonian constraint becomes

$$0 = \mathcal{H} = -\frac{p_R^2}{24R} - 6R + \frac{p_\tau}{R} \tag{L.9}$$

The ADM Hamiltonian is obtained from $H_{ADM} = p_\tau$, or

$$H_{ADM} = \frac{p_R^2}{24R} + 6R^2 \tag{L.10}$$

which is just the Hamiltonian for a simple harmonic oscillator.

The lapse N is fixed by solving Hamilton's equation

$$\tau' = 1 = \frac{\partial(N[H_g + H_m])}{\partial p_\tau} = \frac{N}{R} \tag{L.11}$$

which says that $N = R$; that is, *true* time is just conformal time, which is why I have called it τ.

If we quantize by the replacement $p_\tau \to \hat{p}_\tau = -i\partial/\partial\tau$, and $p_R \to \hat{p}_R = -i\partial/\partial R$, together with a reversal of the direction of time $\tau \to -\tau$ in the super-Hamiltonian constraint (L.9), the Wheeler-DeWitt equation (L.1) will then become (if we ignore factor ordering problems) Schrödinger's equation for the simple harmonic oscillator with mass $m = 12$, spring constant $k = 12$ and angular frequency $\omega = 1$:

$$i\frac{\partial\Psi}{\partial\tau} = -\frac{1}{24}\frac{\partial^2\Psi}{\partial R^2} + 6R^2\,\Psi \qquad (L.12)$$

The wave function of the universe $\Psi(R,\tau)$ in this mini–superspace is a function of two variables, the scale factor of the universe R and the conformal time τ.

If the *final*(!) boundary condition

$$\Psi(0,\pi) = \delta(R) \qquad (L.13)$$

$$\left[\frac{\partial\Psi\,(R,\tau)}{\partial R}\right]_{R=0} = 0 \qquad (L.14)$$

is imposed, then the resulting wave function is that pictured in Figure V.4. (The wave function is assumed to have no support for $R < 0$. However, we cannot get this by imposing the DeWitt boundary condition $\Psi(0,\tau) = 0$, because it contradicts (L.13). But (L.14) is sufficient for self-adjointness of the SHO Hamiltonian on the half-line $R \in [0,+\infty)$; see [2] for a discussion.) The wave function satisfying boundary conditions (L.13) and (L.14) is just the Green's function $G(R,\tilde{R},\tau)$ defined on the entire real line for the simple harmonic oscillator, with $\tilde{R}$ set equal to zero. The wave function is thus

$$\Psi(R,\tau) = \left[\frac{6}{\pi L_P \sin\tau}\right]^{1/2} \exp\left[\frac{i6R^2 \cot\tau}{L^2_P} - \frac{i\pi}{4}\right] \qquad (L.15)$$

where L_P is the Planck length. This wave function is defined only for a finite conformal time: $0 \le \tau \le \pi$. (The initial and final singularities *are* in the domain of the wave function!)

Notice that the magnitude of the wave function (L.15) is independent of the scale factor of the universe R. Since the scale factor plays the role of "spatial position" in the simple harmonic oscillator equation $(L.12)$, we have $\nabla^2 R$ $= 0$, and hence from the discussion on phase trajectories in Section K, we see that the phase trajectories for the wave function $(L.15)$ are all the classical trajectories for a simple harmonic oscillator. That is, the phase trajectories are all of the form

$$R(\tau) = R_{max} \sin \tau \qquad (L.16)$$

which are also all the classical solutions to the Einstein field equations for a radiation-dominated Friedmann universe.

We can also show that the phase trajectories are given by $(L.16)$ by direct calculation. Since in the natural units $L_P = 1$, the phase φ is $\varphi = 6R^2 \cot \tau - \frac{\pi}{4}$, we have $\nabla \varphi = \partial \varphi / \partial R = 12 R \cot \tau$. The tangents are defined by $p_R = \nabla \varphi$, which implies

$$\frac{1}{R} \frac{dR}{d\tau} = \cot \tau \qquad (L.17)$$

using $(L.6)$, $N = R$, and $\tau \to - \tau$. The solutions to $(L.17)$ are $(L.16)$.

With the boundary condition $(L.13)$, *all* radii at maximum expansion, R_{max}, are present; all classical paths are present in this wave function. We thus see that, with the boundary condition $(L.13)$, both the phase trajectories and the wave function begin with an initial singularity and end in a final singularity. In other words, with this wave function, the universe behaves quantum mechanically just as it does classically. The singularities are just as real in both cases.

Now let me give a simple mini-superspace model with an omega point. I shall base this model on the Friedmann classical spacetime, which means, as I showed in Section F, that the pressure in each of the classical histories must be negative. Since this is unphysical (except, as I showed in Section H, when the universal temperature of the universe is near room temperature), I shall not bother to construct a super-Hamiltonian for this quantum universe.

The classical metric for a radiation-dominated Friedmann universe is

$$ds^2 = - \sin^2(\tau)d\tau^2 + \sin^2(\tau)[d\chi^2 + \sin^2(\chi)(d\theta^2 + \sin^2 \theta d\phi^2)] \qquad (L.18)$$

while, as we saw in Example 2 of Section F, a simple classical metric for a Friedmann universe ending in an omega point is

$$ds^2 = -dt^2 + \sin^2(t)[d\chi^2 + \sin^2(\chi)(d\theta^2 + \sin^2\theta d\phi^2)] \quad (L.19)$$

The only difference between $(L.18)$ and $(L.19)$ is the time scale. Therefore, a wave function for a quantum cosmology satisfying the boundary conditions $(L.13)$ and $(L.14)$ and with all phase trajectories ending in an omega point is simply $(L.15)$ with the conformal time replaced by proper time along the phase trajectories.

$$\Psi(R,t) = \left[\frac{6}{\pi L_P \sin t}\right]^{1/2} \exp\left[\frac{i6R^2 \cot t}{L^2_P} - \frac{i\pi}{4}\right] \quad (L.20)$$

The replacement $\tau \to t$ is *not* trivial. With conformal time τ, we know that the time is being measured by changes in the combination $(L.8)$ of Schutz potentials and their moment. The physical quantities which measure proper time t in $(L.20)$ are quite different. I shall not try to compute them since the classical metric $(L.19)$ is not a solution to the Einstein equations with a physically reasonable matter tensor. But the phase trajectories of $(L.20)$ are, like those of $(L.15)$, simply

$$R(t) = R_{max} \sin t \qquad (L.21)$$

We could form a more realistic mini-superspace model with an omega point by joining wave function $(L.15)$ with wave function $(L.19)$ at the time of maximum expansion in all trajectories, just as was done for a classical universe in Example 3 of Section F. Such a mini-superspace model would have past c-boundary with topology S^3 beginning all phase trajectories, and all phase trajectories would end in an omega point.

R *eferences*

[1] Barrow, John D. and F. J. Tipler 1986. *The Anthropic Cosmological Principle.* Oxford: Oxford University Press.
[2] Tipler, F. J. 1986. *Physics Reports* **137**: 231.
[3] Lapchinskii, V. G. and V. A. Rubakov 1977. *Theoretical and Mathematical Physics* **3**: 1076.
[4] Schutz, B. F. 1971. *Physical Review* **D4**: 3559.

M. The Omega Point Boundary Condition on the Universal Wave Function

Life must be prepared to survive arbitrarily close to the final singularity. The definition of "life" given in Section H was based on classical spacetime concepts, and one is certainly correct to be dubious about the validity of these notions close to the final singularity, when the radius of the universe is less than L_P, the Planck length.

But should we regard L_P as the limit for the validity of the idea of space-time? In the 1930s both Bethe and Heitler [1], following the general opinion, argued that "the quantum theory is definitely wrong for electrons of ... high energy (presumably for $E > 137 m_e c^2$)." Their reason: the de Broglie wavelength of an electron of such energy was shorter than the classical radius ($E = hc/\lambda > hc/r_0 = 2\pi(\hbar c/e^2) = 2\pi(137) m_e c^2$). Furthermore, from the 1930s to the end of his life ([2] p. 542), Heisenberg believed that quantum mechanics broke down at a critical length; in the 1930s he argued that this length was h/mc, where m was the mass of the Yukawa meson([2], pp. 360, 407). In the 1920s Bohr himself believed [2] quantum mechanics broke down when applied to regions smaller than 10^{-13} cm. If history is any guide, it is quite possible that classical spacetime concepts may be valid at distances smaller than L_P.

But if not, then I shall outline how to generalize Conditions I–III of Section H to apply in quantum cosmology, provided only that a complex valued wave function of the universe can be defined, and the Second Law of Thermodynamics holds at arbitrarily high energies. It will not be essential to assume that a metric exists at distances smaller than L_P.

I am far more confident that the Second Law of Thermodynamics will remain eternally valid and thus allow the entropic time of Section B to be extended to infinity than I am confident that a spacetime metric will exist at distances smaller than L_P. The Law of Mass Action discussed in Section D and in Chapter IX provides an example in which the Second Law remained valid in the face of a breakdown of Newtonian mechanics. There are numerous other examples. Collectively they provide evidence that we should be ready to give up every other law in preference to abandoning the Second Law. The Omega Point Boundary Condition, which I shall now outline, is imposed in order to ensure the continued and global validity of the Second Law.

Let us first consider a quantum cosmology based on superspace, in which the basic entity is a wave functional $\Psi(\tilde{h},\Phi,S)$ on compact 3-manifolds S with

3-metrics h and nongravitational fields Φ. (I have placed a tilde over the 3-metric h to express the fact that superspace is Riem(S)/Diff(S); the space of all Riemannian metrics mod Diffeomorphisms.) Fix S and write $\Psi(\tilde{h},\Phi) = \mathcal{R}(\tilde{h},\Phi) \, e^{\varphi(\tilde{h},\Phi)}$. The wave functional thus defines *histories*—phase trajectories— in superspace, each history being a path whose tangent is the functional derivative $\delta\varphi/\delta\tilde{h}_{ij}$. In nonrelativistic quantum mechanics (QM), $\psi = Re^{i\varphi}$ often can be chosen so that these phase trajectories (those with $\vec{\nabla}\varphi$ as tangents) are the classical paths for the Hamiltonian, as I showed in Section K. For example, the phase trajectories of the plane wave $\psi = e^{i\vec{k}\cdot\vec{r}}$ constitute all the classical trajectories with momentum $\vec{k}$ of the free particle Hamiltonian, and $\psi(x, t = 0) = \delta(x-a)$ used as the initial wave function of the simple harmonic oscillator will generate a wave function whose phase trajectories in time are all classical trajectories with zero amplitude at $x = a$, as I showed in Section L. But in both QM and quantum gravity, one gets classical trajectories only if one imposes field equations, Schrödinger's and DeWitt-Wheeler for $\psi(\vec{r},t)$ or $\Psi(\tilde{h},\Phi,S)$ respectively. In the absence of such equations (and appropriate boundary conditions), the trajectories serve only as a foliation of the base space—the superspace of all 3-metrics and all 3-manifolds for $\Psi(\tilde{h},\Phi,S)$, with the 3-metrics and manifolds identified under diffeomorphisms—in terms of histories. Each history can be regarded as a spacetime.

I propose to obtain the universal wave function not by separately assuming equations and imposing boundary conditions, but by requiring Conditions I–III to hold on each of the histories in superspace for which $\mathcal{R}$ is nonzero. Thus the histories which "really" exist—those for which $\mathcal{R} \neq 0$—are generated entirely by the requirement that "life" arises in all "real" histories and continues to exist in each such history until its end. This requirement can be regarded as a precise mathematical formulation of Wheeler's idea [3] that the universe is a self-excited circuit: the universe is brought into existence by the activities of "life" in its general sense. This is the *Omega Point Boundary Condition* for the universal wave function.

The nongravitational fields Φ are constrained not by field equations but by Condition III. I propose defining the amount of information in a given 3-geometry $(\tilde{h},S)$ as $I_{max}^{B} - S_P$, where I_{max}^{B} is the RHS of $(C.1)$ and S_P is the entropy of the gravitational and non-gravitational fields, both quantities being computed on the subset of each $(\tilde{h},S)$ in $I^-(\gamma)$ in each history/phase trajectory. Bekenstein [4,5] has developed an algorithm for computing I_{max}^{B}, and it is well known how to compute the nongravitational part of S_P, but, though there are a number of conjectures, it is still not known how to compute the entropy of the gravitational field. At present, I propose to avoid this difficulty by restricting calculation to quantum cosmological models with high symmetry—low-frequency modes for which the gravitational entropy is presumably zero, containing high-frequency gravitational radiation the entropy of which can be calculated in the standard way. What Condition III thus says is that $I_{max}^B - S_P$ diverges *in only one direction*, a direction in which S_P also increases, in each history as it unfolds (the "one direction" restriction is the quantum version of "future"). Imposing the increase of S_P means that we are imposing the Second Law of Thermodynamics. (If $\Psi = \Psi(g,\Phi,M)$ rather than $\Psi = \Psi(\tilde{h},\Phi,S)$, where (M,g) is a spacetime, then one requires $\mathcal{R} = 0$ on any (M,g) for which Conditions I–III do not hold.)

If the phase trajectories can be approximated at arbitrarily small sizes by a classical closed universe history, then I have shown in Section H that the Bekenstein Bound will not prevent the divergence of information stored near the final singularity. An infinite amount of information can be processed and stored in the finite proper time before the final singularity. Using the shear, life can force horizons to disappear, making an infinity of circumnavigations possible, as I showed in Section H.

The increase of $I_{max}^B - S_P$ is clearly a separate condition from the second law and is not implied by it. (But see the last paragraph of Section C!) However, Frautschi [6], Layzer [7,8], and Landsberg [9] have all pointed out that the actual universe to date has obeyed this rule. I propose that it is generally true and that it can be used to define the universal wave function; an equation for Ψ $(\tilde{h},\Phi,S)$ like the DeWitt-Wheeler equation is redundant. Biologists like Brooks and Wiley [10,11] (see also [12]) have shown that a restricted version of $I_{max}^B - S_P$ can be used to define what is meant by "information" in biological systems, and that its increase measures evolutionary progress. The activity of life itself causes the increase of I_{max}^B. Following Wheeler, I suggest this will also occur near the final state.

Thus the worry, expressed by Linde ([13 ,14] and private communication) that quantum fluctuations would necessarily wipe out life at a final singularity is obviated with the Omega Point Boundary Condition, because in this case the universe continues to exist *because* life itself does; quantum fluctuations large enough to destroy life cannot occur because they are prevented by the boundary condition from forming. Thus ultimately, the continued existence of life is required and life-threatening fluctuations suppressed by the Second Law of

Thermodynamics itself. I reached the same conclusion from other premises in Section C.

The preceding analysis was based on canonical quantum gravity, in which it is assumed that the 3-metric h and 3-manifold S are defined for arbitrarily small sizes. But in superstring theory both h and S are macroscopic objects, arising from the superposition of string excitations. However, the Omega Point Boundary Condition can in principle also be imposed on string fields if a "foliation" of the string state space can be made in which on each leaf of the foliation an entropy can be defined, with the direction of increase of entropy defining a "time" direction. Notice that this "time" need not be related to the metric of spacetime at high string excitations; the metric presumably does not exist at these energies. If entropy can be defined, so can an analogue of the Bekenstein Bound I_{max}^B, which is just the logarithm of the number of possible states in a region of phase space; one must first be able to define the total number of states in order to define the entropy. The past light cones used in Conditions I–III of Section H would not exist in this case when the radius of the universe became less than L_P, but this light cone constraint may actually be redundant: the divergence of information defined as $I_{max}^B - S_P$ simply cannot occur as the final state is approached unless the information is effectively integrated by signals of some sort.

References

[1] D. C. Cassidy, *Historical Studies in the Physical Sciences.* **12** (1981) 1 (quote on page 13).

[2] D. C. Cassidy, *Uncertainty: The Life and Science of Werner Heisenberg* (Freeman, New York, 1992).

[3] J. A. Wheeler, IBM J. *Res. Develop* **32** (1988) 4.

[4] J. D. Bekenstein, *Phys. Rev. Lett.* **46** (1981) 623.

[5] M. Schiffer and J. D. Bekenstein, *Phys. Rev. D* **39** (1989) 1109 and *Phys. Rev. D* **42** (1990) 3598.

[6] S. Frautschi, in *Entropy, Information and Evolution*, ed. B. H. Weber, D. J. Depew, and J. D. Smith (MIT Press, Cambridge (US), 1988).

[7] D. Layzer, *Ap. J.* **206** (1976) 559.

[8] D. Layzer, in *Entropy, Information and Evolution*, ed. B.H. Weber, D. J. Depew, and J. D. Smith (MIT Press, Cambridge (US), 1988).

[9] P. T. Landsberg, *Phys. Lett.* **102A** (1984) 171.

[10] D. R. Brooks and E. O. Wiley, *Evolution as Entropy*, Second Edition (University of Chicago Press, Chicago, 1988).

[11] E. O. Wiley, in *Evolutionary Progess*, ed. M. H. Nitecki (University of Chicago Press, Chicago, 1988).

[12] J. S. Wicken, *Evolution, Thermodynamics, and Information* (Oxford University Press, Oxford, 1987).

[13] Linde, A. D. *Physics Letters* **B211** (1988) 29.

[14] Linde, A. D. *Physics Letters* **B227** (1989) 352.

N. *Relativistic Spacecraft*

A relativistic spacecraft is one whose cruising speed is comparable to the velocity of light c. It turns out that for "short" interstellar distances—those between 1 and 10^7 parsecs—there is really no point in going faster than $0.9c$, because at such a speed the transit time relative to the universal rest frame is 90% of the minimum transit time, whereas going faster than $0.9c$ is extremely costly in terms of energy, as I shall show below. Furthermore, the time needed for a von Neumann probe to reproduce will be several years at least, so for a transit distance of a few parsecs the time saved by going faster will be insignificant in comparison to the reproduction time. For "large" interstellar distances—distances comparable to the distance to the other side of the universe, the so-called antipodal point—a spacecraft needs a high initial speed in order to avoid being slowed down during transit by the expansion of the universe. In this section, I shall summarize the basic theory of spacecraft traveling at relativistic speeds. The theory was first developed by Johann Ackeret [1] in 1946, and reinvented in the 1960s by at least three people: Edward Purcell [2], Edwin Taylor and John Wheeler [3].

In any rocket, most of the initial mass is in the form of rocket fuel. If the mass of the payload is M_P and the mass of the entire rocket is initially M_i, then the *mass ratio* is $r \equiv M_i/M_P$. To express this ratio in terms of the final payload velocity v and the exhaust velocity v_S, let me first remind the technically knowledgeable reader of a few facts about special relativity. Defining $\beta \equiv v/c$, $\gamma \equiv (1 - \beta^2)^{-\frac{1}{2}}$, we recall that the total energy E of the spacecraft is given by $E = \gamma mc^2$, where m is the *rest mass* of the spacecraft, which is the mass the spacecraft will have if this mass is measured when the craft is at rest. In this book, *all* masses will be rest masses. In older textbooks on relativity, one will find "masses" which can vary with velocity, but we now know that this is not a good way to think about mass. All modern textbooks in relativity written by professional relativists (e.g., [3]), use the term "mass" to refer only to rest mass, because this is the only concept of mass that is independent of the reference frame.

It will be essential to introduce a less familiar concept, that of the *rapidity* ω defined by

$$\cosh \omega \equiv \gamma \equiv \frac{1}{\sqrt{1 - \beta^2}} = \frac{1}{\sqrt{1 - \frac{v^2}{c^2}}} \qquad (N.1)$$

We also have

$$\sinh \omega \equiv \frac{\beta}{\sqrt{1 - \beta^2}} = \frac{1}{\sqrt{1 - \frac{v^2}{c^2}}} \qquad (N.2)$$

and so $\tanh \omega = \beta = \frac{v}{c}$.

The reason for introducing the rapidity is that rapidities, unlike velocities, add linearly. That is, if v_r is the velocity of a rocket relative to the Earth, v_q is the velocity of some object in the rest frame of the rocket, and v_E is the velocity of the object in the rest frame of the Earth, then $v_E \neq v_r + v_q$. Instead, $v_E = c\left(\frac{\beta_r + \beta_q}{1 + \beta_r \beta_q}\right)$. However, we do have $\omega_E = \omega_r + \omega_q$, since $\tanh(\omega_r + \omega_q) = \frac{\tanh \omega_r + \tanh \omega_q}{1 + \tanh \omega_r \tanh \omega_q}$ is both the standard velocity addition formula and an identity of hyperbolic functions.

To compute the mass ratio, suppose a rocket having initial mass $\tilde{M}$ moves forward by expelling a burst of gas with infinitesimal mass Δm at exhaust velocity v_S (as measured in the rocket's instantaneous rest frame), leaving the rocket with mass M and infinitesimal forward velocity dv. Then $d(\frac{v}{c}) = d\beta = \tanh(d\omega)$.

Conservation of energy in this situation is given by

$$\Delta mc^2 \cosh \omega_s + Mc^2 \cosh(d\omega) = \tilde{M}c^2 \qquad (N.3)$$

and the conservation of momentum by

$$-\Delta mc \sinh \omega_s + Mc \sinh(d\omega) = 0 \qquad (N.4)$$

Since $d\omega$ is infinitesimal, we have $\cosh(d\omega) \approx 1$, and $\sinh(d\omega) \approx d\omega$; putting in these approximations and dividing the momentum equation ($N.4$) by the energy equation ($N.3$) gives

$$\frac{\sinh \omega_s}{\cosh \omega_s} = \tanh \omega_s = \frac{v_s}{c} = \frac{M d\omega}{\tilde{M} - M} \qquad (N.5)$$

But the change in the rocket rest mass is $dM = M - \tilde{M}$, so

$$d\omega = -\frac{v_s}{c}\frac{dM}{M} = -\beta_s \frac{dM}{M} \qquad (N.6)$$

Now rapidities add linearly, so ($N.6$) can be integrated to give

$$\omega = \beta_s \ln\left(\frac{M_i}{M_p}\right) \qquad (N.7)$$

which implies

$$\tanh \omega = \frac{v}{c} = \tanh \ln \left(\frac{M_i}{M_p}\right)^{\beta_s} \tag{N.8}$$

where v is the final velocity of the rocket in the rest frame of the Earth. After a little algebra, this expression gives

$$\frac{M_i}{M_p} = \left[\frac{1 + \frac{v}{c}}{1 - \frac{v}{c}}\right]^{c/2v_s} = \left[\frac{c + v}{c - v}\right]^{c/2v_s} \tag{N.9}$$

Since $\frac{v}{c} = \sqrt{1 - \frac{1}{\gamma^2}}$, then if $\gamma \gg 1$, we have $\frac{v}{c} \approx 1 - \frac{1}{2\gamma^2}$, so the mass ratio is approximately

$$\frac{M_i}{M_p} \approx (2\gamma)^{c/v_s} \tag{N.10}$$

For photon rockets ($v_s = c$), this means that, in the ultrarelativistic limit ($\gamma \gg 1$), the ratio of the initial total energy of the rocket, including the fuel, to the final total energy of the payload is just

$$\frac{M_i c^2}{\gamma M_p c^2} = \frac{2\gamma}{\gamma} = 2$$

Photon rockets are thus a quite efficient means of obtaining a high γ: the total initial mass-energy needed to accelerate the rocket to the final velocity v is only twice the final total energy the payload has in the rest frame of the Earth. However, once the rocket's velocity has reached $0.9c$, it becomes extremely costly to decrease significantly the travel time as measured in the universal rest frame. When $v = 0.9c$, we have $\gamma = 2.3$, whereas $v = 0.99$ corresponds to $\gamma = 7.1$; the total rocket energy must be increased by a factor of 3 in order to decrease the transit time by only 10%. This is expensive, since for photon rockets the mass ratio is 4.4 for a velocity of $0.9c$ but 14.1 for a velocity of $0.99c$.

Since *any* spacecraft acceleration mechanism will require at least $E = (\gamma - 1) mc^2$ of energy to be imparted to the spacecraft, the photon rocket is within a factor of 2 of the most efficient acceleration mechanism.

A high γ spacecraft will be useful only if the spacecraft is going so far that the expansion of the universe becomes significant—as would be the case, for example, if one wished to go to the opposite side of the universe. In such a situation, the spacecraft would appear to be going slower and slower relative to the galaxies farther and farther away, since these galaxies are moving faster and faster away from us, by Hubble's law. If we set $N(t) = 1$, so that t measures universal proper time, we recall from Section B that the FRW metric becomes

$$ds^2 = -dt^2 + R^2(t) \, [d\chi^2 + \Sigma^2(\chi)(d\theta^2 + \sin^2 \theta d\phi^2)] \qquad (B.1a)$$

Since this spacetime is spatially homogeneous and isotropic, a geodesic initially moving entirely in the radial (χ) direction remains without velocity in either the θ or the ϕ directions. Thus a radial geodesic moves in the 2–dimensional space defined by the metric

$$ds^2 = -dt^2 + R^2(t)d\chi^2$$

Since the metric components do not contain χ explicitly, this means that the momentum in the χ direction, p_χ, is a constant of the motion. (This fact is derived in Misner, Thorne, and Wheeler [4], Section 25.2. The rest of the derivation of equation (N.11) will require knowledge of modern general relativistic concepts. See [4], particularly pp. 656–657.) But $p_\chi = g_{\chi\chi}p^\chi = g_{\chi\chi}d\chi/d\lambda$, where λ is the affine parameter if the particle we are following is a photon, and is equal to the particle's proper time per unit rest mass along the particle's trajectory if the particle is timelike (as it would be if it is a spacecraft).

If we compute the momentum in the radial direction in the local Lorentz rest frame of observers at rest in the FRW coordinates—such observers have constant χ, θ, ϕ, and they are the observers at rest with respect to the cosmological background radiation — we get (letting p^χ_{Local} be this momentum):

$$p^\chi_{Local} \equiv p^{\hat\chi} \equiv \langle \omega^\chi, p \rangle = \left\langle g^{1/2}_{\chi\chi} \, d\chi, p \right\rangle = g^{1/2}_{\chi\chi} p^\chi = g^{1/2}_{\chi\chi} \frac{d\chi}{d\lambda}$$

where ω^χ is a local orthonormal basis 1–form, and p is the 4–momentum vector. But since $g_{\chi\chi}d\chi/d\lambda$ is a conserved quantity, and since $g_{\chi\chi} = R^2(t)$, we have shown that $R(t) \, p^\chi_{Local}(t)$ is a constant, independent of cosmic time. Thus

$$\frac{p^\chi_{Local}(t_{now})}{p^\chi_{Local}(t)} = \frac{\gamma_{now} v_{now}}{\gamma(t)v(t)} = \frac{R(t)}{R(t_{now})} \qquad (N.11)$$

where $p^\chi_{Local}(t_{now}) = \gamma_{now} m v_{now}$ is the relativistic momentum the spacecraft has in the rest frame of the stellar system which launches it, and $R(t_{now})$ is the scale factor of the universe the day the spacecraft is launched. (If it is launched in the next billion years, $R(t)$ will not change significantly from what it actually is today.)

This relation actually applies to photons as well as to timelike geodesics; the derivation did not need to assume that the particle whose motion is being analyzed was timelike. In fact, using the well-known relation between the photon momentum and wavelength, namely $p = h/\lambda$, equation $(N.11)$ becomes

$$\frac{\lambda_{now}}{R(t_{now})} = \frac{\lambda_t}{R(t)} \qquad (N.12)$$

which is the standard cosmological redshift formula. For an alternative derivation of equation $(N.11)$ see [5, p. 169].

The crucial thing to note about equation $(N.11)$ is that it says we can in effect use the expansion of the universe itself to slow down the spacecraft; we need not carry along any fuel to accomplish this. This is extremely important for high gamma spacecraft, because if all the velocity of transit had to be killed, the initial mass ratio given above would have to be *squared*. If the spacecraft is to reach the antipodal point at a time when the universe is 3×10^5 its present size, we would need an initial $\gamma_{now} = 5 \times 10^5$ for a photon rocket if the travel is to be relativistic the whole trip. (Having $\gamma(t_{max}) = 2$ is a sufficient condition for the entire trip to be relativistic, where t_{max} is the time of maximum expansion.) If we had to use the rocket to slow down from $\gamma = 5 \times 10^5$, we would have to have an initial mass ratio of 1×10^{12}. Instead, only $(3.7)(2)(5 \times 10^5) = 3.7 \times 10^6$ is necessary. (The extra factor of 3.7 is required to slow the payload from $\gamma = 2$ to $\gamma = 1$.)

However, a realistic relativistic rocket would probably not be a photon rocket, because the only known method of converting mass entirely into energy involves matter-antimatter annihilation. Thus the rocket fuel has to consist of half matter and half antimatter. The reaction $e^+ + e^- \rightarrow 2\gamma$ gives only photons, but there is no known method of storing large amounts of positrons, except as part of anti-atoms. So most of the antimatter mass would be antiprotons, which does not annihilate directly into two photons. Proton-antiproton annihilation generally proceeds [6] by decay into pions:

$$p + \bar{p} \rightarrow m\pi^0 + n(\pi^+ + \pi^-)$$

where $m \approx n \approx 1.60$. None of the pions are stable, and the neutral pion usually decays via the reaction $\pi^0 \to 2\gamma$. The gamma rays from the neutral pions are lost, carrying away energy, but the charged pions will travel about 20 meters before they decay, and thus can provide thrust by having their trajectories bent by magnetic fields so that they go out the rocket exhaust. The neutral pions carry away on the average zero net momentum in the rocket's instantaneous rest frame.

If some of the energy in the annihilation is lost, then equations (N.3) and (N.4) have to be modified. If a fraction $\eta \Delta mc^2$ of the propellent rest mass gets rapidity ω_S, and another fraction $\delta \Delta mc^2$ just disappears in the reaction, then equations (N.3) and (N.4) respectively become

$$\eta \Delta mc^2 \cosh \omega_s + \delta \Delta mc^2 + Mc^2 \cosh(d\omega) = \tilde{M}c^2 \qquad (N.13)$$

$$-\eta \Delta mc \sinh \omega_s + Mc \sinh(d\omega) = 0 \qquad (N.14)$$

Proceeding as in the derivation of equation (N.5), we get

$$\frac{\eta \sinh \omega_s}{\eta \cosh \omega_s + \delta} = \frac{M \, d\omega}{\tilde{M} - M} = -\frac{M \, d\omega}{dM} \qquad (N.15)$$

where I have inserted the change in the rocket rest mass, $dM = M - \tilde{M}$. Integrating equation (N.15) gives

$$\omega = \left[\frac{\sinh \omega_s}{\cosh \omega_s + \frac{\delta}{\eta}}\right] \ln\left(\frac{M_i}{M_p}\right) \qquad (N.16)$$

where now v_s is the velocity of the charged pions in the $p-\bar{p}$ annihilation reaction. Solving equation (N.16) for the mass ratio yields

$$\frac{M_i}{M_p} = \left[\frac{1 + \frac{v}{c}}{1 - \frac{v}{c}}\right]^{c/2v_s[1 + \frac{\delta}{\eta\gamma_s}]} \qquad (N.17)$$

where $\gamma_s = \cosh \omega_s$.

But by conservation of energy we have

$$\eta\gamma_s = \delta$$

which reduces equation (N.17) to

$$\frac{M_i}{M_p} = \left[\frac{1 + \frac{v}{c}}{1 - \frac{v}{c}}\right]^{c/v_s} \tag{N.18}$$

For $\gamma \gg 1$, we have

$$\frac{M_i}{M_p} \approx (2\gamma)^{2c/v_s} \tag{N.19}$$

instead of equation (N.10). Equation (N.19) differs from equation (N.10) by an extra factor of 2 in the exponent.

Conservation of energy gives $2 \times 938 - 4.8 \times 139$ MeV divided more or less evenly among 4.8 pions, so each charged pion has a kinetic energy of 252 MeV. The ratio of kinetic energy to rest mass is $\gamma - 1$, so each pion has $\frac{v_s}{c} = 0.935$. Equation (N.19) thus becomes

$$\frac{M_i}{M_p} \approx (2\gamma)^{2.14} \tag{N.20}$$

With the initial $\gamma_{now} = 5 \times 10^5$ required to reach the antipodal point by the time of maximum expansion, we would need an initial mass ratio of 1×10^{14}. (Remember that an extra factor of 17 is required, because the rocket must be used to reduce $\gamma(t_{max}) = 2$ down to $\gamma = 1$.)

Now the term "payload" in the mass ratio includes not only the payload proper, but also the fuel tanks and the rocket engines. The key to reducing both the mass of the payload proper and the masses of the tanks and engines is nanotechnology [7]. I have argued in Chapter II that the mass of the payload proper need be no greater than 100 grams. If we use molecular-size universal constructors [7] to reshape the rocket and the engines as it accelerates, then in principle, the tanks and the motors can be made out of fuel; the tanks and motors will then make *zero* contribution to the payload mass. If this is done, then a matter-antimatter annihilation rocket capable of traveling, at relativistic velocities the whole way, from the Earth to the other side of the universe by the time of maximum expansion, would have a mass of ten billion metric tons. (If a rocket motor could be devised that annihilated the quarks which make up the protons and antiprotons, then we would have a true photon rocket, and the initial mass of the rocket would only be 400 tons rather than ten billion tons. Unfortunately, it is not known if such a motor is possible even in principle.)

The current cost of five billion tons of antimatter is enormous, as I showed in Chapter II. (The power output of the Sun is $L_\odot = 3.8 \times 10^{26}$ Joules/sec = 42 million tons of mass-energy per second, so synthesizing this much antimatter would require the entire power output of the Sun for 4 minutes, even at 100% efficiency!) A large fraction of this enormous cost is due to the baryon and lepton number conservation law, which requires that a proton be created along with each antiproton. This means that at least half of the energy must go into creating useless protons. The same conservation law restricts nuclear energy to less than 1% efficiency: less than 1% of the rest mass of nuclei can be converted into energy, whereas if the law did not hold, possibly all the mass could be converted into energy.

However, in 1976, Gerard 't Hooft [8] showed that the law can be violated in the Standard Model of particle physics. The predicted violation is tiny, and has never been observed, but if the Standard Model is correct—and all experiments indicate that it is—then this violation must occur. A number of physicists [9–12] since 1976 have discovered ways in which the effect can be enhanced, but our mathematics is too primitive to analyze the details of the effect in the absence of experiments. The SSC—if it's ever built—might be able to study this baryon number violating effect, and quite possibly might show how to use the effect to create antimatter efficiently on macroscopic scales.

Recall that nanotechnology allows us to code one bit per atom in the 100-gram payload, so the memory of the payload would be sufficient to hold the simulations of as many as 10^4 individual human equivalent personalities, at 10^{20} bits per personality. This is the population size of a fair-sized town, as large as the population of "space arks" that have been proposed in the past for interstellar colonization. Sending simulations—virtual human equivalent personalities—rather than real-world people has another advantage besides reducing the mass ratio of the spacecraft: one can obtain the effect of relativistic time dilation without the necessity of high γ by simply slowing down the rate at which the spacecraft computer runs the simulation of the 10^4 human equivalent personalities on board. One needs the large γ in the trip to the universal antipode in order to get there by the maximum expansion time, not to reduce the time experienced on board the spacecraft.

A third advantage of using virtual human equivalent personalities rather than real-world humans is that it solves the problem of radiation shielding. Protons in the interstellar medium have the same γ in the spacecraft's rest frame as the spacecraft has in the medium's rest frame, and the resulting intense radiation from the protons in the interstellar medium has often been cited [2,3] as proving the impossibility of high γ spacecraft. One indeed needs thick shielding:

2 meters thickness of aluminum is required to stop 1 GeV protons ($\gamma = 2$). However, if the spacecraft has a cross-sectional area of 1mm^2, then only 5 grams of aluminum is required. (Molecular-size universal constructors would be required in the shielding to continuously repair the shielding; about 1/5 joules per second of energy would be deposited by the radiation.) For $\gamma = 10^5$ spacecraft, shielding is not practical but almost all the $\gamma = 10^5$ protons would pass right through, so one would simply use the constructors to repair the occasional (heavy) damage. (During the acceleration phase, magnetic fields would have to be used to shield the antimatter from the medium particles.) There are about 10^{-5} protons per cm^3 in the intergalactic medium, so about 5×10^3 joules per second is the kinetic energy of the protons that is passing through each mm^2 of ship surface area per second of ship's time. But the intergalactic medium is being thinned out as $R^{-3}(t)$ by the universal expansion, so this power through the ship could be reduced to the 1/5 joules per second experienced by a $\gamma = 2$ spacecraft in the *interstellar* medium just by waiting to launch the spacecraft until the universe has expanded by a factor of 20, or about 2 trillion years from now.

A fourth advantage of virtual humans in a virtual environment over real humans is that the virtual humans will experience the simulated acceleration of the virtual environment rather than the real acceleration of the rocket. If a rocket accelerates at 155 gravities, real humans would be converted into jelly, while virtual humans on the same rocket would experience their choice of accelerations: the usual 1 gravity or less. Since there is no difference between an emulation and the machine emulated, I predict that no real human will ever traverse interstellar space. Humans will eventually go to the stars, but they will go as emulations; they will go as virtual machines, not as real machines.

A high acceleration can enormously reduce the distance required to accelerate to large gammas. In Newtonian mechanics, a particle uniformly accelerating from zero velocity to a final velocity v must accelerate through a distance s given by $s = v^2/2a$. A straightforward calculation based on Section 6.1 of [4] shows that the relativistic generalization of this formula is

$$s = \frac{c^2}{g} (\gamma - 1) \qquad (N.21)$$

where g is the constant acceleration as measured in the instantaneous rest frame of the rocket, and s is the distance travelled in the rest frame of the stellar system which launches the rocket. If s is measured in light years and g in gravities, equation (N.21) becomes

$$\left(\frac{s}{1 \text{ light year}}\right) = 0.971 \left(\frac{1 \text{ gravity}}{g}\right) (\gamma - 1) \qquad (N.22)$$

So for $\gamma = 5 \times 10^5$, $s = 5 \times 10^5$ light years at 1 gravity, but only 3,000 light years at 155 gravities.

References

[1] Ackeret, Johann 1946. "Zur Theorie der Raketen." *Helvetica Physica Acta* **19**: 103–12. Reprinted in English translation in *Journal of the British Interplanetary Society* (1946) **6**: 116–23.

[2] Purcell, Edward 1963. "Radioastronomy and Communication Through Space," in *Interstellar Communication*, 121–143. New York: Benjamin.

[3] Taylor, Edwin F. and John A. Wheeler 1963. *Spacetime Physics*. San Francisco: Freeman.

[4] Misner, Charles W., Kip S. Thorne, and John A. Wheeler 1973. *Gravitation*. San Francisco: Freeman.

[5] Peebles, P. James E. 1971. *Physical Cosmology*. Princeton: Princeton University Press.

[6] Cassenti, Brice N. 1988. "Energy Transfer in Antiproton Annihilation Rockets." In *Antiproton Science and Technology*. Edited by B. W. Augenstein, *et al*. Singapore: World Scientific.

[7] Drexler, K. Eric 1992. *Nanosystems: Molecular Machinery, Manufacturing, a Computation*. New York: Wiley.

[8] 't Hofft, Gerard 1976. "Symmetry Breaking through Bell–Jackiw Anomalies," *Physical Review Letters* **37**: 8-11.

[9] McLerran, Larry 1989. "Can the Observed Baryon Asymmetry Be Produced at the Electroweak Phase Transition?" *Physical Review Letters*: **62**: 1075–78.

[10] Shaposhnikov, Mikhail E. 1992. "Standard Model Solutions of the Baryogenesis Problem," *Physics Letters* **B277**: 324-30.

[11] Bagnasco, John E. and Michael Dine 1993. "Some Two-Loop Corrections to the Finite Temperature Effective Potential in the Electroweak Theory," *Physics Letters* **B303**: 308–14.

[12] Kunz, Jutta and Yves Brihaye 1993. "Fermions in the Background of the Sphaleron Barrier," *Physics Letters* **B304**: 141–46.

INDEX